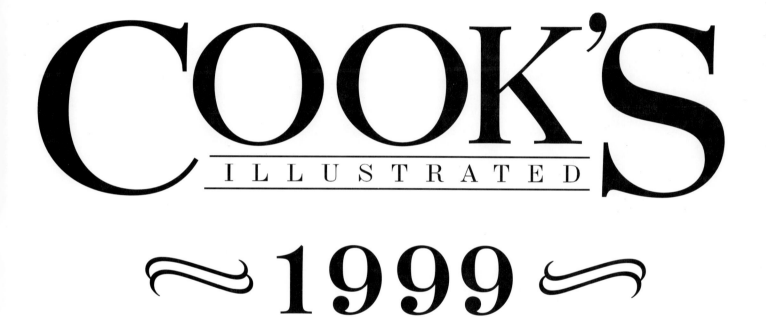

COOK'S
ILLUSTRATED

~ 1999 ~

$29.95

Published by

Boston Common Press Limited Partnership

17 Station Street

Brookline, MA 02445

ISBN: 0-936184-40-X

ISSN: 1068-2821

To get home delivery of future issues of *Cook's Illustrated*, call 800-526-8442 inside the U.S., or 555-247-7571 if calling from outside the U.S.

In addition to the Annual Hardbound Editions, *Cook's Illustrated* offers the following publications:

The *How to Cook* series of single topic cookbooks
Titles include *How to Make A Pie, How to Make An American Layer Cake, How to Stir-Fry, How to Make Ice Cream, How to Make Pizza, How to Make Holiday Desserts, How to Make Pasta Sauces, How to Make Salad, How to Grill, How to Make Simple Fruit Desserts, How to Make Cookie Jar Favorites, How to Cook Holiday Roasts & Birds, How to Make Stew, How to Cook Shrimp & Other Shellfish, How to Barbecue & Roast On The Grill, How to Cook Garden Vegetables, How to Cook Pot Pies & Casseroles,* and *How to Make Soup*. A boxed set of the first 11 titles in the series is available in an attractive, protective slip case. New releases are published every two months, so give us a call for our complete list of available titles.

The Best Recipe
This 560-page book is a collection of over 700 recipes and 200 illustrations from the past seven years of *Cook's*. We've included basics, such as how to make chicken stock, as well as recipes for quick weeknight meals and special entertaining. Let *The Best Recipe* become your indispensable kitchen companion.

Multi-Year Master Index
Quickly find every article and recipe *Cook's Illustrated* has published from the Charter Issue in 1992 through the most recent year-end issue. Recipe names, authors, article titles, subject matter, equipment testings, food tastings, cookbook reviews, wine tastings, and ingredients are all now instantly at your fingertips.

The Cook's Bible and *The Yellow Farmhouse Cookbook*
Written by Christopher Kimball and published by Little, Brown and Company.

To order any of the books listed above, call 800-611-0759 inside the U.S., or 515-246-6911 if calling from outside the U.S.

You can order subscriptions, gift subscriptions, and any of our books by visiting our online store at
www.cooksillustrated.com

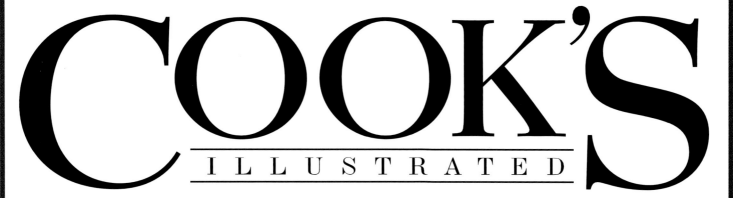

COOK'S
ILLUSTRATED

Testing Roasting Pans
Cheap Hardware Store Brand
Scores Well

New French Onion Soup
Use Red Onions and "Cheater's" Broth

Cream Cheese Brownies
Why Underbaking Makes the Difference

White Rice Tasting
Test Surprise: Boil-in-Bag Brand
Places Second

Twice Baked Potatoes
Triple Baked Shells Give Extra Crunch

Best Italian-Style Meat Sauce
Wine, Milk, and Tomatoes are the Key

Kitchen Quick Tips
Real Bread Pudding
Coq au Vin
Broccoli Rabe
Flatbreads Made Easy

$4.95 U.S./$5.95 CANADA

CONTENTS

January & February 1999

PUBLISHER AND EDITOR
Christopher Kimball

EXECUTIVE EDITOR
Pam Anderson

SENIOR EDITOR
John Willoughby

SENIOR WRITER
Jack Bishop

ASSOCIATE EDITORS
Adam Ried
Maryellen Driscoll

TEST KITCHEN DIRECTOR
Susan Logozzo

TEST COOKS
Dawn Yanagihara
Anne Yamanaka

CONTRIBUTING EDITOR
Stephanie Lyness

ART DIRECTOR
Amy Klee

CORPORATE MANAGING EDITOR
Barbara Bourassa

EDITORIAL PRODUCTION MANAGER
Sheila Datz

COPY EDITOR
India Koopman

MARKETING DIRECTOR
Adrienne Kimball

CIRCULATION DIRECTOR
David Mack

FULFILLMENT MANAGER
Larisa Greiner

CIRCULATION MANAGER
Darcy Beach

MARKETING ASSISTANT
Connie Forbes

PRODUCTS MANAGER
Steven Browall

VICE PRESIDENT PRODUCTION AND TECHNOLOGY
James McCormack

SYSTEMS ADMINISTRATOR
James Burke

PRODUCTION ARTIST
Daniel Frey

SENIOR ACCOUNTANT
Mandy Shito

OFFICE MANAGER
Danielle Shuckra

SPECIAL PROJECTS
Fern Berman

Cook's Illustrated (ISSN 1068-2821) is published bimonthly by Boston Common Press Limited Partnership, 17 Station Street, Brookline, MA 02445. Copyright 1999 Boston Common Press Limited Partnership. Periodical postage paid at Boston, MA and additional mailing offices, UPPS #012487. For list rental information, contact List Services Corporation, 6 Trowbridge Drive, P.O. Box 516, Bethel, CT 06801; (203) 743-2600; fax (203) 743-0589. Editorial office: 17 Station Street, Brookline, MA 02445; (617) 232-1000; fax (617) 232-1572. Editorial contributions should be sent to: Editor, *Cook's Illustrated*. We cannot assume responsibility for manuscripts submitted to us. Submissions will be returned only if accompanied by a large self-addressed envelope. Postmaster: Send all new orders, subscription inquiries, and change of address notices to: *Cook's Illustrated*, P.O. Box 7446, Red Oak, IA 51591-0446. PRINTED IN THE USA.

POTATOES

POTATOES While most of us may be familiar with only a few varieties of potatoes, there are actually hundreds. They can be divided by many different factors including color and length of time to maturity, but for the cook the most important characteristic is the starch content. High starch potatoes such as the widely available Russet or the lesser known All Blue have a rather mealy texture that makes them very good for baking and mashing. Medium-starch varieties, including the Purple Viking, Caribe, and Irish Cobbler, as well as some of the tiny fingerlings—Ozette, Butterfinger, and Peruvian Purple, make the best all-purpose potatoes. Low-starch potatoes, also known as waxy potatoes, remain very firm when cooked and therefore are best boiled, steamed or roasted. Low starch varieties include most red-skinned potatoes such as the All Red and Dark Red Norland. Rose Finn Apple, Ruby Crescent, and Russian Banana fingerlings are also low in starch.

COVER PAINTING: BRENT WATKINSON.   BACK COVER ILLUSTRATION: JOHN BURGOYNE

A FISHER OF CHILDREN

On a cloudy August afternoon, the cry goes up for a fishing party. We dig for worms, rustle through the barn for a net, check the hooks and leaders, grab a few poles, and soon we're off in the old red pickup, headed down to the trout stream through a narrow back road that is closed in winter. Each of my three older children is wearing big rubber boots with red soles and carrying high expectations about who will catch the first fish. The bed of the old truck jostles and shakes independently from the cab as we drive slowly over the narrow dirt track, up over the mountain, and then down again through a dark hollow. Clouds sail low over the mountaintops and a small field behind a white farmhouse disappears into the mist. We rattle by the meadow where the last tribe of local Indians under Chief Chunks once made camp, a stand of curved white birch and poplar edging out into the grass. We drive deeper into the woods until we suddenly emerge onto the main road and turn left toward our fishing hole.

After the thrill of the first casts, we settle into a routine, my oldest, Whitney, taking the project most seriously, checking her lure carefully, a Mepps or perhaps a Marble Spinner or a Sonic Rooster Tail. Caroline, my second daughter, soon loses interest and, removing her boots, wades into the shallow current, looking for rocks and small fish. I crouch down next to Charlie, my only son, helping him cast into the pool, amid cries of "Let me do it." Soon, I am just a spectator, watching my three oldest children off on their own, enjoying the river each in their own way.

Here I sit, a fisher of children, casting about with a great box of lures, applying all of the tricks I have learned in my lifetime to snare each of my children with love but also to prepare them for the rigors of adulthood. As they grow older, they become harder to catch, like wild trout who are easily spooked by the slap of line on water or who have fickle tastes, the fly not perfectly matching the evening hatch. They grow more patient with time, considering the bait before lunging. And once caught, they put up a good fight, often running out the line or snagging it on a rock, the hook spit out and useless.

I must learn to be more clever as the years pass. I sit by the side of this famous trout stream and watch patiently, looking for a single rise in the still pool and choosing my fly carefully. With children as with fish, the approach is everything. One poor cast and the fishing is over for the day, the waders stripped off and thrown back in the pickup for the ride home. Whitney is perhaps the cleverest of my children, an old trout who is always on guard, questioning hidden motives before I know I have them. She will only be caught willingly, taking the offered fly with full knowledge of the consequences. Caroline is carefree but wily, keenly adept at manipulating others with breezy charm and false enthusiasm. She will take the fly that is offered out of sheer lust for life, enjoying the action; the great leaps from the water and the final landing, my hands

Christopher Kimball

holding her gently. She is no loner, no solitary brook trout content in her pool. When I reel her in, I often realize that she has landed me. She is the real fisher in this family, the consummate player, the one who is most attuned to the whims and needs of others. And then there is Charlie who, still young, has enthusiasm and energy for all things. Every offering is worth a nibble and often a lunging strike. And once hooked, he is capable of a great fight, banging his head against the river bottom to dislodge an unwanted barb or running underneath the boat to tangle the line. He is a fisherman's dream, a hot streak of quicksilver, giving the fight of his life on every cast.

And then I think of other fishermen I have met over the years, their voices carrying clearly from a far shore, or perhaps I remember hearing just a whisper of encouragement at my side in the kitchen. They were unexpected visitors who pushed me into deeper currents before I knew I was ready, who used all the guile of an old angler to make me put up a good fight. And, as I sit on the rocky shore, I watch each of my children and hope that they, too, will hear a voice, one that speaks to them about deeper currents. It will not be my voice. It will be an old hand who can cast a thousand yards, the fly kissing the surface of the water lightly, waiting patiently for those who are willing to rise to the occasion.

ABOUT COOK'S ILLUSTRATED

The Magazine Cook's Illustrated is published every other month (6 issues per year) and accepts no advertising. A one-year subscription is $24.95, two years is $45, and three years is $65. Add $6 postage per year for Canadian subscriptions and $12 per year for all other foreign countries. To order subscriptions in the U.S. call 800-526-8442 or 515-247-7571 from outside the U.S. Gift subscriptions are available for $24.95 each.

Magazine-Related Items Cook's Illustrated is available in an annual hardbound edition, which includes an index, for $24.95 each plus shipping and handling. Discounts are available if more than one year is ordered at a time. Back issues are available for $5 each. Cook's also offers a 6-year index (1993-1998) of the magazine for $12.95. To order any of these products, call 800-611-0759 inside the U.S. or 515-246-6911 outside the U.S.

Books Cook's Illustrated publishes a series of single-topic books, available for $14.95 each. Titles include: How to Make A Pie, How to Make An American Layer Cake, How to Stir Fry, How to Make Ice Cream, How to Make Salad, How to Make Simple Fruit Desserts, How to Make Cookie Jar Favorites, How to Cook Holiday Roasts and Birds, How to Make Stew, How to Make Pizza, How to Make Holiday Desserts, How to Make Pasta Sauces, and How to Grill. The Cook's Bible, written by Christopher Kimball and published by Little, Brown and Company, is available for $24.95. The Yellow Farmhouse Cookbook, also written by Christopher Kimball and published by Little, Brown and Company, is available for $24.95. To order any of these books, call 800-611-0759 inside the U.S. or 515-246-6911 outside the U.S.

Reader Submissions Cook's accepts reader submissions for both Quick Tips and Notes From Readers. We will provide a one-year complimentary subscription for each Quick Tip that we print. Send a description of your technique, along with your name, address, and daytime telephone number, to Quick Tips, Cook's Illustrated, P.O. Box 569, Brookline, MA 02447. Questions, suggestions, or other submissions for Notes From Readers should be sent to the same address.

Subscription Inquiries All queries about subscriptions or change of address notices should be addressed to Cook's Illustrated, P.O. Box 7446, Red Oak, IA 51591-0446.

Website Address Selected articles and recipes from Cook's Illustrated and subscription information are available online. You can also order books and other products at www.cooksillustrated.com.

Heat beyond Chiles

We all know that capsaicin makes chiles hot, but what makes black pepper, ginger, mustard, and horseradish hot?

L.A. WATKINS
STONINGTON, CT

➤ According to Dr. Arthur O. Tucker, a spice expert and Research Professor in the Department of Agriculture and Natural Resources at Delaware State University, black pepper, ginger, mustard, and horseradish all contain distinct chemical compounds, sometimes referred to as chemical irritants, that give them their characteristic pungent or hot flavors. Tucker reported that the primary irritant in black pepper, for example, is piperine, while the irritants in ginger include zingerone, gingerols, and shogoals. Brown mustard and horseradish get their heat from yet another type of chemical.

Dr. Bruce P. Bryant, Senior Research Associate at the Monell Chemical Senses Center in Philadelphia, explained that these irritants activate neurons of the somato-sensory system, which conveys the sensations of touch, temperature, and pain. According to Pamela Penzey, purchasing agent for the mail-order spice retailer Penzey's Ltd., black pepper and ginger are pungent rather than strictly hot. This means that their chemical irritants are present in lower concentrations, so they stimulate the temperature-sensitive, but not the pain-sensitive, nerves. Hence, our tongues feel warmth. At higher concentrations, the pain-sensitive nerves are also stimulated, giving rise to both pungency and pain with both mustard and horseradish, which Penzey considers hot.

In her book *Savoring Spices and Herbs* (Morrow, 1996), Julie Sahni writes that the pungency that zingerone imparts to ginger decreases with cooking, giving the dishes cooked with it a mellow, warm quality. In mustard, Sahni reports, the irritants are released by enzymatic reactions that occur when the dry mustard is mixed with liquid. The pungency and heat are most intense during that enzymatic action; when it ends, the flavor of the mustard paste mellows. Adding an acid such as vinegar or lemon juice to the paste abruptly ceases the enzymatic activity and sets the hot flavor. When mustard seed is in its whole, crushed, or powdered form, the irritants are dormant, which is why mustard has no real flavor or aroma until it is steeped in water.

Gewürztraminer

The Gewürztraminer tasting in the May/June 1998 issue noted that many of the wines in the tasting would complement Asian food, but did not mention that Gewürztraminer is one of the very few wines that nicely sets off and complements hot, spicy dishes, such as curries.

GARY SOUCIE
SHAFTSBURY, VT

➤ You're right. Many wine authorities suggest serving Gewürztraminer with spicy foods. We tasted a bottle of our winning Gewürztraminer from that tasting, a 1996 Chateau Ste. Michelle, with the spicy Pork Vindaloo recipe in the *Cook's* master series book "How to Make Stew" (*see* previous page for information) and every taster considered the match ideal.

Vacu-Vin Experiment

My liquor store sells vacuum stoppers which are meant to preserve the flavor of red wine in opened but unfinished bottles. The store clerks, who strike me as knowledgeable, claim that the stoppers do a reasonably good job. Has anyone at *Cook's* tried these? Do you have an opinion about their effectiveness?

MATTHEW KLEIN
NEW YORK, NY

➤ We hadn't considered these vacuum bottle stoppers before, so we set up an experiment to test them. Before we began, we spoke to Timothy Walsh, wine buyer for Marty's Fine Wines in Allston, MA. Walsh explained that oxidation, which results from contact between the wine remaining in a bottle and the air occupying the space vacated by the wine you've poured, deteriorates the flavor of the leftover wine. The vacuum stoppers are designed to mitigate the problem by pumping the air out of the bottle, essentially creating a vacuum. In Walsh's opinion, two to three hours of exposure to air is enough time to really hurt the flavor of the wine, so it is best to put the vacuum stopper into the bottle as quickly after opening it as possible.

For our tests we chose a 1990 Taurino Notarpanaro Rosso del Salento, the Italian "Best Buy" recommended in our November/December 1998 tasting of rich red wines. We bought five bottles, opened and poured two glasses from each of two of the bottles, and allowed the wine remaining in the bottles to stand uncorked for 45 minutes, about the length of time they might sit open on the table during a weeknight dinner. Then we closed one using the vacuum pump, and the other with its cork.

On each of the following three days, five tasters from the *Cook's* staff (none of whose palates, incidentally, were trained or extensively experienced with wine) tasted both of these wines, along with a freshly opened bottle. On all three days, the freshly opened bottle was the most highly regarded, but none of the tasters could distinguish much, if any, difference between the recorked and vacuum-stopped samples. In fact, on the second and third days, the vacuum-stopped wine was the lowest rated, though not far behind the recorked wines.

Surprised, we decided to double-check the results by repeating the tests with another red, and, just for kicks, a white. This time around, we chose a Cline Zinfandel, the 1995 vintage of which was highly recommended in our January/February 1998 tasting of California Zinfandels, and a Kendall-Jackson Vintner's Reserve, the '96 vintage of which was top rated in our March/April 1998 tasting of inexpensive chardonnays. With both wines, the numbers told the same story again. There was very little, if any, discernible taste difference between the recorked and vacuum-stopped wines.

We are left to conclude, then, that the vacuum stoppers make no difference for the average wine drinker. This may not hold true, however, for those whose palates are experienced and well developed.

As an aside, we were discussing this, and other matters, with Dr. Susan Brewer, an Associate Professor of Food Chemistry at the University of Illinois, and she mentioned that you can mimic the effect of the vacuum stopper by inhaling deeply, holding your breath for a moment, and exhaling into the bottle. The carbon dioxide you exhale will force the oxygen out of the bottle, thereby retarding oxidation.

Muscovy Duck

Though I enjoyed Jack Bishop's November/December 1998 recipes for roast duck, I also like duck breast meat cooked medium-rare and sliced. In the article, Mr. Bishop briefly mentioned another type of duck, called Muscovy, which he said is better suited to this type of preparation. Can you provide any more information on Muscovy duck?

ALISON MARKUM
FOXBORO, MA

➤ Jack Bishop focused the roast duck article on Pekin duck, also known as Long Island–style duck, because it is the only choice for supermarket shoppers. If you are willing to order from the butcher or by mail, however, the larger breasted Muscovy duck is another option.

From research for the roast duck article and other projects, Bishop reported that the Muscovy duck, also known as the Barbarie duck, is a South American species favored by many chefs for roasting. There are also two other varieties of duck, but Moulards are rarely sold whole and Mallards are hard to find unless you hunt. We ordered several Muscovy ducks by mail to see how they compared with the Pekin ducks roasted for the article.

The female Muscovy is much more popular than the male. It weighs about four pounds and looks very much like a Pekin duck. We consulted with several chefs and followed their cooking advice, roasting the bird at 350 degrees until an instant-read thermometer inserted in the leg/thigh registered 160 degrees. This took about 1¼ hours. We then poured off the fat, added some water to the pan to prevent smoking, and cranked up the heat to 425 degrees to crisp the skin. The Muscovy had a much gamier flavor, something several of our tasters found unappealing. On the plus side, though, the breast was substantially thicker. In fact, our four-pound Muscovy fed four people easily. The Muscovy seemed moister and less fatty than a Pekin that had been roasted only, without first steaming it, as Bishop recommended. However, the Muscovy was still fattier than a steamed/roasted Pekin. Also, the skin was not nearly as crisp.

We then cooked a Muscovy by the same steaming, carving, and roasting regimen Bishop recommends for Pekin ducks. This Muscovy was less greasy and the skin was crisper. If you want a gamier flavor and don't mind some fat, you can roast a female Muscovy without steaming. If you want a gamier flavor without the fat, though, substitute a Muscovy duck in our steamed-then-roasted master recipe.

To order duck by mail, we recommend New Jersey–based D'Artagnan (800-327-8246), a leading purveyor of poultry and game. They sell whole Muscovy ducks, both female and male (which, though very large at around six pounds, we found to have a strong gamy flavor). The female is much more common and weighs about four pounds. The cost is $5.95 per pound plus shipping. The male weighs six to seven pounds and costs $5 per pound plus shipping. D'Artagnan also sells whole Mallard ducks in the fall and winter. These birds weigh 2 to 2½ pounds and cost $27 each. Whole boneless Moulard duck breasts are also available for $10.95 per pound.

Chocolate Bloom

➤ Reading the chocolate chip tasting article in the September/October 1998 issue made me think of a question. More than once, I've noticed that some of the chips in a bag have odd, whitish blemishes. This seems to happen regardless of the brand, the type of chip (minichips to kisses), or where I purchased them. Honestly, I have always gone ahead and used the chips because I couldn't taste any difference between those with and without the blemishes, but now

I am curious about the cause. Are they safe? Are those chips too old to use, or perhaps contaminated? Should I be throwing the bad-looking chips out?

ELENA MACCARONE
ARLINGTON, VA

➤ To answer your question, we checked with representatives from Nestlé and Ghirardelli, who explained that the whitish haze you see on the surface of some of your chips is not a function of their age. Appearing as a powder or film on the chip, the haze can develop at any time and may be caused by any one of several things. According to Suzanne Wong, senior food technologist at Ghirardelli, it could simply be scuff marks resulting from the chips having been bounced around in the packaging process or during shipping. Another possibility, called bloom, is caused by either the sugar or the fat in the chocolate rising to the surface. Neither scuffing nor bloom presents any reason to worry about the safety of the chips.

Sugar bloom results from extreme temperature changes. In going from a warm humid environment to a cool environment, moisture condenses on the chocolate and dissolves some of the sugar out of it. When the moisture evaporates, it leaves a gray, slightly grainy film that's basically fine sugar crystals. Fat bloom appears when chocolate has been sitting in temperatures above 75 degrees. The fats melt and rise to the surface of the chocolate, creating a gray oily sheen.

Commercial chips seem particularly prone to bloom because retailers have a wide range of storage conditions that are not necessarily sensitive to chocolate, said Tricia Bowles of Nestlé. Despite its looking a bit funny, "there is nothing wrong with it, there is no harm to your health," she said. To prevent bloom from developing on your chips at home, manufacturers recommend that you wrap them tightly and store them in a cool, dry place, but not in the refrigerator.

WHAT IS IT?

This round "pot" is approximately 12 inches across and about 7 inches high. It's hammered copper on the outside, either tin or aluminum on the inside, and has a single hinge connecting the top and the bottom, handles on both sections opposite the hinge, and two clamps to hold it shut on the other sides. Any ideas as to its real purpose in life?

WENDY WEIR
PACIFIC HOUSE, CA

➤ Called a "cataplana," your pan is a workhorse of Portuguese cookery, particularly in the southern resort province of Algarve. Jean Anderson, an authority on Portuguese cooking and author of *The Food of Portugal* (Hearst Books, 1986) told us that cataplanas are made from a variety of metals, though aluminum is especially popular in restaurant kitchens. Most of the cataplanas we see in the United States are clad in copper. Anderson added that the pan is probably of Arab origin, from the period in history—the years 711 to 1249—when the Arabs occupied Portugal.

Both the pan and the dishes cooked in it, Anderson explained, are called cataplanas. She added that stovetop cataplana cooking is successful only on gas burners and with a wok collar or similar device to hold the curved pan steady; electric burners cannot produce sufficient heat. Though many combinations of pork, fish, shellfish, fowl, and vegetables are cooked in cataplanas, perhaps the most widely known such dish (which is, incidentally, pictured on the cover of Anderson's book) is called "Amêijoas na Cataplana." It consists of small clams, ham, and chouriço sausage cooked together in an onion, garlic, and tomato-flavored sauce. The pan, which resembles a huge clamshell, is brought to the table sealed and then opened in front of the diners so they can enjoy the fragrant steam as it pours out. Most recipes we consulted advised that a Dutch oven with a tight-fitting lid is a good substitute for a cataplana, though you do risk losing some degree of panache in the presentation.

If you are after the real thing, The Spanish Table (1427 Western Avenue, Seattle, WA 98101; 206-682-2827) sells copper-clad cataplanas in three sizes: a 6-inch diameter model for $22.00, a 9-inch diameter model for $32.00, and a 13-inch diameter model for $58.00. It also sells a cork base to keep the cataplana steady on the table for $20.00. Incidentally, Chuck Williams, founder of Williams-Sonoma, notes that you can also steady the cataplana with a simple kitchen towel that has been rolled into a tight ring. A recipe for Amêijoas na Cataplana can be found in Anderson's book, *The Food of Portugal*, which is available from two of our favorite cookbook sources, Jessica's Biscuit (The Cookbook People, Box 301, Newtonville, MA 02460; 800-878-4264;) for $12.80 and Kitchen Arts & Letters (1435 Lexington Avenue, New York, NY 10128; 212-876-5550) for $16.00.

Quick Tips

Easier Pounding

Recipes that require pounding chicken or veal into thin cutlets (such as the recipe for chicken Parmesan in the September/October 1998 issue) commonly instruct the cook to pound the meat between sheets of plastic wrap. But some cooks report that the meat slides around and the wrap rips. Karla Anders of Wheeling, Illinois, has even had cutlets land on the floor. Now, instead of plastic wrap, she uses cereal box liners that have been wiped free of crumbs. This thicker, stronger plastic never tears.

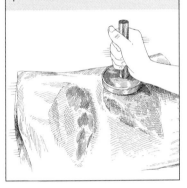

Keeping the Pepper Grinder Clean

Preparing raw cutlets, ground meat, or poultry for cooking can leave the cook's hands greasy and slippery once it is time to season the meat. To avoid dirtying her pepper mill, Test Cook Dawn Yanagihara covers the pepper mill with plastic wrap, which can later be removed and discarded.

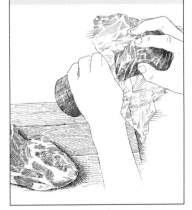

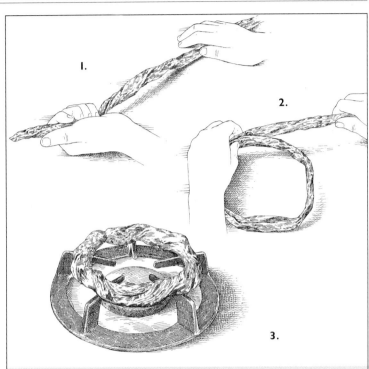

Making a Flame Tamer

If you don't have a commercial flame tamer, you can fashion one by making a thick, slightly flattened ring of aluminum foil and placing it on top of the gas burner.
1. Cut a 3-foot length of aluminum foil and squeeze into a ¾-inch rope.
2. Roll one end to form a ring the size of the burner.
3. Twist remaining foil rope around ring to form flame tamer.

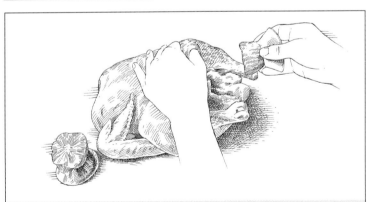

Seasoning the Bird

The flavor of lemon is lovely with chicken or turkey, but squeezing a lemon half or pouring lemon juice directly into the cavity of a bird can result in a messy spill. To limit mess and maximize the amount of lemon juice that actually goes inside the bird, Laurie Pitcher of Eastport, New York, chooses a thin-skinned or somewhat older, more pliable lemon, cuts it in half, and turns the halves inside out. This makes it easy to rub the cavity evenly and neatly.

Pressing Crumb Crusts

Pressing graham cracker crumbs into a pie plate can be a messy proposition, especially when the crumbs start sticking to your warm hands. Barbara Lanoy Picarelli of Novato, California, keeps the process neat by sheathing her hands in plastic sandwich bags.

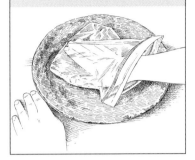

Filling Tube Pans with Batter

Many bakers have known the frustration of batter spilled down the hole in a tube pan. So did Michele Haley of North Berwick, Maine, until she decided to cover the hole with a paper cup.

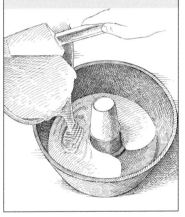

Caramel Safety

Authors Marie Piraino and Jamie Morris made many batches of caramel while developing the story on crème caramel in the September/October 1998 issue. To quickly combat burns that may result from an accident with hot sugar, they recommend keeping a bowl of ice water on hand.

Send Us Your Tip We will provide a complimentary one-year subscription for each tip we print. See page 1 for information.

Spice Storage Trick

It can be frustrating to sort through a sea of spice bottles, lifting and replacing each one, to find what you are looking for. Jenneke Reynolds of New Orleans, Louisiana, has found a way to make this easier, and Eric Aldrich of Hancock, New Hampshire, adds a method for keeping track of the age of your spices.

1. Using stick-on dots, write the name and purchase date on top of spice jars.
2. It is easy to locate and extract the spice you want and to know when it is time to discard spices. Dry spices should be discarded after one year.

No-Fuss Flouring

Hauling out a large flour canister can be a nuisance when all you have to do is dust a cake pan or work surface with flour. Jodi Palmquist of Bloomington, Minnesota, gets around this inconvenience by filling empty glass salt shakers with flour. These small, easy-to-reach shakers can also be filled with powdered sugar.

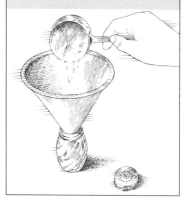

Making Homemade Lemonade Easier

Slicing and mashing the lemons for a full batch of lemonade from the July/August 1998 issue can be a tedious process. Several readers suggested alternatives.

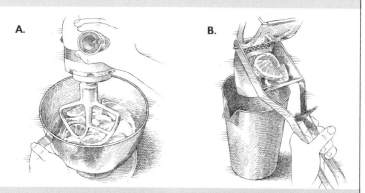

A. To cut down on the effort involved, Kay Norin of Tigard, Oregon, mashes the lemon slices and sugar together in the bowl of her standing mixer, using the paddle attachment. Just be sure to watch the timing, for if you over-mash the lemons, the drink will be bitter. We found 45 seconds on low speed to be just about right. To prevent splatters, drape a kitchen towel over the machine.

B. For those who may not have a standing mixer, Barbara McGuire of Santa Barbara, California, suggests sugaring the slices, letting them sit for 15 minutes or so to soften, and then mashing them in batches in a potato ricer right over the lemonade pitcher.

Easy Cake Handling

When garnishing the sides of a frosted cake with nuts or coconut, it's easy to make a mess. To keep the process neater and make handling the cake easier, Test Kitchen Director Susan Logozzo recommends the following: Cut a cardboard cake round slightly smaller than the cake and place the cake on top of it. Using the cake round, hold the cake over a bowl of chopped nuts or coconut by hand while applying the garnish to the sides of the cake.

Bacon Grease Management

In the South, bacon is a prized, oft-used flavor in everyday cooking, which can mean contending with a lot of drippings. Instead of keeping a bulky jar of drippings in the refrigerator, William Harris of Tallahassee, Florida, freezes them.
1. Melt the collected drippings in the microwave and let the solids settle at the bottom of the container. Then strain grease through a fine-mesh sieve.
2. Pour the liquid fat into an ice cube tray, which should be kept in a separate part of the freezer. Each cube will be approximately one heaping tablespoon.

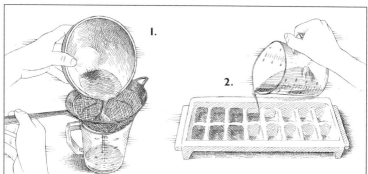

No-Stick Steaming

For Betty Bauer of Wichita, Kansas, and her family, steamed frozen Chinese dumplings and buns are a popular snack, but they often stick to the steamer and tear as she tries to remove them. To prevent this, she now lines her steamer with a sturdy lettuce leaf or two and then lays the food on the lettuce. This same method will work for any steamed pastry item.

Keeping the Stove Top Clean

Everyone knows how fat can splatter from a hot pan. Laurie Latour of Jacksonville, Florida, used to hate cleaning the mess left on the stove top after sautéing—but that was before she started laying a cookie sheet across the burners next to the pan. The cookie sheet, which is easy to clean in the sink or dishwasher, catches most of the grease, leaving the burner plates and stove top relatively clean.

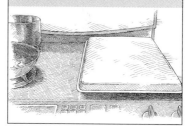

Freshening Stale Bread

The quick tip in our May/June 1998 issue for freshening stale bread in a dampened paper bag reminded Lou Pouschock of Appleton, Wisconsin, of his own method. He boils a 1-inch depth of water in a wide sauté or frying pan, places a splatter screen over the top of the pan, and then puts the bread on the screen. The rising steam softens the bread.

Best Bolognese Sauce

For the richest flavor and the most tender meat, simmer a mix of chuck, pork, and veal in milk, then wine, then canned tomatoes with their juice.

⪴ BY JACK BISHOP ⪵

I lived in Italy 15 years ago and became enamored of Bolognese, a dense, rich meat sauce spooned over fresh fettuccine or cheese ravioli or used to make lasagna. Of course there are scores of delicious meat-based sauces made in Italy and elsewhere, but I think slow-simmering Bolognese (it comes from the city of Bologna, hence the name) is the very best.

Unlike other meat sauces in which tomatoes dominate (think jars of spaghetti sauce with flecks of meat in a sea of tomato purée), Bolognese sauce is about the meat, with the tomatoes in a supporting role. Bolognese also differs from many tomato-based meat sauces in that it contains dairy—butter, milk, and/or cream. The dairy gives the meat an especially sweet, appealing flavor.

Bolognese sauce is not hard to prepare (the hands-on work is less than 30 minutes), but it does require hours of slow simmering. The sauce must be worth the effort. Bolognese should be complex, with a good balance of flavors. The meat should be first and foremost, but there should be sweet, salty, and acidic flavors in the background.

Over the years, I have probably made this sauce a hundred times. While it has never been bad, some recipes have clearly been better than others. I decided to cook Bolognese sauce in earnest (I made more than 20 batches in one week) to decide what makes a truly great version of this classic.

Important Characteristics

All Bolognese recipes can be broken down into three steps. First, vegetables are sautéed in fat. Ground meat is then browned in the pan. The final step is the addition of liquids and slow simmering over very low heat.

In the process, a good Bolognese sauce must acquire three important characteristics. It must be quite thick in order to heighten the richness and intensity of the beef flavor: Every mouthful should be decadent. The sauce should also be smooth, with the meat disintegrated into tiny pieces, so that it will easily coat the pasta.

Before starting this testing, I knew how to make a dense, smooth Bolognese sauce. My goal now was to achieve the third important trait, complex flavor. After an initial round of testing in which I made five different styles of Bolognese, I had a recipe I liked pretty well. I found that I pre-

This rich, smooth, thick sauce is best over fresh pasta; it is especially good with fettuccine or cheese ravioli.

ferred using only onions, carrots, and celery as the vegetables, and that I liked them sautéed in butter rather than oil. I also discovered that a combination of ground beef, veal, and pork made this sauce especially complex and rich tasting. The veal adds finesse and delicacy to the sauce, while the pork makes it sweet.

Settling on the liquid element of the recipe, however, proved more difficult.

Choosing the Right Liquids

The secret to a great Bolognese sauce is the sequential reduction of various liquids with the sautéed meat and vegetables. The idea is to build flavor and tenderize the meat, which has toughened during the browning phase. Many recipes insist on a particular order for adding these liquids. The most common liquid choices I uncovered in my research were milk, cream, stock, wine (both red and white), and tomatoes (fresh, canned whole, crushed, or paste). I ended up testing numerous combinations to find the perfect balance.

Liquids are treated in two ways. In the earlier part of the cooking process, liquids are added to the pan and simmered briskly until fully evaporated,

the point being to impart flavor rather than to cook the meat and vegetables. Wine is always treated this way; if the wine is not evaporated the sauce will be too alcoholic. Milk and cream are often but not always treated this way. Later, either stock or tomatoes are added in greater quantity and allowed to cook off very slowly. These liquids add flavor, to be sure, but they also serve as the "cooking medium" for the sauce during the slow simmering phase.

I tested pouring wine over the browned meat first, followed by milk. I also tried them in the opposite order, milk and then wine. I found that the meat cooked in milk first was softer and sweeter. As the bits of meat cook, they develop a hard crust that makes it more difficult for them to absorb liquid. Adding the milk first, when the meat is not crusty or tough, works better. The milk penetrates more easily, tenderizing the meat and making it especially sweet.

I tried using cream instead of milk but felt that the sauce was too rich. Milk provides just enough dairy flavor to complement the meat flavor. (Some recipes finish the sauce with cream. I found that cream added just before the sauce was done was also overpowering.)

So I settled on milk as the first liquid for the sauce. For the second liquid, I liked both white and red wine. White wine was a bit more delicate and is my choice for the master recipe below. Red wine made a more robust sauce that was also delicious and can be used in the variation with pancetta.

Now I moved on to the final element in most recipes, the cooking liquid. I did not like any of the recipes I tested with stock. Canned beef and chicken stock (I tried both) gave the sauce an odd chemical flavor when reduced so much. I tried using homemade beef stock as well as homemade chicken stock, but I did not think either was worth the considerable effort. As for the tomato paste, I felt that it had little to offer; with none of the bright acidity of canned whole tomatoes and

To achieve the very fine, smooth texture of Bolognese, crumble the ground meats with the edge of a wooden spoon as they cook so no clumps remain.

no fresh tomato flavor, it produced a dull sauce.

I tried tomatoes three more ways—fresh, canned whole, and canned crushed. Fresh tomatoes did nothing for the sauce and were a lot of work since I found it necessary to peel them. (If not peeled, the skins would separate during the long cooking process and mar the texture of the sauce.) Crushed tomatoes were fine, but they did not taste as good as the canned whole tomatoes that I chopped myself. Whole tomatoes have an additional benefit—the packing juice. Since Bolognese sauce simmers for quite a while, it's nice to have all that juice to keep the pot from scorching.

Final Refinements

My recipe was finally taking shape, with all the ingredients in place. But I still wanted to know if it was really necessary to cook Bolognese sauce over low heat and, if so, how long the sauce must simmer.

I found that long, slow simmering is necessary to tenderize the meat and build flavor. When I tried to hurry the process along by cooking over medium heat to evaporate the tomato juice more quickly, the meat was too firm and the flavors were not melded.

I also tried browning the meat and then simmering it in milk in a separate pan. At the same time, I browned vegetables in another, and then quickly reduced the wine and tomatoes over them. When the meat had absorbed all the milk, I added it to the tomato sauce and let it finish cooking for another 30 minutes. The whole process took an hour start to finish. The sauce was good, to be sure, but the flavor was not nearly as complex and the texture not as smooth and creamy.

I finally concluded that generations of Italian cooks have been right: Low simmering over the lowest possible heat—a few bubbles may rise to the surface of the sauce at one time but it should not be simmering all over—is the only method that allows enough time for flavor to develop and for the meat to become especially tender. In fact, the meat begins to fall apart into a creamy mass when the sauce is done. There is no way to speed up this process.

As for the timing, I found that the sauce was too soupy after two hours on low heat and the

meat was still pretty firm. At three hours, the meat was much softer, with a melt-in-the-mouth consistency. The sauce was dense and smooth at this point. I tried simmering the sauce for four hours but found no benefit. In fact, some batches cooked this long over-reduced and scorched a bit.

One final test involved browning the meat. Several sources suggest that deep browning builds flavor, a theory that makes some sense. However, other sources caution about overcooking the beef and suggest adding the first liquid to the pan as soon as the meat loses its raw color. I found this latter warning to be true. Sauces made with fully browned meat had a pleasant browned meat flavor, but the meat itself was not as tender and the sauce was not as smooth. When the first liquid was added to the pan as soon as the meat was no longer rosy, the sauce was more delicate and tender.

In the end, great Bolognese sauce is surprisingly simple to prepare. The ingredients are readily available (you probably have most of them on hand) and the results are definitely worth the slow, but not very taxing, cooking process.

CLASSIC BOLOGNESE SAUCE
MAKES GENEROUS 3 CUPS, ENOUGH TO SAUCE
1 POUND OF PASTA

Don't drain the pasta of its cooking water too meticulously when using this sauce; a little water left clinging to the noodles will help distribute the very thick sauce evenly into the noodles, as will adding an extra 2 tablespoons of butter along with the sauce. Top each serving with a little grated Parmesan and pass extra grated cheese at the table. If doubling this recipe, increase the simmering times for the milk and the wine to 30 minutes each, and the simmering time once the tomatoes are added to 4 hours.

3	tablespoons unsalted butter
2	tablespoons minced onion
2	tablespoons minced carrot
2	tablespoons minced celery
¾	pound meatloaf mix or ¼ pound each ground beef chuck, ground veal, and ground pork
	Salt
1	cup whole milk
1	cup dry white wine
1	can (28 ounces) whole tomatoes packed in juice, chopped fine, with juice reserved

1. Heat butter in large, heavy-

bottomed Dutch oven over medium heat; add onion, carrot, and celery and sauté until softened but not browned, about 6 minutes. Add ground meat and ½ teaspoon salt; following illustration at left, crumble meat with edge of wooden spoon to break apart into tiny pieces. Cook, continuing to crumble meat, just until it loses its raw color but has not yet browned, about 3 minutes.

2. Add milk and bring to simmer; continue to simmer until milk evaporates and only clear fat remains, 10 to 15 minutes. Add wine and bring to simmer; continue to simmer until wine evaporates, 10 to 15 minutes longer. Add tomatoes and their juice and bring to simmer; reduce heat to low so that sauce continues to simmer just barely, with an occasional bubble or two at the surface, until liquid has evaporated, about 3 hours (if lowest burner setting is too high to allow such a low simmer, use a flame tamer or, following illustrations on page 4, a foil ring to elevate pan). Adjust seasonings with extra salt to taste and serve. (Can be refrigerated in an airtight container for several days or frozen for several months. Warm over low heat before serving.)

BEEF BOLOGNESE SAUCE

There is something very appealing about the simplicity of an all-beef sauce; while it may lack some of the finesse and sweetness of the master recipe, its pure beef flavor is uniquely satisfying.

Follow recipe for Classic Bolognese Sauce, substituting ¾ pound ground beef chuck for meatloaf mix.

BEEF BOLOGNESE SAUCE WITH PANCETTA AND RED WINE

All ground beef works best with the pancetta in this sauce. If you can't find pancetta, use prosciutto, but don't use American bacon, which is smoked and will overwhelm the beef. Last, I found that red wine stands up to the more robust flavors in this sauce better than the white wine.

Follow recipe for Classic Bolognese Sauce, adding 2 ounces minced pancetta to butter along with vegetables, substituting ¾ pound ground beef chuck for meatloaf mix, and substituting an equal amount of red wine for white wine.

Use a flame tamer when you need to maintain the barest simmer. Commercial tamers work by adding a layer of metal between the pot and the heating element. You can fashion one that slightly elevates the pot above the flame using a ring of foil. *See* Quick Tips, page 4, for instructions.

French Onion Soup

We found most recipes for this French classic uninspiring.
Here's how we strived to return this soup to its original grandeur.

⇒ BY DAWN YANAGIHARA ⇐

French onion soup seems passé with today's trend toward lighter, healthier fare. But I love it, so if I see it on a menu, I'm inclined to order it. That is, before I remember that I've had one too many crocks of flavorless onions floating in hypersalty beef bouillon topped with globs of greasy melted cheese. The few French onion soups that I sampled in Paris were just the opposite: weak, watery, and nothing to write home about.

I almost never make French onion soup at home because I know what it involves. It's easily a two-day affair, one day making the beef stock and another toiling over the onions to finish the soup. And there's no guarantee that it will turn out to be what I see and taste in my mind. If I'm investing that much time and effort in a soup, I want to know it will be great, that every minute of simmering, slicing, and sautéing can be tasted. I want a dark, rich broth, intensely flavored by a plethora of seriously cooked onions, covered by a crouton that is broth-soaked beneath and cheesy and crusty on top. I was determined to uncover the makings of a French onion soup par excellence.

Take Stock

First, I gathered more than two dozen French onion soup recipes. I weeded out most of the recipes and ended up trying six, each quite different from the others. One soup was bland and watery, and two were excessively winey and—in the words of one taster—tasted like "swill." Those made with chicken broth, both homemade and canned, were, well, too chicken-y and just not right. The one made with the beef broth developed by *Cook's* executive editor Pam Anderson along with Melissa Hamilton (*see* "How to Make Flavorful Beef Soup," January/February 1998) was flavorful, beefy, and full-bodied. This rich broth simmers for only two hours, but I wanted to develop a quicker solution. After plenty of experimentation, I devised a formula for what I call "cheaters" broth.

This soup is best served in fairly deep, oven- and broiler-safe serving bowls instead of traditional flat soup plates, so that the croutons cover the whole top of the bowl.

By combining canned beef and chicken broths with red wine, I came up with a broth that has enough good, rich flavor to make an excellent soup base.

Go, Red, Go!

The next obvious step was to examine the onion factor. In addition to the standard yellow, white, and red onions at the grocery store, I was able to find the reputedly sweet and mild Vidalia onions. After a crying game of slicing many onions and sautéing away, my tasters and I agreed that the Vidalias were disappointingly bland and boring. White onions were candy sweet and one-dimensional. The yellows were only mildly flavorful with just a slight sweetness. Red onions ranked supreme. They were intensely onion-y, sweet but not cloying, with subtle complexity and nuance. A fluke, I thought, so I repeated the test with onions purchased from a different grocery store and got the same results.

Red onions were not, however, without their flaws. First, they were much harsher on the eyes when being sliced. Second, they discolored and made the soup a bluish-gray color so unappetizing that despite the soup's wonderful flavor and tan-

talizing cheese, diners would be hard put to finish the bowl.

To find a solution to the first problem, *Cook's* associate editor Adam Ried and I sliced pound after pound of onions to test tearless onion-cutting tips accumulated over the years. The suggestions ranged from the wacky to the mundane, with my favorite, practicality in mind, being a lit candle (*see* "Cry Me a River," page 10). The second problem, believe it or not, was much easier to solve. I turned to food scientist Shirley O. Corriher, author of *Cookwise* (Morrow, 1997). Her answer was to add some acid, either lemon juice or vinegar, to the soup at the end and watch it regain its color (*see* "Onion Soup Blues," page 9). It was incredible. It sounded like kitchen lore, but when I stirred in one tablespoon of balsamic vinegar, the soup returned to a deep reddish brown. I was transfixed like a child with a chemistry set! And not only did the soup look better, it tasted better. Just that small dose brightened the flavors and made me very happy.

The Long and the Short of It

I was appalled to find out just how much volume and weight the onions lose when they're cooked down. A whopping 3½ pounds of raw, sliced onions weighed in at less than 1 pound after nearly an hour of cooking. After making a few more soups, I concluded that 3 pounds of onions shrank down to just the right amount to yield a nice onion-to-broth ratio.

It was exasperating that the onions took so long—nearly an hour—to caramelize. On top of that, they required frequent stirring to keep them from sticking to the bottom of the pot and burning. I found that adding salt to the onions as they begin to cook helped draw out some of the water and shaved about 10 minutes off the cooking time. But I began to wonder if it was necessary for the onions to be so caramelized. I tried, as one recipe suggested, sautéing them until just softened and colored, but they didn't brown enough to contribute much flavor to the soup. Maybe, I thought, a vigorous sauté over high heat to achieve deep browning might do the trick. Not so. Onions cooked that way did not lose enough liquid and made the soup watery and bland. Besides, there is something wrong with onions in onion soup that have even an iota of crunch. I also tried roasting the onions, thinking that the even, constant heat of

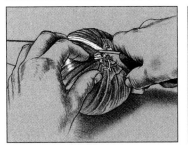

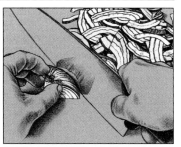

1. Cut off the tip of the blossom end (opposite the root end). Cut the onion in half lengthwise pole to pole.

2. Peel off the papery outer layer of skin. With the flat side facing down, cut each half in half lengthwise.

3. Holding two quarter pieces together, cut crosswise into 1/8-inch thick slices.

4. When you get close to the root end, flip each piece over separately on the other flat side and continue to slice.

the oven might be the answer. Wrong again. Going in and out of the oven to stir the onions is an incredible hassle.

It was inattentiveness that caused me to let the drippings in the pot of a batch of onions go a little too far. The onions themselves weren't thoroughly caramelized, but all the goo stuck on the pot was. I was sure that the finished soup would taste burnt, but I was surprised to find that it was, in fact, as sweet, rich, and flavorful as the soups I had been making with fully caramelized onions. To refine the technique I had stumbled on, I decided that medium-high heat was the way to go and that the drippings should be very, very deeply browned. There's no way around frequent stirring, but this method cut about another 10 minutes off the onion-cooking time, bringing it down to just over 30 minutes.

Soup's On

With all those wonderful, tasty drippings stuck on the bottom of the pot, the deglazing process of adding the liquid and scraping up all the browned bits is crucial. Once the broth is added to the onions, I found that a simmering time of 20 minutes is needed to allow the onion flavor to permeate the broth and for the flavors to meld.

Many French onion soup recipes call for herbs. A couple of sprigs of fresh parsley, some thyme, and a bay leaf simmered in the soup rounded out the flavors and imparted freshness. I also tried just a smidgen of garlic, but its flavor is far too distinct in a soup where onions should take center stage. Another common embellishment is cognac or brandy stirred into the soup at the end. It's a nice touch, I thought, enriching the soup and adding an element of intrigue. A few of my tasters found the soup too boozy, so I leave it to the cook's discretion.

Finally, I tried a little flour as a thickener, stirring it into the onions after they were cooked. It added body to the soup, but it also bogged down its flavor and muddied its appearance, just as I thought it would. The soup was excellent without it. Having arrived at a soup

that was rich, well-balanced, and full of fabulous onion flavor, it was time to move on to the crouton and the cheese, much to my tasters' delight.

Staying Afloat with the Grand Fromage

The first time my husband experienced French onion soup, he was disgusted to find a soggy napkin in his bowl. That "napkin" was the crouton. A mushy, sopping, disintegrating bread sponge was precisely what I wanted to avoid. Some recipes call for placing the crouton in the bottom of the bowl and ladling the soup over it. I disagree. I opt to set the crouton on top, so that only its bottom side is moistened with broth while its topside is crusted with cheese. The crouton can then physically support the cheese and prevent it from sinking into the soup. To keep as much cheese as possible on the surface, I found it best to use two croutons, instead of only one, to completely fill the mouth of the bowl. A baguette can be cut on the bias as necessary to secure the closest fit in the bowl. My tasters and I liked the croutons sliced three-quarters of an inch thick. Any thicker and it was overly bready; any less and it was insubstantial. I tried toasting the baguette slices, but toasted slices became soggy very quickly. Untoasted slices seemed to keep their texture better in the broth.

Some say that the cheese is the raison d'être of French onion soup. Traditionally, French onion soup is topped with Swiss, Gruyère, or Emmenthaler. I also ventured to cross the border to try Parmesan, Asiago, mozzarella, and fontina. Plain Swiss cheese was neither outstanding nor offensive. It was gooey, bubbly, and mild in characteristic Swiss flavor. Both Gruyère and Emmenthaler melted to perfection and were sweet, nutty, and faintly tangy, but they also were very strong and pungent, overwhelming my tasters' palettes and my own. We surprised ourselves by favoring the

To caramelize onions, cook until they become dark and syrupy.

subdued Italian Asiago. Its flavor, like that of Gruyère and Emmenthaler, was sweet and nutty, but without the pungent quality. Parmesan, too, was good, with a pleasant sweetness and saltiness, but without the nuttiness of Asiago. The big losers were mozzarella and Fontina. The first was extremely bland, too chewy, rubbery, and suggestive of pizza topping; the latter was very soft, almost wet and slippery, with no distinctive character.

Both Asiago and Parmesan are dry, not "melting," cheeses, so although we were leaning toward them in flavor, we were left wanting in texture. The obvious answer was to combine cheeses. I tried a layer of Swiss topped with a hefty sprinkling of Asiago. A winning combination, hands down, of chewy goodness and nutty sweetness.

French onion soup recipes generally specify grated cheese for the topping, but I did come across a couple that called for sliced cheese. I was working with two cheeses, one soft and one hard. It was more efficient to slice the soft Swiss cheese and set the slices in a single layer on top of the crouton, covering as much surface as possible. The hard Asiago, on the other hand, was better grated and sprinkled atop the Swiss. The final coup that weakens knees and makes

Onion Soup Blues

When my onion soup turned a sickly blue color, I panicked and called food scientist Shirley O. Corriher. Red onions, she explained, contain anthocyanin, a water-soluble pigment that also causes red cabbage to discolor when cooked. This pigment is present in some other reddish fruits and vegetables as well, such as cherries and radishes. (I recall making a cherry smoothie that turned a drab gray.)

Here's the story: Anthocyanin leaches out of the fruit or vegetable and into the surrounding liquid, if there is any. If the liquid is alkaline, the anthocyanin becomes blue. Add acid and it turns red. Corriher said it can go back and forth endlessly. In the case of my onion soup, if I cooked out the acid of the vinegar, the soup would become blue-gray again, requiring additional acid to regain its color. —D.Y.

French onion soup irresistible is a browned, bubbly, molten cheese crust. The quickest way to brown the cheese is to slip the bowls set on a baking sheet under the broiler, so heat-safe bowls are essential. Bowls or crocks with handles make maneuvering easier. This is no soup for fine china.

FRENCH ONION SOUP GRATINÉE
SERVES 6

Tie the parsley and thyme sprigs together with kitchen twine so they will be easy to retrieve from the soup pot. Slicing the baguette on the bias will yield slices shaped to fill the mouths of the bowls. For a soup that is resplendent with deep, rich flavors, use the Rich Beef Broth from the January/February 1998 issue in place of the canned chicken and beef broths and red wine.

    2   tablespoons unsalted butter
    5   medium red onions (about 3 pounds),
        sliced thin
        Salt
    6   cups low-sodium canned chicken broth
 1¾   cups low-sodium canned beef broth
   ¼   cup dry red wine
    2   sprigs fresh parsley
    1   sprig fresh thyme
    1   bay leaf
    1   tablespoon balsamic vinegar
        Ground black pepper

    1   baguette, cut on the bias into ¾-inch slices
        (2 slices per serving)
 4½   ounces Swiss cheese, sliced ¹⁄₁₆-inch thick
    3   ounces Asiago cheese, grated

1. Melt butter in large soup kettle or Dutch oven over medium-high heat; add sliced onions and ½ teaspoon salt and stir to coat onions thoroughly with butter. Cook, stirring frequently, until onions are reduced and syrupy and inside of pot is coated with very deep brown crust, 30 to 35 minutes. Stir in the chicken and beef broths, red wine, parsley, thyme, and bay leaf, scraping pot bottom with wooden spoon to loosen browned bits, and bring to simmer. Simmer to blend flavors, about 20 minutes, and discard herbs. Stir in balsamic vinegar and adjust seasonings with salt and pepper. (Can be cooled to room temperature and refrigerated in airtight container up to 2 days; return to simmer before finishing soup with croutons and cheese).

2. To serve, adjust oven rack to upper middle position; heat broiler. Set serving bowls on baking sheet and fill each with about 1½ cups soup. Top each bowl with two baguette slices and divide Swiss cheese slices, laying them in a single layer, if possible, on bread. Sprinkle with about 2 tablespoons grated Asiago cheese and broil until well browned and bubbly, about 10 minutes. Cool 5 minutes and serve.

Cry Me a River

Every now and then, something will prompt you to think of a particular song. In the *Cook's* test kitchen, that something occurred every time we had to slice another batch of onions for another pot of soup, and the song that came to mind, of course, was Arthur Hamilton's "Cry Me a River." As we started humming it for the umpteenth time, we began to wonder if we could change our tune to Johnny Nash's "I Can See Clearly Now."

Over the past couple of years, we have compiled more than 20 ideas from reader correspondence, books, and conversations with colleagues all aimed at reducing our tears while cutting onions. What better time than now, we thought, to put all those ideas to the test?

The problem, it turns out, derives from the sulfuric compounds in onions. Dr. Susan Brewer, Associate Professor of Food Chemistry at the University of Illinois, explained that when an onion is cut, the cells that are damaged in the process release sulfuric compounds as well as various enzymes, notably one called sulfoxide lyase. Those compounds, which are separated in the onion's cell structure, activate and mix to form the real culprit, a volatile new compound called thiopropanal sulfoxide. When thiopropanal sulfoxide evaporates into the air, it irritates the eyes, causing us to cry. Some sources we consulted even claim that the irritants produce a very mild form of sulfuric acid in the eyes.

Our tests, which are detailed along with their results in the chart below, ranged from common sense to comical. Overall, the two general methods that we found worked best were to protect our eyes by covering them with goggles or contact lenses or to introduce a flame near the cut onions. Dr. Brewer explained that the flame, which can be produced by either a lit candle or a gas burner, changes the activity of the thiopropanal sulfoxide by completely oxidizing it and probably deteriorates it, as well.   —Adam Ried and Dawn Yanagihara

No More Tears?

Two people, intense criers both, tried each method several times and rated its effectiveness on a scale of 1 to 10, 10 being the most effective and 1 being the least.

METHOD	RESULTS	EFFECTIVENESS
Wear contact lenses	Almost no tears onion after onion, but useless if you don't wear contacts	10
Wear ski or swimming goggles	Very effective, although, it makes you look like a kitchen terrorist	9
Burn a candle near the cutting board	Easy to do, and it worked pretty well	6.5
Place cutting board near a lit gas burner	Worked as well as a candle, but not terribly practical for those with electric burners	6.5
Refrigerate whole onion for 8 hours	Chilled onions; some tears	5
Refrigerate quartered onion for 8 hours	Even colder onions; some tears	5
Freeze onions for 30 minutes	Coldest onions; some tears	5
Hold a slice of bread in your mouth	Looked silly; didn't work consistently	5
Balance a slice of onion on your head	Talk about looking silly, but since it forces you to tilt your head up, your eyes are averted from the fumes and the tears do slow down a little	5
Hold a lit-and-put-out match in your teeth	Looked silly, but it worked better than the unlit match	4
Slice onions under a running faucet	We were so frustrated with the onion slices washing off the board that the tears didn't matter	3
Trim off ends of onion and microwave for 1 minute	Onions began to cook; minor tear reduction	3
Hold a toothpick in your teeth	Looked silly; we cried a lot	2
Work underneath an exhaust fan	Not at all effective under a home exhaust; very good under the test kitchen's professional-caliber exhaust	2
Tie a scarf (bandit style) around nose and mouth	Looked silly; minor tear reduction	1
Soak onion in ice water for 30 minutes	Wet onions; lots of tears	1
Blanch onions for 1 minute	Slimy onions; lots of tears	1
Wipe cutting board with vinegar	Vinegary onions; lots of tears	1
Slice onions next to a running faucet	Didn't work; lots of tears	1
Slice onions in large plastic bag opened at both ends	Awkward and dangerous because bag obstructs view, plus it didn't stop the tears	1
Hold an unlit match in your teeth	Looked silly; we cried a lot	1
Leave root end of onion intact	Didn't work	1

Stir-Fried Vegetables

Resist the twin temptations to toss in every vegetable in the refrigerator and to stir constantly while cooking.

⇒ BY EVA KATZ ⇐

A vegetable stir-fry does not mean digging through the vegetable bin and putting anything and everything into the pan. That makes the process cumbersome and the final products indistinguishable from each other. Instead, I like to keep the number of vegetables down to two or three. This makes it easier to time the cooking and to match the flavors with a complimentary blend of seasonings. The result is a dish with distinctive vegetable flavors that can be served with several Chinese-style dishes or as a side to grilled or roasted meats.

A hot pan allows the vegetables to char and caramelize—leave it on high heat for four or five minutes before you add the oil. It's a temptation when stir-frying (as the name would imply) to stir constantly, but once the vegetables are in the pan, wait 30 to 45 seconds between each round of stirring so the pan can regain its heat.

SPICY STIR-FRIED GREEN BEANS AND SCALLIONS
SERVES 4 AS A SIDE DISH

Try serving a double portion of these beans with rice as an entree.

- 2 tablespoons soy sauce, preferably light
- 1 tablespoon white or rice wine vinegar
- 2 teaspoons sugar
- 1/2 teaspoon hot red pepper flakes
- 2 tablespoons plus 1 teaspoon peanut or canola oil
- 3/4 pound green beans, stemmed and cut on bias into 1 1/2-inch pieces
- 4 scallions, white and bottom portion of green parts, cut into 2-inch pieces
- 3 medium garlic cloves, minced (about 1 tablespoon)

1. Mix soy sauce, vinegar, sugar, hot red pepper flakes, and 1 tablespoon water in small bowl; set aside.

2. Heat 12-inch heavy-bottomed skillet over high heat until extremely hot, at least 4 minutes. Carefully swirl 2 tablespoons oil in pan until bottom is evenly coated (oil will begin to shimmer and smoke almost immediately). Fry green beans, flipping with wide spatula every 30 seconds, until slightly charred and crisp-tender, about 4 minutes. Add scallions; continue cooking in same manner until scallions are charred and beans are tender, 3 to 4 minutes longer.

3. Make a well in center of pan; mash garlic and remaining 1 teaspoon oil in pan with back of spatula. Fry until fragrant, about 5 seconds, and stir into vegetables. Add soy mixture and toss into vegetables to coat; cook until liquid is reduced by about half, about 15 seconds. Serve immediately.

STIR-FRIED CARROTS AND PARSNIPS WITH GINGER, MAPLE, AND ANISE
SERVES 4 AS A SIDE DISH

- 2 tablespoons soy sauce, preferably light
- 2 tablespoons balsamic vinegar
- 1 tablespoon maple syrup
- 1 1/2 teaspoons anise or fennel seeds
- 2 tablespoons plus 1 teaspoon peanut or canola oil
- 3–4 small carrots (about 3/4 pound), cut into 1/2- x 2-inch sticks
- 3–4 small parsnips (about 3/4 pound), cut into 1/2- x 2-inch sticks
- 1 1 1/2-inch piece fresh ginger, minced (about 2 tablespoons)

1. Stir soy sauce, vinegar, maple syrup, and anise or fennel seeds in small bowl; set aside.

2. Follow step 2 of recipe for Spicy Stir-Fried Green Beans and Scallions, frying carrots first for about 2 minutes, then adding parsnips and frying for 5 to 6 minutes longer.

3. Follow step 3 of recipe for Spicy Stir-Fried Green Beans and Scallions, mashing ginger in pan in place of garlic and substituting maple mixture for soy mixture.

STIR-FRIED ASPARAGUS WITH RED PEPPERS AND ALMONDS
SERVES 4 AS A SIDE DISH

- 2 tablespoons soy sauce, preferably light
- 2 tablespoons rice wine vinegar
- 1 tablespoon sherry
- 1/4 teaspoon hot red pepper flakes
- 2 tablespoons plus 1 teaspoon peanut or canola oil
- 1 medium red bell pepper, cored, seeded, and cut into 1-inch square pieces
- 1 pound asparagus, tough ends snapped off and spears cut on the bias into 2-inch pieces
- 1 1 1/2-inch piece fresh ginger, minced (about 2 tablespoons)

- 3 medium garlic cloves, minced (about 1 tablespoon)
- 2–3 scallions, white and green parts, sliced thin (about 1/4 cup)
- 1/4 cup almonds, toasted and chopped

1. Stir soy sauce, rice wine vinegar, sherry, and red pepper flakes in small bowl; set aside.

2. Follow step 2 of recipe for Spicy Stir-Fried Green Beans and Scallions, frying peppers first for about 2 minutes, then adding asparagus and frying for 5 to 6 minutes longer.

3. Follow step 3 of recipe for Spicy Stir-Fried Green Beans and Scallions, mashing ginger and garlic together in pan and substituting rice-wine vinegar mixture for soy mixture. Serve with scallions and almonds sprinkled on top.

STIR-FRIED CABBAGE AND BEAN SPROUTS WITH CILANTRO AND LIME
SERVES 4 AS A SIDE DISH

The Southeast Asian flavors in this dish would complement a grilled flank steak and steamed rice.

- 2 tablespoons Asian fish sauce
- 2 tablespoons juice from 1 lime
- 1/2 teaspoon hot red pepper flakes
- 2 teaspoons sugar
- 1/2 teaspoon salt
- 2 tablespoons plus 1 teaspoon peanut or canola oil
- 1 small head green cabbage (about 1 1/2 pounds), halved, cored, and sliced thin
- 3 medium garlic cloves, minced (about 1 tablespoon)
- 2 cups bean sprouts
- 1/3 cup chopped fresh cilantro leaves
- 1/2 cup unsalted peanuts, toasted and chopped

1. Stir fish sauce, lime juice, hot red pepper flakes, sugar and salt in small bowl; set aside.

2. Follow step 2 of recipe for Spicy Stir-Fried Green Beans and Scallions, frying cabbage for about 4 minutes.

3. Follow step 3 of recipe for Spicy Stir-Fried Green Beans and Scallions, mashing garlic in pan and substituting lime juice mixture for soy sauce mixture. Toss cabbage with bean sprouts and cilantro and serve immediately, or at room temperature, with peanuts sprinkled on top.

Eva Katz, the former Test Kitchen Director of *Cook's Illustrated*, now lives in Brisbane, Australia.

Better Twice Baked Potatoes

Double bake the potato shells, choose the right dairy for the filling, and finish under the broiler to make this common side dish even better.

⇒ BY ADAM RIED WITH ANNE YAMANAKA ⇐

Roasted, baked, mashed, or French fried: No matter how you cook them, it's hard to go wrong with potatoes. Good as all those methods are, though, many would argue that the twice baked potato is at the very apex of potato cookery. And no wonder. This simple dish—essentially just baked russet potatoes from which the flesh has been removed, mashed with dairy ingredients, cheese, and seasonings, mounded back in the shells, and baked again—offers a range of both texture and flavor in a single morsel. Done well, the skin is chewy and substantial without being tough, with just a hint of crispness to play off the smooth, creamy filling. In terms of flavor, cheese and other dairy ingredients make the filling rich and tangy, a contrast to the mild, slightly sweet potato shell.

Twice baked potatoes are not difficult to make, but the two cooking stages do require a time commitment. Our goal, then, was to perfect every stage of the process—from baking the potatoes to readying the shells to preparing the filling to the final baking. Like any cook, if we were going to invest the time in these potatoes, we wanted the best possible results.

Baking Once

In "The Best Baked Potato" (*see* September/October 1995), we identified the type of potato and the procedure that produce the best baked potatoes: russets baked at 350 degrees for 75 minutes. The relatively low heat and the long cooking time create a particularly browned skin and outermost layer of flesh.

With that recipe in hand, we figured the initial baking stage of our work would be a breeze. Wrong. We tested the skins oiled and not oiled, oven temperatures from 350 to 450 degrees, baking times from 60 to 90 minutes, baking in foil for part and all of the cooking time, and cooking in the microwave oven. For our purposes, the best combination turned out to be baking a lightly oiled potato at 400 degrees for 60 minutes. With the 8-ounce potatoes we had decided to use, the flesh was dry, fluffy, thoroughly cooked, and soft for scooping out, while the skins were slightly crisped with an appealing sheen from the oil. In our recipe the longer baking time was unnecessary, because both flesh and skin were destined to be baked a second time. Our method also cut 15 minutes out of a process that could stand to be shortened.

A regular dinner spoon offered plenty of precision and control for scooping the potato flesh from the shells. Take care not to dig so deep that you rip through the skin.

Speaking of saving time, the microwave is worth mentioning. The quicker baked potatoes from the original article, which were microwaved at full power for 2 minutes and finished in a 450-degree oven for 35 minutes, had a somewhat inferior skin and slightly more watery, flat-tasting flesh than their oven-baked counterparts, but not so much as to be disastrous. If you are in a real rush, consider this option to cut the cooking time by another 20 minutes.

Splitting Up and Baking Twice

The baked potato recipe underscored the importance of opening the potatoes right after baking to release as much steam as possible. In keeping with that, we figured it would be best to halve the potatoes and scoop out the flesh immediately after taking them out of the oven. A few steam burns, however, dissuaded us. The potatoes are significantly easier to handle once they have cooled for a few minutes; because the flesh is mixed with wet ingredients, any compromise to the texture from unreleased moisture is negligible.

Once the potato halves had been emptied of their flesh, we noticed they got a little flabby sitting on the counter waiting to be stuffed. Because the oven was still on and waiting for the return of the stuffed halves, we decided to put the skins back in while we prepared the filling. That worked beautifully, giving the shells an extra dimension of crispness. We tried gilding the lily by oiling the skins again before they went back into the oven and even by brushing them with melted butter, but neither idea improved them.

And Broiling Makes Three

Pleased with our chewy, slightly crunchy skins, we now had to develop a smooth, lush, flavorful filling that would hold up its end of the bargain. (Lumpy, sodden, and dull tasting would not do.) Twice baked potatoes usually are filled with a mixture of well-mashed potato, shredded cheese, and other dairy ingredients, including one or more of the usual suspects: butter, sour cream, cream cheese, yogurt, ricotta, cottage cheese, milk, cream, and buttermilk. Various herbs and spices also often show up, as well as diced meats and sautéed vegetables.

To get an idea how we wanted to flavor our filling, we prepared 10 different recipes with various ingredient combinations. In a rare display of accord, all our tasters agreed on a few general observations. First, everyone preferred tangy dairy products, such as sour cream, yogurt, and buttermilk, to sweet ones, such as milk, cream, and ricotta. Second, the use of only one dairy ingredient produced a rather dull, one-dimensional filling. A second ingredient added depth of flavor and complexity. Third, nobody favored too fatty a mouthfeel, a preference that left the addition of large amounts of butter (some recipes use up to a full stick for four potatoes) and cream cheese out of the running. Finally, nobody liked the sweet flavor and coarse texture that diced, sautéed vegetables gave the filling, at least in the Master Recipe. Dozens of further tests helped us refine our filling to a rich, but not killer, combination of sharp cheddar, sour cream, buttermilk, and just two tablespoons of butter. We learned to season the filling aggressively with salt and pepper; for herbs, the slightly sharp flavor of scallions or chives was best.

With the filling mixed and mounded back into the shells, our last tests centered on the final baking. We wanted to do more than just heat the filling through; we aimed to form an attractive brown crust on it as well. We tried several combinations of oven temperature and rack setting but found that simply leaving the oven rack adjusted to the upper middle, where it had been

TECHNIQUE | THE RIGHT SLICE

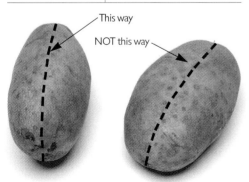

This way

NOT this way

Most potatoes have two relatively flat, blunt sides and two curved sides. Halve the baked potatoes lengthwise so the blunt sides are down once the shells are stuffed, making them much more stable on the pan during the final baking.

when the potatoes were first baked, and setting the oven to broil was easiest and most effective. After 15 minutes, the potatoes emerged browned, crusted, and ready for the table.

MASTER RECIPE FOR TWICE BAKED POTATOES
SERVES 6 TO 8

To vary the flavor a bit, try substituting other types of cheese, such as Gruyère, fontina, or feta, for the cheddar. Yukon gold potatoes, though slightly more moist than our ideal, gave our twice baked potatoes a buttery flavor and mouthfeel that everyone liked, so we recommend them as a substitution for the russets.

- 4   russet potatoes (7 to 8 ounces each), scrubbed, dried, and rubbed lightly with vegetable oil
- 4   ounces sharp cheddar cheese, shredded (about 1 cup)
- ½   cup sour cream
- ½   cup buttermilk
- 2   tablespoons unsalted butter, room temperature
- 3   medium scallions, white and green parts sliced thin (about ½ cup)
- ½   teaspoon salt
       Ground black pepper

1. Adjust oven rack to upper middle position and heat oven to 400 degrees. Bake potatoes on foil-lined baking sheet until skin is crisp and deep brown and skewer easily pierces flesh, about 1 hour. Setting baking sheet aside, transfer potatoes to wire rack and let sit until cool enough to handle, about 10 minutes.

2. Following illustration at left and using an oven mitt or folded kitchen towel to handle hot potatoes, cut each potato in half so that blunt sides will rest on work surface. Using a small dinner spoon, scoop flesh from each half into medium bowl, leaving a ⅛-inch to ¼-inch thickness of flesh in each shell. Arrange shells on lined sheet and return to oven until dry and slightly crisped, about 10 minutes. Meanwhile, mash potato flesh with fork until smooth. Stir in remaining ingredients, including ground black pepper to taste, until well combined.

3. Remove shells from oven and increase oven setting to broil. Holding shells steady on pan with oven mitt or towel-protected hand, spoon mixture into crisped shells, mounding slightly at the center, and return to oven. Broil until spotty brown and crisp on top, 10 to 15 minutes. Allow to cool for 10 minutes. Serve warm.

TWICE BAKED POTATOES WITH PEPPERJACK CHEESE AND BACON

Fry 8 strips (about 8 ounces) bacon, cut crosswise into ¼-inch pieces, and cook in medium skillet over medium heat until crisp, 5 to 7 min-

utes. Remove bacon to paper towel–lined plate to drain; set aside. Follow Master Recipe for twice baked potatoes, substituting pepperjack cheese for cheddar and stirring reserved bacon into filling mixture.

TWICE BAKED POTATOES WITH INDIAN SPICES AND PEAS

Heat 2 tablespoons butter in medium skillet over medium heat; sauté one medium onion, chopped fine (about 1 cup), until soft, 3 to 4 minutes. Add 1 teaspoon finely grated gingerroot, 3 minced medium garlic cloves, 1 teaspoon each ground cumin and ground coriander, and ¼ teaspoon each ground cinnamon, ground turmeric, and ground cloves; cook until fragrant, about 30 seconds more, taking care not to brown garlic or ginger. Off heat, stir in 1 cup thawed frozen peas; set aside. Follow Master Recipe for twice baked potatoes, omitting cheese and butter and stirring reserved spiced peas into filling mixture.

TWICE BAKED POTATOES WITH CHIPOTLE PEPPER AND ONION

For a slightly smoky aftertaste with just a hint of heat, limit the chipotle pepper to 1 tablespoon. For a little bit of upfront heat, increase the chipotle to 1½ tablespoons.

Heat 2 tablespoons butter in medium skillet over medium heat; sauté one medium onion, chopped fine (about 1 cup) until soft, 3 to 4 minutes, and set aside. Follow Master Recipe for twice baked potatoes, omitting butter and adding 1 to 1½ tablespoons minced canned chipotle peppers in adobo sauce, reserved sautéed onion, and 2 tablespoons chopped fresh cilantro leaves to filling mixture.

TWICE BAKED POTATOES WITH MONTEREY JACK AND PESTO

Follow Master Recipe for twice baked potatoes, substituting Monterey Jack cheese for the cheddar, reducing buttermilk to ¼ cup, omitting butter, and adding ¼ cup prepared or homemade basil pesto (*see* "Pesto at its Best," July/August 1996) to filling mixture.

TWICE BAKED POTATOES WITH SMOKED SALMON AND CHIVES

This variation makes a fine brunch dish.

Follow Master Recipe for twice baked potatoes, omitting cheese and scallions and stirring 4 ounces smoked salmon, cut into ½-inch pieces, and 3 tablespoons minced fresh chives into filling mixture. Sprinkle finished potatoes with additional chopped chives as garnish just before serving.

Why Make Coq au Vin?

That was our question until we rediscovered (and then streamlined) this timeless recipe for home cooks.

⇒ BY STEPHANIE LYNESS ⇐

I remember discovering coq au vin in the late 1960s when French food was taking hold in my mother's kitchen, as it was in the rest of America. This classic fricassee of cut-up chicken cooked in a red-wine sauce and finished with a garnish of bacon, tiny glazed pearl onions, and sautéed mushrooms was a giant step away from chicken cooked under a blanket of cream of mushroom soup. Some years later I ran into this dish again at cooking school in France. But if I've cooked coq au vin in the 15 years since then I don't remember: although it's as familiar to me as almost any dish in my repetoire, it simply isn't a dish that I make at home.

Why not, I wondered? As I thought back, I discovered that after falling in love with coq au vin at age 14, those versions of the dish that I had cooked and tasted since then had universally disappointed me. In high school it was enough that coq au vin taste exotic. These days, if I'm going to peel all those baby onions, I want to be thrilled with the results. And I didn't see why I couldn't be. At its best, coq au vin should be hugely tasty, the acidity of the wine rounded out by rich, salty bacon and sweet, caramelized onions and mushrooms. The chicken should act like a sponge, soaking up those same dark, rich flavors. I set about creating a recipe that would satisfy my appetite for a really great coq au vin.

From Serviceable to Sensational

I started out by cooking and tasting a number of recipes from French cookbooks. As I cooked, I noticed that the recipes fell into two categories: those that were simpler and more provincial in character, and one that was more complicated and promised to be a more refined taste. The recipes in the first category were versions of a straightforward brown fricassee. Tasting these simpler versions, I recognized them as the serviceable coq au vins of recent memory. The sauces were good but not extraordinary. The chicken tasted mostly like chicken. In short, the recipes weren't special enough to merit the time they demanded.

I moved on to testing a much more complicated recipe from Madeleine Kamman's *The New Making of a Cook* (William Morrow, 1998). This two-day affair was also a brown fricassee, but with a much more elaborate sauce. The recipe began by combining red wine with veal stock and browned vegetables and reducing this mixture by about

The bacon-mushroom-onion garnish is cooked separately so the flavor remains distinct from the wine-soaked chicken.

half. The chicken was then browned and the pan deglazed with the reduced wine mixture. Once the chicken was cooked, the sauce was strained, bound first with a beurre manié (a paste of mashed butter and flour), and then with a bit of chicken liver pureed with heavy cream; the bound sauce was finished with flambéed cognac.

Although it was built on the same basic model as the others, this dish was in a whole different league. It was what a good coq au vin ought to be—the sauce beautifully textured, clear flavored, and rich without being heavy or murky. The chicken was drenched in flavor. Though I was able to make it in just one day instead of the two that Kamman posited, the recipe unquestionably demanded more time, more last-minute fussing, and a lot more dishes (in addition to a blender) than the recipes I'd made before.

What Makes the Difference?

This recipe got my attention. What was going on that made it so good? Were all of those steps actually necessary, or could I isolate one or two that really made the difference? Clearly there was something to be learned here about how to make a great red wine sauce, but in this recipe even the chicken tasted better. Why?

As I compared Kamman's recipe with the oth-

ers, two techniques stood out. First, Kamman bound her sauce differently—with a beurre manié and chicken liver—rather than sprinkling the meat or vegetables with flour at the beginning. Kamman also used all chicken legs instead of both legs and breasts as the other recipes did. Finally, Kamman's recipe was the only one that reduced the wine with the stock and aromatics before adding the chicken; the others used raw wine.

I first tested a coq au vin bound with a beurre manié and compared it with one in which the vegetables were sprinkled with flour. I liked using the beurre manié far better because it gave me more control over the thickness of the sauce. With the latter technique, I was forced to choose a measurement of flour without knowing what the final measurement of liquid would be.

I found that I also agreed with Kamman's use of legs only. Not only do the legs add more flavor to the sauce because they cook longer than the breasts, but, as Kamman points out, the breasts don't cook long enough in the wine to take on much wine flavor; they taste insipid compared with the legs. Further testing demonstrated that thighs worked as well as whole legs.

Finally, I tested a recipe in which the wine was reduced by half before it was cooked with the chicken against a recipe in which the wine was added to the pan raw and reduced at the end, after the chicken was cooked. There was a readily discernable difference in taste between the two: the first sauce, in which the wine had been reduced early on, was much less astringent, tasting full and round; the other tasted raw and somewhat sweet in comparison. The better sauce tasted more of chicken as well, so the flavor was more interesting and complex. There was even a noticeable difference in the taste of the chicken itself. The chicken in the first test tasted better because it tasted of the cooked, reduced wine; the other had the harsh, sweet flavor of raw wine. In addition, it was a boon not to have to reduce the sauce at the end when I had other things to do.

A Really Great Coq au Vin

Having determined that beurre manié, dark meat, and a preliminary reduction of the wine were key to the success of my dish, I ran some final tests to find out if the addition of cognac, chicken liver, or tomato paste improved the sauce enough to merit the extra trouble. While cognac was a refinement that I could taste, I liked the sauce well enough without it. The chicken liver mellowed the taste of the sauce by balancing the acidity of the wine, and it added body; but since its addition required two more steps and I liked the sauce without it, I nixed the liver. Tomato paste, however, was simple to whisk in, and, as it furnished some of the extra flavor and body that a true veal stock would add, I decided to use it.

Kamman's recipe also called for using pork brisket or pancetta in lieu of bacon, neither of which is smoked, as bacon is; I wondered whether it was worth the extra trouble to find either. Finally, I played with the proportions of chicken stock and wine to arrive at a sauce with a wine flavor that was rich and full but not overpowering.

This, at last, was a relatively simple coq au vin that was truly worth making.

A BETTER COQ AU VIN
SERVES 4

If you have the time to blanch and skin them, fresh pearl onions are terrific. Simply cut an "x" in the root end, blanch them in boiling water for 30 seconds, remove them with a slotted spoon, and refresh them in a bowl of ice water. Then slice off the very tip of the roots with a paring knife and squeeze the onions gently from the blossom end. They will pop right out of their skins.

4	whole chicken legs (about 3 pounds), carefully trimmed of all fat, cleaned, dried, and thighs and drumsticks separated
	Salt and ground black pepper
1	bottle (750 ml) medium-bodied, fruity red wine, such as Oregon Pinot Noir, Zinfandel, or a light Rhone valley wine
2½	cups chicken stock or low-sodium canned chicken broth
6	ounces bacon (preferably thick-cut), cut crosswise into ¼-inch pieces
6–7	tablespoons unsalted butter, at room temperature
1	large carrot, roughly chopped
1	large onion, roughly chopped
2	medium shallots, peeled and quartered
2	medium garlic cloves, skin on and smashed
1	teaspoon dried thyme leaves, 10 parsley stems, and 1 bay leaf (bouquet garni)
1½	teaspoons tomato paste
24	frozen pearl onions (evenly sized), thawed, or fresh pearl onions (see above)
½	pound small white mushrooms, washed and halved if medium sized, quartered if large
2–3	tablespoons all-purpose flour
2	tablespoons minced fresh parsley leaves

1. Generously sprinkle chicken pieces with salt and ground black pepper; set aside. Bring red wine and chicken stock to boil in large, heavy saucepan; reduce heat to medium-high and simmer until reduced to about 4 cups, about 20 minutes.

2. Meanwhile, fry bacon in large Dutch oven or deep, heavy-bottomed sauté pan over medium heat until fat has rendered and bacon is golden brown, about 5 minutes. Remove bacon with slotted spoon to paper towel–lined plate to drain; set aside. Heat 1 tablespoon butter with rendered bacon fat; add carrot, onion, shallots, and garlic and sauté until lightly browned, 10 to 15 minutes. Following illustration 1, below, press vegetables against side of pan with slotted spoon to squeeze out as much fat as possible; transfer vegetables to pan with reduced wine mixture (off heat) and discard all but 1 tablespoon fat from Dutch oven or sauté pan.

3. Return Dutch oven or sauté pan to burner over medium-high heat and add another 1 tablespoon butter. When butter is melted, add chicken (in batches if necessary to avoid overcrowding) and cook until well browned all over, turning once or twice during cooking, 12 to 16 minutes. Remove chicken to a plate; set aside. Pour off all fat from Dutch oven or sauté pan; return to heat and add wine-vegetable mixture. Bring to boil, scraping up browned bits from bottom of pan with wooden spoon (see illustration 2, below.) Add browned chicken, bouquet garni, and tomato paste to boiling wine mixture; return to boil, then reduce heat to low and simmer gently, partially covered. Turn chicken once during cooking, until tender and infused with wine flavor, 45 to 60 minutes.

4. While chicken and sauce are cooking, heat another 2 tablespoons butter in medium skillet over medium-low heat. Add pearl onions and cook, stirring occasionally and reducing heat if butter starts to brown too fast, until lightly browned and almost cooked through, 5 to 8 minutes. Add mushrooms, season with salt, cover, increase heat to medium, and cook until mushrooms release their liquid, about 5 minutes. Remove cover, increase heat to high, and boil until liquid evaporates and onions and mushrooms are golden brown, 2 to 3 minutes more. Transfer onions and mushrooms to plate with bacon; set aside.

5. When the chicken is cooked, transfer to serving bowl or platter; cover with aluminum foil to keep warm. Following illustration 3, below, strain sauce through fine mesh sieve set over large measuring cup, pressing on solids with wooden spoon to release as much liquid as possible; sauce should measure 2 to 3 cups. Return sauce to pan; skim as much fat as possible off surface. Counting 1 tablespoon each of butter and flour for each cup of sauce, mash 2 to 3 tablespoons each butter and flour in small bowl or plate to make a beurre manié, as shown in illustration 4. Bring sauce to boil and whisk in beurre manie until smooth. Add reserved chicken, bacon, onions and mushrooms; adjust seasoning with salt and ground black pepper to taste, reduce heat to medium-low and simmer very gently to warm through and blend flavors, about 5 minutes. Check seasoning one more time and adjust with additional salt and ground black pepper if necessary; add parsley. Transfer chicken to serving platter; pour sauce over chicken. Serve immediately.

STEP-BY-STEP | KEY STEPS TO COQ AU VIN

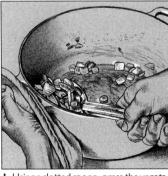

1. Using a slotted spoon, press the vegetables against the side of the pan to remove the fat after sautéing them.

2. Add wine-vegetable mixture, then use a wooden spoon to scrape up the caramelized material on the bottom.

3. After the vegetables have been cooked in the wine-broth liquid, press them in a strainer to release the juices.

4. Mash together equal amounts of butter and flour, then whisk into the simmering sauce to thicken it.

Kitchen Efficiency

Next to washing your hands, one of the first and fundamental lessons of cooking school is ***mise en place,*** a French term that means having all your ingredients and equipment prepared and in place before proceeding with a recipe. While ***mise en place*** (pronounced MEEZ-ahn-plahs) can be a trying lesson in efficiency for the disorganized, it makes cooking simpler and more enjoyable, and it improves the success rate of a recipe. While every cook's methods are as individual as his or her kitchen, the following tips on kitchen efficiency, which were compiled from interviews with professionally trained chefs, cookbook authors, and avid home cooks, can be adopted by anyone in a home kitchen. They are organized according to kitchen work spaces. By Maryellen Driscoll

AT THE CUTTING BOARD

Cook's former test kitchen director Eva Katz recommends always using the largest cutting board available and placing a damp towel underneath to keep the board from slipping. The smaller the cutting board space, the more clumsy and accident-prone your work is likely to be.

If the trash can or compost bin is not nearby, keep a wide-mouthed container or bowl by your cutting board to discard scraps as you work.

If you are chopping a lot of ingredients, assemble enough small bowls or containers next to your work space to hold them all.

Melissa Hamilton, a regular contributor to *Cook's,* suggests using a damp paper towel to cover bowls of ingredients, such as chopped fresh parsley, that are not going to be used immediately and need to be kept fresh.

In our test kitchen, the central work space is on an island across from the stove, so test cook Dawn Yanagihara always places her prepared bowls of ingredients on a cookie sheet. This way everything can be transferred over to the stove at once. If the ingredients must be added in a specific order, such as for a stir-fry, she assembles them in that order.

Regularly clean up scraps with the side of your knife or with a dough scraper kept at hand. Slice the messiest ingredients, such as tomatoes, last.

IN THE BAKING ARENA

Store flours and sugars in wide-mouth canisters so you can comfortably dip and sweep to measure and so that overflow spills back into the canister instead of onto the counter.

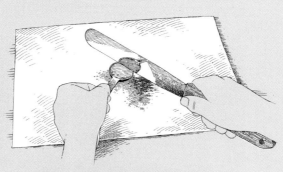

Publisher and Editor Christopher Kimball measures ingredients such as spices, leaveners, flour, and salt over a piece of paper towel, wax paper, or parchment (not over the mixing bowl). Spills can then be slid back into their containers easily.

Illustration: John Burgoyne

IN THE BAKING ARENA

To keep track of how many eggs you have cracked, put broken shells back into the carton as you are working.

When measuring liquid ingredients for baking, pour liquids into clear measuring cups set on the counter and lean down to read them at eye level. Because holding a cup up will jostle or tilt the liquid, it can destroy the accuracy of measurement that might make all the difference when baking.

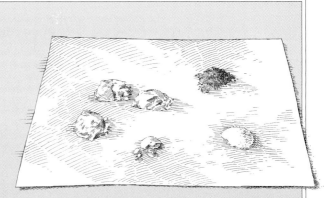

When a recipe calls for a number of dry ingredients to be added simultaneously, place ingredients in separate spoonful mounds on a sheet of parchment. This way you can see not only what but also how much you have measured, which prevents you from losing track if you're interrupted.

AT THE STOVE TOP

Store pot holders within immediate reach of the stove for safety as well as convenience. Also, so that you don't have to go looking for a towel to wipe your hands or clean up a spill, keep a towel tucked into the waistband of your apron or slung over your shoulder.

Senior writer Jack Bishop stores bottles of vinegar and soy sauce near the stove. He lines a shelf with a paper bag, which he can easily replace when it becomes dirty and sticky.

Store your most commonly used cooking utensils, such as spatulas, wooden spoons and tongs, in a canister by the stove, so you don't have to fish through a drawer to find them.

Keep a small bowl of salt next to the stove. It's easier to control the amount of salt you're using if you pinch rather than shake it. A bowl is also easy to dip into with a measuring spoon.

Keep a small stainless steel pitcher of oil next to the stove top and store the remaining large tin or bottle away from light and heat to preserve its freshness.

Turn pot handles toward the back of the stove to protect both children and adults from accidental burns and spills.

Keep another, smaller container by the stove for those small, hard-to-find, and perhaps breakable items, such as candy thermometers, instant-read thermometers, cake testers, and scissors.

Tender Shrimp Scampi

Low-heat cooking—closer to braising than sautéing—creates plump, tender shrimp with plenty of delicious, natural-tasting liquid.

≥ BY MARK BITTMAN ≤

Our version of shrimp scampi is quite simple, with no breading, batter, or deep frying to obscure the fresh flavor of the shrimp itself.

In my childhood, we ate shrimp scampi at a number of different restaurants in New York's Little Italy. Unlike most dishes served in these strictly Italian-American establishments, scampi was neither tomato-based nor deep-fried. In fact, it was—or seemed—about as simple a dish as there could be: shrimp in a light sauce, smacking of garlic and lemon, garnished with parsley.

It was nearly 30 years from the time I left home until I had another satisfactory restaurant encounter with shrimp scampi. In the intervening time, I was served everything from batter-dipped, deep-fried shrimp drenched in bad oil to boiled shrimp and tomato sauce on a bed of pasta. Even back in Little Italy the shrimp were often fried to crispness and drenched in butter or olive oil. It took a trip to Venice to remind me what a simple pleasure this dish could be—the shrimp lightly cooked and moist, the seasonings fresh and minimal, the surrounding liquid light, plentiful, natural tasting, and delicious.

When it came time to re-create that dish, I found it a challenge to cook the shrimp in a way that produced that wonderful juice, which is so good for dunking bread or for moistening rice or even pasta. I tried adding every liquid I could think of that might fit the bill: white wine (of course), lemon juice, more olive oil, fish and chicken stock, even water. The wine and lemon juice added too much acidity; the extra oil made the dish, well, too oily; the stocks and water diluted the flavor of the shrimp. During all of these trial runs, I also played with the heat level. I found that an overly high heat not only caused the garlic to become overdone and bitter but also toughened the shrimp.

As I lowered the heat for cooking, I noticed that the liquid given off by the shrimp lingered in the pan. Could this be the elusive liquid I was searching for? I set out to do everything I could to focus on these shrimp juices, cooking slowly, as if I were braising in the olive oil and natural juices. In fact, because the goal is to preserve the liquid and the tenderness of the shrimp rather than create crispness, the technique is actually closer to braising than sautéing.

Once I started moving in this direction, everything fell into place. With lower heat, the garlic becomes tender and mild-flavored rather than bitter, the olive oil retains its freshness, and the shrimp remains moist and tender—there's little danger of overcooking. I added the lemon juice and parsley at the last possible minute, almost as a garnish, and both kept their sparkle as well. An unexpected benefit of this technique was that it opened up some great possibilities for variations on the basic recipe.

Finally, a serving suggestion. Although this dish goes very well with rice, it is really at its best with bread. Make it in a cast-iron skillet, and bring the pan to the table; serve the shrimp with a spoon, and use the bread to sop up remaining juices from both plate and skillet—there are few greater pleasures.

SIMPLE SHRIMP SCAMPI
SERVES 4

Cayenne pepper replaces ground black pepper in this recipe, but use it sparingly, only to give the faintest hint of spiciness.

- 1/4 cup extra-virgin olive oil
- 4 medium garlic cloves, minced
- 2 pounds large shrimp (21 to 25 count per pound), peeled, deveined, and rinsed
- 1/4 cup minced fresh parsley leaves
- 2 tablespoons juice from 1 lemon
  Salt
  Cayenne pepper

Heat oil and garlic in 10-inch skillet over medium heat until garlic begins to sizzle. Reduce heat to medium-low and cook until fragrant and pale gold, about 2 minutes. Add shrimp, increase heat to medium and cook, stirring occasionally, until shrimp turn pink, about 7 minutes. Be careful not to overcook or the shrimp will become tough. Off heat, stir in parsley, lemon juice, and salt and cayenne pepper to taste. Serve immediately.

SCAMPI–STYLE SHRIMP WITH CUMIN, PAPRIKA AND SHERRY VINEGAR

This dish is deeply flavorful but has slightly less heat than either of the other two versions.

Follow recipe for Simple Shrimp Scampi, sautéing 1 teaspoon ground cumin and 2 teaspoons paprika with garlic, omitting cayenne, and substituting an equal amount of sherry vinegar for lemon juice.

SPICY SCAMPI–STYLE SHRIMP WITH ORANGE ZEST AND CILANTRO

Because it is spicy, this dish is best served with white rice.

Follow recipe for Simple Shrimp Scampi, sautéing 1 teaspoon finely grated orange zest and 1/4 teaspoon red pepper flakes with garlic, omitting cayenne, and substituting 2 tablespoons minced fresh cilantro leaves for parsley.

Taming Broccoli Rabe

Blanching in plenty of salted water before further cooking helps remove bitterness and makes broccoli rabe tender.

⇒ BY ANNE YAMANAKA ⇐

A good friend of mine loves the big, bold, in-your-face flavor of broccoli rabe. He simply sautés it up with a little olive oil and a lot of garlic, grabs some bread, and voila! it's ready to eat. I've tried cooking broccoli rabe that way; it's delicious, but I find it a little overwhelming as well. For me, a perfect plate of broccoli rabe should be intensely flavored but not intensely bitter; I also want to taste the other ingredients and flavors in the dish. So I set my sights on developing a dependable, quick method of cooking this aggressive vegetable that would deliver less bitterness and a rounder, more balanced flavor.

I began my testing by braising the broccoli rabe, figuring that a slow simmer in liquid might mellow its harshness. Unfortunately, it turned an unattractive army-issue green and remained far too bitter for my taste. I then turned my attention to an article by Pam Anderson and Karen Tack, "How to Quick-Cook Strong-Flavored Greens" (January/February, 1996). During their kitchen investigations Anderson and Tack discovered that parcooking the greens helped to carry off some of the bitter flavor. Armed with that information, I knew I had three options: steaming, shallow blanching, or deep blanching, all of which would be followed by a quick sauté with olive oil and garlic.

Steaming produced little change in the broccoli rabe. It was still too intense for both me and my fellow tasters. Blanched in a small amount of salted boiling water (1 quart of water for about 1 pound of broccoli rabe), the rabe was much better. In fact, some tasters liked the rabe prepared that way best. But the bitterness was still overwhelming for me, so I increased the boiling salted water to three quarts. Sure enough, the broccoli rabe was delicious; it was complex, mustardy, and peppery as well as bitter, and the garlic and olive oil complemented rather than competed with its flavor. Depending on personal taste, you can reduce the amount of blanching water for stronger flavor or, to really to tone down the bitterness, increase it.

As I was testing the different cooking methods, I had to decide how much of the stem to use and whether to peel it. Some recipes I referenced included the stems, some did not. After considerable testing, I found that the lower 2 inches or so were woody and tough, while the upper portions of the stems were tender enough to include in the recipes. When I used only the upper portions, there was no need to go through the laborious task of peeling the stems. Cutting the stems into pieces about 1 inch long made them easier to eat and allowed them to cook in the same amount of time as the florets and the leaves.

Now that I had a cooking method I liked, I was ready to add other flavors to the recipe. That was much more difficult than I had imagined. Ingredients I was sure would go well with this vegetable, such as olives, citrus zest, and strong vinegars, tasted extremely harsh when paired with the rabe. I found that anything highly acidic or bitter in flavor clashed with the strong flavor of the vegetable. Unexpectedly, I discovered that ingredients that are sweet (sun-dried tomatoes, sweet red peppers), salty (anchovies, soy sauce), spicy (any hot fresh or dried pepper), pungent (garlic, onions), or nutty complement the broccoli rabe, balancing and rounding out its sharp edge.

BLANCHED BROCCOLI RABE
MAKES ABOUT 3½ CUPS

Using a salad spinner makes easy work of drying the cooled blanched broccoli rabe.

- 1   bunch broccoli rabe (about 14 ounces), washed, bottom 2 inches of stems trimmed and discarded, remainder cut into 1-inch pieces
- 2   teaspoons salt

1. Bring 3 quarts water to boil in large saucepan. Stir in broccoli rabe and salt and cook until wilted and tender, about 2½ minutes. Drain broccoli rabe and set aside.

2. Cool empty saucepan by rinsing under cold running water. Fill cooled saucepan with cold water and submerge broccoli rabe to stop the cooking process. Drain again; squeeze well to dry and proceed with one of the following recipes.

BROCCOLI RABE WITH GARLIC AND RED PEPPER FLAKES
SERVES 4

This recipe and the following one can be turned into main course pasta dishes. Increase the oil to 4 tablespoons and toss the broccoli rabe with 1 pound of pasta, cooked al dente. Season to taste with salt and ground black pepper, and serve with grated Parmesan cheese.

- 2   tablespoons extra-virgin olive oil
- 3   medium garlic cloves, minced
- ¼   teaspoon red pepper flakes
- 1   recipe Blanched Broccoli Rabe
     Salt

Heat oil, garlic, and red pepper flakes in medium skillet over medium heat until garlic begins to sizzle, about 3 to 4 minutes. Increase heat to medium high, add blanched broccoli rabe, and cook, stirring to coat with oil, until heated through, about 1 minute. Season to taste with salt; serve immediately.

BROCCOLI RABE WITH SUN-DRIED TOMATOES AND PINE NUTS

Follow recipe for Broccoli Rabe with Garlic and Red Pepper Flakes, adding ¼ cup oil-packed sun-dried tomatoes, cut into thin strips, along with garlic and red pepper flakes. Add 3 tablespoons toasted pine nuts to skillet along with broccoli rabe.

BROCCOLI RABE WITH ASIAN FLAVORS

Adapted from a recipe in Chris Schlesinger and John Willoughby's *Lettuce in Your Kitchen* (Morrow, 1996).

Mix 1 tablespoon soy sauce, 1½ teaspoons rice wine vinegar, 1 teaspoon Asian sesame oil, and 1 teaspoon sugar in small bowl; set aside. Follow recipe for Broccoli Rabe with Garlic and Red Pepper Flakes, substituting vegetable oil for olive oil and adding ½ teaspoon finely grated fresh ginger along with garlic and red pepper flakes. Add reserved soy sauce mixture to skillet along with broccoli rabe.

Broccoli rabe, which is actually a form of turnip green, is also known as rapini, cime de rape, rape, raab, and brocoletti.

Making Flatbread at Home

Is flatbread worth making at home? By cooking the dough in a stovetop skillet and reserving extra dough for future meals, our answer is a resounding yes.

≥ BY SUSAN LOGOZZO ≤

A couple of years ago, I had a memorable meal at a local Afghan restaurant. The food was superb, the wine list diverse and affordable, and the surroundings inviting. But what really captured my attention was the bread. Arriving at the table warm and wrapped in a cloth napkin, it was a flatbread, about a quarter-inch thick, soft and tender yet chewy, and with a wonderful flavor. I watched the baker, who was right in the dining room, stretch the dough onto a paddle and slip it into a brick oven. When I asked the waiter about it, he said, "Oh, it's our everyday bread in Afghanistan, just flour, water, yeast, and salt—nothing special."

But it was special to me, and I decided that I wanted to find a home recipe that approximated this flavorful flatbread. When I began investigating, I found that the world of flatbreads is vast indeed (see "What Are Flatbreads?" page 21). After researching and experimenting with many different kinds of flatbreads, I knew what I wanted: a bread that was soft and tender yet chewy and with a slightly wheaty, mellow flavor. And I wanted a bread easy enough for home cooks to make while dinner is cooking.

My criteria made it easy to dismiss whole categories of flatbreads right from the beginning. First, I eliminated doughs that used starters (because of the time element); unleavened doughs (which were paper thin and very good but not the style I wanted); doughs made with eggs (I wanted a more rustic type of bread); and doughs that used hard-to-find ingredients. I also knew the bit of tang and moistness I wanted probably would come from yogurt.

Even with those guidelines, I still had about 20 representative recipes, so I started testing to find one that would work best for me and for the home cook.

Flour First

Flour was the main ingredient in all the bread recipes, so it was my starting point. I tried a range

When pan grilling, turn the bread after 30 seconds, cook fully on the second side, then flip again to finish the first side. This technique prevents large bubbles, which cause uneven cooking.

of flour mixtures, from all whole wheat to all white, from all-purpose to bread flour. I found the combination of whole wheat and bread flour to be the best. In my research, I found some recipes that called for "chapati flour," a finely milled whole wheat flour that contributes to a more delicate texture. In my last round of testing, I passed my supermarket whole wheat flour through a fine sieve, which removed some rougher bran flakes. To my surprise, this step resulted in an even more tender texture, meaning I could take advantage of the flavor of whole wheat flour without the heaviness.

Mixing, Rising, Baking

Because I wanted a simple bread that I didn't have to wait hours for, I was pleased to discover that 30 to 45 minutes was sufficient rising time. Because the bread is rolled or stretched rather thin, it does not require a long time to develop the complex structure necessary to produce the large holes and crunchy, crisp crust that are important in many loaf-style breads. The yeast and minimum rising time still create the tiny air pockets and the structure necessary to deliver a tender, chewy texture. Generally speaking, flat-

breads are rolled or stretched before cooking, so only a brief rest, instead of a long proofing stage, is required, which saves a lot of time.

Another great discovery I made along the way was that the dough will keep in the refrigerator for a couple of days, so you can pinch off a piece whenever you want fresh bread. Let the dough come to room temperature and then proceed with the rolling and cooking.

I also found that dividing the dough into eight pieces, shaping each piece into a ball, and then rolling and stretching it was the best way to manipulate the dough. A few minutes of rest between these steps helped to prevent the dough from shrinking back and wrinkling. The dough is also very forgiving—if the stretched dough is thinner in spots or a little uneven, it simply adds an interesting dimension to the cooked bread.

Based on the style of bread I wanted, I had two options for cooking methods, stovetop or oven. I liked cooking the breads on the stovetop because I could watch the dough bubble and color and turn it as necessary to control the cooking. Stovetop cooking also resulted in bread that was close to the Afghan-style bread I had in mind when I began my flatbread odyssey.

I found it best to preheat the pan for five minutes over medium-high heat. Cast iron is the best choice because of its ability to retain heat and cook evenly without burning, although any preheated heavy-bottomed pan will do the job.

I discovered that when I fully cooked the bread on one side first, large, unwieldy bubbles formed on the surface. When I turned the bread over to cook the second side, it was "suspended" on the bubbles and not lying flat in the pan. As a result, the bread did not cook evenly. To solve that problem, I cooked the first side for 30 seconds, at which point small bubbles appeared. I then flipped it, cooked the other side for a couple of minutes, then flipped it back to the first side to finish cooking. The result was an evenly cooked and evenly colored bread.

Baking in the oven produced good results, but the type of bread that resulted was quite different. The dough puffed beautifully in the oven, baking crisp on the bottom and softer on top. Because of the intense heat and the flat shape of the dough, a sudden burst of steam in the center literally blows up the bread. As it cools, it deflates slightly and you have a perfect pocket bread. That was not my goal, but it was so good, I have added it here as a variation. Brushing the rolled circles with a little oil and placing them on an outdoor grill also produced great results.

PAN–GRILLED FLATBREAD
MAKES EIGHT 6- TO 7-INCH BREADS

Make sure you let the pieces of dough rest after forming them into balls and again after rolling them into 4-inch circles; otherwise, they will shrink back and not hold their shape. Only one flatbread will fit in a skillet, so speed up the cooking process by using two skillets. Alternatively, you can give the breads an appealing smoky essence by brushing them lightly with oil and cooking them on the grill, over a medium fire, following the same cooking times and techniques.

1	package (2¼ teaspoons) dry active yeast
1	cup warm water (110 to 115 degrees)
1	tablespoon olive oil, plus extra for brushing
2	teaspoons sugar
¼	cup plain yogurt
1½	teaspoons salt, plus extra for sprinkling
½	cup whole wheat flour, sieved (before measuring) to remove coarse flakes of bran
2	cups bread flour plus additional as needed
2	tablespoons sesame seeds, optional

1. In either the workbowl of a food processor fitted with stainless steel blade or, if working by hand, a medium mixing bowl, sprinkle yeast over warm water. Add oil, sugar, and yogurt and pulse to mix, about four 1-second bursts, or, if working by hand, mix with wooden spoon until well combined. Add salt, sieved whole wheat flour, and 2 cups bread flour; process until smooth, about 15 seconds, scraping down sides of bowl as necessary, or, if working by hand, mix with wooden spoon until flour is incorporated, about 3 minutes. Process dough (adding more flour as necessary until dough just pulls completely away from sides of bowl) until soft and satiny, about 30 seconds, or, if working by hand, turn dough out of mixing bowl onto very lightly floured work surface and knead until smooth and elastic, 12 to

15 minutes. Squeeze dough gently with full hand; if dough is sticky, sprinkle with flour and knead just to combine. Place dough in medium bowl or straight-sided plastic container, cover with plastic wrap, and place in warm, draft-free spot until dough doubles in size, 30 to 45 minutes. (At this point, dough can be punched down, wrapped tightly in plastic wrap, and refrigerated up to 2 days.)

2. Turn dough onto lightly floured work surface and, if it is sticky, sprinkle very lightly with flour. Following illustrations 1 through 4 below, cut, shape, and roll dough. If using sesame seeds, brush tops of circles lightly with water, sprinkle each circle with ¾ teaspoon seeds, and gently roll over with rolling pin once or twice so seeds adhere to dough.

3. Five to 10 minutes before cooking flatbreads, heat large, heavy skillet (preferably cast iron) over medium-high heat until hot. Working one at a time, lift dough circles, gently stretch about one inch larger, and place on the skillet. Cook until small bubbles appear on surface of dough, about 30 seconds. With tongs, flip bread and cook until bottom is speckled and deep golden brown in spots, about 2 minutes. Flip bread over again; cook until bottom is speckled and deep golden brown in spots, 1 to 2 minutes longer.

4. Transfer bread to wire rack and cool for about 5 minutes (brush bread lightly with olive oil and sprinkle with salt to taste, if desired). Wrap breads loosely in clean kitchen towel and serve warm. Or wrap breads tightly in foil and store at room temperature up to 2 days; reheat in 300-degree oven until warm, about 15 minutes.

BAKED PUFFED FLATBREAD

Follow steps 1 and 2 of recipe for Pan-Grilled Flatbread to make and shape dough. About 30 minutes prior to cooking, adjust oven rack to lowest position, line rack with unglazed baking tiles, pizza stone, or preheated baking sheet and heat oven to 500 degrees. Bake dough rounds on pre- heated tiles or pizza stone until bread is puffed and golden brown on bottom, 5 to 6 minutes. Transfer breads to wire rack to cool for 5 minutes; wrap in clean kitchen towels and serve warm or at room temperature.

What Are Flatbreads?

Although some varieties, such as the familiar pita, puff when baked or fried, flatbreads are defined simply by their "flatness." The world's oldest style of bread, they can be made from any grain, be leavened or unleavened, and are shaped by rolling or stretching. Unlike European- or American-style loaf breads, which have either a fine crumb or large chewy holes, flatbreads come in a wide range of textures and shapes, from large, crisp, crackery rectangles to smaller, softer rounds to paper-thin, spongy ovals. Usually ripped or cut apart, flatbreads are also used to mop up stews and gravies. Among the better-known types of flatbread are the following:

Chapati A flat, pancakelike, unleavened whole wheat griddle bread.
Lavash Leavened white flour dough baked into a thin round; sometimes soft, sometimes crisp.
Naan Flattened round of yeast-leavened dough cooked against the walls of a tandoor oven so it puffs slightly and browns on one side.
Pappadam Unleavened dough made with lentil flour, flavored with various herbs and spices, and grilled or deep fried so it is paper thin and crisp.
Paratha A flat, flaky, unleavened whole wheat bread made by rolling dough paper thin, brushing with melted ghee (clarified butter), and folding several times to create layers.
Pita Leavened whole wheat or white dough rolled into a thin round and baked on stone so it puffs to form a pocket.
Poori, or puri Unleavened whole wheat dough rolled into thin rounds, deep fried, and puffed.
Roti An unleavened bread cooked on a griddle and finished over an open flame, which causes it to puff.   —S.L.

TECHNIQUE | FORMING FLATBREAD ROUNDS

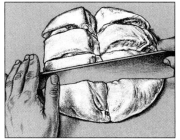

1. Use a chef's knife to divide the dough into 8 equal portions.

2. Roll each portion of dough on work surface to form a round ball.

3. Roll each ball out into a 4-inch circle, let rest for 10 minutes, then roll into a 6-inch circle.

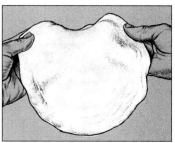

4. Lift and stretch each dough round slightly to form a 7-inch round circle before placing it in the skillet.

In Search of Real Bread Pudding

Real bread pudding should be a lot more than baked custard with a top layer of bread.
It should be crisp but soft, simple in flavor and construct, and mostly about bread.

≥ BY CHRISTOPHER KIMBALL ≤

Bread pudding is a bit like baked beans; both have origins deep in the culinary past and, over time, so many styles have emerged that the "real thing" is difficult to uncover even if a modern cook might find it worth the effort. Yet, as with all cooking, recipes are not entirely subjective. They do have beginnings, they are often born out of necessity or a chance mixture of readily available ingredients, and, especially with sturdy old favorites, they can show, as a nineteenth century Vermonter might say, "good proofs of usefulness."

Bread pudding is just such a recipe. This dessert, which is found in virtually all European home cooking (often referred to as *Brotpudding*), is simply a mixture of bread, milk and/or cream, sugar, eggs, and flavorings. So what's to discover? Well, the styles vary tremendously, from a baked custard with slices of French bread on top (as with the famous Coach House Bread Pudding, one of James Beard's favorite recipes) to a rich, treacly pudding with sauce, really more of a pudding cake.

My previous encounters with bread puddings had been decidedly mixed. Since I was not yet exactly certain which style appealed to me most, I decided to work my way through every version I could find, from recipes snagged on the Internet to buttermilk bread puddings to recipes from many cookbooks, including *Joy of Cooking*, *The New Basics*, and *The Wooden Spoon Dessert Book*. For months, I ordered bread pudding for dessert whenever it was on the menu, a Herculean task not appreciated a whit by my wife, who was getting back into shape after the arrival of our fourth child and was in no mood to be tortured by a dinner partner who could shamelessly gum a thousand calories in mere seconds. I consumed every conceivable sort of bread pudding, from those in which the bread seemed to have melted into the custard, to dry slices of bread that

Unlike most bread pudding recipes, in which all of the bread is soaked in liquid before going in the oven, we place some on top of the pudding just before baking. The result is a nicely crisp, beautifully browned top layer.

were slightly moistened, sweetened, and baked, to puddings shot through with a surfeit of ingredients, including raisins, pecans, orange zest, coconut, and, in one less than memorable instance, pineapple chunks.

This massive intake of calories yielded some valuable clues. I discovered that I wanted a real contrast between the crust and the filling in both texture and flavor; without this contrast, I found this to be a dull little dessert, all pudding and no chew. I also knew that the choice of bread was going to be crucial, as some loaves simply melted into the custard whereas tough, rustic breads seemed too muscular to succumb to the soft embrace of milk, cream, and eggs. The consistency of the "pudding" was also important, my tastes tending to land halfway between a custard and

a sauce. The balance between bread and filling was going to be critical as well. Some recipes were dry from too much bread; others used so little that it disappeared during baking. The pudding and the bread needed to be distinct but well integrated; I was not favorably inclined toward bread puddings that were nothing more than egg custards topped with bread. I wanted a modest amount of sugar, not something that would indulge the indefatigable sweet tooth of my hyperactive three-year-old son. Finally, I decided to dispense with a sauce since the pudding would be plenty rich without it and it added extra work in a recipe that calls out for simplicity.

Near the end of my trials and at the point at which my wife had mastered the stony watchfulness of a predator, apparently ready to lunge with total abandon at my last tender spoonful of silky custard, we dined at the Deer's Head Inn in the Adirondacks. There I had a bread pudding epiphany. The deep golden brown top of this excellent, plain dessert was made up of crispy pieces of bread with great chew. Underneath, instead of the usual layer of thin custard, was an interesting, not-too-sweet pudding/custard, some of the bread having been soaked and dissolved into the filling. This was a humble bread pudding that spoke loudly of bread, with a crusty top and a thick creamy bottom layer.

Back in our test kitchen, we started building my ideal recipe. First, we tackled the bread. We tried rustic Italian, a fine-textured French pullman loaf, Pepperidge Farm raisin bread, super-

TECHNIQUE | BREAD TIPS

1. To cut squares of bread, stack four slices, cut into 3 equal sections, then turn board and repeat.

2. Place the reserved squares of bread on top of the mixture and brush with melted butter.

market Italian bread, challah, brioche, and potato bread. The winners were the French loaf (this was not a baguette but more of a dense sandwich loaf), the fine, dense texture holding up well during cooking, and a bakery-quality American-style loaf of bread. Other more tender loaves such as challah and brioche were too soft and spongy. Additional testing discovered that a dense, bakery-style white bread purchased from a local baker was best, although Pepperidge Farm Hearty White will do in a pinch if you depend entirely on supermarket bread. Avoid really tough rustic loaves with heavy crusts and excessive chew, since this type of bread will not soften sufficiently during soaking and baking.

In the course of our testing we also discovered that there was no point in removing the crusts other than for appearance, that using stale or dried bread did not make a difference, and that we preferred cubes over sliced bread since they were easier to measure (8 cups is a more precise measurement than 8 slices) and to work with, as large slices tended to curl at the corners when baked. Finally, we tested buttering the bread and found that this added an excessive amount of fat and was unnecessary. However, we did discover that the key to a crisp, crunchy top layer was to separate two cups of the cubed bread and place them on top of the pudding just before baking. Brushing these cubes with melted butter added a rich color to the dessert. In order to provide more contrast between the topping and the filling, I also decided to sprinkle the pudding with cinnamon and two tablespoons of sugar just before it was placed in the oven. This gave the bread topping a flavor distinct from that of the nutmeg-laced custard.

The next issue was the custard. As stated above, I wanted a richer, silkier feel to the filling, not simply a thin egg custard. It turned out after many tests that half milk and half cream was about right. For eggs, another factor that affects the texture of the custard, we finally agreed on four whole eggs plus one yolk for a rich pudding, although many recipes use only two or three eggs. The amount of sugar was a matter of some dispute in the tasting, some preferring a full cup whereas I preferred a more modest amount, ¾ cup. A low oven temperature, 325 degrees, was best. Although a water bath seemed to provide a slightly improved texture, we opted not to include it in the final recipe since it was more work.

As our testing neared its end, I tried an unusual experiment. I placed two cups of the custard/bread mixture, before baking, into a food processor and pureed it, then mixed it back with the other ingredients. This resulted in a sauce rather than a custard, which some tasters liked and others didn't. If you are looking for real comfort food—"baby food" in one taster's estimation—this technique works nicely. For the major-

ity, and I include myself in this category, the master recipe is fine as is.

Determining just when to remove the pudding turned out to be a bit of a trick. Overcooking results in a dry, unappealing custard and undercooking makes for a very loose sauce. After two score or more of tests, we determined that the bread pudding should "wobble like a Jello-mold." (Remember that it will continue to cook after it's removed from the oven.) Another tip is to remove the pudding from the oven before it has a chance to inflate and rise up high in the pan. Actually, it is done just when this process begins, when the edges of the pudding start their upward climb. A knife inserted in the center should not come out clean but be partially coated with half-set custard.

RICH BREAD PUDDING WITH CRISP CINNAMON-SUGAR TOPPING
SERVES 8 TO 10

A firm white American-style bakery loaf bread gives the best texture to this pudding. In a pinch, however, use Pepperidge Farm Hearty White Bread. Avoid chewy, crusty European-style breads because they do not soften properly in the custard. For an extra-creamy bread pudding with a sauce beneath a crisp top layer, remove about 1 cup of soaked bread and 1 cup of soaking liquid to a food processor or blender and puree them until smooth, about 10 seconds. Add the puree back to the rest of the mixture and stir to combine before transferring it to the baking dish. If desired, serve this pudding with softly whipped cream.

Cinnamon Sugar
  2 tablespoons sugar
  ½ teaspoon cinnamon

Bread Pudding
  4 large eggs
  I large egg yolk
  ¾ cup sugar
  2½ cups whole milk
  2½ cups heavy cream
  3 tablespoons bourbon
  I tablespoon vanilla extract
  ¾ teaspoon fresh ground nutmeg
  ¼ teaspoon salt
  12 ounces (about ½ loaf) good quality American-style white bread, sliced ⅜-inch thick and cut into 1½-inch square pieces (about 8 cups)
  1½ tablespoons unsalted butter, melted, plus extra for greasing pan

1. *For the cinnamon sugar:* Mix sugar and cinnamon in small bowl; set aside.
2. *For the pudding:* Adjust oven rack to lower middle position and heat oven to 325 degrees. Butter 13-by-9-inch baking dish.
3. Whisk eggs, yolk, and sugar in a large bowl

to blend well. Whisk in milk, cream, bourbon, vanilla extract, nutmeg, and salt. Stir in 6 cups prepared bread; mix thoroughly to moisten. Let stand 20 minutes.

4. Pour mixture into prepared baking dish. Scatter remaining 2 cups bread pieces on top, pushing down gently to partially submerge. Brush exposed bread with melted butter and sprinkle with cinnamon sugar. Bake until pudding is deep golden brown, is beginning to rise up sides of baking dish, and jiggles very slightly at the center when shaken, about 45 to 50 minutes. Let cool until set but still warm, about 45 minutes. Serve.

RICH BREAD PUDDING WITH RAISINS AND WALNUTS

Follow recipe for Rich Bread Pudding, increasing bourbon to ⅓ cup. Soak ¾ cup raisins in bourbon until moistened and plumped, 20 to 25 minutes. Stir plumped raisins, any remaining bourbon, and 1 cup chopped walnuts into soaked bread mixture before transferring to baking dish.

Rich, Lush Cream Cheese Brownies

The secret to moist, but not wet, cream cheese brownies is the correct proportion of ingredients and a touch of underbaking.

≷ BY PAM ANDERSON ≶

Not that many years ago, our sweets were pretty straight-forward—chocolate-chip cookies, cheesecake, vanilla ice cream, chocolate bars. At some point, however, we must have decided that, if one dessert is good, two would be even better. Cheesecake, chocolate-chip cookies, and candy bars began to turn up in our ice cream; ice cream in our chocolate bars; and chocolate bars in our cheesecake and pecan pie. I imagine this is how cream cheese brownies originated. For many dessert lovers, nothing could be better than a rich, fudgy brownie with generous dollops of cheesecake baked inside.

An aficionado of both cheesecake and brownies, I set out to combine the two desserts into one perfect bar. For me, the ideal cream cheese brownie would be distinctly a brownie, but with a swirl of cream cheese filling in every bite. I wanted the brownie portion of the bar to have a rich, soft texture that would complement the lush cream cheese filling, yet at the same time contrast its soft interior with a thin, crisp (but not over-baked) crust. These brownies would taste intensely chocolate, with a tangy filling that could hold its own against such a dominant partner.

I set out to refine the brownie part of the recipe first. After extensive research, I identified three brownie styles—chewy-gooey, dense-and-fudgy, and mild-and-cakey. I made a batch of each style, observing that all three exhibited both assets and liabilities: Cakey brownies offered structure and crumb but lacked the intense chocolate hit of the other two styles. Fudgy brownies packed a lot of chocolate flavor, but their heavy, almost candylike structure was too dense for the soft cream cheese filling. Chewy brownies, although oozing with an irresistible gooey quality, still required a little crumb definition. My ideal brownie would be a mix of the three styles—intensely chocolate flavored, like a fudgy brownie; rich and soft, like a chewy brownie; and offering some crumb definition, like a cakey brownie.

Having used Jack Bishop's recipe (*see* "Basic Brownies Are Best," March/April 1994) over the last few years, I knew that his brownies embodied many of the characteristics for which I was search-

Because these brownies are part cheesecake, they should be stored in the refrigerator. We like them served at a cool room temperature.

ing. They were thin, moist squares, with a pleasant chocolate flavor and a fine, tender crumb—in other words, classic brownies. Add cream cheese batter to the equation, however, and the chief assets of Jack's brownies became liabilities. When paired with dense, tangy cream cheese, the brownie's fine cake-flour crumb did not provide enough structure to suspend the filling; its otherwise pleasant chocolate flavor lacked intensity; and, finally, the amount of batter did not produce a high enough bar for cream cheese brownies. To make this brownie batter more suitable for its cream cheese partner, I needed to strengthen its structure, infuse it with more chocolate flavor, and give it a bit more height.

To this end, I increased Jack's recipe by half (for added height), used all-purpose flour instead of cake flour (for strengthened structure), and threw in an extra ounce of unsweetened chocolate (for a more intense chocolate flavor). Baking the increased amount of batter (1½ times the original recipe) in the same size pan solved the height problem. The extra height, however, accentuated the brownie's cakey qualities. Desiring a denser, softer texture, I made the brownies again, this time returning the flour and baking powder to the original amounts, but leaving the eggs and vanilla at the increased quanti-

ties. This equation created a dense but relatively dry brownie. The increased amount of unsweetened chocolate, while making the brownie more intensely flavored, also caused it to taste bitter.

From previous chocolate experiments, I deduced that the unsweetened chocolate might be at the root of my harsh, bitter brownies. In her book *The Cake Bible* (Morrow 1988), Rose Levy Beranbaum calculates the interchange of unsweetened and sweetened chocolates: "For every ounce of unsweetened chocolate, substitute 2 ounces semisweet or bittersweet chocolate and subtract 2 tablespoons sugar and ⅔ teaspoon butter."

Using her theory, I made three pans of brownies—one with all unsweetened chocolate, another with all bittersweet chocolate, and a third with a combination of the two. Confirming previous results, the brownies made with unsweetened chocolate alone were dry and crumbly, with a slightly bitter finish. On the other hand, the brownies created with all bittersweet or all semisweet chocolate were too soft and gooey (*see* "The Chocolate Exchange," page 25). A combination of unsweetened and either of the sweetened chocolates corrected the texture and flavor deficiencies and delivered a perfect cream cheese brownie base—intensely chocolate, soft, lush, with just a hint of structure.

The Rest Is Cream Cheese

Fortunately, the cream cheese filling was much simpler to develop than the brownie batter. I was looking for an intensely flavored filling, but I found that other common cheesecake ingredients like sour cream, butter, and cream simply diluted the intense cream cheese flavor I was after. As it turned out, I only needed to add an egg yolk, ¼ cup sugar, and a couple of drops of vanilla extract to an 8-ounce package of cream cheese to achieve the flavor and texture I was seeking.

To determine the best way to incorporate the filling into the batter, I experimented with four options: I spread a thin layer of cream cheese filling between two layers of brownie batter. I sandwiched dollops of the cream cheese filling between the two layers of brownie batter. I sandwiched dollops of the cream cheese filling between two layers of brownie batter, then swirled them with a knife. Finally, twice I alternated a layer of brownie batter with a layer of cream cheese filling dollops that I swirled with a knife. The final technique—which

NO-STICK CREAM CHEESE BROWNIES

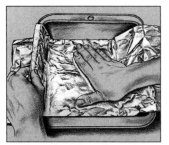

I. Fit a 16-by-8-inch sheet of foil in bottom of greased pan, leaving overhang to use as handles to remove baked brownies. Coat with cooking spray.

2. Pour half the brownie batter into prepared pan; then drop half the cream cheese mixture, by spoonfuls, over the batter.

3. Repeat with remaining batter and cream cheese mixture. Use a knife or spoon handle to gently swirl the batter and cream cheese filling.

4. After brownies have cooled in the pan for 5 minutes, use the foil sling handles to remove them from the pan; place on a wire rack for further cooling.

The Chocolate Exchange

While developing this brownie recipe, I substituted semisweet or bittersweet chocolate for unsweetened chocolate, and vice versa. Obviously, because each ingredient is very different, butter and sugar compensations had to be made. Using standard calculations to interchange unsweetened and sweetened chocolates and working from the same recipe for both versions, I expected my brownies to look and taste identical, regardless of the type of chocolate I used. So I was puzzled when the brownies made with unsweetened chocolate were drier in texture and slightly more bitter tasting than brownies made with bittersweet or semisweet chocolate, which turned out moist and gooey. For an explanation, I turned to an expert at the Van Leer Chocolate Company, who pointed to two differences in the chocolate's processing.

First, unlike unsweetened chocolate, bittersweet and semisweet chocolates contain lecithin, a sticky emulsifier that is responsible for chocolate's creamy mouthfeel. It makes sense that these smoother, creamier sweetened varieties would bake into gooier, chewier brownies. Because unsweetened chocolate contains no lecithin, brownies made with this ingredient tend to be drier and more crumbly.

Second, during the manufacture of sweetened chocolates, sugar and chocolate are heated together so that the sugar dissolves and the cocoa butter melts, bonding the two together. Unsweetened chocolate contains no sugar, so larger quantities of granulated sugar are mixed with the chocolate just before baking. These undissolved sugar granules remain distinct and separate in the batter. Sugar is hygroscopic (readily takes up and retains moisture), which causes the undissolved granules to absorb moisture during baking, resulting in a drier, more crumbly brownie. Because brownies are so rich in chocolate, the types of chocolate used in the cream cheese brownie batter create dramatic differences in the recipe. Chocolate exchanges exhibit less visible results in recipes where chocolate makes up a smaller proportion of total ingredients. —P.A.

created a visible swirl of light on dark and evenly distributed the filling throughout the brownies—was the winner.

This ultra-thick brownie, with its delicate filling, needed to be baked at a relatively low oven temperature. Brownies baked at 350 degrees had burned edges or turned out hard and inedible, requiring the crusts to be trimmed. At 325 degrees, however, the problem was solved: The brownies baked evenly. By putting a foil sling coated with cooking spray in the bottom of the pan before I added the batter, I was able to remove the brownies from the pan almost immediately after baking, which made cooling, cutting, and serving the brownies a breeze.

CREAM CHEESE BROWNIES
MAKES 16 2-INCH BROWNIES

Knowing when to remove a pan of brownies from the oven is the only difficult part about baking them. If you wait until an inserted toothpick comes out clean, the brownies are overcooked. But if a toothpick inserted in the middle of the pan comes out with fudgy crumbs, remove the pan immediately. If you are a nut lover, you can stir 1 cup toasted walnuts or pecans into the brownie batter. To melt the chocolate and butter in a microwave oven, microwave chocolate alone at 50 percent power for 2 minutes. Stir chocolate; add butter; and continue microwaving at 50 percent for another 2 minutes, stopping to stir the mixture after 1 minute. If chocolate is not entirely melted, microwave an additional 30 seconds at 50 percent power.

2/3	cup all-purpose flour
1/4	teaspoon salt
1/2	teaspoon baking powder
2	ounces unsweetened chocolate
4	ounces bittersweet or semisweet chocolate
1	stick (8 tablespoons) butter
1 1/4	cups sugar
2 1/2	teaspoons vanilla extract
3	large eggs, plus 1 yolk
8	ounces cream cheese, at room temperature

1. Adjust oven rack to lower-middle position, and preheat oven to 325 degrees. Whisk flour, salt, and baking powder in a small bowl; set aside. Coat an 8-inch-square baking pan with cooking spray, and, following illustration 1, fit an 8-by-16-inch sheet of aluminum foil in bottom of pan. (Foil overhangs both sides of the pan; use as handles to remove baked brownies from pan.) Coat foil with cooking spray.

2. In a medium heat-proof bowl set over a pan of almost simmering water, melt chocolate and butter, stirring occasionally until mixture is smooth. (Alternatively, melt chocolate and butter in microwave oven. *See* instructions above.) Remove melted chocolate mixture from heat; whisk in 1 cup sugar and 2 teaspoons vanilla; then whisk in 3 eggs, one at a time, fully incorporating each before adding the next. Continue whisking until mixture is completely smooth. Add dry ingredients; whisk until just incorporated.

3. In a small bowl, beat cream cheese with remaining 1/4 cup sugar, 1/2 teaspoon vanilla, and egg yolk until of even consistency.

4. Pour half the brownie batter into prepared pan. Following illustration 2, drop half the cream cheese mixture, by spoonfuls, over batter. Repeat layering with remaining brownie batter and cream cheese filling. Following illustration 3, use blade of a table knife or a spoon handle to gently swirl batter and cream cheese filling, creating a marbled effect.

5. Bake until edges of brownies have puffed slightly, center feels not quite firm when touched lightly, and a toothpick or cake tester inserted into center comes out with several moist, fudgy crumbs adhering to it, 50 to 60 minutes.

6. Cool brownies in pan on a wire rack for 5 minutes. Following illustration 4, use foil sling handles to lift brownies from pan. Place brownies on wire rack; allow them to cool to room temperature. Refrigerate until chilled, at least 3 hours. (To hasten cooling, place brownies in the freezer for about 1½ hours.) Cut into squares and serve. (Do not cut brownies until ready to serve. Whole bar can be wrapped in plastic wrap, then foil, and refrigerated up to 5 days.)

"Boil-in-a-Bag" Rice Surprises Tasters

Standard long-grain white rice won high ratings compared with instant or precooked varieties. The big surprise was Uncle Ben's strong showing with a boil-in-bag product.

⇒ MARYELLEN DRISCOLL ⇐

Essentially, white rice is brown rice made convenient. Developed thousands of years ago, the technique of stripping the germ and bran layers from brown rice to get white rice saves 30 minutes in cooking time. In today's busy world, that can make a big difference. Yet rice manufacturers have made cooking long-grain white rice even more of a snap with five-minute instant varieties and boil-in-bag options. At *Cook's,* we could not help but wonder whether so much convenience could still taste good. We decided to find out with a blind taste test.

To avoid comparing apples and oranges, we limited the candidates in our tasting to nationally distributed brands or major regional brands of plain, nonaromatic, long-grain white rice products. This gave us a lineup of 13 products, including standard, instant, converted, and boil-in-bag.

To understand the differences in these products, it helps to first know what they have in common. To begin with, all the rices in our tasting were long-grain, which means that each kernel is four to five times longer than its width when uncooked. (Other common types of rice include medium- and short-grain.) Long-grain white rice is characteristically "fluffy" and is the least sticky of the white rices. In part, this is because it contains a high percentage of amylose, a starch that keeps grains separate after cooking.

All the rices were also milled using the standard milling process in which the hull is removed and then the grains are rubbed together by machine to remove the bran and germ. (Rice with bran and germ left intact is brown rice.) These two processes create standard white rice. Converted and instant rice, however, are subjected to more processing.

The additional processing for converted rice is done before the milling. Unmilled rice is soaked in hot water, then steamed and dried in the husk. This is far from a modern technique, dating back about 1,500 years in India, where rice was put in large pots of water, soaked, steamed, and laid out in the sun to dry. Still practiced today in rural parts of India, this method makes it easier to remove the hull. According to Dr. Jon Faubion, Director of Scientific Activities for the American Association of Cereal Chemists, for modern cooks the primary advantage of this processing is that the rice remains firmer and more separate when it's cooked. Faubion explained that some of the starch in the outer portion of the kernel becomes gelatinized when it's steamed in the husk. The rice kernel then dries harder than its original state and nutrients are retained as they seep from the bran into the kernel. The harder starch makes it more difficult for water to penetrate, so it takes about five minutes more time for converted rice to cook. The result is not only firmer, more separate rice but rice with a tan-yellow tint and a stronger flavor than standard rice.

On the opposite end of the spectrum is instant rice. To make it, milled rice is fully precooked and then dried very fast. This creates cracks or channels that facilitate the movement of water into the kernel as it cooks on the stove. You can actually see this if you look closely at kernels of instant rice, which tend to be light and porous, like miniature puffed rice. This process makes cooking rice as effortless as making instant soup—stir into boiling water, cover, and let rest off heat for five minutes.

The compromise between the firm, separate kernels of converted rice and the convenience of instant rice seems to be boil-in-bag products. These modern innovations are made by precooking converted rice. In other words, these rices are parboiled prior to hulling, then precooked and dried after hulling and the removal of the bran and germ. The idea is that the parboiling will create rice grains with a firmer texture more resistant to coming apart, so that even though they are also precooked they will remain firm and separate during the 10-minute final cooking.

The Results

When it came to tasting, our panel decided that in the case of white rice, less is definitely more. The first-place rice, as well as those that came in third, fourth, and fifth, were all standard rices that had not been subjected to any special processing to make them cook faster or end up with grains that were unusually separate.

This result was not unexpected. What really surprised us, though, was the second-place finish of Uncle Ben's Boil-in-Bag rice, along with the sixth-place showing of Kraft's Boil-in-Bag. In both cases, the idea behind the dual processing of these rices really paid off. Testers found the grains of Uncle Ben's, in particular, to be firm, perfectly unbroken, and nicely moist.

The converted rice, on the other hand, did not fare as well. While the version by Uncle Ben's just managed to edge into the recommended category, tasters found that the converted product by Canilla had a strong undesirable aftertaste and yellow appearance that dropped it into the "not recommended" category.

As for instant rices, our tasters were anything but impressed. Both of the brands sampled in our tasting—Uncle Ben's and Kraft Minute—carried "chemical" and "metallic" flavors. Tasters also found these products unpalatably mushy, and noted that the individual kernels tended to fall apart and fray.

So if you aren't opposed to preparing your rice in a plastic pouch, a boil-in-bag rice might be the best option when you're looking for convenience. The trade-off, however, is that you get less rice for your dollar and you cannot cook these rices along with other seasonings or ingredients. The recommended standard long-grain white rices take a total of only 30 to 35 minutes to prepare (including resting time) and require minimal attention, so the rest of your meal can be prepared as they cook. They also make for a more affordable kitchen staple.

Rice on the Stalk

Grain of Rice

Hull
Bran
Polish
Kernel
Germ

The hull and bran layers, and the germ on a grain of rice are removed to make white rice. For brown rice only the hull is removed.

TASTING LONG-GRAIN WHITE RICE

We selected 13 plain, nonaromatic, long grain white rice products that were distributed nationally or were major regional supermarket brands. The rices were tasted plain. For instant, converted, or boil-in-bag products, we followed their package directions for cooking times. For seasoning and for cooking standard varieties, we followed the *Cook's* master recipe for long grain white rice from the May/June 1996 issue, halving the oil and salt so as not to intrude upon the rice's natural flavors. A panel of 16 tasters numerically rated each product according to flavor, texture, and overall liking and described any outstanding characteristics. Rices are listed in order of preference based on their average scores. Prices are based on purchases made in supermarkets across the country.

RECOMMENDED

Peak Long Grain Enriched Rice

➤ **$1.29 for 32 ounces**

"Overall pleasant," this rice was noteworthy for its full flavor—described as slightly nutty and buttery with a hint of sweetness. Its texture was light, fluffy, and firm. The long, slender grains of rice clung somewhat but were neither mushy nor excessively sticky. "Tastes great by itself," seemed to be the consensus. Sold in supermarkets in the South and Southeast.

Uncle Ben's Boil-in-Bag Enriched Long Grain Rice

➤ **$1.99 for 15.8 ounces**

This parboiled/precooked rice comes in perforated plastic pouches that cook up in boiling water in just 10 minutes. Startlingly simple if you are not averse to the plastic-pouch concept. Our tasters' first impressions of this rice were that it was strong on looks. "The grains are perfect (smooth, unbroken)," "good color," firm, "very long, thin grains." It was not as strong on flavor; one taster best described it as "neutral." Notably moist but not watery with only minor stickiness. Sold in supermarkets nationwide.

Canilla Fancy Extra Long Grain Enriched Rice

➤ **$1.29 for 48 ounces**

Despite the package touting this rice as extra long, tasters characterized the grains as stubby (yet slender). The flavor was nutty, somewhat buttery, and, in general, "good." The texture was firm, light, fluffy, and tender, yet had a contradictory chewy-mushy quality. One taster wrote, "I like the in-between quality." Sold nationwide in urban supermarkets.

Carolina/Mahatma Extra Long Grain Enriched Rice*

➤ **$1.59 for 32 ounces**

This rice was somewhere in between clingy and separate. The grains were somewhat pasty and dry, and there was some fraying at the tips, which one taster described as a "natural food appearance." Offsetting these characteristics were its pleasantly "al dente texture" and "clean flavor." This rice is sold under the Mahatma label in the South, Southeast, Southwest, and Pacific markets. In the Northeast it is sold under the Carolina label.

*Carolina/Mahatma and Hinode brand rices tied.

Hinode California White Long Grain Enriched Rice*

➤ **$1.79 for 32 ounces**

For those who like their long-grain white rice more sticky than fluffy, this brand would be their pick. It has a "nice flavor but not overwhelming" that some tasters described as "neutral." A few tasters picked up on a starchy aftertaste, and the grains broke up during the cooking process. Sold in supermarkets on the West Coast, in the Northwest, and in Arizona and Hawaii.

Kraft Minute Brand Boil-in-Bag

➤ **$1.99 for 14 ounces**

Making rice cannot get much easier and quicker than this: Submerge an unopened bag of rice in boiling water for five minutes, drain, and tear open bag to serve. The end result is a moist, fluffy rice that's tender but a little bit on the mushy side. Tasters' description of its flavor ranged from "mild," "sort of wheaty," and slightly buttery and nutty to "innocuous" and "boring." The grains were distinctly stubby. Sold in supermarkets nationwide.

Uncle Ben's Converted Enriched Long Grain Rice

➤ **$2.49 for 32 ounces**

This rice was lauded for having a lot of flavor character and great potential for pilaf. "[It] has a hint of chicken stock flavor or a richness that masks itself as chicken stock" and "[it's] very tasty." The grains were very moist, firm, plump, separate, and "not chalky or mushy." The color was slightly off, which is typical of converted rices. This rice takes a little longer to simmer than traditional white rice—about 20 minutes—and costs a bit more, too. Sold in supermarkets nationwide.

NOT RECOMMENDED

Success Enriched Precooked Natural Long Grain Rice

➤ **$1.79 for 14 ounces**

This boil-in-bag variety was just a little too much of nothing. One taster described it as having "a weird, hollow flavor." Another described it as "flat." Half the tasters detected off flavors described as "bleach," "chemical," or "artificial." This rice was extremely light and fluffy with very separate but dry grains. "You can feel the individual grains (it's not a mushy blob) but it's not too firm." The grains were also a pale brownish-yellow color, typical of converted rice.

Comet Enriched Long Grain Rice

➤ **$1.39 for 28 ounces**

Considering the brand name, it was ironic that one of the tasters described this rice as tasting like "instant astronaut food." Marked down for chalky off flavors and a soggy, undercooked texture. As one taster wrote, "It's not a bad rice—just not great." Sold in supermarkets in the South and Southwest and on the West Coast.

Golden Canilla Long Grain Enriched Parboiled Rice

➤ **$2.09 for 48 ounces**

An aftertaste described as "bitter," "metallic," "smoky," and "chemical" proved the demise of this converted rice. The grains were separate and plump but soggy and slightly greasy with a distinct yellowish tinge. Sold nationwide in urban-based supermarkets.

Kraft Minute Brand Instant Enriched Long Grain White Rice

➤ **$3.49 for 28 ounces**

The simplicity of this quick-cooking rice could not make up for its "complete lack of any rice flavor." This soggy, mushy, clumpy "snowcone" white rice "tastes more like boiled rice water," said tasters. A chemical or metallic aftertaste was also criticized. The grains disintegrated in your mouth before you could begin to chew. Sold in supermarkets nationwide.

Uncle Ben's Enriched Long Grain Instant Rice

➤ **$1.99 for 14 ounces**

This instant rice was "the strongest tasting rice I've ever eaten," commented one taster. Unfortunately, the powerful flavors were characterized as "chemical," "metallic," "processed," and "artificial." The rice was also mushy, so its texture was unable to compensate for the overpowering off flavors. Sold in supermarkets nationwide.

Blue Ribbon Extra Long Grain Enriched Rice

➤ **79 cents for 32 ounces**

Soggy and mushy on the outside yet crunchy on the inside, "this rice is confused," wrote one taster. "The flavor isn't good enough to compensate for the weird texture." Many of the grains were broken and had a powdery mouthfeel. Available in the Southeast.

Testing Large Roasting Pans

Good weight and great handles make a $180 pan our top choice, but for occasional use an old-fashioned model does most things perfectly well—at one-tenth the price.

⇒BY ADAM RIED WITH ANNE YAMANAKA ⇐

Twelve people were coming to my apartment for the first Thanksgiving dinner I'd ever hosted, and it was meticulously planned...or so I thought. In the kitchen on Thanksgiving morning, as I prepped the side dishes, my friend hoisted the 15-pound bird out of the refrigerator and asked me to hand him the roasting pan. Suffice it to say that his request prompted a mad dash to the convenience store, and the day's turkey was roasted, somewhat less than satisfyingly so, in a disposable foil pan.

That memory drove this *Cook's* testing of large roasting pans. Though most cooks haul out their roasting pan infrequently, when you do need this type of pan, nothing else will do.

Like other pieces of cookware, roasting pans come in various materials and sizes, and prices can range from about $2 for a disposable pan to well above $200 for a copper one. First, we had to determine the size of pan we wanted to test. Because their call to duty usually involves a large roast, we went for the largest pans that would fit in our 23-inch-wide range ovens and still leave at least two inches of space between the oven walls and the pan. That's the space recommended by roasting authorities to ensure proper air circulation around the food. Most of our pans were medium to large, ranging from 15 to 18 inches long. (It's important to measure your oven before purchasing a roasting pan. We discovered that our wall ovens were four inches shorter in width than our freestanding range ovens.)

Materials, all of which we included in our testing, seemed to be variations of steel or aluminum, including enameled steel, stainless steel, stainless steel with an aluminum core, nonstick-coated heavy aluminum, lightweight aluminum, and hard anodized aluminum. We also saw, but decided not to test, pans made of lined copper, which were simply too expensive; cast iron, which when loaded with a turkey weighed almost as much as a midsize sedan; and Pyrex, ceramic, and stoneware, all of which seem better suited to lasagna and casseroles than to the heavy-duty use a roasting pan gets. In addition, the Pyrex, ceramic, and stoneware pans could not be heated

directly on the stove top, which would preclude deglazing the pan drippings to make a gravy once the roast was removed.

True to the nomenclature of this pan, roasting—in our case, 12-pound turkeys—was our most important test. We paid particular attention to the depth and evenness of the browning, the maneuverability of the pan in terms of lifting it and its heavy contents in and out of a hot oven, and the condition of the pan drippings from which the gravy would be made. We also assessed the pan's stove top performance by searing a pork loin over medium-high heat. Admittedly, though, this test was less significant in our eyes than roasting the turkeys.

We also tested the pan's browning ability by roasting vegetables. This test carried the least weight, however, because vegetables could just as easily be roasted in a rimmed baking sheet or jelly roll pan. Ease of cleaning, which is detailed in the chart below, was the last point we examined.

Handles and Heft

The turkey tests highlighted the importance of the handles on these pans. When you are lifting a heavy pan with a 12-pound bird in and out of a hot oven, grip counts, and lack of it can be disastrous. The All-Clad, Calphalon, and Roshco Nonstick pans all had the strong, riveted, upright handles we liked best. The Granite Ware, Roshco Lasagna•Roast pan, and Progressive International all had side loop handles, which do provide grip, though not as much as our preferred design. The

other problem with the loop handles is that the combination of their position on the sidewalls of the pan and the large size of the pan can bring your forearms perilously close to the hot oven walls. Least successful in this department were the Farberware pan, which has a wide rim you can grab, and the Mirro Comet, which has no handles at all.

We were surprised to find that the height of the sidewalls mattered less than the type of rack we used. The Farberware, the Roshco Lasagna•Roast pan, and the Progressive International all came with flat racks, which allowed the turkey to sit too low in the pan, compromising air flow around the bird and therefore its browning. In all of the other pans, we used—and vastly preferred—our own adjustable V-rack, which allowed for good browning of the turkey skin. That said, honors for the best roasted turkeys went to the All-Clad and the Granite Ware. The lesson we learned, then, is to chuck any flat rack that may come with the pan and use an adjustable V-rack instead.

We also learned something important about nonstick finishes. As we expected, our nonstick pan, the Roshco, was very easy to clean. A problem we didn't foresee, though, was how much the rack would slide around in the pan. If we tilted the pan even slightly while moving it, the turkey in the rack slid sharply to one side, which threw off our balance and nearly landed the hot turkey in our laps. In our minds, this unnerving problem, combined with the somewhat pale, poorly caramelized pan drippings this pan produced, outweighs the

The Roasting Pans We Tested

All-Clad
Best handles, best weight, best performer overall.

Calphalon
Second-best at roasting, best on the stove top.

Granite Ware
For most uses, a solid performer at a great price.

Roshco Nonstick
Easy-to-clean nonstick surface caused turkey to slide dangerously.

Roshco Lasagna•Roast
Mediocre performer on several key tests.

Farberware
Buckled, browned poorly, and hard to maneuver.

Mirro Comet
Buckled on stove top and in oven, flimsy and hard to clean.

Progressive
Performed poorly on virtually every test.

RATING ROASTING PANS

RATINGS
★★★
GOOD
★★
AVERAGE
★
POOR

Eight large roasting pans were tested and evaluated according to the following criteria. All tests were performed in the same 23- x 14-inch gas KitchenAid home ranges in our test kitchen.

MATERIALS: Materials for each pan are listed.

PRICE: Prices listed at Boston-area retail outlets, in mail-order catalogs, or at Manufacturer's Suggested Retail promotional price.

SIZE (MEASUREMENTS AND SIDEWALL HEIGHT): Length and width of the pans plus height of sidewalls, measured from inside of bottom surface to top inside edge of pan wall.

WEIGHT: Not including rack or lid, if available.

HANDLES: Strong, upright, riveted handles were preferred over side-mounted loop or lighter, fold-down types.

TURKEY TEST: A 12-pound turkey was roasted on the rack that came with the pan (if no rack came with the pan, we used an adjustable V-rack). Turkey with crisp, evenly colored skin and dark, well-caramelized pan drippings earned best ratings.

STOVE TOP-WORTHINESS: Assessed by searing a pork loin at medium-high heat. Pans that seared the meat evenly and deeply, without burning or buckling, earned highest ratings.

BROWNING: Assessed by roasting root vegetables. Pans that produced a dark brown, even crust without burning or smoke earned highest ratings.

TESTERS' COMMENTS: Observations about unusual or noteworthy aspects of the pans and their performance.

Brand	Price	Materials	Size	Weight	Handles	Turkey Test	Stove Top	Browning	Cleanup	Testers' Comments
BEST PAN **All-Clad** Stainless Steel Roti, Model #5016	$180.00	Stainless steel exterior and interior with aluminum core	16" x 13" 3" high	8 lbs.	★★★	★★★	★★	★★	★★	This expensive pan had a nice, heavy feel and great handles. Turkey browned and crisped beautifully, although stove top performance was a bit quirky. Cleaned relatively easily.
Calphalon French Roast Pan, Model G6818HC	$152.00	Hard anodized aluminum	18" x 14" 3" high	7 lbs., 4 oz.	★★★	★★	★★★	★★★	★★	The turkey was fine, and both pork loin and vegetables browned deeply and evenly. However, turkey drippings scorched a bit, and the dark surface color obscured the drippings in the pan.
BEST BUY **General Housewares Corporation** Granite Ware Extra Large Capacity Covered Oval Roaster	$17.99	Enameled steel	16" x 12" 4¾" high	3 lbs., 11 oz.	★★	★★★	★★	★★★	★★	This pan's good performance with turkey and roasted vegetables surprised us. But it tends to burn food when used on the stove top, and it's not particularly easy to clean. For the price, though, it can't be beat. Make sure your rack fits in the oval shape.
Roshco SilverStone Nonstick Coated Lasagna/ Roast Pan, Item # 90104	$49.99	Nonstick coated aluminum; nonstick coated V-rack included	15½" x 11¾" 3" high	5 lbs., 4 oz	★★★	★★	★★	★★	★★★	Nonstick surface was much easier to clean than the other pans, but it also caused the rack to slide around in the pan whenever we moved it. Could be dangerous, not to mention frustrating.
Roshco Lasagna•Roast Pan, Model #93104	$19.99	Porcelain enamel on steel; flat wire rack included	15¼" x 11¼" 3½" high	4 lbs., 9½ oz.	★★	★	★★★	★★	★★	This pan is too small for turkeys larger than 12 pounds. Vegetables browned poorly; pork loin well.
Farberware Classic Series Large Roaster, Model #59007	$39.99	Stainless steel; flat wire rack included	20½" x 13½" 2½" high	2 lbs., 9 oz.	★	★★	★	★★	★	This pan buckled badly on stove top and browned pork loin poorly. It also felt flimsy under the weight of the turkey, was difficult to maneuver because of the handle design, and was a bear to clean.
Mirro Comet Bake & Roast Pan, Item #C8077	$8.99	Aluminum	17¼" x 11½" 2¼" high	12½ oz.	None	★	★★	★★	★	Buckled seriously and permanently on stove top and in oven. Light, flimsy, and hard to handle under the weight of a turkey, and very difficult to clean.
Progressive International 12-Quart Stainless Steel Roaster, Model SHDR-30	$39.99	Stainless steel; flat wire rack included	17¼" x 12¼" 4" high	2 lbs., 8 oz.	★★	★	★	★★	★	Buckled on the stove top and seared the pork loin very unevenly, failed to brown the turkey evenly, and was hard to clean.

benefit of easy cleaning.

Finally, we found that for size we preferred the 16-inch pan. The larger ones were too bulky and, with their large surface area, also tended to burn pan drippings more readily.

Stove top Abilities

For deglazing and making gravy, a good roasting pan should be stove top-worthy, meaning it can be used over direct heat without burning its contents or warping out of shape.

The key to good performance here, we discovered, was the weight of the pan. We seared pork loins over medium-high heat in each pan and found that heavier pans, those of roughly 3½ pounds or more, including the All-Clad, Calphalon, Granite Ware, and both Roshcos, resisted buckling and felt sturdy. Buckling was a problem with some of the other pans, including the lighter, thinner Farberware, Mirro Comet, and Progressive International.

The key to searing the meat deeply and evenly was to carefully modulate the burner setting. (Medium-high heat turned out to be too much for most of our pans, but with more careful heat regulation, the All-Clad, Granite Ware, Calphalon, and both Roshcos all seared meat acceptably.)

Conclusions

For the occasional roaster, we recommend the ubiquitous speckled enameled steel Granite Ware pan, which is even available in good hardware stores. In its favor, this pan turned in a beautiful turkey and admirable roasted vegetables. Its handles, however, are not ideal, and you'll have to watch it on the stove top, but for $20 or less, it does a nice job and is a good buy. If, on the other hand, you are a frequent roaster who puts a pan through its paces, it may be worth dropping the money on the $180 All-Clad. This pan was sturdy, had the best handles of the lot, and delivered an exemplary roasted turkey.

For a Few Dollars More: The Best $20 Reds

While the best Bordeaux are out of the price range of most Americans, the second tier is not only affordable but wonderful. BY MARK BITTMAN

There is a good argument to be made that quality Bordeaux wines costing less than $20 are the great bargains of the red wine world. This is especially true given that almost all decent red wines, regardless of their origin, now weigh in the $10 to $15 range. For a few dollars more, you can obtain some of the qualities for which many of the best French reds are known: an appealing bouquet, strong fruit backed by moderating acidity, a high level of complexity, and a certain austerity that is almost always lacking in all the other red wines of the world, no matter how highly praised.

Why would anyone spend good money to purchase "austere" wine? Because when applied to red wines, *austere* refers to lushness and fruitiness tamed not only by acid but by sterner flavors and aromas, those that are good but not bright: leather, cigars, and chocolate, for example. The combination of fruit, acid, and those dark flavors produces wines that complement rich, meaty foods as no other wines can.

At their absolute best, Bordeaux reds are so wonderful that they really should be sipped and savored. But those wines are out of reach for most casual wine drinkers, commanding prices of well over $50 a bottle and often more than twice that. Fortunately, the best of the $20 Bordeaux are also terrific food wines, capable of turning a simple grilled steak into a luxury meal by creating a magical synthesis.

This tasting featured what we hoped would be 14 such wines, and the majority of them lived up to our expectations. The best, and this includes all three wines in the "highly recommended" category, would do well in tastings of wines costing up to $35 or even $50. Two of these, Larose-Trintaudon and Greysac, are perennial favorites among bargain-hunting lovers of Bordeaux. The third, le Cadet de Larmande, is the second label of Chateau Larmande, one of the great properties of St. Emilion.

In fact, many of these wines are either second labels of great wines—made from grapes that simply didn't meet the highest standard—or wines that have long been officially recognized as very good if not great; these are the so-called cru bourgeois, wines that don't measure up to the grand

crus, at least not officially, but command ongoing attention.

Generally, cru bourgeois and second-label wines are ready to drink at an earlier age than their more expensive cousins, which require lengthier cellaring. That plus the fact that the vintages represented here—1994 and 1995—are both good (the '95 is considered the better vintage, but the '94 is perhaps underrated) contributed to a tasting in which all but the bottom couple of wines were roundly enjoyed. (And even those losers garnered a fair number of positive comments.)

For red wines, you simply cannot do any better in this price range.

THE JUDGES' RESULTS | BORDEAUX

The wines in our tasting—held at Mt. Carmel Wine and Spirits in Hamden, Connecticut—were judged by a panel made up of both wine professionals and amateur wine lovers. The wines were all purchased in the Northeast; prices will vary throughout the country.

Within each category, wines are listed based on the number of points scored. In this tasting, comments on the "Highly Recommended" wines were almost entirely positive; those labeled "Recommended" garnered mostly positive comments; the "Recommended with Reservations" group had decidedly mixed comments.

HIGHLY RECOMMENDED

95 Chateau Larose-Trintaudon, Cru Bourgeois, Haut-Médoc, $18. The decisive winner, with all but one taster ranking it in the top four. "Lush nose," "great character." (This is a large-production wine and should be easy to find.)

95 Chateau Greysac, Cru Bourgeois, Médoc, $18. An old standard that clearly had a great year: "Full, rich, and classy." "Real quality, just delicious stuff."

95 le Cadet de Larmande, St-Emilion, $20. Tied for strong second with Chateau Greysac, above. "Mellow," "forward," and "mouth-filling." "Fruity, round, and altogether pleasant."

RECOMMENDED

94 Chateau Fourcas-Hosten, Listrac Médoc, $19. "Dark and intense," but "too young to be enjoyed right now; will be great."

95 Chateau Tronquoy-Lalande, St-Estèphe, $20. "Pleasant," but "lightweight." "Slightly smoky" and "nicely balanced."

94 Domaines Prats, St-Estèphe, $18. "Light," but with "a little authority." "Some fruit, but could be riper."

95 Chateau La Cardonne, Médoc, $18. "Needs time, but strong, rich, and good." "Intense and luscious."

95 Chateau d'Agassac, Cru Bourgeois, Haut-Médoc, $17. "Rich and warm, the real thing." "Lean but intense, a quality wine."

RECOMMENDED WITH RESERVATIONS

95 Chateau Plagnac, Médoc, $16. "Not much nose, but nice body" and "decent flavor." A least-common-denominator-type wine, neither loved nor disliked by anyone.

94 Les Fiefs de Lagrange, St-Julien, $19. "Sophisticated" with a "lush nose," but "thin" and "a bit harsh."

95 Chateau Potensac, Médoc, $20. "Soft and simple," but "nicely approachable." (Unless, of course, you agree with the taster who thought it smelled "like nail polish remover."

95 Chateau Pitray, Cotes de Castillon, $9. "Mushroomy nose, pleasant and complex." "Light and easy drinking, but lacks charm."

95 Chateau Jonqueyres, Bordeaux Superieur, $10. "Thin, with little structure." One found it "soft and easy to drink."

95 Chateau Les Hauts de Pontet, Pauillac, $20. Nose is "musty," taste is "bland," but texture is "pleasant" and finish is "nice." At this price, outclassed in this tasting.

Recipe Database Software Falls Short

Unfortunately, existing software programs are only moderately successful at helping the home cook keep track of recipes easily and efficiently. BY CHRISTOPHER KIMBALL

L
ike most home cooks, I am terribly disorganized when it comes to meal planning. I find or develop recipes I think are great, then either forget them forever or recall them only through serendipity, perhaps while flipping through the pages of a long-forgotten cookbook or scanning the recipe files on my hard drive. Changes in recipes are noted in margins in an unreadable script, or the recipes themselves, printed out on computer paper, are stained with pan juices and then lost altogether. Meal planning, the art of carefully balancing a group of recipes, is often done in mere minutes.

So the notion of creating a computer database of favorite recipes has great appeal. After all, manipulating data is exactly what computers do best. So I set out to find some Windows software that would help me organize my recipes in a sensible and usable fashion. Much to my dismay, I discovered that few programs have been written specifically to perform this task. I found only four such offerings, two of which were almost identical.

I started by entering the same recipe, Fennel Tangerine Slaw, in all the programs as a mini road test and immediately ran into trouble. None of the programs could identify a "medium fennel bulb." If I simply listed "fennel bulb" to solve this problem, then I had to decide whether the term "medium" was in fact a term of measurement or a trailing description of the ingredient. In addition, listing two ingredients, such as "tangerines or clementines," on the same line confused all the programs. This, of course, is the essential conflict of database programming. In order for the program to massage data—print shopping lists, provide nutritional information, offer search engines that search by ingredient—the user must input information in a specific format, which can be cumbersome, to say the least.

The other big problem is that designers often get carried away with the potential of the computer without assessing the relative value of simplicity over complexity. Just because a computer *can* handle unlimited entry fields doesn't mean it should. *The Micro Cookbook 5.0,* for instance, lists 21 separate fields when entering a new ingredient, including information on saturated fat, carbohydrates, fiber, sodium, and calcium. Other programs are not as demanding as this one, but all are still less streamlined than I would have liked.

Perhaps the most irritating feature was the prepackaged recipes, from a few hundred to 5,000, which are difficult or impossible to get rid of, mercilessly appearing on one's screen like yesterday's newspaper. To make matters worse, the software folks got cute and entitled chapters "Tempting Fresh and Fun" or "Seasoned with Love Calendar" or "Tasty Tidbits." A large red button marked "Delete Recipe Inventory" would have been much appreciated. My last complaint is that most of these programs demand that you organize recipes into cookbooks and chapters, unnecessarily complicating the process. It would be fine as an add-on feature, but unfortunately it is usually hard-wired into the basic organization of the software.

The good news is that all the programs offer shopping lists, menu and calendar planning, and the ability to quickly search the database by ingredients or other criteria. Despite my misgivings about the perils of data entry, creating a computer cookbook of one's favorite recipes makes sense, with the Mangia program making more sense than the others.

Cook'n
➤ DVO Enterprises, $29.95

This was the best of the lot in terms of entering recipe information. The recipe-entering software was simple and straightforward. The program did not recognize simple ingredients such as "garlic cloves" or "salt and ground black pepper," but as with all the programs, ingredients can be added to the dictionary for future use and the list of ingredients is rather extensive. It also provides nutrition information without getting carried away. The bad news is that this program is rigidly structured by cookbooks and chapters, and new recipes can be entered only in specific places, such as in the "Treats from the Heart" cookbook. There is no simple pull-down menu that says "Add New Recipe."

Micro Cookbook 5.0
➤ IMSI, $29.95

This program is relatively downscale and very health-conscious. It includes extremely detailed ingredient listings specifying RDA levels of Vitamin A, iron, and calcium, to mention just a few categories. The most disturbing aspect of this software is that specific brand name products such as "Healthy Choice Fat Free Pasteurized Processed Cheese Singles" are promoted in the ingredient lists. This program is relatively friendly toward those who wish to add recipes, since this feature can be accessed from the top menu and you need to use only one screen to enter data, but I felt as if these recipes were written and edited by the Campbell's Soup Kids.

Mangia
➤ Sierra On Line, $29.95

This is the smartest and most sophisticated of the recipe programs and would garner high ratings indeed if the entry screen was less complicated. But first things first. The initial screen offers a series of file folders that can be configured by course, main ingredient, season, and so on. The recipes are held in these files, an intuitive arrangement that makes for easy browsing. The program also contains a powerful search engine with 10 criteria available for selection. The big downfall is that the recipe entry is unduly complicated. There are 10 separate screens for entry, including the title of the recipe and a description, the published source and author, the yield and serving amounts along with cooking times, the ingredients (each of which has four entry categories: amount, ingredient, condition when measured, and remarks), instructions, notes, information on nationality, course, season, method, ratings, and compatibility. (Of course, one need not enter all this data, but the screens are unavoidable). I also found, on more than one occasion, that two letters were typed on the screen for every keystroke. Hheellpp!! The typographic style of the recipes was a bit fussy, with roman, bold, and italic type all merged together, an arrangement that made the layout less than ideal. That being said, *Mangia* is blessed by containing only a few hundred recipes, some of them from this magazine. This is clearly the software of choice. (For purposes of full disclosure, please note that an earlier version of this software was sold to *Cook's Illustrated* subscribers by this magazine. We have no ongoing relationship with Sierra, the parent company, at this time.)

Most of the ingredients and materials necessary for the recipes in this issue are available at your local supermarket, gourmet store, or kitchen supply shop. The following are mail-order sources for particular items. Prices listed below were current at press time and do not include shipping or handling unless otherwise indicated. We suggest that you contact companies directly to confirm up-to-date prices and availability.

Roasting Pans

The All-Clad Roti (French for "roast") pan proved the best of the eight roasting pans we put through their paces in our test kitchen. Admittedly, this pan is expensive. The 16" x 13" pan with 3" tall sides typically sells for about $200. We found it by mail order for $180 through **A Cook's Wares (211 37th Street, Beaver Falls, PA 15010-2103; 800-915-9788)**. A close second to the All-Clad was the Calphalon French Roast Pan. This pan should not be confused with the more widely available · Calphalon Commercial Roaster, which is a lighter pan with hanging handles that are difficult to grasp. The 18" x 14" French Roast Pan that we tested, model G6818HC, can be purchased at a discount for $130 from **Kitchen Arts (161 Newbury Street, Boston, MA 02116; 617-266-8701)**. They also carry a smaller version—16" x 13"—for $112 (model G6816HC). Kitchen Arts prices include freight costs. If you are looking for less of an investment, Granite Ware Extra Large Capacity Covered Oval Roaster performed well when roasting both a turkey and vegetables. This roasting pan is sold in many hardware stores. For information on a nearby store that carries Granite Ware or to order directly by mail, call the manufacturer, **General Housewares Corporation (1536 Beech St., Terre Haute, IN 47804; 800-545-4411, ext. 11, or ask for customer service)**. This 16"x 12" oval pan sells for $16.50 when ordered from the manufacturer.

Flatbread Griddle

When testing flatbread recipes we pulled out the Chef's Design reversible cast aluminum griddle model 3535. This 20" x 10½" griddle fits over two stovetop burners so that you can cook two to three flatbread discs at once. Five minutes is all it takes to preheat this griddle on a gas burner, while electric burners take a bit longer. The griddle looks similar to a cast-iron variation but is not such a chore to lift (6 pounds versus 10). The smooth side that we used for the flatbreads has a shallow channel running along two edges for catching drippings. The back side is ridged for a grilled effect. Two opposing corners are designed as handles. The Chef's Design griddle model 3535 can be ordered directly from its manufacturer, **The Wisconsin Aluminum Foundry (P.O. Box 246, Manitowoc, WI 54221-0246; 920-682-8627)**. The cost of $39 includes shipping.

Onion Soup Crocks

Our onion soup recipe is so simple (as well as delicious) that you might want to have a set of the traditional French-style onion soup crocks on hand for making it. **Kitchen Etc. catalog services (Department TM, 32 Industrial Drive, Exeter, NH 03833; 800-232-4070)** sells a set of four crocks for $19.99. These 16-ounce ceramic crocks are broiler safe, have a 2½" handle for easy removal from under the broiler, and come with lids. A glaze of three shades of brown makes these crocks reminiscent of old-fashioned bean pots.

Flour Containers

In the story on kitchen efficiency on page 16, we recommend storing flour in a wide-mouthed container. **King Arthur Flour's Baker's Catalog (P.O. Box 876, Norwich, VT 05055-0876; 800-827-6836)** sells buckets specifically designed for storing flour. The buckets come in two sizes and are made of a food-safe acrylic that is strong, flexible, and opaque, so that you can easily monitor your flour supply. The large bucket is 12" in diameter, 15" high, and can hold a 25-pound bag of flour. It sells for $17.95. The small size is 9" in diameter, 11" high, and can hold a 10-pound bag of flour. It sells for $7.95. Both buckets have handles on each side as well as snap-on lids with tabs to facilitate opening and sealing.

Wooden Blending Spoon

In the bolognese sauce recipe on page 7, the edge of a wooden spoon is used to break the ground meat into tiny pieces. In the *Cook's* test kitchen, we used a blending spoon for this task. This utensil resembles a traditional wooden spoon but is only about ¼" thick and is completely flat except for a gentle taper at the oval end. We particularly like using it for sauces because it easily reaches inside the bottom edge of a saucepan, and, since there's no concave bowl to the spoon, food tends to stick less. **Sur La Table (1765 Sixth Avenue South, Seattle, WA 98134-1608; 800-243-0852)** sells this style of spoon in boxwood, a dense, golden-grained wood that will not splinter or pick up flavors. The 10" spoon (item #3379) sells for $4.95. The 14" spoon (item #3383) sells for $5.95.

Heat Diffuser

On page 4 we show how to make a heat diffuser out of a coil of tin foil. But if you make a lot of delicate sauces or if you find the lowest flame of your stovetop still seems to burn rice, a heat diffuser is a worthwhile and inexpensive purchase. **Sur La Table catalog division (1765 Sixth Avenue South, Seattle, WA 98134-1608; 800-243-0852)** sells a heat diffuser by Mouli (item #0252) for just $7.95. Made in France, this tin steel disk with an 8¼" diameter is ridged and perforated so that it distributes burner heat slowly and evenly. It has a loop handle that folds in for easy storage and is wrapped in rubber to protect hands.

UNITED STATES POSTAL SERVICE™ — Statement of Ownership, Management, and Circulation (Required by 39 USC 3685)

1. Publication Title: Cook's Illustrated
2. Publication Number: 1 0 6 8 – 2 8 2 1
3. Filing Date: 10/1/98
4. Issue Frequency: Bi-Monthly
5. Number of Issues Published Annually: 6
6. Annual Subscription Price: $24.95
7. Complete Mailing Address of Known Office of Publication: Boston Common Press, 17 Station Street, Brookline, MA 02445
   Contact Person / Telephone: 617-232-1000
8. Complete Mailing Address of Headquarters or General Business Office of Publisher: Same as Above
9. Full Names and Complete Mailing Addresses of Publisher, Editor, and Managing Editor
   Publisher: Christopher Kimball, Boston Common Press, 17 Station Strye Brookhomein, MA 02402
   Editor: Same as Publisher
   Managing Editor: Barbara Bourassa, Boston Common Press, 17 Station St., Brookline, MA 02445
10. Owner:

Full Name	Complete Mailing Address
Boston Common Press Limited Partnership	500 Boylston St. #1880, Boston, MA 02116
(Christopher Kimball)	

11. Known Bondholders, Mortgagees, and Other Security Holders Owning or Holding 1 Percent or More of Total Amount of Bonds, Mortgages, or Other Securities. If none, check box ☑ None

Full Name	Complete Mailing Address
N/A	

12. Tax Status (For completion by nonprofit organizations authorized to mail at special rates) (Check one)
   The purpose, function, and nonprofit status of this organization and the exempt status for federal income tax purposes:
   ☑ Has Not Changed During Preceding 12 Months
   ☐ Has Changed During Preceding 12 Months (Publisher must submit explanation of change with this statement)

PS Form 3526, September 1998 (See Instructions on Reverse)

13. Publication Title: Cook's Illustrated
14. Issue Date for Circulation Data Below: Sept/Oct 1998

15. Extent and Nature of Circulation	Average No. Copies Each Issue During Preceding 12 Months	Actual No. Copies of Single Issue Published Nearest to Filing Date
a. Total Number of Copies (Net press run)	345,349	341,473
b. Paid and/or Requested Circulation (1) Sales Through Dealers and Carriers, Street Vendors, and Counter Sales (Not mailed)	45,433	49,738
(2) Paid or Requested Mail Subscriptions (Include advertiser's proof copies and exchange copies)	247,189	238,390
c. Total Paid and/or Requested Circulation (Sum of 15b(1) and 15b(2))	292,622	288,128
d. Free Distribution by Mail (Samples, complimentary, and other free)	4,457	4,389
e. Free Distribution Outside the Mail (Carriers or other means)	317	200
f. Total Free Distribution (Sum of 15d and 15e)	4,774	4,589
g. Total Distribution (Sum of 15c and 15f)	297,396	292,717
h. Copies not Distributed (1) Office Use, Leftovers, Spoiled	7,093	3,537
(2) Returns from News Agents	40,860	45,219
i. Total (Sum of 15g, 15h(1), and 15h(2))	345,349	341,473
Percent Paid and/or Requested Circulation (15c / 15g x 100)	98.4	98.4

16. Publication of Statement of Ownership
   ☑ Publication required. Will be printed in the Jan/Feb 1999 issue of this publication.
   ☐ Publication not required.

17. Signature and Title of Editor, Publisher, Business Manager, or Owner
   Date: 10/1/98

I certify that all information furnished on this form is true and complete. I understand that anyone who furnishes false or misleading information on this form or who omits material or information requested on the form may be subject to criminal sanctions (including fines and imprisonment) and/or civil sanctions (including multiple damages and civil penalties).

PS Form 3526, September 1998 (Reverse)

RECIPE INDEX

Simple Shrimp Scampi **PAGE 18**

French Onion Soup Gratinée **PAGE 10**

Broccoli Rabe with Sun-Dried Tomatoes and Pine Nuts and
Pan-Grilled Flatbread **PAGES 19 AND 21**

A Better Coq au Vin **PAGE 15**

Twice Baked Potatoes with Smoked Salmon and Chives **PAGE 13**

Fettuccine with Classic Bolognese Sauce **PAGE 7**

PHOTOGRAPHY: CARL TREMBLAY   STYLING : MYROSHA DZIUK

Dark Red Norland

Russian Banana

Peruvian Purple

Irish Cobbler

Purple Viking

Ruby Crescent

All Red

Ozette

All Blue

Rose Finn Apple

Butterfinger

Caribe

POTATOES

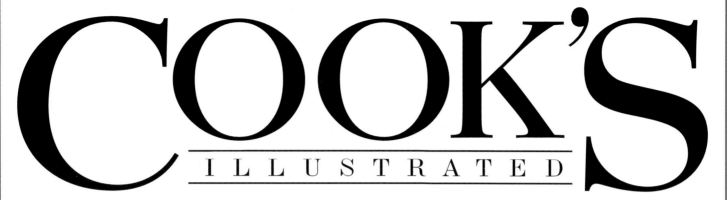

COOK'S
ILLUSTRATED

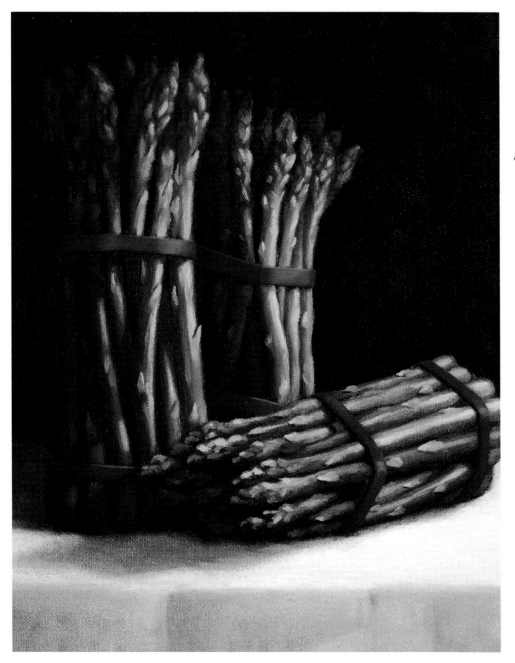

Double Chocolate Pudding
The Secret? Cocoa Powder and Bittersweet Chocolate

Quick Pan-Seared Salmon
A Crisp Crust without Overcooking

The Best Split Pea Soup
Putting the Ham Back

Updating Chicken Fricassee
Faster and Lighter

Testing Graters
Rating Flat, Box, Electric, and Rotary Graters

Moist and Tender Yellow Cake
Tasting Jarred Tomato Sauces
How to Dice Vegetables
The Best Egg Salad
Vietnamese Noodle Soups
Pantry Pasta Sauces

$4.95 U.S./$5.95 CANADA

CONTENTS

March & April 1999

PUBLISHER AND EDITOR
Christopher Kimball

EXECUTIVE EDITOR
Pam Anderson

SENIOR EDITOR
John Willoughby

SENIOR WRITER
Jack Bishop

ASSOCIATE EDITORS
Adam Ried
Maryellen Driscoll

TEST COOKS
Dawn Yanagihara
Anne Yamanaka
Bridget Lancaster

CONTRIBUTING EDITOR
Stephanie Lyness

ART DIRECTOR
Amy Klee

CORPORATE MANAGING EDITOR
Barbara Bourassa

EDITORIAL PRODUCTION MANAGER
Sheila Datz

COPY EDITOR
India Koopman

EDITORIAL INTERN
Sarah Moughty

MARKETING DIRECTOR
Adrienne Kimball

CIRCULATION DIRECTOR
David Mack

FULFILLMENT MANAGER
Larisa Greiner

CIRCULATION MANAGER
Darcy Beach

MARKETING ASSISTANT
Connie Forbes

PRODUCTS MANAGER
Steven Browall

**VICE PRESIDENT
PRODUCTION AND TECHNOLOGY**
James McCormack

SYSTEMS ADMINISTRATOR
James Burke

PRODUCTION ARTIST
Daniel Frey

SENIOR ACCOUNTANT
Mandy Shito

OFFICE MANAGER
Mary Connelly

SPECIAL PROJECTS
Fern Berman

CABBAGES The cabbage family is particularly large and varied. Americans are most familiar with the headed European cabbages, including red, green, and the curly leafed savoy. Brussels sprouts are another of the European-derived members of the cabbage family. Among the scores of Asian cabbages are the ubiquitous two-tone bok choy along with green Shanghai bok choy, as well as several types of headed cabbages, including napa and Chinese. All of these cabbages are relatively mild with only a touch of bitterness. Other members of the cabbage family, including mustard cabbage, have more peppery flavors.

COVER PAINTING: BRENT WATKINSON, BACK COVER ILLUSTRATION: JOHN BURGOYNE

Cook's Illustrated (ISSN 1068-2821) is published bimonthly by Boston Common Press Limited Partnership, 17 Station Street, Brookline, MA 02445. Copyright 1999 Boston Common Press Limited Partnership. Periodical postage paid at Boston, MA and additional mailing offices, UPPS #012487. For list rental information, contact List Services Corporation, 6 Trowbridge Drive, P.O. Box 516, Bethel, CT 06801; (203) 743-2600; fax (203) 743-0589. Editorial office: 17 Station Street, Brookline, MA 02445; (617) 232-1000; fax (617) 232-1572. Editorial contributions should be sent to: Editor, *Cook's Illustrated*. We cannot assume responsibility for manuscripts submitted to us. Submissions will be returned only if accompanied by a large self-addressed envelope. Postmaster: Send all new orders, subscription inquiries, and change of address notices to: *Cook's Illustrated*, P.O. Box 7446, Red Oak, IA 51591-0446. PRINTED IN THE USA.

THE DAIRY BAR

Last summer, our family stopped one lazy Saturday afternoon at Shaw's Dairy Bar, each of my kids begging for a soft-serve ice cream cone. It's a small establishment, just south of our country town, the menu offering its own special shorthand. There were "Wing Zings," kielbasa with kraut, meatball grinders, foot-long dogs, barnburgers, corn dogs, Michigan dogs, cheese sticks, buckets of chicken, and onion rings. If you were there for dessert, you could choose a "Frozen Eat-It-All Sandwich" or slush puppies, or the soft-serve ice cream, which comes in eight flavors, including banana ripple. You could order chocolate, rainbow, or krunch-kote sprinkles on top, but I knew that my two girls would go for a big cone of the bubble gum ice cream, swirled with pink flavoring on a stocky cone. My wife remembers the original bubble gum ice cream with real pieces of Bazooka in it. The trick was to avoid eating any of the cone since it stuck to the gum, which could be chewed and blown after the ice cream was finished.

Built onto the side of the Dairy Bar is a small shed called the "Dining Area," with red painted benches running around the inside walls. Three teenage boys were sitting there, waiting patiently for something to happen, smirking, talking with a bit more animation than was called for by the content of their conversation. Napkins stained with the blood red of ketchup and smears of chocolate ice cream sprang fitfully across the well-worn grass in the lively breeze. Whole families sat in vans in the parking area, licking and sucking swirled towers of freshly exuded confection, silent, intent in their pleasure. Pickups and motorcycles passed by but without the intensity of destination, just out for the ride.

Our family sat at one of the tables, tongues extended, licking great furrows in the custardy soft-serve, cool, creamy gobs sliding slowly across the tongue and then continuing deliciously toward the back of the throat. And then I began to notice the play of the branches in the large oak nearby, the breeze a fine thing on a hot summer afternoon. Distracted, I began to look at the people around us. An older couple was seated at a picnic table, the man's bright tortoise-shell glasses framed in stark relief by his nearly bald and perfectly round head. His features were small and simple, his expression reflecting his total focus on the matter at hand, a partially eaten onion ring, only the bottom half remaining, the milky white insides pulled halfway out of the crisp brown ring on the first bite. Other folks were the type who appear whitewashed in the dead of winter, the sort of strangers one might avoid in the supermarket checkout or down at the country store; old bachelors who talk about shooting their neighbors and women who stop washing their hair, their dark tresses limp and stringy. But on this day last summer, everyone looked refreshed. A lazy eye or a slight tic at the corners of the mouth had been dissolved by the warmth of the sun and the childlike

Christopher Kimball

pleasure of the Dairy Bar.

Each of us has food memories. For some, the velvety mouth-kissing texture of a well-made crème caramel enjoyed at a small Paris bistro haunts the memory, while others call to mind the crunch of biting through the deep-fried crust of mahogany-colored southern fried chicken. Pleasures once experienced are readily recalled, brought to mind in an absent moment. And over a lifetime we come to know how food is supposed to taste, whether a tomato sauce is properly balanced, whether a loaf of bread is pleasantly yeasty or overproofed.

And for those of us who cook as well as eat, we have the power to live in the moment, not just in the past, able and willing to fry the chicken or proof the bread. Each new bite of a familiar recipe brings us back in time, reconnecting to our past, but it also enlarges the present, filling our heads and kitchens with yeasty thoughts and aromas out of time. Cooks know that they can find paradise wherever they look, in a sharp piece of Vermont cheddar or in the sizzle of a good steak when it hits the cast-iron skillet. Some of us even find it in a napkin skittering across a well-worn lawn or in the summer's first bite of ice cream, our mouths filled with the familiar chew of krunch-kote sprinkles, our minds empty save for summer's rare pleasures.

ABOUT COOK'S ILLUSTRATED

The Magazine Cook's Illustrated is published every other month (6 issues per year) and accepts no advertising. A one-year subscription is $29.70, two years is $55, and three years is $75. Add $6 postage per year for Canadian subscriptions and $12 per year for all other foreign countries. To order subscriptions in the U.S. call 800-526-8442 or 515-247-7571 from outside the U.S. Gift subscriptions are available for $24.95 each.

Magazine-Related Items Cook's Illustrated is available in an annual hardbound edition, which includes an index, for $24.95 each plus shipping and handling. Discounts are available if more than one year is ordered at a time. Back issues are available for $5 each. Cook's also offers a 6-year index (1993-1998) of the magazine for $12.95. To order any of these products, call 800-611-0759 inside the U.S. or 515-246-6911 outside the U.S.

Books Cook's Illustrated publishes a series of single-topic books, available for $14.95 each. Titles include: *How to Make A Pie, How to Make An American Layer Cake, How to Stir Fry, How to Make Ice Cream, How to Make Salad, How to Make Simple Fruit Desserts, How to Make Cookie Jar Favorites, How to Cook Holiday Roasts and Birds, How to Make Stew, How to Make Pizza, How to Make Holiday Desserts, How to Make Pasta*

Sauces, How to Grill, and *How to Cook Shrimp and Other Shellfish. The Cook's Bible*, written by Christopher Kimball and published by Little, Brown and Company, is available for $24.95. *The Yellow Farmhouse Cookbook*, also written by Christopher Kimball and published by Little, Brown and Company, is available for $24.95. To order any of these books, call 800-611-0759 inside the U.S. or 515-246-6911 outside the U.S.

Reader Submissions Cook's accepts reader submissions for both Quick Tips and Notes From Readers. We will provide a one-year complimentary subscription for each Quick Tip that we print. Send a description of your technique, along with your name, address, and daytime telephone number, to Quick Tips, Cook's Illustrated, P.O. Box 470589, Brookline, MA 02447. Questions, suggestions, or other submissions for Notes From Readers should be sent to the same address.

Subscription Inquiries All queries about subscriptions or change of address notices should be addressed to Cook's Illustrated, P.O. Box 7446, Red Oak, IA 51591-0446.

Website Address Selected articles and recipes from Cook's Illustrated and subscription information are available online. You can also order books and other products on our website: www.cooksillustrated.com.

Cornichons

Pam Anderson's article about preparing beef tenderloin in the November/December 1998 issue was timed just right for our annual holiday party. The meat was perfect, and we served it with a horseradish cream sauce, as it is my family's preference. But we were curious about the recipe for Parsley Sauce with Cornichons and Capers that was included in the article. What are cornichons?

LYNN RINNETA
LA CROSSE, WI

➤ Cornichons (pronounced kor-nee-SHOHNs) are basically tiny French pickles, traditionally served as an accompaniment to pâté and smoked meats and fish. They are made from a European variety of cucumber called gherkins, which feature thin skins and tiny seeds and seed cavities, and are usually picked slightly immature, at only one to two inches long. Cornichons are characteristically crisp and tart, which means their flavor is an excellent contrast with rich meats.

Jarred cornichons are common and should be available in well-stocked supermarkets or gourmet shops. In a taste test we ran between jarred cornichons and those sold in bulk, however, tasters agreed unanimously that the bulk cornichons were crisper and had a brighter, sharper flavor. To order bulk cornichons by mail, try Formaggio Kitchen (244 Huron Avenue, Cambridge, MA 02138; 617-354-4750). For $6.50 per pound, plus shipping costs, Formaggio sells a French brand of cornichons, Maitre Provi, which have been pickled along with tiny onions in a brine of water, salt, white wine vinegar, and mustard seeds.

Boston Lemon Tea Cakes

During my childhood in Brookline Village, Massachusetts (very near your office, I think), we used to get wonderful little cakes called Boston Lemon Tea Cakes from a local bakery. They were individual sponge cakes, about the size of a small muffin and tender as could be, split in half and spread with a creamy lemon filling, then sandwiched back together and dusted with confectioners' sugar. I remember them so fondly, and since no bakery I have ever checked has them, I've often wished I knew how to make them.

With these cakes in mind, I was struck by the recipe for Sponge Cake with Rich Lemon Filling in *Cook's* September/October 1998 issue. This recipe is the closest I've ever seen to the treats of my youth, so I wondered if it could be adapted to make individual cakes?

JOAN THOMAS
HARLEYSVILLE, PA

➤ The bakery to which you refer is gone, but you can use our Foolproof Sponge Cake recipe to make individual "Boston Lemon Tea Cakes." We tried it in the test kitchen and found the little lemon-filled cakes to be charming. Follow the cake recipe, substituting two very generously greased and floured muffin tins—ours had cups of ½ cup capacity—for the parchment-lined 8- or 9-inch cake pans. Bake the cakes in a preheated, 350-degree oven, with the racks at the lower middle position, until the cake tops are light brown and feel firm and spring back when touched, 10 to 12 minutes. Use a serrated knife to split the cakes in half neatly through their equators, spread about 2 tablespoons of rich lemon filling in the center, and replace the tops. A little confectioners' sugar sieved over them, as you suggest, gives the cakes an elegant appearance. The full recipe of batter produced 20 individual cakes.

Grinding Cinnamon at Home?

Maryellen Driscoll's article about tasting cinnamon in the November/December 1998 issue was a real eye-opener. Even though cinnamon is one of my favorite spices, I never realized that what I've been using isn't really cinnamon at all. One issue that the article did not cover, however, is grinding your own cinnamon from sticks. I usually buy my spices whole and then toast and grind them as needed for recipes. A few cookbooks I've consulted recommended grinding your own cinnamon, too, but not all of them. Does *Cook's* have an opinion?

KARLA PASCHKIS
CAMBRIDGE, MA

➤ We asked a number of the spice merchants who helped with the cinnamon-tasting article if they would grind their own cinnamon from sticks, and their message was quite clear and simple—no.

According to Pamela Penzey, purchasing agent for the mail-order spice retailer Penzey's, Ltd., the ruddy, scrolled twigs we know as cinnamon sticks are cut from the cinnamon/cassia tree's newer, upper branches. The bark on these high branches carries less flavor than the bark from the larger, older base branches, which is stripped to provide cinnamon (both cassia and True Ceylon) for grinding. In addition to having a slightly lighter flavor, the bark from these high branches is more expensive, about $6 for one ounce in a local grocery store, because of the labor necessary to retrieve it from the treetop.

Once the bark has been taken from the tree's lower branches, it is left to dry for 24 hours. The outer layer is then scraped off so that the ground cinnamon will taste less sharp and biting. The remaining inner layer of bark, which is relatively thick and light-colored, curls as it dries, and winds up looking much like a giant cinnamon stick, about 18 inches long. To preserve freshness, these large sticks of bark are shipped to the United States as is for spice merchants to grind. Many of the major spice suppliers grind the cinnamon cryogenically, a process in which the cinnamon is ground at very low temperatures to retain its flavorful volatile oils. This is done because heat releases and disperses these important oils. The friction from the spice grinder produces heat, which is another reason why our sources did not recommend grinding sticks at home.

Nonetheless, we tried grinding Penzey's Indonesian cassia sticks to compare their flavor with the pre-ground version you can purchase. We snapped the sticks in half and then into thirds before grinding them in a coffee grinder and straining the rough ground product through a sieve. Sure enough, the grinding did warm up the cinnamon. Then we conducted a taste test with equal amounts of our home-ground sticks and pre-ground cinnamon in small bowls of applesauce. The home-ground sticks, which were nowhere as fine as the pre-ground powder, gave the applesauce an unpleasant, gritty mouthfeel. Compared with the pre-ground version, the flavor of our home-ground was extremely weak and slightly woody.

That said, cinnamon sticks certainly do have their place in the kitchen. They are preferable when infusing flavor into hot liquids, where ground cinnamon will clump and lend a gritty texture to the liquid. Sticks also stay fresher longer—three to four years.

The Neiman Marcus Cookie Recipe Legend, Part II

I was very interested in the Neiman Marcus Cookie Recipe legend mentioned in the September/October 1998 issue "Notes from Readers" section. Many years ago, I was given a similar recipe called "Mrs. Fields $250.00 Cookies" and was told it came from Mrs. Fields Cookies. No mention was made of Neiman Marcus. But the story was the same, about a woman who was unexpectedly charged $250 for the recipe and who then distributed it widely as a means of revenge.

BOBBIE LOVE
KAPAA, HI

➤ Many readers responded to the Neiman Marcus Cookie legend piece. Like you, Lynn Kouf of Darby, Montana, encountered the same tale about Mrs. Fields rather than Neiman Marcus. Several other readers reported a version of this story that once circulated about yet another cookie maker, Famous Amos.

Attributing the story to urban legend, three more readers, including Matthew Marciano of Sanibel, Florida, Lori Meltzer of Arlington, Massachusetts, and Marcia Coakley of Brockton, Massachusetts, all turned to the Internet to investigate the myth's origins. All three readers discovered the same thing. According to the Web sites they consulted, "The same story circulated in the late 1930s about a lady who dined at the Waldorf Astoria Hotel in New York City. She liked the Red Velvet Cake so much that she asked for the recipe. When she received her hotel bill, she had been charged $100 for the recipe." Though the cost of the recipe seems to have been adjusted for inflation, the mechanics of the tale remain the same. Regardless of its origin, Neiman Marcus representatives consider the story to be a hoax.

Umami

I enjoyed reading the article "White Mushrooms Revisited" in the September/October 1998 issue of *Cook's*. The "inherent, deep," "meaty," "mushroom" flavor that the authors sought and described is considered by some to be an example of umami.

Umami has been described as the flavor of richness, such as in caramelized proteins or in tomatoes. Others describe it as the savoriness of raw oysters or mushrooms. Still others regard it as a pungency, as in seaweed. *Webster's New World Dictionary of Culinary Arts* lists umami as "One of the five primary sensations comprising the sense of taste; refers to the savory taste of protein." The most common description of the umami flavor, however, is glutamate.

DAVID KAMEN
REGO PARK, NY

➤ The authors' research and innumerable conversations with home and professional cooks proved that most people find it difficult to describe the flavor of mushrooms. Invariably, one adjective that was used was "meaty."

This trait of mushroom flavor can, as you said, be linked to the Japanese word *umami*. As you noted, umami describes a "meaty" or "brothy" flavor that the Japanese and other Asians have long considered a fifth basic taste along with the traditional Big Four of sweet, sour, salty, and bitter. Western scientists have also begun to accept the legitimacy of umami. According to Dr. Gary Beauchamp, director of the Monell Chemical Senses Center in Philadelphia, "There is a growing consensus that umami is in fact distinct, that there is something different about it from all other tastes."

The "umami" taste is produced by a common amino acid known as glutamate. Glutamate is present in relatively high amounts in all protein, including meat and dairy products, and also in certain vegetables. In mushrooms, the glutamate content is high enough to lend that familiar meaty flavor. Umami also works to make food more palatable in general. "Umami stimulates appetites in all cultures across the board," says Steve Roper of the University of Miami. "Indeed, it seems very likely that glutamate drives the appetite for protein, just as the sweet taste drives the appetite for carbohydrates and the salt taste for minerals."

Product Choices for Tasting and Testing Reviews

I have tried all the tunas you reviewed in the July/August 1998 tuna tasting. It is a shame that you limited your selection to the obvious corporate choices. None of them come close to the tuna I've been buying at Trader Joe's.

REMY CHEVALIER
WESTON, CT

➤ We frequently hear from readers whose favorite food or piece of equipment did not appear in our rating of that item. Selecting the particular foods and pieces of equipment to include in our tasting and testing stories is a challenging, and carefully considered, process. To use the tuna tasting as an example, we found that the Trader Joe's chain has stores only on the East and West Coasts. Because our readership is national (in fact, international), we try to avoid using regional brands in these articles when there are more than enough national brands available, as was the case in the canned tuna tasting. The recent butter tasting (*see* "Freshness, Not Fat, Make the Best Butter," May/June 1998) was a different matter, because Land O' Lakes was the only brand with extensive national distribution. Often we will include items that are available by mail order when appropriate.

Unfortunately, there are bound to be some great products that go unrecognized in our tests because they just don't have the wide-scale distribution we require for our readership.

Shaving Strips of Parmesan

Though you did not test this in your September/October 1998 rating of all-purpose vegetable peelers, I use mine to shave strips from wedges of Parmesan or Romano (or other hard) cheese to garnish salads and pasta.

LINDA WATERMAN
LOS ANGELES, CA

➤ To determine which peeler was best for this job, we shaved strips from a wedge of Parmesan with both the winner of our peeler rating, the Oxo Good Grips straight peeler, and the best of the "Y," or harp type peelers (with the blade perpendicular to the handle), the Kuhn Rikon. Certainly both peelers did the job, but we felt that the Kuhn Rikon "Y" peeler offered both a good bite into the cheese and an extra measure of control, which made it easier to produce strips of uniform size and thickness.

Erratum

➤ In the November/December 1998 Notes from Readers letter titled "Apple Pie Airspace," we cited the wrong issue date for our article "All-Season Apple Pie." The correct date of the issue in which that article appeared was November/December 1997. We apologize for the confusion.

Quick Tips

Steaming the Skins Off Roasted Peppers

The accepted technique for steaming roasted peppers so that the skins will peel off is to place them in a closed brown paper bag. But what if there are no such bags handy? Diane Lanctot of San Francisco, California, places her roasted peppers in a covered saucepan to steam. The cleanup is a breeze, and this eliminates having to first locate, and then discard, the paper bag.

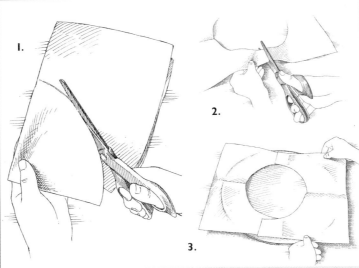

Lining Cake Pans and Plates

We have previously run Quick Tips for both cutting correctly sized rounds of parchment paper for lining cake pans (*see* September/October 1998) and for using strips of parchment for lining the cake plate to keep it clean while you frost or decorate the cake (*see* May/June 1997). It occurred to Suzanne Jewell of Post Falls, Idaho, that you could save parchment paper and extra effort by combining the two tips.

1. Cut out the proper size lining sheet by tracing the bottom of the cake pan onto the center of a large sheet of parchment, folding the sheet into four equal quarters, and cutting along the outline of the quarter circle that resulted.

2. Cut the remainder of the sheet in half so that it makes an adjustable circle.

3. This outer circle will fit perfectly around the cake on the plate, so the plate rims will stay neat while you frost or decorate.

Cleaning Up Dough

Our previous advice about removing dough from counters and bowls inspired other readers. Greg Im of Woolwich, Maine, uses an old credit card to scrape dough from a counter (illustration A).

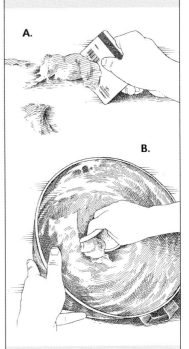

Paul Bech of Swarthmore, Pennsylvania, uses a plastic yogurt container or coffee-can lid to remove dough from bowls (illustration B). The curve of these circular lids fits the contours of the bowls perfectly.

Steadying Oysters on a Baking Sheet

When preparing an oyster dish that requires baking the shucked oysters in their shells, the shells often tip and spill the liquor out. Instead of using a bed of Kosher salt to steady them, as many recipes recommend, A. David Boccuti of Arlington, Massachusetts, uses the freshly removed top shells of the oysters, placed rough side up, to prop up the bottom shells and prevent them from tipping.

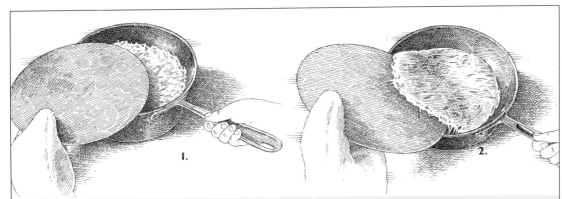

Flipping Hot Foods

Many recipes, such as that for Classic Hash Browns in the September/October 1998 issue, call for inverting food onto a plate in order to flip it so the uncooked side is down. Alison Richards of Boulder, Colorado, has found that the removable bottom of a tart pan works very well for this task.

1. Using an oven mitt or pot holders, slide the tart pan bottom over the skillet and invert the skillet.

2. The tart pan bottom is lightweight, and easy to handle, and it has no rim or curvature, so the food slides easily off of it and back into the skillet.

Send Us Your Tip We will provide a complimentary one-year subscription for each tip we print. See page 1 for information.

Makeshift Rolling Pin

Rented vacation condos or cottages often have poorly equipped kitchens, as Shinei Tsukamoto of San Ramon, California, found when he went searching for a rolling pin in the kitchen of a rented ski condo in Colorado. Finding no such thing, he reached for a chilled, unopened bottle of white wine with straight sides, which provided both good weight and a cold temperature for rolling his pie dough.

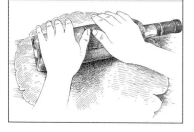

Removing Stencils from Cake Tops

Using stencils to decorate unfrosted cakes with a dusting of powdered sugar or cocoa can be fun. But removing the stencil without marring the design can be tricky because the stencils generally do not have handles for easy grasping. Mary Anne Spinner of Chicago, Illinois, suggests this method of dealing with the problem.

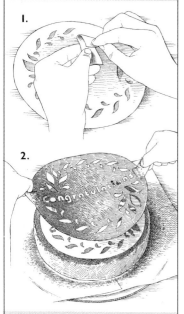

1. Create tabs by folding 2-inch lengths of masking tape halfway back on themselves, pinching the middle sections together.
2. Stick the ends to either side of the stencil and use the pieces of tape as handles to grasp and lift the stencil straight up and off.

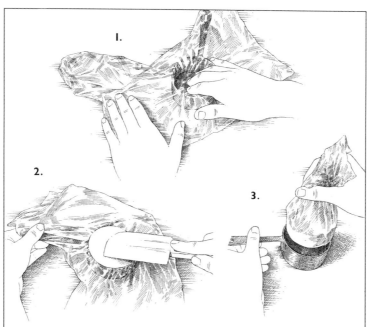

Mess-Free Measuring Cups

Frequent pie bakers have experienced the frustration of trying to thoroughly clean measuring cups that have contained a solid fat such as shortening or lard. Dale Chao of Concord, California, has found a way to avoid this problem.
1. Line the measuring cup with plastic wrap before adding the fat.
2. Push the fat into the cup with a spatula or wooden spoon to be sure the cup is completely full.
3. When you remove the fat, the measuring cup stays clean—and you can even wrap the fat in the plastic to chill it before cutting it into the flour for the pie dough.

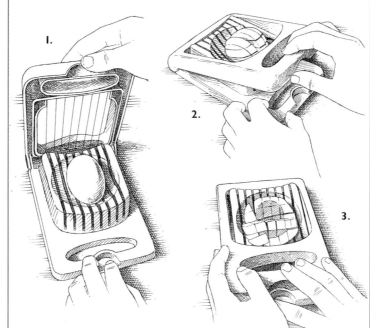

Perfectly Cubed Hard-Cooked Eggs

For her ideal egg salad (*see* page 15), Maryellen Driscoll found that 3/8-inch cubes of hard-cooked egg worked best. She eventually located a mozarella slicer that quickly made cubes of just the right size (*see* "Sources", page 32, for ordering information).
1. Place the egg in the depression in the slicer and slice it lengthwise.
2. Turn the egg a quarter turn and slice lengthwise again.
3. Rotate the egg 90 degrees and slice widthwise.

Quick and Easy Way to Decorate a Frosted Cake

Once a layer cake is frosted (*see* page 24 for step-by-step instructions), use the back of a tablespoon to make decorative swirls on the top.

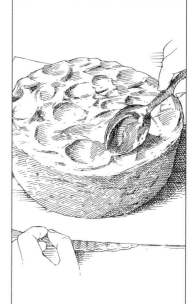

Draining Ground Meat

Many cooks who use ground meat in their recipes want to drain off the excess fat that accumulates in the pan as the meat browns. Pat Brown of Telluride, Colorado, tilts the pan so the fat will accumulate on one side and blots it with wadded-up sheets of paper towel that she holds with tongs. This way, no meat spills from the pan, and a maximum amount of fat is removed. If using a gas burner, be sure to keep the oily paper away from the flame.

Why Not Chicken Fricassee?

Almost entirely forgotten by modern cooks, this simple dish of chicken poached in broth makes its own sauce.

⇒ BY CHRISTOPHER KIMBALL ⇐

Chicken can be roasted, sautéed, grilled, fried, stir-fried, oven-fried, baked, poached, and smoked, but these days we rarely think about a simple fricassee. Why? Well, for one thing, most of us mistake it for some outdated Cordon Bleu preparation. In fact, a chicken fricassee is nothing more than chicken poached in stock, after which a simple sauce is made from the liquid. It's simple, it's flavorful, and it's easy. So why is it also forgotten?

For many versions of this recipe, the answer is quite simple: They are either too time consuming or no longer appeal to the modern palate. It has been 20 years since I last made a coulibiac of salmon (fish baked in a casing of brioche dough), filled pounded beef fillets with duxelles (finely minced mushrooms sautéed with butter and brandy), or even made homemade fettuccine, the flaccid strands draped over chair backs in the dining room to dry. But certain recipes do deserve a second life. I have found much to recommend turnip slaw, hermit bars, applesauce cake, and many other dishes that have passed out of favor for no good reason, so it seemed high time to resurrect chicken fricassee. It is neither time consuming to make nor a culinary dinosaur.

The process did involve solving some problems, however. The first was to define the parameters of the recipe. The fricassee has had a long history and many different interpretations. In short, though, a French fricassee was chicken (or sometimes vegetables) cooked in a white sauce. Over time, this dish evolved to become chicken poached in a clear liquid, usually chicken stock but sometimes water and/or wine. When the chicken was done, it was removed from the pan and then a sauce was made from the poaching liquid. This simple definition was my starting point.

But I had other considerations as well. I did not want an extremely rich sauce, preferring instead something lighter and more modern. I was also keen on developing a recipe that could

We make our chicken fricassee with a generous amount of sauce, so be sure to serve plenty of rice or bread to soak it up.

be put together as quickly and simply as possible, making it a candidate for weeknight cooking. This would mean shortening cooking times and using the minimum number of pans and ingredients. I also wanted to make sure that the skin was not unappealing, which would require either sautéing or using skinless pieces of chicken. Producing moist chicken was going to be important, as was producing a flavorful, well-balanced sauce that was neither too rich nor too acidic.

As usual at *Cook's Illustrated*, we started off with a blind taste test, choosing the lightest, most promising fricassee recipes we could find. The first was a classic French preparation in which the chicken pieces were lightly sautéed in butter and then simmered in equal amounts of chicken stock and white wine, which was finished with a bit of heavy cream. The resulting sauce was judged too acidic, and the chicken's skin was unappealing. The second recipe, taken from the *Joy of Cooking*, was similar to the first except that the cooking liquid was a combination of

water and chicken stock. This recipe also called for three large carrots and two large celery stalks. The sauce was thin and vegetal, with a carrot flavor so strong that it was unwelcome. The third recipe, the worst of the lot, called for 45 minutes of cooking in chicken stock, much too long to produce moist meat.

After these initial forays, we made three decisions: Chicken stock rather than water or wine was the preferred poaching liquid, we favored a light hand when finishing the sauce with cream, and the remaining ingredients had to be added with a high degree of parsimony.

Now we were ready to create our own recipe. First, though, I had to decide whether I preferred a brown or white fricassee, the difference being a matter of whether the chicken is sautéed before being poached. A quick test confirmed that sautéing develops flavor and renders fat from the skin, some of which is used to flavor the sauce. We prefered full-fledged sauté to the light sauté used in some of the recipes selected for the blind tasting; the higher heat made the skin crisper and the dish more flavorful.

At this point we had a working recipe. A whole chicken is cut up, seasoned liberally with salt and pepper, and sautéed in olive oil and butter. The chicken is then simmered in stock for about 20 minutes and removed from the liquid. Meanwhile, onions and mushrooms are sautéed in a second pan, and a sauce is then made with the poaching liquid, the vegetables, and a bit of heavy cream to finish. I decided to thicken the sauce using a basic roux, which is simply melted butter and flour whisked together over high heat.

The first test of this master recipe produced very good results. The skin was appealing, and the sauce had a nice, rich flavor; by poaching the

TECHNIQUE | SAVING THE "OYSTER"

When cutting the chicken into parts, be careful to save the "oyster" when you remove the leg and thigh from the bird. With chicken breast down, closely follow the contour of the hip bone to remove this tender disk-shaped muscle.

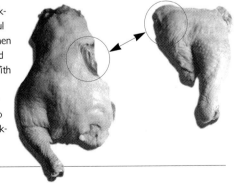

chicken in stock we had created a wonderful double stock. But there were still some problems. The sauce was a bit too fatty, and it was also a bit flat, in need of some bite and contrast. I then substituted a half cup of white wine for the same amount of stock, using the wine to deglaze the pan after sautéing the onions and mushrooms. This helped, but I found that an additional squirt of lemon juice just before serving was also necessary for balance. I then tried substituting half and half for the cream, a change that made the sauce more balanced as well as livelier. We also tried making the sauce with no dairy. This version was acceptable, but the sauce lacked the silky feeling provided by the half and half and did not balance as nicely with the wine and lemon juice.

The other big issue was the chicken itself. Since I like a choice of white or dark meat, I prefer buying a whole chicken and cutting it up myself. However, chicken thighs work well, as do other selected parts of the bird, such as the breasts. You can use skinless chicken parts if you like, but if you do so I suggest that you eliminate the sautéing step, simply starting the recipe by poaching in the chicken stock. Note that this will result in a very good but somewhat less flavorful dish. I also learned that it was best to simply let the cooked chicken rest in a covered bowl rather than keeping it warm in an oven. A great deal of liquid escapes from the meat when left in a warm oven, resulting in dry chicken. Finally, be sure to add back to the sauce any accumulated juices from the resting chicken.

SIMPLE CHICKEN FRICASSEE WITH MUSHROOMS AND ONIONS
SERVES 4

If you own a large Dutch oven that can hold all the chicken in a single layer without crowding, use it to brown all the pieces at once. If not, divide the task between a smaller Dutch oven and the same skillet that you will use to sauté the vegetables. This eliminates the need to brown in batches in one pot and shortens the cooking time by about 10 minutes. Dark meat fans can substitute eight bone-in, skin-on thighs for the whole chicken.

1	chicken, 3 to 4 pounds, cut into 2 wings, 2 legs, 2 thighs, and breast quartered (*see* illustration) Salt and ground black pepper
4	tablespoons butter
2	tablespoons olive oil
2½	cups chicken stock or low-sodium canned chicken broth
1	medium onion, chopped fine
10	ounces white mushrooms, washed and left whole if small, halved if medium, quartered if large
½	cup dry white wine
3	tablespoons flour
1	cup half and half
1	teaspoon minced fresh thyme leaves
1½	tablespoons juice from one lemon
¼	teaspoon fresh grated nutmeg
¼	cup minced fresh parsley leaves

1. Season chicken with salt and pepper. Heat 1 tablespoon each olive oil and butter in both a Dutch oven and medium skillet over medium-high heat. When foam subsides, add chicken pieces skin side down and cook until well browned, 4 to 5 minutes on each side. Spoon off all but 2 tablespoons fat from Dutch oven. Add chicken from skillet, arranging pieces in a single layer as much as possible. Add stock, partially cover, and bring to boil. Reduce heat to low and simmer until chicken is fully cooked, 20 to 25 minutes. Remove Dutch oven from heat, transfer chicken to bowl; cover with foil and set aside.

2. While chicken is simmering, drain off all but 1 tablespoon fat from the now-empty skillet. Add onion, mushrooms, and ¼ teaspoon salt; sauté over medium-high heat, stirring occasionally, until mushroom liquid evaporates and vegetables begin to brown, 6 to 8 minutes. Add wine; cook until almost all liquid evaporates, 2 to 3 minutes. Transfer to small bowl and set aside.

3. Heat remaining 2 tablespoons butter in now-empty skillet over medium heat until foaming. Add flour and whisk until golden in color, about 1 minute. Add half and half, whisking vigorously until smooth. Immediately whisk this mixture into hot chicken cooking liquid in Dutch oven. Bring to a boil over medium-high heat; reduce heat to medium-low and simmer, stirring frequently, until thickened to the consistency of heavy cream, 6 to 8 minutes. Stir in mushroom mixture, thyme, lemon juice, and nutmeg; season with salt and pepper to taste. Transfer chicken to pot and simmer until heated through, 2 to 3 minutes. Stir in 2 tablespoons parsley. Transfer chicken pieces to serving or individual plates, spoon sauce over and sprinkle with remaining parsley.

SIMPLE CHICKEN FRICASSEE WITH PEAS AND CARROTS

Follow recipe for Simple Chicken Fricassee with Mushrooms and Onions, substituting 1 small carrot, diced small, for mushrooms. Sauté until vegetables begin to brown, 3 to 4 minutes. Reduce heat to low, add wine, cover, and cook until carrots are tender, 10 to 12 minutes. Stir in ½ cup thawed frozen peas, increase heat to medium-high, and cook until almost all liquid evaporates, 1 to 2 minutes. Transfer to small bowl; set aside. Continue with recipe, substituting peas and carrot mixture for mushrooms.

TECHNIQUE

CUTTING UP THE CHICKEN

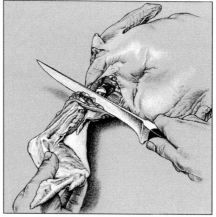

Removing the Wings By removing the wings with the chicken breast-down, you will avoid cutting off a piece of the breast.

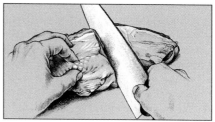

Quartering the Breast Cut the breast in half crosswise, then cut each half in half.

Simple Pan-Seared Salmon

The ultimate weeknight dinner, this salmon is on the table less than 15 minutes from the time the pan hits the stove.

⇒ BY ADAM RIED WITH ANNE YAMANAKA ⇐

Salmon may not seem the stuff of comedy, but my friend Greg and I used to crack up over it. Not a week goes by where we don't talk two or three times, and since we are both interested in food, the conversation invariably turns to what the other is making for dinner that night. For months on end, as if it were a practical joke, the answer was always the same for both of us: "Salmon."

But it was no joke. Greg and I had both clued into the fact that salmon is readily available, flavorful, supremely quick and easy to cook, and uniquely satisfying; in other words, the perfect weeknight meal for family or guests.

The cooking options for salmon are many. Steamed, poached, and baked are all good, and grilling is fantastic (*see* "How to Grill Salmon," July/August 1997). Now I was in search of an almost effortless indoor technique that would exploit salmon's high oil content and natural moistness while also indulging my taste for fish that comes out of the pan with a crisp, even, deeply golden crust. So I zeroed in on pan-cooking over a relatively high heat on the stove top. Requiring little time and equipment, this method heightens the flavor of the fish and produces an appealing contrast in texture.

Or at least it does when the fish is cooked right. In the past I had struggled to attain the perfect degree of doneness. My fish was often overcooked to the point of being dry and chalky as I tried to create a nice, healthy crust, or, in an effort to protect against overcooking, I ended up with a wimpy crust. At least my travails had shown me what areas to explore. Should I use fat in the pan? If so, what kind and how much? Should the fillets be dredged in flour, bread crumbs, or the like for added crispness? And, of course, I had questions about the type of pan to use, the degree of heat required, and cooking times. Getting all of that right would lead to fish with a crisp, uniform crust and moist, firm flesh within.

Fat First

The amount and type of fat to use was a real wild card in our research. There were recipes using

Forget the rules about 10 minutes per inch of thickness. Fillets take about 4½ minutes on the first side, 3½ on the second.

everything from butter to canola oil in quantities ranging from five tablespoons down to no fat at all for four fillets.

We chose the extreme first, cooking four fillets with no fat in the pan. Though salmon supplies plenty of its own fat and a nonstick pan eliminates sticking problems, these fillets developed uneven, blotchy, unappealing crusts, especially on the skin side. Some fat in the pan, we thought, would improve matters. So we cooked four fillets in amounts ranging from one to three tablespoons of canola oil, moving in one-half tablespoon increments. These larger amounts might work well for lean fish, but for a fatty fish such as salmon even one tablespoon of oil was too much. Eventually, we found that a mere teaspoon of fat in a large skillet was all we needed to promote a deep, even crust on both sides of the fillets.

We also experimented with the different types of fat suggested in our research. Salmon is extremely rich to begin with, so butter simply pushed it over the top, not to mention the fact that it burned. The flavor of olive oil seemed at odds with the fish, and a butter–olive oil combination offered no advantage. Cooking spray was

sub-par. Peanut oil worked nicely, as did both canola and vegetable oil. Because these two oils are more of a staple than peanut oil and are neutral in flavor, they were our first choice. Some recipes suggested oiling the fillets themselves instead of the pan, but this practice diminished the crust we were looking for.

While we were at it, we also tried dredging the fish in a coating meant to cook up crisp, including seasoned flour, bread crumbs, and corn meal, but we disliked them all for uneven browning, dull flavor, and pasty texture.

Pan Scan

Without a doubt, the type of pan and the heat setting would be important variables. The good news concerning pans was that every one of the four we tried—including a cheap, thin stainless steel model, heavy-bottomed stainless steel and nonstick models, and our faithful cast iron skillet—produced a decent crust. Though the nonstick pan ensures easy cleanup and no sticking, the crust it developed was marginally less deep than the others, and the necessary preheating of the pan is not kind to the nonstick finish. The heavy stainless steel and cast iron pans produced exemplary crusts, while the lighter, cheaper pan scorched almost fatally during cooking. While any one of them will work, our favorites were the heavy stainless steel and cast iron models. Whichever pan you choose, make sure it is large enough to accommodate the fillets comfortably; the edges of the fillets should not touch, as this could cause some steaming, instead of searing, to

TECHNIQUE | CUTTING THE FISH

Try to get all your fillets from the thicker end of the fish, so they all have the same thickness and therefore will cook in the same amount of time.

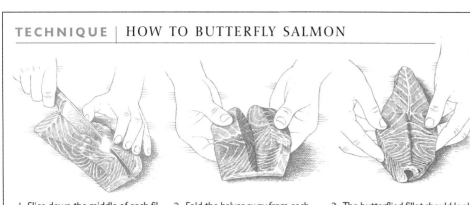

1. Slice down the middle of each fillet, cutting down to but not through the skin.

2. Fold the halves away from each other so that each side lies flat. The skin should act as a hinge.

3. The butterflied fillet should look like a salmon steak.

occur. We found a 12-inch skillet to be just right.

Preheating the pan and choosing the right heat for cooking the fish were also critical. We tried preheating the pan for lengths of time ranging from one to five minutes and found that three minutes over high heat did the trick, regardless of whether the stove is gas or electric. But the high heat was too much once the fish was in the pan, cooking it too fast and producing billows of smoke, so we reduced the heat to medium-high. Because the pan loses some heat when the fish is added, we waited about 30 seconds before reducing the flame so the pan could regain some of the lost heat.

The Finish Line

Timing, of course, was also crucial. We did not want to overcook the salmon. Because our fillets were consistently between 1 inch and 1¼ inches thick, we decided to start by following the old kitchen maxim of 10 minutes per inch of thickness. The fish overcooked. It overcooked at 9 minutes, too. At 8 minutes, though, it undercooked ever so slightly. Fortunately, as with many cuts of meat, we learned that salmon fillets have enough residual heat to continue cooking briefly after they come out of the pan. In fact, we found that a 1-minute rest before serving brought the 8-minute fillets to a perfect medium with no danger of overcooking.

Though many sources suggest shaking the pan after adding the salmon to prevent sticking, we found this step to be unnecessary. Provided that the pan is hot enough and the fat is shimmering, we decided it is best to just drop the fillet in the pan skin side down and leave it be until the fish turns opaque and milky white from the bottom to about halfway up the fillet. Then simply slide a thin, flexible metal spatula between the pan bottom and the skin, and flip it quickly so the flesh side is down; make sure not to move the fish for the first two minutes. After that, you can lift it gently at the corner with the spatula to check the bottom crust. We also suggest peeking inside the fillet with the tip of a paring knife. The center should still show traces of bright, translucent orange. If it is completely opaque and the orange

color is a little duller, as it is toward the exterior of the fillet, the fish is overcooked.

SIMPLE PAN-SEARED SALMON
SERVES 4

With the addition of the fish fillets, the pan temperature drops; compensate for the heat loss by keeping the heat on medium-high for 30 seconds after adding them. If cooking two or three fillets instead of the full recipe of four, use a 10-inch skillet and medium-high heat for both preheating the pan and cooking the salmon. A splatter screen helps reduce the mess of pan-searing. Serve salmon with the chutney (right), a fresh salsa, an herb-spiked vinaigrette, or squirt of lemon or lime.

4 skin-on salmon fillets, each about 6 ounces and 1 to 1¼ inches thick
Salt and ground black pepper
1 teaspoon canola or vegetable oil

1. Heat a 12-inch heavy-bottomed skillet for 3 minutes over high heat. Sprinkle salmon with salt and ground black pepper.

2. Add oil to pan; swirl to coat. When oil shimmers (but does not smoke) add fillets skin side down and cook, without moving fillets, until pan regains lost heat, about 30 seconds. Reduce heat to medium-high; continue to cook until skin side is well browned and bottom half of fillets turns opaque, 4½ minutes. Turn fillets and cook, without moving them, until they are no longer translucent on the exterior and are firm, but not hard, when gently squeezed: 3 minutes for medium-rare and 3½ minutes for medium. Remove fillets from pan; let stand 1 minute. Pat with paper towel to absorb excess fat on surface, if desired. Serve immediately.

PAN-SEARED BUTTERFLIED SALMON

Some folks savor crisp salmon skin as a treat, while others simply won't eat it. For those who do not fancy the skin, butterflying the salmon fillets is an excellent idea. This is not recom-

mended for skin lovers, because the skin is never exposed to the heat, so it never crisps. For those who want to avoid the skin, however, the advantage is that both sides of the flesh get a good sear, so there is twice as much of the brown, flavorful crust.

Following illustrations 1 through 3, above, butterfly salmon fillets. Follow cooking instructions for Simple Pan-Seared Salmon, cooking fillets for one minute less on the first side.

PAN-SEARED SALMON WITH SESAME SEED CRUST

For heightened sesame flavor, rub the fish fillets with Asian sesame oil instead of canola or vegetable. If you pair this variation with butterflied fillets, double the quantity of sesame seeds and coat both sides of each fillet.

Spread ¼ cup sesame seeds in a pie plate. Follow recipe for Simple Pan-Seared Salmon, rubbing fillets with 2 teaspoons canola or vegetable oil, sprinkling with salt and ground black pepper, then pressing flesh sides of fillets in sesame seeds to coat. Continue with recipe, being careful not to break sesame crust when removing fillets from pan.

SWEET AND SOUR CHUTNEY WITH ONIONS AND WARM SPICES
MAKES ABOUT ⅓ CUP, ENOUGH FOR 4 SALMON FILLETS

Since it takes several minutes to make this chutney, prepare it before cooking the salmon. A little of this intensely flavored condiment goes a long way.

1 teaspoon fennel seeds
½ teaspoon ground cumin
½ teaspoon ground coriander
¼ teaspoon ground cardamom
¼ teaspoon paprika
¼ teaspoon salt
2 teaspoons olive oil
½ medium onion, chopped fine (about ½ cup)
¼ cup red wine vinegar
1 tablespoon sugar
1 tablespoon minced fresh parsley leaves

Mix fennel, cumin, coriander, cardamom, paprika, and salt in small bowl; set aside. Heat olive oil in medium skillet over medium heat; sauté onion until soft, 3 to 4 minutes. Add reserved spice mixture; sauté until fragrant, about 1 minute more. Increase heat to medium-high and add vinegar, sugar, and 2 tablespoons water; cook until mixture reduces by about one-third and reaches a syrupy consistency, about 1½ minutes. Stir in parsley and serve chutney as a topping for pan-seared salmon fillets.

Ham and Split Pea Soup

An agreeably cheap cut of pork proved to be the secret to a modern but full-flavored version of this classic soup.

≥ BY PAM ANDERSON WITH GABRIELLE HAMILTON ≤

Ham was as central to my culinary past as the boneless, skinless chicken breast is to my present. There was hardly a month that went by that my mother didn't roast one of those big, water-added grocery store hams. She'd stick it in the oven and roast it for hours. The thick rind would crisp up, the fat would render, and the added water would evaporate, leaving the meat irresistibly rich and dense. For days we'd have sliced ham for dinner, ham sandwiches for lunch, and fried ham for breakfast. Finally, when the ham was picked nearly clean, it was time to make a pot of soup.

My mom's bean and pea soups were hardly recipes. She simply dropped the ham bone in a pot, dumped in a package of overnight-soaked beans or peas, and covered them with water. This simple concoction cooked until the meat fell off the bone, the fat discreetly melted into the broth, and the peas or beans became creamy enough to thicken the soup. Minced fresh onion and cornbread were the only accompaniments.

I still love these bean and pea soups made with ham broth—particularly those with split peas—but times have changed. Except for the occasional holiday, I rarely buy a bone-in ham, opting more often for the thin-sliced deli stuff. But convenience has its price. With every one of my deli ham purchases I lose another pot of split pea soup. I've tried to figure out ways to cheat the soup of its crucial ham bone and sometimes have almost convinced myself of success, until I remember the tender shreds of flavorful ham in my mother's soup. Was it possible to duplicate this wonderful soup without buying a huge ham? I decided to find out.

The Proof's in the Broth

To confirm or disprove my belief that ham broth is crucial to split pea soup, we made several pork broths and pork-enhanced canned chicken broths. In addition to making broth from a meaty ham bone, we made them from smoked pork necks, pork hocks (fresh and smoked), and smoked ham shanks. We also made cheater broths: kielbasa simmered in canned chicken broth, kielbasa simmered in water, bacon simmered in chicken broth, and bacon simmered in water.

Broths made with hocks—fresh as well as smoked—were more greasy than flavorful. In addition, the hocks gave up very little meat, making it necessary to purchase an additional portion of ham

A bone-in picnic shoulder yields plenty of meat for the soup.

to fortify the soup. Ham shanks, which include the hock, made a pleasant but lightweight broth that was a tad greasy and salty—both fixable problems had the broth been more stellar. Though not widely available, pork necks made a fairly flavorful but salty broth. All four cheater broths failed. Both the kielbasa- and bacon-enhanced chicken broths tasted strongly of overly processed meat, while the water-based versions tasted weak.

Not surprisingly, the broth made from the bone of a big ham was the winner. It was meaty and full flavored, rich but not greasy, nicely seasoned without being overly salty, and smoky without tasting artificial. Unlike any of the other broths, this one sported bits of meat. And not just good meat—great meat. The tender pieces of ham that fell away from the bone during cooking were not just a nice byproduct of the broth. They were the glory of my split pea soup.

But was there a way around buying half a ham (with an average weight of about 8 pounds) just to make a pot of soup? I made a trip to the grocery store to find out. After checking out the ham and smoked pork cases at two different stores, I discovered the picnic from the pork shoulder. Unlike what we generally refer to as ham, which comes from the back legs of the animal, the picnic comes from the shoulder and front legs (*see* illustration, page 11). Smaller than a ham, the half-picnic

weighs only 4½ pounds. After making a couple more pots of soup, we found that the picnic pork shoulder—with its bones, fat, rind, and meat—made outstanding stock, and after two hours of simmering, the meat was meltingly tender yet potently flavorful.

Since we did not need the full picnic half for our pot of soup, we pulled off and roasted two of its meatier muscles (*see* illustrations, page 11) and used the remaining meat, bone, fat, and rind to make the soup. At around 99 cents a pound, picnic shoulders are usually cheaper than a ham, and at my grocery store picnics were even cheaper than pork hocks, shanks, and neck bones. Here, I thought, was the modern solution. Rather than buy a ham for eating (and eating and eating) with a leftover bone for soup, instead purchase a picnic for soup, and roast the remaining couple of pounds for eating.

Although not as widely available as picnic shoulder, picnic pieces also work well, coming in portions of 2 to 2½ pounds that are ideal for the soup. Simply throw the whole piece in the pot and make your soup.

No Soaking, Please

To determine whether or not the split peas needed to be soaked before cooking, we made soups with split peas treated in three ways. We made the first pot with peas that had been soaked overnight, the second with peas that had been soaked in boiling water for 10 minutes, and the third with peas that were not soaked at all.

Surprisingly (and happily), the unsoaked peas cooked the quickest, and the soup made from these peas tasted the best of the three. The peas disintegrated into the stock, forming a deliciously thick and creamy soup.

In contrast, the peas soaked overnight tasted washed out and bland. Since these water-plumped peas were fully swelled, there could be no marriage between the broth and peas. The soup made with the parboiled peas was a slight improvement; these blanched peas tasted good—

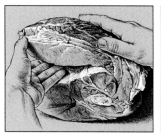

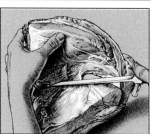

1. With your fingers, loosen the large comma-shaped muscles on top of the picnic half.

2. Use a knife to cut the membrane separating the comma-shaped muscles from the rest of the roast.

not washed out and bland like those soaked overnight—but there was still too much of a distinction between stock and peas.

Order in the Pot

Now that we had figured out an inexpensive way to get a ham bone and had discovered that preparing the split peas meant no more than snipping the bag and dumping them into the pot, we were ready to start making soup.

There are several ways to make ham and split pea soup. You can throw all the ingredients—ham bone, beans, and diced vegetables—into a pot and simmer until everything is tender. Or you can sauté the vegetables, then add the remaining ingredients and cook the soup until the ham and peas are tender. Alternatively, you can cook the ham bone and peas (or give the ham bone a little bit of a head start) until ham and peas are tender and then add raw, sautéed, or caramelized vegetables to the pot, continuing to cook until the vegetables are tender and the flavors have blended.

Although we had hoped to keep the soup a straightforward one-pot operation, we found out pretty quickly that dumping everything in at the same time resulted in gloppy, overcooked peas and tired mushy vegetables by the time the ham was tender. For textural contrast in this smooth, creamy soup, we ultimately preferred fully—not overly—cooked vegetables.

Our best soups were those in which the vegetables spent enough time in the pot for their flavors to blend, but not so long that they had lost all of their individual taste. Of the soups with vegetables added toward the end of cooking, we preferred the one with the caramelized vegetables. The sweeter vegetables gave this otherwise straightforward meat and starch soup a richness and depth of flavor that made the extra step and pan worth the trouble.

To cook the peas, ham, and vegetables to perfection, we couldn't get around adding them to the pot at different times. After many experiments, we concluded that our ideal pot of soup started with a meaty picnic bone that we simmered about two hours, until the meat was fall-off-the-bone tender. We then fished out the ham and, after waiting for it to cool, shredded the meat, discarding bone, rind, and excess fat. Meanwhile, we added the peas to the pot, along with some thyme for flavor, and simmered until the peas started to break down, about 45 minutes. Finally, we added the caramelized vegetables and the shredded ham to the pot and simmered until the vegetables crossed the border from crisp to tender. At this point the peas were smooth and creamy but had not yet turned the stock gloppy.

Many bean and pea soup recipes call for an acidic ingredient—vinegar, lemon juice, fortified wines such as sherry or Madeira, Worcestershire sauce, or sour cream—to bring balance to an otherwise rich, heavy soup. After tasting all of the above, we found ourselves drawn to balsamic

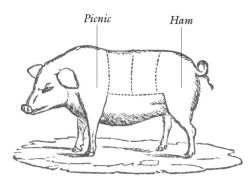

Picnic   Ham

vinegar. Unlike any of the other ingredients, balsamic's mildly sweet, mildly acidic flavor perfectly complemented the soup.

Now all I needed was minced red onion and a skillet of cornbread, and I'd be back home again.

HEARTY HAM AND SPLIT PEA SOUP WITH POTATOES
SERVES 6

Use a small 2½-pound smoked picnic portion ham if you can find one. Otherwise, buy a half-picnic ham and remove some meat, which you can save for use in sandwiches, salads, or omelets (see illustrations 1 and 2 above). If you like caraway, toast 1½ teaspoons of caraway seeds in a small skillet over medium-high heat, stirring frequently, until fragrant and browned, about 4 minutes, and substitute them for the dried thyme. The finished soup will continue to thicken as it stands but can be thinned with some water when reheated. To cut 45 minutes off the cooking time of the soup, simmer the ham 1½ hours, then add the split peas to the pot. When the ham is tender, after about 45 minutes more of simmering, remove it and shred; continue with the recipe.

1 piece (about 2½ pounds) smoked, bone-in picnic ham (see illustrations at left)
4 bay leaves
1 pound (2½ cups) split peas, rinsed and picked through
1 teaspoon dried thyme
2 tablespoons olive oil
2 medium onions, chopped medium
2 medium carrots, chopped medium
2 medium celery stalks, chopped medium
1 tablespoon butter
2 medium garlic cloves, minced
  Pinch sugar
3 small new potatoes, scrubbed and cut into medium dice
  Ground black pepper
  Minced red onion (optional)
  Balsamic vinegar

1. Bring 3 quarts water, ham, and bay leaves to boil, covered, over medium-high heat in large soup kettle. Reduce heat to low and simmer until meat is tender and pulls away from bone, 2 to 2½ hours. Remove ham meat and bone from broth; add split peas and thyme and simmer until peas are tender but not dissolved, about 45 minutes. Meanwhile, when ham is cool enough to handle, shred meat into bite-sized pieces and set aside. Discard rind and bone.

2. While ham is simmering, heat oil in large skillet over high heat until shimmering. Add onions, carrots, and celery; sauté, stirring frequently, until most of the liquid evaporates and vegetables begin to brown, 5 to 6 minutes. Reduce heat to medium low; add butter, garlic, and sugar. Cook vegetables, stirring frequently, until deeply browned, 30 to 35 minutes; set aside.

3. Add sautéed vegetables, potatoes, and shredded ham to soup; simmer until potatoes are tender and peas dissolve and thicken soup to the consistency of light cream, about 20 minutes more. Season with ground black pepper. Ladle soup into bowls, sprinkle with red onion, if using, and serve, passing balsamic vinegar separately.

TECHNIQUE | SHREDDING THE MEAT

Once the meat is cooked and has cooled, use your fingers to shred it into bite-sized pieces.

Pantry Pasta Sauces with Garlic and Oil

Finely pressed or minced garlic is the key to a flavorful pasta sauce
that can be varied to create quick meals.

≫ BY JACK BISHOP ≪

If you have garlic and olive oil on hand, you have the makings of a basic sauce for pasta. Italians call this sauce *aglio e olio*, garlic and oil, and they prepare it for late-night snacks or quick dinners when the refrigerator is bare.

Although this pantry sauce is easy to make, I did have a number of questions. How much garlic is right for a pound of pasta, and how should it be prepared and/or cooked to keep it from burning? How much oil will coat a pound of pasta? Is extra-virgin oil necessary?

After several tests, I determined that one-third cup of oil was enough to sauce a pound of spaghetti. (Oil-based sauces are best with long, thin pasta shapes. They coat the long strands from end to end, and the sauce does not pool up on the noodles and become greasy, as can happen with stubby pasta shapes.) I found an extra-virgin oil to be worth the extra pennies. The sauces I made with pure olive oil were bland and severely downgraded by tasters. As for the garlic, four medium cloves deliver enough flavor without overwhelming the pasta.

The next task was to fully cook the garlic to tame its sharpness but at the same time to avoid burning it, which turns it bitter. This is not necessarily easy, since in hot oil garlic can go from perfectly golden to burned in seconds.

I tried preparing the garlic several ways, including slicing, crushing, mincing, pressing, and pureeing. The larger the pieces, the more likely they were to burn and become acrid. As Christopher Kimball found in his "Twenty-Minute Tomato Sauce" story (*see* May/June 1997), putting peeled cloves through a press is the best way to get the pieces very small. If you don't own a press, you can mince the garlic by hand, sprinkle it with salt, and continue mincing and pressing on the garlic until it forms a smooth puree.

As an added precaution against burning, I found it helpful to dilute the pressed or pureed garlic with a little bit of water, a tip Stephanie Lyness discovered when cooking spices to make curry. I also found it imperative to heat the oil and garlic together, rather than heating the oil first and then adding the garlic. Letting the garlic gradually heat up ensures even cooking, as does the use of medium-low heat.

Because there is so little sauce and that sauce may be just barely warm, these pastas tend to cool off very quickly. Heating pasta bowls in a 200-degree oven for 10 minutes keeps the pasta warm, right down to the last noodle. Just make sure to warn everyone that the bowls are hot, and use oven mitts to bring them to the table.

SPAGHETTI WITH GARLIC AND OLIVE OIL
SERVES 4

The garlic is quickly and easily pureed with a garlic press. Alternatively, you can mince it with a chef's knife, sprinkle with ¼ teaspoon salt, and continue to mince to a paste, but be sure to reduce the amount of salt cooked with the oil and garlic to ½ teaspoon. Diluting the garlic with a bit of water before sautéing ensures a mild, even garlic flavor and helps to prevent burning. Although not a pantry item, parsley adds a fresh herbal flavor and should be used if you have some on hand. If you like, cook ¼ teaspoon red pepper flakes (or more to taste) along with the garlic and oil for this recipe only (not for the variations).

- 4   medium garlic cloves, peeled, processed through garlic press and mixed with 1 teaspoon water (*see* note above)
- ⅓   cup extra-virgin olive oil
       Salt
- 1   pound spaghetti or linguine
- ¼   cup minced fresh parsley leaves (optional)
       Ground black pepper

1. Heat oil, garlic, and ¾ teaspoon salt in small skillet over medium-low heat. Cook, stirring frequently, until garlic turns golden but not brown, about 5 minutes; remove pan from heat.

2. Meanwhile, bring 4 quarts water to boil in large pot. Add 1 tablespoon salt and pasta; cook until al dente. Reserving ¼ cup cooking liquid, drain pasta and return to pot. Add garlic mixture, reserved pasta cooking liquid, and optional parsley; toss well to coat. Adjust seasoning with salt and ground black pepper to taste. Serve immediately.

LINGUINE WITH LEMON AND PINE NUTS

Toast ¼ cup pine nuts in small dry skillet over medium heat, stirring frequently, until golden and fragrant, about 5 minutes; set aside. Follow recipe for Spaghetti with Garlic and Olive Oil, adding pine nuts and 1 teaspoon grated lemon zest to pasta along with garlic mixture.

SPAGHETTI WITH FRIED CAPERS AND ANCHOVIES

To keep the capers from splattering during frying, thoroughly pat them dry with paper towels before adding them to the skillet.

Heat olive oil in small skillet over medium-high heat until shimmering; add ½ cup rinsed and dried capers and cook, stirring occasionally, until capers crisp, darken, and pop open, about 4 minutes. Remove capers with slotted spoon and drain on paper towels. Off heat, let oil cool about 3 minutes. Follow recipe for Spaghetti with Garlic and Olive Oil, reducing salt to ½ teaspoon and using caper cooking oil to sauté 4 anchovy fillets, rinsed and minced, along with garlic; decrease cooking time to about 3 minutes. Add capers to pasta along with garlic mixture.

LINGUINE WITH PECORINO AND BLACK PEPPER

Follow recipe for Spaghetti with Garlic and Olive Oil, reducing salt to ½ teaspoon and adding ½ cup grated Pecorino Romano cheese and 2 teaspoons lemon juice to pasta along with garlic mixture. Omit parsley and season with 1 teaspoon ground black pepper.

LINGUINE WITH WALNUTS, GARLIC, AND OIL

The finely chopped walnuts, sautéed with the garlic and oil, make for an especially rich sauce.

Follow recipe for Spaghetti with Garlic and Olive Oil, cooking ⅔ cup finely chopped walnuts along with garlic.

SPAGHETTI WITH GREEN AND BLACK OLIVES

Follow recipe for Spaghetti with Garlic and Olive Oil, reducing salt to ½ teaspoon and adding ⅓ cup each pitted and chopped green and black olives and 1 tablespoon lemon juice to cooked garlic mixture.

The Best Way to Hard-Cook an Egg

An egg with a perfectly creamy yolk, tender white, and no green ring results from a simple bring-it-to-a-boil method.

➢ BY MARYELLEN DRISCOLL ➣

I have always considered hard-cooking an egg to be a crapshoot. There's no way to watch the proteins cook under the brittle shell of an uncracked egg, and you certainly can't poke it with an instant-read thermometer, as you would a piece of meat.

In the past, I have turned to my old edition of the *Joy of Cooking* for instructions on how to hard-cook an egg. Unfortunately, however, my eggs often would end up overcooked, with whites the texture of a rubber eraser, yolks unpalatably chalky, and an off-green ring marrying the two. Other times I have tried to wing it, with results on the opposite end of the spectrum—undercooked eggs more appropriate for breakfast. Of course, there were the haphazard victories. At those times the yolk cooked through yet remained moist and creamy, the whites were firm yet tender, and the green ring was nowhere to be seen.

I decided I had to solve this basic cooking problem once and for all, no matter how much time and attention it took. In my quest, I wanted to avoid using any out-of-the-ordinary equipment (such as the hen-shaped egg cooker I saw in an advertisement). I also wanted to end up with a method that entailed little or no fuss (no instant-read thermometers, no matter how much of a nerd I can be about mine). And, most of all, my method had to result in the most consistent results with the least margin of error.

Green Eggs and . . .

I quickly discovered several facts about an egg's composition that proved relevant to the hard-cooking process. To begin with, the egg white, or albumen, consists primarily of water and layers of protein. Each of the protein layers cooks at a somewhat different rate, but, generally, they all begin to coagulate at 144 degrees Fahrenheit. Yolks begin to coagulate at a higher temperature (around 149 degrees) because of their high fat content. The green ring that can appear around the yolk results from excessive or prolonged heat. Under such conditions the iron in the yolk reacts with the sulfur in the white to produce ferrous sulfide, which is recognizable by the discoloring. (High iron levels in household tap water can also promote discoloring, since the water seeps into the egg during boiling.)

With this information in mind, I began to collect techniques for hard-cooking eggs from vari-

For a perfect hard-cooked egg every time, stop at a boil and never simmer.

ous cookbooks. There appeared to be two main camps. The first and most common method: Cover eggs with cold water in a saucepan, bring water to a boil, drop to a simmer, remove the eggs after anywhere from 5 to 20 minutes of simmering (depending on the cookbook used), and cool in ice water or under running water. The other camp starts with boiling water. The eggs are lowered into the bubbling water, which is then reduced to a simmer. Recipe times for simmering the eggs ranged from 15 to 20 minutes before they were placed in an ice water bath or under a running faucet to cool.

I tested the first method—the cold water start—by allowing the eggs to remain in the simmering water for different lengths of time, pulling them out at 5-minute intervals for up to 20 minutes after the water began simmering. Surprisingly, 5 minutes produced the best hard-cooked egg. The white was tender, the yolk was cooked through yet creamy, and there was no discoloring. At 10 minutes the yolk began to toughen and dry out,

with slight indications of discoloring. After 15 minutes one taster described the egg as "way gone," after 20 minutes, "nearly indestructible."

Next I tested the "boiling start" method in the same way, pulling the eggs from the water after they had simmered for 10, 15, and 20 minutes. At 15 minutes the yolk was just slightly undercooked. At 20 minutes the yolk edge had begun to pick up a green tinge, though slight. There seemed to be hope between 15 and 20 minutes, but having to lower the eggs into boiling water was beginning to annoy me. The process is awkward, and, typically, at least one egg would crack. I learned that this occurs because all eggs have an air pocket that rapidly expands when abruptly exposed to high heat. Consequently, the shell may crack. Many cookbooks suggest preventing this problem by poking a thumb tack through the large end of the egg where the air hole typically sits (*see* illustration, page 14). When I tried this, however, the results were inconsistent.

Not fully satisfied with either of these two methods, I wondered if there was yet another way to approach hard-cooking an egg. I hypothesized that if meat (another protein) toughens when boiled but tenderizes when braised (cooked in a small amount of liquid on low heat), maybe egg proteins would respond similarly. Backing up this theory was a section I read in Harold McGee's *On Food and Cooking* (Scribner's, 1984), where he states that cooking eggs at 185 degrees (a bare

TESTING | BAD, GOOD, AND UGLY

Just one minute of cooking time can make the difference between a dark-yolked, undercooked egg (left), a perfectly hard-cooked egg (center), and an overcooked egg with a green ring around the yolk (right).

simmer) for 25 to 35 minutes will render tender whites. To the contrary, I found not only that the eggs came out tough and dry but also that the temperature was difficult to maintain on the burner I was using. I had to keep a thermometer in the water to guide my adjustments of the gas flame in and around medium-low.

This juggling act revealed a hole in all of the above methods: Each involves simmering. While most cooks know what a boil looks like, their definition of a simmer varies. And simply calling for the lowest heat is misleading, because it can vary from stove to stove. (I once had a burner on which I couldn't drop the flame low enough for a simmer.) In a knee-jerk reaction, I decided to try the opposite approach and straight-out boil the eggs. I liked the idea of being able to maintain a constant temperature no matter what the capacity of the stove (discounting those at high altitudes). The result was cracked eggs that gave off a strong, unpleasantly "eggy" smell. Another problem was the cooking time; the eggs cooked so fast that there was little margin of error.

Going under Cover

At this point I swallowed my pride and called the American Egg Board in Park Ridge, Illinois, for a recommendation. The Egg Board recommends starting the eggs in cold water and bringing it to a boil. Then, instead of simmering, the board suggests removing the pan from the heat and covering it, leaving the eggs to rest for 15 minutes. I tried this and found the egg white to be somewhat rubbery, but the yolk, except for a greenish tinge around its edge, was just right. I felt confident that I was onto something. The technique involved neither simmering nor immersing in boiling water, both of which had proved problematic. In a second testing of the Egg Board's method I pulled the eggs out at staggered times. The egg pulled after a 10-minute rest was voted by my tasters as the best of the bunch.

Despite my success, I still had to wonder if this technique would forgive the fact that different burners, different stoves, and even different pans change the amount of time necessary to bring the

Taking a Crack at Hard-Cooked Eggs

Some days when working on this story I would go home with raw thumbs after having fought to peel the shell from one too many eggs. Other times the shells would slip off effortlessly. The ease of peeling seemed privy to whimsy.

I had read about all sorts of tricks to make peeling eggs easy, and I worked my way through pretty much every one of them. I tried adding salt to the cooking water, then baking soda, then vinegar; I poked a hole through the shell; I cracked the shell before cooling in ice water; I tossed the cooked eggs into a freezer before peeling them. I even tried plunging them into ice water for a minute, then putting them back into boiling water for 10 seconds, and back yet again into the ice water for a final rest. None of these methods offered consistent results.

I read in a number of sources that the fresher the egg, the harder it is to peel, and that this is somehow related to the egg's pH level. To check this out, I called Dr. Patricia Curtis, a food scientist at North Carolina State University in Raleigh. She explained that an egg becomes more alkaline with age because carbon dioxide and moisture escape from the egg through its porous shell. As this occurs, an air pocket develops, typically at the large end of the egg between two fine membrane layers that separate the shell from the white (*see* illustration, right). But after testing this theory, I frankly did not see a whole lot of difference in ease of peeling between old and new eggs. In any case, this is a moot question for most consumers, since any egg you buy at a supermarket will be old enough to have an air pocket.

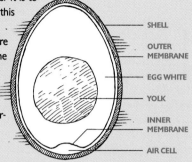

- SHELL
- OUTER MEMBRANE
- EGG WHITE
- YOLK
- INNER MEMBRANE
- AIR CELL

I finally called Linda Braun, consumer services director of the American Egg Board, who asked a simple question: Was I by any chance trying to peel large chunks of shell off at a time? I had to plead guilty. Braun suggested that I try cracking the egg all over, breaking the shell into tiny pieces, then peeling off these little bits, starting from the end with the air cell so I could get under the membrane without digging into the white. With the shell broken into so many little pieces, the membrane was pliable and—as I found in many, many successful tries—often peeled away from the egg in a clean spiral, leaving the egg with a scar-free exterior. While Braun warned me that this method was not foolproof, after all the peeling tests I ran, I concluded that it was nonetheless the most consistent "trick" of all.   — M.D.

same amount of water to a boil. To make matters even more complex, there is no established standard for the amount of water needed when hard-cooking an egg. Basically, the eggs should be covered by an inch of water, which means that a three-quart pan with a seven-inch diameter will require less water than one with an eight-inch diameter and thus take less time to reach a boil. One last variable that concerned me was the ability of some pans to retain heat better than others. This meant that the water temperature during the rest period could vary.

To test the reliability of this method under all of these conditions, I decided to forge on to further extremes despite the raised eyebrows of a few co-workers. Taking every brand of two-and-one-half and three-quart saucepans in the test kitchen and at home (all of varying quality), I tested the Egg Board's method, giving all the pans a 10-minute rest, on both the small and large gas burners in the test kitchen and the small and large electric burners I have at home. Although each pan differed in the amount of time it took to boil water (as much as a 12-minute difference) and in the amount of heat lost when resting with a cover, I repeated success. Each egg consistently displayed a

bright, creamy yolk worthy of boasting (and so I did) and tender whites that barely required chewing. I could finally go to sleep at night without dreaming about eggs.

Throughout all my tests I transferred my hot eggs to an ice water bath to cool. I also tried cooling the eggs under running water as well as leaving them out at room temperature to cool. Cooling under the tap took many minutes and seemed a waste of water. Leaving the eggs out at room temperature allowed them to continue cooking. The ice water bath was undoubtedly the most efficient way to halt the cooking process.

FOOLPROOF BOILED EGGS
MAKES 6 EGGS

You may double or triple this recipe as long as you use a pot large enough to hold the eggs in a single layer, covered by an inch of water.

6 large eggs

Place eggs in medium saucepan, cover with 1 inch of water, and bring to boil over high heat. Remove pan from heat, cover, and let sit for 10 minutes. Meanwhile, fill a medium bowl with 1 quart water and 1 tray of ice cubes (or equivalent). Transfer eggs to ice water bath with slotted spoon; let sit 5 minutes. Following illustrations 1 and 2, peel and use as desired, or proceed with one of the salad recipes on page 15.

STEP-BY-STEP | FOOLPROOF PEELING

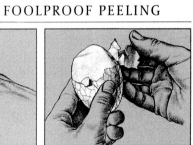

1. Tap the egg all over against the counter surface, then roll it gently back and forth a few times on the counter.

2. Begin peeling from the air pocket end. The shell should come off in spiral strips attached to the thin membrane.

Exceptional Egg Salad

First we figured out the perfect dicing method, then we tried mixing eggs with everything from buttermilk to cream cheese for the best egg salad.

⇒ BY MARYELLEN DRISCOLL ⇐

Egg salad is one of those simple, spur-of-the-moment comfort foods that I have always failed miserably at making. It typically turns out to be too pasty. The overall flavor is drab. The mayonnaise excessive. The onions too biting. The hardest part for me, though, has always been cooking the eggs properly. So once I had nailed down a foolproof method for hard-cooking an egg (*see* "The Best Way to Hard- Cook an Egg," page 13), I was ready to move on to other aspects of building the perfect egg salad.

First and foremost was the chopping technique. I had been raised to break up the eggs with a fork. I quickly found, however, that both a fork and a pastry blender, which had also been recommended to me, mashed the eggs so much that, when blended with mayonnaise, they became unpleasantly pasty. In addition to being reminiscent of baby food, this egg salad was quick to ooze out from between the slices of bread in a sandwich. After experimenting with various options, I found that dicing the eggs into half-inch cubes gave the salad the full mouthfeel I had been seeking and also held up well in a sandwich.

Of course, dicing eggs into uniformly shaped cubes is not as easy as it may sound. Hard-cooked eggs can be tough to slice through. I found that even the broad side of a paring knife inevitably drags through and crumbles the yolk, bringing me back once again to that pasty consistency. Meeting with no success after trying a variety of knives to dice the eggs, I tried both spraying the knives with cooking spray and coating them with mayonnaise before dicing. Neither of these efforts did the trick. Looking around the kitchen for other options, I decided to try a wire cheese knife. After one egg, I was sold. This knife sliced right through the egg cleanly and easily, leaving the yolks chunky.

Because I knew I would be dicing up dozens upon dozens of eggs for this story, I wanted to be able to dice up large quantities of eggs faster than the cheese knife allowed. My temporary solution was to cut every other wire off of an egg slicer, an adaptation that gave me cubes measuring three-eighths of an inch. Ultimately, I found a slicer for fresh mozzarella that is constructed in the same style as an egg or mushroom slicer but with wires spaced a perfect three-eighths of an inch apart (*see* Resources, page 32). After a quick pass through the egg's width and length, and then, after a quarter turn, another pass through the length, I had perfect dice in fewer than 10 seconds. (*see* Quick Tips, page 5 for exact technique).

With the slicing method set, I turned to the binder. Although most egg salad recipes call for binding the eggs with mayonnaise—"egg on egg," a friend of mine likes to joke—I wanted to reconsider this. While nearly every recipe I found used mayonnaise, some called for combining it with cream cheese, yogurt, light cream, cottage cheese, sour cream, or even buttermilk. I tried them all.

A few of my tasters were surprised to find they liked the addition of a little cottage cheese or cream cheese to the mayonnaise. But the loudest applause went to the egg salad made with just plain mayonnaise. Simple enough. Still, I did want to add a little more complexity and life to the mix. Some lemon brightened things up, while a bit of mustard added depth. I preferred the sweetness of a red onion for the master recipe but also liked scallions and shallots for some of the variations. Yellow onion was simply too harsh. Minced celery and parsley added an element of freshness, and I finally had an egg salad that was truly a source of comfort rather than disappointment.

Dicing the hard-cooked eggs gives the salad a pleasing, chunky texture.

CLASSIC EGG SALAD
MAKES ABOUT 2½ CUPS, ENOUGH FOR 4 SANDWICHES

I	recipe Foolproof Boiled Eggs (page 14), peeled and diced medium
¼	cup mayonnaise
2	tablespoons minced red onion
I	tablespoon minced fresh parsley leaves
½	medium celery stalk, chopped fine (about 3 tablespoons)
2	teaspoons Dijon mustard
2	teaspoons juice from I lemon
¼	teaspoon salt
	Ground black pepper

Mix all ingredients together in medium bowl, including ground black pepper to taste. Serve. (Can be covered and refrigerated overnight.)

EGG SALAD WITH RADISH, SCALLIONS, AND DILL

Follow recipe for Classic Egg Salad, substituting 1 tablespoon minced fresh dill for parsley, 1 medium thin sliced scallion for red onion, and adding 3 medium radishes, minced (about 3 tablespoons).

CURRIED EGG SALAD

Follow recipe for Classic Egg Salad, substituting 1 tablespoon minced fresh cilantro for parsley and adding 1½ teaspoons curry powder. Omit salt.

CREAMY EGG SALAD WITH CAPERS AND ANCHOVIES

Follow the recipe for Classic Egg Salad, adding 1 small garlic clove, minced, 2 tablespoons chopped capers, and 1 minced anchovy fillet. Omit salt.

CREAMY EGG SALAD WITH BACON, SHALLOTS, AND WATERCRESS

In medium skillet over medium heat, fry 4 slices bacon (about 4 ounces, cut into ¼-inch pieces), until brown and crisp, about 5 minutes. Transfer bacon with slotted spoon to plate lined with paper towel; pour off all but 1 tablespoon of fat from pan. Add 2 large shallots, chopped medium, and sauté until softened and browned, about 5 minutes. Follow recipe for Classic Egg Salad, omitting celery and salt, substituting sautéed shallots for red onion, and adding bacon and ¼ cup watercress leaves, chopped coarse.

Chef's Dicing Tips & Techniques

Vegetables grow in anything but perfect cube shapes. This presents some definite challenges when you need to cut a vegetable into uniform dice for purposes of even cooking and/or aesthetic appeal. To learn the best and most efficient way to dice, we turned to Chef Alain Sailhac, the executive dean of culinary studies at the French

Culinary Institute in New York City, where technical precision is part and parcel of classic French culinary training. We decided to start with the basics—potatoes and carrots—to underscore the primary approach to turning odd-shaped vegetables into even-shaped dice.

For each vegetable, we included two techniques—quick "rough" dicing as well as precise dicing, which is used when appearance is paramount.

The knife position for dicing most vegetables begins with the tip of the blade pointed down and the butt end raised. To avoid slipping, Sailhac particularly advised that vegetables be dried before cutting, especially woody or awkward-shaped vegetables. The cutting board should also be dry, with no oil on it.

Chef Alain Sailhac, along with chef instructors Jacques Pépin, André Soltner, and Jacques Torres, recently published *The French Culinary Institute's Salute to Healthy Cooking* (Rodale Press, 1998).

TIP: MODIFIED CLAW HOLD

Because of the potato's rounded shape, the traditional "claw" grip of the hand guiding the knife must be adjusted. With the back of the index and middle finger still guiding the knife blade, extend the pinkie finger and thumb to polar ends of the potato to hold it steady.

Illustration: John Burgoyne

TERMS AND SIZES

Very small dice	Small dice	Medium dice	Large dice
1/8" × 1/8" × 1/8"	1/4" × 1/4" × 1/4"	1/2" × 1/2" × 1/2"	3/4" × 3/4" × 3/4"

QUICK ROUGH DICING

The following techniques make for fuss-free prep suitable for most dishes.

Potatoes

Because they are rounded, potatoes can be awkward to dice. They can also be slippery on the cutting board when peeled and sticky to cut through because of their high starch content.

I.

1. Cut a peeled potato lengthwise into quarters.

2. Make two stacks with curved slices on top of each so that the base of each stack is flat and steady. Cut each stack lengthwise into quarters.

3. Turn stacks 90 degrees and cut horizontally to complete dice.

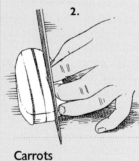

Carrots

Root vegetables such as carrots and parsnips can be tricky to dice because of their tapered shape. Their fibrous, woody composition can also make them tough and slippery to cut through.

I. Holding the top to steady the peeled carrot, cut through the center two-thirds of the carrot's length.

2. Turn the carrot around and, holding onto the halved tapered end, cut down the center length of the top, starting where the first cut began.

3. With cut side facing down on the board, cut each half in half lengthwise to make quarters.

4. Line up the carrot quarters next to one another and cut horizontally into rough dice.

PRECISE DICING

On special occasions when presentation is emphasized, the following straightforward steps will give you perfect dice.

Potatoes

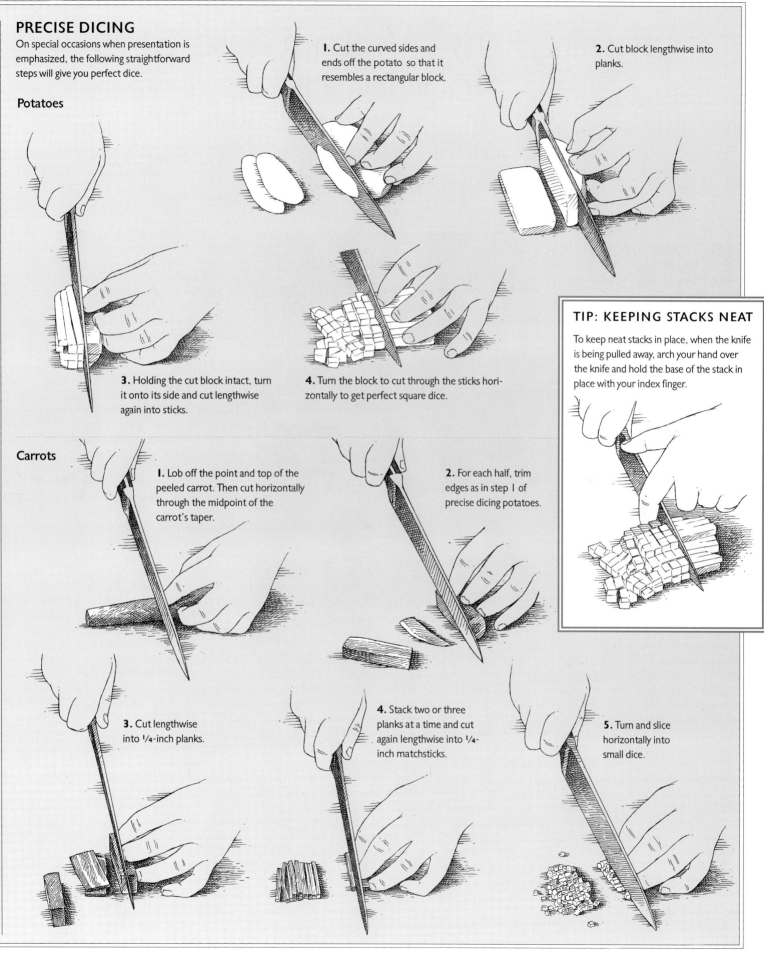

1. Cut the curved sides and ends off the potato so that it resembles a rectangular block.

2. Cut block lengthwise into planks.

3. Holding the cut block intact, turn it onto its side and cut lengthwise again into sticks.

4. Turn the block to cut through the sticks horizontally to get perfect square dice.

Carrots

1. Lob off the point and top of the peeled carrot. Then cut horizontally through the midpoint of the carrot's taper.

2. For each half, trim edges as in step 1 of precise dicing potatoes.

3. Cut lengthwise into ¼-inch planks.

4. Stack two or three planks at a time and cut again lengthwise into ¼-inch matchsticks.

5. Turn and slice horizontally into small dice.

TIP: KEEPING STACKS NEAT

To keep neat stacks in place, when the knife is being pulled away, arch your hand over the knife and hold the base of the stack in place with your index finger.

Shortcutting Vietnamese-Style Noodle Soups

The secret to making super-quick, Asian-style noodle soups is to enliven canned chicken broth with classic Vietnamese flavorings.

∋ BY STEPHANIE LYNESS ∈

Eating out recently in a Vietnamese restaurant, I had a fabulous beef noodle soup. The soup was based on a homemade broth (made with meat, not just bones), flavored with something that tasted indescribably exotic to my French-trained palate. The broth was rich flavored but not heavy and was filled with fettuccine-width rice noodles, paper-thin and barely cooked slices of beef, thin rounds of raw onion, angled scallion slices, crisp bean sprouts, and lots of whole fresh mint and coriander leaves. I'd ordered other dishes but wished I hadn't because the soup was satisfying enough to be a whole meal.

Later, I couldn't stop thinking about that soup. It seemed like such a terrific strategy for an everyday, home-cooked, one-pot meal that tasted anything but everyday. But I kept running into the inescapable fact that making a broth of that caliber is impractical because it has to cook for several hours. Even a chicken stock would take at least three hours to make, including prep time.

Faced with this dilemma when I'm cooking a French-style soup, I can usually substitute canned broth, even though it doesn't taste homemade and I don't particularly like its taste. Because French soups are typically set up something like a stew—sauté aromatics, add broth and whatever major ingredient, season with herbs, and simmer at least half an hour to cook the ingredients through and marry the flavors—by the time the soup is cooked, the flavor of the broth has been substantially transformed by the ingredients cooked in it. In fact, I can often dispense with the canned broth entirely and use just water because the soup-making process itself is similar to that for making a quick stock from scratch. I wondered whether this system would hold true for Asian soups.

An Alternative Approach to Soupmaking

As I researched my beef soup in Asian cookbooks, I discovered that it belonged to a genre of noodle soup that appeared in a number of Asian—partic-

Adding herbs and other flavoring elements at the last minute creates a soup with many clear, distinct tastes.

ularly Southeast Asian—cuisines. These soups were based on a model that differed from French soupmaking in important ways. In contrast with the simmering and marrying that characterizes French soups, the Asian soups were collections of raw and cooked ingredients—one or several different proteins, noodles, vegetables, handfuls of fresh herbs and other aromatics—that were combined in the hot broth like a garnish at the last minute, with little or no secondary cooking. So whereas a leek and potato soup cooks leeks, potatoes, and chicken stock together until the edges of the flavors soften and merge, Asian soups are structured in a way that allows the flavorings to remain distinct and separate.

These Asian soups are tremendously flavorful despite their short cooking time because the ingredients themselves are so potent. The minimal cooking allows the flavors to remain clean and bright, just as they do in a stir fry. It seemed to me, then, that this model could be just as well suited to the use of canned broth as the French, and for entirely different reasons. The use of strong flavorings would punch up and disguise the pallid flavor of the broth. And because the Asian approach doesn't call for long simmering to marry and transform flavors, the soups promised to be extraordinarily quick to make. Now it was time to put my research to the test in the kitchen.

A Basic Asian-Style Broth

I started by working to develop a broth to serve as the master recipe for several noodle soups. (*Cook's Illustrated* tests have shown that canned chicken broth is far superior to canned beef broth, so I worked with chicken broth.) I had noticed that some Vietnamese soup recipes infused stocks with aromatics—garlic, spices, and lemon grass—so I adopted that technique. I cooked the broth for 20 minutes with chopped garlic and fresh ginger. The flavor of the broth was immeasurably improved, but I wanted to do less work. So instead of chopping, I carefully crushed medallions of ginger with the back of a knife handle and whole garlic with the flat side of a chef's knife before simmering in the canned stock; the resulting broth tasted just as good.

With this base to build on, I experimented with other ingredients to figure out how to get the taste I was looking for. I found that soy and fish sauces added much-needed body and depth of flavor to the broth; fish sauce, in particular, added just the right combination of salt and a musky sweetness. In an effort to approximate the taste of the original beef soup, I infused the broth with cinnamon sticks and star anise as well as the ginger and garlic; the spices were responsible for the exotic taste I so admired.

I also experimented with lemon grass to determine how best to use it. First I chopped it and cooked it in the broth from the beginning. Then I did the same with larger pieces of lemon grass, bruised with the dull edge of the knife. As a last test, I minced the lemon grass and added it fresh at the end of the process. I settled on bruising, which is both fast and efficient.

I was making headway, but I wasn't there yet.

Those which tasted best to me (particularly those made with coconut milk) were also rich and heavy; the heaviness didn't jibe with my memory of the original soup. The flavors also tasted jumbled and all over the map. I couldn't identify a distinctive sensibility or flavor palate clearly telling me that this was the food of a particular culture.

Dried Rice Noodles

In my research I found dried rice noodles sold in two different styles: a thick, flat, fettuccine-width noodle and a very thin, thread-like noodle. It's confusing to try to buy these noodles by name; because they're used in several Asian cuisines (including Chinese, Thai, and Vietnamese), they're marketed under several different Asian names. The English names are no more helpful because they're not standardized; you'll find the thicker noodles sold as "rice sticks" and the thread-like noodles sold as both "rice sticks" and "vermicelli." To further confuse matters, thin cellophane noodles made from mung beans are also marketed as "vermicelli." So don't bother with the names, just look for the shape of the noodle—all of the packages I've seen have been obligingly transparent.

Thin rice vermicelli, above.
Thick "rice sticks," below.

The literature I have read indicates that rice noodles are made from rice flour and water. But some of the packages I've seen list cornstarch in the ingredients as well as rice flour. Michael Moriguchi, the general manager of Seasia, an importer of rice noodles in Seattle, Washington, explained why. In the fabrication of the noodles, rice flour may be stretched with or completely replaced by cornstarch, a cheaper ingredient. Noodles made with cornstarch break apart and stick together more readily than noodles made only with rice flour, so, if you have a choice, buy noodles made without cornstarch. —S.L.

Eventually, I found that the key to the soups lay in the Asian model I'd identified earlier. The trick was to season the broth as if I were making a salad. Using blasts of strong, separate flavors—salty, pungent, hot, acid, and spiced—I could create a specifically Asian mixture of tastes. Although the tastes are harsh enough to be almost dissonant to my Western palate, when used in combination they create a mix of flavors that's satisfying precisely because the dissonance tears brassily through the mouth and doesn't warm the belly. The delight of these soups lies in a careful balance of individual flavors and not in a comfortable, Western-style harmony that basically involves one blended flavor. And given the heat of the Southeast Asian climate, it makes sense to me that this food was not designed to warm and comfort.

The Noodles

Satisfied with the broth, I turned my attention to the noodles. In my local Asian food market, I found dried rice noodles the width of fettucine as well as the thinner rice vermicelli. I also found a translucent cellophane noodle made with mung bean starch. I brought all of them home to play with. First I tried boiling them. The boiled noodles had a tendency to get mushy and, if left in the soup for any length of time, to break apart. So I tried soaking for 15 minutes and then briefly submerging in boiling water. This worked better but required two pots.

Ultimately, I settled on soaking alone because it was less complicated and worked just as well. I simply drained the noodles when they had softened to the point that they were tender but still had tooth. The only problem was that the noodles sometimes stuck together and then failed to soften properly. I was able to avoid this dilemma by stirring the noodles occasionally, especially at the beginning. Although I've chosen combinations of noodles and flavorings that I particularly like, the vermicelli and wider noodles can be used interchangeably. I didn't like the cellophane as well as the rice noodles in these soups, so I didn't use them.

Variations on a Theme

Having solved the problems of the canned broth and the flavorings, I was able to develop variations on the broth using chicken, shrimp, and beef. The cinnamon/star anise combination that worked so well with the beef seemed unlikely to work with chicken and shrimp, so I omitted the cinnamon. Lime juice and extra fish sauce compensated for its loss and gave me the tearing quality I was looking for. As did the quantity of fresh herbs—I used cilantro and mint, but basil may be used as well—which are crucial for these soups and more effective in whole leaf than chopped. Finally, I also discovered that because the noodles are so bland and smooth, some crunchy vegetables, such as bean sprouts and Asian cabbages, are needed for texture.

QUICK VIETNAMESE-STYLE BROTH
MAKES ABOUT 5 CUPS

Two of the three noodle soups found here use a variation on this aromatic broth; each is tailored to best suit the flavors in the soup. Therefore, make the broth while the noodles are soaking, noting the adjustments to each broth in the ingredient list.

- 5   cups canned low-sodium chicken broth
- 4   medium garlic cloves, smashed and peeled
- 1   2-inch piece fresh gingerroot, peeled, cut into 1/8-inch rounds, and smashed (*see* illustration, page 20)
- 2   3-inch cinnamon sticks
- 2   pods star anise
- 2   tablespoons Asian fish sauce
- 1   tablespoon soy sauce
- 1   tablespoon sugar

Bring all ingredients to boil in medium saucepan over medium-high heat. Reduce heat to low; simmer partially covered to blend flavors, about 20 minutes. Remove solids with slotted spoon and discard. Cover and keep hot over low heat until ready to serve.

STEP-BY-STEP | ASSEMBLING THE SOUP

1. Divide the noodles and sprouts or cabbage among the bowls.

2. Add the meat, seafood, or chicken, then ladle in the broth.

3. Sprinkle on the herbs and other flavorings of choice.

VIETNAMESE–STYLE BEEF NOODLE SOUP
SERVES 4

For this soup and the two that follow, be sure to have all the vegetables and herbs ready at hand.

8	ounces thick rice noodles
1	recipe Quick Vietnamese-Style Broth
	Salt
12	ounces sirloin steak, sliced crosswise into 1/4-inch strips
	Ground black pepper
1	tablespoon vegetable oil
2	cups bean sprouts (about 5 ounces)
1	jalapeño chile, sliced thin
2	scallions, white and green parts, sliced thin on an angle
1/3	cup loose-packed basil leaves, torn in half if large
1/2	cup loose-packed fresh mint leaves, torn in half if large
1/2	cup loose-packed fresh cilantro leaves
2	tablespoons chopped roasted unsalted peanuts
	Lime wedges

1. Bring 4 quarts water to boil in large pot. Off heat, add rice sticks, and let sit until tender, 10 to 15 minutes. Drain and distribute among four bowls.

2. Meanwhile, make Quick Vietnamese-Style broth, seasoning with additional salt if necessary.

3. Season steak with salt and pepper. Heat oil in medium skillet over medium-high heat until shimmering. Add half of steak slices in single layer and sear until well-browned, 1 to 2 minutes on each side; set aside. Repeat with remaining slices.

4. Following illustrations 1 to 3, page 19, assemble soup and serve immediately, passing lime wedges separately.

HOT AND SOUR NOODLE SOUP WITH SHRIMP AND TOMATO
SERVES 4

Lemon grass is an essential ingredient in Southeast Asian cooking; it lends a subtle fragrant lemon essence without harsh citrus notes. Use fresh lemon grass if you can find it. Otherwise, try two pieces of water-packed lemon grass, bruised, or 1/2 teaspoon grated lemon zest.

6	ounces rice vermicelli
1	recipe Quick Vietnamese-Style Broth, cinnamon omitted, Asian fish sauce increased to 3 tablespoons, sugar decreased to 1 teaspoon
1	stalk lemon grass, bruised (see illustration, above)
12	ounces shrimp, shelled, shells reserved
1	jalapeño chile, sliced thin
1/4	cup juice from 4 or 5 limes
	Salt
2	cups bean sprouts (about 5 ounces)
1	medium tomato, cut into 12 wedges
2	scallions, white and green parts, sliced thin on an angle
1/2	cup loose-packed fresh mint leaves, torn in half if large
1/2	cup loose-packed fresh cilantro leaves

1. Bring 4 quarts water to boil in large pot. Off heat, add rice vermicelli, and let sit until tender, 5 to 10 minutes. Drain and distribute among individual serving bowls.

2. Meanwhile, make Quick Vietnamese-Style

TECHNIQUE
BRUISING THE AROMATICS

Using the handle or back of a chef's knife, smash the ginger, garlic, and lemon grass to release flavor.

Broth, simmering lemon grass and reserved shrimp shells with broth for 15 minutes. Add jalapeño and simmer 5 minutes longer; strain, return broth to pot, and bring back to simmer over medium heat. Add shrimp and simmer until opaque and cooked through, about 2 minutes. Remove with slotted spoon; set aside. Add lime juice, and season broth to taste with additional salt if necessary. Cover and keep hot over low heat.

3. Following illustrations 1 to 3, page 19, assemble soup and serve immediately.

VIETNAMESE–STYLE NOODLE SOUP WITH CHICKEN AND NAPA CABBAGE
SERVES 4

8	ounces thick rice noodles
1	recipe Quick Vietnamese-Style Broth, cinnamon omitted, Asian fish sauce increased to 3 tablespoons, sugar decreased to 2 teaspoons
12	ounces boneless, skinless chicken thighs, trimmed of excess fat
	Salt
1/2	medium napa cabbage, rinsed and sliced thin crosswise (about 4 cups)
2	scallions, white and green parts, sliced thin on an angle
1/2	cup loose-packed fresh mint leaves, torn in half if large
1/2	cup loose-packed fresh cilantro leaves
2	tablespoons chopped roasted unsalted peanuts
	Lime wedges

1. Bring 4 quarts water to boil in large pot. Off heat, add noodles, and let sit until tender, 10 to 15 minutes. Drain and distribute among individual serving bowls.

2. Meanwhile, make Quick Vietnamese-Style Broth, simmering chicken thighs in the broth until cooked through, about 10 minutes. Remove chicken with slotted spoon and set aside; when cool enough to handle, slice thinly. Continue to simmer broth 10 minutes longer. Strain broth, return to pot; season to taste with additional salt if necessary. Cover and keep hot over low heat.

3. Following illustrations 1 to 3, page 19, assemble soup and serve immediately, passing lime wedges separately.

Fresh Lemon Grass Is Always Greener

Lemon grass is an integral part of Southeast Asian cooking, imparting a rich, ethereal, lemony essence to many dishes. Most often it is trimmed to the lower third, the tough outer leaves stripped away, and the soft inner core chopped or minced. Or, if it is eventually to be removed, as in a broth, the stalk—leaves and all—can simply be bruised and used as is. This is the approach that we took, for example, in making the broth for Hot and Sour Noodle Soup with Shrimp and Tomato.

Fresh lemon grass is a staple in many Asian grocery stores, but it is not always available everywhere. We did find it in both dried and waterpacked form at our local grocer, however, and decided to investigate. So we cooked them into broths and compared them with broths made with fresh lemon grass and lemon zest. Here are our findings.

Fresh lemon grass was the most aromatic, infusing the broth with a delicate, lemony freshness that made it the clear favorite. The next best was the **water-packed lemon grass**. Although it lacked the crispness and clarity of fresh, this version still maintained lemon grass characteristics. **Grated lemon zest** finished a remote third. Better zest than dried lemon grass, though. While the broth made with lemon zest was flat and one-dimensional compared with those made with fresh or water-packed lemon grass, it was still, at the very least, lemony. **Dried lemon grass** was the dog, with a dull, "off" herbal quality; the broth made with it lacked not only freshness but any lemon flavor. —Dawn Yanagihara

Fresh lemon grass

Water-packed lemon grass

Grated lemon zest

Dried lemon grass

Refreshing Celery Root Salads

We discover how to avoid the twin problems of these salads—blandness and a dressing that overpowers the celery root—and also figure out the best way to grate this vegetable.

> BY ANNE YAMANAKA <

I admit I've never been a big fan of celery root. That is, I wasn't until recently, when I was introduced to celery root rémoulade, a classic French bistro side dish of raw, grated, or finely julienned celery root dressed in a mustardy, creamy emulsion. Unlike cooked purees or gratins, celery root salads maintain the vegetable's pristine white appearance, its crunchy, coleslaw-like texture, and (most important) its refreshing, herbal flavor, which tastes like a combination of mint, anise, mild radish, and celery.

My interest sparked, I began to research and experiment and soon found that fresh celery root salads are straightforward and easy to make. The hardest part of the process was figuring out how to prepare the root vegetable itself: the best and quickest way to peel the bumpy, uneven outer layer and the proper method for cutting or grating it so that it retained some resistance and crunch in the final salad.

To begin, I wanted to find a fast and efficient way to rid the celery root of its dirty, unattractive outer layer and rootlets. After fumbling around with vegetable peelers, different types of knives, and various peeling methods, I settled on the following procedure. First I lopped off about ⅜ inch on both the root end (the side where there is a mass of rootlets) and the stalk end (the opposite side). Then I sat the vegetable root on either flat end and used a paring knife to cut the outer layer of flesh from top to bottom, rotating it as I cut off its entire circumference.

Now that I had a quick, safe, and easy peeling method, I was ready to explore cutting and grating techniques. I prepared and compared a basic recipe for celery root rémoulade using five different cutting or grating techniques: one cut into fine matchsticks by hand; one using the coarse side of a box grater; one using the fine side; a batch prepared using a rotary grater (or Mouli), and one batch using the grating attachment in the food processor. The salads prepared with the coarse side of the box grater and with the food processor proved to be the best. The celery root developed contrasting textures, softening on the outside while maintaining a good crunch, and, unlike the batches made with the rotary grater or the fine side of the box grater, the celery root did not leach out its water. I also liked the ease and speed of using the food processor. It produced nicely grated celery root in a matter of seconds, while cutting the root by hand took considerable time and effort.

Finding the right dressing was the next step. I wanted to develop a dressing that would highlight, not mask, the celery root's fresh, clean, straightforward flavor. I tried several different dressings, including a simple vinaigrette as well as several that were finished with dairy—one with sour cream, one with heavy cream, and one in which crème fraîche was the dominant ingredient. My tasters and I agreed that the vinaigrette finished with sour cream complemented the celery root the best, contributing a fuller, rounder, and creamier flavor while maintaining the salad's fresh, piquant taste.

The final touches to the master recipe were a matter of personal taste. I added apples for more crunch and acidity as well as a touch of sweetness, thereby giving the salad a necessary spark. Mustard and lemon juice are classic ingredients for celery root rémoulade. Through testing I found that celery root salads need not be limited to the classic rémoulade flavors. My variations include nuts, fruit, herbs, and fragrant spices to complement the salad.

CELERY ROOT SALAD WITH APPLE AND PARSLEY
SERVES 4 TO 6 AS A SIDE DISH

Although not always available, fresh tarragon complements the flavor of celery root. If you can find it, stir in 2 teaspoons minced fresh tarragon along with the parsley. Add a teaspoon or so more oil to the dressed salad if it seems a bit dry.

Creamy Dijon Dressing
- 2 tablespoons juice from 1 lemon
- 1½ tablespoons Dijon mustard
- 1 teaspoon honey
- ½ teaspoon salt
- 3 tablespoons neutral-flavored oil, such as vegetable or canola
- 3 tablespoons sour cream

Salad
- 1 medium celery root (13–14 ounces), peeled (*see* illustration) and rinsed
- ½ medium tart apple, cored and peeled
- 2 scallions, sliced thin
- 2 teaspoons minced fresh parsley leaves
- Salt and ground black pepper

1. *For the dressing:* In medium bowl, whisk together lemon juice, mustard, honey, and salt. Whisk in oil in slow, steady stream. Add sour cream; whisk to combine. Set aside.

2. *For the salad:* If using food processor, cut celery root and apple into 1½-inch pieces and grate with shredding disc. (Alternatively, grate on coarse side of box grater.) You should have about 3 cups total. Add immediately to prepared dressing; toss to coat. Stir in scallions and parsley (and tarragon, if using; *see* note above). Adjust seasonings with salt and pepper. Refrigerate until chilled, about 30 minutes. Serve.

CELERY ROOT SALAD WITH PEAR AND HAZELNUTS

For this salad, toast the hazelnuts in a small dry skillet over medium-high heat until fragrant, about 5 minutes. Rub toasted nuts in a clean kitchen towel to remove as much skin as possible.

Follow recipe for Celery Root Salad with Apple and Parsley, substituting ½ firm pear, grated, for apple and adding ¼ cup hazelnuts that have been toasted and skinned and then chopped along with herbs.

CELERY ROOT SALAD WITH RED ONION, MINT, ORANGE, AND FENNEL SEED

Follow recipe for Celery Root Salad with Apple and Parsley, substituting 2 tablespoons finely chopped red onion for scallion and adding 2 teaspoons minced fresh mint leaves, ½ teaspoon grated orange zest, and 1 teaspoon fennel seed along with parsley.

CELERY ROOT SALAD WITH APPLE, CARAWAY, AND HORSERADISH

Follow recipe for Celery Root Salad with Apple and Parsley, adding ½ teaspoon caraway seeds and 1½ teaspoons prepared horseradish along with herbs.

In Search of the Best Yellow Cake

We were looking for a moist, tender cake that was both foolproof and full-flavored.
By changing mixing methods and ingredient ratios, we achieved our goal.

⇒ BY STEPHEN SCHMIDT ⇐

Yellow cake has always been a broad category, but most of the recipes for making it are very similar. For example, in *The Boston Cook Book,* published in 1884, Mary Lincoln, one of Fannie Farmer's colleagues at the Boston Cooking School, outlines several recipes for yellow cake. But she singles out one as "the foundation for countless varieties of cake, which are often given in cook books under different names." Mrs. Lincoln's master cake formula turns out to be similar to what we today call a 1-2-3-4 cake, made with one cup of butter, two cups of sugar, three cups of (sifted) cake flour, and four eggs, plus milk and small amounts of baking powder, vanilla, and salt.

As it turns out, things have not changed much since more than a century ago: When analyzed, most of the yellow cake recipes in today's cookbooks are 1-2-3-4 cakes or something very similar.

So when I set out in search of the perfect yellow cake, the first thing I did was bake a 1-2-3-4 cake. It's not that I hadn't used this recipe before. At one time in my life, all of the cakes I baked, whether yellow, white, chocolate, or whatever, were based on this formula, and I thought they were just fine. But as time went on and I tried other recipes, I realized that the formula fell short of perfection. This summer I baked a 1-2-3-4 yellow cake in a sheet pan to make a giant strawberry "shortcake" for a crowd of picnickers. I was unpleasantly surprised. The cake was overly sweet, bland, and crumbly, and I really didn't like it. But I was rushed when I made it, and the kitchen was hot, the oven did not heat evenly, and the pan was pitted and warped. Perhaps I hadn't given the cake a fair trial.

This time I proceeded with more care and deliberation. I made sure that the ingredients were at the proper temperature (around 65°F) for optimal aeration and emulsification; I measured everything with scrupulous accuracy; I dispatched each step of the mixing process carefully; and I baked the cake in conventional layer pans, in my more or less reliable oven. The result? Basically, I felt the same way about this cake as I had about my summer shortcake. It wasn't a bad cake, it just wasn't very interesting. Instead of melting in the mouth, the cake seemed crumbly, sugary, and a little hard. The crust was tacky and separated from the underlying cake. Above all, the cake lacked flavor. It did not taste of butter and eggs, as all plain cakes ought to, but instead

This soft, fine-grained cake has the rich taste of butter and eggs.

seemed merely sweet.

Before tinkering with the ingredients, I decided to try a different mixing method. I had mixed my 1-2-3-4 cake the classic way, first beating the butter and sugar until light and fluffy, then adding the eggs one at a time, and finally adding the dry ingredients and milk alternately. Now I wanted to try mixing the batter by the so-called two-stage method, developed by General Mills and Pillsbury in the 1940s and recently popularized by Rose Levy Beranbaum in *The Cake Bible* (Morrow, 1988).

In the two-stage method (*see* "It's All in the Mix," page 24), the flour, sugar, baking powder, and salt are combined, the butter and about two-thirds of the milk and eggs are added, and the batter is beaten until thick and fluffy, about a minute. Then, in the second stage, the rest of the milk and eggs are poured in and the batter is beaten about half a minute more. The two-stage method is simpler, quicker, and more nearly foolproof than the conventional creaming method, and I have successfully adapted many conventional cake recipes to it over the years. But I had never tried it with the 1-2-3-4 cake.

When I did try it, the results exceeded my expectations. The two-stage method is often touted for the tender texture it promotes in cakes, and my two-stage 1-2-3-4 cake was indeed tender. But, more important, its consistency was improved. Whereas my conventionally mixed 1-2-3-4 cake had been crumbly, this cake was fine-grained and melting, and, interestingly enough, it did not seem overly sweet. Even the crust was improved. It was still a bit coarse, but only slightly sticky. This was a cake with a texture that I truly liked.

The problem, though, was the taste. The cake still didn't have any. In fact, oddly enough, it seemed to have less taste than the conventionally mixed version. Certainly it had less color. The 1-2-3-4 cake, it seemed, conformed to a typical cake pattern—as the texture lightened, the taste and color faded.

After trying to remedy the taste deficit by playing around with the ingredients in many ways—primarily adjusting the amounts and proportions of the sugar and eggs—I finally recalled a recipe called Bride's Cake in Mrs. Rorer's *New Cook Book,* published exactly a century ago. This is basically an egg white pound cake—made of a pound each of flour, sugar, butter, and egg whites—with a cup of milk and a little chemical leavening added. It had long been on my mind to try this recipe. I thought it might produce a very nice cake, one with the rich flavor and fine grain of a pound cake and the lightness of a butter cake. What would happen, I wondered, if I made Mrs. Rorer's cake with whole eggs instead of egg whites? It seemed worth a try.

I cut all of Mrs. Rorer's ingredients by half—that is, I made a half-pound cake, so that the batter would fit into two standard 9-by-1½-inch round layer pans—and when mixing the batter I followed the two-stage method.

The resulting cake was richer, more flavorful, and generally more interesting than any of the

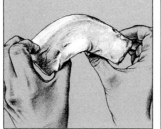

1. The butter (shown here without wrapper) is properly softened when it bends with little resistance and does not crack or break.

2. For accurate measuring, sift flour until mounded into the measuring cup set on parchment or waxed paper. Use a straight-sided utensil to level the flour.

3. When dry ingredients and butter begin to form clumps, after 30 to 40 seconds of mixing, add 1 cup of liquid and beat until liquid is fully absorbed.

1-2-3-4 cakes I had baked, but it was not perfect. The layers were low, and the cake was just a tad dense and rough on the tongue (though not rubbery, thank goodness). I had several options. I could try to open up the crumb by adding more milk and baking powder; I could try to lighten the cake up with an extra egg or a couple of extra yolks; or I could try to increase the volume and tenderize the texture by adding a few more ounces of sugar. I tried all three strategies. The last one—the extra sugar—did the trick. This cake was fine-grained, soft, and melting, and it tasted of butter and eggs. This cake had elegance and finesse, but it was still sturdy enough to withstand the frosting process.

Both the 1-2-3-4 cake and my improved yellow cake based on Mrs. Rorer's recipe are made with a half pound each of butter and eggs. But while the 1-2-3-4 cake contains three cups of sifted cake flour and one cup of milk, my improved yellow cake contains just two and one-quarter cups of sifted cake flour and only one-half cup of milk. So, while the 1-2-3-4 cake contains, by weight, three ounces *more* flour and milk than butter and eggs, my yellow cake contains three ounces *less* flour and milk than butter and eggs. This difference in basic proportions, as it turns out, makes a tremendous difference in texture and taste.

RICH AND TENDER YELLOW LAYER CAKE
MAKES TWO 9-INCH CAKES

To quickly bring the eggs and milk to room temperature (65°F), submerge them in a bowl of warm water for about 10 minutes after mixing them together. Adding the butter pieces to the mixing bowl one at a time prevents the dry ingredients from flying up and out of the bowl.

- 4   large eggs, room temperature
- 1/2   cup whole milk, room temperature
- 2   teaspoons vanilla extract
- 2 1/4   cups sifted plain cake flour (*see* illustration 2, above, and "To Sift or Not to Sift," above left)
- 1 1/2   cups sugar
- 2   teaspoons baking powder
- 3/4   teaspoon salt
- 1/2   pound (2 sticks) unsalted butter, softened (*see* illustration 1), each stick cut into 8 pieces

1. Adjust oven rack to lower-middle position and heat oven to 350 degrees. Generously grease two 9-by-1½-inch cake pans with vegetable shortening and cover pan bottoms with rounds of parchment paper or wax paper. Grease parchment rounds, dust cake pans with flour, and tap out excess.

2. Beat eggs, milk, and vanilla with fork in small bowl; measure out 1 cup of this mixture and set aside. Combine flour, sugar, baking powder, and salt in bowl of standing mixer fitted with paddle attachment; mix on lowest speed to blend, about 30 seconds. With mixer still running at lowest speed, add butter one piece at a time; mix until butter and flour begin to clump together and look sandy and pebbly, with pieces about the size of peas, 30 to 40 seconds after all butter is added. Add reserved 1 cup of egg mixture and mix at lowest speed until incorporated, 5 to 10 seconds. Increase speed to medium-high (setting 6 on KitchenAid) and beat until light and fluffy, about 1 minute. Add remaining egg mixture (about ½ cup) in slow steady stream, about 30 seconds. Stop mixer and thoroughly scrape sides and bottom of bowl. Beat on medium-high until thoroughly combined and batter looks slightly curdled, about 15 seconds longer. (To mix using hand mixer, whisk flour, sugar, baking powder, and salt in large bowl. Add butter pieces and cut into the flour mixture with a pastry blender. Add reserved 1 cup of egg mixture; beat with hand mixer at lowest speed until incorporated, 20 to 30 seconds. Increase speed to high, add remaining egg mixture, and beat until light and fluffy, about 1 minute. Stop mixer and thoroughly scrape sides and bottom of bowl. Beat at high speed 15 seconds longer.)

3. Divide batter equally between prepared cake pans; spread to sides of pan and smooth with rubber spatula. Bake until cake tops are light golden and skewer inserted in center comes out clean, 20 to 25 minutes. (Cakes may mound slightly but will level when cooled.) Cool on rack 10 minutes. Run a knife around pan perimeter to loosen. Invert cake onto large plate, peel off

Dip and sweep measuring created a mounded cake (left); sifting the flour into the measuring cup yielded a perfectly level cake (right).

FROSTING THE CAKE

1. Using 4 rectangular pieces of parchment paper, form an empty square on top of a cake platter.

2. Place cake on parchment. Place about one cup of icing in the center of the bottom cake layer and, with an icing spatula, spread the icing to the edge of the cake, then level the icing.

3. Place second cake layer on top, making sure layers are aligned. Frost the top in the same manner as the first layer.

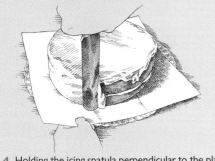

4. Holding the icing spatula perpendicular to the platter, frost the sides of the cake. Smooth the frosting on the top to level the ridge that forms around the edge.

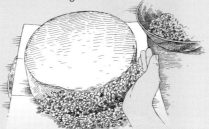

5. Lightly press nuts on sides of cake, letting the excess fall onto the parchment. Allow about one cup of nuts to work with; some will be left over once the parchment is removed and the excess is poured off.

6. Carefully pull out the pieces of parchment from beneath the cake.

parchment, and re-invert onto lightly greased rack. Cool completely before icing.

COFFEE BUTTERCREAM FROSTING
MAKES ABOUT 3 CUPS

If you prefer not to use the raw egg in this recipe for safety reasons, substitute 3 tablespoons of milk. Keep in mind, however, that the texture will be less smooth.

1 1/2	tablespoons instant coffee
1 1/2	tablespoons water
1 1/2	tablespoons vanilla extract
3/4	pound (3 sticks) unsalted butter, softened
3	cups confectioners' sugar
1	large egg, beaten, or 3 tablespoons milk (*see* note above)

1. Dissolve coffee in water and add vanilla in small bowl; set aside. Beat butter in bowl of electric mixer fitted with paddle attachment on medium speed until fluffy, about 1 minute. Reduce speed to low and add sugar 1 cup at a time, beating 15 seconds between each addition. Increase speed to medium and beat until smooth, about 3 minutes, scraping sides and bottom of bowl as necessary.

2. Add coffee mixture and egg or milk; beat on low speed to combine. Scrape sides and bottom of bowl with rubber spatula. Increase speed to medium and beat until fluffy, 3 to 4 minutes. (Buttercream may be covered and kept at room temperature for several hours or refrigerated in an airtight container for a week. Bring to room temperature before using.)

ORANGE BUTTERCREAM FROSTING

Follow recipe for Coffee Buttercream Frosting, omitting instant coffee and vanilla, substituting 3 tablespoons orange juice for water, and adding 1 tablespoon grated orange zest along with egg or milk.

LEMON BUTTERCREAM FROSTING

Follow recipe for Coffee Buttercream Frosting, omitting instant coffee and vanilla, substituting 1 1/2 tablespoons lemon juice for water, and adding 1 1/2 tablespoons grated lemon zest along with egg or milk.

CHOCOLATE CREAM FROSTING
MAKES ABOUT 3 CUPS

1 1/2	cups heavy cream
16	ounces semisweet chocolate, chopped fine
1/3	cup corn syrup
1	teaspoon vanilla extract

Place chocolate in heatproof bowl. Bring heavy cream to boil in small saucepan over medium-high heat; pour over chocolate. Add corn syrup and let stand 3 minutes. Whisk gently until smooth; stir in vanilla. Refrigerate 1 to 1 1/2 hours, stirring every 15 minutes, until mixture reaches spreadable consistency.

Stephen Schmidt's *Master Recipes* was recently reissued by Clear Light Publishers.

It's All in the Mix

Those who are experienced in baking cakes will likely recognize that the "two-stage" mixing method used here is unorthodox. Probably the most familiar mixing method is one in which the butter and sugar are creamed, the eggs beaten in, then the dry and liquid ingredients added alternately. Another, slightly more complicated method involves separating the eggs and folding beaten whites into the batter.

We were curious as to the effects these different mixing methods would have on this particular cake, so we made one cake with each method. The standard creaming method yielded a cake relatively coarse in texture and crumb, with a weak structure that readily crumbled. The cake made with separated eggs, on the other hand, rose impressively in the oven, then fell upon cooling; this cake's texture was cottony and the crumb open. Finally, the cake made according to the two-stage method baked into a delicate but sturdy cake with a fine, tight, even crumb. Another big selling point of this mixing method is its simplicity—there was no need to alternate wet and dry ingredients, separate eggs, or beat and fold in egg whites. A simple and superior cake. —Dawn Yanagihara

Double Chocolate Pudding

For the silkiest texture and richest chocolate flavor, sift the dry ingredients together before you start, and use a combination of bittersweet chocolate and cocoa powder.

≥ BY LISA YOCKELSON ≤

On a map of desserts, chocolate pudding can be located as the chocolate version of a classic cornstarch custard. Typically, a cornstarch custard is made by cooking a mixture of sugar, cornstarch, eggs (or egg yolks), a bit of salt, and a dairy liquid in a saucepan on the stove top until thickened. Butter (which is optional) and vanilla extract are added off the heat.

For me, the choicest chocolate pudding should taste deeply of chocolate and of dairy ingredients, be thickened to a soft suppleness, and sweetened just enough to support the chocolate bouquet. The correct balance of dairy and chocolate should make the dessert rich but not cloying and exceptionally smooth on the tongue.

With voluptuous as the key word, I set out to create a pudding that would bring together all of these factors. I determined that a pudding based on three cups of liquid would yield enough for six ramekin-size servings. Before I actually began cooking batch after batch of pudding, though, I revisited my research into cream pie fillings. Those fillings required working out a delicate balance of starch thickener to liquid and correcting some unnerving problems regarding the combining, stirring, and cooking of ingredients.

During what I now refer to as my "cream pie obsession," I'd leap out of bed at 3 AM, go into the kitchen, and attempt to solve such prickly matters as how to introduce a buttery finish into a pudding filling. After several weeks of cream pie obsession, I had learned that the making of a pudding mixture, whether destined to be poured into a baked pie crust or into individual bowls, requires observing similar watchpoints. Overall, I concluded that a pudding mixture needs to be pampered by sifting the dry ingredients (sugar, cornstarch, and cocoa powder) before combining them with the liquids to make the liquid-thickener amalgamation as smooth as possible in the beginning. I also learned that to achieve a gorgeous texture, it is important to monitor the strength of the heat beneath the saucepan and to use a reasonably slow hand to stir (not whisk or beat) the pudding mixture as it approaches the thickening point, then continue to slowly stir the pudding as it cooks for two minutes. More vigorous beating can break down the starch granules built up during the thickening process. I also found that it helped to strain the finished pudding through a fine-meshed sieve for a suave, smooth texture.

With these points in mind, I began to consider my stove-top pudding. I just love dairy ingredients, so you can understand why I was thrilled to have tested a dozen or more variations on this theme. I made puddings with all milk, two-thirds milk and one-third heavy cream, two-thirds milk and one-third light cream, half milk and half heavy cream, half milk and half light cream, and all light cream. The clear winner was the leaner blend of milk and light cream, which was rich but not overwhelming and unified the chocolate.

Now I was ready to begin building the chocolate taste. I started with three ounces of unsweetened chocolate alone, but that proved inadequate. An ounce or two more of semisweet chocolate added only a nuance of flavor; an ounce or two of bittersweet chocolate raised the chocolate meter slightly, but not enough. At this point, I turned to cocoa powder to see if it would develop, sharpen, and polish the chocolate flavor. Fortunately, it did. I eventually settled on using two tablespoons of cocoa powder in the pudding, along with a combination of unsweetened and bittersweet chocolate.

One nagging problem remained: Although the density, dairy ingredients, and chocolate intensity were right on the mark, the pudding finished with a certain chalkiness on the tongue. Executive editor Pam Anderson urged me to create a pudding that had all the characteristics of an ultrasmooth chocolate pot de crème and, to that end, to try using bittersweet chocolate in place of the unsweetened variety.

I replaced the unsweetened chocolate with bittersweet, adjusting the sugar to balance out the chocolate's sweetness. Now the pudding was smooth and silky. There are two reasons for the pudding's successful textural change with the use of bittersweet chocolate. First, unsweetened chocolate has a lower percentage of cocoa butter than the bittersweet variety. Second, bittersweet chocolate contains some milk solids and lecithin (an emulsifier), both of which create a smoother, creamier texture and mouthfeel.

So never mind if you had a My-T-Fine childhood. You will find that homemade chocolate pudding, creamy and hand-stirred in a saucepan on the stove top to a bubbly conclusion, is a wonderful indulgence.

DOUBLE CHOCOLATE PUDDING
SERVES 4 TO 6

To melt the chocolate, chop and place it in a heatproof bowl set over a pan of almost simmering water, stirring once or twice until smooth. You can also melt the chocolate in a microwave at 50 percent power for 3½ minutes, stopping to stir after 2 minutes. If the chocolate is not yet completely melted, heat up to 30 seconds more at 50 percent power. Serve the pudding with whipped cream, if desired.

- 2 tablespoons Dutch-processed cocoa powder
- 2 tablespoons cornstarch
- ⅔ cup sugar
- ⅛ teaspoon salt
- 1 cup light cream
- 3 large egg yolks
- 2 cups whole milk
- 6 ounces bittersweet chocolate, melted (*see* note above) and cooled slightly
- 1 tablespoon unsalted butter, softened
- 2 teaspoons vanilla extract

1. Sift cocoa powder, cornstarch, sugar, and salt into large heavy-bottomed saucepan. Slowly whisk in light cream, followed by yolks, then milk. Stir in chocolate. (Chocolate will form clumps that smooth with cooking.)

2. Bring mixture to boil over medium-high heat, stirring constantly with whisk, scraping bottom and sides of pot. Pudding will gradually darken and thicken. Reduce heat to medium and cook, stirring gently but constantly with wooden spoon until pudding very thickly coats spoon or instant-read thermometer registers about 200 degrees, 1½ to 2 minutes.

3. Pass pudding through fine-mesh strainer into medium bowl, pressing with rubber spatula. Leave residue in strainer. Stir butter and vanilla into pudding. Serve warm or directly cover surface of pudding with plastic wrap, cool 30 minutes, and refrigerate.

Lisa Yockelson is a food journalist and the author of *Layer Cakes and Sheet Cakes* (HarperCollins, 1996).

Jarred Pasta Sauces Earn Low Ratings

A quick homemade spaghetti sauce that uses canned tomatoes is worlds better than most popular jarred varieties.

⇒ BY MARYELLEN DRISCOLL ⇐

My cousin Karen, a five-foot-nine-inch head-turner with the metabolism of a speeding bullet, is legendary for her lack of cooking ability. So when I told her that I was doing a taste test story on jarred tomato-based pasta sauces, she said, "I can tell you which brand is the best, since I eat it at least two times a week and have never even considered making my own." She predicted not only the top jarred sauce in our tasting but also the second- and third-place sauces. She also knew which to avoid at all costs. Now, there's a true voice of experience.

Non-cooks like my cousin as well as some of the best cooks I know use jarred tomato sauces. As a result, sales of these convenience sauces have nearly doubled in the past 10 years, now standing at $1.1 billion dollars a year, according to Information Resources, a Chicago company that tracks sales trends. At my local supermarket there are a dozen brands to choose from, each brand having up to a half-dozen variations.

Here at *Cook's*, we decided to sort through the choices to determine those worth recommending—if any.

Because there are so many brands and types of jarred tomato-based sauces, we decided to stick to the basics, meaning the most widely distributed supermarket brands as well as a few of the more popular brands in specialty food stores. We also restricted our tasting to marinara-style sauces containing tomatoes, garlic, herbs (usually basil and/or oregano), and sometimes onions.

From supermarkets we included jarred sauces by Barilla, Classico, Five Brothers, Newman's Own, Prego, and Ragú, all of which are nationally distributed. From specialty food stores we selected sauces by Enrico's, Muir Glen, Rao's, Rusticella d'Abruzzo, and Timpone's. We also decided to throw in a ringer, a quick home-cooked tomato sauce (made from canned tomatoes) that was developed for the May/June 1997 issue of *Cook's*. Nineteen tasters rated the sauces on a variety of flavor components, including sweetness, acidity, freshness, and strength of herb flavor. They were also rated for consistency and overall likability.

Freshness Is All

While tasters clearly expressed varied preferences when it came to the ideal consistency of the sauces, they all agreed on the driving component—freshness of flavor. In this department, the *Cook's* quick home-made sauce was the only one considered to taste "extremely fresh" and the only one that tasters really liked. The three highest-rated jarred sauces, on the other hand, tasted only "somewhat fresh." While the *Cook's* recipe is not merely a matter of opening a jar, it involves minimal ingredients—primarily basic pantry goods, including canned tomatoes—and takes about the same amount of time to make as it does to cook a pot of pasta.

We found several probable reasons for the stale taste of most of the jarred sauces. Apart from those which placed first and third (Barilla and Classico, respectively), all of the supermarket jarred tomato sauces listed tomato puree as their main ingredient and diced tomatoes second. In the *Cook's* rating of canned crushed tomatoes (*see* the March/April 1997 issue), we found that tomato puree "diminishes the fresh tomato flavor." This results from the fact that puree is a concentrate requiring higher temperatures and longer cooking times to process than simple cooked tomatoes, whether whole or diced.

The freshness and purity of other ingredients in a sauce also contribute to the success of the final product, said Kamal Dagher, vice president of product development at Barilla America. Barilla, a market leader in pasta and jarred sauces in Italy, uses primarily fresh ingredients that are diced at the plant. Some other producers use dried spices and even dried vegetables.

Barilla America's Dagher also noted that the longer a sauce cooks, the less fresh it tastes. Barilla's sauce is minimally cooked, really just enough to prevent the growth of bacteria. The problem for many manufacturers, however, is not excessive cooking but the prolonged time that a sauce stays hot before it is jarred and cooled, said Dagher. To avoid this, Barilla expedites the final stage by rapidly cooling the sauce and filling the jars.

A few of the sauces tried to make up for their deficiency in tomato flavor with excessive sweetness. These efforts failed, though. Our tasters typically labeled these sauces as "kids' food." Notably, Barilla and Classico were the only supermarket brands to put onions before sugar (or corn syrup in some cases) on their list of ingredients.

Many of the higher-priced specialty food store sauces contained neither tomato puree nor a morsel of added sugar. Tasters found that these products lacked flavor or that what flavor they had was undesirable. This was not surprising, since we found when developing the *Cook's* recipe below that a small amount of sugar was important in reducing sour notes and heightening the tomato flavor.

Somewhat surprisingly, tasters also found that a "homemade" appearance was not an indicator of good taste; sauces that tried to look rustic turned out to have little flavor or strong off flavors. Timpone's, for example, contained whole cloves of flavorless garlic and soggy basil leaves. The orange-tinted sauce from the famous restaurant Rao's (sounds like Ray-ohs) stumped some tasters as the most mysterious, while others thought they recognized it as Chef Boyardee. At twice the price of most supermarket brands, none of these products merited even an acceptable rating among tasters.

Simply put, jarred tomato-based pasta sauces do not taste great. Some are not bad; many are. The good news is that there is an easy homemade alternative that offers superior flavor and requires minimal effort or skill. Even my cousin could handle this one.

SIMPLE TOMATO SAUCE
DRESSES ¾ POUND PASTA: SERVES 3

1	28-ounce can diced or whole tomatoes (not packed in puree or sauce)
2	medium garlic cloves, peeled
3	tablespoons extra-virgin olive oil
2	tablespoons coarsely chopped fresh basil leaves (about 8 leaves)
¼	teaspoon sugar
1½	teaspoons salt

1. If using diced tomatoes, go to step 2. If using whole tomatoes, drain and reserve liquid. Dice tomatoes either by hand or in work bowl of food processor fitted with metal blade (three or four pulses at ½ second). Tomatoes should be coarse, with ¼-inch pieces visible. If necessary, add enough reserved liquid to tomatoes to total 2 cups.

2. Process garlic through garlic press into small bowl; stir in 1 teaspoon water. Heat oil and garlic in 10-inch sauté pan over medium heat until fragrant but not brown, about 2 minutes. Stir in tomatoes; simmer until thickened slightly, about 10 minutes. Stir in basil, sugar, and salt, and cook, stirring constantly, for 1 minute. Serve over pasta.

TASTING JARRED TOMATO SAUCES

Our tasting included the most widely distributed national brands in supermarkets and specialty food stores nationwide. Also, all of the sauces were marinara style. For those brands which offered two marinara-style sauces, we included the one with flavorings most similar to the others in the tasting. Nineteen tasters, including *Cook's* staff and students from the Boston University culinary arts program, were served sauce samples in small cups served warm. Bowls of ziti were also served to taste along with the sauce if desired. The sauces were rated on a variety of flavor components: sweetness, acidity, freshness, and strength of herb flavor. They were also rated for consistency and overall likability. The sauces are listed below in order of preference.

HIGHLY RECOMMENDED

Cook's Simple Tomato Sauce
➤ About $2.50 for 28 ounces

This homemade tomato sauce was included as a ringer in the tasting because it can be cooked up as fast as a pot of pasta and uses basic pantry ingredients, with the exception of fresh basil. Tasters responded to its freshness of flavor with an enthusiasm that they could not conjure up for any of the other sauces.

ACCEPTABLE

Barilla Marinara Pasta Sauce
➤ $2.39 for 26 ounces

This tangy, thick tomato sauce was the best of the jarred sauces. With lots of oregano punch, the flavor was fresher than most, with a fair level of acidity and sweetness. Tasters liked the thick and yet smooth consistency of this sauce. "Lots of substance," one taster noted. Available in supermarkets nationwide.

Five Brothers Fresh Tomato and Basil Pasta Sauce
➤ $2.19 for 26 ounces

"Although very sweet, this one has a fresh flavor," one taster stated. It carried a strong vegetal flavor that one taster likened to V-8 and a few to ketchup. The sauce consisted of big chunks of tomato in a somewhat watery sauce. Available in supermarkets nationwide.

Classico Tomato and Basil Pasta Sauce
➤ $2.59 for 26 ounces

"Rather uninteresting" seemed to be the consensus. This sauce was notably acidic, very "tomato-y," and had strong herb flavors. It had a smooth paste texture with some small chunks. Available in supermarkets nationwide.

NOT RECOMMENDED

Rao's Homemade Marinara Sauce
➤ $5.28 for 15.5 fluid ounces

Along with a recent cookbook, the famous East Harlem New York restaurant Rao's released a jarred version of its marinara sauce, and for a pretty price. Some tasters said it was reminiscent of Chef Boyardee or tomato soup. Those who took to this unusual sauce picked up on complex, smoky undertones reminiscent of meat. Available in specialty food stores or by mail order (call 1-800-HOMEMADE).

Enrico's Traditional Italian Style Pasta Sauce
➤ $5.49 for 15.5 ounces

Tasters were bored by this natural food company's sauce. It was "lackluster," as one *Cook's* editor put it. The sauce lacked freshness, depth, and character. To its credit, there were no off flavors. The texture was thick, pasty, and smooth. Available in natural food stores nationwide.

Newman's Own Venetian Pasta Sauce
➤ $1.99 for 26 ounces

One of the more inexpensive brands, this sauce was rejected by tasters for its extreme sweetness, a bitter aftertaste, and texture like "watered-down tomato paste." Wrote one taster, "I can't taste any flavor other than sugar and tomatoes." Available in supermarkets nationwide.

Timpone's Mom's Spaghetti Sauce
➤ $3.99 for 14 ounces

The oddest and most disturbing aspects of this sauce were the flavorless whole cloves of garlic and whole basil leaves in it. With such a homemade appearance, "you expect a lot of flavor—then when it hits your mouth, it falls flat," wrote one taster. The texture was described as chunks in a watery and oily sauce. Available in specialty and natural food stores.

Prego Traditional Spaghetti Sauce
➤ $1.89 for 28 ounces

This sauce bordered on cloying. "Kids will like this one," noted one taster. Many tasters likened it to ketchup with an overdose of oregano. It contained two to three times as much sweetener as most other sauces. The texture was thick, smooth, and pasty. Available in supermarkets nationwide.

Ragú
➤ $1.59 for 27.7 ounces

More than one taster likened Ragú to Spaghetti-os sauce. Pizzeria sauces and tomato soup were also mentioned. Tasters complained of excessive saltiness. Its thin, smooth texture was the least popular among all of the sauces. Herb flavors were completely absent. Available in supermarkets nationwide.

Muir Glen Tomato Basil Pasta Sauce
➤ $2.59 for 25.5 ounces

This brand name was a winner in our canned crushed tomato tasting (*see* the March/April 1997 issue), but the sauce offered fewer diced tomatoes and more of a heavy tomato puree, a formula that failed to lend "even a hint of freshness," said one taster. Tasters complained that this sauce was too spicy, with a burnt flavor. Available in some supermarkets and in natural food stores nationwide.

Rusticella d'Abruzzo Tomato Sauce
➤ $5.49 for 9.8 ounces

This expensive little import was primarily turned down for strong off flavors that many tasters described as plastic and burnt. The taste of olive oil was excessive for many. As for consistency, this sauce contained chunks of tomato suspended in an oily liquid. Available in specialty food stores.

Grate Expectations

Many graters are awkward or so dull they are hardly worth using. Here's what worked in our test kitchen.

≥ BY ADAM RIED ≤

When I was growing up, the average American's idea of Parmesan cheese was that familiar little green can. In fact, the old box grater in my mother's 1965 kitchen may never have seen an intact wedge of Parmesan. But now, more than 30 years later, Italian cooking is red hot in America, and so is good-quality Parmesan cheese...sold in wedges, not in cans, green or otherwise.

As a result, hard-cheese graters have become nearly essential equipment in the 1999 home kitchen. A quick look through most cookware stores bears this out, as cheese graters now come in several distinct designs. Unfortunately, many of them don't work all that well. With some designs you need Herculean strength to move the cheese over the teeth with sufficient pressure for grating; with others you eventually discover that a large portion of the grated cheese has remained jammed in the grater instead of sitting where it belongs, on your food. Whether you are dusting a plate of pasta or grating a full cup of cheese to use in a recipe, a good grater should be easy to use and efficient.

We rounded up 15 different models and set about determining which was the best grater. Pre-testing eliminated 4 of these models, which left us with 11 graters in five basic configurations. First were the flat graters, including The Cheese Grater, the AMCO, and the Bradshaw. Each of these consists of a flat sheet of metal that is punched through with teeth and attached to some type of handle. Next were the familiar upright box graters, including the FarberWare and the Progressive International Pro Grip Comfort Ultra Tower, which offer different size holes on each of their sides to allow for both fine grating and coarse shredding. A third type was the rotary grater, including the Moulinex Mouli, the Zyliss, and the Oxo Good Grips. With this design, you put a small chunk of cheese in a hopper and use a handle to

The Cheese Graters We Tested

BEST GRATER

The Cheese Grater
Very sharp teeth and solid handle make this a breeze to hold and use.

Moulinex Mouli
The metal arm provides good leverage, sharp teeth grated easily.

Progressive International Pro Grip
Ball handle and feet are nice touches, but bulky for storage.

FarberWare Nonstick
Not good for tableside grating, but offers several texture options.

AMCO
Design not bad in general, but avoid this particular brand.

Bradshaw
Effective enough, but outclassed by several others.

Zyliss
Teeth were sharp, but it won't take long until your hand aches.

Oxo Good Grips
Least favorite of the rotary graters because of bulky, clumsy feel when handling.

Kyocera Dish
Clumsy grater design with very, very sharp teeth....Watch your knuckles.

Progressive International
Graham Kerr Dish
So much effort for so little cheese.

Imetec
Loud, bulky, expensive, and useless.

press it down against a crank-operated grating wheel. Porcelain dish graters were our fourth type, including the Kyocera and the Progressive International Graham Kerr model. These are porcelain dishes with raised teeth in the center and a well around the outside edge to collect the grated cheese. Last was our electric model, the Imetec Pronto Parmesan, which uses an electric motor to push and rotate small chunks of cheese against a grating disk.

The Cheese, the Whole Cheese, and Nothing but the Cheese

The testing process for the graters was quite straightforward. All we had to do was grate cheese, and lots of it. After going through more than 10 pounds of the stuff, we found some graters consistently easy to use. Most, however, were not. In fact, using several of these graters amounted to nothing less than a full upper-body work-out. Success, we observed, was due to a combination of sharp grating teeth, a comfortable handle or grip, and good leverage for pressing the cheese onto the grater.

Overall, the runaway star of the show was the best of the flat graters. Called simply The Cheese Grater, it is sold through a New York company, Cooking by the Book. Essentially the shape and size of a standard ruler (about 12 inches long by 1 inch wide), The Cheese Grater's design is based on a small, maneuverable wood-working tool called a rasp. Rasps have lots and lots of tiny, sharp, raised teeth that remove wood smoothly and efficiently. The rasp-like Cheese Grater was both the most aggressive and most controlled of the bunch, grating large quantities of cheese smoothly and almost effortlessly. The black plastic handle, which we found more comfortable than any of the others, also earned high praise.

Another small flat model with a handle, the AMCO Cheese Grater, disappointed us. Generally, this design comes with both flat and curved grating surfaces. In pre-testing everyone preferred the flat because it is easier to move cheese over a flat surface than a curved one.

RATING CHEESE GRATERS

We tested each grater with pieces of room temperature, hard Parmesan cheese, which had been left unwrapped in the refrigerator for one month to harden even further. The degree of effort required to grate was our single, most important consideration. We also rated each grater on grip comfort, ease of cleaning, dishwasher safeness, and texture of cheese after grating. Other observations, such as perceived sharpness of the blade, whether the grater felt sturdy or flimsy in use, and the shape of the grater as it might affect portability (bringing it to the table to grate directly from a block of cheese onto a diner's plate) and storage, are noted in the Testers' Comments.

Brand	Price	Type	Material	Grating Effort	Grip Comfort	Clean-up	Dish-washer	Cheese Texture	Testers' Comments
BEST GRATER **The Cheese Grater**	$16.00	Flat	Metal	★★★	★★★	★★★	No	Very flaky and feathery	A real winner with super-sharp teeth, a stable, comfortable handle, and a shape that's great for both table use and storage. Blade is a bit narrow and it cannot go into the dishwasher, but that's a small price to pay for its other virtues.
Moulinex Mouli Grater	$16.99	Rotary	Metal	★★★	★★★	★★★	Yes	Thick, separate shreds	Much stronger and more stable than plastic rotary models and therefore smoother and easier to use. Shape makes for easy tableside grating but awkward storage.
Progressive International Pro Grip Comfort Ultra Tower Grater	$12.00	Three-sided box/ pyramid	Metal	★★	★★★	★★	Yes	Fine, short shreds	Black plastic feet make this grater very stable when used and the teeth feel reasonably sharp, so tough cheese rinds are no problem. The shape looks great but has its downsides: This grater is hard to clean on the inside and awkward for both tableside grating and storage.
FarberWare Deluxe Nonstick Grater	$7.99	Box	Metal	★★	★★★	★★★	Yes	Fine and powdery	Felt like Old Faithful, but this grater had a hard time with tough, rubbery rinds, and the shape was too bulky for easy storage.
AMCO Cheese Grater	$7.99	Flat	Metal	★★	★★★	★★★	Yes	Uneven, from powder to short shreds	Good for table use and storage because of compact size and shape, but teeth are dull, meaning that considerable pressure is required to grate the cheese.
Bradshaw International Good Cook Stainless Grater	$2.19	Flat	Metal	★★	★★	★★★	Yes	Short, thick shreds	This familiar old design is stable to use as long as you set it over the mouth of a bowl. Without the bowl, it can be hard to use. Teeth are sharp, and it stores easily.
Zyliss Cheese Grater	$14.99	Rotary	Plastic	★	★★	★	Yes	Tiny, feathery shreds	Because the plastic bends too much, the level of pressure is diminished and hand strain sets in almost immediately. Good for table use but bulky for storage.
Oxo Good Grips Rotary Cheese Grater	$14.99	Rotary	Plastic	★	★	★	Yes	Uneven, from powder to thick shreds	Grip was bulky and awkward, so it was difficult to exert enough pressure on the cheese for efficient grating. OK for table use, but tricky to disassemble for cleaning and storage.
Kyocera Porcelain Dish Grater	$39.95	7" diam. dish	Porcelain	★	★★	★★	Yes	Compact and slightly granular	No-skid rubber base provides great stability. The teeth are extremely sharp—we did several nasty numbers on our knuckles—and rubbery cheese was a problem.
Progressive International Graham Kerr's Porcelain Grating Dish	$6.99	6³⁄₈-" diam. dish	Porcelain	★	★★	★★	Yes	Fine and powdery as dust	To say that grating with this dish was difficult is a definite understatement. What's worse, all that work provided very little grated cheese. The teeth were not particularly sharp, and without a no-skid base the dish slid all over our work surface.
Imetec Pronto Parmesan	$39.99	Recharge-able electric	Plastic	★★★	★	★	No	Very uneven, from dust to large chunks	The three words that best describe this tool are "piece of junk."

Because it is compact and has a good handle, I've been pleased with a flat version I've had at home for years. Unfortunately, though, the AMCO was a particularly poor example of this type of grater, with teeth so dull the cheese slid right over them. Avoid this brand.

Among the rotary graters in our group, the Moulinex Mouli was popular. We had pre-tested this stainless steel model against the same grater made of plastic and found the metal to be significantly better. The metal arm is rigid enough to do some of the work of pushing the cheese down onto the grating drum. The arms on the plastic models, including the Zyliss we tested, flexed too much against the cheese, thus requiring extra pressure to force the cheese down. Hand strain set in quickly. Even more pain occurred because the crank handle grazed my other hand with every turn. Though the Oxo Good Grips Rotary model was designed to let you use more of your hand to push the cheese against the drum, the same phenomenon held true because the plastic was too flexible. In fact, most testers were forced to use two hands on this one. Another fault that plagued all three rotaries was their inability to grate the piece of cheese entirely. There was always a little nub left jammed up against the grating drum. Because good Parmesan often costs around $15 a pound, I didn't want to waste any of it.

A new take on the old box grater design, the Progressive International Pro Grip Comfort Ultra Tower Grater, impressed us with a comfortable handle and black plastic feet for stability. The two porcelain dish graters were duds. After laboring over the Progressive International Graham Kerr Grating Dish, I thought I'd have the biceps of Charles Atlas. The teeth, which are shaped like tiny pyramids with sharp edges, were quite ineffective. The alleged advantage of the $40 Kyocera Dish was its cone-shaped teeth. They were indeed sharp, to the dismay of my knuckles, but we found it no easier to grate cheese in this dish than in the other, save for the no-skid base, which was a significant improvement. This dish is not worth the money.

The last grater in the group, the electric Imetec Pronto Parmesan, was a loser of monumental proportions. True, the grating effort required was next to nothing, but so were the results. My 102-year-old grandfather could have grated cheese faster and more efficiently than this thing. After all of this grater's wheezing and laboring, it was even difficult to clean. All this, and expensive to boot.

The Quest for Inexpensive Chardonnay

We looked for good—not great—Chardonnays that cost less than $12 and were available nationally; there aren't many. BY MARK BITTMAN

The quest for a decent, inexpensive, and light Chardonnay continues. Once again, we went looking for a wine akin to a Chablis, a wine with a flavor not completely overwhelmed by oak and with a balance of fruit and acid that allows it to serve as both an aperitif and a good accompaniment to light foods. Our search was limited by two major factors: price (we wanted to stay below $12, and nearly succeeded) and availability (we wanted the wines to be sold throughout the United States). We also excluded those wines we already knew to be dominated by the flavor of oak.

The news is not especially heartening. Even allowing for some flaws, even allowing for lowered expectations, I wouldn't feel comfortable recommending any but the top three wines. The reasons are simple: Most of the wines lacked acidity, tasted of raw oak, had weak fruit, or smacked of technical manipulation, including the addition of ingredients other than grapes and yeast.

Chardonnay is the grape responsible for making one of what are generally acknowledged to be two of the world's great white wines (the other is Riesling, used predominantly in Germany and Alsace). The top white Burgundies—with names like Chablis, Montrachet, and Meursault—are made from Chardonnay, as are most of the very good and even great white wines from the United States. At their best, Chardonnays have an enticing aroma, wonderful body, and a terrific balance between fruit and acidity; often, but not always, the subtle flavor of oak is present as well. Most very good Chardonnays cost upward of $30 a bottle, and many go for twice that much and even more.

But you don't expect all wines to be great, and Chardonnays need not be great to be good. Nevertheless, certain elements must be present to make a Chardonnay pleasant tasting. The first is a good bouquet; one that smells artificial, or downright bad, does not encourage further pursuit. Many of the wines we tasted featured the aroma of artificially flavored pineapple candy (some even tasted that way).

Second is the balance between ripe fruit and acidity. This really begins with the grape; those grown in hot climates (as are many of the inexpensive grapes from California) become intensely sweet but retain little acidity. This imbalance can be partially remedied by adding acidity directly to the wine (usually in the form of citric acid crystals), but often the cure is worse than the disease. In any case, when either fruit or acid dominates, the tasting experience is diminished. Many of the wines in this tasting were so fruity as to be candy-like; in others, the acid taste was reminiscent of artificially flavored lemonade. If neither fruit nor acid is perceptible, which was the case in some of these wines, the wine is flat.

Finally, there is the question of wood. Many (but not all) great wines are aged or even fermented in wood barrels, a process that contributes a certain roundness and rich flavor. But wood aging is expensive; the barrels themselves cost a great deal of money, and aging or fermenting wines in them is much more of a hassle than doing so in enormous stainless steel vats. In an attempt to mimic the preferably subtle qualities of wood, producers go to all kinds of extremes, including adding wood chips to vats of wine. This procedure usually produces a wine in which the flavor of oak dominates—all the more so if the wine is not a strong one to begin with, which is exactly the case with inexpensive wines.

It's difficult to make a good, inexpensive Chardonnay, especially in the quantities necessary to meet national distribution in a vast country like the United States. So let's look on the optimistic side and say that the discovery of even three winemakers that seem to have risen to this challenge is good news.

THE TASTERS' RESULTS | INEXPENSIVE CHARDONNAY

The wines in our tasting—held at Mt. Carmel Wine and Spirits in Hamden, Connecticut—were judged by a panel made up of both wine professionals and amateur wine lovers. All of the wines were purchased in the Northeast; prices will vary throughout the country. Within each category, wines are listed based on the number of points scored. In this tasting, the "Highly Recommended" wine had almost all positive comments. Those wines labeled "Recommended" garnered mostly positive comments, and the "Recommended with Reservations" group got decidedly mixed comments. The wines in the "Not Recommended" category received few or no positive comments.

HIGHLY RECOMMENDED

1996 St. Francis CALIFORNIA **$11.**
The only wine that was wholeheartedly endorsed by all tasters: "This wine, unlike the others, has some stature and finesse." "Rich fruit and decent acidity."

RECOMMENDED

1997 Drouhin La Foret FRANCE **$9.**
"Clean nose, clean fruit, nice finish."

1997 Fetzer Sundial CALIFORNIA **$8.**
An old standby in inexpensive Chardonnay, and, if not great, not at all bad: "Clean, fruity, and quite pleasant."

RECOMMENDED WITH RESERVATIONS

1995 Chateau St. Jean CALIFORNIA **$13.**
"Nose is oaky, and fruit is pleasant," but overall flavor is "one-dimensional" and "flabby."

1997 Glen Ellen Proprietor's Reserve CALIFORNIA **$6.**
Another standard, this one with "decent," "clean" flavor but "little character."

1997 Meridian CALIFORNIA **$10.**
"Nice" flavors, if "somewhat sweet." Generally "inoffensive."

1997 Beringer Founder's Estate CALIFORNIA **$10.**
A tossup between those who found "pure fruit" and others who said "tastes phony—like chemicals."

1997 Napa Ridge Coastal Vines CALIFORNIA **$8.**
"Acceptable" wine with "nice fruit" and "decent balance." "Lacks acidity."

1996 Latour Ardeche FRANCE **$7.**
"White, wet, and has alcohol." "Poor fruit."

NOT RECOMMENDED

1997 Domaine de Bernier FRANCE **$8.**
1996 Callaway CALIFORNIA **$10.**
1996 Chateau Ste. Michelle WASHINGTON **$11.**
1996 Louis Martini CALIFORNIA **$10.**
1997 Columbia Crest WASHINGTON **$13.**
1997 Hess Select CALIFORNIA **$12.**

The Pie and Pastry Bible

Although this book often uses two steps where one would do nicely, it still belongs in the kitchen of every serious baker. BY CHRISTOPHER KIMBALL

Rose Levy Beranbaum's first book, *The Cake Bible*, was a huge success. It sold hundreds of thousands of copies and established her as a highly respected culinary authority. It also established her as a cook with more than a dash of obsessiveness, a kind of Woody Allen of baking who infused home cooking with her borderline neurotic attention to detail. Her new book, *The Pie and Pastry Bible*, has been much anticipated, since it has the same heft and gravitas of the original Bible. We were anxious to learn whether this second production would be another stand-alone masterpiece—a *Godfather, Part II*, if you like—or just an also-ran sequel. In addition, the last 10 years have seen a wealth of "Bible" books, including one by this author, so the bar has been raised in terms of expectations.

Clearly, Beranbaum's obsession with baking has not diminished. This was foretold in the foreword by her editor, Maria Guarnaschelli, who says about her own early married life, "I especially liked to make desserts—the more complex, the better." Rose and Maria remind me of two quantum physicists studying the intricacies of the atom's nucleus. As soon as one of them discovers a muon, another unknown particle shows up in the particle accelerator to be catalogued. This attention to detail is two-edged. As a home cook, I find the ingredient lists, which often run to a full page and are presented in chart form, to be useful. But they are also unnecessarily complex in that each ingredient is listed three times, by volume, in ounces, and in grams. Serious bakers do measure by weight rather than volume, but only a glutton for obscure details would want to know that two teaspoons of cornstarch weigh six grams, since this information has no practical value. It would be easier on the eye and the cook, it seems to me, to simply offer weight measures for those ingredients, such as flour, which really need it.

The Pie and Pastry Bible
Rose Levy Beranbaum
Scribner's, 690 pages, $35

This marriage of unnecessary complexity and thorough research abounds in *The Pie and Pastry Bible*. I am fascinated by the author's discussions of which flours to use in pastry crusts (pastry flour and bleached all-purpose are recommended) as well as why one would want to add baking powder and vinegar to a crust. (For my part, I can taste the vinegar in the crust and find the flavor unwelcome.) Yet, as I glide along on her philosophical wings, I find that her recipes become increasingly complex, much like a government building designed by committee. A good example is her apple pie. To solve the problem of excess juices and to add extra flavor (a problem that might have been solved by testing different apple varieties), the author first sugars the cut apples, then lets them sit for 30 minutes, pours off the syrup, caramelizes it on top of the stove, and then finally adds it back to the pie before baking. In addition, she uses a very high oven temperature of 425 degrees throughout the baking of the pie, which means that the edges need to be covered with foil to avoid burning. (We found this to be a problem with many of her pies.) Here is the simplest of recipes gone astray. I found myself wishing that Beranbaum would stop trying to reinvent every recipe, remaking it in her own image. (Do we really need, for example, to bake meatloaf in a cheddar cheese pastry crust?)

That brings us to the recipe testing. We made a total of 21 recipes, of which 13 received very good reviews, a more than respectable percentage in our experience. Beranbaum's brioche is first rate, as are her cheese puffs (gougères), and the quick puff pastry was a total winner, perhaps the best recipe in the book. Her pie crust is a lot more work than most standard recipes, but it blind bakes perfectly and tastes great. Still, given the incredible attention to detail and recipes that often ran two or three pages, I was a bit disappointed that more of the recipes were not slam-dunk winners. After all, many of these recipes involved a lot of extra work, and my rule is simple—if it's harder, it has to be better. Coconut cream pie was turned into a coconut ice cream pie, which required steeping the cream and milk with shredded coconut for more than an hour (why not just use coconut milk?) and then freezing it before proceeding; scones were not simply thrown together like biscuits but had to be turned much like puff pastry (yes, they were terrific); and whole wheat croissants, which also received high ratings, took two to three days to make. Several of the recipes fell short by any standard. Buttermilk Chess Pie, for example, was too lemony and separated into a curdled top with a slippery bottom custard. A hot fudge sauce came out thin, not sticky as promised. The Pumpkin Chiffon Pie never really set up properly, was cloyingly sweet, and the beaten egg whites began to weep.

Along the way, I picked up a handful of minor quibbles. I wondered, for instance, why certain topics received intense scrutiny while others seem to have escaped the author's appetite for testing. A few recipes also called for mail-order-only ingredients such as Tahitian vanilla beans and Cobasan (a stabilizer made from sorbitol and glucose and available only in one-quart amounts), although in fairness I must say that most of the recipes in this book are made from supermarket ingredients. Finally, I found the inclusion of savory recipes a bit jarring, even though they technically qualify as pastry. On page 461 one finds Bite Size Peanut Butter Napoleons. On page 471, one tucks into Beef Wellington.

In the end, however, one cannot help but be impressed by Beranbaum's thoroughness and depth of knowledge. Despite my reservations, anyone who takes baking seriously ought to buy this book. And the choice between simplicity and complexity may be a matter of personal style. I am reminded of the debate between Albert Einstein and the great physicists of his day. Einstein was in search of an elegant solution to the universe, a great unifying theory through which one might glimpse the hand of God, while others delved into quantum mechanics, content with an increasingly complex, yet astonishingly accurate, view of the world. As far as we know, Einstein was wrong—but it doesn't stop many of us from seeking out simplicity as a guiding principle, even in the kitchen.

RESOURCES

Most of the ingredients and materials necessary for the recipes in this issue are available at your local supermarket, gourmet store, or kitchen supply shop. The following are mail-order sources for particular items. Prices listed below were current at press time and do not include shipping or handling unless otherwise indicated. We suggest that you contact companies directly to confirm up-to-date prices and availability.

Cheese Graters

For the rating of cheese graters on page 28, only 2 of the 11 graters lived up to our highest standards. Our favorite, The Cheese Grater, is reminiscent of a metal ruler lined with sharp grating teeth and is attached to an easy-to-grip black handle. It is made of stainless steel but is not dishwasher safe. The Cheese Grater typically sells for $16. To inquire about stores that carry it or to order by mail, call **Cooking by the Book, Inc. (13 Worth Street, New York, NY 10013; 212-966-9799).**

The runner-up in our tests was the stainless steel Moulinex Mouli Grater (not to be confused with the tin model). Moulinex of France is touted as the original manufacturer of the rotary cheese grater. We found that those companies which have tried to mimic the Mouli do not approach the original's ease of use, sharp teeth, and sturdy grip. The Mouli is available for only $12.95 from **The Gooseberry (Route 7A, Manchester Center, VT 05255; 802-362-3263).**

"Egg"/Mozzarella Slicer

We became attached to a gadget designed for slicing fresh mozzarella balls when making batch after batch of egg salad. This slicer is designed like a wire egg or mushroom slicer, but the metal wires are spaced twice as far apart (3/8 inch) as they are in an egg slicer, so it makes perfect-sized dice for egg salad. The fine, taut wires make a particularly clean slice through the crumble-prone yolk. More important, the 18 slices needed to dice up a hard-cooked egg are done in just a few seconds with this gadget. The slicer we used is made by Leifheit, a German housewares manufacturer. It comes in white, is made of a sturdy plastic, and measures 4½ by 6½ inches and is 1½ inches deep. The round, concave base is 3 inches in diameter — plenty large enough for an egg, a ball of mozzarella, a large white mushroom, or even a cooked beet. The Leifheit mozzarella slicer can be ordered from **Kitchen Arts (161 Newbury Street, Boston, MA 02116; 617-266-8701) for $14.95, including freight.**

Lemon Grass

For the Hot and Sour Noodle Soup with Shrimp and Tomato per recipe on page 20, we found that bruising the lemon grass was the best method of imparting its pungent, lemony flavor to the broth. Lemon grass, a stiff, fibrous grass, is available in Asian markets and many supermarkets. If you cannot find it and wish to use only fresh, the cost of shipping can be prohibitive because it is a perishable item. **Melissa's World Variety Produce, Inc. (P.O. Box 21127, Los Angeles, CA 90021; 800-588-0151; www.melissas.com)**, will ship fresh lemon grass. Call for information on availability. Fresh lemon grass will dry out after about two weeks in the refrigerator, but it does store well in the freezer for up to six months. On page 20, we found that water-packed lemon grass in a jar is the next best thing to fresh. Melissa's sells a seven-ounce jar for $4.19. While on the subject of lemon grass, husband and wife team Harry and Catherine Matthewson bottle and sell a Barrel-Aged Lemon Grass Vinegar, which we think is worth trying. Made from a rice vinegar base infused with the flavors of fresh lemon grass, garlic, and ginger, it goes particularly well with chicken or shrimp. Handsomely packaged in a tall, narrow 250-ml bottle, the vinegar can be purchased for $3.50 per bottle from their company, **Black Swan, Inc. (P.O. Box 58, Olalla, WA 98359; 800-228-8954; info@blackswaninc.com).**

Rice Noodles

For the Asian noodle soup recipes on page 20, we use two kinds of rice noodles, and their names are often used interchangeably. Rice vermicelli is a long, translucent, hair-like noodle; the other variety of rice noodle we use is also translucent, but is flat, like fettuccine. Both are sold in Asian markets and increasingly in supermarkets and natural food stores. If you cannot locate rice noodles in your area, **The CMC Company (P.O. Box 322, Avalon, NJ 08202; 800-262-2780)** sells both varieties at $2.75 per 16-ounce package. The CMC Company also sells water-packed lemon grass (*see* above) at $5.20 for a 7-ounce jar.

Fish Spatula

Flipping a salmon fillet in a fry pan can be a bit of a juggling act. Either the spatula is too stiff to angle over the raised pan edge and under the fillet without bending and breaking the fillet, or the spatula is too short and the fillet flakes into two or more pieces in the process of lifting and flipping. We avoided both of these problems when developing the recipe for pan-seared salmon fillets (page 9) by using a spatula that is especially pliable so that it can flex under a fillet. It is also shaped like a whole fillet—with one side edge straight and the other slanting out and widening at the top—giving it a reasonable fit for flipping. **Sur La Table (Catalog Division, 1765 Sixth Avenue South, Seattle, WA 98134-1608; 800-243-0852)** sells this style of spatula (item #0503) for $13.95. The spatula blade is stainless steel, 6 inches long and 3 inches at its top width. The wood handle is 4½ inches long. Made in Sweden.

Back Cover Potatoes

The back cover of our January/February 1999 issue included a number of potatoes varied in both color and size. Some of these varieties are not widely distributed in stores. We received our samples from the fields of **Ronniger's Seed & Potato Co. (P.O. Box 307, Ellensburg, WA 98926; 509-925-6025)**. Ronniger's sells 74 varieties of seed potatoes as well as a diverse assortment of garlic cloves and onion bulbs for home gardeners. Its mail-order catalog may be purchased for $2.

Icing Spatulas

When developing frostings for the yellow cake recipe on page 24, we continually reached for a straight icing spatula with an 8-inch blade over the variety of lengths and angles of spatulas we have in the test kitchen. This spatula is long enough to make a nice clean sweep across the top of a cake without being so long that it's awkward to control. We also prefer the convenience of spatulas that can go straight into the dishwasher (the popular wood-handled ones cannot). The Ultra Spatula, sold by **New York Cake & Baking Distributor (56 West 22nd Street, New York, NY 10010; 800-942-2539)**, has a high-grade polypropylene handle so that it is dishwasher safe and easy to grip. The stainless steel blade comes in various lengths (as short as 4½ inches and as long as 14 inches), both straight and angled. The 8-inch blade straight spatula we prefer sells for $5.99.

Cooking Mitt

Our test cooks have been using a particularly colorful potholder mitt in the test kitchen for months. At first we were reluctant to recommend this item because of its cost: $19.95. But after about six months of use, this potholder has become the most prized in the kitchen, valued for its comfortable fit, flexibility, and ease of feel when gripping hot baking sheets or pans. Made of thick 100% wool in bright swaths of red and yellow, it is shaped like a hand puppet, which makes it easy to fold your thumb forward toward your fingers for gripping. The mitt can be purchased through **King Arthur Flour's Bakers Catalogue (P.O. Box 876, Norwich, VT 05055-0876; 800-827-6836; www.kingarthurflour.com)** It can be hand-washed. You can expect some shrinkage, but it should be insignificant.

RECIPE INDEX

Hot and Sour Noodle Soup with Shrimp and Tomato **PAGE 20**

Simple Pan-Seared Salmon and Sweet and Sour Chutney with Onions and Warm Spices **PAGE 9**

Rich and Tender Yellow Layer Cake with Lemon Buttercream Frosting **PAGES 23 AND 24**

Classic Egg Salad **PAGE 15**

Double Chocolate Pudding **PAGE 25**

Hearty Ham and Split Pea Soup with Potatoes **PAGE 11**

PHOTOGRAPHY: CARL TREMBLAY   PROP STYLING: MYROSHA DZIUK

Savoy Cabbage

Chinese Cabbage

Mustard Cabbage

Bok Choy

Napa Cabbage

Red Cabbage

Green Cabbage

Brussels Sprouts

Shanghai Bok Choy

CABBAGES

NUMBER THIRTY-EIGHT

MAY & JUNE 1999

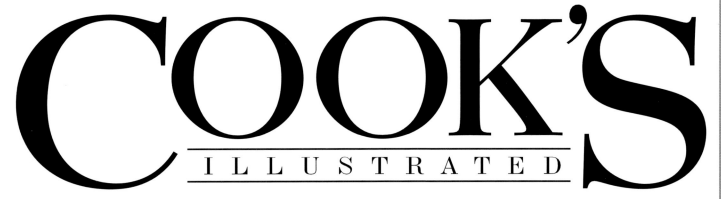

COOK'S
ILLUSTRATED

Rating All-Purpose Flours
Which Brands Perform Best Overall?

Pasta Primavera Simplified
A Fancy Restaurant Dish Comes Home

How to Buy a Gas Grill
Which Features Really Matter?

Oven-Fried Chicken
Not Just Crispy, It's Crunchy

Discovering Great Gumbo
Complex Flavor in Less Time

Improving Custard Pie
Crisp Crust, Foolproof Filling

Authentic Guacamole
Quick Sauces for Sautéed Chicken
Creamy Blue Cheese Dressing
A "New" White Wine?
Roasted Rack of Lamb

$4.95 U.S./$5.95 CANADA

CONTENTS

May & June 1999

COOK'S ILLUSTRATED

PUBLISHER AND EDITOR
Christopher Kimball

EXECUTIVE EDITOR
Pam Anderson

SENIOR EDITOR
John Willoughby

SENIOR WRITER
Jack Bishop

ASSOCIATE EDITORS
Adam Ried
Maryellen Driscoll

TEST COOKS
Dawn Yanagihara
Anne Yamanaka
Bridget Lancaster

CONSULTING EDITORS
Jasper White
Jim Dodge

CONTRIBUTING EDITOR
Stephanie Lyness

ART DIRECTOR
Amy Klee

CORPORATE MANAGING EDITOR
Barbara Bourassa

EDITORIAL PRODUCTION MANAGER
Sheila Datz

COPY EDITOR
India Koopman

EDITORIAL INTERN
Sarah Moughty

MARKETING DIRECTOR
Adrienne Kimball

CIRCULATION DIRECTOR
David Mack

FULFILLMENT MANAGER
Larisa Greiner

MARKETING ASSISTANT
Connie Forbes

PRODUCTS MANAGER
Steven Browall

VICE PRESIDENT
PRODUCTION AND TECHNOLOGY
James McCormack

SYSTEMS ADMINISTRATOR
Richard Cassidy

PRODUCTION ARTIST
Daniel Frey

CONTROLLER
Mandy Shito

OFFICE MANAGER
Mary Connelly

SPECIAL PROJECTS
Fern Berman

OLIVES: There are literally hundreds of different varieties of olives, but all can be categorized by two factors: their ripeness when picked, and the manner in which they are cured. Green olives, picked before they are fully ripe, tend to have fruitier and somewhat lighter flavors, while ripe olives—which range in color from dark brown to purple to deep black—have deeper, more fully developed flavors. Most olives are brine-cured, which involves fermenting them in a strong salt solution. Others are oil-cured, a process that gives them a wrinkled appearance and a sharper flavor. As for particular names, olives may be named after their type of cure, their place of origin, or their actual varietal name. The most important thing to remember about these little fruits, though, is that they vary wildly from batch to batch and year to year: Actually tasting them is the only proof.

COVER PAINTING: BRENT WATKINSON   BACK COVER ILLUSTRATION: JOHN BURGOYNE

Cook's Illustrated (ISSN 1068-2821) is published bimonthly by Boston Common Press Limited Partnership, 17 Station Street, Brookline, MA 02445. Copyright 1999 Boston Common Press Limited Partnership. Periodical postage paid at Boston, MA and additional mailing offices, USPS #012487. For list rental information, contact The SpecialISTS, 1200 Harbor Blvd. 9th Floor, Weehawken, NJ 07087; (201) 865-5800; fax (201) 867-2450. Editorial office: 17 Station Street, Brookline, MA 02445; (617) 232-1000; fax (617) 232-1572. Editorial contributions should be sent to: Editor, *Cook's Illustrated*. We cannot assume responsibility for manuscripts submitted to us. Submissions will be returned only if accompanied by a large self-addressed envelope. Postmaster: Send all new orders, subscription inquiries, and change of address notices to: *Cook's Illustrated*, P.O. Box 7446, Red Oak, IA 51591-0446. PRINTED IN THE USA.

WHY I COOK

I cook because a hot baking powder biscuit is an invitation that no guest can refuse, drawing one downward to a seat at the kitchen table where neighbors trade closely held secrets. I cook because cooks are alchemists, transforming flour and apples into a shotgun marriage of tart Macouns and rich, flaky crusts. I cook because I am the king of my small domain, working without kind words of advice or the helpful suggestion, free to do it my way and at my own pace. Cooking is the amalgamation of a life, the gathering up of tiny bits of experience and knowledge, rolled into a perfect circle of dough or kindly spooned into a worn casserole. I have found nothing clearer in objective or intent than the execution of a recipe, a lockstep of beginnings and endings as comforting as the hollow punctuation of chalk on a grammar school blackboard. This imparts purpose and clarity, delivering blessed structure to the tumble of hours during a long Saturday afternoon.

Cooking is about making do with the crudest of tools, rolling dough with a wine bottle or baking a blueberry cobbler on a covered grill when the power fails after an evening's thunderstorm. Cooks overcome inconvenience and muddle through to the end without complaint, changing plans for want of an ingredient or plunging wildly in a new direction inspired by a whiff of freshly picked rosemary or the burst of flavor from a ripe tomato. We are easily led, I think, susceptible to the whims of life for the sake of pleasure, hedonists seeking out what is pure and undiscovered.

But our pursuit of pleasure eventually leads to simplicity, not excess. Good cooks are well con-nected to the past and are unre-pentant in their love of the famil-iar. Good recipes stand the tests of time and are offered without a thought for the despotism of modern fashion. As we grow in experience, we relish the taste of bourbon sipped from a tin cup by a campfire more than the rarest cognac. We crave a crisp Baldwin in autumn and the taste of hot maple syrup from the first run in March, lungs filled with moist, sweet smoke. We run our fingers through the slow, undulating pour of honey from September's hives and shove them in our mouth, tongues seeking out the distinct notes of golden-rod and wildflower. In our hands, dough comes alive with an elastic bounce that confirms our sus-picions about the breadth of life, which reaches down into the most everyday objects. We are common people, we cooks, but we are blessed with a keen tongue and a sharp eye to uncover life's secrets, growing by the side of the brook or unfurling in the strengthening spring sunlight.

Like lovers, we bring our skills and knowledge with us wherever we go, daring to stand naked in front of the world without props or frivolous trappings. Good cooks offer pleasure readily, seemingly without effort, needing no more than a sizzle or a whiff. We are neither artists nor arti-sans but proud workers, content with the ring-ing of spoons on old soup bowls and the view down the table of heads bowed over hot suppers. And we feel obliged to give our thanks, our

Christopher Kimball

blessings to the food and the table, knowing that we are somehow part of a grander plan.

I suppose that I cook, after all, because I have to. It is not sport or intellectual curiosity that drives me so much as the need to use one's hands upon occasion, to put aside the keyboard, the steering wheel, and the tele-phone in favor of the knife and the onion. I can feel the world rush by my kitchen window and leave me undisturbed, my atten-tion absorbed by proofing dough or roasting chicken. When we take up the knife, we leave behind all that we don't need, all that is con-stantly pressed upon us for our time and consid-eration. Cooking is one of the last acts of defi-ance, a time when the phone rings unanswered and the outside world is left to make do with the answering machine.

Each of us cooks because we secretly recog-nize each other as we pass in the street, bakers or barbecuers, knowing that we live a secret life within arm's length of the stove, simply passing time as best we can the rest of the day. We har-bor the cherished hope that when the world comes to its senses that we will know something of value, something that we can pass on to future generations. Perhaps that torch will never be passed, I don't know, but each of us does our part with a lick of the spoon or a swirl of batter, small faces wide-eyed with the fantastic promise of the kitchen.

ABOUT COOK'S ILLUSTRATED

The Magazine Cook's Illustrated is published every other month (6 issues per year) and accepts no advertising. A one-year subscription is $29.70, two years is $55, and three years is $75. Add $6 postage per year for Canadian subscriptions and $12 per year for all other foreign countries. To order subscriptions in the U.S. call 800-526-8442 or 515-247-7571 from outside the U.S. Gift subscriptions are available for $24.95 each. Rather than put ™ or ® in every occurrence of trade-marked names, we state that we are using the names only in an editorial fashion and to the bene-fit of the trademark owner, with no intention of infringement of the trademark.

Magazine-Related Items Cook's Illustrated is available in an annual hardbound edition, which includes an index, for $24.95 each plus shipping and handling. Discounts are available if more than one year is ordered at a time. Back issues are available for $5 each. Cook's also offers a six-year index (1993–1998) of the magazine for $12.95. To order any of these products, call 800-611-0759 inside the U.S. or 515-246-6911 outside the U.S.

Books Cook's Illustrated publishes a series of single-topic books, available for $14.95 each. Titles include How to Make a Pie, How to Make an American Layer Cake, How to Stir Fry, How to Make Ice Cream, How to Make Salad, How to Make Simple Fruit Desserts, How to Make Cookie Jar Favorites, How to Cook Holiday Roasts and Birds, How to Make Stew, How to Make Pizza, How to Make Holiday Desserts, How to Make Pasta Sauces, How to Grill, and How to Cook Shrimp and Other Shellfish. The Cook's Bible, written by Christopher Kimball and published by Little, Brown and Company, is available for $24.95. The Yellow Farmhouse Cookbook, also written by Christopher Kimball and published by Little, Brown and Company, is available for $24.95. To order any of these books, call 800-611-0759 inside the U.S. or 515-246-6911 outside the U.S.

Reader Submissions Cook's accepts reader submissions for both Quick Tips and Notes from Readers. We will provide a one-year complimentary subscription for each Quick Tip that we print. Send a description of your technique, along with your name, address, and daytime telephone num-ber, to Quick Tips, Cook's Illustrated, P.O. Box 470589, Brookline, MA 02447. Questions, sug-gestions, or other submissions for Notes from Readers should be sent to the same address.

Subscription Inquiries All queries about subscriptions or change of address notices should be addressed to Cook's Illustrated, P.O. Box 7446, Red Oak, IA 51591-0446.

Web Site Address Selected articles and recipes from Cook's Illustrated and subscription infor-mation are available online. You can also order subscriptions, gift subscriptions, or any of our books by visiting www.cooksillustrated.com.

Equipment Test Follow-Up

The editors of *Cook's Illustrated* are looking for information about several cookware items tested in past issues of the magazine. If you have purchased and regularly used any of the standing mixer or espresso machine models listed below, we'd love to know what you think of them. What are your specific likes and dislikes? How have they stood up over time? Are they easy to clean? Which features have you found to be particularly useful or unnecessary? In general, are you satisfied with the item? Any information would be helpful and greatly appreciated. Please mail responses to Equipment Follow-Up, *Cook's Illustrated*, 17 Station Street, Brookline, MA 02445.

Standing Mixers: Rival Select KM210B, KitchenAid K5SS, and KitchenAid K45SS

Espresso Machines: Krups Novo 2000 Plus, Briel Estoril ES-33, and Estro 410

Nut-Topped Coffee Cakes

The yeasted coffee cakes in the November/December 1998 issue of *Cook's* were very good and well worth a little extra effort. We enjoyed the versions with both the sweet cheese and berry fillings for holiday brunches, but I was not successful when I improvised by using nuts as a topping. Is there a technique for getting the nuts to stick well to the cake?

DONNA LOWRY
WARWICK, RI

➤ Nuts make a great topping for this dough, and the author, Susan Logozzo, developed a two-step technique to ensure that they will adhere. First, start by combining the nuts with sticky ingredients, such as butter and corn syrup rather than using them on their own. As added insurance, line the bottom of a well-buttered pan with the topping mixture and nuts, then position the dough over them. This way, you bake the cake as you might a fruit upside-down cake, with the topping on the bottom. Once the cake is baked, invert it so that the topping is on the top.

The recipe below includes both of these techniques. The finished cake is ring shaped, with a hollow center. We found, however, that common high-sided tube pans, the type of pan you would typically choose for such cakes, interfere with air circulation around the dough while baking. Our solution was to invert an ovenproof ramekin in the center of a standard 9 by 2-inch round cake pan. This recipe makes enough topping for half of a recipe of the yeasted dough, so if you have a full recipe and want to bake two cakes, double the topping recipe.

UPSIDE-DOWN COFFEE CAKE WITH ORANGE-ALMOND TOPPING
MAKES ONE 9-INCH ROUND CAKE

Orange-Almond Topping
2   tablespoons unsalted butter, plus extra for pan and ramekin
1/3   cup sugar
3   tablespoons light corn syrup
2   teaspoons grated zest and 1/4 cup juice from 1 medium orange
1   cup sliced almonds

Cake
1/2   recipe rich coffee cake dough (*see* November/December 1998 *Cook's Illustrated*, page 12)

1. *For the topping*: Bring butter, sugar, corn syrup, and orange zest and juice to boil, stirring constantly, in medium saucepan over medium heat; continue to boil and stir until mixture is uniform in texture and glossy, about 1 minute. Remove from heat; stir in almonds.

2. *For the cake*: Meanwhile, butter the sides of a 9 by 2-inch round cake pan and the outside of a 3½-inch ovenproof ramekin. Invert ramekin in center of pan; spread topping evenly on pan bottom, around ramekin.

3. Roll chilled and rested dough into 8-inch circle; using fingers, stretch a 3½-inch hole in center and position in pan, around ramekin and over topping. Cover loosely with plastic wrap and let rise until doubled in size, about 2 hours. (After this final rise, unbaked cake can be refrigerated overnight and baked the next morning).

4. Adjust oven rack to middle position and heat oven to 350 degrees. Bake until deep golden brown and/or an instant-read thermometer inserted into cake registers 190 degrees, 25 to 30 minutes. Invert cake on cooling rack, lift off pan, and remove ramekin from center of cake using tongs. Scrape any topping stuck to bottom of pan with rubber spatula and replace on top of cake. Cool cake at least 20 minutes and serve.

Serving Oysters

I know that oysters are supposed to be served "chilled," but just what is "chilled"? Restaurants seem to refrigerate oysters and then serve them on a bed of ice. In keeping with a personal and completely arbitrary rule of thumb, I take them off the ice and let them come to more or less the temperature of the water they grew in. So, just what is the proper serving temperature for oysters?

SKY COLE
RIDGEFIELD, CT

➤ The answer to your question is not absolute. Consulting editor, chef, and seafood expert Jasper White, whose most recent book is *Lobster at Home* (Scribner, 1998), said that "proper" serving temperature is really a matter of taste. White made a comparison of oysters and beer. Just as some people prefer to drink ice cold beer, others like theirs somewhat warmer. "The same," he said, "goes for oysters." White noted that many Americans, including himself, prefer ice cold oysters, while some Europeans allow the chill to wear off. Mark Bittman, another noted seafood authority and author of both *Fish: The Complete Guide to Buying and Cooking* (Macmillan, 1994) and the *Cook's* wine-tasting column, shares White's preference, declaring: "I never had an oyster that seemed too cold." Bittman added that the bed of ice on which oysters are served in restaurants not only chills them but also steadies them to prevent the oyster liquid from spilling out of the open shell.

Blanching Bitter Greens

I had tried broccoli rabe only once or twice before I read your recent article (*see* "Taming Broccoli Rabe," January/February 1999) and, like the author, found it unpleasantly bitter. As your article promised, though, blanching rids the rabe of excess bitterness. Can you tell me why blanching improves the flavor so much more than other methods, such as steaming, braising, or sautéing?

EMILY MARSHALL
NAPA, CA

➤ Shirley Corriher, food scientist and author of *CookWise* (Morrow, 1997), explained that natural acids in the rabe cause the harsh, bitter flavor. The heat of cooking, said Corriher, weakens the walls of the plant's cells to the point at which some of them collapse. When the cell walls break, the acids in the plant leak out.

In effect, the large quantity of water used to blanch the rabe cleans it off by washing away those natural acids. When you pour the water down the drain, the acids go with it. In addition, the rabe gets a second rinsing when you shock it in cold water to stop the cooking. Braising, steaming, or sautéing, on the other hand, accomplish none of this because so little liquid, or none at all, is present to wash away the acids. So essentially, blanching in lots of water leaves the rabe cleaner, at least with regard to bitter-tasting acids, than the other techniques.

Fluffy and Sticky Rices

I have noticed big differences in the textures of various white rice dishes I've eaten at home and abroad. Some rice is very sticky and holds together in clumps, while other types, particularly the kind of "standard" white rice that many Americans eat, are loose and separate. Your January/February 1999 rice tasting alluded to this, and I wondered if you could offer any more detail.

BOB TRACY
ST. PAUL, MN

➤ According to the USA Rice Federation, there are thousands of varieties of rice in the world, grown on every continent except Antarctica. In the United States, rice is generally classified in three categories: long, medium, and short grains. As the names suggest, the categories are differentiated primarily by the size and shape of the uncooked grains, but they also have different cooking characteristics.

Kimberley Park of the USA Rice Federation explained that rice contains two starches, amylose and amylopectin. The ratio of these starches determines the textural properties—from separate and fluffy to sticky and gummy—of the rice when it is cooked. Though there are exceptions to the rule, it is generally recognized that rice with a higher amylose content cooks into grains that are separate, light, and fluffy. Uncooked, those grains appear somewhat translucent. Rice with a lower amylose content cooks into grains that are more moist and tender, with a greater tendency to cling together. Uncooked, these grains appear more opaque.

Generally, long-grain rice has long, slender kernels that are four to five times longer than they are wide. Long-grain rice contains the highest percentage of amylose, which sources at the USA Rice Federation and the Texas A&M University Rice Experiment Station estimate to be roughly 23 to 26 percent. Medium-grain rice kernels are two to three times longer than they are wide. The cooked grains are moist and tender, and they cling together. Medium-grain rice is estimated to contain approximately 15 to 19 percent amylose and is typically used in recipes that call for a creamy consistency, such as rice pudding and paella. Short-grain rice kernels are almost round. When cooked, this rice tends to be even more moist, tender, and sticky than medium grain. Short-grain rice, which is commonly used for sushi, is estimated to contain roughly 12 to 17 percent amylose.

Duplicating Panko Bread Crumbs

I agree fully with your preference for Panko breadcrumbs in the story "Chicken Parmesan Simplified" (see September/October 1998, page 10). These are the only commercial breadcrumbs I've found that retain the airy texture of the original bread. My attempts to duplicate that light, consistent texture at home were mostly unsuccessful until I tried the grating attachment on my food processor. These homemade crumbs were nearly as light, airy, and consistent as the Panko.

MIKE GRANEY
JAMAICA PLAIN, MA

➤ Though there are instances when it's best to have coarse, irregular bread crumbs that lend texture to gratins, pasta dishes, and sautés, the light, even texture of Panko is indeed unique. We have found it to be unbeatable for breading vegetables and cutlets. Your idea of using the grating disk on the food processor to replicate this texture was a good one. The crumbs we made using your method were much more airy and consistent than those made using the food processor's all-purpose blade, the large holes on a box grater, or our chef's knife. In fact, chicken cutlets coated with the homemade crumbs and sautéed came out every bit as crisp and appealing as the Panko-coated cutlets. We particularly recommend this if you have trouble locating Panko at your local grocery store.

Bundt Pan History

Though I know *Cook's* was not 100 percent satisfied with quick breads that are baked in tube pans, I appreciate the time savings and have been baking mine this way since I read about your experiments in the September/October 1998 issue's "Notes from Readers." Actually, I use a Bundt pan, which is donut shaped just like a tube pan, but also fluted with an interesting design. The last time I pulled out my Bundt pan, I started wondering about its origins. Does anyone at your magazine know who came up with this unique design?

KYLE MARCELLA
LOS ANGELES, CA

➤ A representative from Nordic Ware, a division of Northland Aluminum Products and holder of the registered trademark on Bundt pans, provided a detailed history of the pan. In short, Bundt pans were based on Kugelhopf molds, used to bake a favorite Eastern European yeasted cake. In 1950, members of the Hadassah Society's Minneapolis chapter asked the founder of Nordic Ware, H. David Dalquist, to produce out of aluminum a pan similar to the Kugelhopf mold, which was commonly made of cast iron. Dalquist obliged, manufacturing pans for the Hadassah members as well as several more to sell in area department stores. Sales were slow until the 1960s, when the *Good Housekeeping Cookbook* published a photograph of a pound cake that had been baked in a Bundt pan, and a finalist in the 1966 Pillsbury Grand National Bake-Off called for a Bundt pan in her popular recipe for Tunnel of Fudge Cake. Additional boosts came along in 1972, the year that the grand-prize winner as well as 11 out of 100 top winners in the Pillsbury Bake-Off called for Bundt pans in their recipes. It was also in 1972 that Pillsbury released its Bundt cake mixes. Sales reached $25 million in the first year, making the Bundt cake one of Pillsbury's most successful new product introductions ever.

Clarifications

Representatives from Uncle Ben's contacted us to clarify our use of the phrase "converted" rice in the January/February 1999 article "'Boil-in-a-Bag' Rice Surprises Tasters." It turns out that the term "converted" is a registered trademark of Uncle Ben's and should not be used to describe a type of rice. Instead, we should have said "parboiled."

In the March/April 1999 testing of cheese graters titled "Grate Expectations," we assessed the AMCO Cheese Grater as having a decent design but dull teeth, and concluded that you should "avoid this particular brand." In the event that some readers may have been confused by our comment, we meant that you should avoid this brand of cheese grater, not necessarily the entire AMCO product line.

WHAT IS IT?

We took a trip to upstate New York last fall and found this device in a cabin where we spent a couple of nights. It was in a cabinet with a number of other tools, some obviously for cooking, but others not. We couldn't figure this one out, but we suspect it was used in the kitchen. Do you know what it is?

GAYLE AND MIKE BONEEN
SEDALIA, MO

➤ You found a pyramid toaster designed to toast bread without electricity over a wood stove or an open flame such as a camp stove or campfire. Also sometimes called a stove-top toaster, it is usually about 6 inches across the base, 4 or 5 inches tall, and made of either thin tin or stainless steel. The design features holes in the base and perforations in two of the four sides to allow the heat through. Wire frames, which fasten the base and sides together, jut out near the bottom to hold two slices of bread on the perforated sides of the pyramid. When you place the toaster over a heat source, the sides of the bread facing the walls get toasted. A different design, called the folding toaster, dispenses with the sides and forms an open pyramid with four wire frames that hold one slice of bread each. For easy storage, all four frames fold flat against the base.

Both types of toaster are available by mail from the Cumberland General Store Catalog (#1 Highway 68, Crossville, TN 38555; 800-334-4640; www.cumberlandgeneral.com). Tin pyramid toasters cost $11.90, stainless steel models cost $20.00, and the folding toaster costs $10.25.

Quick Tips

Perfect Bread Slices

With their heavy crusts, artisan breads can pose a challenge when it comes to slicing neatly. Often, the bread knife fails to cut all the way through the thick bottom crust, leaving you to literally yank the slice free from the loaf, often tearing it in the process. To get around this problem and cut perfect slices, Olivia MacLeod of Portland, Oregon, turns the loaf on its side and cuts it. This way, she cuts through both crusts simultaneously.

What's in the Freezer?

Practically every cook with a freezer has put something in there at one point or another only to forget about it completely and throw away the freezer-burned mystery parcel months later. Maureen Gamble of Overland Park, Kansas, threw out her last package when she started keeping a simple list of the foods she froze clipped to the freezer door. Now she knows what's in there, and actually uses it.

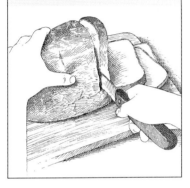

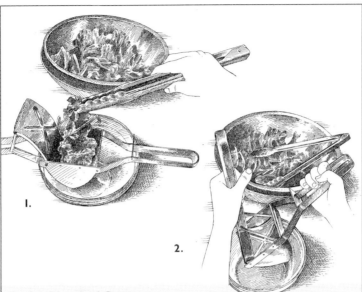

Drying Blanched Greens

Many greens benefit from a quick cooking in water (blanching) before they are sautéed with flavorings. In these cases, though, it is important to squeeze as much water as possible out of the cooked greens before adding them to the pan. Jim Leal of San Francisco, California, has found a way to do this quickly and efficiently.

1. Place wet greens in the hopper of a potato ricer.
2. Close the handle and squeeze the water from the greens.

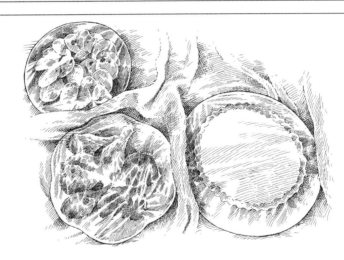

Transporting Platters of Prepared Food

Driving around a curve a little too fast or stopping suddenly can mean disaster for a platter of food that you are transporting in your car. Amanda Hewell of Olympia, Washington, has found a way to thwart this potential disaster—she simply lines the trunk of her car with a large, damp beach towel before placing the platters in the trunk. The towel prevents the platters from slipping; bunching the towel between the platters also provides extra cushioning and stability.

Pouring Oil Smoothly

Many large households buy olive oil in gallon containers, pouring some into a smaller can or bottle for daily use. But pouring from the huge container can be a problem, especially when the oil glugs and sloshes out .

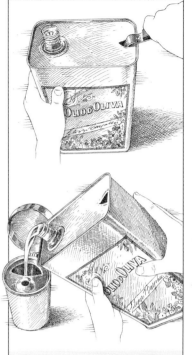

1. To even out the flow while pouring, use a can opener to punch a hole in the top of the container opposite the pouring spout.
2. Having thus evened out the pressure in the container, the oil will pour in a smooth, continuous flow.

Securely Stacking Batches of Cookies

When baking numerous batches of cookies, it's easy to run out of counter space. Instead of trying in vain to spread out, Melissa Hamilton of Lambertville, New Jersey, places rolled balls of foil in the corners of the cooled baking sheets, which allows her to stack one sheet on top of the next without damaging the cookies.

Send Us Your Tip We will provide a complimentary one-year subscription for each tip we print. See page 1 for information.

Testing Avocado Ripeness

A soft avocado may be a bruised fruit rather than a ripe one. To test for ripeness, try to flick the small stem off the avocado. If it comes off easily and you can see green underneath it, the avocado is ripe. If it does not come off or if you see brown underneath after prying it off, the avocado is not useable.

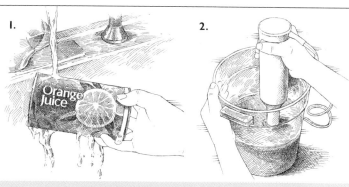

Shortcutting Frozen Orange Juice Preparation

When the craving for orange juice hits, waiting for a can of frozen concentrate to thaw before mixing it with water can be frustrating. Todd Datz of Holliston, Massachusetts, has found a way to avoid the wait.
1. Run the can of frozen concentrate under hot water so it will melt just enough to release from the can.
2. Use an immersion blender to mix the still-frozen block of concentrate with water. The action of the blender results in smooth, even juice with no waiting.

Getting All That Lobster

Instead of cracking lobster and crab shells in order to pick out the meat, Deborah Cherkas of San Jose, California, cuts them open with kitchen shears and pulls the shells away. This way, she is certain to get all the meat.

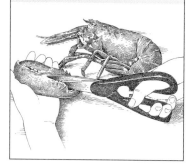

Many Cookies, One Cookie Sheet

Baking batch after batch of cookies can be a frustrating exercise, especially when you have only one cookie sheet on hand. Stephanie Hersh of Boston, Massachusetts, makes the most efficient use of a single cookie sheet.
1. She loads up a sheet of parchment paper with balls of dough, places it on a baking sheet, and places that in the oven.
2. While that batch is baking, she loads up a second sheet of parchment paper.
3. When the baked cookies come out of the oven, she simply whisks the parchment and its cargo onto a cooling rack. After cooling the baking sheet with a quick rinse and dry, it's ready for the next prepared batch.

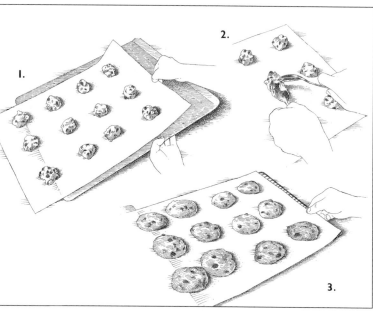

Spill-Free Pouring

A number of recipes for baked goods call for tiny amounts of strongly flavored liquids such as peppermint extract or citrus oils. Linda Burpee of Deming, Washington, uses an ordinary drinking straw to neatly remove a drop or two from the bottles.

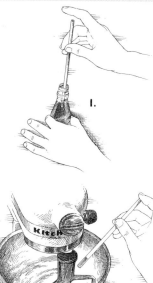

1. Dip the tip of the straw just below the surface of the liquid in the bottle, and place your finger over the open top end. This traps a small amount of liquid.
2. To release the liquid, just remove your finger.

Scrubbing Root Vegetables

Maria Reidelbach of New York, New York, uses rough-textured "bathing" or "exfoliating" gloves to quickly and easily clean root vegetables such as potatoes, carrots, and beets.

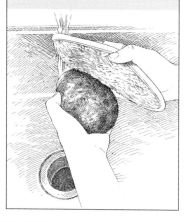

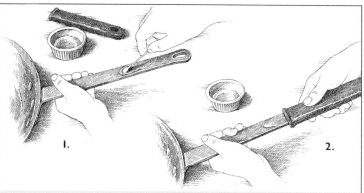

Removing Skillet Handle Covers

Many skillets now come with a removable rubber grip over the handle, but often the grip proves itself to be anything but removable. Tired of struggling to get the grip off for cleaning, Ted Giffin of Carlsbad, Texas, developed this solution.
1. Before placing the cover on the handle, lightly apply a very small amount of cooking oil to the metal handle.
2. The grip slides on and off with ease.

Discovering Great Gumbo

After making more than 75 gumbos, we perfected a method for cutting the stirring time in half while avoiding a separated roux, a common but hard-to-solve problem.

⊱ BY ADAM RIED ⊰

I had always heard about gumbo, the legendary soup/stew of Louisiana that is famous not only for its complex flavor but for its temperamental nature, but my experience with it was limited. That changed after I took a quick trip to southern Louisiana. In just over 48 hours, I covered a couple of hundred miles of bayou country, downed 15 bowls of gumbo, cooked alongside four native cooks, and interviewed two more. After returning, I dug up and studied about 80 recipes, and before long I learned that gumbo, like all great folk recipes, is open to plenty of individual interpretation.

Generally speaking, though, gumbo usually includes some combination of seafood, poultry, or small game along with sausage or some other highly seasoned, cured smoked pork. Also present is the Creole/Cajun "holy trinity" of onion, bell pepper, and celery. Quite often, gumbos are thickened with okra or ground dried sassafras leaves, known as filé (pronounced fee-LAY) powder. Last, but very important, most gumbos are flavored with a dark brown roux. To me, at least, this roux is the heart of a good gumbo.

In classic French cooking, a roux is nothing more than flour cooked gently in some type of fat to form a paste that is used to thicken sauces. If the flour is just barely cooked, you have a white roux; if cooked to a light beige, you have a blond roux. When it reaches the color of light brown sugar, you have brown roux. Creole and Cajun cooks push that process to the outer limit. When they make roux, they keep cooking until the flour reaches a shade of very dark brown, sometimes just short of black. This breaks down the starches in the flour to the point where the roux offers relatively little thickening power. Instead, it imbues gumbo with a complex, toasty, smoky flavor and a deep, rich brown color that define the dish. The problem is that the flour can burn very easily, and the only safeguards against that are relatively low heat and constant stirring. This means that it often takes as long as an hour of constant stirring and careful attention to make a dark roux. Few of the cooks I asked said they'd be willing to go to this trouble, so I had to shorten that time if I wanted a more practical recipe for gumbo.

My goals for this project were falling into place, and there were three. First, the roux was key. I wanted to feature its flavor over the cacoph-

Gumbo tastes even better the next day, after the flavors have had a chance to meld. Make it ahead if you have the opportunity, but stir in the parsley and scallions just before serving.

ony of other herbs and spices and to streamline its preparation. Once I had mastered the roux, I would have to determine the components and flavorings of the stew. As a starting point, I chose to feature shrimp over chicken or game and to include sausage, which was absolutely necessary, in my opinion. Finally, I would have to decide whether to use okra or filé as a thickener, knowing that either would bring not only viscosity but also a distinct flavor to the gumbo.

Dark Roux Primer

The distinctive taste, color, and aroma of dark roux is a central characteristic of Creole and Cajun food. Most of the recipes I saw called for cooking the roux over low heat while stirring constantly for anywhere from 40 to 60 minutes, or, as St. Martinsville, Louisiana, food writer and instructor Marcelle Bienvenu taught me: "About the time it takes to drink two cold beers." Since the roux truly does need to be stirred constantly as it cooks to avoid burning the flour, which will give the mixture a noticeable bitter taste, time was the first issue I had to tackle. As a group, the editors at *Cook's* decided on 20 minutes as our limit for stirring. Any

longer than that, we reasoned, and most cooks would probably skip over this dish. Just as important, my tasters discerned little difference in flavor between gumbos made with the traditional low-heat, long-cooking roux and those with roux that were cooked faster and hotter.

To hit that 20-minute mark, I knew I'd have to increase the heat and probably preheat the oil before adding the flour, too. I also thought I'd try a microwave roux, instructions for which I'd seen along the way. For my testing, I began with the widely used one-to-one ratio of all-purpose flour to vegetable oil, using one-half cup of each.

Some cooks recommend heating the oil until it smokes and then cooking the roux over high heat. Though this method produced a very dark roux, about the color of bittersweet chocolate, in less than 10 minutes the sizzle and smoke was too much for me. The process felt out of control, and the specter of burned roux loomed large.

So I slowed things down a bit, preheating the oil over medium-high heat for only about two minutes (to well below the smoke point) before adding the flour, then lowering the heat to medium to cook the roux. At my 20-minute stopping point, the roux had cooked to a deep reddish brown, about the color of a shelled pecan or a dirty penny. It had started to smoke once or twice, but it cooled fairly quickly when I removed it from the heat, stirred it for a minute, then returned it to the burner. In all, the process was much less nerve-wracking than the high-heat methods I had tried, and it yielded absolutely acceptable results. Unfortunately, though, another problem popped up at this point. I began to have trouble incorporating the simmering stock into the roux. Occasionally, the roux and stock would mix smoothly, but sometimes they wouldn't, and the result was little globs of brown flour floating in a layer of oil at the surface of the liquid. Nonetheless, I pressed on testing the roux.

I experimented with a number of fats—including bacon fat, sausage fat, butter, and different types of oil—and ended up preferring the flavor and ease of vegetable oil. I tried different ratios of fat to flour, varying them by as much as six tablespoons up and down from the half-cup starting point, but none improved on the original 1-to-1 ratio in terms of either taste or performance. Switching the all-purpose flour from a high-protein, unbleached northern brand to a slightly lower-protein, bleached national brand improved the texture of the gumbo slightly, making it a little smoother and more satiny. The gumbo's consistency also benefits from a thorough skimming of the foam from the surface of the liquid, both just after it has come to a boil and throughout the simmering time.

The microwave roux seemed vaguely promising until the day I turned the test kitchen into a scene from a *Lethal Weapon* movie by putting a superheated, microwave-safe bowl with its smoking hot contents down on a damp counter. The bowl did not merely shatter; it exploded, literally raining glass shards and globs of fiery hot roux into every corner of the room. We were very lucky that no one was hurt, and sure enough, a quick call to the test kitchens at Corning Consumer Products confirmed that they do not recommend heating oil in any Pyrex product for 10 minutes on high in the microwave.

Smooth Move

Throughout the roux testing, the occasional separation of the flour and oil upon the addition of simmering liquid continued to perplex me. All along, I had followed the instructions in most of the recipes I'd studied to add simmering stock, which is about 200 degrees, to a hot roux-vegetable mixture, also about 200 degrees.

But there is another, if less popular, school of thought. Food scientist and author of *On Food & Cooking* (Collier, 1984) Harold McGee, *Cook's* consulting editor and restaurateur Jasper White, and legendary New Orleans restaurateur Leah Chase had all advised cooling either the roux or the stock before combining them. Sure enough, cooling the stock (which took less time than cooling the roux) did the trick. Room-temperature stock, at about 75 degrees, mixed into the hot roux beautifully; stock at about 150 degrees also mixed in very well and was only slightly less smooth than its cooler counterpart. In terms of the timing in the recipe, then, I decided to make a concentrated shrimp stock and cool it rapidly by adding ice water rather than making the full amount and allowing it to cool at its own slow

pace. This quick-cooling technique brought the stock to about 110 degrees within minutes, and the gumbo made with this concentrated, then diluted stock easily passed muster with my tasters.

McGee, along with Shirley Corriher, author of *CookWise* (Morrow, 1997), explained the success. Both said that the key to smooth incorporation was to thoroughly mix the roux into the liquid before the starch in the flour in the roux had a chance to swell up and gelatinize. Though much of the starch would be broken down by the high heat of the oil before the stock was added, McGee and Corriher estimated that the remaining starch would gelatinize somewhere around 160 degrees. Adding 200-degree stock to 200-degree roux would thus cause instant gelatinization. The result was disastrous: the globules of flour stuck together in gluey clumps before they could be dispersed throughout the liquid. By adding cooler stock, the roux and the stock had time to blend thoroughly before the whole mixture came up to temperature and the starch gelatinized, resulting in the smooth consistency I was looking for.

Season to Taste

The rest of the recipe development process focused on testing the wide range of ingredients and flavorings I encountered on my trip and in the research. First, I experimented with the liquid. My testing thus far had been done with a simple shrimp stock, made by simmering the shells in water. I tried boiling the shells in chicken stock instead of water, combining equal parts shrimp and chicken stock, adding bottled clam juice to the shrimp stock, and adding small amounts of white wine and beer to the gumbo. The clam juice, suggested by *Cook's* executive editor Pam Anderson, did the trick, adding a depth of flavor that supplemented the 20-minute roux.

Two big flavoring questions concerned toma-

toes—some say that gumbo just isn't gumbo without them—and garlic. Well, my tasters said that gumbo was just fine without tomatoes, but they gave the thumbs up to garlic, six cloves of it, in fact. Other seasonings in gumbo range from elaborate mixtures of herbs, spices, and sauces down to nothing more than salt. My tasters and I tried what seemed like a hundred seasoning

TESTING | ROUX GONE RIGHT...AND WRONG

Lukewarm stock and constant stirring are keys to the right consistency. The roux in the spoonful of gumbo at right is dispersed smoothly in the liquid. The second roux has broken, with globs of browned flour floating in oil.

variations and finally settled on a simple combination of dried thyme and bay leaves. Our experiments with different proportions of onion, bell pepper, and celery in the holy trinity notwithstanding, the ratio proposed by both Marcelle Bienvenu and accomplished home cook Paul Begnaud from Scott, Louisiana, about ½ part celery to 1 part pepper to 2 parts onion, tasted best to all of my tasters. We did, however, switch from the traditional green bell pepper to red peppers, preferring their sweeter, fuller flavor.

Next I considered the level of spicy heat, usually provided by either cayenne pepper alone or in combination with a hot pepper sauce such as Tabasco. The gumbos I tasted in Louisiana were only subtly spicy, with the pepper heat very much in the background. Both Marcelle Bienvenu and Vance Roux, assistant professor in the culinary program at Delgado Community College in New Orleans, put it well. They explained that you want to feel a slight heat in the back of your throat after you've swallowed a couple of spoonfuls. A mere one-quarter teaspoon of cayenne did the trick for my tasters, all of whom favored the powder over the vinegary taste of bottled hot sauce.

Last, my tasters and I considered whether to thicken the gumbo with okra or filé powder. I think both are probably acquired tastes. Thus far, everyone had been satisfied without either, and because both added distinct—and to some unwelcome—flavors, we decided to reserve them for the variations on the master recipe.

By the time I was finished cranking out pot after pot of gumbo, its once exotic southern flavor and aroma had become familiar, even comforting. With my early travails now just a memory, I'm hooked on its deep, smoky flavor, and

With flour just added to the oil, the roux at left is very light in color. After about 10 minutes of cooking, the mixture browns to about the color of peanut butter (center). The completed dark roux, at right, is a deep reddish brown, almost the color of dark chocolate.

gumbo now makes regular weekend appearances on my stove top at home.

CREOLE–STYLE SHRIMP AND SAUSAGE GUMBO
SERVES 6 TO 8

Making a dark roux can be dangerous. The mixture reaches temperatures in excess of 400 degrees. Therefore, use a deep pot for cooking the roux and long-handled utensils for stirring

Thickening the Gumbo

In a Creole or Cajun dark roux, most of the starch in the flour breaks down in the cooking, so it does more to flavor the stew than thicken it. That leaves the task up to one of two other traditional southern ingredients, okra and filé powder.

Okra pods, said to have been brought to the southern United States from Africa by the slave trade, are slender, green, usually about three inches in length, ridged in texture, tapered in shape, and often slightly fuzzy. The interior of the pods is sticky and mucilaginous, so once they are cut open, they thicken any liquid in which they are cooked. Okra's flavor is subtle, with hints of eggplant, green bean, and chestnut. In our gumbo testing, we could detect no taste difference between fresh and frozen.

The other possible thickener, filé powder, is made of ground dried sassafras leaves. It is said to have been introduced to the settlers of southern Louisiana by the native Choctaw Indians. Filé, also referred to in Louisiana as gumbo filé, adds both a gelatinous thickness and a subtle, singular flavor to gumbo. Though difficult to describe precisely, the flavor is distinctly earthy, with notes of straw, bay, marjoram, and oregano. Filé is as much a hallmark of authentic Louisiana cooking as dark roux and the holy trinity of onion, bell pepper, and celery. Filé is used in one of two ways. Diners can either sprinkle a little bit onto their portion of gumbo right at the table, or the cook can stir some into the pot at the very last moment of cooking or even once the pot has come off the heat. In our tests, we preferred the latter method, which mellowed the flavor of the filé somewhat. In stores that carry it, pale green filé powder is generally sold in tall, slender, one-ounce jars. For information about ordering filé powder by mail, *see* Resources, page 32.

One thing on which most Creole and Cajun cooks agree is that you should never use okra and filé together because the gumbo will get too thick, or even gummy. —A.R.

it, and be careful not to splash it on yourself. One secret to smooth gumbo is adding shrimp stock that is neither too hot nor too cold to the roux. For a stock that is at the right temperature when the roux is done, start preparing it before you tend to the vegetables and other ingredients, strain it, and then give it a head start on cooling by immediately adding ice water and clam juice. So that your constant stirring of the roux will not be interrupted, start the roux only after you've made the stock. Alternatively, you can make the stock well ahead of time and bring it back to room temperature before using it. Spicy andouille sausage is a Louisiana specialty that may not be available everywhere; kielbasa or any fully cooked smoked sausage makes a fine substitute. Gumbo is traditionally served over white rice.

1 1/2	pounds small shrimp (51 to 60 count), shelled, and deveined (if desired), shells reserved
1	cup (one 8-ounce bottle) clam juice
3 1/2	cups ice water
1/2	cup vegetable oil
1/2	cup all-purpose flour, preferably bleached
2	medium onions, chopped fine
1	medium red bell pepper, chopped fine
1	medium rib celery, chopped fine
6	medium garlic cloves, minced
1	teaspoon dried thyme
1	teaspoon salt
1/4	teaspoon cayenne
2	bay leaves
3/4	pound smoked sausage, such as andouille or kielbasa, sliced 1/4 inch thick
1/2	cup minced fresh parsley leaves
4	medium scallions, white and green parts, sliced thin
	Ground black pepper

1. Bring reserved shrimp shells and 4 1/2 cups water to boil in stockpot or large saucepan over medium-high heat. Reduce heat to medium-low; simmer 20 minutes. Strain stock and add clam juice and ice water (you should have about 2 quarts of tepid stock, 100 to 110 degrees); discard shells. Set stock mixture aside.

2. Heat oil in Dutch oven or large, heavy-bottomed saucepan over medium-high heat until it registers 200 degrees on an instant-read thermometer, 1 1/2 to 2 minutes. Reduce heat to medium and stir in flour gradually with wooden spatula or spoon, working out any small lumps. Continue stirring constantly, reaching into corners of pan, until mixture has a toasty aroma and is deep reddish brown, about the color of an old copper penny or between the

colors of milk chocolate and dark chocolate, about 20 minutes. (The roux will thin as it cooks; if it begins to smoke, remove from heat and stir constantly to cool slightly.)

3. Add onion, bell pepper, celery, garlic, thyme, salt, and cayenne; cook, stirring frequently, until vegetables soften, 8 to 10 minutes. Add 1 quart reserved stock mixture in slow, steady stream, stirring vigorously. Stir in remaining quart stock mixture. Increase heat to high; bring to boil. Reduce heat to medium-low, skim off foam on surface, add bay leaves, and simmer uncovered, skimming foam as it rises to the surface, about 30 minutes.

4. Stir in sausage; continue simmering to blend flavors, about 30 minutes longer. Stir in shrimp; simmer until cooked through, about 5 minutes longer. Off heat, stir in parsley and scallions, adjust seasonings to taste with salt, ground black pepper, and cayenne; serve.

SHRIMP AND SAUSAGE GUMBO WITH OKRA

Fresh okra may be used in place of frozen, though it tends to be more slippery, a quality that diminishes with increased cooking. Substitute an equal amount of fresh okra for frozen; trim the caps, slice the pods 1/4-inch thick, and increase the sautéing time with the onion, bell pepper, and celery to 10 to 15 minutes.

Follow recipe for Creole-Style Shrimp and Sausage Gumbo, adding 10 ounces thawed frozen cut okra to roux along with onion, bell pepper, and celery.

SHRIMP AND SAUSAGE GUMBO WITH FILÉ

Follow recipe for Creole-Style Shrimp and Sausage Gumbo, adding 1 1/2 teaspoons filé powder along with parsley and scallions after gumbo has been removed from heat. Let rest until slightly thickened, about 5 minutes. Adjust seasonings and serve.

TECHNIQUE | MAKING THE ROUX

A long-handled, straight-edged wooden spatula is best for stirring the roux. Be sure to scrape the pan bottom and reach into the corners to help avoid burning. The cooking roux will have a distinctive toasty, nutty aroma. If it smells scorched or acrid, or if there are black flecks in the roux, it has burned.

Easy Pan Sauces for Chicken

Use the flavor developed during sautéing to make quick, tasty sauces.

⇒ BY EVA KATZ ⇐

The concept of a pan sauce is simple. The juices that escape from the meat (in this case, chicken) during cooking reduce, caramelize, and sometimes harden. These bits, which are basically caramelized proteins that chefs refer to as "fond," provide a concentrated flavor upon which to build a sauce. The flavors are created by a process known as the Maillard reaction. Named for a French chemist, this reaction (also more simply known as browning) takes place whenever a carbohydrate and a protein are heated together. The molecules break apart as they are heated, then combine and recombine over and over, forming hundreds of distinctly flavored compounds.

To release these flavors into a sauce, a liquid is used to wash and dissolve these bits off the bottom of the pan. This "deglazing" can be done with many different liquids—wine, water, juice, brandy, stock, vinegar, or a combination. The liquids are then boiled and reduced to thicken the sauce. For a silky, rich-textured sauce, butter can be added at the end. Chicken with pan sauce is quick enough for every-night eating, but it is also dressed up enough for special occassions.

SAUTÉED CHICKEN BREAST CUTLETS
SERVES 4

To minimize the amount of time the cutlets wait in the oven, prepare the sauce ingredients before sautéing the chicken.

Rinse and thoroughly dry 4 boneless, skinless chicken breasts (this should be about 1½ pounds total). Generously season both sides of each breast with salt and pepper and dredge one at a time in ¼ cup flour placed in a shallow dish; shake gently to remove excess flour and set aside. Heat 1½ tablespoons each butter and vegetable oil in 12-inch heavy-bottomed skillet over high heat, swirling to melt butter. When foam subsides and butter begins to color, place cutlets in skillet, skinned side up. Reduce heat to medium-high and sauté without moving until nicely browned, about 4 minutes. Turn cutlets over and cook on other side until meat feels firm when pressed and clotted juices begin to emerge around tenderloin, 3 to 4 minutes. Transfer cutlets to plate, cover loosely with foil, and keep warm in 200-degree oven while preparing one of the following sauces.

LEMON SAUCE WITH PROSCIUTTO AND SAGE

- 2 medium garlic cloves, sliced thin
- 15 medium whole fresh sage leaves
- 2 tablespoons juice from 1 lemon
- 1 cup chicken stock or low-sodium canned chicken broth
- 3 tablespoons butter, softened
- 1 slice prosciutto (¼-inch thick, about 1½ ounces), diced fine
  Salt and ground black pepper

Follow recipe for Sautéed Chicken Breasts, leaving fat in skillet. Set skillet over medium heat. Add garlic and sage leaves; sauté until garlic is fragrant and sage crisps, 1 to 2 minutes. Add lemon juice and bring to boil, scraping up browned bits from bottom of skillet with wooden spoon. Add chicken stock, increase heat to medium-high and bring to boil, stirring occasionally, until reduced to ¼ cup, about 8 minutes. Off heat, swirl in butter, and add prosciutto. Season to taste with salt and pepper. Spoon sauce over cutlets; serve immediately.

SWEET AND SOUR SAUCE WITH CHERRY TOMATOES AND CILANTRO

- 2 medium shallots, minced
- ½ jalapeño chile, minced
- 1½ teaspoons ground cumin
- 1 teaspoon sugar
- 2 tablespoons cider vinegar
- 6 tablespoons juice from 2 oranges
- 1 tablespoon juice from 1 lime
- 1 cup cherry tomatoes, quartered
- ¼ cup chopped fresh cilantro leaves
  Salt and ground black pepper

Follow recipe for Sautéed Chicken Breasts, discarding all but 1 tablespoon of fat from skillet. Set skillet over medium heat. Add shallots, chile, and cumin; sauté until fragrant, about 1 minute. Add sugar and cook until shallots begin to caramelize, 1 to 2 minutes. Stir in vinegar and orange and lime juices; increase heat to medium-high and bring to boil, scraping up browned bits from bottom of skillet with wooden spoon. Boil sauce, stirring occasionally, until thickened and reduced to about ¼ cup, 2 to 3 minutes. Stir in tomatoes and cilantro; season to taste with salt and pepper. Spoon sauce over cutlets; serve immediately.

WHITE WINE SAUCE WITH GRAPES AND TARRAGON

- 2 medium shallots, minced
- 1 tablespoon chopped fresh tarragon leaves
- ½ cup dry white wine
- 1 cup seedless green grapes, each grape halved lengthwise
- ½ cup chicken stock or low-sodium canned chicken broth
  Salt and ground black pepper

Follow recipe for Sautéed Chicken Breasts, leaving fat in skillet. Set skillet over medium heat. Add shallots; sauté until softened, about 1 minute. Add tarragon, wine, and grapes; increase heat to medium-high and bring to boil, scraping up browned bits from bottom of skillet with wooden spoon. Cook until reduced and syrupy, 4 to 5 minutes. Add chicken stock and boil, stirring occasionally, until thickened and reduced to ¾ cup, about 4 minutes. Season to taste with salt and pepper. Spoon sauce over cutlets; serve immediately.

MUSTARD AND CREAM SAUCE WITH ENDIVE AND CARAWAY

- 1 medium head endive, cut diagonally into ¼-inch slices
- 2 medium shallots, minced
- 2 tablespoons cider vinegar
- 1 teaspoon caraway seeds
- ½ cup chicken stock or low-sodium canned chicken broth
- ½ cup heavy cream
- 1 teaspoon Dijon mustard
  Salt and ground black pepper

Follow recipe for Sautéed Chicken Breasts, leaving fat in skillet. Set skillet over medium heat. Add endive and shallots; sauté until softened and lightly browned, 3 to 4 minutes. Add cider vinegar and bring to boil, scraping up browned bits from bottom of skillet with wooden spoon. Add caraway seeds, stock, and cream; increase heat to medium-high and boil, stirring occasionally, until slightly thickened and reduced to generous ½ cup, about 5 minutes. Stir in Dijon mustard; season to taste with salt and pepper. Spoon sauce over cutlets; serve immediately.

Simplifying Pasta Primavera

Is it possible to streamline this two-hour, six-pot restaurant recipe for home cooks?

≥ BY JACK BISHOP ≤

Unlike most dishes, pasta primavera has a clear pedigree: it was created at Le Cirque, New York's famed French restaurant, in the 1970s. Patrons told restaurateur Sirio Maccioni that they wanted healthier, lighter dishes, so he created a pasta dish loaded with fresh vegetables. He dubbed his invention spaghetti primavera—"primavera" is the Italian word for spring—and it quickly became a New York sensation.

I used to make this recipe frequently. I loved the flavors, and it was always a winner with company. But eventually I decided it was just too much work. For one thing, the recipe calls for blanching each green vegetable in a separate pot to retain its individual character; if the same pot is used for each vegetable, this first step takes almost an hour. If that weren't enough of a bother, once the vegetables are blanched, you need five more pots—one to cook the vegetables in garlicky olive oil; one to sauté mushrooms; one to make a fresh tomato sauce flavored with basil; one to make a cream sauce with butter and Parmesan; and one to cook the pasta.

None of the tasks involved is difficult, but the timing is complicated and better suited to a professional kitchen, where different cooks can handle different jobs. But I love this dish. I wanted to find out if I could simplify the cooking process while keeping the fresh vegetable flavors.

Researching Recipes

I began combing through my Italian cookbooks, both those written in English and in Italian. I was intrigued by a couple of older Italian recipes for pasta dishes with the word "primavera" in the title. These dishes were substantially different from the original version. The directions read like those used to make a slow-simmering meat sauce. In these old-fashioned recipes, the vegetables were either sautéed or stewed together in just one pot. How sensible and how Italian, I thought. I was sure I had discovered the secret to simpler, home-style primavera. I prepared several of these

Our version of this American classic uses half the number of pans and takes half the time, but it still has great flavor.

recipes, some where the vegetables were stewed and others where they were sautéed.

When I cooked the vegetables in a covered pan, they quickly dissolved into a thick porridge. The lid trapped moisture, and the vegetables, instead of browning and gaining flavor, just fell apart—they tasted like overcooked minestrone. Sautéing the vegetables in an open pan was better, but my tasters felt that freshness was missing from this dish. Yes, this was pasta with lots of vegetables, but it didn't have the crisp-tender vegetables, each with its own distinct shape and flavor, that everyone expected from something called pasta primavera.

Having reached a dead end, I returned to Le Cirque's original recipe. I would still blanch the vegetables to keep them crisp, but I knew I could do better than six pots and two hours.

Simplifying a Classic

The first issue was to decide which vegetables were a must for primavera sauce and which could be dropped. Despite its name, this dish as originally conceived contains many non-spring vegetables, including broccoli, green beans, and zucchini. Only the peas, snow peas, and asparagus are truly spring vegetables.

I began testing other spring vegetables and soon realized why they were not included. Artichokes were way too much work to prepare, and leeks tasted better when sautéed rather than blanched, which meant an extra pan and more work. I usually like fennel, but its sweet, anise flavor overwhelmed that of the other vegetables. I also decided to jettison the broccoli (my tasters liked this vegetable the least in this sauce) and snow peas (the pea family was already represented by shelled peas). I was left with four spring/summer vegetables—asparagus, peas, zucchini, and green beans. I went still further and tried eliminating a couple of these vegetables and increasing the quantity of those remaining, but this compromise did not save any time, and my tasters felt that the name "primavera" connotes a variety of vegetables, not just two or three.

I found I could blanch all the green vegetables together in a single pot. I had to add them at different times to make sure each was properly cooked, but after some trial and error I devised a cooking regimen—adding the green beans first, followed by the asparagus, then the zucchini, and ending with the peas. Since I was cooking all the vegetables together, I needed a larger pot, which I found I could reuse (without washing) to cook the mushrooms and tomatoes.

I tried adding the cooked vegetables directly to the drained pasta, but they were watery and bland. Clearly, they needed to be sautéed to build flavor. A couple of minutes in a hot skillet with some garlicky butter proved essential.

In the original recipe, the mushrooms are sautéed, then added to the green vegetables, and then sautéed again. I wondered if I could instead keep the mushrooms in the pan and build the tomato sauce on top of them. This worked fine. I tried cooking the mushroom-tomato sauce (as well as the green vegetables) in butter and in olive oil. Tasters preferred the sweet, rich flavor of the butter, which worked better with the cream.

Next, I focused on the tomatoes. I concluded that this dish would need fresh tomatoes for flavor and juiciness. Plum tomatoes are not as watery as fresh round tomatoes and are best in this dish. I found it unnecessary to seed the tomatoes, but the peels had to go since they separated from the chopped tomatoes and curled up into unappetizing bits (*see* "Peeling Plum Tomatoes," right).

Finally, I found that the separate cream sauce (with butter, cheese, and cream) could be combined with the mushroom-tomato sauce. I reduced some cream over the mushroom-tomato mixture and discovered that this worked perfectly well. There was plenty of butter in the sauce already, and I found that cheese could just as easily be sprinkled on at the table. So instead of three pans—one for mushrooms, one for tomato sauce, and one for cream sauce—I had cooked them together in one pan.

At this point, my recipe was just as delicious as the original and I was down to just three pans. I had also reduced total preparation and cooking time by more than half. This pasta primavera may not be Tuesday night supper, but when you want a fancier pasta dish, there's no reason to run screaming in the other direction when someone suggests primavera sauce.

PASTA PRIMAVERA

SERVES 6 AS A MAIN DISH OR 8 TO 10 AS A FIRST COURSE

    Salt
 6 ounces green beans, cut into ³/₄-inch pieces
    (about 1 ¹/₄ cups)
12 medium asparagus spears, tough ends snapped
    off, halved lengthwise, and cut diagonally into
    ³/₄-inch pieces
 1 medium zucchini, cut into ¹/₂-inch dice
 1 cup frozen peas, thawed
 6 tablespoons unsalted butter
 8 ounces white mushrooms, sliced thin
    (about 4 cups)
 4 large plum tomatoes (about 1 pound), peeled,
    cored, and chopped medium (about 2 cups)
¹/₄ teaspoon red pepper flakes (optional)
¹/₂ cup heavy cream
 1 pound dried egg fettuccine
    (see "Finding the Right Pasta")
 2 medium garlic cloves, minced
¹/₄ cup shredded fresh basil leaves
1 ¹/₂ tablespoons juice from 1 lemon
    Parmesan cheese, grated

1. Bring 6 quarts water to boil in large stockpot for pasta. Bring 3 quarts water to boil over high heat in large saucepan for green vegetables; add 1 tablespoon salt. Fill a large bowl with ice water; set aside. Add green beans to boiling water in saucepan; cook 1¹/₂ minutes. Add asparagus; cook 30 seconds. Add zucchini; cook 30 seconds. Add peas; cook 30 seconds. Drain vegetables and immediately plunge them into ice water bath to stop cooking; let sit until chilled, about 3 minutes. Drain well and set aside.

Finding the Right Pasta

Le Cirque's recipe for primavera sauce calls for spaghetti. However, I found that the vegetables cling better to wider fettuccine noodles. There are three kinds of fettuccine sold in most supermarkets—dried noodles made without eggs, dried noodles made with eggs, and fresh noodles made with eggs. I decided to test the nationally available brands to see which kind (and brand) works best in this recipe.

CONTADINA

BARILLA

RONZONI

DELVERDE

DeCECCO

"Fresh" Contadina fresh fettuccine (sold in the refrigerator case at supermarkets) cooked up flaccid and gummy. This pasta has little egg flavor (it's made with whites instead of the customary whole eggs, no doubt so it can be labeled "cholesterol-free"). At $5/pound, this pasta is no bargain. Unless you are willing to make your own fresh fettuccine or can shop at a store that makes fresh pasta daily, dried fettuccine works better in this dish.

Dried Without Eggs I tried dried fettuccine made without eggs from Barilla (Italy's number one brand). The pasta was decent, although I did have some trouble with the ends of these wide noodles sticking together. Also, the cream sauce did not cling especially well to the noodles.

Dried With Eggs Finally, I tried several brands of dried egg pasta. The first, from Ronzoni, didn't have much egg flavor, and the texture was very similar to the eggless Barilla pasta. Dried egg pasta from two other producers, Delverde and DeCecco, was by far the best choice. Each brand cooked up springy yet tender and had a pleasant egg flavor that works well with the cream and butter in the sauce. These noodles are more porous than pasta made without eggs, so they do a better job of absorbing some of the sauce. You pay for the higher quality (a pound of either pasta costs $3 to $4), but this is a small investment to make for such a dramatic difference in outcome.   —J.B.

2. Heat 3 tablespoons butter over medium-high heat until foamy in now-empty saucepan. Add mushrooms and sauté until browned, 8 to 10 minutes. Add tomatoes and red pepper flakes (if using), reduce heat to medium, and simmer until tomatoes begin to lose their shape, about 7 minutes. Add cream and simmer until slightly thickened, about 4 minutes; cover to keep warm and set aside.

3. Add 1 tablespoon salt and the pasta to boiling water in stockpot and cook until pasta is al

TECHNIQUE | PEELING PLUM TOMATOES

Most chefs and cookbook authors suggest dunking tomatoes in boiling water for 10 to 20 seconds, refreshing the tomatoes in ice water to stop the cooking process, and then peeling the skins off with your fingernails. I found that a sharp vegetable peeler can remove the skins from firm plum tomatoes far more easily.

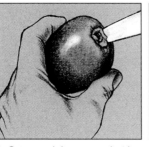

1. Cut around the stem end with a small sharp knife and remove the core.

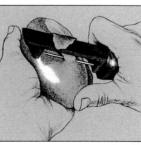

2. Starting at the core end, slide the vegetable peeler down to remove the skin in wide strips.

dente (refer to package directions; cooking times vary with different brands). While pasta is cooking, heat remaining 3 tablespoons butter in large skillet until foamy. Add garlic and sauté until fragrant and very lightly colored, about 1 minute. Add blanched vegetables and cook until heated through and infused with garlic flavor, about 2 minutes. Season to taste with salt; set aside. Meanwhile, bring mushroom-tomato sauce back to simmer over medium heat.

4. Drain pasta and add back to now-empty stockpot. Add mushroom-tomato sauce to pot with pasta and toss well to coat over low heat. Add vegetables, basil, and lemon juice; season to taste with salt and toss well. Divide portions among individual pasta bowls. Serve immediately, passing cheese separately.

LIGHTER PASTA PRIMAVERA

While not as delectably rich as the version above, this primavera, with considerably less saturated fat, is still delicious.

Follow recipe for Pasta Primavera, replacing 4 tablespoons of the butter with olive oil, using 2 tablespoons to sauté the mushrooms in step 2, and 2 tablespoons to sauté the garlic in step 3. Substitute canned low-sodium chicken broth for heavy cream, swirling 2 tablespoons softened butter into the mushroom-tomato sauce before pouring over pasta.

Roasted Rack of Lamb

Can you forgo an initial browning on top of the stove without sacrificing a great crust?
And how do you make a flavorful pan sauce without trimmings?

≥ BY STEPHANIE LYNESS ≤

The word "mouthwatering" must have been invented to describe rack of lamb. The meat is ultra-tender and luscious tasting, more refined in flavor than almost any other cut of lamb, but no less satisfying.

But, at $17 to $18 a pound, there's hardly a cut of meat more expensive. And like other simple but fabulous dishes (roast chicken comes to mind), there's nothing to cooking it except that there's no disguising imperfection. I want the meat to be perfectly pink and juicy, the outside intensely browned to boost flavor and provide contrasting texture, and the fat to be well enough rendered to encase the meat in a thin, crisp, brittle shell.

With all of this in mind, I set out to find a foolproof way to roast this extravagant cut. And because it's such an good choice for a party, I wanted a sauce to serve with it. A traditional jus is easy to make from pan drippings if your butcher gives you bones from butchering and trimming the rack. But you don't get bones if you buy a rack from a supermarket or one that's been packaged in cry-o-vac, and two racks on their own, cooked only to medium-rare, just don't produce enough jus to feed four people. I had to figure out a new way to make a sauce.

Stove-Top Searing

Since good exterior caramelization is critical to the taste of any roast meat, I needed to find out whether the rack would brown adequately in the oven or would need to be browned on top of the stove first. I hoped for the former; I like the ease of simply shoving the rack into the oven. So I decided to test four racks that had been trimmed and frenched (rib bones cleaned of meat and fat for an attractive presentation) at four different temperatures in a preheated oven: 425 degrees, 475 degrees, 500 degrees, and, finally, 200 degrees.

Unfortunately, none of the high oven temperatures gave me the quality of crust I was looking for, even when I preheated the roasting pan. I knew that the conditions of my remaining test—roasting at 200 degrees—would not make for a nicely browned lamb; the meat wouldn't form a crust at such a low temperature. So I started this test by searing the fat side of the rack in a little vegetable oil in a skillet on top of the stove to get a crust before putting it in a 200-degree oven. The slow-roast technique was a

Rack of lamb is a cut most of us save for entertaining, so it is particularly important that it be cooked just right.

bust: the meat was no more tender than when cooked at a high heat, it had a funny, murky taste and mushy texture that I didn't like (see "Why Is Slow-Roasted Rack of Lamb Mushy?" next page), and it took much too long to cook. But the searing technique was terrific. The only refinement I needed was to find a way to brown the strip of eye meat that lies below the bones on the bony side of the rack. After some experimentation I came up with the system of leaning two racks upright one against the other in the pan; this allowed me to brown all parts of the meat before roasting.

Now I went back to testing oven temperatures. Once the rack was seared, I roasted it at 350, 425, and 475 degrees. I ended up taking the middle road. At 425 degrees, the lamb tastes at least as good (if not better) than when cooked at a lower temperature, and there was more room for error than when cooked at a higher heat.

Too Much Fat?

But now I was running into an unexpected problem. Surprisingly, the racks I was cooking were too fatty even for my taste. They looked great when they came out of the oven, but once carved the chops were covered with a layer of fat that was browned only on the exterior. Some chops also had a second layer of internal fat, separated by a thin piece of meat, called the cap, that didn't get browned at all. I didn't want to forfeit this little flap of meat (particularly at the price I paid for it), but there seemed no help for it: I needed to get rid of some of the fat. So I trimmed the flap and all the fat underneath it (see step 2, below), leaving only a minimal amount at the top of the eye and covering the bones to give the cut its characteristic rounded shape.

The meat tasted great, needing only one final adjustment: I removed the silver skin that I had exposed in trimming the fat because it curled during roasting (see step 3, below).

TECHNIQUE | PREPARING THE RACK OF LAMB

1. Using a boning or paring knife, scrape the ribs clean of any scraps of meat or fat.

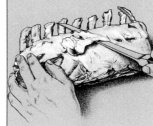

2. Trim off the outer layer of fat, the flap of meat underneath it, and the fat underneath that flap.

3. Remove the silver skin by sliding the boning knife between the silver skin and the flesh.

Saucing the Lamb

Satisfied with my roasting technique, I was now ready to work on a sauce. I wanted a separate sauce, ready just as soon as the lamb was done, so that I wasn't starting from scratch with the pan drippings at the last minute. First I made a separate jus (a very concentrated, reduced stock made with meat, onions, carrots, garlic, and a little water),

To get a good crust on the rack of lamb, brown it on both sides on top of the stove before placing it in the oven. Leaning one rack against the other, as shown, allows you to brown all parts of the meat.

using lamb stew pieces on the bone bought separately at the supermarket. The jus tasted good, but making it was too much work; I didn't want to complicate a simple meal.

So I went back to the pan drippings. I transferred the rack to a second pan after browning on top of the stove, I could make a pan sauce while the lamb roasted. This was, indeed, the solution to my problem. As it turned out, I got the best results by preheating the roasting pan in the oven so that it was hot when the lamb hit it. That done, I had what I was looking for: a near-foolproof way to cook a perfect rack of lamb and a sauce to boot.

SIMPLE ROASTED RACK OF LAMB
SERVES 4 TO 6

Have your butcher french the racks for you; inevitably, the ribs will need some cleaning up, but at least the bulk of the work will be done. Should you choose to make one of the accompanying pan sauces, have all the ingredients ready before browning the lamb and begin the sauce just as the lamb goes into the oven. This way, the sauce will be ready with the meat.

- 2 racks of lamb (each 8 to 9 ribs, weighing 1 1/4 to 1 1/2 pounds), rib bones frenched, and meat trimmed of fat and silver skin (*see* illustrations 1 to 3, page 12)
  Salt and ground black pepper
- 2 tablespoons vegetable oil

1. Adjust oven rack to lower-middle position, place shallow roasting pan or jelly-roll pan on oven rack, and heat oven to 425 degrees.
2. Season lamb with salt and pepper. Heat oil in heavy-bottomed 12-inch skillet over high heat until shimmering. Place racks of lamb in skillet, meat-side down in the center of the pan, with ribs facing outwards (*see* photo, above); cook until well-browned and nice crust has formed on surface, about 4 minutes. Using tongs, stand racks up in skillet, leaning them against each other to brown the bottoms; cook until bottom sides have browned, about 2 minutes longer.

3. Transfer lamb to preheated roasting pan. (Begin pan sauce, if making.) Roast until instant-read thermometer inserted into the center of each rack registers about 135 degrees, 12 to 15 minutes, depending on size of rack. Cover meat loosely with foil and let rest about 10 minutes. Carve, slicing between each rib into individual chops, and serve immediately with an additional sprinkling of salt and pepper or with one of the following sauces.

RED WINE PAN SAUCE WITH ROSEMARY
MAKES ABOUT 3/4 CUP

- 2 medium shallots, minced
- 1 cup dry red wine
- 2 1/2 teaspoons minced fresh rosemary leaves
- 1 cup canned low-sodium chicken broth
- 2 tablespoons butter, softened
  Salt and ground black pepper

Pour off all but 1 1/2 tablespoons fat from skillet used to brown lamb; place skillet over medium heat. Sauté shallots until softened, about 1 minute. Add red wine and rosemary; increase heat to medium-high and simmer until dark and syrupy, about 7 minutes. Add chicken broth; simmer until reduced to about 3/4 cup, about 5 minutes longer. Off heat, swirl in butter; season to taste with salt and pepper, and serve with lamb.

ORANGE PAN SAUCE WITH MIDDLE EASTERN SPICES
MAKES ABOUT 3/4 CUP

- 2 medium shallots, minced
- 1 teaspoon ground cumin
- 1/4 teaspoon ground black pepper
- 1/4 teaspoon ground cinnamon
- 1/4 teaspoon ground cardamom
- 1/8 teaspoon cayenne
- 2 teaspoons sugar
- 3 tablespoons red wine vinegar
- 1/4 cup juice from 1 medium orange
- 1 1/2 cups canned low-sodium chicken broth
- 1 tablespoon minced fresh cilantro leaves
  Salt

Pour off all but 1 1/2 tablespoons fat from skillet used to brown lamb; place skillet over medium heat. Sauté shallots until softened, about 1 minute. Stir in cumin, pepper, cinnamon, cardamom, cayenne, and sugar; cook until fragrant, about 1 minute. Stir in vinegar, scraping up browned bits on bottom of pan. Add orange juice, increase heat to medium-high, and simmer until very thick and syrupy, about 2 minutes. Add chicken broth and simmer until slightly thickened and reduced to about 3/4 cup, 8 to 10 minutes. Off heat, stir in cilantro, season to taste with salt and serve with lamb.

SWEET AND SOUR MINT SAUCE
MAKES ABOUT 1/4 CUP

This simple sauce should be made before you begin cooking the lamb so the sugar has time to dissolve while the lamb cooks.

- 1/2 cup loosely packed fresh mint leaves, chopped
- 1/4 cup red wine vinegar
- 1 tablespoon sugar
  Salt

Stir together mint, vinegar and sugar in small bowl. Let stand about 20 minutes to allow sugar to dissolve. Season to taste with salt, and serve with lamb.

Why Is Slow-Roasted Rack of Lamb Mushy?

Cook's testers have often found that roasting beef at a very low temperature results in particularly tender, luscious meat. But when I roasted rack of lamb at 200 degrees, the meat just got mushy. I talked to several people about this phenomenon. The most convincing argument was suggested to me by Alfred Bushway, a professor in the Department of Food Science and Human Nutrition at the University of Maine, and Susan Brewer, associate professor of food chemistry at the University of Illinois. They explained that at optimum temperatures, naturally occurring enzymes in the meat break down protein. (This is why a piece of meat becomes more tender if you "hang" it over a period of days.) Different enzymes target different components of the meat. According to Brewer, one enzyme in particular has been shown to target myosin, a substance that gives meat its firm texture. This enzyme becomes active between 95 and 135 degrees, when it chops myosin to pieces. In a 200-degree oven, the internal temperature of the rack would be at this optimal temperature long enough for the enzyme to do its work. Because a rack of lamb starts out so tender, given its young age and relatively high fat content, the result is meat that is just too tender—in other words, mushy. —S.L.

Creamy Blue Cheese Dressing

This complex mix of tart and sweet, acidic and creamy is a matter of perfect balance and an unusual mix of ingredients. Best of all, it can be made in just two minutes.

≥ BY DAWN YANAGIHARA WITH ANNE YAMANAKA ≤

If I were to dress a salad with my preferred amount of dressing, it would be blue cheese soup with a lettuce garnish. I just can't get enough of the stuff. This would surprise my parents, since we were an Italian dressing family. My first encounter with blue cheese dressing occurred as the result of a dorm-room delivery of Buffalo wings during my freshman year in college in upstate New York. I still often have a hankering for Buffalo wings, which is in part really a craving for blue cheese dressing in amounts that a salad just can't deliver.

Recently, I found a local pizza delivery joint that not only makes great wings but also serves up a pretty good blue cheese dressing. It's creamy and tangy, with a hint of sweetness and a few blue cheese crumbles at the bottom of the disposable plastic cup. I spoon it down using the wing as a utensil, but I know it isn't as good as it could be, because it isn't cheesy enough. But even at that, it is miles better than bottled blue cheese dressings from the grocery store. To me, those bottled brews are virtually inedible. Harsh mayonnaise-like concoctions, they are either as sweet as candy or painfully vinegary and sour. In both cases, the result is a one-dimensional dressing completely lacking in that necessary blue cheese punch.

I'd never made blue cheese dressing at home because I always thought of it as a restaurant offering. But I finally decided it was time to do a little research and development in the test kitchen.

We began by scouring cookbooks for blue cheese dressing recipes. They were all similar: no revelations, just a mixture of blue cheese with a creamy component, such as mayonnaise or sour cream or a combination of the two, thinned with either heavy cream or buttermilk or sometimes bulked up with cottage cheese. Very often the richness of the dressing was offset with a smidgen of vinegar or lemon juice.

We gathered our recipes and tried them out. In the initial tasting, a common complaint was that there wasn't enough blue cheese flavor. We found that the secret to the proper flavor and texture lay in the creamy components. Cottage cheese was the one entirely unwelcome ingredient. It watered

Allow about three tablespoons of dressing for each individual salad portion of about two and one-half cups loosely packed greens. Be sure to toss well before serving.

down the dressing, and its flabby and bland curds did nothing for the flavor. After much tasting, we concluded that three creamy ingredients were necessary: mayonnaise to give the dressing body, sour cream to supply tang, and buttermilk to both thin out the dressing and support the role of the sour cream. Our challenge was to find the right balance of the three to achieve both good flavor and the right consistency. We tinkered around, and where some recipes call for as much as a half-cup of mayonnaise to a half-cup of crumbled blue cheese, we found only two tablespoons of mayonnaise to be necessary. That, in combination with three tablespoons of sour cream and three tablespoons of buttermilk, and our dressing was right on. A combined total of one-half cup of sour cream, buttermilk, and mayonnaise to one-half cup of crumbled blue cheese put the blue cheese on center stage and kept our dressing from tasting like a gussied-up, thinned out sand-

wich spread. It was cheesy with a pleasant, creamy tang and fluid enough to gently coat sturdy, leafy greens.

Realizing that buttermilk isn't often at hand in most households, we tried cream in place of it, but the flavor of the dressing fell flat under the cream's weight. Milk is a better substitute, though it makes a somewhat lighter dressing.

At this point our dressing was good and tasty, but needed a kick in the pants. We added a smidgen of sugar for sweetness and white wine vinegar for a little zing. That was it. The dressing now had high and low notes that titillated the taste buds, was jam-packed with blue-cheesy flavor, and was delicious whether eaten with a spoon, on a chicken wing, or even on a salad.

Our next step was to investigate different kinds of blue cheese. We were stunned to find that a cheese that made a good dressing didn't necessarily make for good eating. A dressing made with an inexpensive domestic blue cheese—not a $15-per-pound French Roquefort—was our final choice. In general, we found that any rich, creamy blue cheese makes a good dressing. Dry cheeses, such as Spanish Cabrales, should be avoided (see "Which Blue Cheese Makes the Best Dressing?," next page).

Finally, we had to decide on a mixing method. Some of the recipes we researched called for making the dressing in a blender or food processor, but we wanted to make our dressing in the simplest way possible with the fewest number of dirty dishes. We took to mashing the crumbled blue

STEP-BY-STEP | CHEESE PROCESSING

1. Crumble the blue cheese into small pieces with a fork.

2. Using the same fork, simply mash the cheese together with the buttermilk, leaving some small chunks.

cheese and buttermilk together with a fork to break up the cheese a bit (*see* "Cheese Processing," previous page). This was an easy means of getting the texture we liked—creamy, with a few small crumbles of cheese, just enough to give the dressing some tooth. What we had here was a super-simple, ultra-tasty blue cheese dressing.

RICH AND CREAMY BLUE CHEESE DRESSING

MAKES ³⁄₄ CUP, ENOUGH TO DRESS ABOUT 10 CUPS
OF LOOSELY PACKED GREENS, SERVING 4

In a pinch, whole milk may be used in place of buttermilk. The dressing will be a bit lighter and milder in flavor, but will still taste good. We dressed a variety of different salad greens and found that delicate ones, such as mesclun and butter lettuce, became soggy under the weight of the dressing. Sturdy romaine and curly leaf lettuce were our two favorites. Remember that aggressive seasoning with salt and pepper is necessary because the dressing will be dispersed over the greens.

2¹⁄₂	ounces crumbled blue cheese (about ¹⁄₂ cup) (*see* illustration 1, page 14)
3	tablespoons buttermilk
3	tablespoons sour cream
2	tablespoons mayonnaise
2	teaspoons white wine vinegar
¹⁄₄	teaspoon sugar
¹⁄₈	teaspoon garlic powder
	Salt and ground black pepper

Mash blue cheese and buttermilk in small bowl with fork until mixture resembles cottage cheese with small curds (*see* illustration 2, page 14). Stir in remaining ingredients. Taste and adjust seasoning with salt and pepper. Can be covered and refrigerated up to 14 days.

TYPES OF BLUE CHEESES

Cabrales is crumbly, chalky, and complex in flavor, delivering a spicy, peppery kick and a long finish. Deeper in color than the other cheeses we tasted, it is yellow-brown with a cast of gray and streaked with fine lines of gray-green mold. Good eating for those who like a very strong blue cheese flavor.

➤ **Cabrales** ($14.95/pound)
ASTURIAS, SPAIN
Type of milk used: goat's, sheep's, or cow's milk or a mixture thereof

This ivory-colored cheese is pocked throughout with dark green-blue mold, and it is very pungent. With a texture so creamy and buttery that it is almost spreadable, it tastes salty, sweet, and a bit tangy.

➤ **Roquefort** ($14.59/pound)
ROQUEFORT SUR SOULZON, FRANCE
Type of milk used: sheep's milk

This very approachable blue cheese was by described by one taster as "mellow" and "refreshing for blue cheese." It is rich, salty, slightly bitter, sweet, and buttery. A great cheese for about half the price of Roquefort.

➤ **Bleu d'Auvergne** ($7.59/pound)
AUVERGNE, FRANCE
Type of milk used: pasteurized cow's milk

Blue Stilton can be identified by its reddish-gold rind and butter-colored interior speckled with blue-green veins. It is a fairly firm cheese—sliceable, yet crumbly in texture—with a well-balanced, salty flavor that is buttery, nutty, and sweet.

➤ **Blue Stilton** ($11.99/pound)
LEICESTERSHIRE, NOTTINGHAMSHIRE, AND DERBYSHIRE, ENGLAND
Type of milk used: pasteurized cow's milk

Gorgonzola Naturale was by far the creamiest and softest of all the cheeses included in the tasting. Described as "sweet" and "smooth," this cheese is fairly mild, with a distinguishing "musty" odor. Look for the Gorgonzola labeled Marca d'Oro, which means it is made with the highest quality milk, but be sure to eat it quickly, since it has a shelf life of only about two weeks.

➤ **Gorgonzola Naturale** ($9.99/pound)
LOMBARDY, ITALY
Type of milk used: cow's milk

Creamy, fresh, and smooth, with a tangy bite of blue cheese flavor, Maytag Blue was very popular among our tasters. This fairly dense cheese is ivory-white in color (the palest of all), with minimal green-blue pockets of mold.

➤ **Maytag Blue** ($11.99/pound)
MAYTAG DAIRY FARMS, NEWTON, IOWA
Type of milk used: cow's milk

Danish Blue is straightforward and cheddar-like. It has a strong salty and tangy presence, is slightly crumbly in texture, and is spotted with silvery blue pockets. Readily available and the least expensive of the cheeses tested, Danish Blue is a great value. It is especially recommended for use as an ingredient in a recipe, such as our blue cheese dressing.

➤ **Danish Blue** ($4.99/pound)
DENMARK
Type of milk used: pasteurized cow's milk

This supermarket-brand blue cheese was extremely crumbly and almost feta-like in texture. The simple flavor and "wet" texture that made it flounder as a table cheese made it an excellent addition to our blue cheese dressing. It produced a dressing that coated our salad perfectly and did not overpower the other ingredients.

➤ **Stella Blue Cheese** ($5.69/pound)
WISCONSIN
Type of milk used: cow's milk

How to Freeze Summer Fruits

We froze six kinds of popular summer fruits, using up to seven different methods, then thawed them six months later to find out what worked best. BY MARYELLEN DRISCOLL

Freezing is one of the most effortless methods for preserving fruits. It requires no special equipment or extraneous preparation. But as pure as the process might seem, a few months of freezer storage can destroy all the fresh summer succulence a fruit once embodied. Sweet strawberries can turn to sour mush, and peaches frozen at their peak of ripeness thaw into brown, slippery waste. I wanted a sure-fire way to take my favorite summer fruits from the local "u-pick" farm and store them in the freezer with minimal (albeit reasonable) loss of flavor, color, and texture.

The testing for this story began last summer. We froze six kinds of summer fruits—strawberries, raspberries, cherries, blueberries, peaches, and nectarines—using the methods most commonly recommended in books on preserving. Each fruit was frozen with no additions whatsoever as well as mixed with sugar, sugar syrup, or one of these two combined with ascorbic acid.

After six months in the test kitchen freezer, the fruits were thawed and rated in a series of blind tastings.

Unfortunately, our test results did not provide us with a blanket technique for freezing all fruits. But we did find certain consistencies across the board. Most important, we found that all of the fruits turned mushy, picked up strong off flavors, or experienced significant flavor loss if not frozen in sugar or a sugar syrup. The probable reason for this, according to Kenneth Hall, professor of nutritional sciences at the University of Connecticut, is that sugar both enhances fruity flavor and retards solubility, so the fruit stays firmer. Freezing in sugar syrups offers a third advantage, explained Hall, by creating a physical barrier between the fruit and oxygen. Oxidation is often the culprit when off flavors develop in frozen fruits. Oddly, however, those fruits which froze best mixed with sugar did not preserve well at all with sugar syrup, and vice versa. No form of sugar was able to salvage the cherries, which verged on inedible with every method used.

While canning fruits destroys the troublesome organisms that trigger chemical reactions causing fruits to spoil, freezing fruits at home does not. Home freezers simply do not get cold enough to completely stop the enzymatic actions that cause fruit to go bad over time, according to Diane Barrett, a fruit-processing specialist in the Department of Food Science and Technology at the University of California at U.C. Davis. There are other drawbacks to freezing fruits in a standard home freezer. The gradual freezing process forms large ice crystals in the fruit that can tear cell walls and reduce firmness, and the fluctuating temperatures of a freezer's defrost cycle will contribute to freezer burn. All of this does not mean, however, that Barrett does not freeze fruits at home. She simply advises, "People should try to use their frozen foods as soon as possible." After a year in the freezer, it's best to start over with a fresh crop.

Presented here are recipes and tips for freezing each of the fruits tested (except for cherries, which should be eaten fresh). A series of master steps outline the general technique recommended to avoid freezer burn, oxidation, and other potentially harmful effects of freezing fruits.

MASTER STEPS FOR FREEZING FRUITS

1. For freezer bags: Fit a labeled and dated quart-size zipper-lock freezer bag into a 2-cup liquid measuring cup. For easy filling, fold over the mouth of the bag.

2. If using a sugar syrup, fill the bag with 2 cups (1 pint) of prepared fruit and pour sugar syrup over to cover. If tossing the fruit in sugar, spoon 2 cups of the fruit-sugar mixture into bag.

3. Remove as much air as possible from the bag before sealing.

4. Lay the bags flat in a single layer on a cookie sheet to freeze. Do not crowd; make sure there is plenty of space for air to circulate between the bags for the first 24 hours in the freezer.

5. For plastic freezer containers: Label and date the containers. Follow step 2, above, for filling leaving at least ½" headspace for expansion. Run a paring knife around the interior sides of the container to work out air pockets. Crumple wax paper on top of the fruit to minimize exposure to air, seal the container, and freeze.

6. To thaw: Defrost the fruit overnight in the refrigerator. If desired, transfer the fruit to a colander and gently rinse with the sink sprayer to remove excess syrup and sugar. If the fruit is not going to be cooked, it is preferable to eat it while it is semi-frozen and still has a fairly firm texture.

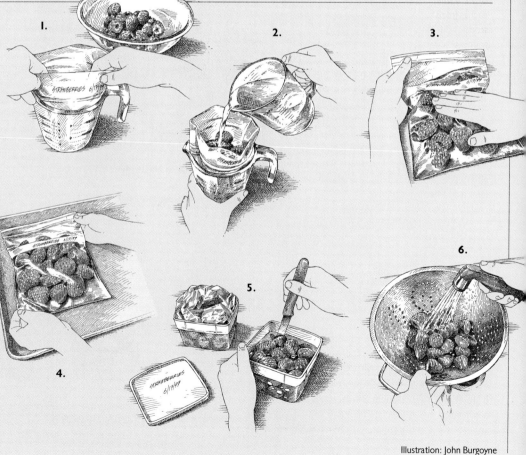

Illustration: John Burgoyne

PREPARING THE FRUIT

For Berries

A sugar syrup was the hands-down winner with raspberries and strawberries, helping to preserve their bright color, fresh flavor, and texture. Blueberries, however, tasted best when mixed with plain sugar. All berries should be gently rinsed and dried as follows to avoid bruising which imparts off flavors. Hull and halve strawberries, if large, before rinsing. Dry blueberries only partially so that the sugar will adhere to them.

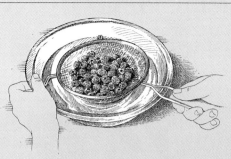

I. Place berries in a sieve or colander and submerge in a large bowl of water.

2. Drain and air dry on a cooling rack, placing a dishcloth, paper towels or a jelly roll pan underneath to catch drips.

FREEZING FRUIT WITH SIMPLE SUGAR SYRUP

Simple Sugar Syrup: Makes 5¾ cups, enough for 4 pints of raspberries or strawberries or 4 medium nectarines (about 6 cups, sliced). Heat 3 cups sugar and 4 cups water in medium saucepan over medium-high heat, stirring occasionally, until sugar has fully dissolved, about 5 minutes. Cool to room temperature.

Raspberries and Strawberries: Prepare 4 pints berries according to steps 1 through 3, right. Following master steps 1 through 5 for freezing, cover each pint of berries with 1¼ cups sugar syrup.

Nectarines: Prepare 4 medium nectarines according to steps 1 and 2 for nectarines (about 6 cups, sliced). Following master steps 1 through 5 for freezing, cover every 2 cups nectarine slices with 1¾ cups sugar syrup.

3. If the wires in your cooling rack are far apart enough to let small berries fall through, place a layer of paper towels on top of the rack.

For Peaches

Peaches froze best with the help of some ascorbic acid. Mixing this anti-browning agent with sugar was strongly preferred over using sugar syrup, which created an unfavorably mushy texture. The fruit's plentiful juices dissolved into the sugar to create an ample protective coating. Because peaches are tender at their peak, the process of peeling, pitting, and slicing can make them soft and slippery. To avoid this problem, place whole unpeeled peaches into the freezer until semifrozen, 1½ to 2 hours. If you are using cling peaches, the halves will be difficult to separate; peel them whole and use the slicing technique shown in step 2 for nectarines.

I. Halve the peach by cutting it from pole to pole at a 90-degree angle to the crease, twist halves to separate and pop out the pit.

2. The brief freezing process significantly loosens the skin from the flesh, so you can peel away the skin with your fingers.

3. Slice over a bowl containing a mix of sugar and ascorbic acid.

For Nectarines

Nectarines fared best in a sugar syrup without the addition of ascorbic acid (though the two combined was a close runner-up). Unlike peaches, nectarines tossed in sugar turned mushy. As with peaches, chill whole unpeeled nectarines until semifrozen, 1½ to 2 hours. If the nectarines do not twist off the pit or peel with the same ease as peaches, follow the steps at right.

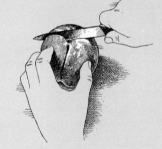

I. Peel with a vegetable peeler.

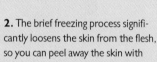

2. Using a paring knife, slice the flesh directly off the pit. For large batches, slice into a bowl of sugar syrup to prevent browning.

FREEZING FRUIT WITH SUGAR

Blueberries: Prepare 4 pints blueberries according to steps 1 through 3 for berries, but dry only partially so sugar will adhere. Gently toss blueberries with 2 cups sugar to coat. Follow master steps 1 through 5 to freeze.

Peaches: Stir together 1½ tablespoons Fruit Fresh (or other similar ascorbic acid–based product) and 1½ cups sugar in large bowl. Prepare 4 medium peaches according to steps 1 and 2 for peaches and slice as in step 3 directly over bowl containing sugar. Toss gently to combine; let stand until peach slices begin to release their juices, 5 to 10 minutes. Follow master steps 1 through 5 to freeze.

Oven-Fried Chicken

We found the secret to oven-fried chicken that is not just crispy but actually crunchy.

⇒ BY PAM ANDERSON WITH GABRIELLE HAMILTON ⇐

I've always thought of oven-fried chicken as ersatz fried chicken—only for those who were afraid to mess up their kitchen or consume too much fat or who had to cook for a large crowd. Although there was certainly nothing wrong with this chicken, there often wasn't a lot that was right with it. Depending on the liquid or crumb coating, this chicken could be bland, soggy, rubbery-skinned, greasy, artificially flavored, dry, or crumbly. Was it possible, I wondered, to make oven-fried chicken that had real crunch and good flavor, a quick weeknight alternative to the real thing?

After looking at scores of recipes, it seemed that good oven-fried chicken depends on the right flavorings, oven temperature, and baking time. But most crucial of all are the coatings—both the moist one that helps the crumbs stick and the dry one that provides texture and crunch.

Since the moist coating comes first, we started there. A review of oven-fried chicken recipes revealed that this first coat could be as lean as water or milk, as rich as cream or butter, and as thick as mayonnaise, yogurt, or even sour cream. Before testing, we assumed this wet dunk did little more than help the crumbs adhere to the chicken. After testing, however, it became clear that this initial coat plays a larger role. A good first coat, we discovered, should offer flavor, season the meat without tasting too obvious, attract the right proportion of crumbs to form an impressive uniform crust, and, finally, help the crust stay crunchy during baking.

Eggs for the Legs

To find the best moist coating, we baked 13 drumsticks. The dry coating was constant but the moist coatings were all different: water, whole milk, evaporated milk, cream, buttermilk, yogurt, sour cream, milk beaten with egg, egg beaten with lemon juice, and egg with Dijon mustard. In addition, we tried legs coated with ranch dressing, mayonnaise, and butter.

When made with the right coatings, oven-fried chicken has real crunch and excellent flavor.

Since many oven-fried chicken recipes start by rolling chicken parts in butter, I thought the fat coatings would perform well. Not so. All of them—butter, mayonnaise, and ranch dressing—created a slick surface that prevented the crumbs from adhering properly. In addition, none of the fats did anything to crisp up the crumbs.

With the exception of buttermilk and evaporated milk, moreover, none of the dairy coatings impressed us. While the sour cream–coated chicken sported an impressively thick crust, its distinct, rich flavor overpowered the chicken. Yogurt, on the other hand, tasted downright sour and made for a thick, hard, dry crust. Milk and milk beaten with egg couldn't hold their crumbs. Chicken parts with these wet coatings baked up wimpy-crumbed and wimpy-flavored. Buttermilk and evaporated milk did attract decent crusts and give a subtle flavor dimension to the chicken, but they didn't result in the crispness we wanted.

The egg beaten with lemon did result in a crisp coating. Unfortunately, it also contributed too

much lemon flavor with an overcooked egg aftertaste. But a change of just one ingredient made all the difference. Chicken coated with beaten egg and Dijon mustard was our favorite. This not-too-thick, not-too-thin moistener not only attracted a uniform, impressive layer of crumbs, it also gave the meat a wonderfully subtle flavor. And unlike many of the wet coatings, which made the crumbs either soggy or barely crisp, this one took the crumbs to an almost crunchy level.

So Many Coatings

For consistency, we had used dry breadcrumbs in all of the moist coating tests, but we constantly remarked on their lackluster texture and flavor. Now it was time to put those dry breadcrumbs to the test.

Considering that there's an oven-fried chicken recipe on the back of many boxes of crackers and most good-for-you cereals, we had scores of options. We started with 20 dry coatings or combinations, all from published recipes.

Cornflakes, unprocessed bran, and bran flakes (each used straight and mixed with flour) as well as Grape-Nuts and oatmeal took care of the cereal category. Saltines, cracker meal, and Ritz crackers were our nod to the cracker aisle. Stuffing mix (both bread and cornbread) as well as dry and fresh breadcrumbs (mixed with Parmesan cheese, too) took care of bread. Flour and cornmeal, including a mix of the two, were also on our list. And, of course, who could overlook the venerable old Shake 'n Bake?

After baking and tasting them all, there wasn't a single one we thought was perfect. Of the cereal coatings, cornflakes made the best, offering good color and crunch but too much sweet corn flavor for our taste. Ditto for bran flakes, but its distinct flavor was even more pronounced. Unprocessed bran looked like kitty litter, while Grape Nuts looked (worse) like hamster food: those crunchy little pellets. Oatmeal tasted raw and chewy.

Crackers didn't work, either. Both saltines and Ritz were too soft; the Ritz, in addition, were too sweet. Cracker meal

TESTING | COATING WARS: THE FINALISTS

(Left to right) Only certain brands of bagel chips made good coatings. Corn flakes were crunchy but offered too much sweet corn flavor. Plain bread cubes for stuffing made a respectable crumb coating, but Melba toast took first prize.

delivered a bland blond shell. In the bread department, stuffing mix scored well in crunch but struck out in flavor. Fresh bread crumbs, on the other hand, tasted great but lacked the crunch we had come to like. The addition of Parmesan cheese did nothing to improve the texture.

The meals and flours, as to be expected, did not show well. Cornmeal tasted raw, and it chipped off the chicken like flecks of old paint. My grocery store's house brand of Shake 'n Bake was vile, tasting of liquid smoke and bad hot dogs. To be fair, we tried the real thing, but it was only a step up from bad.

A Toast to Melba

Although this first round of tests did not produce a strong winner, it became clear what we wanted—a coating that was crunchy (not just crisp) and flavorful (but not artificial tasting) and that baked up a rich copper brown.

With a clear ideal in mind, I found a whole new range of coating possibilities in the specialty/international cracker section of my grocery store. Melba toast, pain grillé (French crisp toast), Swedish crisps, Lavash (crisp flat bread), two varieties of bread sticks, two brands of bagel chips, Italian toasts, and pita chips presented new options. I also located some almost plain croutons and dry bread cubes for stuffing.

This series of tests delivered oven-fried chicken that was much closer to our ideal. Many of the coatings were good but not great, offering good flavor or texture or color, but only one was consistently good.

The rather surprising winner, it turned out, was Melba toast. It scored the best in all three major categories—texture, flavor, and color.

The Rest of the Story

Over the course of testing, we found that we much preferred legs and thighs to breasts because they don't dry out as quickly. For chicken breast lovers, however, egg and mustard/Melba toast coatings work well. We also discovered that we didn't like the skin on oven-fried chicken. Unlike fried chicken, in which hot oil causes the fat to render and the skin to crisp up, oven heat simply softens the skin and makes it rubbery.

Oven temperature was simple. We started baking at 400 degrees, and all our chicken parts were cooked through and rich golden brown in about 40 minutes. As a check, we baked one batch at 375 degrees and another at 425 degrees. At the lower oven temperature the chicken was too blond, and at the higher oven temperature the chicken looked and tasted overly brown by the time it was done.

A wire rack set over a foil-covered jelly-roll or shallow baking pan allows heat to circulate around the chicken during baking, resulting in crisp chicken without turning. The foil, of course, protects the pan, making cleanup a breeze.

THE BEST OVEN–FRIED CHICKEN
SERVES 4

For those who like breast meat, use a whole cut-up chicken instead of drumsticks and thighs. Be careful not to over-crush the Melba toast; crumbs that are too fine will leave the chicken wanting in crunchiness. If you own a spray bottle for oil (see "The Battle of the Misters," below), skip the step of tossing the Melba toast crumbs in oil. Instead, once the chicken is coated with crumbs, spray the pieces evenly with oil.

¼	cup vegetable oil
1	box (about 5 ounces) plain Melba toast, processed to sand and pebble texture (*see* illustration below)
2	large eggs
1	tablespoon Dijon mustard
1	teaspoon dried thyme
¾	teaspoon salt
½	teaspoon ground black pepper
½	teaspoon dried oregano
¼	teaspoon garlic powder
¼	teaspoon cayenne (optional)
4	chicken leg quarters, separated into drumsticks and thighs, skin removed (*see* illustration above right), and patted dry with paper towels

1. Adjust oven rack to upper-middle position and heat oven to 400 degrees. Line sheet pan with foil and set large flat wire rack over sheet pan.

2. Drizzle vegetable oil over Melba toast crumbs in a shallow dish or pie plate; toss well to coat. Mix eggs, mustard, thyme, salt, pepper, oregano, garlic powder, and optional cayenne with a fork in a second shallow dish or pie plate.

3. Working one piece at a time, coat chicken on both sides with egg mixture. Set chicken in Melba crumbs, sprinkle crumbs over chicken, and press to coat (illustration 2). Turn chicken over and repeat on other side. Gently shake off excess and place on rack. Bake until chicken is deep nutty brown and juices run clear, about 40 minutes.

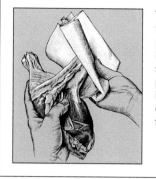
The Battle of the Misters

The Best Mister

When challenged to find the most effective way to evenly coat the chicken pieces with oil, the test kitchen staff at *Cook's* tested four different oil sprayers: Quick-Mist and Misto (two of the newer air-pumped sprayers), a plastic spray bottle, and vegetable oil Pam. All the refillable sprayers were filled with vegetable oil.

The QuickMist fared the best. Only 15 pumps were necessary to create the pressure needed to keep the oil at a constant spray. The mist of oil created was the finest, making it easy to coat the chicken evenly. Conveniently, the QuickMist also held a mist for the longest period of time, making the task of pumping less repetitive.

Pam came in a distant second. While no pumping is necessary, the spray produced tended to be very concentrated in the center, with splatters of oil on the outside.

The Misto, the other air-pumped sprayer we tested, had surprisingly different results from the QuickMist. While the number of pumps required to pressurize the sprayer was the same, the spray did not last as long, requiring more frequent pumping. It was also difficult to produce a fine mist, and once again the spray was concentrated in the center and splotched on the outside.

The worst of the bunch was the ordinary spray bottle. The spray was the most uneven of all, and to ensure coverage we had to overspray. This constant squeezing of the bottle caused our hands to fatigue quickly, and the nozzle tip gave us little control of the mist.
                                                    —Bridget Lancaster

TECHNIQUE | COATING THE CHICKEN

1. To make Melba toast crumbs, place the toasts in a heavy-duty plastic freezer bag, seal, and pound with a meat pounder or other heavy blunt object. Leave some crumbs the size of pebbles in the mixture.

2. Working one piece at a time, lay the chicken in the Melba crumbs. Press a mix of sand and pebble crumbs onto the chicken, flip and repeat on the remaining side, then shake off excess crumbs.

Authentic Guacamole

The keys to velvety, chunky-textured guacamole are the right avocado and a minimum of mashing.

⇒ BY ADAM RIED ⇐

Guacamole has traveled a long road. Once a simple Mexican avocado relish, it has become one of America's favorite party dips. Unfortunately, the journey has not necessarily been kind to this dish. The guacamole I'm served in restaurants, and even in friends' homes, often sacrifices the singular, extraordinary character of avocados—the culinary equivalent of velvet—by adding too many other flavorings. Even worse, the texture of the dip is usually reduced to an utterly smooth, listless puree.

I wanted my guacamole to be different. First, it should highlight the dense, buttery texture and loamy, nutty flavor of the avocado. Any additions should provide bright counterpoints to the avocado without overwhelming it. Just as important, the consistency of the dip should be chunky rather than perfectly smooth.

Since good guacamole must begin with good avocados, I began my research with an avocado tasting. I focused on the two most familiar market varieties, the small, rough-skinned Hass (also spelled Haas), grown primarily in California and Mexico, and the larger, smooth-skinned Fuerte, grown mostly in Florida. The tasters were unanimous in their preference for Hass, compared with which the Fuerte tasted "too fruity," "sweet," and "watery."

Regardless of their origin, many supermarket avocados are sold rock hard and unripe. Because these fruits ripen off the tree, that's fine; in two to five days, your avocados are ready to eat. I tested all the common tricks to accelerate ripening, from burying the avocados in flour or rice to enclosing them in a brown paper bag, with and without another piece of fruit. I also tried putting them in different areas in the kitchen: light spots and dark, cool spots and warm. In the end, I found that most of these tricks made little difference. The fastest ripening took roughly 48 hours and occurred in a warm, dark spot, but the advantage was minor. From now on, I won't think twice when tossing hard avocados into the fruit bowl on the counter. In my mind, it's as good an option as any, and easier, too.

Determining ripeness was also straightforward. The skins of Hass avocados turn from green to dark, purply black when ripe, and the fruit yields slightly to a gentle squeeze when held in the palm of your hand.

Now having the proper ripe avocados, I turned to the mixing method. Most guacamole recipes direct you to mash all the avocados, and some recipes go so far as to puree them in a blender or food processor. After making dozens of batches, I came to feel that neither pureeing nor simple mashing was the way to go. Properly ripened avocados break down very easily when stirred, and I was aiming for a chunky texture. To get it, I ended up mashing only one of the three avocados in my recipe lightly with a fork and mixing it with most of the other ingredients, then dicing the remaining two avocados into substantial ½-inch cubes and mixing them into the base using a very light hand. The mixing action breaks down the cubes somewhat, making for a chunky, cohesive dip.

Other problems I encountered in most recipes were an overabundance of onion and a dearth of acidic seasoning. After extensive testing with various amounts of onion, my tasters found that two tablespoons of finely minced or grated onion gave guacamole a nice spike without an overwhelming onion flavor. I also tried guacamoles with various amounts of fresh lemon and lime juice. The acid was absolutely necessary, not only for flavor but also to help preserve the mixture's green color. Tasters preferred two tablespoons of lime juice for the three-avocado guacamole.

CHUNKY GUACAMOLE
MAKES 2½ TO 3 CUPS

To minimize the risk of discoloration, prepare the minced ingredients first so they are ready to mix with the avocados as soon as they are cut.

- 3 medium-sized, ripe avocados (preferably Hass)
- 2 tablespoons minced onion
- 1 medium garlic clove, minced
- 1 small jalapeño chile, minced (1 to 1½ teaspoons)
- ¼ cup minced fresh cilantro leaves
- ¼ teaspoon salt
- ½ teaspoon ground cumin (optional)
- 2 tablespoons juice from 1 lime

1. Halve one avocado, remove pit, and scoop flesh into medium bowl. Mash flesh lightly with onion, garlic, jalapeño, cilantro, salt, and cumin (if using) with tines of a fork until just combined.

2. Halve and pit remaining two avocados, and prepare according to illustrations 1 and 2 below. Gently scoop out avocado cubes into bowl with mashed avocado mixture.

3. Sprinkle lime juice over diced avocado and mix entire contents of bowl lightly with fork until combined but still chunky. Adjust seasoning with salt, if necessary, and serve. (Can be covered with plastic wrap, pressed directly onto surface of mixture, and refrigerated up to one day. Return guacamole to room temperature, removing plastic wrap at the last moment, before serving).

GUACAMOLE WITH BACON, SCALLIONS, AND TOMATO

Retired cooking teacher and *Cook's* friend Bernice Sisson inspired this variation.

Follow recipe for Chunky Guacamole, substituting 3 large scallions, sliced thin (about ⅓ cup), for onion and adding 6 slices cooked, drained, and crumbled bacon with 1 teaspoon rendered fat and half a medium tomato, seeded and diced small.

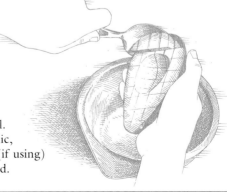

1. Use dishtowel to hold avacado steady. Make ½-inch cross-hatch incisions in flesh with a dinner knife, cutting down to but not through skin.

2. Separate diced flesh from skin using spoon inserted between skin and flesh, gently scooping out avocado cubes.

Really Good Custard Pie

The secret to a delicate, foolproof custard pie lies in the chemistry of cornstarch and eggs.

≥ BY CHRISTOPHER KIMBALL ≤

One of my Vermont neighbors, Jean, inherited a recipe from her mother, Dorothy, which in turn came from her Aunt Nellie Newton. It is a simple custard pie made with fresh cream from a Jersey cow, sugar, nutmeg, and one egg. The trick with this recipe is to use a very low oven and an extremely long baking time (more than six hours), which produces an extraordinarily delicate, light custard, rich from the intense flavor of the Jersey cream.

Having enjoyed this pie for years, I began to think about why I preferred it to the more traditional custard pie, which is made with a higher proportion of eggs. To figure this out, we baked up a sampling of custard pies in our test kitchen. I was quickly reminded of their shortcomings. Many had a tough, overbaked outer ring of custard (the perimeter overbakes by the time the center is set), a soggy, milk-soaked pie crust, and an eggy taste that is less than delightful for a dessert. Although this dessert was relatively simple to make, clearly it was not foolproof. Experience counts.

Yet my neighbor's custard pie was problematic as well. It took forever to bake, often did not set up right, and was lacking in flavor when made with supermarket cream. Worst of all, the crust was soggy after such a long baking time. Although I was clear about what I wanted—a custard pie recipe with a crisp crust, a tender yet flavorful filling, and a relatively foolproof cooking method—I was far short of my goal and needed to test each variable to end up with a "really good" custard pie.

The first question was, which type of liquid is best? I tried, in order of ascending cholesterol count, skim milk, whole milk, half and half, light cream, and heavy cream. The skim milk gave the custard a hollow taste and a thin texture; the whole milk provided good flavor but did not set up that well; the half and half was good; the light cream was a bit fatty; and the heavy cream was much too much of a good thing. I played a bit more with proportions and settled on two cups of milk to one cup heavy cream. (Half and half runs about 10 percent butterfat, milk around 4 percent, and heavy cream is between 36 percent and 40 percent. So a mixture of two parts milk to one part heavy cream is about 15 percent butterfat, richer than half and half, but less heavy than light cream, which is about 30 percent butterfat.)

Before I pursued this recipe any further, however, I had to deal with the issue of the crust. When making other custard-based pies, such as

This pie has a crisp crust, an evenly silky filling with no overbaked spots, and true custard flavor rather than an eggy taste.

pumpkin, the *Cook's* test kitchen has found the best method is to prebake the crust, add a hot filling, and then finish the baking in the oven. I was certain this would work well for a simple custard pie since the crust would already be light brown and crispy and the oven time would be dramatically reduced. I tried this method and found that it took much too long to cook the filling, well over a half-hour. This meant that the pie dough could not be prebaked to the point where it was browned and crispy without overcooking during the long oven time. The result? A soggy crust. Since I wanted to prebake the crust as much as possible, I had to get the filled pie in and out of the oven fast. So the question became, how could I speed up the thickening process?

I naturally turned to the issue of the thickener itself. After some reflection, I thought that a combination of cornstarch and eggs might be best. The reason for this pairing lies in understanding the science of thickeners. Most custards are made with eggs, sugar, and milk. As eggs are heated, individual protein molecules begin to unfold and stretch out. (Think of a bird's nest of dried pasta; when it is cooked, the individual strands of pasta unwind and stretch out.) Once unfolded, the molecules become more likely to bond, and as they bond, water molecules become trapped

between them. The problem with egg custards, however, is that overcooking (that is, overheating) results in more frenzied, tighter bonding that forces the water molecules out of this fragile framework, resulting in weeping. Cornstarch works differently, in a two-stage process. In stage one, the starch granules start to absorb water molecules and swell up, which causes some thickening of the sauce or custard. In stage two, amylose and amylopectin chains (these are starch molecules) leak out of the starch granules into the surrounding liquid. This results in a tangled mesh that entraps water molecules, resulting in more thickening.

When cornstarch is added to an egg custard mixture, the viscosity is greater—in other words, the mixture becomes thicker. This causes heat to be transmitted more evenly throughout the custard, which neatly solves the problem of the overcooked perimeter. At the same time, eggs also add flavor and provide emulsification, which ensures a longer-lasting custard mixture less likely to "weep" in the refrigerator the next day. Finally, it is a well-known fact among bakers that cornstarch helps prevent eggs from curdling. One theory is that swelling starch granules make it more difficult for egg proteins to bond, the immediate cause of curdling. A good balance between cornstarch and eggs should therefore produce the best and most foolproof custard pie.

Having thought this through, I started a new round of tests using cornstarch along with the eggs. (I later discovered that custard pies that use both eggs and cornstarch do exist; most often from the South, they are referred to simply as custard pies or sometimes silk pies.) At first, I added two tablespoons of cornstarch to two cups of milk, one cup of cream, and three whole eggs. The pie had difficulty setting up properly, so I increased the cornstarch to three tablespoons, which worked fine. The pie was evenly cooked throughout, including the edges, and had a delicate, light texture, a major improvement, I thought, on a standard eggs-only custard pie. I also tried four

WHEN THE CUSTARD IS DONE

Scrape along the bottom of the pot with a wooden spoon or spatula; when a bit of custard adheres to the edge of the spoon, your custard is done.

tablespoons, which produced a gloppy, Jell-O-like product. For the eggs, I tried a half-dozen variations and eventually settled on three whole eggs, which was just right.

Now the issue was finding the best way to assemble the filling. I thought that preheating the milk/cream mixture made a lot of sense since it could be done quickly without fear of overcooking the eggs. Once back at the stove, I heated the custard until it started to thicken. Now, here was one of my least favorite directives in all of cooking—determining when a custard has been cooked properly. Is it supposed to look like heavy cream or like pudding? Why does it often take twice as long as the recipe indicates?

I had a leg up on this problem since I was using both eggs and cornstarch. The latter would speed up the thickening and make it much easier to detect. But I was still afraid of using too much heat. As a result, I was taking forever to get the custard up to the point at which it started to thicken. I also did not want to have to stand by the stove for 20 minutes, stirring constantly. So, I decided that until the custard got close to thickening, more heat could be used and constant stirring was not critical. I also decided to use an instant-read thermometer, which I thought would be of great help in determining exactly what was going on with the custard mixture.

In fact, this worked like a charm. I used a medium-low heat until the custard got up to 155 degrees. I stirred occasionally but not constantly. Once the mixture reached that temperature, I stirred constantly but gently with a wooden spoon. At 170 degrees, the custard on the edge of my wooden spoon thickened to a loose paste; this meant that the custard in contact with the bottom of the saucepan was starting to set up. At this point, I noticed that the custard looked a bit clumpy, with small curds in the mix. At first I thought that the mixture had curdled, but in fact it was not a problem. The pie came out just fine. I poured the hot, thickening custard into the hot prebaked pie shell and found that it took only 12

to 15 minutes at 375 degrees to finish the baking. I removed the pie from the oven when the custard still wobbled a bit when lightly shaken but felt mostly set, not very loose.

To finish off the testing, I fiddled with the sugar and settled on two-thirds of a cup—this was enough to add flavor but less than the three-quarters of a cup or more called for in most recipes. I liked the addition of nutmeg, but only a quarter of a teaspoon. After experimenting to find the best lemon and orange variations, I was done. I think Aunt Nellie would be proud of the result.

RICH, SILKY CUSTARD PIE
SERVES 8

For a flaky and tender pie pastry with detailed instructions on how to prebake it, *see* "The Secrets of Prebaking Pie Shells" in the September/October 1997 issue of *Cook's Illustrated*. The prebaked pie shell can be made ahead, but it should be heated in a 375-degree oven until hot, about 5 minutes, before the custard filling is poured into it. Or, if you prefer to prebake the pie shell and make the pie in one continuous process, begin heating the milk and cream for the custard when the foil and pie weights are removed; the filling should be ready at the same time as the shell is ready to be filled. (The oven rack position and temperature for prebaking the pie shell remain the same for the filled pie.) It is a given: Your pie shell will shrink as it bakes. With minimal shrinkage, all the custard will fit into the shell, but if you experience more severe shrinkage you will have some leftover filling.

2 cups whole milk
1 cup heavy cream
3 large eggs
2/3 cup sugar
3 tablespoons cornstarch
2 teaspoons vanilla extract
1/4 teaspoon fresh grated nutmeg
1/8 teaspoon salt
1 prebaked 9-inch pie shell (*see* note above)

1. Adjust oven rack to lower-middle position and heat oven to 375 degrees. Heat milk and cream in medium saucepan over medium-low heat until steaming, about 6 minutes. Meanwhile, whisk together eggs, sugar, cornstarch, vanilla, nutmeg, and salt in medium bowl.

2. Heat prebaked pie shell in oven until hot, about 5 minutes. Meanwhile, whisk steaming milk and cream into egg and cornstarch mixture in slow, steady stream. Return egg and milk mixture to saucepan and cook over medium-low heat, stirring constantly with wooden spoon, scraping bottom of pan, until custard begins to thicken and forms a ridge on tip of spoon when bottom of pan is scraped and spoon is lifted (*see*

FILLING THE PIE SHELL

The hot filling needs to go directly into a hot prebaked pie shell. If you have made the pie shell in advance, heat it up before adding the filling.

illustration, left), 6 to 8 minutes. (If using thermometer, stir occasionally until custard reaches 160, then constantly.) Leaving pie plate on oven rack, pour custard into hot pie shell. Bake until custard has set around edges but jiggles slightly in the center when shaken, 12 to 15 minutes. Cool to room temperature, 2 hours. Cut into wedges and serve.

LEMON CUSTARD PIE

Follow recipe for Rich, Silky Custard Pie, decreasing vanilla to 1 teaspoon, substituting 1½ tablespoons grated lemon zest for the nutmeg, and whisking 1½ tablespoons lemon juice into egg and cornstarch mixture.

ORANGE CUSTARD PIE

Follow recipe for Rich, Silky Custard Pie, decreasing vanilla to 1 teaspoon, substituting 1½ tablespoons grated orange zest for the nutmeg, and whisking 1½ tablespoons orange juice into egg and cornstarch mixture.

A Too-Slippery Pie

In her classic cookbook, Fannie Farmer offers a recipe for a slipped custard pie, which calls for prebaking a pie crust and then baking the filling separately in an identical buttered pie plate. The cooled filling is then gently coaxed out of its pie plate and into the waiting crust. Our test kitchen tried it and found that first, one needs to use a smaller pie plate for the filling than for the crust, otherwise the filling is too big. Second, once the custard starts to slip, look out! It's impossible to stop, making the prospect of a nice-looking, perfectly fitting custard filling a remote possibility at best. —C.K.

All-Purpose Flour: Does the Brand Matter?

We set out to learn if there was a single all-purpose flour that could best handle most any recipe. Six months later, we had the answer.

∋ BY MARYELLEN DRISCOLL ∈

Muffins are maddening. When I see a photo in a cookbook or magazine of a big, fat muffin split in half, with steam wafting from a cupcake-tender interior, I am onto that recipe at once. Yet the trail of crumbs in my kitchen inevitably seems to lead to a muffin of half the stature and double the density. Whenever this happens my knee-jerk reaction is to blame the recipe. Then I typically backpedal through a rigmarole of questions: Was my oven temperature off? Did I overmix the batter? Was the baking powder old? Until recently, though, I would not have suspected the brand of flour as a potential culprit.

All-purpose flour is such a simple kitchen staple. Yet it is a fundamental building block for many home-baked goods. In our efforts here at *Cook's* to make a poor recipe great or a great recipe even better, we typically take this into account. We test not only amounts of flour, sifted versus unsifted, and bleached versus unbleached; we also try various specialty flours. Often we find that they can make a real difference. For some serious bakers, this is not a problem. They simply stock their pantries with a variety of flours—cake, all-purpose, bread, high gluten, and so on. But for most home cooks this option is neither reasonable nor desirable. We wanted to know if there was a single all-purpose flour that would be best for those who keep only one kind of flour in the pantry. So we stocked our test kitchen shelves with many bags of many brands of all-purpose flour and started a bake-off that eventually stretched over some six months.

What's the Difference?

Before we began testing, we turned to experts in both grain science and baking science to find out what we should be looking for. Many of these sources, including Jim Pritchett of the Kansas Wheat Commission, began by pointing out that all-purpose flour is not necessarily a premium product. Most wheat that is milled is made into specialized flours used on a large-scale commercial level. All-purpose is designed to be used in a wide range of recipes written for home cooks who do not have the kind of high-intensity mixers or the expertise necessary to use the specialized flours made for commercial bakeries. The amount of baked foods made in the home kitchen pales beside that purchased on a retail level. Even in supermarkets, consumers spend annually about $500 million more on baking mixes than they do on all-purpose flour, according to the Food Marketing Institute.

Nevertheless, there are a number of choices a flour company must make when milling all-purpose flour that will influence the way its product

TESTING | HIGH PROTEIN, LOW PROTEIN

The same recipe can turn out very differently when made with different flours. A muffin made with high-protein flour, left, was compact, with a rather coarse crumb. The muffin on the right, made with low-protein flour, spread much more and had a soft, cakelike crumb.

performs in recipes. For starters, there is the essence of the flour, the wheat itself. All-purpose flour is typically made from either hard red winter wheat, soft red winter wheat, or a combination of the two. Of the flours we used in the taste tests, five were made from hard winter wheat, one was made of soft wheat, and three were a mix of soft and hard.

Perhaps the primary difference between these types of wheat—and consequently in the flours made from them—is the variation in protein content. Hard winter wheat is about 10 to 13 percent protein, and soft wheat about 8 to 10 percent. Mixtures of the two wheats are somewhere in between. You can actually feel this difference with your fingers; the hard wheat flours tend to have a subtle granular feel, while soft wheat flours feel fine but starchy, much like corn starch.

We found that a number of cookbooks offer guidelines on which kinds of recipes are best suited for low-protein versus high-protein all-purpose flours. High-protein flours are generally recommended for yeasted products and other baked goods that require a lot of structural support. The reason is that the higher the protein level in a flour, the greater the potential for the formation of gluten. The sheets that gluten forms in dough are elastic enough to move with the gas released by yeast but also sturdy enough to prevent that gas from escaping, so the dough doesn't deflate. Lower-protein flours, on the other hand, are recommended for chemically leavened baked goods. This is because baking powder and baking soda are quick leaveners. They lack the endurance of yeast, which can force the naturally resistant gluten sheets to expand; consequently, the gluten can overpower quick leaveners, causing the final baked product to fall flat.

A second important difference in flours is whether they are bleached or not. Technically, all all-purpose flours are bleached. Carotenoid pigments in wheat lend a faint yellowish tint to freshly milled flour. But in a matter of about 12 weeks, these pigments oxidize, undergoing the same chemical process that turns a sliced apple brown. In this case, yellowish flour changes to a whiter hue (though not stark white). Early in this century, as the natural bleaching process came to be understood, scientists identified methods to chemically expedite and intensify it. Typically, all-purpose flours are bleached with either benzoyl peroxide or chlorine gas. The latter not only bleaches the flour but also alters the flour proteins, making them less inclined to form strong gluten. Neither chemical, however, poses any health risks, according to Dr. Jon Faubion of the American Association of Cereal Chemists. Today consumers prefer chemically bleached flour over unbleached because they associate the whiter color with higher quality. In our tests, some of the baked goods made with bleached flour were such a pure white that they actually looked startlingly unnatural and "commercial" versus homemade.

When I spoke with food science consultant Shirley Corriher about flours, she suggested a test that would demonstrate vividly yet another significant difference between higher- and lower-protein flours: their ability to absorb moisture. We mixed two cups of each of the two flours with the highest and lowest protein content, King Arthur and White Lily, respectively, with one cup of water in a food processor. The King Arthur flour (left) quickly absorbed the water and took on the form and appearance of a potential bread dough, while White Lily (right) resembled a wet paste or even cottage cheese. This doesn't necessarily make one kind of flour better than the other. But what it does mean for home cooks is that they can follow a recipe to a T and still end up with a product that looks different from a cookbook or magazine photo of the finished recipe simply because a different brand of flour was used. —M.D.

Test Results

Of all the product taste tests *Cook's* has run, these flour tastings were undoubtedly the most difficult. The differences in flavor between the various versions of the selected recipes were usually extremely subtle. For example, tasting nine different plain muffins in which the only ingredient difference was the brand of flour required shrewd discrimination on the tasters' part. The most obvious differences were often in appearance.

That is not to say, however, that the tests were inconclusive. As difficult as it was for tasters to pick up differences, they were remarkably consistent in their observations. The performance of each of the flours tested, however, was not so consistent. All of the flours baked up well enough in most of the recipes. And some baked up better than that—at times. Failure also occurred, sometimes without apparent reason.

While the protein guidelines make eminently good sense, to our surprise, the results of our tests did not always correspond. The biscuit test did reveal a certain progression from light, cake-like biscuits produced by the lowest-protein flours to coarser, heavier biscuits produced by the higher-protein flours. But our tasters liked all of the biscuits, except for one that had stale flavors. Another trend we noticed was that lower-protein flours spread more in tests of chocolate chip cookies and muffins. In the pie crust test, however, six of the nine flours revealed no correlation between protein content and texture or flavor.

This was no surprise to Dr. Finlay MacRitchie, who specializes in wheat protein analysis at the department of grain science at Kansas State University. "Pro-teins are different from one wheat variety to another and therefore from one flour to another." There are about 100 different proteins in flour. "The quality can vary considerably," said MacRitchie.

According to Joe Caron, spokesman for King Arthur Flour, this is exactly why his company's high-protein flour performed so well in nearly every taste test. Because flour is not a high-profit commodity, he said, manufacturers mill from strains of wheat that offer the greatest yield of flour from a given amount of grain. "Yield is often at cross-purposes with good baking properties," said Caron. King Arthur purchases wheat for its protein quality (not its yield). It then extracts a smaller percentage of flour from the kernel of wheat than the industry average (65 percent versus 72 percent). This is done so that the flour is made more from the center of the wheat berry, avoiding the area where the bran and germ come in contact with the endosperm. (White flour is milled from the endosperm, the inner portion of the berry. *See* "Becoming Flour.") While the protein content is actually higher on the outside of the endosperm, the quality is better at the center. "The center is whiter in color and sweeter in flavor and has a better mix of the gluten-forming proteins glutenin and gliadin," said Caron. MacRitchie agreed that increasing the extraction can compromise the baking performance of a flour.

The flour quality can decline with increased extraction because more of the endosperm bordering the bran is used. This increases the risk of introducing non-endosperm parts of the berry that can compromise the effectiveness of the protein. A perfect example of this, he pointed out, would be whole wheat flour, which consists of the whole berry—the endosperm, bran, and germ. Coarse bran flakes will tear through strands of gluten, which is why whole wheat bread tends to be denser and smaller than bread made from white flour.

Extracting flour close to the bran also results in a higher mineral component known as ash, said Caron. This not only can take away from the flavor but also lends a gray tint to the flour. Bleaching can easily resolve this, which is why so many companies bleach their flour, said Caron. "The bleach is disguising poorer flour." None of the industry experts interviewed for this story could confirm this. Nor could they confirm the belief at King Arthur that bleaching strips flour of flavor and leaves an acidic residue that is detectable to a sensitive palate.

As an overall category, though, the four bleached flours in our tests in fact did not perform as well as the unbleached flours and were regularly criticized for tasting flat or carrying "off" flavors, often described as metallic. These characteristics, however, were more difficult to detect in recipes that contained a high proportion of ingredients other than flour. Coincidentally, our cake tests and chocolate chip cookie tests (both sugary recipes) were the two tests in which off flavors carried by the bleached flour went undetected or were considered faint.

Despite the variations and subtleties, however, the good news is that we did end up with two flours we can recommend wholeheartedly. Both King Arthur and Pillsbury unbleached flours regularly baked up highly recommended baked goods, producing a more consistent range of preferred products than the other seven flours in the taste tests. There is an old bakers' saying that "all-purpose flour is good for everything but not real good for anything." After months of tests, we would have to differ. It can be awful at some things and really good at others. It depends on which flour and which recipe. If you are going to have only one flour in the house, though, our advice is to choose one of these two.

Becoming Flour

During the milling process, the whole wheat berry is first stripped of the outer layer, or bran. The remaining inner kernel is then subjected to a series of grindings and siftings. Bulky particles of bran and wheat germ are used for food products such as cereals, while the smaller particles, called mids, are sold as animal feed. The innermost section, or endosperm, is further ground and sifted into varying grades of flour. —M.D.

WHOLE WHEAT BERRY

BRAN

"MIDS"

FLOUR

TASTING ALL-PURPOSE FLOUR

The two all-purpose flours that consistently turned in above-average performances are listed at the top of the chart as best all-around. They were not, however, without flaws, nor were they the best at all or even many of the tests. The other seven flours are listed in alphabetical order because each has its individual strengths. Our tasters consisted of a team of *Cook's* editors and test cooks. We emphasize that often the differences in flavor were extremely subtle. Likewise, the textural differences often were not dramatic. Those flours labeled "enriched" have vitamins and minerals added to boost their nutritional value. None contained bromate, a controversial additive that gives extra lift to a baking dough. The yeast bread recipe was for a basic white loaf, and the pie pastry recipe was for a flaky pastry. A first-place finish in any category is noted with a ★.

BEST ALL-AROUND

King Arthur Unbleached Enriched All-Purpose Flour
➤ **$1.83/5-pound bag**
Content: Made from hard red winter wheat with a protein content of 11.7 percent
Pie pastry ★ Crisp, thin, flaky, and tender; light toasty flavor
Biscuits ★ Buttery, fresh flavor; crispy, crunchy exterior; hearty
Cake Tender yet sturdy; somewhat dry; slightly above average overall
Muffins Good flavor but downgraded significantly for coarse texture
Chocolate chip cookies Clean flavor; soft, chewy texture
Icebox cookies Crispy; tight crumb; good flavor
Yeast bread Second-place finish; chewy, sturdy texture with a coarse crumb; yellow hue; above average flavor

Pillsbury Unbleached Enriched All-Purpose Flour
➤ **$1.59/5-pound bag**
Content: A combination of hard red winter and soft red winter wheats with a protein content of 10 to 11.5 percent
Pie pastry Flaky ; clean, toasty flavor; above average
Biscuits Second-place finish; medium tender, a bit more bready than cakey; flavorful
Cake Second-place finish; delicate yet sturdy, not particularly tender; flavorful
Muffins Second-place finish; tender; particularly good flavor
Chocolate chip cookies Second-place finish; thick, moist, and chewy; clean flavor
Icebox cookies Very crispy bordering on tough; best flavor
Yeast bread Somewhat tough, decent chew, bland flavor

THE OTHERS (LISTED IN ALPHABETICAL ORDER)

Gold Medal Enriched Bleached Presifted All-Purpose Flour
➤ **$1.49/5-pound bag**
Content: Hard red winter wheat with a protein content of 10.5 percent. Bleached with benzoyl peroxide.

Pie pastry A metallic flavor but tender, very flaky, and crisp
Biscuits Metallic flavor, somewhat dense
Cake: Not among the best because of a mealy texture; it still scored well
Muffins Average
Chocolate chip cookies Crispy, good flavor
Icebox cookies ★ Tie; pleasant, buttery flavor; crisp yet tender texture
Yeast bread Somewhat chewy, tight crumb, not great

Gold Medal Unbleached All-Purpose Flour
➤ **$1.53/5-pound bag**
Content: Hard red winter wheat with a protein content of 10.5 percent

Pie pastry Thick, tough, and somewhat off in flavor
Biscuits Tender but a bit mushy; particularly good flavor
Cake Average
Muffins Average
Chocolate chip cookies ★ Good flavor, moist, soft
Icebox cookies Average
Yeast bread ★ Buttery and clean, "not too doughy," somewhat tender and somewhat chewy, with a medium crumb

Heckers/Ceresota Unbleached Enriched Presifted All-Purpose Flour
➤ **$1.79/5-pound bag**
Content: Made from hard red winter wheat with a protein content of 11.5 to 11.9 percent

Pie pastry Crumbly or "sandy" in texture; uneven in color
Biscuits Off flavor, somewhat tender
Cake Somewhat coarse crumb; leaned more toward the tough side
Muffins Well liked; somewhat hearty with good chew and pleasant flavor
Chocolate chip cookies Crisp exterior; tender, chewy interior; good flavor
Icebox cookies ★ Tie; flavorful with a buttery taste and good crunch
Yeast bread: Sweet, clean, buttery flavor; light and soft

Hodgson Mill Unbleached All-Purpose Flour
➤ **$2.99/5-pound bag**
Content: Made from hard red winter wheat with a protein content of 11 percent

Pie pastry Well-liked buttery, toasty flavor; nice flaky texture
Biscuits Downgraded for an "off," stale flavor; average tenderness
Cake Somewhat dry, tough, and dense; uneven crumb
Muffins ★ Moist, cakelike, light
Chocolate chip cookies Flat, dry, tough
Icebox cookies Crisp, clean buttery flavor; somewhat coarse texture

Yeast bread Clean, clear, subtly toasty flavor; chewy and sturdier than others

Martha White Enriched Bleached Pre-Sifted All-Purpose Flour
➤ **$1.59/5-pound bag**
Content: Made from mostly soft winter wheat but also hard winter wheat with a protein content of about 9 percent. Bleached with chlorine gas.

Pie pastry Medium tenderness, average overall
Biscuits Slight off flavor; cakey texture; very soft
Cake Somewhat coarse and tough; average flavor
Muffins Average flavor; cakelike texture
Chocolate chip cookies Thick, crumbly texture; puffy; average flavor
Icebox cookies Sweet and buttery; "nothing outstanding or offensive"
Yeast bread Like "store-bought white" bread; fine, dense crumb, spongy, dry, flavorless

Pillsbury Bleached Enriched All-Purpose Flour
➤ **$1.50/5-pound bag**
Content: Made from a combination of hard and soft red winter wheat with a protein content of 10 to 11.5 percent. Bleached with chlorine gas.

Pie pastry Very tender but not flaky; flat in flavor

Biscuits Somewhat chewy and dense; clean, slightly wheaty flavor
Cake ★ Even, tender crumb, slight tang to what tasters considered the cake with the best flavor and texture
Muffins Average; lackluster flavor
Chocolate chip cookies Chewy; OK flavor
Icebox cookies Flavor "like old cloth"; "worst of the bunch"
Yeast bread Stale flavor; soft and gummy texture

White Lily Enriched Bleached Plain All-Purpose Flour
➤ **$1.79/5-pound bag**
Content: Made from soft winter wheat with a protein content of 8 to 9 percent. This southern flour is especially intended for traditional southern baked goods, in particular, biscuits. A small trace of phosphate is added, which acts as a leavener when mixed with buttermilk (a primary ingredient in biscuits).

Pie pastry Sandy and soft like shortbread; off, sour flavor
Biscuits Extremely fluffy, tender, and light
Cake Notably tender and delicate; good flavor
Muffins Off flavor; cupcakey; fluffy
Chocolate chip cookies Thin; crisp; OK flavor
Icebox cookies Described as "play-doughy" and "rubbery"; sour flavor
Yeast bread Cottony texture; lacking chew; off flavor; bright white

Searching for the Ideal Gas Grill

We find that hotter is not always better, proper fat drainage is key, and lava rocks are problematic.

⇒ BY JACK BISHOP ⇐

Along with the major kitchen appliances, a grill is likely to be one of the most expensive and important equipment purchases any cook makes. For more and more Americans, buying a grill means buying a gas grill. Last year 6 out of 10 grills purchased were fueled by small liquid propane tanks. The reason for the ascendancy of gas over charcoal is not hard to figure out—ease of use.

But you pay for all that convenience. Even modest gas grills cost almost $200, and many hardware stores regularly stock models that cost three times as much. For people with money to burn, there are grills that cost almost as much as a car.

With this in mind, I spent several weeks cooking on six grills priced between $200 and $600. (I also tested a mega-grill; see "Burning Money on a $3,000 Grill?" page 28). My butcher looked at me in awe as I went through 7 turkeys, 7 slabs of ribs, 56 chicken thighs, 14 pounds of ground chuck, and 28 steaks in the course of one particularly busy week.

I cooked all this food (and more) on widely available models from the four leading manufacturers of gas grills. Char-Broil, the biggest player in the market, also sell grills under the Thermos and Coleman brand names. Both Char-Broil and Sunbeam, which has the second largest market share, make grills for large retailers, such as Sears and K Mart, which may slap their own brand names on the grills. Weber is the dominant force in the midpriced ($300 to $600) market, where most experts say the real growth in sales is occurring. Finally, I included a grill from Ducane, a company that manufactures mostly high-priced grills ($600 and above). The model I selected is one of the cheapest the company makes.

Sizing Things Up

I started my testing with a ruler and a thermometer. I measured the surface area of the grills, the height of the lids, and the size of the warming racks and prep areas. I measured how high and how low I could get each grill to run. I also noted various design features that seemed promising or frivolous. (My observations for each grill are summarized in the chart on page 27.)

From this initial inspection, I noticed a number of design differences in the grills. Some have a much smaller cooking area than others, and size did not seem related to cost. Clearly, these small grills would have trouble holding lots of steaks or a really big turkey. In the end, I weighted my ratings to favor larger grills. If you don't entertain for large crowds, size won't be as important to you.

As I worked with the grills, I came to appreciate a number of features. A built-in thermometer

The Gas Grills We Tested

Weber Genesis
Ideal grill for a crowd. Three burners offer a lot of control.

Weber Spirit
Much like Genesis, but smaller and with two burners.

Char-Broil Saber
A few annoying flaws knock this good grill down to third place.

Sunbeam Grillmaster
Low price, but heats unevenly and needs better thermometer.

Char-Broil MasterFlame 2
Runs too hot and often burns food.

Ducane
Very uneven heating and no way for fat to escape.

RATING GAS GRILLS' DESIGNS

I tested six gas grills fitted with liquid propane gas tanks according to the criteria listed below.

PRICE: Suggested retail price. You may be able to get a better price on these grills, especially at discount stores. For instance, my local Home Depot sells the Weber Genesis for $479 and the Weber Spirit for $359.

ASSEMBLY TIME: I had a mechanically inclined teenager who works at a local hardware store assemble the grills. Mechanically challenged individuals (like myself) will need more time than indicated in the chart, but the times listed offer a good basis for comparison. My advice is to spend the $25 that most stores charge to assemble the grill for you.

EASE OF ASSEMBLY: Grills with parts that fit together easily and with clearly written

manuals are rated good. Grills with very badly written manuals and/or missing or broken parts are rated poor.

COOKING SPACE: Area of main cooking surface.

NUMBER OF BURNERS: Most grills tested have two burners. One grill has three.

MAXIMUM SUSTAINED TEMPERATURE: Measured with all burners on high and lid down for 20 minutes. When a lot of food is added to the grill, maximum and minimum temperatures will be lower.

MINIMUM SUSTAINED TEMPERATURE: Each grill was preheated, the lid was opened to dissipate heat, one burner was turned to low, the other burner(s) was turned off, the lid was closed, and the temperature was measured over the next hour.

DESIGN NOTES: Noteworthy features and serious flaws.

Brand	Price	Assembly Time	Ease of Assembly	Cooking Space	Number of Burners	Max. Temp.	Min. Temp.	Design Notes
BEST GRILL								
Weber Genesis 1000	$549	40 minutes	Good	413 sq. inches	3	560°	230°	Disposable drip pan does excellent job of draining fat. No annoying lava rocks. Built-in thermometer and gauge on gas tank.
Weber Spirit 500	$429	30 minutes	Good	338 sq. inches	2	550°	220°	Same features as Weber Genesis, but on a smaller scale
Char-Broil Saber 2910	$399	2½ hours	Poor	408 sq. inches	2	590°	240°	Holes in lid let rain water run through grill, causing grate to rust and drip cup to fill. Fat drains well into cup, but cup, which is too small, is hard to empty. Built-in thermometer but no gas gauge. Very large warming rack.
Sunbeam Grillmaster 455	$199	3 hours	Poor	388 sq. inches	2	700°	350°	Fat drains into drip can (not provided), so flare-ups are not too bad. Built-in thermometer registers low and high only and did not move much from middle reading in my testing. No gas gauge.
Char-Broil MasterFlame 2 8910	$199	2 hours	Poor	384 sq. inches	2	800°	410°	Holes in bottom of grill allow some fat to drip onto grass, but better design is needed to channel fat out of cooking chamber and into a drip pan. Built-in thermometer registers low, medium, and high (not actual numbers) and is not very useful. No gas gauge.
Ducane 1204S	$593	1½ hours	Good	310 sq. inches	2	620°	320°	No holes in bottom of grill, so fat just sits there waiting to ignite. For the money, should have thermometer and gas gauge. Does come with grill cover and observation ports (little holes in front of grill) that let you see if burners are lit.

that registers real numbers (not just low, medium, and hot) is essential. A gauge that tells you how much gas is left in the tank is also a plus.

I was most curious about the various features that are supposed to improve flavor and/or drain grease. Four grills came with lava rocks—ceramic briquettes that look like charcoal. According to the manuals, lava rocks absorb and distribute the heat evenly. They are also said to flavor the food, something I found hard to believe but figured was worth testing.

The two Weber grills do not have lava rocks. Instead, flavorizer bars (made from steel coated with porcelain-enamel) are supposed to vaporize falling juices on contact, creating steam that flavors the food. The bars are shaped like an upside-down V to channel fat down into the bottom of the grill and eventually into a drip pan attached to the underside of the cooking chamber.

Cooking with Gas

After two days of reading manuals and measuring and heating up the grills, I was itching to cook. For my tests, I chose foods that would illustrate as many grilling techniques as possible. (*See* the

EQUIPMENT | ANATOMY OF A GRILL

When shopping for a grill, make sure the model you choose has a temperature gauge that registers real numbers, not just low, medium, and high. A fuel gauge, which lets you know when the tank is running low, is another helpful feature.

A warming rack can be useful, but you may want to remove it before grilling for full access to the cooking grill surface. Weber grills, our top choices, have flavorizer bars—we prefer them to lava rocks—that help direct fat down into the drip pan. To avoid constant flare-ups, make sure to buy a grill with some system for draining fat.

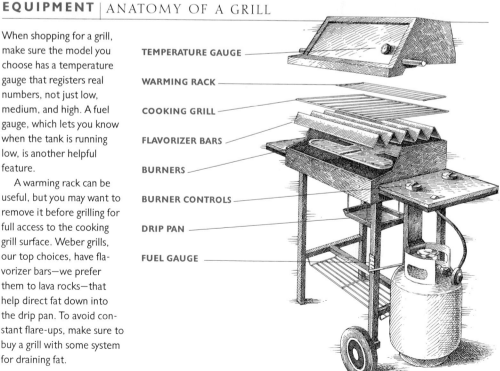

TEMPERATURE GAUGE

WARMING RACK

COOKING GRILL

FLAVORIZER BARS

BURNERS

BURNER CONTROLS

DRIP PAN

FUEL GAUGE

chart on page 29 for details of the tests.) I grilled zucchini, bread, hamburgers, chicken thighs, steaks, ribs, and a turkey on each grill, repeating some tests several times to confirm results.

The more I cooked, the closer I got to defining a set of criteria by which to judge the grills. First of all, the heat should be evenly distributed across the entire surface of the grill. I was shocked to see steaks steaming on one side of the Ducane grill and searing nicely on the other. Once I moved a thermometer around the grill surface, I had my explanation. This grill consistently ran 100 degrees hotter on the right side than the left.

I had thought that grills able to produce more heat would do well in my tests. However, the grill able to maintain the hottest temperature—the

Burning Money on a $3,000 Grill?

I admit the notion of spending thousands of dollars on a grill strikes me as odd. Can a luxury grill really work all that much better than a regular grill that costs $500? It seems a lot of American consumers think so. Sales in this segment of the grill market are blazing hot.

To see what all the fuss is about, I cooked on a Weber Summit 450 (suggested retail price $2,950) for a couple of months. This huge stainless steel grill comes with four burners, a side burner (where you can simmer a pot of beans or make rice), and tons of storage cabinets and trays. The cooking area, however, is no bigger than that on the top-rated Weber Genesis.

So how does it cook? I ran all the tests outlined on page 29 on the Summit, and it performed as well if not better than all the other grills. The Summit heats to 725 degrees, but unlike the blistering Char-Broil MasterFlame, this is controlled heat. Steaks were beautifully seared and chicken cooked without flare-ups. Four-burner control makes cooking ribs or turkey a breeze since there are so many ways to manipulate the heat.

Is this grill worth $3,000? It doesn't work six times better than the $500 Weber Genesis. But it does look six times better. So if money is no object and design really matters to you, this might be the grill for you.   —J.B.

Char-Broil MasterFlame, which heated to 800 degrees (100 degrees hotter than any of the others) with both burners set to high—actually posed something of a problem. For one thing, steaks and burgers burned before the meat was cooked through in the center, despite the fact that I was cooking the meat only to medium-rare. Setting the burners at medium delivered better results, but this is counterintuitive. Most cooks will want to sear over high heat. The 550 degrees put out by the "coolest" grill (the second-placed Weber Spirit) was more than enough heat to develop a thick crust on steaks and burgers.

As I suspected, the grills able to sustain very low temperatures were better suited to barbecuing ribs. Again, the Char-Broil MasterFlame, as well as the Ducane and the Sunbeam, was tough to regulate down (even with one burner off and the other at low) to the ideal barbecuing temperature of 275 degrees.

Perhaps the most shocking conclusion I came to during my long days (and nights) of grilling concerns the cause of flare-ups. Despite going through two tanks of gas on each Weber, I never once experienced a severe flare-up on either grill. Sure, fat would drip down and flame for a brief second. However, just as quickly as a flame would rise from the bottom of the grill, it would go out. While I'm not sure that the flavorizer bars add flavor to the food (spice rubs and wood chips are better suited to that task), their sloped shape does an excellent job of channeling fat down into the drip pan.

On all the other grills tested, flare-ups were an issue, especially when trying to cook chicken thighs and sometimes with burgers and steaks. Several times I ignited the chicken, causing the skin to blacken, and had to throw the pieces out. One time the flames got so bad (they were shooting up at least a foot from the grill surface for a good 30 seconds) that my wife considered calling the fire department.

Why did I have this problem on every grill but the Webers? I began to suspect the lava rocks at the bottom of the four other grills. I decided to remove them and try the chicken again. On the grills equipped with some means of draining fat away (both Char-Broils and the Sunbeam), the results were better. It seems that the lava rocks soak up dripping fat and then catch fire as soon as there is some sort of flare-up. (By the way, I did not detect any change in flavor when cooking without the lava rocks, and the heat seemed just as evenly distributed as when the rocks were in place.)

My theory about lava rocks causing flare-ups is supported by another observation. Several times I moved flaming chicken parts to the cool side of the grill (not over a lit burner), and the lava rocks on the hot side still flamed from below for several minutes. It wasn't the chicken that was on fire; rather, the lava rocks had caught fire even though the burner underneath them was cool.

Lava rocks are not the sole reason for flare-ups.

Four Tips for Better Gas Grilling

During the course of testing, I discovered some tricks for getting the best performance from a gas grill.

1. Remove the warming rack before lighting the grill unless you know you are going to need it. On most grills the rack is very close to the cooking surface, and it can be hard to reach foods on the back of the grill without burning your hands on the hot metal.

2. Preheat the grill with all burners turned to high (even if you plan on cooking over low heat) and the lid down for at least 15 minutes. Once the grill is blazing hot, scrape the grate clean with a brass bristle brush, then adjust the burners as desired.

3. To add wood flavor, wrap unsoaked chips in aluminum foil, tear several small holes in the foil to allow smoke to escape, and place the packet directly over the primary burner—depending on the grill, this is the one that must be lit first or the one you plan to leave on. Then light the grill as directed in tip 2. Once the chips start to smoke heavily, turn the heat to the desired level and place the food on the cool part of the grill.

4. Whether cooking by direct or indirect heat, keep the lid down. With charcoal grills, residue from the briquettes can build up on the inside of the lid and give quickly cooked foods an off flavor. Gas burns clean, so having the lid down concentrates the heat when searing and keeps the temperature steady when slow-cooking.

Poor design doesn't help either. In the Ducane, for instance, grease gets trapped in the bottom of the grill. I consider a drainage system mandatory. The bottom of the cooking chamber should be sloped so that fat runs through an opening in the center and into a drain pan below.

Ranking the Grills

I had some trouble deciding which grill should take first place. Both the Weber Genesis and Spirit performed admirably in most tests. The Genesis had trouble grill-roasting a midsized turkey because when just one of its three burners is lit the temperature hovers around 300 degrees. However, it does fine when grill-roasting foods that will fit between the back and front burners; when both are lit they can boost the temperature to 400 degrees or more.

The Spirit performed better on the turkey test because the single lit burner heats up the much smaller volume under the lid to 375 degrees. However, the smaller cooking area is a problem when trying to cook a lot of food at once, such as two racks of ribs. In the end, I gave the Genesis the top rating because the larger cooking area and three burner controls offer the cook more flexibility.

COOKING ON THE GRILLS

The chart on page 27 focuses on design features. This chart explains how each of the grills performed under various real-life grilling conditions. The details of the tests are explained below.

ZUCCHINI AND BREAD: I grilled ½-inch-thick slices of lightly oiled zucchini as well as 1-inch-thick slices of plain Italian bread. For both tests, I covered the entire grill surface with food and then flipped all the pieces at the same time to judge evenness of cooking. Grills that evenly browned zucchini and bread are rated good. Grills with significant hot or cold spots are rated fair. Grills with severe hot or cold spots are rated poor.

HAMBURGERS: I grilled eight burgers over high heat for 10 minutes, turning them once, to test for sticking to the grill surface and flare-ups. Sticking was not a problem on any grill. Grills that cooked burgers without flare-ups are rated good. Grills subject to modest flare-ups are rated fair. Grills subject to severe flare-ups and that burned the exterior of the burgers before they were cooked through are rated poor.

CHICKEN THIGHS: I grilled eight chicken thighs to test for flare-ups. The thighs were seared over high heat for 2 minutes per side. Thighs were then moved over low heat and cooked, turning once, until done, about 15 minutes. Grills that cooked without significant flare-ups are rated good. Grills that flared during the searing phase but not over low heat are rated fair because the danger of charring exists but can be avoided with some quick work. Grills that flared during searing and low-heat cooking and that charred the chicken are, inevitably, rated poor.

STEAKS: I grilled four boneless strip steaks over high heat for nine minutes, turning them once, to test for caramelization of the exterior and formation of a good crust. Grills that produced a richly browned crust are rated good. Grills that produced a slightly burned crust are rated fair because it would be possible to get a good crust by lowering the heat. Grills that produced a pale crust are rated poor.

RIBS: I set a packet of wood chips in foil over a lit burner and placed one rack of ribs on the part of the grate with no burner lit below. The lit burner was regulated to maintain cooking temperature near 275 degrees when possible. Ribs were cooked until meat started to separate from bones, 2 to 3 hours, depending on the grill. Grills that cooked evenly and slowly at proper temperature are rated good. Grills that cooked a bit too high and thus charred exterior a bit are rated fair. Grills that cooked much too high and burned exterior of meat are rated poor. Note that on smaller grills, it would be necessary to barbecue a second rack of ribs on the warming tray attached to the back; this is a bit awkward and is reflected in the ratings.

TURKEYS: I cooked one 14-pound turkey in a V-rack as per ribs, with one burner on, other burner(s) off, and one packet of chips. Lit burner was regulated to maintain cooking temperatures between 350 and 375 degrees. Turkey was flipped once. Grills that are large enough to cook a turkey without burning legs and wings on one side (because bird is too close to lit burner) are rated good. Grills that are a bit too small or were unable to maintain the desired temperature are rated fair.

Brand	Zucchini & Bread	Hamburgers	Chicken Thighs	Steaks	Ribs	Turkey
BEST GRILL **Weber** Genesis 1000	★★★ Extreme corners are a bit cool	★★★ No sticking or flare-ups	★★★ No flare-ups means nicely browned skin	★★★ Good searing	★★★ Longest cooking time, but ribs are nice and smoky	★★ With only one burner lit, grill runs a bit cool; small turkey could be cooked in center of grill with front and back burners on for more heat
Weber Spirit 500	★★★ A bit cooler in center when burners are not set to high	★★★ No sticking or flare-ups	★★★ No-flare-ups means nicely browned skin	★★★ Good searing	★★ Main cooking grate is too small for two slabs; must use warming rack	★★★ Because grill is smaller, using only one burner heats grill 75 degrees higher than on Genesis for better results
Char-Broil Saber 2910	★★ Front third is much cooler than rest of grill; left side is hotter than right	★★★ No sticking or flare-ups	★★ Removing lava rocks helps minimize flare-ups, but be vigilant when searing	★★★ Good searing	★★★ Large cooking area and warming rack really come in handy	★★★ Large cooking area makes it possible to cook even a large turkey
Sunbeam Grillmaster 455	★ Corners are much cooler and left side is hotter than right	★★★ No sticking or flare-ups	★★ Minor flare-ups when searing, but overall very good	★★★ Steaks on hotter left side cook fast, so be vigilant	★★ Can't use hot left burner for slow cooking; even right burner runs a bit too hot	★★★ Plenty of room for decent sized turkey
Char-Broil MasterFlame 2 8910	★★ Front is much cooler than rest of grill	★ Flare-ups and high heat burned exterior; better when cooked over medium	★ Even when cooked over unlit burners, thighs flamed because lava rocks were on fire	★★ Some flare-ups a problem, and exterior became too crisp	★ Unable to cook low and slow; ribs were lightly charred before cooking through	★★★ Quickest cooking time
Ducane 1204S	★ Left side is at least 100 degrees cooler than right side	★★ Some flare-ups, and burgers cooked on left side didn't brown as well	★ Towering inferno with flames leaping a foot off grill; great for blackened chicken	★ Steaks cooked on hot right side were fine; steaks cooked on left were pale	★★ Runs a bit hotter than desired; must use warming rack to cook second slab	★ Smallest cooking grate and lowest lid make for tight squeeze; best for very small turkeys

As for the other grills, only the Char-Broil Saber is any real competition for the Webers. It's big, has a number of nice features, and performed well on most tests. If there were fewer flare-ups, a sealed lid to prevent rain water from running through it, and more even heating, I would love this grill. As is, it's certainly a good choice.

If you are on a budget, the Sunbeam Grillmaster is a decent choice for the money. However, this grill heats unevenly (the left side is noticeably hotter than the right), it runs a bit too hot for real barbecuing, and the thermometer is useless since it doesn't register the temperature numerically. (During my testing, the gauge was almost always in the middle anyway.) But for $199 you get what you pay for, and I liked this model better than the inexpensive Char-Broil grill tested.

Finally, the Ducane grill proves that more money doesn't always buy a better product. With so many significant flaws (uneven heating, no drainage system for fat, no thermometer), it richly deserves its last-place rating.

A "New" White Wine?

Few people know about Pinot Blanc, but the overall quality is terrific, and prices are fairly low. BY MARK BITTMAN

Pinot Blanc is largely ignored in favor of its more famous and widely admired cousin, Chardonnay. But if there is a discovery to be made in the wine world, this is it. Taken as a whole, the wines we tasted were more enjoyable than any comparably priced selection of whites we've sampled in six years of tastings for this magazine. In fact, the wines were so good that tasters had an unusual amount of trouble ranking them—"I hate to leave this one off my list," was a common complaint.

Although the Pinot Blanc grape is considered to be a good one, no wine scholar would ever rank it with Chardonnay and Riesling, generally acknowledged to be the two great white wine grapes. It falls into the large and vaguely defined second tier, with grapes such as Sauvignon Blanc and Chenin Blanc. So it isn't easy to come up with an explanation for the nearly uniform high quality of these wines.

Tim Chegwidden, who has sold wine for 20 years and was at the tasting, has a theory. "Because almost everyone buys Chardonnay, wineries can get away with making less-than-brilliant Chardonnay up to the $15 level or even higher," he theorized. "People buy Chardonnay because it's Chardonnay; restaurants pour Chardonnay because customers demand it. But since Pinot Blanc is a tough sell, you have to put everything you've got into it to distinguish yourself, even at lower price levels." This analysis, Mr. Chegwidden admits, is intuitive. But it makes sense to me.

Or it could be that it's simply easier to make good Pinot Blanc. Most of the Pinot Blancs we tasted had three characteristics, all agreeable and, for white wines in the $20-and-under range, remarkable. All had a subtle but pleasant nose, a distinct fruitiness offset by adequate acidity, and a relatively full body.

Of course the wines were not all the same. Some (the powerful but expensive Arrowood and Zind Humbrecht were good examples of this) were remarkably rich. Others (Lockwood and Trimbach, for example) were notably well balanced. But there was a similarity of flavor and body in all the wines here except for the Italians, which were thin and generally outclassed.

The Pinot Blanc grape is probably native to eastern France, most specifically, Burgundy, where it still makes up parts of some wines that drinkers assume to be 100 percent Chardonnay; this is especially true of the wines of Savigny-les-Beaune, so we included one in the tasting. The blend is a good one, and several of the wines here tasted as if they contained both Pinot Blanc and Chardonnay. Most of the best Pinot Blanc has traditionally come from Alsace, where it is sometimes called Klevner. It has long been popular, too, in Central Europe (where it is known as White Pinot) and northern Italy (Pinot Bianco). A reasonably priced Austrian wine did well in our tasting; Italian wines did not.

But if our results are any indication Alsace must now share honors with California; our two top wines were made there. Both Alsatian and Californian wines showed great consistency, which allows me to make this recommendation: To explore Pinot Blanc, start with some of the least expensive wines of our tasting—the Lockwood, Domaine Schlumberger, and Mirassou. You may find your personal winner right there. If not, proceed up the list until you do.

THE TASTERS' RESULTS | PINOT BLANC

The wines in our tasting—held at Mt. Carmel Wine and Spirits in Hamden, Connecticut—were judged by a panel made up of both wine professionals and amateur wine lovers. The wines were all purchased in the Northeast; prices will vary throughout the country.

Within each category, wines are listed based on the number of points scored. In this tasting, the "Highly Recommended" wines had almost all positive comments; those labeled "Recommended" garnered mostly positive comments; the "Recommended with Reservations" group had decidedly mixed comments. The sole "Not recommended" wine was not only roundly trounced but is relatively expensive.

HIGHLY RECOMMENDED

1997 Steele Bien Nacido Vineyard SANTA BARBARA $18. "Serious," "complex" wine that was enjoyed by every taster. A true winner.
1997 Lockwood MONTEREY $13. Some tasters noticed "a bit of Chardonnay" in here, but almost all liked this wine for its "clean fruit," "good body," and "sweet nose." An excellent buy.

RECOMMENDED

1994 Zind Humbrecht ALSACE $25. Sweeter than most, with a tiny bit of fizz. If you didn't find "too much sugar" you might consider it "a blockbuster."
1996 Domaine Schlumberger ALSACE $11. The least expensive Alsatian wine we tasted, "very clean," with "the right amount of wood and good flavor." Great buy.
1996 Trimbach ALSACE $13. Some found "a lovely, spicy nose" and a "clean, dry, and crisp" wine. Others found it "a tad too tart."
1996 Arrowood RUSSIAN RIVER (SONOMA) $34. A tad on the sweet side. "Good but lacks complexity." Given the price, there are many preferable choices here.
1996 Jadot Savigny les Beaune BURGUNDY $26. "Some Chardonnay" and "a lot of oak." Loved by some but not all.

1996 Hopler Burgenland AUSTRIA $12. "Complex, alive, and steely," with "strong fruit." Easily mistaken for an Alsatian wine.
1996 Hugel "Cuvee les Amours" ALSACE $13. One taster loved this wine, calling it "lovely, clean, and delicious." The general consensus: "More than decent."
1996 Mirassou "White Burgundy" MONTEREY $10. Another wine that garnered favorable comments but few high ratings. "Not a big wine, but a good one."
1996 Chalone MONTEREY $23. "A little on the sweet side," but "pretty nice flavor."

RECOMMENDED WITH RESERVATIONS

1997 Casarsa FRIULI, ITALY $5. "Good pinot fruit, but lacks finish." In another tasting this might do well, and it's worth a shot at this price.
1997 J. Lohr MONTEREY $13. "Nose of wet cardboard," taste is "almost chemical." It did have one admirer, who found it "well balanced."

NOT RECOMMENDED

1996 Foradori Vigneto Sgarzon TRENTINO, ITALY $32. "Lean, lacking, and out of balance"—especially at this price.

TV Dinners

Can the stars of TV cooking shows really cook? We tested recipes from three popular TV-inspired cookbooks to find out. BY CHRISTOPHER KIMBALL

When the TV Food Network was first launched, I was skeptical of the notion of marrying entertainment with cooking, worried that the media was on the road to creating the culinary equivalent of the singing cowboy. As it turns out, the enthusiasm for cooking that the Two Fat Ladies, Emeril Lagasse, and Mario Batali transmit over the airwaves is both real and infectious. For that I offer a hearty vote of thanks. But the question still remains, can they cook? Armed with their respective cookbooks, we went into the *Cook's* test kitchen to find out.

The Two Fat Ladies Ride Again
Clarissa Dickson Wright and Jennifer Paterson
Clarkson Potter, 192 pages, $25

This book is richly illustrated with color food photography plus many black-and-white shots of the "fat ladies" riding their motorcycle, having tea, shopping, or sitting about taking a load off. The 150 or so recipes are blessedly not trendy, consisting mostly of English mainstays such as kedgeree and jugged kippers. Desserts are your best bet here since the heart-stopping level of fat is often worth it. All in all, I find these two ladies, fat or otherwise, hard not to like. As the introduction states, "In an industry where women's success...is mostly defined by youthful good looks...Jennifer and Clarissa's success is an enormous achievement." Hear! Hear!

PROS: You will not find another cookbook just like it. Like them or hate them, these ladies dance to their own drummer.

CONS: The design is truly offensive, with a shade of orange that should have been made illegal after the 1950s. You won't find many recipes to fit into your weeknight repertoire; the food is clearly British and will not be to the liking of most health-conscious American cooks. Recipe directions are too often cursory, resulting in food that does not cook up as promised.

RECIPE TESTING: We made 11 recipes, and only 3 of them passed our "make again" hurdle. A butterscotch tart didn't taste much like butterscotch and was rubbery, orange gobbet cakes were bland, and chicken recipes often resulted in inedible skin. But the chocolate whiskey cake was a

hit, as were the cheese beignets. Overall, the recipes were imprecise and could have done with more seasoning and better testing.

Emeril's TV Dinners
Emeril Lagasse with Marcelle Bienvenu and Felicia Willett
William Morrow, 268 pages, $25

You either love Emeril or hate him; this cookbook will not change your mind. It includes not only recipes but plenty of candid black-and-white shots of Emeril and the cast of his TV program doing what they do best—putting on a show. The whole thing feels a bit like a fan club cookbook. The food, however, is not simple. If you are looking for easy "TV dinners," you'll be out of luck; but if you like Emeril and his food, well, go for it.

PROS: There is a lot of Emeril in this book, and, for Emeril fans, that's a good thing. The food is, even at its most complicated, interesting, and practiced cooks will get plenty of fresh ideas.

CONS: There is a lot of Emeril in this book.... You get the point. For the most part, this is restaurant cooking, since few home cooks are going to make tempura soft-shell crabs with oriental salad and citrus gastrique or whole roasted squabs stuffed with eggplant and bacon dressing. Emeril likes an abundance of fat, which often throws recipes out of balance. Heavy cream and a bowl full of egg yolks are not uncommon.

RECIPE TESTING: It wasn't easy to find recipes we wanted to make from this book (we made only six since the editors found the recipes in the other books more appealing). But there were a few good ones even if they were usually hard to make. To our surprise, a goat cheese and leek cake was easy and delicious (a caveat: Emeril touts this as a vegetarian dish, but it contains a half-pound of bacon!). His biscuits were light and fluffy but lacking in flavor. An eggplant and garlic soup requires that you roast garlic, spread it on eggplant, and then roast the eggplant for what turned out to be only a fair soup. An old-fashioned chocolate pudding was too sweet and lacking in chocolate flavor. A lasagna of exotic mushrooms was a four-star disaster: The cheese drowned the mushrooms, it was soupy, and it didn't cook in the time prescribed. A smoked trout hash was outstanding but required making a tomato/red

wine reduction, whipping up a hollandaise, deep-frying diced potatoes, and, finally, doing a bit of sautéing and poaching for good measure. On balance, we'd rather eat at his restaurant than cook from his book.

Simple Italian Food
Mario Batali
Clarkson Potter, 288 pages, $30

Mario Batali presents a wide array of recipes from his two villages—Borgo Capanne, the tiny mountainside town in Italy where he was born, and Greenwich Village in Manhattan, where he subsequently moved to start a restaurant. The design of the book is maddening. Recipes are often printed over faded, peach-colored photographs, which makes them hard to read. The typography is also unhelpful, with key ingredients printed in a large bold type that makes the recipes harder, not easier, to follow. The recipes themselves are not at all simple, but do represent the sort of food you would in fact make in a small Italian town with plenty of time and local ingredients.

PROS: Overall, the food in this cookbook is more appealing than the recipes in the other two books. Another bonus is that Batali comes across as a likable, straightforward cook who is not a media invention.

CONS: Too many hard-to-find ingredients and too many difficult recipes. If you are used to the more accessible cooking of Marcella Hazan, you will find this book a bit of a stretch for your culinary patience and skills.

RECIPE TESTING: Out of seven recipes tested, we would make only two again. A balsamic-glazed chicken had a whopping quarter-cup of chopped rosemary, the stuffing didn't flavor the meat at all, the skin never crisped properly, and the vinegar trickled down off the bird into the roasting pan, where it burned. Chicken livers cooked with dried apricots, an odd combination to say the least, and a turnip risotto that required major preparation were both bland. A basic tomato sauce, on the other hand, was fine, and a rolled flank steak was actually quite good and suitable for midweek supper. A sweet-and-sour tuna and chicken thighs with saffron, green olives, and mint were both disappointing.

RESOURCES

Most of the ingredients and materials necessary for the recipes in this issue are available at your local supermarket, gourmet store, or kitchen supply shop. The following are mail-order sources for particular items. Prices listed below were current at press time and do not include shipping or handling unless otherwise indicated. We suggest that you contact companies directly to confirm up-to-date prices and availability.

Gas Grills

The top two gas grills in the rating on page 26 are readily available at many national retail chains, including Home Depot and True Value stores. However, not every outlet within a chain necessarily carries both or either model—the Weber Genesis 1000 or the Weber Spirit 500—so we recommend that you call the store beforehand. You may also call **Weber (800-446-1071)** for information on the nearest store that carries these gas grills. If ordering by mail is your best option, you can purchase the Genesis for $479.99 and the Spirit for $359.99 from **The BBQ Pit (925 West Armitage Avenue, Chicago, IL 60614-4296; 888-469-3237; www.webergrills.com)**. The Genesis 1000 is fitted with a bottom storage rack, locking casters, and a wood side and swing-up table. Its three individually controlled burners light with the touch of a button and generate 36,000-BTU-per-hour output. The Spirit has two individually controlled burners that generate 22,000-BTU-per-hour output. It is fitted with a bottom storage rack and a molded thermoplastic side table. Both grills carry a 10-year limited warranty and are sold in black or red. Both are sent unassembled if ordered by mail.

Magnetic LP Fuel Indicator for Gas Grills

It is not uncommon and certainly not fun to be in the midst of grilling up a big dinner and have the fuel in your propane tank run out. The two winning models in our gas grill rating avoid this problem with a built-in LP gas gauge. None of the other models had this feature. If you own a gas grill that does not have a fuel gauge, **The Grill Lovers Catalog (P.O. Box 1300, Columbus, GA 31902; 800-241-8981; www.grilllovers.com)** sells an LP fuel indicator for just $6.99 (item #4184682). The gauge magnetically attaches to the side of the propane fuel tank and is reusable. The manufacturer advises keeping the gauge out of direct sunlight.

All-Purpose Flour

Among the all-purpose flours in our rating on page 23, Pillsbury (bleached and unbleached) and Gold Medal (bleached and unbleached) are available throughout the country. King Arthur is widely distributed in the Northeast and in many states east of the Mississippi, but is sold in select stores nationwide. Check the company's Web site (listed below) for information on the nearest store to you that carries King Arthur flour. It is also available by mail order for $2.95 for a 5-pound bag, $5.75 for a 10-pound bag, and $13.50 for a 25-pound bag through **King Arthur Flour's Baker's Catalogue (P.O. Box 876, Norwich, VT 05055-0876; 800-827-6836; www.kingarthurflour.com)**. White Lily is distributed throughout the South. A 5-pound bag may also be purchased by mail order for $7 from **White Lily (P.O. Box 871, Knoxville, TN 37901; 800-264-5459; www.whitelily.com)**. The other three flours in our tasting are more limited in availability. Heckers all-purpose flour can be found in New York, New Jersey, and southern parts of New England. The same flour is sold under the Ceresota label in Chicago and Philadelphia and their surrounding areas. Hodgson Mill flour is found in many natural food stores and some supermarkets across the country. Martha White is available throughout the South.

Andouille Sausage

While you can get away with making the gumbo recipe on page 6 with kielbasa or any other fully cooked smoked sausage, andouille sausage best completes this mainstay of New Orleans cuisine. Compared with the familiar kielbasa sausage, andouille (pronounced an-DOO-ee) carries even more of a smoky and spicy heat in its flavor. While andouille is becoming increasingly available, it is not yet a simple find in markets beyond the Louisiana border. But it can be easily ordered through the mail from **Aidells Sausage Company (1625 Alvarado Street, San Leandro, CA 94577; 800-546-5795; www.aidells.com)**. You can order four packs of 16 links total (about 4 pounds worth) for $30 plus a $12 shipping and handling fee.

Filé Powder

Just like andouille sausage, filé powder or okra can be left out of a good bowl of gumbo, but it will not quite be representative of the traditional stew. Filé powder, made from the dried, ground leaves of the sassafras tree, most obviously acts as a thickener, adding almost a gelatinous texture to gumbo. It also contributes flavors that can be difficult to pin down. Our test cooks described it as "earthy" or tasting subtly of "straw." Retail availability of filé powder is just as elusive as its flavor characteristics. We could not find it in supermarkets or specialty food stores in the Boston area. It can be ordered by mail. **Creole Delicacies (533 St. Ann Street, New Orleans, LA 70116; 800-786-0941)** sells filé powder in 1-ounce plastic shakers for $2.49 and 5-ounce shakers for $5.98. The alternative thickener, okra, can be found fresh in the produce section or in the frozen foods section of most supermarkets.

QuickMist

To help mimic the crisp and crunchy coating of fried chicken in our oven-fried chicken recipe on page 18, we toss the pulverized Melba toasts with a quarter-cup of oil. We recommend vigorously tossing them after drizzling on the oil to get an even coating. A preferred alternative is to coat the chicken with dry crumbs and then spray the oil onto the chicken. Unfortunately, many oil sprayers fail to emit an even, light mist. This was not the case with the QuickMist, a nonaerosol kitchen spray bottle made exclusively for Williams-Sonoma. This popular item is available for $19 in Williams-Sonoma stores nationwide and through its catalog service **(Mail Order Department, P.O. Box 7456, San Francisco, CA 94120-7456; 800-541-2233)**. You can fill and refill the QuickMist canister with any kind of oil you prefer.

Cabrales Blue Cheese

Of the eight samples in our blind tasting of blue cheeses (*see* page 15), the Cabrales blue cheese stood out with a pronounced spicy, peppery kick that lingered on the tongue. It is a pungent cheese best suited for the more daring blue cheese lovers. Cabrales is considered Spain's best-known blue cheese and is ripened in natural limestone caverns in the rugged mountainous region of Asturias. Its texture is complex: creamy yet dry and crumbly; soft yet grainy, verging on crunchy. **Formaggio Kitchen (244 Huron Ave., Cambridge, MA 02138; 888-212-3224)** sells a Cabrales DO blue cheese for $19.95 per pound. The initials "DO" certify that the cheese was made in the right town, with the right milk, and in the right fashion, according to Ihsan Gurdal, owner of the specialty foods store. Depending on how it is aged, the taste of Cabrales blue cheese can range from sweet with a sharp finish to very heavy with a strong earthy flavor. It can also range in color from a light blue to extremely dark, almost black. This is not a cheese for slathering on a slice of bread. Gurdal recommends pairing it with an aged Rioja wine or a sherry and some fruit.

RECIPE INDEX

Pasta Primavera **PAGE 11**

Creole-Style Shrimp and Sausage Gumbo **PAGE 8**

Rich, Silky Custard Pie **PAGE 22**

The Best Oven-Fried Chicken **PAGE 19**

Chunky Guacamole **PAGE 20**

Simple Roasted Rack of Lamb **PAGE 13**

PHOTOGRAPHY: CARL TREMBLAY STYLING : MYROSHA DZIUK

Dalmatia

Hondralia

Calamata

Cassis de Beaux

Sicilian Colossal

Canned "California"

Oil Cured

Calabrese

Nicoise

Alfonso

Lucques

Gaeta

OLIVES

Picholine

NUMBER THIRTY-NINE

JULY & AUGUST 1999

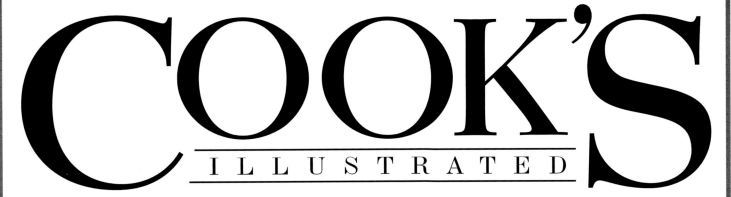

COOK'S
ILLUSTRATED

Perfect Chilled Lemon Soufflé
The Secret to Bright Lemon Flavor

How to Grill Flank Steak
Marinate? High Heat? We Investigate

Rating Inexpensive Chef's Knives
How to Buy a Great Knife for Less Than $50

Best Grilled Chicken Wings
A Two-Level Fire Makes Them Crispy

Hot-Smoked Salmon
Moist, Smoky Salmon on Your Backyard Grill

Hot Dog Tasting

Best Way to Grill Corn

Foolproof Iced Tea

Three-Bean Salad Revisited

Summer Pudding

Best Picnic Wines

$4.95 U.S./$5.95 CANADA

CONTENTS

July & August 1999

PUBLISHER AND EDITOR
Christopher Kimball

SENIOR EDITOR
John Willoughby

SENIOR WRITER
Jack Bishop

ASSOCIATE EDITORS
Adam Ried
Maryellen Driscoll
Dawn Yanagihara

TEST KITCHEN DIRECTOR
Kay Rentschler

TEST COOKS
Anne Yamanaka
Bridget Lancaster

CONSULTING FOOD EDITOR
Jasper White

CONSULTING EDITORS
Jim Dodge
Pam Anderson
Stephanie Lyness

ART DIRECTOR
Amy Klee

CORPORATE MANAGING EDITOR
Barbara Bourassa

EDITORIAL PRODUCTION MANAGERS
Sheila Datz
Nate Nickerson

COPY EDITOR
India Koopman

EDITORIAL INTERN
Sarah Moughty

MARKETING DIRECTOR
Adrienne Kimball

CIRCULATION DIRECTOR
David Mack

FULFILLMENT MANAGER
Larisa Greiner

MARKETING ASSISTANT
Connie Forbes

PRODUCTS MANAGER
Steven Browall

CIRCULATION ASSISTANT
Carrie Horan

VICE PRESIDENT
PRODUCTION AND TECHNOLOGY
James McCormack

SYSTEMS ADMINISTRATOR
Richard Cassidy

PRODUCTION ARTIST
Daniel Frey

CONTROLLER
Mandy Shito

OFFICE MANAGER
Mary Connelly

SPECIAL PROJECTS
Deborah Broide

For list rental information, contact The SpeciaLISTS, 1200 Harbor Blvd. 9th Floor, Weehawken, NJ 07087; (201) 865-5800; fax (201) 867-2450. Editorial office: 17 Station Street, Brookline, MA 02445; (617) 232-1000; fax (617) 232-1572. Editorial contributions should be sent to: Editor, *Cook's Illustrated*. We cannot assume responsibility for manuscripts submitted to us. Submissions will be returned only if accompanied by a large self-addressed envelope. Postmaster: Send all new orders, subscription inquiries, and change of address notices to: *Cook's Illustrated*, P.O. Box 7446, Red Oak, IA 51591-0446. PRINTED IN THE USA.

HEIRLOOM TOMATOES

HEIRLOOM TOMATOES Most of the tomatoes we are familiar with are hybrid varieties bred for easy shipping rather than flavor or texture. But over the past 20 years or so, many pre-hybrid "heirloom tomatoes" have been making a comeback. Adapted to grow in particular microclimates, they come in all shapes and colors, from the creamy Great White Beefsteak to the lemon-yellow Wonder Light and the brick-red Debarao. Instead of being "all-purpose," many of these heirlooms are ideally suited for a particular culinary use. The blood-red Moskvich, for example, matures early and has sweet flesh that is great for eating out of hand, while the creamy texture of the persimmon-orange Flamme makes it ideal for sauces, and the tart flavor of the lime-emerald Green Zebra is wonderful in salads.

COVER PAINTING: BRENT WATKINSON.   BACK COVER ILLUSTRATION: JOHN BURGOYNE.

BINGO NIGHT AT THE FIRE STATION

Last August, our family drove over to the next town, which was having its annual fireman's parade and carnival. Although it was past five, the sun was still hard at work, and we walked slowly onto the main stretch of road that passes for a town center, the firehouse being the center of attraction at one end, the Congregational church at the other. In front of the firehouse, hundreds of folding lawn chairs had been set up, brought by eager townspeople and visitors, the frayed bands of yellow and green tightly stretched across aluminum frames, having to support the weight of farmers grown fat on a diet of potatoes, meat, and bread. Across the street sat another hundred spectators, a collage of long white dresses, tank tops, gray beards, green work pants held up by suspenders, kids with freckles the size of blueberries, and solemn-faced women who looked like dowagers in the orchestra section of an opera house, double-chinned and demanding a fine performance.

Behind the firehouse, the food stands were open for business in whitewashed cabins with stained counters, offering homemade fries, hot dogs, hamburgers, and fried dough. The fries were good, dumped onto dark-stained paper bags, glistening with hot oil, and then shoveled into small cardboard containers almost too hot to carry. The fried dough was slathered with melted butter, sprinkled with a thick layer of sugar and cinnamon, and eaten hot, the sugar sticking like sand to the lips and fingers. Inside a tent were games of chance, and in the hall itself, bingo cards had been laid out with dried corn kernels for markers. The board in back, where the on-duty volunteers were listed, was filled with good local

names such as Morey and Truehart, Mackey and Tifft, Putnam and Zinn. I had known Morey's father, Merritt, a man who'd rather tell a story than eat supper. He used to live just down the road on the corner, right where the game wardens set up "Bambi," a remote control buck used to lure unsuspecting hunters who then get arrested for shooting from a car.

Soon enough, the parade started with the fire trucks from the adjoining towns. Kids with big ears that stuck out like custom side-view mirrors waved from the high cabs, locals cheered at the sight of a next-door neighbor, and small candies were thrown from the backs of trucks for the children, a spray of tightly wrapped sweets skidding across the pavement, skittering underneath the chairs. A few local bands marched their way through town, the musicians wearing heavy red woolen uniforms that hung limply in the sun, sweat beading up on their foreheads and then running down, pooling up over bushy eyebrows and then diverted off to the side of the face as if by a waterbar. Homemade floats displayed hunting scenes, complete with pine trees, the mounted heads of bucks, two or three boys dressed in full camouflage with Black Bear bows, and, always, the banner, advertising "The Vermont Predator" or perhaps something less bloodthirsty, such as "Hunt and Fish the Green Mountains of Vermont."

In these small towns, everyone has a place, the volunteer firemen, the sheriff, the carpenters, the

Christopher Kimball

selectmen, the farmers, and the kids marching next to their fathers in the band. These little towns are not home to a World Series baseball team or a football stadium, nor do they have summer theater or fancy weddings. They are dusty towns, too small and too poor even for the Junior League. Bingo night occurs only once per year, on the day of their big parade, when firemen and trombone players and young couples with brightly waxed muscle cars slowly make their way down Main Street to the fire hall, where they are cheered and counted, where each of them is somebody in a town that nobody has much heard of.

As our children grow older and shake the dust from their shoes, they will be anxious to be rid of the sight of french fries left in the dirt next to the ball toss and large doughy women in bright green shorts surrounded by small dirty faces. But many years from now, on a hot night in August, it will be bingo night once again, and they will hear the blast of the horn on top of the fire truck. Each of their names will be posted on the firehouse wall that evening, with the Moreys and Tiffts, the town knowing that they are willing and able to do their duty if called to action. It is a gift to know that a seat is reserved for each of us, that a homecoming is ours for the asking. We just need to stop and listen for the sound of the band on a hot night in August, calling us to sit elbow to elbow with our neighbors, asking if we are ready to accept the luck of the draw with good faith and fellowship.

ABOUT COOK'S ILLUSTRATED

The Magazine *Cook's Illustrated* (ISSN 1068-2821) is published bimonthly (6 issues per year) by Boston Common Press Limited Partnership, 17 Station Street, Brookline, MA 02445. Copyright 1999 Boston Common Press Limited Partnership. Periodical postage paid at Boston, MA and additional mailing offices, USPS #012487. A one-year subscription is $29.70, two years is $55, and three years is $75. Add $6 postage per year for Canadian subscriptions and $12 per year for all other foreign countries. To order subscriptions in the U.S. call 800-526-8442; from outside the U.S. call 515-247-7571. Gift subscriptions are available for $24.95 each.

Magazine-Related Items *Cook's Illustrated* is available in an annual hardbound edition, which includes an index, for $24.95 each plus shipping and handling. Discounts are available if more than one year is ordered at a time. Back issues are available for $5 each. *Cook's* also offers a six-year index (1993-1998) of the magazine for $12.95. To order any of these products, call 800-611-0759 inside the U.S. or 515-246-6911 outside the U.S.

Books *Cook's Illustrated* publishes a series of single-topic books, available for $14.95 each. Titles include *How to Make a Pie, How to Make an American Layer Cake, How to Stir-Fry, How to Make Ice Cream, How to Make Salad, How to Make Simple Fruit Desserts, How to Make Cookie Jar Favorites, How to Cook Holiday Roasts and Birds, How to*

Make Stew, How to Grill, How to Make Pizza, How to Make Holiday Desserts, How to Make Pasta Sauces, How to Barbecue & Roast on the Grill, How to Cook Shrimp & Other Shellfish, and *How to Cook Garden Vegetables. The Cook's Bible,* written by Christopher Kimball and published by Little, Brown and Company, is available for $24.95. *The Yellow Farmhouse Cookbook,* also written by Christopher Kimball and published by Little, Brown and Company, is available for $24.95. To order any of these books, call 800-611-0759 inside the U.S. or 515-246-6911 outside the U.S.

Reader Submissions *Cook's* accepts reader submissions for both Quick Tips and Notes from Readers. We will provide a one-year complimentary subscription for each Quick Tip that we print. Send a description of your technique, along with your name, address, and daytime telephone number, to Quick Tips, *Cook's Illustrated,* P.O. Box 470589, Brookline, MA 02447. Questions, suggestions, or other submissions for Notes from Readers should be sent to the same address.

Subscription Inquiries All queries about subscriptions or change of address notices should be addressed to *Cook's Illustrated,* P.O. Box 7446, Red Oak, IA 51591-0446.

Web Site Address Selected articles and recipes from *Cook's Illustrated* and subscription information are available online. You can also order books and other products at www.cooks illustrated.com.

Hard-Cooked Egg
Starting Temperature

Your March/April 1999 article "The Best Way to Hard-Cook an Egg" was admirably researched, but the recipe ignored one crucial variable: starting temperature of the eggs. Prior to cooking, are they at room temperature or just out of the refrigerator and chilled?

ELIZABETH MORGAN
RICHARDSON, TEX.

➤ We heard from several readers who had the same question, and we regret any confusion the recipe may have caused. All of our recipes, including the Foolproof Boiled Eggs, start with chilled eggs right from the refrigerator. If we ever do use eggs that are not cold, we specifically note that in the recipe and include directions for a quick method of warming the eggs to room temperature. One technique we like is to place the eggs in a small microwave-safe bowl and warm them in the microwave at 30 percent power for 10 seconds. Letting the eggs simply sit on the counter to come to room temperature is not only time-consuming but also an invitation for accelerated bacterial growth.

Super-Chilling Summer Drinks

I have a very efficient way to chill cans and bottles of soft drinks and beer for summer picnics or other outdoor celebrations. Like most people, I use a large container filled with ice, into which I nestle the cans and bottles. The difference is that I first mix the ice with a liberal amount of salt. This not only cools the drinks faster, it also keeps them cold longer than plain ice.

KIMBERLY HO
IRVINE, CALIF.

➤ We tested your method using ½ cup of kosher salt per quart of ice and found it very effective. In side-by-side buckets, we chilled six cans of Coke in salted ice and six in plain ice. The starting temperature in the bucket of plain ice was 33 degrees, while the salted ice started at 36 degrees. After just 15 minutes, though, the plain ice was 32 degrees, while the salted ice had dropped to 26 degrees. We continued to measure the temperatures every 15 minutes for the next hour, and the salted ice was consistently 5 or 6 degrees colder than the plain ice. In fact, after an hour in the salted ice bath, the Coke inside the cans was only 24 degrees, and turning to slush itself. This method works because salt lowers the freezing temperature of water. It is for this same reason that salt is always used when packing ice around the canister in the old-fashioned churns used to make ice cream.

No More Tears, 10 More Ways

Regarding your recent article about the tears shed while cutting onions (see "Cry Me a River," January/February 1999, page 10), there is a very effective system I've been using for years to eliminate the tear problem. I place a small electric fan to the side of the cutting board so that the airflow over the board will blow the fumes away from me. Make sure not to blow the fumes into another object that can deflect them back toward you.

ADAM BAUER
MOOR PARK, CALIF.

➤ When doing the testing for the "Cry Me a River" section of our article on onion soup, we tried 22 different ways to stem the flow of tears while chopping onions. Since then we've received 10 more ideas from readers, so back to the cutting board we went.

Two testers were pretty impressed with the effect of placing a small fan next to the cutting board, which was the most popular suggestion, coming also from Ann Bowes of Westmoreland, New Hampshire, Patricia Cornetta of Portsmouth, New Hampshire, Steve Edwards of Barnet, Vermont, and S. J. Silverman of Houston, Texas. Each tester was able to chop three large onions before the fumes felled us, which they eventually did. We would note, though, that all other cooks in the kitchen, including those who were not participating in our tests, also succumbed to the tears because the fumes were being circulated around the room. For that reason, this method didn't win us any friends, but we would still give it a rating of 6 out of 10.

Leslie Allen of Mill Valley, California, suggested moving the whole operation outdoors. We had good luck with this trick, chopping onion after onion with only minor irritation. Despite the obvious seasonal, regional, and logistical limitations of this method, we would give it an 8.

Other suggestions, which met with much less success in our tests, were to work quickly using a very sharp knife, to wash the knife blade frequently, to breathe exclusively through the mouth while chopping, and to keep the mouth tightly shut while chopping. Each of these methods rated only a 1. Two other suggestions—to whistle constantly while chopping and to slice off the root and blossom ends and allow the juices to run out before chopping—rated in the 4 to 5 range, which means they probably aren't worth the effort.

The funniest suggestion we got is meant to serve as a remedy once the tears start to flow rather than as a preventive measure. Kelly Sautter of Simi Valley, California, said that sticking her head in the freezer provides immediate relief once her eyes begin to sting. To the great amusement of the other test cooks, we tried this and found that it took about 30 seconds for the stinging to subside, whereas it took about 45 seconds to feel relief after simply leaving the room.

All in all, we'll stick with our original conclusions, which were to wear eye protection in the form of contact lenses or ski or swimming goggles or to chop the onions near the flame of a candle or lit gas burner. Both methods are effective, easy, and available regardless of location or equipment. The one technique we found that might work better came from Michael Burwen of Los Altos, California, who said, "and about avoiding onion tears, the only method I have found 100 percent effective is to con someone else into chopping them."

Grilling Duck

I was encouraged by your article "Roast Duck without the Fat" (see November/December 1998, page 8). The article did not mention brining, as have many of your chicken and turkey articles. Is it not recommended for duck? Also, I wondered whether this steamed duck would make a nice grilled meat, or would there still be enough fat to warrant a burning permit?

ANDREA TWOMBLY
ATTLEBORO, MASS.

➤ We have tried brining duck, and while the results were certainly acceptable, we felt the process was not as beneficial for duck as it was for turkey, chicken, or Cornish hens. Brining offers two main advantages, but both relate primarily to the white meat on a bird. First, brining seasons the meat. While this is helpful for the dark meat, too, it is paramount for the white meat, which is often bland without sufficient seasoning. But duck has no white meat, and since its meat is so juicy and flavorful from the bird's abundant natural fat, this point is moot. Second, brining protects delicate white meat from overcooking and drying out in the time necessary to cook the dark meat properly. Again, with no white meat and plenty of fat, this becomes a nonissue.

Now on to your second question. We did try grilling steamed duck parts and had great success, particularly when using the two-level fire method outlined in "How to Grill Chicken Wings" on page 12 of this issue. We did experience flare-ups while grilling the pieces over a medium fire, but starting them off over a low fire for 15 minutes on the skin side and about 5 minutes on the other side allowed the fat to render slowly and evenly, thus avoiding the inferno effect. Then we moved the pieces over to a hot fire for about 5 minutes, skin side down, to crisp up. The result was moist, tender, smoky duck with crisp skin and no excess fat.

Ceramic Grating Dishes

I was surprised by one aspect of your March/April 1999 review of hard cheese graters (*see* "Grate Expectations," page 28). Two of the alleged cheese graters, the Kyocera Dish and the Progressive International Graham Kerr Grating Dish, are clearly not cheese graters. These dishes are specifically engineered to grate ginger and collect its juice. Neither of these models should have been part of the test.

CARA HALL
HERMOSA BEACH, CALIF.

➤ It is certainly true that many graters intended exclusively for ginger are made of ceramic and fashioned as dishes, like the Kyocera and Progressive International Graham Kerr models we tested. But both the retail catalog from which we bought our Kyocera dish and the Kyocera company itself promote this ceramic grater as suitable for ginger as well as for other foods. In the case of the Progressive International Graham Kerr dish, the packaging says that it is "perfect for grating hard cheese, chocolate, carrots, ginger, lemon peel, and more." For a magazine determined to find the best kitchen equipment and appliances, we simply couldn't resist putting such wide claims to the test. Insomuch as we were testing cheese graters and wanted to consider the widest possible range of models, it would not have made sense to exclude the ceramic graters from our lineup.

Cheese Grater Lineage

"Grate Expectations," the article testing hard cheese graters in the March/April issue of *Cook's*, was well done. I was especially interested in the connection between the winner of this test, The Cheese Grater, and the woodworking tool called a rasp. I checked the rasp we had in our garage workshop, and, while it was similar, our rasp was solid metal with raised, bumpy teeth on a curved surface, whereas The Cheese Grater was described as "a flat sheet of metal that is punched through with teeth." I don't question the connection between these two tools, but what I am curious to know is whether The Cheese Grater's design was based on some particular type of rasp.

LESLIE LOCKE
LAUREL, MISS.

➤ Yes, the basis for The Cheese Grater is a line of rasps called Microplanes, which were developed and are made by Grace Manufacturing in Russellville, Arkansas. Unlike your solid rasp, which provides no escape route for the wood shavings, leaving them to jam up between the teeth, the Microplane's teeth remain clear because the continued planing action works the wood shavings through the perforations in the metal, so they fall out the back side. Discussing the use of a Microplane rasp versus other versions of the instrument, Giles Parker of Rockler Woodworking and Hardware in Cambridge, Massachusetts, noted its impressively sharp teeth and commented: "They are ideal for fine tasks such as shaping a curved chair leg or arm."

Mike Jayroe, a marketing representative at Grace Manufacturing, related the story of how his company's rasps came to be used in the kitchen for grating and zesting. According to Jayroe, the wife of a Canadian hardware store owner was baking an orange cake and, out of sheer frustration with her old grater, began to use a new rasp her husband had brought home from their store. That tool, a Rigid Microplane designed for a hacksaw, worked beautifully, so they changed the product description in their hardware store and mail order catalog.

Grace Manufacturing currently has three Microplanes that do double duty in woodworking and grating/zesting, and it has two more designed specifically for kitchen use. For more information, including ordering instructions, contact Grace Manufacturing (614 SR 247, Russellville, AR 72802; 501-968-5455; www.microplane.com).

Grinding Nuts Manually

One of my family's favorite cookies, especially around the holidays, has always been nut crescents, so I read your article (*see* "Nut Crescent Cookies," November/December 1998, page 24) with great interest. I have found that the best way of preparing walnuts or pecans is to grind them manually in a Mouli rotary grater (*see* "Grate Expectations," March/April 1999, page 28). As you mentioned, these oily nuts quickly turn into nut butter if overprocessed in a food processor or blender, and chopping them finely by hand is just too much work for me. The Mouli grater, however, is fast, easy, and yields a finely ground, dry product with enough larger pieces remaining to give the cookies their characteristic texture.

DENISE PERKINS
NAPERVILLE, ILL.

➤ Generally speaking, rotary graters are intended to grate nuts and chocolate as well as hard cheese. Following your suggestion, we tested the stainless steel Moulinex Mouli (the second-place finisher in our March/April 1999 testing of graters), fitted with the finer of its two grating wheels, with nuts. The Mouli made quick, easy work of the two cups of walnuts called for in the Nut Crescent Cookie recipe, breaking them down into a dry, flaky meal, just as you say. Also, we never felt in danger of accidentally overprocessing the nuts. For cooks who do not have a food processor to grind the nuts for this recipe, the Mouli is an excellent alternative.

For these cookies, though, a perfectly dry texture turns out to be less crucial. We went on to make side-by-side batches of cookies, one with walnuts ground in the Mouli and the other with nuts ground in the food processor. The majority of tasters detected a slightly richer nut flavor and a more delicate, tender texture in the cookies made with nuts from the food processor because the heat from the grinding process released a little more of the nut's oils than did the manual grinding. So if you have a food processor, that remains our first choice for grinding the nuts in this recipe.

WHAT IS IT?

My sister purchased this device at a yard sale and challenged me to figure out what it is. I admit that I don't know. "Slice-a-Slice" is imprinted on the face of it, as is the place of manufacture, Duncannon, Pennsylvania. Do you know what it is and its purpose?

Dennis Anderson
Spokane, Wash.

➤ It's all in the name with this gadget. The Slice-a-Slice was designed to do just that: halve a pre-cut slice of bread vertically to make two extrathin slices. We learned this from another reader, Susan Steel of North Fort Myers, Florida, who also wrote to inquire about the Slice-a-Slice. Steel knew what it was—she purchased one new more than 50 years ago, and, since it is now worn down, she wanted to know if they are still available. They are not.

To use Slice-a-Slice, open the metal plates, insert a single slice of bread between them, and close the plates so they hold the bread in place firmly. Then simply cut the slice of bread from the top down, using the two plates as a guide.

Duncannon, Pennsylvania, antique dealer Jimmy Rosen has two Slice-a-Slices, in their original packaging, in the collection at his Old Sled Works Antique and Craft Market. The instruction booklet touts a number of "good things made with very thin bread," including "melba toast, party sandwiches, canapés, tart cases, patty shells, bread pudding, combination sandwiches, and thin bread and butter."

Quick Tips

Squeeze Bottle Uses

Sharon Denner of Great Neck, New York, has found a quick, easy, neat way to handle and apply smooth barbecue sauces or marinades to foods during the last few minutes on the grill. Instead of brushing the food with sauce from a bowl, she puts her sauce into a leftover pull-top spring water squeeze bottle and squirts the sauce onto the food. This method saves time on cleanup, too, since there is neither a bowl nor a brush to wash, and unused sauce can be refrigerated in the bottle.

Jar-Opening Assistant

Many cooks have a kitchen drawer full of the thick rubber bands used to bind together bunches of broccoli or keep a lobster claw shut. Geré Nelson of Brownfield, Maine, found that those rubber bands can provide much-needed extra grip when it's time to pry off a lid that is stuck to its jar. Simply slip the band around the jar lid and turn to open.

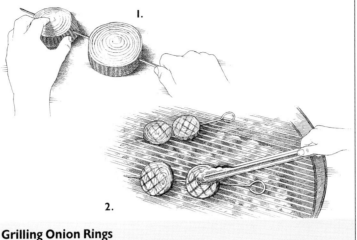

Grilling Onion Rings

Onion slices can be difficult to handle and cook evenly on the grill. A vegetable grilling basket can solve the problem, but not everyone, including Marilyn Chattman of Mountain Lakes, New Jersey, owns one. She came up with this alternate solution.

1. Cut thick slices (at least ½ inch) of large red or Spanish onion and skewer them all the way through with a slender bamboo skewer, which is about the same thickness as a toothpick, or a thin metal skewer.

2. The skewered onion slices remain intact as they grill, and, best of all, they can be flipped easily with tongs.

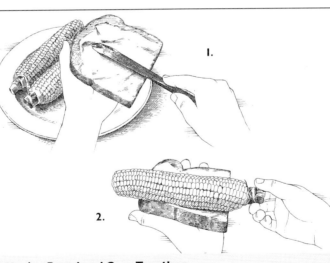

Buttering Bread and Corn Together

Using a knife to butter an ear of corn can be messy and frustrating, as the melting butter slides off the knife and down the ear. Then you have to fish under the corn with the knife to pick up the remaining butter and try again... and again. Loryn Kipp of Manchester, Maine, has an easier way.

1. She uses the knife to apply a thick layer of butter to a slice of bread she's eating with her meal anyway.

2. She then rolls the hot ear of corn over the buttered bread, which neatly gives the corn an even coating of warm butter.

Blending Natural Peanut Butter

Fans of natural peanut butter, tahini, and other natural nut butters know that the butter often separates into a dense, solid mass beneath a layer of oil that has risen to the surface. Before spreading, the oil and the solids have to be reblended, which is often a difficult, messy task. Phoebe Harper of Kula, Hawaii, discovered that she could skip the mixing step by turning the sealed jar upside down until the oil once again rose to the top. Flip the jar right side up again, and the butter is ready to spread.

Distributing Goodies Evenly in Cookie Dough

Many readers may have noticed that the last few cookies baked from a batch of chocolate chip cookie dough never seem to have as many chips or nuts in them as the first few cookies. To avoid this common problem, Stephen Tao of Los Angeles, California, suggests reserving some of the chips and other goodies and mixing them into the dough after about half of it has been scooped out for cookies. This way, the last cookies will have as much good stuff as the first.

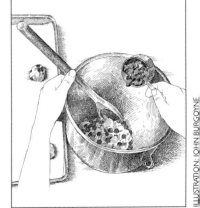

Send Us Your Tip We will provide a complimentary one-year subscription for each tip we print. See page 1 for information.

ILLUSTRATION: JOHN BURGOYNE

Makeshift Cake Platter

Many cake platters are too small to accommodate square or rectangular sheet cakes or kid's character cakes. When Wendi Krause of Pittsburgh, Pennsylvania, needs a larger cake plate, she does the following:

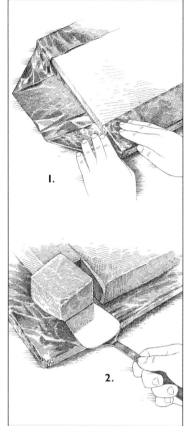

1. Wrap a cutting board tightly with aluminum foil.
2. Invert the board, so the seam side is down, place the cake, and serve.

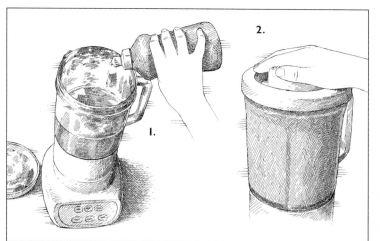

Quick-Cleaning the Blender

Washing dishes is never fun, but washing a blender jar that has been sitting around with food residue in it can be especially irritating. Beau Brush of East Amherst, New York, recommends this method to get a head start on the process.
1. Fill the dirty blender bowl half-full with hot water and add a couple of drops of liquid dish soap.
2. With the top firmly in place, turn the blender on high for 30 seconds. Most of the residue pours right out with the soapy water, and the blender jar need only be rinsed or washed lightly by hand.

Cutting Corn from the Cob

Cutting the kernels from long ears of corn can be tricky. Associate editor Dawn Yanagihara makes the task easier and safer by cutting the ear in half and standing the half ears on their cut surfaces, which are flat and stable. Not only is the corn more stable on the work surface, it is also easier to control the knife down the length of only half an ear.

Making Even-Sized Balls of Cookie Dough, Redux

Our November/December 1998 tip for making even-sized balls of cookie dough prompted two readers to offer alternative methods for the same task. Janet Noble of Hopkins, South Carolina, suggests this method:
1. Roll the dough into a cylinder of even diameter.
2. Then cut the cylinder in half, and each half in half, and each quarter in half, and so on.

Maya Klein of El Cerrito, California, has an approach that is useful when the recipe indicates a particular yield of cookies:
1. Form the entire mass of dough into a flat rectangular block with even edges and a smooth top.
2. Cut the dough into uniformly sized pieces. For example, if the recipe indicates a yield of 4 dozen cookies, cut the block into 6 equal strips in one direction, crossed by 8 equal strips going in the other direction.

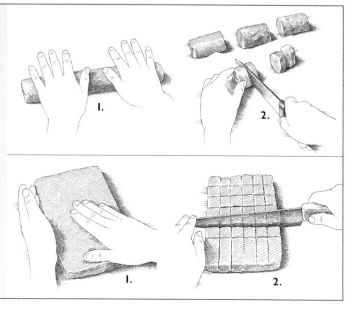

Keeping Bean Sprouts and Jícama Fresh

Audrey Bauer of University Heights, Ohio, found a method that keeps bean sprouts crisp and fresh for up to five days. She simply submerges the sprouts in a container of water, then refrigerates them. Scott Saifer and Julie Adibzadeh of Berkeley, California, discovered that this also works very well with cut-up jícama.

Halving Peaches and Nectarines, Take Two

Nancy Stutzman of Boston, Massachusetts, saw the tip in our July/August 1998 issue about an easy way to halve peaches and nectarines. Her method is similar, and just as easy.

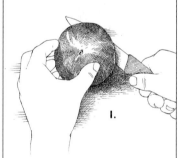

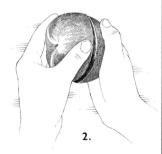

1. Position the knife at a right angle to the crease in the fruit and cut along its equator, across the crease.
2. Grasp the halves and twist them apart, exposing a large portion of the pit, which is easy to pop free from the flesh.

Grilled Corn Perfected

Grilling corn typically involves a compromise between flavor and texture—but we found a way around this dilemma.

⇒ BY MARYELLEN DRISCOLL ⇐

During childhood summers spent at our grandparents' house on the short New Hampshire coastline, my sisters and I could anticipate a few benchmark events every August. The first was when our mother would finally wade past her ankles and lose her hairdo to the willful Atlantic waves. Then there was the neighborhood party line spreading word of the first corn for sale up on old Route 1. That inevitably led to the most intriguing moment of them all: would our grandmother's false teeth hold out another year as she insisted on eating her corn on the cob?

I can't think of any vegetable that garners as much widespread anticipation, ritual, and celebration as the ear of corn. And because it so suitably arrives during the heyday of the grilling season, it often just doesn't make sense to boil up a pot of water in the kitchen when you are already outdoors firing up the grill.

I cannot say I have ever grilled an ear of corn that I did not like. But I can say that before tackling this story I had never grilled an ear of corn that met my ideal. I wanted my grilled corn to retain the juiciness of boiled without sacrificing the toasty caramelization and smoke-infused graces of the grill.

To steer my way toward this ideal balance of texture and flavor, I started my tests by cooking bare ears of corn directly over a medium-high fire. The outcome seemed too good to be true. The lightly caramelized corn was still juicy but came with a toasty hit of grilled flavor and a sweet corn essence to chase it down. In fact, it was too good to be true. It turned out that the corn I had used was fittingly called Fantasy, a supersweet variety. (There are basically three types of hybrid sweet corn on the market today, categorized by sugar content of immature kernels. Supersweet corn has the highest sugar concentration, as high as 16 percent. Sugar-enhanced corn contains about 12 to 14 percent sugar. Normal sweet corn contains

A single layer of husk protects the corn during grilling and is easily removed, along with the blackened silks, once the corn is done.

only 8 to 12 percent.) When I tried grilling a normal sweet corn variety in the same manner, the outcome was a flavorless, dry, gummy turn-off. The end result was no better with sugar-enhanced corn. The direct heat was just too straightforward for the fleeting flavors and tender texture of the normal sweet and sugar-enhanced corn. Placing the corn off to the side of the fire so that it would cook indirectly proved no better; the kernels dried out before they could cook.

At this point I realized that my goal should be to come up with a technique that would work no matter what type of sweet corn is used. This struck me as particularly important because you cannot tell the type of corn you have purchased by its appearance. Nowadays corn marketed as "Butter and Sugar" often indicates only that it has bicolored kernels. Actually, the variety Butter and Sugar is less commonly grown on a commercial level. All three sweet corn types contain varieties that come in all yellow, all white, or the popular so-called Butter and Sugar, alternating white and yellow kernels. During the off season, you can be fairly certain that the corn in your supermarket is supersweet. During harvest season it

varies. And I have never seen a supermarket specify the corn type. Even at some farm stands the sales help can enthusiastically report the variety's catchy name, such as Seneca Dancer or Calico Bell, but have no clue as to what that means. With the three types of sweet corn consisting of hundreds of varieties being grown in fields across the United States, I did not want a recipe that could send a cook trekking across the countryside in search of a particular type. The technique needed to be all-purpose.

With this new information in mind I went on to test another popular grilling technique: throwing the whole ear on the grill as is, husk and all. I tried this with all three types of sweet corn and at various heat levels. With each test, I soaked half of the ears in water beforehand and left half unsoaked. My tasters (friends and coworkers) and I agreed that the husk-on method makes for a great-tasting ear of corn, and a particularly crisp, juicy one. But if it were not for the sticky charred husks that must be awkwardly peeled away at the table if you serve the corn hot, you would think you were eating boiled corn. The presoaked corn in particular just steams in the husk and picks up absolutely no grilled flavor. The grilled flavor picked up by the unsoaked corn in my tests was "wimpy," as one taster aptly noted. This no-nonsense method for grilling corn certainly has its place. It just was not what I was seeking.

I took a few excursions off the path of this basic technique, such as peeling back the husk to remove the silk and then folding the green husks back up to make a jacket for the corn. Many recipes call for then tying the husks back together near the tip with string (fussy) or a strand of husk (futile). I also tried just pulling the husk back up to cover the corn loosely. This helped some in that it gave the corn a little more exposure at the tip to the grill— but not enough. So it's simpler to leave the ear untouched if you are going to grill husk-on.

Since grilling with the husk off was too aggressive for non-supersweet varieties and grilling with the husk on was no different from boiled corn, I turned to a compromise approach I'd read of in a favorite grilling cookbook: begin grilling with the husk on, and once the corn is cooked, remove the husk and return the ear to the grill to get a bit of browning. Again, however, the corn lost too much moisture and the grilled flavor proved shallow. (Presoaking insignificantly minimized dry-

The Best Way to Store Corn

While the general rule of thumb is to buy and eat corn the same day it has been harvested, many of us have to break that rule pretty often. So I decided to check out a variety of methods for overnight storage. I chose Silver Queen corn, one of the more perishable varieties.

What I found is that the worst thing you can do to corn is leave it sitting out on the counter. Throwing it into the refrigerator without any wrapping is nearly as bad. Storing it in an airtight bag helps, but the winning method—no contest—entailed wrapping the corn (husk left on) in a wet paper bag and then in a plastic bag (any shopping bag will do) and refrigerating it. After 24 hours of storage I found that corn stored this way was still juicy, sweet, and fresh tasting, and not starchy.

To understand how corn loses its fresh flavor and why this storage technique seemed to help delay the loss of flavor, I spoke to Dr. Donald Schlimme of the University of Maryland's food science department.

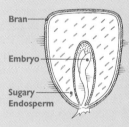

He explained that the kernels on the ears of corn that we savor each summer are really immature seeds. Their role is to carry embryos into the next growing season, when they will germinate and the growth cycle will repeat itself. To survive the rigors of winter, the seed has to "toughen up." (A hard kernel of popping corn is an example of this.) One way in which corn does this is by converting the simple sugars in the milky interior into starch. This alters the kernels' consistency from succulent to doughy to hard. Picking the ear from the stalk prematurely triggers this process. Refrigeration helps to slow the rate of biochemical changes, particularly the conversion of sugar to starch. Covering the ears in dampened paper and then plastic helps in another way: it slows down the rate of moisture loss from the kernels and promotes retention of succulence. —M.D.

ing.) The greatest drawback of this method was trying to remove the husks without burning your hands. With a grill full of corn, it would never have worked. This method was awkward, time-consuming, and messy.

Since none of the normally prescribed methods for grilling corn were providing the balance of flavor and texture I was seeking, I decided to follow a whim. I removed the outer half of the corn's husk before placing the ear over the fire. There was enough coverage to let the corn steam, thus keeping it juicy. But because the barrier between the flames and the corn had been reduced, there was also some slight caramelization.

The final adjustment proved simple: I peeled the husk off down to the final layer that wraps around the ear. This inner layer is much more moist and delicate than the exterior ones—you can practically see the kernels through the husk. This gave the corn a "jacket" that was thick enough to prevent dehydration yet thin enough to allow a medium-high fire to gently toast the kernels. After about eight minutes (rolling the corn one-quarter turn every two minutes), I could be certain that the corn was cooked just right because the husk picked up a dark silhouette of the kernels and began to pull back at the corn's tip. It was a simple visual indicator of completion that I particularly appreciated while using one of the most unpredictable and difficult-to-control cooking mediums—the grill.

GRILLED SWEET CORN
SERVES 4 TO 8

If you are using a gas rather than a charcoal grill, turn all burners to high, close the lid, heat the grill until hot, 10 to 15 minutes, and follow steps 2 and 3 below. If you are certain that you have a supersweet variety of corn, remove the husks entirely, then follow instructions below, grilling until kernels are light caramel brown, about 5 to 7 minutes.

> 8   ears fresh corn, husks on
>   Salt and ground black pepper
>   Butter

1. Ignite about 6 quarts charcoal and burn until coals are completely covered with thin coating of light-gray ash. Spread coals evenly over grill bottom; heat to medium-high (you can hold your hand 5 inches above grill surface for 3 seconds); position grill rack.
2. Meanwhile, following illustration 1 below, remove all but innermost layer of husk from each ear of corn (kernels will be covered by, but visible through, last husk layer). Use scissors to snip off long silk ends at tips of ears (*see* illustration 2).
3. Grill corn, turning ears every 1½ to 2 minutes, until kernels have left dark outlines in the husk and husks are charred and beginning to peel

---

TECHNIQUE
WHEN IS IT DONE?

When the corn is properly grilled, the husk will pick up a dark silhouette of the kernels and begin to pull away from the tip of the ear.

away at tip to expose some kernels (*see* illustration above), 8 to 10 minutes. Transfer ears to platter; remove and discard charred husks and silk. Season corn with salt and pepper and butter to taste, if desired; serve immediately.

GRILLED CORN SALSA
MAKES ABOUT 2 CUPS

Serve this salsa with tortilla chips or, better yet, as a condiment for grilled seafood or chicken.

> 2   ears grilled corn, kernels cut from cobs
>   (about 1 cup)
> 1   medium red bell pepper, diced small
> 1   medium scallion, sliced thin
> 1   small garlic clove, minced
> ½   medium jalapeño chile, minced
> 1½   tablespoons corn or vegetable oil
> 1½   tablespoons juice from 1 lime
> 1   teaspoon ground cumin
> 1   tablespoon chopped fresh cilantro leaves
> ⅛   teaspoon salt

Place all ingredients in medium bowl, toss well, and serve.

STEP-BY-STEP | PREPARING CORN FOR THE GRILL

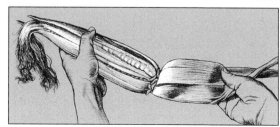

1. Remove all but the innermost layer of the husk.

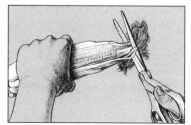

2. Use scissors to snip off the tassel.

"Hot-Smoked" Salmon

Make moist, nicely crusted salmon with a hint of smoked flavor in any covered grill—in just two hours.

⇒ BY A. CORT SINNES ⇐

As a child growing up in a Scandinavian household, I was subjected to all manner of smoked and pickled fish. I liked all of it—from pickled herring in sour cream to gravlax. But my favorite was the smoked salmon, a store-bought rarity. With the acquisition of my own house and my own grill, I was anxious to figure out how to make smoked salmon at home. The store-bought stuff was simply inconsistent in quality and also expensive.

My initial goal was to replicate the not-too-dry, not-too-moist, flavorful, just-smoky-enough salmon I remembered having as a kid. I started testing with a small electric smoker I had received as a Father's Day present. The results were OK, but too moist and too smoky for my taste—more like lox than what I had come to know as smoked salmon.

I then decided to do the rest of the testing in a covered kettle grill, since this is the most common piece of equipment used by outdoor cooks. I started off trying to make the covered grill act like a cold smoker. I used very few coals, adding them as I went along, often putting out the fire with handfuls of wet smoking chips. The results were disappointing—the salmon was lacking in flavor, and the texture was a bit too wet.

Patience is supposed to be a virtue, but in this case impatience turned out to be the key to success. I simply got tired of messing with the process of cold-smoking. In fact, at this point I realized that cold-smoking, which occurs in a range of 75 to 110 degrees, is simply not practical for home cooks. It takes a very long time, requires both skill and patience, and can be disastrous if health precautions are not followed carefully. Therefore, I decided to use a greater number of briquettes in the initial fire. This eliminated the need to add more coals during the smoking process, and the larger fire was less likely to go out when I added more wet smoking chips. Most of all, however, the hotter fire cooked the fish more, giving it a more pleasing, flakier texture.

I continued to refine this method over many months of trial and error. Eventually, I had perfected a procedure that yields a salmon that has many of the attributes of good smoked salmon but that is also moister, crustier, and a whole lot easier to make. Since it is somewhere between classic smoked salmon and traditional barbecue, I call it "hot-smoked." The difference between hot-

We found that brining the salmon before cooking keeps the texture moist, while smoking adds deep flavors.

and cold-smoked salmon is largely one of texture: the cold-smoked salmon is more "silky," like lox, whereas hot-smoked salmon will actually "flake."

But the drawback of this method—and the reason why salmon is usually cold-smoked—is that the fish became dry. I found the solution to this problem in Mark Bittman's article "A New Way to Prepare Shrimp" in the July/August 1994 issue of *Cook's*. In it, he details the benefits of brining shrimp before cooking them: "By denaturing protein strands, salt changes the structure of the flesh and allows it to trap more water. This excess water gives us the sensation of plumper, firmer, and juicier meat." If it worked with shrimp, I could see no reason why it wouldn't work with salmon, so I gave it a try.

Now I was getting somewhere. I experimented with various brining times and eventually settled on three to four hours for a salmon fillet weighing two-and-a-half to three pounds. Any longer and the flavor of the brine was too intense; any shorter and it didn't produce the desired results as far as texture was concerned. This brined, hot-smoked salmon definitely had the texture I had been longing for, but I was still looking for more flavor to complement its smokiness.

I then remembered the marinated cucumbers my Finnish grandmother used

to make: thin slices of cucumbers and white onions in a sugar and salt water brine. If a combination of sugar and salt intensified the flavor of relatively flavorless cucumbers, I reasoned, it could do the same for salmon. In fact, it worked like a charm, adding another level of flavor. (I later discovered that traditional European methods for smoking salmon—whether hot or cold—dictate that the fish must be immersed in a salt or salt-and-sugar brine before smoking.)

Again, I experimented with various salt/sugar/water ratios for the brine; with different brining times (from 2 to 24 hours); and with all manner of smoking woods (alder wood, apple, hickory, and oak). I eventually settled on the recipe below, which calls for three hours of brining in a solution of one cup each of sugar and salt to seven cups of water and which favors alder wood chips for the distinctive flavor they give the fish. (*See* "What Makes the Best Smoke?" on page 9.) The salmon it produces is just smoky enough, has a moist yet flaky texture, and gets a nice boost to its natural flavors from the brining.

Hot-smoked salmon can be served warm off the grill as well as chilled, and works as both a traditional hors d'oeuvre and, somewhat surprisingly, an entrée. For hors d'oeuvres it is absolutely delicious as is or accompanied by melba toast (or any other flat bread or cracker), finely chopped white onion, capers, and lemon wedges.

TECHNIQUE | BRINING THE FISH

To prepare for brining the salmon, place a one-gallon zipper-lock plastic bag in a large, narrow container or pitcher. To facilitate filling the bag, fold the bag over the mouth of the container.

1. Slide the salmon off the foil and onto the grill. To make it easier to remove the salmon from the grill, position the fillet with the long side perpendicular to the grill rods.

2. Use two spatulas to transfer the cooked fish from the grill to a cookie sheet or cutting board.

3. To serve, cut through the pink flesh, but not the skin, to divide into individual portions.

4. Slide a spatula between the fillet and skin to remove individual pieces, leaving the skin behind.

If you serve the salmon as an entrée, simple wedges of lemon will suffice, or you might try a sour cream, dill, and cucumber sauce.

HOT-SMOKED SALMON
SERVES 4 TO 6

Alder wood is best for this recipe, but hickory or mesquite chips are also fine. The grill rack must be hot and thoroughly clean before you place the salmon on it; otherwise the fish might stick.

- 1 cup kosher salt (or ½ cup table salt)
- 1 cup sugar
- 1 skin-on salmon fillet (about 2½ pounds), pin bones removed with tweezers or needle-nose pliers
- 2 tablespoons vegetable oil
- 1½ teaspoons sweet paprika
- 1 teaspoon ground white pepper

1. Dissolve salt and sugar in 2 cups hot water in gallon-sized zipper-lock plastic bag, about 20 minutes. Add 5 cups cold water and salmon, seal bag, and refrigerate until fish is fully brined, about 3 hours.

2. About 45 minutes prior to cooking, open bottom grill vents and ignite about 4 quarts charcoal in pile on one side of grill; burn until completely covered with thin coating of light-gray ash, 20 to 30 minutes. Meanwhile, assemble wood chip pouch by wrapping 2 cups wood chips on 18-inch square sheet heavy-duty aluminum foil; seal to make pouch. Prick top of pouch at least six times with knife tip to allow smoke to escape; place on top of ash-covered coals.

3. Meanwhile, remove salmon from brine and blot dry completely with paper towels. Place fillet, skin side down, on 30-inch sheet heavy-duty foil; rub both sides of fillet, especially skin side, with oil. Dust fillet top with paprika and pepper.

4. Set grill rack in place; open grill lid vents and cover, positioning lid with vents opposite wood pouch to draw smoke through grill. Heat rack thoroughly, at least 5 minutes; clean with wire brush. Following illustration 1, above, slide salmon off foil and onto rack opposite fire so that long side of fillet is perpendicular to grill rods. Barbecue until cooked through and heavily flavored with smoke, 1½ hours.

5. Following illustration 2, above, use two spatulas to remove salmon from grill. Serve either hot or room temperature, cutting through flesh but not skin to divide into individual portions and sliding spatula between flesh and skin to remove individual pieces, leaving skin behind. (Can be wrapped in plastic and refrigerated up to 2 days.)

HOT-SMOKED SALMON ON A GAS GRILL

Here is a way to mimic the indirect heat method of cooking on a charcoal grill. Since some gas grills require that one burner be ignited before the other(s), make sure that the foil tray containing the wood chips is placed over the burner that will remain on.

Follow recipe for Hot-Smoked Salmon, making the following changes: Soak wood chips for 15 minutes and drain. Following illustrations 1 through 4, below, make foil tray for wood chips and position on top of burner that will remain on. Turn all burners to high, close lid, and heat grill until chips smoke heavily, about 20 minutes. Turn off burner(s) without chips. Position salmon over cool part of grill and barbecue until cooked through and perfumed heavily with smoke, 1½ hours. Serve as directed.

A. Cort Sinnes is the author of several cookbooks, including *The Gas Grill Gourmet* (Harvard Common Press, 1996).

What Makes the Best Smoke?

For years, alder wood has been the top choice for smoking salmon, a tradition begun eons ago with the American Indians of the Pacific Northwest. Apple wood is often recommended as a close second. (If you use apple wood from your own trees, make sure no chemical pesticides or fungicides have been applied to them). If you can't find either alder or apple smoking chips, the more widely available oak or hickory will do fine. In a blind tasting I found that alder wood does, to my taste, actually produce a superior product. But beyond that exception, I think it's darned near impossible to tell the difference between mesquite, hickory, apple, or any other hardwood chips or chunks. I recommend that you choose whichever is most readily available.

Whatever smoking wood you choose, wrap the chips or chunks in heavy-duty aluminum foil, forming it into a tight packet. By poking a few holes into the top and placing the packet directly on top of the hot coals, you'll avoid the tedious step of soaking the chips as well as the problem of having the wet chips extinguish the fire. The foil wrapping has the additional advantage of meting the smoke out over a longer period of time. —A.C.S.

STEP-BY-STEP | MAKING A WOOD CHIP TRAY FOR A GAS GRILL

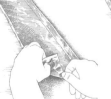

1. Make a 1-inch fold on one long side of a 12 x 18-inch piece of heavy-duty foil. Repeat three more times and turn the fold up to create a sturdy side that measures about 1 inch high. Repeat the process on the other long side.

2. With a short side facing you, fold in both corners as if wrapping a gift.

3. Turn up the inside inch or so of each triangular fold to match the rim on the long sides of the foil tray.

4. Lift the pointed end of the triangle over the rim of foil and fold down to seal. Repeat the process on the other short side.

Great Iced Tea in 15 Minutes

A hybrid technique based on traditional brewing and sun-tea steeping results in smooth, full-flavored tea—quickly.

≥ BY PAM ANDERSON WITH DAN MACEY ≤

Sweet tea is to Southerners what wine is to the French. Winter or summer, my family drank it with supper almost every night. And since I despised milk as a child, my mother even put it in my thermos for lunch. I have helped make and have made thousands of gallons of my mom's iced tea. In addition to my mom's tea, I have drunk hundreds of glasses in homes and restaurants over the years—some that merely quenched thirst or washed down a meal, others that put an "Ahhhh" in my voice and a smile on my face.

For me, great tea is strong but not bitter, richly colored, not cloudy and dark, and pleasantly, but not toothachingly, sweet. Was it the brewing method, steeping time, type of water, or ratio of ingredients that would consistently ensure the perfect glass of iced tea? I decided to find out.

Brewing Lessons

To begin with, I decided that I would limit myself to finding the best method for making iced tea using supermarket tea bags, since this is what my parents and most people I know always use. Brewing a pot of iced tea from premium loose teas seemed a bit too refined, and I also figured that it might require a different brewing method.

Because I was certain the brewing method was the key to good tea, that's where I started my investigation. The overwhelming number of iced tea recipes I turned up were variations of the back-of-the-box method. Pour X quarts of boiling water over X number of tea bags and let steep for X minutes or hours. The number of tea bags ranged from one bag per cup to one bag per quart, while steeping times ranged from three minutes to overnight. Of course there was also sun tea—a method of slowly extracting flavor from a tea bag by using the sun's heat and light. And although I had never tried it, I had seen recipes for "refrigerator tea"—steeping tea bags in a pitcher of water in the refrigerator overnight.

I started with the time-honored method— pouring boiling water over tea bags and letting them steep for 5 minutes. After testing this method again and again with different numbers and brands of bags, I found that all the teas made

To make it even easier to have a quick glass of iced tea, keep ice-filled glasses in the door of the freezer.

by this method were bitter and downright unpleasant to drink, especially without sugar and lemon. Not quite willing to give up on this method yet, I tested various steeping times, ranging from a minute to an hour, with even less success. The 1-minute steeped tea wasn't bitter, but it didn't have any flavor either. At 3 minutes, the tea was starting to taste a little bitter but still had very little flavor. At 5 minutes, the bitterness was noticeable, and at 10 minutes it was overwhelming. At 15 minutes and beyond, the tea was more medicine-like than beverage. I even tried boiling the tea bags themselves, but that method led to the worst result of all: a bitter, caramel-colored liquid with no distinctive tea flavor.

Though perfectly acceptable, the low-tech teas—both sun and refrigerator—required more tea bags, were relatively light in color, and tasted rather one-dimensional. The refrigerator tea had the added disadvantage of turning cloudy overnight.

No Special Purchase Required

At this point, I turned from tradition to modernity, in the shape of the microwave. As it turns out, this modern convenience actually made an exceptional pitcher of iced tea. With my first attempt, I microwaved four tea bags in four cups of water in a two-quart Pyrex measuring cup, covered, until it was very hot, about eight minutes. I immediately removed the tea bags and stirred in a quart of ice. The resulting tea was on the weak side, but it was not bitter. A little stronger, I thought, and this had a lot going for it. The equipment was simple, the technique was simple and fast, and the tea was not bitter. In an attempt to extract more flavor from the tea bags without picking up the bitterness, I upped the microwave time and tacked on some steeping. It worked. With 9 to 10 minutes of microwaving and 3 minutes of steeping, I had great iced tea—from start to finish—in about 15 minutes.

As long as I gave it a good rinse, my coffee maker was happy to do double duty as a tea maker, too. In the past, I had always put the tea bags in the coffee basket, the hot water simply flowing over the bags. With no steeping time, the tea was obviously weak. Moving the tea bags from the basket to the carafe made all the difference. With this arrangement, the bags spent some time in hot (not boiling) water and the resulting tea was strong, smooth, and clear.

When I told the other *Cook's* editors about my new method, they asked whether it could be duplicated on the stove top in a saucepan. As I thought about it, I realized that there was one primary difference between the newfangled and traditional methods: both the microwave recipe and the coffee maker used subboiling water.

So I tried it, bringing the same amount of water and tea bags to a hot, steamy-but-not-boiling state over medium-low heat, then covering and steeping the bags for three minutes. It worked just fine.

Why do these methods work when traditional steeping doesn't? The experts I interviewed all agreed that tea contains bitter-tasting tannins, many of which are not extracted until the boiling point. All the methods I had found to be successful relied on slow, steady heat and hot, but not boiling, water, thereby extracting a lot of flavor from the leaves without releasing their bitter tannins.

It's the Little Things That Make a Difference

For consistent results, I had performed all of the tests thus far with spring water. But was it necessary? After tasting teas made with running tap water, filtered tap water, and spring water, I think so. The tea made with spring water was the clear favorite, giving the tea the freshest, cleanest, clearest look and taste.

Should you sweeten iced tea? Unless you can't, I think you should. Much like salt, sugar rounds out flavor and brings the tea alive. Even for "unsweetened" tea, I recommend a tablespoon of sugar per quart. For lightly sweetened tea, figure two tablespoons per quart, and for sweet tea allow three tablespoons per quart. (Many Southerners, I know, will not be satisfied with anything less than one-quarter cup per quart).

In addition to sweetening the tea with sugar, I tried regular honey, dry honey, and natural cane sugar. No surprise. The taste of honey was too distinct, taking away from the great tea flavor I had worked so hard to get. Like regular honey, Honey Sweet (a mix of dry honey, fructose, and maltodextrin) also contributed too much flavor, though more of fruit than honey.

The surprise for me was the natural cane sugar. Before tasting it, I would have bet it didn't matter. The tea sweetened with regular sugar tasted "off" with a quick sweet hit and a hollow finish. By comparison, the natural cane sugar tea had a pure sweet flavor that enveloped my mouth and lingered. I am reminded once again that when making a simple concoction such as iced tea, little things matter.

I used to like to junk up my tea with a lot of extras. Now I know why—to mask the bitterness. With my new brewing methods, however, I found these flavors very easily overwhelmed the tea. To subtly incorporate them, I turned to the old mint julep technique, bruising a small number of mint leaves or coins of fresh ginger with a wooden spoon or the broad side of a chef's knife, respectively. This action releases fresh oils, which when steeped with the tea bags add fresh yet subtle flavor.

QUICK, SIMPLE, FULL–FLAVORED ICED TEA
MAKES 1 1/2 QUARTS, SERVING 4 TO 6

Depending on the quality of your tap water, you may want to use bottled spring water to make both the tea itself and your ice cubes. Doubling this recipe is easy, but use a large saucepan and expect the water to take a few minutes longer to reach the proper temperature. For a slightly stronger iced tea, reduce the amount of ice to 3 cups. Garnish with a thin lemon wedge to squeeze into the tea, if you like.

- 5   tea bags of your choice
- 1   quart spring water (*see* note above)
- 1 to 6 tablespoons sugar, natural cane or regular granulated (depending on desired sweetness)
- 1   quart ice (*see* note above), plus additional cubes for glasses

Heat tea bags and water in medium nonreactive saucepan over medium heat until dark colored, very steamy, and small bubbles form on bottom and sides of pan (an instant-read thermometer will register about 190 degrees), 10 to 15 minutes. Off heat, steep for 3 minutes (no longer or tea may become bitter). Remove and discard tea bags; pour tea into pitcher. Stir in sugar, if using, until dissolved; stir in ice until melted. Serve in ice-filled glasses.

TECHNIQUE
EASY TEA BAG REMOVAL

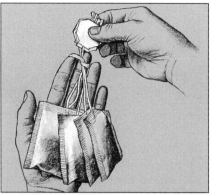

To solve the problem of how to remove tea bags from the tea when it is finished, simply tie their strings together as shown before making the tea.

MICROWAVE ICED TEA

Using a 2-quart Pyrex measuring cup makes this tea a one-pot drink from brewing to pouring. Exact heating time will depend on the power of your microwave and the starting temperature of the water.

Follow recipe for Quick, Simple, Full-Flavored Iced Tea, heating tea bags and water in 2-quart Pyrex measuring cup or other large microwave-safe bowl covered with microwave-safe dinner plate, on high power until dark colored, very steamy, and water starts to move but not boil (an instant-read thermometer will register about 190 degrees), 8 to 10 minutes. Remove from microwave and steep 3 minutes (no longer or the tea may become bitter). Remove plate; remove and discard tea bags. Stir in sugar, if using, until dissolved; stir in ice until melted. Serve in ice-filled glasses.

MINTED ICED TEA

Follow recipe for either Quick, Simple, Full-Flavored Iced Tea or Microwave Iced Tea, heating and steeping 1/4 cup fresh mint leaves, bruised with a wooden spoon, along with tea bags and water. When steeping is complete, remove tea bags and strain tea through fine-mesh sieve to remove mint.

GINGERED ICED TEA

Follow recipe for either Quick, Simple, Full-Flavored Iced Tea or Microwave Iced Tea, heating and steeping 1-inch piece fresh ginger, sliced into thin coins and smashed with broad side of large chef's knife, along with tea bags and water. When steeping is complete, remove tea bags and strain tea through fine-mesh sieve to remove ginger.

Equipment: Machine Tea

In addition to standard brewing, I tested two devices that are specifically designed for brewing tea.

I was particularly skeptical of Details The 3-Quart Iced Tea Pot by Mr. Coffee, a culinary white elephant in my mind. Much like a drip coffee maker, this device heats up water and directs it into a steeping basket—in this case, one filled with tea bags. The hot tea drips into a pitcher of ice, resulting in cold tea. I was surprised to find that it made a very decent glass of iced tea. If I hadn't found a better way, this appliance might have gotten my vote.

A more elaborate and expensive unit (about $100 retail), TeaMate Electric Tea Maker by Chef'sChoice International, is designed for brewing hot tea, although it works for iced tea, too. The operating principle is similar to the Mr. Coffee teapot except that while the water is heating, the glass carafe is warming and tea leaves (or bags) are steaming. A portion of the subboiling water steeps the leaves to make a concentrate that combines with the remaining hot water and flows into the carafe. The machine makes a flawless cup of hot tea and a perfect glass of iced tea. If you're a steady tea drinker, it might be worth a look.   – P.A.

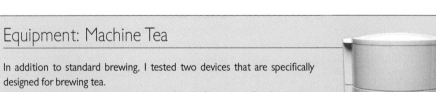

Chef'sChoice International
TeaMate Electric Tea Maker

How to Grill Chicken Wings

The problem with chicken wings is their thick, rubbery skin. Here's how to make crisp wings with moist meat and smoky flavor.

≥ BY ANNE YAMANAKA AND BRIDGET LANCASTER ≤

Let's face it. Chicken wings are usually enjoyed as restaurant food. While we have no problem ordering these tasty bites while dining out, at home chicken wings end up at best as a base for a good stock and at worst in the trash bin. But chicken wings are flavorful, inexpensive, and great for casual summer entertaining, especially when cooked on the grill. Cook these wings incorrectly, though, and you have greasy meat surrounded by a charred, rubbery, thick coating of skin that is hardly appealing. We wanted to develop a foolproof grilling technique that ensured a great wing experience at home—a recipe that would produce crisp, thin, caramelized skin, tender and moist meat, and a smoky grilled flavor that was well-seasoned throughout. We also wanted our chicken wings to be eater-friendly without being tedious or time-consuming for the cook.

Preparing the Wings

Our journey began on the cutting board. Wings are made up of three parts: the meaty, drumstick-like portion that is closest to the breast section of the bird; the two-boned center portion that is surrounded by a band of meat and skin; and the small, almost meatless wingtip. After cutting and grilling wings several different ways, we concluded that wingtips are not worth the effort. They contribute almost no meat and get charred well before the other two parts are even close to being cooked through.

Wingtips discarded, we pushed the meat up the bones of the separated meatier parts to replicate the lollipop-shaped wings favored by traditional chefs. But this took too much time and effort for casual summer fare. So we decided that the best method would be to separate the two usable portions of the wings at the joint and discard the wingtips. The resulting pieces are small enough to be eaten as finger food and are much less awkward to get a hold on than a whole wing. Best of all, you don't have to spend a whole lot of time in the kitchen.

Firing Up the Grill

Our first round of grilling tests was disappointing. Grilling the wings directly over the coals at temperatures ranging from high heat to low heat produced wings that were mediocre at best. Those cooked over medium-high and high heat charred quickly, and the skin remained thick and tough. Grilling the wings over medium and medium-low heat produced better wings; the skin was crisper and thinner. But the wings still lacked the great-tasting caramelized crust that we were after.

It was at this point that we tried the indirect heat method, that is, building a fire on one half of the grill, placing the meat on the opposite side, then covering until cooked through. The result was a very moist interior, but the meat had an off flavor that most tasters identified as "chemical." In addition, the skin was flaccid and had a very unappealing grayish tint.

Compiling our information from these initial tests, we concluded that a more sophisticated grilling technique was necessary; perhaps even a second method of cooking was in order. We tried blanching the wings for various amounts of time before throwing them on the grill for crisping and browning, but this technique, while producing thinner, crisper skin, also yielded wings with less flavor and drier meat. Blanching was also time-consuming and added extra clean-up.

So far, the best wings were those cooked directly over the coals at a medium-low heat level (a single layer of charcoal). Although they were

TECHNIQUE

BUILDING A TWO-LEVEL FIRE

To build a two-level fire, spread hot coals in a single layer over the entire grill. Then pile up unlit coals on half of the grill, adding enough to reach within two or three inches from the grill grate.

acceptable, we felt that the texture and flavor would be greatly improved with a crisper, darker exterior. At this point we decided to try what had worked in the *Cook's* approach to several other grilled dishes: a two-level fire. We grilled the chicken wings using two different methods. One batch was browned over medium-high heat and then moved to the other side of the grill to continue cooking slowly, while the other was started on medium-low to cook slow and then moved to medium-high heat to get a final quick crisping and browning. While both batches were good, the one cooked first over medium-low heat and then moved to medium-high heat was superior. More fat was rendered from the skin with this cooking method, and the result was a thin, delicate crust.

A Well-Seasoned Wing

Now we were close to the wings we had envisioned, but one thing was missing—perfect seasoning. The wings we had been testing were simply sprinkled with salt and pepper before grilling. They were tasty, but since most of the salt and pepper was lost through the grill grate as the fat rendered from the skin of the wings, we wanted to find a way to season the interior meat, not just the surrounding skin.

Prompted by past experience, we thought that brining might improve the flavor as well as the texture of our chicken wings. We used a brining solution from John Willoughby and Chris Schlesinger's article in *Cook's Illustrated* from July/August 1996, "Grilling Chicken Legs and Thighs," in which equal parts by volume of sugar and kosher salt are added to water.

Tasting the wings as they came hot off of the grill, we happily discovered that the brined chicken wings were not only tasty and well-seasoned throughout but that the brining process also added several unexpected bonuses. The brined chicken meat was noticeably plumper before grilling and more tender after cooking, and it also developed a crisper, more caramelized skin. Brining took our wings to a higher level altogether.

At last we had the wings of our dreams... smoky from the grill, tender, well-seasoned, and, most important of all, blessed with crispy, deep brown skin. In fact, they were better than any restaurant wings.

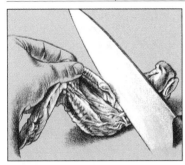  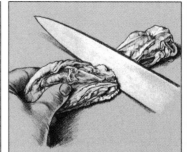 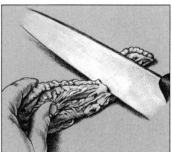

1. With a chef's knife, cut into the skin between the two larger sections of the wings until you hit the joint.

2. Bend back the two sections to pop and break the joint.

3. Cut through the skin and flesh to completely separate the two meaty portions.

4. Hack off the wingtip and discard.

CHARCOAL-GRILLED CHICKEN WINGS
MAKES 24 WING PIECES, SERVING 4 TO 6

Use a grill that is large enough to hold all the wings over roughly one-half of the rack surface. Brine the wings while the grill fire heats up to save time. Serve the wings as is, with a squeeze of lemon or lime, or with one of the sauce recipes that follow.

- ¾ cup kosher salt (or 6 tablespoons table salt)
- ¾ cup sugar
- 12 whole chicken wings (about 2½ pounds), separated into sections following illustrations 1 to 4 above, wingtips discarded
  Ground black pepper

1. In gallon-sized zipper-lock plastic bag, dissolve salt and sugar in 1 quart water. Add chicken; press out as much air as possible from bag and seal; refrigerate until fully seasoned, 30 minutes. Remove from brine, rinse well under running water, dry thoroughly with paper towels, and season with pepper.

2. Meanwhile, build two-level fire in grill by igniting 1 large chimney (or about 6 quarts) of charcoal briquettes; burn until completely covered with thin coating of light-gray ash. Empty coals into grill and spread in even layer over bottom; place another three-quarters chimney full (or scant 4 quarts) of fresh briquettes over one-half of lit coals (pile should come to within about 2½ inches of grill rack). (If using hardwood charcoal, ignite about 10 quarts of charcoal and, once it is completely covered with gray ash, use fireplace tool to push about ¾ of it to one side of grill.) Position grill rack over coals; heat until very hot, about 10 minutes.

3. Grill chicken pieces over lower-heat area (with single layer of coals), turning once, until color is light spotty brown, skin has thinned, and fat has rendered, 8 to 10 minutes. Using tongs, move chicken pieces to high-heat side of grill; grill, turning constantly to prevent charring, until wings are dark spotty brown and skin has crisped, 2 to 3 minutes longer. Transfer to serving platter and serve immediately, with one of the dipping sauces below, if desired.

GAS-GRILLED CHICKEN WINGS

We prefer grilling over charcoal for the smoky flavor it imparts. But a gas grill is easy to use, and it yields a flavor that's almost as good.

Follow step 1 in recipe for Charcoal-Grilled Chicken Wings. Turn all burners on grill to high, close lid, and heat grill until hot, 10 to 15 minutes. Adjust one burner to medium and grill chicken pieces over it, turning once, until color is light spotty brown, skin has thinned, and fat has rendered, 15 to 20 minutes. Using tongs, move chicken pieces over burner still set on high, turning constantly to prevent charring, until wings are dark spotty brown and skin has crisped, 5 to 7 minutes longer.

BASIC BARBECUE SAUCE
MAKES 3 CUPS

This is one of our favorite barbecue sauces, published originally in John Willoughby and Chris Schlesinger's story "How to Grill Bone-in Chicken Breasts" (see July/August 1997, page 15). Extra sauce can be refrigerated in an airtight container for up to two weeks, or frozen.

- 2 tablespoons vegetable oil
- 1 medium onion, minced
- 1 can (8 ounces) tomato sauce
- 1 can (28 ounces) whole tomatoes with juice
- ¾ cup distilled white vinegar
- ¼ cup packed dark brown sugar
- 2 tablespoons molasses
- 1 tablespoon paprika
- 1 tablespoon chili powder
- 1 teaspoon salt
- 2 teaspoons ground black pepper
- ¼ cup juice from 1 medium orange

1. Heat oil in large heavy-bottomed saucepan over medium heat until hot and shimmering (but not smoking). Add onion; sauté until golden brown, 7–10 minutes, stirring frequently. Add remaining ingredients. Bring to boil, reduce heat to low, and simmer, uncovered, until thickened, 2 to 2½ hours.

2. Puree sauce, in batches if necessary, in blender or workbowl of food processor. Transfer to bowl or cover in airtight container.

HOISIN-SESAME DIPPING SAUCE
MAKES ABOUT ½ CUP

- 2 tablespoons hoisin sauce
- 1 tablespoon rice wine vinegar
- 1 teaspoon sesame oil
- 1 tablespoon soy sauce
- 1 tablespoon vegetable oil
- 1 2-inch piece fresh ginger, minced (about 2 tablespoons)
- 2 medium garlic cloves, minced
- 2 tablespoons chopped fresh cilantro leaves

Mix hoisin sauce, rice vinegar, sesame oil, soy sauce, and 2 tablespoons water in small bowl; set aside. Heat vegetable oil in small saucepan over medium heat; sauté ginger and garlic until fragrant but not browned, about 30 seconds. Stir in hoisin mixture; cook until flavors meld, about 2 to 3 minutes. Off heat, stir in cilantro. Serve warm or at room temperature.

SPICY PEANUT DIPPING SAUCE
MAKES ABOUT ¾ CUP

- 5 tablespoons creamy peanut butter
- 2 teaspoons Asian fish sauce
- 2 tablespoons juice from 1 lime
- ¼ cup unsweetened coconut milk
- 1 tablespoon honey
- 1 1-inch piece fresh ginger, minced (about 1 tablespoon)
- 2 medium garlic cloves, minced
- ½ teaspoon red pepper flakes
- 1 teaspoon curry powder (optional)

Combine all ingredients in jar of electric blender; blend until smooth.

How to Grill Flank Steak

Several tenets of common wisdom about this flavorful steak were tried and found true, but one holds no water.

⇒ BY JOHN WILLOUGHBY ⇐

Thanks to fajitas, flank steak has become the darling of Tex-Mex fans from New York to California and everywhere in between. Also jumping on the flank steak bandwagon are the many lovers of "London broil." While this is actually a recipe rather than a cut of meat, many cooks think of it as synonymous with flank.

But there are good reasons for the popularity of flank steak in addition to mere culinary fashion. Like other steaks cut from the chest and side of the cow (*see* "Three Flat Steaks," page 15), flank has rich, full, beefy flavor. Also, because it is very thin, it cooks quite quickly. This makes it an ideal candidate for grilling.

Although this is a pretty straightforward proposition, I still had some questions about what was exactly the best way to go about it. The questions were whether the meat should be marinated, how hot the fire should be, and how long the meat should be cooked. I also wanted to check out my favorite technique for grilling, rubbing the food with spices before putting it on the fire.

Virtually every recipe I found for flank steak called for marinating. Most experts ballyhooed this as a way to tenderize the meat as well as add flavor. I am not generally a fan of marinating, and Jack Bishop's findings in "Do Marinades Work?" (*see Cook's,* July/August 1993) made me even less enthusiastic. But since it is so universal a recommendation I decided to check it out.

I made an acid-based marinade and marinated strips of flank steak for 24 hours, 12 hours, 6 hours, 3 hours, 1 hour, and 30 minutes, respectively. Just for good measure, I also followed the method that Rick Bayless uses for skirt steak fajitas in *Authentic Mexican* (Morrow, 1989), simply brushing the steak with lime juice right before cooking it.

The results were just as I expected. The steak marinated for 24 hours was not only gray and mushy on the outside but actually had a slimy texture. The steak marinated for 12 hours was slightly slimy, while the rest seemed basically unchanged in texture but had taken on various shades of dark purplish gray on the outside. As for tenderness,

For tender meat, it is crucial that you slice this steak very thin, against the grain and on the bias.

when the cooked steaks were sliced thin against the grain there was virtually no difference.

While marinating had little effect on the meat's texture, it did affect the flavor somewhat. The pieces of meat that had been marinated for 24 hours and for 12 hours had a more distinct taste of lime and garlic than the others. The difference, however, was relatively minor. In fact, in the first round of testing my favorite was the steak just brushed with juice before cooking. To my mind, therefore, the small difference in flavor did not make it worth dealing with the real issue around marinating: remembering to put the steak in the marinade hours ahead of cooking time. Since I seldom plan a meal that far in advance, this was not a practical approach for me; I was not disappointed to find it superfluous.

With that precept verified, I turned to what I considered a much more promising method of enhancing flavor: using spice rubs, which produce a flavorful crust on the outside of the steak.

Just to be fair, I rubbed one steak with spice rub 8 hours before cooking it, one an hour before cooking it, and one just before I put it over the flames. A fourth steak was cooked exactly like the others, but with no spice rub at all. Again, the results were not unexpected. The three spice-

rubbed steaks all had about the same amount of flavor, and all developed almost identical dark brown, very flavorful crusts. The plain steak did not develop nearly as nice a crust, but cooked in approximately the same amount of time. I noticed no differences in tenderness among the steaks.

Since spice rubs create an excellent crust with plenty of intense flavor, they are my first choice for flank steaks. However, they are not good for folks who like their steak medium, because if you leave the steak on long enough to get it that done, the spices burn. You even have to be a bit careful to keep them from burning if you like your steak medium-rare. But if you don't mind exercising that small degree of care, spice rubs are great.

Everyone is in the same camp on one aspect of cooking flank steak, and it is the right camp: These are steaks that should be cooked over high heat for a short period of time. I tried lower heat and longer times, but inevitably the meat ended up being tough.

Because flank steak is too thin for you to check its temperature with a meat thermometer, you need to resort to the most primitive (but ultimately the most effective) method of checking for doneness: Cut into the meat and see if it is done to your liking. Remember that carryover heat will continue to cook the steak after it comes off the grill. So if you want the steak medium-rare, take it off the heat when it looks rare, and so on. (Because cooking flank steak beyond medium-rare toughens it, I advise against it. In fact, I would say that if you like your meat more than medium, you might want to consider choosing another cut.)

A final but very important step with flank steak, as with all red meats, is allowing it to rest after it comes off the heat. In his book *On Food and Cooking* (Macmillan, 1984), food scientist Harold McGee explains why this is necessary. As the proteins in meat heat up during cooking they coagulate, which basically means they uncoil and bond with each other. When the proteins coagulate, they squeeze out part of the liquid that was trapped in their coiled structures and in the spaces between the individual molecules. The heat from the cooking source drives these freed liquids toward the center of the meat.

This process of coagulation explains why experienced chefs can tell how done a piece of meat is by pushing on it and judging the amount of resistance: the firmer the meat, the more done it

Three Flat Steaks

Like flank steak, the other two cuts most similar to it—skirt steak and hanger steak—have also recently undergone a transformation from neglected to fashionable.

These three recently popular steaks share the distinction of coming from the chest and side of the animal. Hanger and flank both come from the rear side, while skirt comes from the area between the abdomen and the chest cavity (*see* diagram, right). In addition to location, these steaks share certain other basic qualities: all are long, relatively thin, quite tough, and grainy, but with rich, deep, beefy flavor.

Of course, there are also differences between these flavorful steaks. Hanger, a thick muscle that is attached to the diaphragm, derives its name from the fact that when a cow is butchered, this steak hangs down into the center of the carcass. Because it is a classic French bistro dish, this cut is highly prized by restaurants and therefore difficult to find in butcher shops. To my mind this is no great loss, however, since the hangers that I sampled had the toughest texture and least rich, beefy flavor of these three cuts.

Fortunately, flank steak is quite easy to find in any butcher shop or supermarket. Easily recognizable by its longitudinal grain, flank has great beef flavor and is

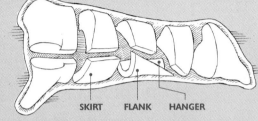

SKIRT   FLANK   HANGER

quite tender if cooked to rare or medium-rare and sliced thin against the grain. Unfortunately, largely because of the popularity of fajitas and "London broil," flank has become a relatively expensive cut, running about $5 a pound in local markets.

The skirt steak, which was the cut originally used in fajitas, can also be hard to locate in supermarkets or butcher shops. This is a real pity, because the skirt steak is a beefeater's dream come true. It has more fat than the hanger or flank, which makes it juicier and richer; at the same time, it also has a deep, full, beefy flavor that outdoes either the flank or the hanger. If you can get your hands on a skirt steak, by all means do so. You will not be sorry. —J.W.

---

is. But the coagulation process is apparently at least somewhat reversible, so as you allow the meat to rest and return to a lower temperature after cooking, some of the liquid is redistributed and reabsorbed by the protein molecules as their capacity to hold moisture increases. As a result, less juice will run out when you cut into the meat, which in turn makes for much juicier and more tender meat.

This is common wisdom among cooks, but to be sure it was correct I cooked two more flank steaks, sliced one up immediately after it came off the fire, and allowed the second to rest for 10 minutes before slicing it. Not only did the first steak exude almost 40 percent more juice when sliced as the second, it also looked grayer and was not as tender. So in this case, it is crucial to follow conventional wisdom: Give your steak a rest.

CHARCOAL-GRILLED FLANK STEAK
SERVES 4 TO 6

Flank steak is best when cooked rare, or medium-rare at most. It is also very important for the meat to rest after it comes off the grill.

- 1   flank steak (about 2½ pounds)
  Salt and ground black pepper

1. Ignite about 7 quarts charcoal and burn until coals are completely covered with thin coating of light-gray ash, 20 to 30 minutes. Pile coals on one-half of grill bottom, position grill rack and heat until very hot (you can hold your hand 5 inches above grill surface for 2 seconds).

2. Generously sprinkle both sides of steak with salt and pepper; place directly over coals and grill until well-seared and dark brown on first side, 5 to 7 minutes. Flip steak using tongs; continue grilling on second side until interior of meat is slightly less done than you want it to be when you eat it, 2 to 5 minutes more for medium-rare (depending on heat of fire and thickness of steak). Transfer meat to cutting board; cover loosely with foil, and let rest 5 to 10 minutes. Slice very thin, on bias against the grain; adjust seasoning with additional salt and pepper and serve immediately.

GAS-GRILLED FLANK STEAK

Turn all burners on gas grill to high, close lid, and heat grill until hot, 10 to 15 minutes. Follow step 2 of Charcoal-Grilled Flank Steak, grilling steak covered for 4 to 6 minutes on first side and 3 to 5 minutes on second side.

LATIN SPICE–RUBBED GRILLED FLANK STEAK

Mix 2 tablespoons each ground cumin and chili powder, 1 tablespoon each ground coriander and kosher salt (or 1½ teaspoons table salt), 2 teaspoons ground black pepper, and ½ teaspoon each ground cinnamon and hot red pepper flakes in small bowl. Follow recipe for either Charcoal-Grilled or Gas-Grilled Flank Steak, rubbing steak all over with spice mixture before cooking and watching meat carefully to ensure that spice rub darkens but does not burn.

CLASSIC FAJITAS
SERVES 8

Although it was originally made with skirt steak, this combination of steak and vegetables grilled and then wrapped in warm tortillas is the dish that put flank steak on the culinary map in the United States. The ingredients go on the grill in order as the fire dies down: steak over a hot fire, vegetables over a medium fire, and tortillas around the edge of the medium to low fire just to warm them. *See* "Easy Summer Salsas," July/August 1996, page 21, and "Authentic Guacamole," May/June 1999, page 20, for Classic Red Table Salsa and Chunky Guacamole recipes.

- 1   flank steak (about 2½ pounds)
- ¼   cup juice from 2 medium limes
  Salt and ground black pepper
- 1   very large onion, peeled and cut into half-inch slices
- 2   very large red or green bell peppers, cored, seeded, and cut into large wedges
- 16   10-inch flour tortillas
- 1   recipe Classic Red Table Salsa (*see* note above)
- 1   recipe Chunky Guacamole (*see* note above)

1. Follow master recipe for either Charcoal-Grilled or Gas-Grilled Flank Steak, sprinkling steak with lime juice along with salt and pepper.

2. When charcoal fire has died down to medium or gas grill burners are adjusted to medium (you can hold your hand 5 inches above grill surface for 4 seconds), grill onions and peppers, turning occasionally, until onions are lightly charred, about 6 minutes, and peppers are streaked with dark grill marks, about 10 minutes. Remove onions and peppers from grill and cut peppers into long, thin strips; set aside. Arrange tortillas around edge of grill; heat until just warmed, about 20 seconds per side. (Do not dry out tortillas or they get brittle; wrap tortillas in towel to keep warm.) Remove to platter; set aside.

3. To serve fajitas: Arrange sliced meat and vegetables on large platter; serve immediately, with tortillas, salsa, and guacamole passed separately.

SCIENCE | MUSCLE STRUCTURE

Flank steak is a long, flat piece of meat with a very pronounced, distinctive longitudinal grain.

Tomato Basics

Many dishes are much better made with peeled and seeded tomatoes.
These step-by-step instructions show you the easiest way to accomplish both tasks,
as well as how to dice tomatoes both roughly and precisely.

Imagine slicing a perfect summer tomato. You wouldn't dream of sacrificing the sweet band of skin encircling the flesh or of forfeiting the pleasure of one of the slippery little bundles of seeds that elude your fork to the very end. A cherry tomato salsa without skins or seeds? Why bother? Likewise, there is no cause to peel tomatoes destined to be stuffed and baked, since the skin provides needed structure. Nor do you need to peel tomatoes when you are cooking a sauce or soup that you intend to puree or sieve later.

But there are plenty of situations in which you do need to peel and/or seed tomatoes. To confirm this, we made two tomato sauces with diced tomatoes, one in which the tomatoes had been peeled and seeded, and the other in which they had been diced as is. In the "as is" sauce, the skins separated from the tomatoes and curled up into sinewy little scrolls that were unpleasant in terms of both flavor and texture. The seeds, which are quite bitter, trailed off into the sauce unnecessary and unwanted. Removing the skins and seeds prepares the way for simple and delicious sauces as well as for dicing and julilenning tomatoes destined for garnishing.

By following the steps below, you can accomplish these culinary tasks in the easiest and most efficient way. A sharp serrated paring knife makes short work of coring and seeding. For chopping or dicing use a sharp 8- or 10-inch chef's knife in a rocking motion.

CORING

Tomatoes are almost always cored. That is, the tough stem end is removed and discarded. We suggest coring before peeling, as peeled tomatoes are more difficult to handle. Coring also provides a practical point of departure when it's time to peel.

PEELING

We found that peeling tomatoes is easiest after a quick blanch, even for small jobs. A vegetable peeler—especially a dull one—can be slow and cumbersome and tends to mangle soft, ripe fruit. Holding an individual tomato over a burner gets the job done, but the potential for damage to the tomato flesh is greater. A quick dip in boiling water followed by a plunge in ice water does just what it should: it loosens the skin without allowing the heat to reach the flesh of the tomato.

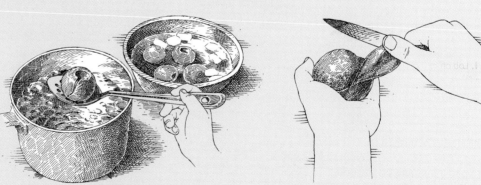

Place the tomato on its side on the work surface. Holding the tomato stable with one hand, insert the tip of a paring knife about 1 inch into the tomato at an angle just outside of the core. Use the paring knife with a sawing motion, at the same time rotating the tomato toward you until the core is cut free.

1. Place cored tomatoes in boiling water, no more than five at a time. Boil until skins split and begin to curl around the cored area of the tomato, about 15 seconds for very ripe tomatoes or up to 30 seconds for firmer, underripe ones. Remove tomatoes from water with a slotted spoon or mesh skimmer and place in a bowl of ice water until cool enough to handle.

2. With a paring knife, peel the skins away using the curled edges at the core as your point of departure. (The bowl of ice water fulfills a helpful second function—the skins will slide right off the blade of the knife if you dip the blade into the water.)

Illustration: John Burgoyne

CHOPPING WHOLE UNSEEDED TOMATOES

Whether peeled or unpeeled, whole (and therefore necessarily unseeded) tomatoes can be chopped following these steps. The shape of the resulting tomato pieces will be irregular, but that's fine for uses in which precision and uniformity are not important.

Whole round tomatoes

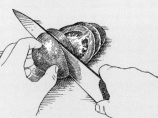

1. Place the tomato cored side down on a cutting board and cut into slices of desired thickness.

2. Set aside the end pieces. Stack the slices in pairs of two and cut into strips.

3. Turn strips one-quarter turn and cut them crosswise into cubes.

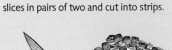

4. Place the end pieces skin side down and cut into strips; make one-quarter turn and cut crosswise into rough cubes.

Whole plum tomatoes

1. Lob off one of the long sides to make a flat side.

2. Place the tomato cut side down and slice lengthwise into slices of desired thickness. To chop, follow steps 2–4 for whole round tomatoes, above.

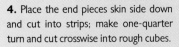

SEEDING

Seeding rids tomatoes of excess liquid and bitter seeds. This technique works for both peeled and unpeeled tomatoes.

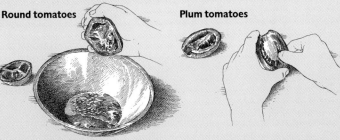

Round tomatoes   **Plum tomatoes**

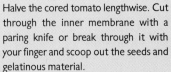

Halve the cored tomato along the equator. If it is ripe and juicy, gently give it a squeeze and shake out the seeds and gelatinous material. If not, scoop them out with your finger or a small spoon.

Halve the cored tomato lengthwise. Cut through the inner membrane with a paring knife or break through it with your finger and scoop out the seeds and gelatinous material.

CHOPPING SEEDED TOMATOES

Seeded tomatoes can be chopped into much more evenly sized pieces than unseeded tomatoes. Use this technique when having pieces of a relatively regular size is important.

Round tomatoes

1. Lay a tomato half cut side down on the cutting board. Steady the top of the tomato with one hand and, with a chef's knife held parallel to the work surface, slice into the lower portion of the tomato half using a wide sawing motion.

2. Slide the uncut portion of the tomato off the bottom slice. Repeat until all desired slices are made. To chop, follow steps 2 through 4 for whole round tomatoes, above left.

Plum tomatoes

Lay a tomato half cut side down on the cutting board. Slice lengthwise into strips of desired width. To chop, follow step 3 in the instructions for whole round tomatoes, above left.

PERFECT-DICING TOMATOES

Cutting tomatoes into perfect dice involves a bit more waste—tomatoes are, after all, round fruit. Perfectly diced tomatoes are ideal for garnish, and you can save the scraps for soups or stocks. This technique works for both peeled and unpeeled round and plum tomatoes.

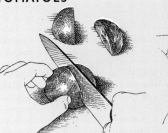

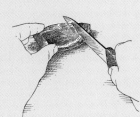

1. Cut the cored tomato into quarters.

2. Use a paring knife to remove the inner flesh, pulp, and seeds.

3. Trim ¼ to ½ inch off the top and bottom of each quarter to form roughly even rectangles.

4. Cut into even strips. Follow step 3 for whole round tomatoes, above left, to chop.

Classic Three-Bean Salad Updated

Can this recipe from the '50s be improved with modern ingredients and techniques? The answer is yes, and no.

≥ BY BARBARA BOURASSA WITH DAWN YANAGIHARA ≤

I grew up with my mom's three-bean salad: a sweet, vinegary dressing mixed with canned green, yellow, and kidney beans and a bite of red onion. Her trick, she said, was to cook the vinegar, sugar, and oil together. I never thought much about that trick until I tried to develop my own version of three-bean salad, and then I discovered she was really onto something.

When I began researching the origins of this picnic standby, I discovered that most of the recipes for it have remained essentially unchanged since the 1950s. Given the evolution of the ingredients and cooking techniques used over the last 50 years, I wondered if this classic salad could benefit from some updating.

My goal was a fresh taste (something other than canned beans came to mind), dressed with a light, sweet, and tangy dressing that united the subtle flavors of the beans without overpowering them. To that end, my testing divided itself into three categories: improving the flavor and the texture of the beans; determining the right mix of vinegar and oils for the marinade; and addressing the question of sweetness, which was handled differently in almost every recipe I looked at. (Although I did find a few recipes that did not include a sweetener, sugar in one form or another seemed to differentiate three-bean salad from a simple oil and vinegar vegetable salad.)

I decided to first test boiling, blanching, and steaming the green and the yellow beans. Not surprisingly, the less time the beans are cooked, the better they stand up in the dressing. My 10- and 20-minute boiled beans were soft and flavorless, but those blanched for one and two minutes each weren't cooked enough. I eventually settled on boiling the beans for five minutes. This was long enough to remove their waxy exterior and thereby allow the marinade to penetrate, but not long enough to break down their cell structure and make them mushy. After draining the beans, I plunged them into cold water to stop the cooking. My steamed beans held up fairly well, but they didn't have the crunch of the boiled and shocked beans.

Next I moved on to the kidney beans. None of the recipes recommended cooking dried beans—they all called for canned. Just to be sure, I cooked up two batches of beans, then marinated them overnight. Not only were the canned beans a lot easier to use, but they tasted just as good.

With the beans ready for dressing, I moved on to the marinade. As with many of the recipes I found, my mom's recipe was vague: it didn't tell you what type of vinegar to use, or what type of oil. After testing eight oil varieties and seven types of vinegar, I found that I preferred canola oil for its mild flavor and red wine vinegar for its tang.

When I was ready to test types of sugar, I went back to Mom's recipe. It was at this point that I discovered the key to dramatically improving the flavor of the dressing. I tried cooking vinegar mixed with brown sugar, with honey, and with white sugar over medium heat. The white sugar version won hands down: the cooking process created a syrup with its own unique flavor—sweet and tangy at the same time. It turns out that Mom's instincts on heating the ingredients were right on the mark. Heat, as well as the type of sugar used, make all the difference between a so-so marinade and a tasty one.

On doing some investigating, I found out that the heating process causes several different chemical reactions that alter the flavor of the dressing. For starters, the heated mixture is actually chemically sweeter, according to Diane A. Dooley, associate professor of food science and human nutrition at the University of Hawaii at Manoa. Table sugar is sucrose, or a chemical combination of two simpler sugars, glucose and fructose. When you heat table sugar in an acid (such as vinegar), some of the bonds between the two sugars are broken, resulting in free fructose and free glucose. Because free fructose is about 30 percent sweeter than sucrose, the resulting mixture is sweeter, too.

"Adding heat is like adding a new substance to the mixture," says Stanley Segall, professor of food science and nutrition at Drexel University in Philadelphia. "The heat changes the chemical makeup of the mixture, creating products that didn't exist before, and these products add flavor." This change is known as the Maillard reaction, named after its French discoverer. In addition, the chemical change of the sugar that takes place during heating adds flavor, Segall says. Although these reactions would take place on their own given enough time, cooking the dressing before pouring it over the beans gives you more flavor upfront, which the beans in turn absorb as they marinate.

CLASSIC THREE-BEAN SALAD
SERVES 8 TO 10

- 1 cup red wine vinegar
- ¾ cup sugar
- ½ cup canola oil
- 2 medium garlic cloves, minced
- 1 teaspoon salt
  Ground black pepper
- 8 ounces green beans, cut into 1-inch-long pieces
- 8 ounces yellow wax beans, cut into 1-inch-long pieces
- 1 15.5-ounce can red kidney beans, rinsed and drained
- ½ medium red onion, chopped medium
- ¼ cup minced fresh parsley leaves

1. Heat vinegar, sugar, oil, garlic, salt, and pepper to taste in small nonreactive saucepan over medium heat, stirring occasionally, until sugar dissolves, about 5 minutes. Transfer to a large nonreactive bowl and cool to room temperature.

2. Bring 3 quarts water to boil in large saucepan over high heat. Add 1 tablespoon salt and green and yellow beans; cook until crisp-tender, about 5 minutes. Meanwhile, fill medium bowl with ice water. When beans are done, drain and immediately plunge into ice water to stop cooking process; let sit until chilled, about 2 minutes. Drain well.

3. Add green and yellow beans, kidney beans, onion, and parsley to vinegar mixture; toss well to coat. Cover and refrigerate overnight to let flavors meld. Let stand at room temperature 30 minutes before serving. (Salad can be covered and refrigerated up to 4 days.)

THREE-BEAN SALAD WITH CUMIN, CILANTRO, AND ORANGES

Separate two medium oranges into segments, remove membrane from sides of each segment, then cut each segment in half lengthwise. Set aside. Follow recipe for Classic Three-Bean Salad, substituting ¼ cup lime juice for ¼ cup red wine vinegar, and heating 1 teaspoon ground cumin with vinegar mixture. Substitute minced fresh cilantro leaves for parsley and add halved orange segments to vinegar mixture along with beans.

Italian-Style Tomato Pasta Salads

Raw tomato sauce is a refreshing alternative to traditional dressings for pasta salad—but is it necessary to peel and seed the tomatoes? and what about marinating?

≥ BY JACK BISHOP ≤

Pasta salad is a purely American invention. Most Italians would never dream of eating chilled pasta. Of course, the fact that Italians may scoff at the notion is no reason not to enjoy a good pasta salad, especially one dressed with a light vinaigrette rather than leaden mayonnaise. (For more information, *see* "Pasta Salad Made Right," July/August 1998).

While Italians may not understand the concept of pasta salad, they don't always eat pasta piping hot, either. In the summer, they often toss pasta with a raw tomato sauce and cool the dish to room temperature. This "salad" can be taken on picnics, served at barbecues, or eaten on a sultry night when the thought of hot food is unappetizing. I've eaten these salads dozens of times while living and traveling in Italy. They are usually quite good, but I have encountered a recurring problem, which is that the raw tomatoes often make a rather watery sauce.

With this issue in mind, I formulated a list of questions to answer in my testing. Do the tomatoes need to be peeled and/or seeded? Should they be salted? Is there a way to add some garlic without overwhelming everything else? Should the ingredients be marinated for a while? Working with a classic recipe of chopped tomatoes, olive oil, basil, a little raw garlic, salt, and pepper, I began to make some observations.

When I use fresh tomatoes in a cooked sauce, I prefer to peel them. The tiny bits of skin separate from the tomato flesh and are not terribly appealing in terms of flavor or texture. But when preparing pasta salads by tossing raw tomato sauce with hot pasta, I noticed that while the heat did soften the tomatoes slightly, make their texture more appealing, and bring out their flavor, the skins were still firmly attached to each tomato cube. Therefore, I see no need to remove the skin.

The seeds are another matter. The tiny seeds are bitter (try tasting them alone), but within the context of a pasta salad their sharpness is hard to detect. The more pressing issue is the liquid that surrounds them. When I made two salads—one with seeded tomatoes, the other with unseeded—I was surprised that they were so different.

The unseeded tomatoes shed a lot of liquid that sat at the bottom of the bowl when the sauce was tossed with the hot pasta. The pasta salad tasted watery and bland. When I looked at the juices at the bottom of the bowl, I noticed that tiny droplets of oil were dispersed in this liquid. The sauce made with seeded tomatoes was meatier and more flavorful. Although each batch contained the same amount of seasonings, the salad made with seeded tomatoes tasted more like olive oil, garlic, basil, and salt because the oil, which carries all these flavors, was clinging to the noodles, not being dispersed in a watery mess underneath the pasta.

Next, I wondered if marinating the ingredients would affect the final outcome of the sauce. After half an hour, the tomatoes were giving off a lot of clear liquid, with a little oil dispersed in it. After an hour, I tossed the sauce with hot pasta, and I did not like the results. The tomatoes had given up a lot of their flavorful juices, which again sat at the bottom of the bowl. I also thought that the garlic flavor had intensified and become overpowering. For these reasons, it is best to assemble the raw tomato sauce while the pasta is cooking.

A last series of tests concerned timing. When should the sauce and pasta marry? Was it better to oil the drained pasta, let it cool, and then sauce it, as several cookbooks I looked at suggested? I tried this method but did not like the results. The oil formed a barrier that prevented the pasta from absorbing the flavors of the tomato sauce. The sauce also slipped off the noodles. I vastly preferred tossing the hot pasta with the raw sauce that included the oil. The pasta and the sauce elements were unified this way, and the heat of the pasta also "cooked" the tomatoes and garlic a bit.

Once the pasta and sauce are combined, you have several options. You can eat the pasta right away—it's warm but not piping hot at this point. Or you can wait half an hour or so until the pasta salad is at room temperature, then eat it or cover the bowl tightly with plastic wrap and set aside for up to four hours. After four hours, the pasta will start to soften. The refrigerator does nothing for this pasta salad; it irrevocably damages the flavor and texture of the ripe tomatoes.

PASTA SALAD WITH FRESH TOMATOES AND BASIL
SERVES 6 TO 8 AS A SIDE DISH

Use only the ripest, most flavorful round tomatoes you can find. Avoid plum tomatoes because they are too firm and tend not to soften, even with the heat of the just-cooked pasta. The tomatoes can be diced a couple hours in advance, but to prevent the garlic from becoming too pungent and the salt from drawing out the tomatoes' juices, wait until the pasta is cooking to add the seasonings to the tomatoes. Short, stubby pasta shapes such as orecchiette, fusilli, and farfalle (bow ties) are the best choice to catch juicy bits of sauce.

	Salt
1	pound pasta (*see* note above)
2	pounds ripe tomatoes, cored, seeded, and cut into 1/2-inch dice
1/4	cup extra-virgin olive oil
1	medium garlic clove, minced
1/4	cup shredded fresh basil leaves
	Ground black pepper

1. Bring 4 quarts water to boil in large soup kettle. Add 1 tablespoon salt and pasta. Cook until pasta is al dente (refer to package directions; cooking times will vary with different shapes). Drain well.

2. While pasta is cooking, toss together tomatoes, olive oil, garlic, basil, 3/4 teaspoon salt, and pepper to taste in large bowl. Add drained pasta to tomatoes and toss well. Serve immediately, or, if desired, cool to room temperature before serving, about 30 minutes. (Can be covered with plastic wrap and kept at room temperature for up to 4 hours.)

PASTA SALAD WITH TOMATOES, OLIVES, AND CAPERS

Follow recipe for Pasta Salad with Fresh Tomatoes and Basil, adding 1/3 cup pitted and sliced black kalamata olives (or other brine-cured black olives) and 2 tablespoons drained capers to tomatoes along with oil and garlic and reducing salt to 1/4 teaspoon.

PASTA SALAD WITH TOMATOES AND FRESH MOZZARELLA

Follow recipe for Pasta Salad with Fresh Tomatoes and Basil, adding 6 ounces fresh mozzarella cheese, cut into small dice, to tomatoes along with oil and garlic.

The Perfect Chilled Lemon Soufflé

This dessert, an American take on the classic Bavarian cream, runs the gamut from rubbery orbs to lemony foams. The perfect version, however, is a divine marriage of custard and soufflé.

⇒ BY CHRISTOPHER KIMBALL ⇐

There are recipes that arrive at the kitchen door one day, with no letter of introduction, and then go on to quietly claim a room in the house of American culinary history. Chilled lemon soufflé is such a recipe. Based on a classic Bavarian cream, it is most often a mixture of a custard base, gelatin, whipped cream, beaten egg whites, sugar, and lemon flavorings. But like any good mongrel American classic, "chilled lemon soufflé" covers a wide range of recipes, from baked pudding cakes, which are then cooled and served at room temperature, to nothing more than lemon juice, sugar, and beaten whites, with no egg yolks and no whipped cream.

Despite its various guises, how should it taste? For me—and I have happily eaten lots of them—chilled lemon soufflé is an unusual marriage of cream and foam, of sweet and sour, of high lemony notes and lingering, rich custard. It starts at the tip of the tongue with the sharp tingle of lemon zest and then slides slowly down the throat, filling the mouth with cream and pudding and a soft, long finish. At least that's what it is supposed to do. The question is, how can a home cook make this delicate balance of ingredients and technique turn out just right? I set out to test as many recipes as possible to find out.

For starters, I hauled out all the recipes that I could find and quickly discovered that there are five basic approaches to this dessert. The most elaborate begins with a custard base that is then combined with gelatin, whipped cream, and beaten egg whites. Many recipes, however, leave out the custard, using only beaten egg yolks and sugar as the base, while some classic French versions of this dish also leave out the egg whites. Other recipes omit the egg yolks, using just sugar, lemon juice, whipped cream, and beaten egg whites. If the whipped cream is eliminated in a further act of reductionism, you have what is known as a lemon snow pudding. I also looked up recipes for lemon mousse and found that mousse is usually made without gelatin, the key ingredient in chilled lemon soufflé.

I began my testing with the simplest approach, just beaten egg whites, gelatin, sugar, and lemon juice. The result was a foamy confection, much like being served a mound of beaten egg whites. This dessert needed some fat for texture and fla-

Like savory soufflés, this dessert has a very airy, foam-like texture.

vor. I then thought I would try a recipe with whipped cream as well. This was quite good, rated number one by some of my tasters. It had lots of lemon punch but a somewhat airy, foamy texture that called for a bit more fat. Next, I added beaten egg yolks to the mixture, perhaps the most common approach to chilled lemon soufflé, but the texture of this version of the dessert was tough. I tried a second variation on this theme and was still unsatisfied with the texture. I then left out the egg whites and produced a dense, rubbery lemon dome, the sort of dessert that might hold up nicely in Death Valley in July. Finally, I started with a custard base made with sugar, egg yolks, milk, lemon juice, and gelatin and then added this to the whipped cream and beaten whites. This was highly rated, but the lemon flavor was a bit muted.

Reviewing my testing results, I decided that a compromise might be reached between the two test winners. The lemon juice/whipped cream/beaten egg-white dessert was light and lemony but too foamy; the custard base dessert had a better finish and mouthfeel but was lacking the bright, clear flavor of lemon. I worked up a new master recipe that called for softening one package of gelatin over a half cup of lemon juice. (I tried two packages of gelatin and ended up with a rubbery orb.) Next, a cup of milk was heated with sugar while I beat two egg yolks with an extra two tablespoons of sugar. The milk and the beaten yolks were combined on top of the stove and heated until the mixture began to steam. Finally, the cooled custard was folded into three-quarters cup of whipped heavy cream, and six beaten egg whites folded into the result. This was the best variation to date, but it still needed a few refinements.

First, I cut back the whites to five from six to

Getting the Peel Off

Once I decided that fresh lemon zest was a better choice for flavoring than oils or extracts, I wanted to test the best method for removing it from the fruit. First, we should define the term "zest": The zest is the outer peel of the lemon, without any of the white pith. (A zester, one of the tools tested below, is a hand-held instrument with small holes in the blade that removes the peel in thin strips.)

Cooks from our test kitchen tried five tools: a flat, moderately coarse grater; a flat, very fine grater; the finest side of a box grater; a zester (the zest was then minced with a knife); and a vegetable peeler (the zest was then minced). After making a chilled lemon soufflé using each method, we declared the coarsely grated zest the winner. This method produced the most lemon oil by breaking down the skin of the lemon. The fine grater, on the other hand, produced a light, flaky, dry zest. The box grater version was light on lemon flavor, since so much of the zest was lost in the grater. The zester also produced a dry, flaky product, and it required a fair amount of pressure to pull the zester across the outside of the lemon. Finally, we found the vegetable peeler to be difficult to use—it was easy to take too much of the bitter white peel—and the resulting zest was bland. The conclusion? The lemon zest really needs to be bruised to break down the cells enough to release oils. It takes a tough grater to make flavorful zest.

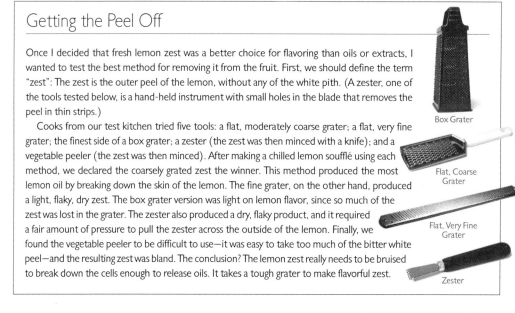

Box Grater

Flat, Coarse Grater

Flat, Very Fine Grater

Zester

Getting to Lemon: Zests, Oils, and Extracts

I have always wondered about the differences in flavor that result from using lemon zest, lemon oil, and lemon extract. For starters, I tried making the chilled lemon soufflé three different ways, using each of these flavorings. I quickly discovered that the worst of the lot was the extract, which had a very dull flavor indeed. The oil produced good lemon flavor, but it was monochromatic; it lacked highs and lows. The zest, on the other hand, provided a wider range of lemon flavor from bitter to sweet, which made the dessert more complex and therefore more interesting. The front of the tongue immediately picks up a sharp bite of lemon that then mellows in the back of the mouth as the soufflé melts across the palate. I then wondered how specific brands of these three ingredients would work, not only in this dessert but also in a pound cake and buttercream. Here are the results.

Lemon Zest

The hands-down favorite, with more bite, more depth, and more lemon flavor.

Boyajian Pure Lemon Oil

Natural oil pressed from fresh lemons. This product has a true lemon flavor without any mysterious chemical undertones. The hands-down favorite if not using zest.

The Spicery Shoppe Natural Lemon Flavor

Soybean oil, oil of lemon, natural flavorings, and alpha tocopherol. The desserts did have a pleasant lemon flavor but did not have the fresh lemony taste of those made with lemon oil.

Scott's Pure Lemon Extract

Oil of lemon, water, and alcohol. The alcohol was quite noticeable and the flavor inferior.

Durkee Imitation Lemon Extract

Alcohol (82%), water, oil of lemon, artificial flavor, and artificial color. There was a strong alcohol/chemical taste. To make matters worse, it had only a hint of lemon flavor. Not recommended.

So if you want the complex tang of lemon, go for the zest! If, however, you are looking for a milder, less aggressive lemon flavor, we recommend the pure lemon oil. The extracts are a very distant third place, since they are mostly alcohol.   C.K.

STEP-BY-STEP | CREATING A SOUFFLÉ TOP

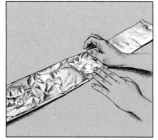  

1. Cut a piece of foil 3 inches longer than the circumference of the soufflé dish and fold it lengthwise into fourths.

2. Wrap the foil strip around the upper half of the soufflé dish and secure the overlap with tape. Tape the collar to the soufflé dish.

3. Carefully remove the collar before serving.

---

give the dessert a bit less air and more substance. Next, I added just one-quarter teaspoon of cornstarch to the custard mixture to prevent the yolks from curdling too easily. (For more information on this technique, *see* "Really Good Custard Pie," May/June 1999). I then wondered if either lemon oil or lemon extract might be better than zest, so I made a side-by-side comparison. I settled on the zest, since it produced a more complex range of flavors. (*See* "Getting to Lemon: Zests, Oils, and Extracts," above). I also discovered that to maintain a more consistent texture it was better to whisk a small part of the beaten egg whites into the

custard base before folding the mixture together.

Many recipes call for using individual ramekins, but most home cooks do not have these on hand. I thought that a soufflé dish was best (after all, this is a chilled lemon soufflé), and, to make it look even more like its baked cousin, I added a simple collar of aluminum foil and increased the recipe to the point where it would rise above the rim of the dish, much like a real soufflé. I was also curious about how well this dessert would hold up in the refrigerator. After one day, it was still good but slightly foamy, losing the creamy, tender undercurrent that is the hallmark of this dessert. After two days, it quickly deteriorated. This is one dessert that is best served the day it is made.

CHILLED LEMON SOUFFLÉ
SERVES 4 TO 6

To make this lemon soufflé "soufflé" over the rim of the dish, use a 1-quart soufflé dish and make a foil collar for it, following illustrations 1 and 2 above before beginning the recipe. For those less concerned about appearance, this dessert can be served from any 1½-quart serving bowl. For best texture, serve the soufflé after 1½ hours of chilling. It may be chilled up to 6 hours; though the texture will stiffen slightly because of the gelatin, it will taste just as good.

- ½ cup lemon juice from 2 or 3 lemons, plus
  2½ teaspoons grated zest (grate before juicing)
- 1 ¼-ounce packet unflavored gelatin
- 1 cup whole milk
- ¾ cup sugar
- 5 large egg whites, plus 2 yolks, at room temperature
- ¼ teaspoon cornstarch
- ¾ cup heavy cream

1. Place lemon juice in small nonreactive bowl; sprinkle gelatin over. Set aside.

2. Heat milk and ½ cup of the sugar in medium saucepan over medium-low heat, stirring occasionally, until steaming and sugar is dissolved, about 5 minutes. Meanwhile, whisk

together yolks, 2 tablespoons sugar, and cornstarch in medium bowl until pale yellow and thickened, 3 to 5 minutes. Whisking constantly, gradually add hot milk to yolks. Return milk and egg mixture to saucepan and cook, stirring constantly, over medium-low heat until foam has dissipated to a thin layer and mixture thickens to consistency of heavy cream and registers 185 degrees on instant-read thermometer, about 4 minutes. Strain into medium bowl; stir in lemon juice mixture and zest. Set bowl of custard in large bowl of ice water; stir occasionally to cool.

3. While custard mixture is chilling, in bowl of standing mixer fitted with whisk attachment (or in large mixing bowl if using hand mixer), beat egg whites on medium speed until foamy, about 1 minute. Increase speed to medium-high; gradually add remaining 2 tablespoons sugar and continue to beat until glossy and whites hold soft peaks when beater is lifted, about 2 minutes longer. Do not overbeat. Remove bowl containing custard mixture from ice water bath; gently whisk in about ⅓ of egg whites, then fold in remaining whites with large rubber spatula until almost no white streaks remain.

4. In same mixer bowl (washing not necessary), with mixer fitted with whisk attachment, beat cream on medium-high speed until soft peaks form when beater is lifted, 2 to 3 minutes. Fold cream into custard and egg-white mixture until no white streaks remain. Pour into prepared soufflé dish or bowl. Chill until set but not stiff, about 1½ hours (can be refrigerated up to 6 hours, *see* note above); remove foil collar, if using, and serve.

CHILLED LEMON SOUFFLÉ WITH WHITE CHOCOLATE

The white chocolate in this variation subdues the lemony kick. The difference is subtle, but the sweeter, richer flavor and texture was popular among tasters.

Follow recipe for Chilled Lemon Soufflé, adding 2 ounces chopped white chocolate to warm custard before adding lemon juice mixture and zest. Stir until melted and fully incorporated.

Summer Pudding

The ideal summer pudding, a simple marriage of berries and bread, is all in the details.

≥ BY DAWN YANAGIHARA ≤

If any food speaks of the summer, summer pudding does. Ripe, fragrant, lightly sweetened berries are gently cooked to coax out their juices, which then soak and soften slices of bread to make them meld with the fruit. Served chilled, summer pudding is incredibly fresh and refreshing. Last summer, I came home from a farmer's market with half a flat of strawberries that I'd purchased for a dollar. Not enough to preserve, I thought, but a great chance to make a summer pudding. With some raspberries, blueberries, and old bread from the freezer, I easily threw one together. I was pleased with this first attempt, but the pudding was a bit too sweet for me, and the bread seemed to stand apart from the fruit, as if it were just a casing. Improving upon it, I knew, would be an easy task. I wanted sweet-tart berries and bread that melded right into them.

In a typical summer pudding, berries fill a bowl or mold of some sort that has been neatly lined with crustless bread. Well, trimming the crusts is easy, but trimming the bread to fit the mold, then lining the bowl with it, is fussy. After having made a couple of puddings, I quickly grew tired of this technique—it seemed to undermine the simplicity of the dessert. I came across a couple of recipes that called for layering the bread right in with the berries instead of using it to line the bowl. Not only is this bread-on-the-inside method easier, but a summer pudding made in this fashion looks spectacular—the berries on the outside are like brilliant jewels. Meanwhile, the layers of bread on the inside almost melt into the fruit.

My next adjustment to this recipe was losing the bowl as a mold. I switched instead to a loaf pan. Its rectangular shape requires less trimming of bread slices, and, once unmolded, the pudding better retains its shape. When I tried making individual summer puddings in ramekins, I found them to be hardly more labor-intensive in assembly than a single large pudding. Sure, you have to cut out rounds of bread to fit the ramekins, but a cookie cutter makes easy work of it, and individual servings transform this humble dessert into an elegant one. The individual puddings are also easily served—simply unmold one onto a plate. No slicing or scooping involved.

With the form set, I moved on to the ingredients. For the four pints of berries I was using, three-quarters of a cup of sugar was a good

Summer berry puddings can be made in individual servings, as shown, or in a large loaf pan.

amount. Lemon juice, I found, perked up the berry flavors and rounded them out. I then sought alternatives to cooking the fruit in an attempt to preserve its freshness. I mashed first some and then all of the berries with sugar. I tried cooking only a portion of the fruit with sugar. I macerated the berries with sugar. None of these methods worked. These puddings, even after being weighted and chilled overnight, had an unwelcome crunchy, raw quality. The berries need a gentle cooking to make their texture more yielding, more puddinglike, if you will. But don't worry—five minutes is all it takes, not even long enough to heat up the kitchen.

Next I investigated the bread. I tried six different kinds as well as pound cake (for which I was secretly rooting). Hearty, coarse-textured sandwich bread and a rustic French loaf were too tough and tasted fermented and yeasty. Soft, pillowy sandwich bread became soggy and lifeless when soaked with juice. The pound cake, imbued with berry juice, turned into wet sand and had the textural appeal of sawdust. A good-quality white sandwich bread that had a medium texture, somewhere between Wonder bread and Pepperidge Farm, was good, but there were two very clear

winners: challah and potato bread. Their even, tight-crumbed, tender texture and light sweetness were a perfect match for the berries. Challah, available in the bakery section of most grocery stores, is usually sold in unsliced braided loaves and therefore makes for irregular slices. I sidestepped this complication and chose to go with potato bread, which tastes every bit as good as challah in this recipe but comes in convenient bagged and sliced loaves, like sandwich bread.

Most summer pudding recipes call for stale bread. And for good reason. Fresh bread, I found, when soaked with those berry juices, turns to mush. You might not think this would be so noticeable with the bread layered between all those berries, but every single taster remarked that the pudding made with fresh bread was soggy and gummy. On the other hand, stale bread absorbs some of the juices and melds with the berries yet still maintains some structural integrity. I tried different degrees of staleness. A day-old loaf was still too fresh, yet bread left out long enough to become completely dry cracked and crumbled easily under the cookie cutter or bread knife. I found that simply leaving slices out overnight until they were dry to the touch but still somewhat pliable resulted in bread that was easy to cut and also tasted good in the pudding.

Probably the oddest thing about summer pudding is the fact that it is weighted as it chills. What, I wondered, does this do for the texture? And how long does the pudding need to chill? I made several and chilled them with and without weights for 4, 8, 24, and 30 hours. The puddings chilled for 4 hours tasted of underripe fruit. The bread was barely soaked through, and the berries barely clung together. At 8 hours the pudding was at its peak: the berries tasted fresh and held together, while the bread melted right into them. Twenty-four hours and the pudding was still good, though a hairsbreadth duller in color and flavor. After 30 hours the pudding was well past its prime and began to smell and taste fermented.

No matter how long they chilled, the summer puddings without weights were loose—they didn't hold together after unmolding. The fruit was less cohesive, and the puddings less pleasurable to eat.

No pound cake, no butter. Just bright, fresh summer berries made into the perfect summer dessert. Topped with a healthy dollop of whipped cream, what could be better?

INDIVIDUAL SUMMER BERRY PUDDINGS
SERVES 6

Stale the bread for this recipe by leaving it out overnight. Otherwise, put the slices on a rack in a single layer into a 200-degree oven for 50 to 60 minutes, turning them once halfway through. For this recipe, you will need six 6-ounce ramekins and a round cookie cutter of slightly smaller diameter than the ramekins. If you don't have the right size cutter, use a paring knife and the bottom of a ramekin (most ramekins taper toward the bottom) as a guide for trimming the rounds. If you use challah, the second choice for bread, cut it into ½-inch-thick slices. If neither potato bread nor challah is available, use a good-quality white sandwich bread with a dense, soft texture. Whipped cream is the perfect accompaniment to summer pudding.

- 2 pints strawberries, rinsed, hulled and sliced
- 1 pint raspberries
- ½ pint blueberries
- ½ pint blackberries
- ¾ cup sugar
- 2 tablespoons juice from 1 lemon
- 12 slices stale potato bread, challah, or other good-quality white bread (*see* note above)

1. Heat strawberries, raspberries, blueberries, blackberries, and sugar in large nonreactive saucepan over medium heat, stirring occasionally, until berries begin to release their juice and sugar has dissolved, about 5 minutes. Off heat, stir in lemon juice; let cool to room temperature.

2. While berries are cooling, cut out 12 bread rounds, following illustration 1 (above).

3. Spray six 6-ounce ramekins with vegetable cooking spray and place on rimmed cookie sheet. Following illustrations 2 to 6, assemble, cover, and weight summer puddings. Refrigerate puddings for at least 8 and up to 24 hours.

4. Remove weights, cookie sheet, and plastic wrap. Run a paring knife around ramekin perimeters, unmold, and serve.

SUMMER BERRY PUDDING
SERVES 6 TO 8

To ensure that this larger pudding unmolds in one piece, use a greased loaf pan lined with plastic wrap. Because there is no need to cut out rounds for this version, you will need only 8 bread slices, depending upon their size.

Follow recipe for Individual Summer Berry Puddings through step 1. While berries are cooling, follow illustration 1 (right) to trim bread, spray loaf pan with vegetable cooking spray, and line pan with plastic wrap. Place loaf pan on rimmed cookie sheet. Following illustrations 2 and 3, assemble, cover, and weight summer pud-

Individual Puddings

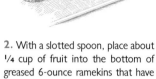

1. For individual summer puddings, cut out rounds of bread with a cookie cutter.

2. With a slotted spoon, place about ¼ cup of fruit into the bottom of greased 6-ounce ramekins that have been placed on a cookie sheet.

3. Lightly soak rounds of bread in the juices left in the saucepan, then place on top of the fruit in the ramekins.

4. Divide the remaining fruit among the ramekins (about ½ cup more per ramekin).

5. Lightly soak rounds of bread and place on top of fruit; bread should sit above ramekin lip. Top with remaining juices, and cover the ramekins loosely with plastic wrap.

6. Place a second cookie sheet on top, then weight with several heavy cans.

One Large Pudding

1. Remove the crusts from bread slices and trim them to fit in a single layer in the loaf pan. It will take approximately 2½ slices to form one layer. Line a 9 x 5-inch greased loaf pan with plastic wrap. Make sure that the plastic wrap lies flat against the surface of the loaf pan, leaving no air space.

2. Place the loaf pan on a rimmed cookie sheet and use a slotted spoon to place about 2 cups of fruit into the bottom.

3. Lightly soak enough bread slices for one layer in juice and place on top of fruit. Repeat with two more layers of fruit and bread. Top with remaining juices, cover loosely with plastic wrap, and weight with a second cookie sheet and several heavy cans.

4. To unmold, remove outer plastic wrap and invert onto serving platter. Lift off loaf pan; remove plastic wrap lining and serve.

Creamy Party Dips

Using fresh ingredients and the right base reminds us of how good these classics can be.

⇒ BY EVA KATZ ⇐

One big difference between cookbooks from the '60s and '70s and cookbooks from the '90s is the dip recipes. The former have lots of creamy party dips based on sour cream and mayonnaise, while newer cookbooks have recipes for more eclectic sorts of dips made with pureed beans, roasted vegetables, and exotic ingredients such as pomegranate molasses and tahini. Yet there is something very satisfying about dipping a crisp carrot stick or salty potato chip into a cool, savory, creamy dip, and, in fact, these old standbys can be just as delicious as their ethnic competitors. However, the richness of both sour cream and mayonnaise can easily dominate a dip that is seasoned too timidly. Therefore, these dips need to be seasoned with gusto. That means mostly fresh ingredients, and plenty of them.

After playing around with these dips for quite a while, I found that a combination of mayonnaise and sour cream is the ideal medium for carrying fresh and vibrant flavors. This combination also has the perfect consistency for dipping and scooping. As for the ratio, I found equal portions to be ideal. The mayonnaise adds body and richness, while the sour cream brings a bright freshness to the dip. I also found that "lite" mayonnaise and sour cream fare pretty well in these dips. They tend to taste a bit flatter and result in a dip that is slightly less creamy and silky, but they are certainly worth trying.

Preparing these dips at least one hour ahead of time or even a day in advance allows the flavors to blend. They are also best served cool rather than at room temperature.

CLAM DIP WITH BACON AND SCALLIONS
MAKES ABOUT 2 CUPS

- 4 strips (about 4 ounces) bacon, cut into 1/4-inch pieces
- 3/4 cup sour cream (regular or light)
- 3/4 cup mayonnaise (regular or light)
- 1 teaspoon juice from 1 lemon
- 1 teaspoon Worcestershire sauce
- 2 6 1/2-ounce cans minced clams, drained
- 2 medium scallions, sliced thin
  Salt and ground black pepper
  Cayenne pepper

1. Fry bacon in small skillet over medium heat until crisp, 6 to 8 minutes. Transfer bacon with slotted spoon to paper towel–lined plate; cool.

2. Whisk together sour cream, mayonnaise, lemon juice, and Worcestershire sauce in medium bowl. Stir in minced clams, scallions, and bacon. Season to taste with salt, pepper, and cayenne. Chill until flavors meld, about 1 hour. (Dip can be covered and refrigerated for up to 2 days.)

SMOKY, SPICY AVOCADO DIP WITH CILANTRO
MAKES ABOUT 2 1/4 CUPS

Chipotle chiles en adobo are dried, smoked jalapeños packed in a tomato-vinegar sauce. If unavailable, substitute 1 medium jalapeño, 1 teaspoon ketchup, 1/4 teaspoon liquid smoke, and 1/4 teaspoon hot red pepper sauce (such as Tabasco) for the chipotles in this recipe.

- 3/4 cup sour cream (regular or light)
- 3/4 cup mayonnaise (regular or light)
- 1 ripe avocado, halved, pitted, and flesh scooped from skin
- 1 tablespoon juice from 1 lime
- 1/2 cup cilantro leaves
- 1 1/2 chipotle chiles en adobo, plus 1 teaspoon of adobo sauce
- 2 medium scallions, sliced thin
  Salt and ground black pepper

In bowl of food processor, process sour cream, mayonnaise, avocado, lime juice, cilantro leaves, and chipotle chiles with adobo sauce until smooth and creamy and cilantro leaves are chopped fine, scraping down sides of bowl once or twice. Transfer mixture to medium bowl; stir in scallions. Season to taste with salt and pepper. Chill until flavors meld, about 1 hour. (Dip can be covered and refrigerated for up to 2 days.)

GREEN GODDESS DIP
MAKES ABOUT 1 3/4 CUPS

- 3/4 cup sour cream (regular or light)
- 3/4 cup mayonnaise (regular or light)
- 2 medium garlic cloves, chopped
- 1/4 cup parsley leaves
- 2 teaspoons fresh tarragon leaves, chopped
- 1 tablespoon juice from 1 lemon
- 2 anchovy fillets
- 1/4 cup fresh chives, minced
  Salt and ground black pepper

In bowl of food processor, process sour cream, mayonnaise, garlic, parsley, tarragon, lemon juice, and anchovy fillets until smooth and creamy, scraping down sides of bowl once or twice. Transfer mixture to medium bowl; stir in chives. Season to taste with salt and pepper. Chill until flavors meld, about 1 hour. (Dip can be covered and refrigerated for up to 2 days.)

SPINACH DIP WITH FETA AND GARLIC
MAKES ABOUT 2 1/2 CUPS

Feta cheese is quite salty. Taste the dip and season to taste with additional salt if you find it necessary.

- 3/4 cup sour cream (regular or light)
- 3/4 cup mayonnaise (regular or light)
- 4 ounces feta cheese, crumbled
- 2 medium garlic cloves, minced
- 1/2 teaspoon grated zest from 1 lemon
- 1 10-ounce package frozen chopped spinach, thawed and thoroughly squeezed dry
  Ground black pepper

In bowl of food processor, process sour cream, mayonnaise, feta cheese, garlic, and lemon zest until smooth and creamy, scraping down sides of bowl once or twice. Transfer mixture to medium mixing bowl; stir in spinach. Season to taste with pepper. Chill until flavors meld, about 1 hour. (Dip can be covered and refrigerated for up to 2 days.)

SMOKED SALMON DIP WITH DILL AND HORSERADISH
MAKES ABOUT 2 CUPS

- 3/4 cup sour cream (regular or light)
- 3/4 cup mayonnaise (regular or light)
- 3 ounces smoked salmon
- 2 teaspoons juice from 1 lemon
- 1 teaspoon prepared horseradish
- 2 tablespoons minced fresh dill
  Salt and ground black pepper

In bowl of food processor, process sour cream, mayonnaise, salmon, lemon juice, and horseradish until smooth and creamy, scraping down sides of bowl once or twice. Transfer mixture to medium mixing bowl; stir in dill. Season to taste with salt and pepper. Chill until flavors meld, about 1 hour. (Dip can be covered and refrigerated for up to 2 days.)

Weight Is Key for Inexpensive Chef's Knives

Though choosing a knife is highly subjective, several important factors can help guide your choice in the lower-cost field.

⫧ BY ADAM RIED ⫨

The big surprise in *Cook's* last test of chef's knives (*see* "Slicing through Knife Myths," March/April 1994, page 27) was the high rating of an inexpensive model, which finished ahead of several other expensive, well-respected, name-brand contenders. While fancy, hand-crafted chef's knives from the best-known makers can cost between $80 and $100, there is no shortage of less expensive choices for cooks on a budget. In fact, many such knives are priced well below $50. Considering the wide selection of inexpensive knives and the good performance of that budget choice in the first knife testing, we began to wonder about the others in this class. To satisfy our curiosity, we organized this full-scale test of eight-inch chef's knives under $50.

Local and regional knife experts Shane Levens of Stoddard's in Boston and Terri Alpert of Professional Cutlery Direct in Madison, Connecticut, helped us identify which knives to test, and a cadre of top Boston-area restaurant chefs (*see* "The Testers," page 26) conducted the testing. Tests included heavy work such as cutting hard butternut squash and root vegetables as well as light, fine work such as mincing parsley and ginger (*see* chart on page 27 for full details). With price and blade size as our main determinants, the final lineup included knives from Forschner, Friedr. Dick, Dexter/Russell, Henckels, Chicago Cutlery, LamsonSharp, and Farberware.

Knife Manufacturing Primer

The price difference between our budget choices and more expensive knives arises primarily from their method of manufacture. More expensive knives are generally made through a process called forging. Bob Topazio, vice president and general manager of Forschner, described a few of the basic steps involved in making a forged knife. The starting point is a very, very roughly knife-shaped piece of steel, usually about ½ inch thick, called a billet. The billet is heated to above 2,000 degrees F., at which point it is nearly molten, and placed in a forging hammer. Using between 250 and 500 tons of pressure, the forging hammer continually slams the red hot billet down into a die, which further refines its shape toward that of a finished knife. From that point, excess metal is ground away and the nascent knife is tempered (heated and cooled repeatedly to strengthen the steel), sharpened, and finished, sometimes in up to 50 steps, and finally given a handle. The process is labor-intensive and therefore expensive, which accounts for the high cost of forged knives.

Because the knives in our group are meant to cost less, they are made with a less involved process called stamping. Topazio said that stamped knives begin with a large "ribbon" of fairly thin steel. This ribbon is fed through a press that punches out knife-shaped "blanks." As with forged knives, the blanks are then tempered, sharpened, and finished, but the whole process costs less because so much of it is handled by machines.

The telltale sign of a forged knife is the presence of a thick steel bolster, also sometimes called the shank or the shoulder, between the blade and the handle. Topazio explained that the bolster, which is formed from the original billet, serves three purposes. First, it keeps the user's hand away from the blade, protecting the fingers from being cut. Second, it adds weight to the knife, simply by virtue of its extra width and mass. Third, it helps to balance the blade with the handle. The bolster can also present a disadvantage. We found in our testing of electric knife sharpeners (*see* "Do Electric Knife Sharpeners Really Work?" March/April 1997, page 27) that a bolster that extends all the way to the heel of the blade (the bottom of the cutting edge closest to the handle), as most of them do, can block the heel from traveling through the slots in the sharpener. This means that the very rear portion of the blade does not get sharpened. Because they start life as flat sheets of metal, our less expensive stamped knives have no bolsters, which means the entire length of the blade can be sharpened.

The Importance of Personal Preference

Wading through the testers' completed questionnaires about each knife made one thing abundantly clear: subjectivity reigns when choosing a chef's knife. Each of our testers had ample experience choosing and using knives, yet their choices turned out to be highly personal. Individual perceptions of a particular knife's weight, balance, and overall construction quality varied. For instance, almost all the testers complimented the handle on the

The Chef's Knives We Tested

Forschner (Victorinox) Fibrox
Winning knife had excellent factory edge and good weight.

Friedr. Dick Pro-Dynamic
Praised for good design and comfortable handle.

Dexter/Russell SofGrip
Most testers found blade a bit too flexible.

Zwilling J.A. Henckels
No Stain Rostfrei
Blade has good rigidity but lacks curvature.

Chicago Cutlery
Walnut Tradition
Balance not great, blade dulled easily.

LamsonSharp Hi Carbon
Tiring to use because of handle-heavy balance.

Farberware Millennium
Slick, space-age handle requires tiring overgripping.

Forschner, save for one who found it a little too thin for optimal comfort. Likewise, one tester commented that the handle on the Dexter/Russell "had a great fit in my hand," while another said that it "felt weird. Nothing really obvious, just weird." Such differences in perception were common and may stem, in part, from the fact that every cook has differently sized and shaped hands. Preferences were more than just whim; there can be actual physical matches or mismatches between particular knives and your hand.

TESTING

BLADE FLEXIBILITY AND CURVATURE

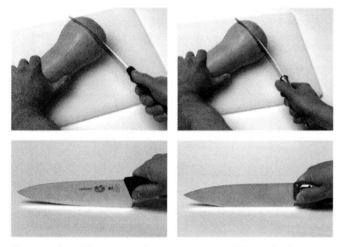

Testers preferred the control and accuracy of more rigid blades, like the one at top left. The blade at top right flexed too much in heavy cutting. Testers also preferred the easy rocking ability of blades with a longer, gentler curve toward the tip, shown at bottom left, versus blades like the one at bottom right, which curve more abruptly near the tip.

What does this subjectivity mean when you're shopping for a knife? Above all, you should hold it in your hand for a while before buying it. Then ask yourself a series of questions. Is the handle comfortable? Does it feel secure and make a tight seal in your hand? Do the handle and blade feel well-balanced? Do the shape and material of the handle feel good? Does the knife feel natural, like an extension of your hand? Do you have the impression that the knife is well made? Does the weight suit you? Answers to these questions are highly individual; the person standing next to you might well have answers that are different from yours.

A Few Consistent Factors

Disagreements aside, our chefs' preferences did reveal some patterns that can help guide your own choice of knife. First, handles made of lightly textured plastic, such as those on the Forschner, Friedr. Dick, Dexter/Russell, and Henckels, were preferred over those made of wood or other materials. In their comments on the wooden-handled Chicago Cutlery and

LamsonSharp knives, our testers said repeatedly that they disliked wooden handles because they tended to collect grease and dirt and to become slippery when wet or greasy. The odd metal handle of the Farberware, with its plastic frame and rubber finger grips, earned universal scorn for being bumpy, unnatural feeling, and slick when wet.

Weight was another important factor. While expensive forged knives usually weigh about 8 to 10 ounces, budget choices such as ours lack bolsters and have thinner blades, so they weigh less. Topazio said that stamped knives could, theoretically, be made heavier, like forged knives, by starting with thicker steel, but "it would not be cost-effective." The extra labor required to grind down to the edge would drive the cost up closer to that of forged knives. Obviously, that would erode the market position of stamped knives.

At 6.8 ounces, the Forschner was the heavyweight of our group, and was preferred because of it. Weight aids a knife in its work by helping the blade move through food with a little less exertion on the user's part, and this was apparent in the Forschner. Especially in heavy work, as in our test of cutting hard vegetables such as butternut squash, this knife required less force to cut through the food. In fact, the knives placing first, second, third, and fourth in this test were also the first, second, third, and fourth heaviest. In this budget class of knives, weight clearly counts. In addition, our testers generally felt that the heavier knives were better balanced in their hands, thus causing less hand, wrist, and arm fatigue after long hours of work.

Blade rigidity also emerged as an element in the knife rankings. While working with a couple of the knives, *Cook's* consulting food editor Jasper White pointed out that blade flexibility is a desirable trait in knives used to fillet fish but not in an all-purpose chef's knife. He demonstrated relative rigidity and flexibility by placing the tip of the knife against a work surface at about a 20-degree angle and pressing gently down on the handle. The Forschner, Friedr. Dick, and Henckels blades were rigid enough to stay straight under the pressure, the Dexter/Russell was slightly less rigid, and the Chicago Cutlery, LamsonSharp, and Farberware blades bent visibly. This excessive flex diminishes control and accuracy when cutting through hard

foods and could even cause the knife to slip, which several testers noted. Fearing that he might cut himself, one seasoned chef declined to cut up a pineapple with the Chicago Cutlery knife because of the blade, which he described as "flimsy" and "hard to control." The blades of the LamsonSharp and the Farberware received similar comments.

The last characteristic that mattered a great deal to our chef testers was blade curvature. All of the blades curve up from the heel to the tip, but some start angling up much closer to the heel than others. Though it can be hard to detect by simply looking at the blades, this means that more of the total edge is curved, which facilitates the rocking motion that makes for comfortable and efficient mincing and fine chopping. This is especially true for mincing garlic, ginger, and leafy herbs, which all must be broken down into tiny pieces.

Most chefs agreed that the longer, rounder curve of the Forschner and the Friedr. Dick blades lent themselves to easy rocking and thus to fine, even mincing. Opinion was divided about the curve of the Henckels, Chicago Cutlery, and Dexter/Russell blades. For instance, about mincing parsley with the Dexter/Russell, one chef said, "The relatively straight blade made this easy job more difficult than it had to be," while a second chef declared, "Perfect. Really nice chop." Almost without exception, though, the LamsonSharp and Farberware blades were considered a little too straight for easy rocking and ideal mincing performance.

Conclusions

There is no getting around the fact that choosing

RATING INEXPENSIVE CHEF'S KNIVES

Chefs and/or prep cooks in five top Boston-area restaurants performed specific tests, outlined below, and used the knives in their daily work for about one month.

RATING: The number, based on a scale of 1 (the worst) to 10 (the best) is an average of the scores assigned by the testers.
PRICE: Suggested retail. Actual prices may vary. *See* Resources, page 32, for specific price and availability of top-choice models.
WEIGHT: The heavier the better.
HANDLE: Handles that formed a tight, secure seal in users' hands and resisted slipping out of wet or greasy hands were preferred.
BLADE: Blades with sufficient rigidity and curvature, as well as a very sharp

factory edge, were preferred. Ease of edge correction using a sharpening steel and ability to hold the edge were also considered.
CHOPPING HARD VEGETABLES (Butternut squash, rutabaga, horseradish): Knives requiring minimal force on the cook's part were preferred.
MINCING ONION: Sharp knives that cut evenly and accurately, with no mashing or bruising of the onion, were preferred.
SLICING TOMATO: Same criteria as for mincing onion.
MINCING PARSLEY: Blades capable of fine, even cuts and good rocking motion were preferred.
MINCING GINGER: Same criteria as for mincing parsley.
TESTERS' COMMENTS: General observations, including comfort, balance, perceived solidity and construction quality, and promotion of hand fatigue.

Brand	Rating	Price	Weight	Handle	Blade	Chopping Hard Veg.	Mincing Onion	Slicing Tomato	Mincing Parsley	Mincing Ginger	Testers' Comments
BEST CHEF'S KNIFE **Forschner (Victorinox)** Fibrox, Model 40520	6.75	$28.40	6.8 oz.	★★★	★★★	★★★	★★	★★★	★★★	★★★	"Felt solid" compared to other knives in the group. Praised by some for its ability to "keep a good edge" and by all for its "decent weight and balance." "Sweet knife" summarized one tester.
Friedr. Dick Pro-Dynamic Hi Carbon, No Stain, Model No. 5447-21	6.30	$28.80	6.5 oz.	★★	★★★	★★★	★★★	★★	★★★	★★★	Overall design and construction considered good, with one chef noting that this knife "felt good in my hand, like a natural extension." Another declared that it "could use a heavier blade." Comfortable and generally easy to use, didn't promote hand fatigue.
Dexter/Russell SofGrip Stain Free, High Carbon, Model SG145-8	6.00	$27.25	6.1 oz.	★★	★★	★★	★★	★★	★★	★★	Sentiments varied from "great handle" to "I hated this knife... the handle was quite uncomfortable." Everyone agreed, however, that the "blade was not very stiff," which made for less than ideal performance on hard veggies.
Zwilling J.A. Henckels No Stain Rostfrei, Model # 32208-204	5.60	$32.00	6.1 oz.	★★	★★	★★	★★	★★	★★	★★	Light overall weight and a relatively straight blade that dulled quickly held this knife back.
Chicago Cutlery Walnut Tradition, Item # 42SP	4.60	$44.00	5.5 oz.	★★	★★	★	★★	★★	★★	★	Several chefs noted poor balance between very light blade and heavy handle. An "extremely deep" blade also added to a generally awkward feel. Cutting action was "smooth enough. Not stellar."
LamsonSharp Hi Carbon, No Stain, Model No. 650	3.50	$44.00	6.0 oz.	★★	★	★	★	★★	★	★★	Cutting edge deemed "sharp enough" by most testers. For one tester, the blade literally broke in half after the second day of use. Design won no fans. Blade rocked poorly.
Farberware Millennium	3.00	$26.99	5.1 oz.	★	★	★	★★	★★	★	★	The lightweight of the group, a fact that every tester noted—and disliked. "Felt flimsy, and unsafe" in all but the very lightest work.

a chef's knife is a highly personal matter. Different cooks might disagree about the handle, balance, performance, and overall design of various knives, but our top two knives, the Forschner and the Friedr. Dick, elicited fewer quibbles than any of the others.

The Forschner blazed through heavy work with hard squashes and rutabagas, earning comments such as "Cuts quickly and exactly" and "Makes fast work of dicing," while the rigid blade of the Friedr. Dick required only "moderate force" to do its work. On lighter chores, such as mincing onion or slicing tomato, both knives were admired for their smoothness and accuracy. The Forschner moved one tester to say, "It slices a tomato like you could on a [meat slicing] machine." The curvature of their blades was also a boon in fine work such as mincing parsley and

ginger, with chefs making notes such as "great rocking motion" for the Friedr. Dick.

So, if you are knife shopping on a tight budget, be comforted by the fact that you can purchase a reliable, good-quality knife without emptying your pockets. The solid-feeling, reasonably heavy, rigid knives from Forschner and Friedr. Dick offer most users a great blend of comfort and performance, each for less than $30.

Searching for the Top Dog

Two tasting panels—one of adults and one of children—disagree on the top wiener but found consensus on the dog of dogs.

⇒ BY MARYELLEN DRISCOLL ⇐

Hot dogs are convenient, inexpensive, easy to prepare, easy to transport, and loved by kids. These reasons alone seem enough to explain why Americans will be eating about 150 million hot dogs this Fourth of July weekend, according to the National Hot Dog and Sausage Council. I could offer three more motivations: relish, ketchup, and mustard.

Between local, regional, and national brands of dogs made from turkey, chicken, beef, pork-and-beef, and no meat at all, there are dozens of dogs from which to choose. The choices can be overwhelming, but making the right one is critical: No one wants to eat a sub-par wiener.

Our most gung-ho dog tasters.

At *Cook's*, we decided to weed out the winners from the losers with a blind taste test. We stuck with all-beef hot dogs that were nationally available. (Although we did do a small, separate blind tasting of meatless dogs; *see* "Why Dogs Need Meat," at right.) We also included a deli-style hot dog, sold in links and made with natural casings. To make doubly certain that we approached this tasting properly, two tasting panels were formed. The first comprised 15 adults; the second consisted of a dozen third- and fifth-grade children. To be realistic, and to make sure we did not spoil their dinner, we served the kids' panel just four brands of hot dogs. They included the top two finishers from the adult tasting, a veggie dog, and the second-to-last-place hot dog.

Nothing Frank about It

Before the taste test, we decided to get our facts straight on the topic. While hot dogs can seem like the ultimate of processed foods, "there is nothing gross about a hot dog," according to Dr. Kathryn L. Kotula, a professor of food science at the University of Connecticut. The primary ingredient of hot dogs is meat trimmings, the same meat that would go into hamburger or other sausages. Trimmings should not be confused with variety meats—hearts, kidney, liver, etc. If variety meats are used, which nowadays is uncommon for hot dogs, the manufacturer is required by federal law to clearly state on the front of the package "with variety meats" or "with meat byproducts." The byproducts must also be listed individually on the label along with the other ingredients. Hot dogs can contain nonmeat binders, such as nonfat dry milk, cereal, dried whole milk (no more than 3.5 percent, according to the U.S. Department of Agriculture), or isolated soy protein (no more than 2 percent). These must also be identified in the ingredients list.

Other hot dog ingredients include water (added in the form of ice) and curing or preserving agents—salt, nitrite, sugar, spices, and seasonings (typically coriander, garlic, ground mustard, nutmeg, and white pepper). Nitrite is a chemical that interacts with muscle pigment, myoglobin, to create the hot dog's characteristic pink color. It also lends a characteristic flavor. Most important, though, it prevents the growth of *Clostridium botulinum*, which can cause botulism, and other potentially harmful microbes.

The process of making hot dogs is a source of intrigue for most eaters. Basically, meat trimmings are ground into a paste and then placed in a high-speed mixer along with spices, ice chips (to keep the meat cold), and curing ingredients. This forms a thick liquid that is pumped into casings. Most brands use inedible plastic casings, which are later removed. Traditional natural casings are costly and therefore less common. The filled casings are moved to a smokehouse, where they are fully cooked. Finally, they are showered in cool water, sent to an automatic peeler to be stripped of the casings (if not natural casings), and vacuum-sealed. While this is the basic process, varying ingredients and styles of processing in different brands create differences in flavor and texture, according to Kotula. Factors include what type of meat and seasonings are used, how long the meat is chopped, under what conditions, and which techniques for emulsifying and smoking are used.

The Top Dogs

What seemed to make or break a hot dog for our panels of tasters was meaty flavor with a balance of seasonings. They also required decent chewability. The deli-style dog was indisputably the top pick among the adult tasters. The manufacturer, a supermarket chain in the Northeast, was reluctant to give away any recipe secrets as to what made this hot dog stand out. A spokesman did say it was formulated after an old-fashioned style hot dog with natural casings and "quality ingredients." The children were not quite as enthusiastic about the deli-style dog. The flavor and chew were a little too adult for their tastes.

The kids chose Ball Park franks as their favorite (the second-place finisher among adults). For similar reasons as the adults, they decisively rejected the loser dog, John Morrell, and were horrified by the veggie dog.

All but one of the hot dogs that fell into the Not Recommended category were unpalatably mushy and weak on beef flavor. The very worst of all the dogs was a brand purchased at a large natural foods chain store. The meat was uncured and contained no nitrites. Unlike its cohorts in the Not Recommended bin, it had chew. This was not much help, however, as tasters likened it to both leather and a spicy rubber sausage.

Since manufacturers were reluctant to give away trade secrets, we turned to food scientists for insight into what can make or break a hot dog. Aside from the obvious differences in products, such as the amount and type of spices used, there are more complex differences. The heart of

Why Dogs Need Meat

With so many kinds of meatless hot dogs now on the market, we decided to conduct a small blind tasting of the brands we found in supermarkets and natural food markets. We sought to answer one very simple question: Are any of them any good? The answer was a resounding no. For the most part these products have an extremely processed effect, often tasting like plastic or rubber, with texture like that of a rubbery paste, according to tasters. "Holy yuck," summed up one adult taster, while a kid commented that even the top-rated veggie dog "tastes like a beefy, rotten apple."

a hot dog's flavor intensity is carried in the fat, says Dr. M. Susan Brewer of the University of Illinois' Cooperative Extension. So less fat often means less flavor. This was obvious in the flavorless low-fat product and the tofu dogs we tasted, but we found no particular correlation between fat and flavor in the regular dogs. As for texture, Brewer pointed out that the addition of nonmeat binders, such as nonfat dry milk and cereal starches, will make a hot dog less firm. Significantly, the leading two hot dogs did not contain any such binders.

In sum, all of the recommended dogs have their individual strengths and characteristics. Whichever one is to your particular liking, the same food safety guidelines that apply to raw meats also apply to cured meats. Always keep these meats refrigerated and cold, and fully reheat them before eating. Once the package is open, you should use the dogs within two to three days or freeze it, says Kotula.

TASTING HOT DOGS

The samples in our blind taste test were all from nationally distributed brands except one. The deli-style links were purchased at the deli counter at a regional supermarket that identifies its product as an old-fashioned style hot dog. The hot dogs were pan-fried and served warm. Bread and water were served on the side for the adults to cleanse their palates. The 12 children, all 8 or 10 years old, ate their hot dogs plain in a bun and were served only four franks: those which placed first, second, and next to last in the regular tasting, plus the winning veggie dog. The tasters were asked to rate each product on appearance, flavor, texture, and overall likeability. The hot dogs are listed below in order of preference.

RECOMMENDED
Deli-Style All-Beef Hot Dogs
STOP & SHOP SUPERMARKET DELI-COUNTER BRAND
$3.69 for 1 pound / 6 franks

Buying the old-fashioned deli-style frank will get you twice the dog for about 25 cents more per link. For a group of adults, it is worth the price for this "substantial," "gutsy," "nice meaty dog." The "juicy beef flavor" was balanced with moderate saltiness, sweetness, smoky flavors, and spice, including a distinctive garlic note. The natural casing was described as "a bit toothy" verging on tough, but was mostly well-liked. For the young tasters, this hot dog was "too grown-up." "It was too spicy, and I didn't like it at all." Stop & Shop is a regional chain located in New England and parts of New York. These hot dogs contain no nonmeat binders.

BALL PARK Bun Size Beef Franks
$3.29 for 1 pound / 8 franks

This was the top choice for the young tasters. One girl wrote, "It tastes like heaven in a bun." The familiarity of these famously plump hot dogs went over well with the adults as well, who made these franks their second choice. They were "how a hot dog should be" with "quintessential hot dog flavor"—somewhat beefy, extremely salty, and a bit on the mushy side. Contains no nonmeat binders.

NATHAN'S Famous Beef Franks
$3.29 for 1 pound / 8 franks

This dog had "medium plumpitude," lots of juice, some greasiness, and "good, straightforward beef flavor." Smoky flavors were mild, as were spices. It was "a little soft and watery, but c'mon, it's a hot dog," wrote one taster. No sugar is added to this hot dog, which does contain nonmeat binders.

HEBREW NATIONAL Kosher Beef Franks
$2.99 for 12 ounces / 7 franks

The general consensus was that this hot dog was good but not great. It was "puny" in size compared with the other three recommended dogs. Tasters liked it because it had an "honest beef taste" and was "not horribly salty," sweet, or spicy. The texture was firm and chewy. A number of tasters did pick up some flavors they described as "off." This is a kosher product, meaning it is made from beef slaughtered according to Jewish law and inspected by a rabbi. No sugar is added to this hot dog, which does contain nonmeat binders.

NOT RECOMMENDED
OSCAR MAYER Beef Franks
$3.29 for 1 pound / 10 franks

The texture of this hot dog, described as "spongy" and "mealy" was probably the worst thing about it. Quite salty, it had decent smokiness but no strong beef flavor, thus making it "drab, insubstantial, lacking." Only hot dog to contain beef stock.

KAHN'S Beef Franks
$3.29 for 1 pound / 10 franks

This was another disappointingly soft, mushy hot dog. There was "only faint meatiness to it." One taster asked if it was made of turkey (it was pale in color). Another two thought they tasted cereal. No nonmeat binders were listed in its ingredients.

HEALTHY CHOICE Low Fat Beef Franks
$3.29 for 14 ounces / 8 franks

This low-fat hot dog's "brick red" appearance was an immediate turn-off. "Looks like a hot dog found in a can of Spaghetti O's," wrote one taster. The dogs were very sweet and "feeble flavored," yet had a distinctive off flavor that one taster described as medicinal. This product contained only 2.5 grams of fat versus the average hot dog's 13 to 15 grams. In addition to the standard ingredients, these franks also contained potato starch, nonfat dry milk, and yeast.

ARMOUR Premium Beef Hot Dogs
$2.49 for 1 pound / 10 franks

"Leave the sweetness to the relish," wrote one taster of these dogs, which had a sugary sweetness. Off flavors likened to metal or cereal were also criticized, and the "pasty" texture was no compensation for the flavor problems. Contains potato starch and soy protein.

JOHN MORRELL Beef Franks
$2.49 for 1 pound / 10 franks

Even the kid tasters did not fall for this dog. "It just isn't that great," wrote one. Adult tasters found it "sickly sweet." Otherwise, it had "no real character" and the texture of "compacted mush." As one taster said, "I would need lots of ketchup and relish to eat this one." Contains nonmeat binders.

PURE FARMS Uncured Beef Wiener
$4.49 for 1 pound / 6 franks

Labeled "uncured" and "no nitrites," this natural foods brand hot dog stood out as the oddball. Tasters described the dark brown exterior and grayish brown interior as "diseased-looking" and "like liverwurst." It carried a hard pepper punch and some other unusual "earthy" spicy flavors, but little to nothing of a beef taste. The texture was leathery, rubbery, and "chewy like chewing gum." One diplomatic taster wrote, "Interesting, but a dog is a dog and this just isn't one."

The Best Picnic Wines

We tested more than 30 wines that seemed appropriate for picnics and found that we could actually recommend 16 of them. BY MARK BITTMAN

What kind of wine should you bring to a picnic? Chances are there will be a variety of foods, ranging from bland to spicy. Some of it will undoubtedly contain vinegar, soy sauce, or some other well-known wine killer. Chances are also good that you're going to be drinking the wine in a super-informal situation—if not out of plastic cups then certainly not in full-attention tasting mode.

All of this serves to narrow the field somewhat, but not enough for our tasting to focus on one particular kind of wine. There are, however, generalizations that can be made: A picnic wine should be informal, inexpensive, chillable, perhaps lightly sweet or at least fruity—either feature cuts through strong flavors like soy better than bone-dry wines—and not too high in alcohol. You'll be drinking this, after all, not sipping it. All of that suggests some parameters, but, again, not a specific wine type.

To come up with some solid suggestions for a number of wines like this, we had to break our usual pattern and taste from a variety of categories and price ranges. We assembled four different groups: inexpensive, fairly fruity whites; more expensive, but still unpretentious, whites, presumably with more complex character; inexpensive, simple, quaffable rosés; and a few pricier, better rosés. In each category, we looked not to rank the wines as usual but to look for wines that were appealing enough to be enjoyed by anyone. In the course of this tasting, we sampled more than 30 wines and feel comfortable recommending about half of them—a total of 16—in four categories.

The best wines here are the more expensive whites, some of which—especially the 1995 Domaine des Baumard, a wine made with Chenin Blanc, and the Domaine Schlumberger, a Gewürztraminer—are astonishingly good, close to great. And they'd be enjoyable not only on a picnic but at a formal dinner or at a time when you want to really savor what you're drinking.

But unless I were picnicking with a group of really sophisticated wine drinkers (more sophisticated than me and my friends, to be sure), I'd look first to the inexpensive whites. All of these—and remember that in our opinion, at least, there are no losers listed here—are good bargains, and

many of them were pleasant surprises. It's not news to experienced wine drinkers that a decent Vinho Verde, the simple, slightly spritzy white of Portugal, is a good buy. But many will be surprised by the attractive Muscat from Portugal or the somewhat complex Ugni Blanc from Gascony. At these prices, you can try a few different wines and pick your own favorite.

RATING THE WINE | PICNIC WINE

The wines in our tasting—held at Mt. Carmel Wine and Spirits in Hamden, Connecticut—were judged by a panel made up of both wine professionals and amateur wine lovers (in this tasting, there was a heavier-than-usual representation of the latter). The wines were all purchased in the Northeast; prices will vary throughout the country.

Within each category, wines are listed in ascending order of price; there are only recommended wines here (those our panel would not recommend are not listed at all), but our favorite in each category is marked with a ★.

INEXPENSIVE WHITES, $10 AND UNDER

★ **NV Casal Garcia Vinho Verde** PORTUGAL **$5.** Spritzy, simple, and a great buy.

1997 Domaine de Pouy Ugni Blanc GASCOGNE, FRANCE **$6.** Also some spritz, but this wine has a little complexity, too. Very pleasant; made from the grape used to produce Armagnac.

1997 Monmousseau Vouvray FRANCE **$8.** There are readily identifiable Vouvrays, and then there are wines like this—simple, light, and fruity. A good buy.

1996 Joao Pires Muscat Terras do Sado PORTUGAL **$10.** Delightful wine, with the lovely fruitiness typical of the Muscat grape. Taste will surprise newcomers, but most will find it instantly enjoyable.

MORE EXPENSIVE WHITES, OVER $10

1996 Apremont Vin de Savoie, Pierre Boniface FRANCE **$11.** A good, solid entry, drier than many of the wines here. Competes better with wines in the first group than those listed here.

1996 King Estate Pinot Gris OREGON **$11.** Clean, straightforward wine with some personality. Not a mistake, if not especially exciting.

1997 Pine Ridge Chenin-Viognier CALIFORNIA **$11.** I just wish this vaguely interesting but somewhat simple wine were inexpensive enough to place in the first category—at $6 or $8, it would be a steal. At this price, there are better.

1997 Chateau St. Jean Gewürztraminer SONOMA **$12.** Excellent value in a very sound, good wine, with typical Gewürztraminer spiciness and nice acidity.

1996 Trimbach Riesling ALSACE **$16.** Class act, with

intensity of flavor and real complexity. Unbeatable at this price.

1996 Trimbach Gewürztraminer ALSACE **$17.** Great character, fun wine, and the perfect match for spicy food. Worth the money.

★ **1995 Domaine des Baumard, Savennieres** FRANCE **$17.** The wine of the tasting, extremely intense and really, really delicious. It's a good food wine, but perhaps wasted at a picnic. Try it.

1995 Domaine Schlumberger Gewürztraminer "Fleur" ALSACE **$20.** Very complex, powerful wine that can stand up to any food. Its intense, unusual flavors may be too much for novice wine drinkers.

INEXPENSIVE ROSÉS, $10 AND UNDER

NV Rene Barbier Mediterranean Rosé PENEDES, SPAIN **$5.** A perennial success in our rosé tastings. It's drinkable and costs five bucks—what more can you ask?

★ **1997 Chateau Saint-Jean Coteaux d'Aix en Provence Cuvée Natacha** FRANCE **$8.50.** Dry and crisp, exactly the kind of house wine you'd be served when eating outside on the Riviera.

1997 Bonny Doon Vin Gris de Cigare Pink Wine CALIFORNIA **$9.** The American version of the wine above. Take your pick.

MORE EXPENSIVE ROSÉS, OVER $10

★ **1996 Chateau de Trinquevedel, Tavel** FRANCE **$15.** This wine, vintage after vintage, has never appeared in one of our rosé tastings without sweeping the field. Highly recommended, and an all-purpose choice.

Satisfy Your Sweet Tooth

Three new dessert books by well-known authors run the gamut from needlessly complicated to sublimely simple. BY CHRISTOPHER KIMBALL

Desserts are much like weddings. You can plan for months, shred a year's salary, and end up too exhausted to enjoy it. On the other hand, you can choose to have just a few friends over, find a quiet spot for a simple ceremony, and enjoy the day. Either course of action can be easily defended, but if you are really going to put on the dog, it had better be worth it. The same is true of desserts.

These three dessert cookbooks run the gamut from the extreme to the sublime, some recipes starting out "Day One" and others requiring just a few minutes of throw-it-all-together preparation. After two months of cakes, cookies, ice cream, pies, crumbles, and tarts, we concluded that the simplest recipes are often the best.

Dessert Circus at Home
Jacques Torres

William Morrow, 304 pages, $28

This 300-page dessert book is aptly named—it looks much like a circus. The book is divided into an eclectic group of chapters, and there are a wealth of saturated color photographs of the desserts, plus the occasional candid shot of the chef and a fair number of step-by-step photos as well. The photograph of the bûche de Noël says it all. This over-the-top yule log is decorated with meringue Santas and mushrooms, chocolate trees and fences, piped ivy and flowers, shaved chocolate, and powdered sugar. The recipe is five pages long and contains 24 ingredients.

PROS: If you like complicated desserts, the sort of fanciful creations that only the French have truly mastered, this is the book for you. Torres even managed to turn a lemon upside-down cake, perhaps one of the simplest American desserts, into a three-day tour de force. It looked great.

CONS: Many of the desserts look a lot better than they taste, the directions are often unclear or incomplete, virtually all of the recipes are unnecessarily complex, and the amount of work required to make most of these desserts far outweighs the quality of the end result. Do we really need to make a disc of tempered chocolate to use as a layer in a banana cream pie?

RECIPE TESTING: These are among the most complicated recipes we have ever tested in our kitchen, yet many received modest marks for flavor. That banana cream pie was a model of pointless complexity; the lemon upside-down cake had a nice lemon curd cream, but the cake itself was curiously dull and the recipe hugely time-consuming; the caramel-walnut soufflé used a base from another recipe, which was a holy terror to make; the muffins were chalky with a very dry crumbled topping; and the chocolate babkas did not proof as promised.

Chocolate
Nick Malgieri

HarperCollins, 464 pages, $40

This 400-page-plus cookbook is, if nothing else, comprehensive. I can't imagine that Malgieri has left anything out. It contains recipes for cakes, cookies, creams, custards, soufflés, ices, pies, tarts, pastries, sauces, and showpiece desserts. It is also chock-full of color photographs and the occasional step-by-step photo. The bûche de Noël photo again tells the story. Unlike Torres, Malgieri has faithfully reproduced the classic confection with génoise, chocolate ganache, and simple meringue mushrooms. No meringue Santas or chocolate trees for Mr. Malgieri!

PROS: There are lots of recipes, and most of them are appealing. Thankfully, Malgieri is not a culinary lotus-eater, far removed from the reality of the American kitchen. He includes plenty of simpler recipes, suitable for the home cook.

CONS: Although half of the recipes we tested were excellent, we did have our problems. We found that flavors were often muted, as with a Chocolate Rum Raisin Cake, and on two occasions we found a cake or cookie to be a bit too dry and crumbly. As recipe testing goes, however, a .500 batting average is more than respectable.

RECIPE TESTING: Malgieri comes up with some real winners here. The Chocolate Banana Coffee Cake was wonderful, a chocolate gelato was easy to make and intense, chocolate thumbprint cookies were well-liked, and the Chocolate Mocha Heart had a terrific coffee buttercream, although the cake itself was a bit dry. Less successful were the Easy Fudgy Loaf Cake, which contained only two ounces of chocolate so it was barely brown, to say nothing of fudgy, and the Orange Chocolate Chip

Cookies, which were disappointingly dry with an overwhelming bitter orange flavor.

Sweet Simplicity: Jacques Pépin's Fruit Desserts
Jacques Pépin

Bay Books, 224 pages, $29.95

We tested these recipes in galley form, so I can offer no comments about the quality of the book's packaging. However, it contains about 150 recipes organized by type of fruit, and the operating philosophy here is simplicity of technique and flavor. It is not uncommon to see recipes with only two or three steps (an obvious blessing), and, for the most part, the recipes are refreshing both in taste and concept. Grapefruit Gratin and Quick Plum and Almond Cake are hard to ignore, although Pépin occasionally ventures into more troublesome territory with entries like Crepe Soufflés in Grapefruit Sauce. Well, nobody is perfect.

PROS: Great cooks are reductionists, stripping away what is unnecessary to find classic culinary marriages. Frozen raspberries are thrown in a gratin dish, topped with buttered and sugared stale croissant crumbs, baked, and then finished with a dollop of sour cream. The three components make a world-class dessert that takes five minutes to assemble. In addition, Pépin has come up with new techniques that are both simple and often dazzling. (Did you know you can make very good ice cream out of frozen banana slices without an ice cream machine?) One tester wrote, "If I had the time, I would systematically make every recipe."

CONS: There aren't many. Two recipes had flavor combinations that were controversial with the staff, but perhaps that is culinary niggling.

RECIPE TESTING: A blueberry crumble was great, pears in chocolate were unanimously judged "fabulous," and a simple, baked apple tart was a snap and delicious (halved apples filled with apricot jam are placed on pastry dough, the edges are rolled up, and then the free-form tart is baked). The banana-mint ice cream was smooth and creamy (made with frozen banana slices put through a food processor), and the raspberry gratin was perfection—the ideal marriage of simplicity and complementary flavors and textures.

RESOURCES

Most of the ingredients and materials necessary for the recipes in this issue are available at your local supermarket, gourmet store, or kitchen supply shop. The following are mail-order sources for particular items. Prices listed below were current at press time and do not include shipping or handling unless otherwise indicated. We suggest that you contact companies directly to confirm up-to-date prices and availability.

Top-Rated Chef's Knife

Preferred over some forged knives in a *Cook's* rating of chef's knives five years ago, the Forschner Fibrox chef's knife, model 40520, ranked tops when rated along with other stamped knives of its class (*see* page 27). Made by Victorinox of Switzerland (inventors of the Swiss Army Knife), the Forschner knife is made of a high-carbon stainless steel, like all of the knives in this issue's test. It has a tang that extends most of the way (seven-eighths) through the handle for balance. The handle is made of a black, textured synthetic material, which most of our testers found particularly comfortable to grip. The knife, which has a blade 8 inches long, can be purchased by mail order for $28.40 from **Professional Cutlery Direct (170 Boston Post Road, Suite 135, Madison, CT 06443; 800-859-6994; www.cutlery.com).** The purchase code is FORSCI97. The runner-up in the rating, the Friedr. Dick Pro-Dynamic 8-inch chef's knife, model 5447-21, can also be ordered through Professional Cutlery Direct. The purchase code is FDCI97, and it sells for $28.80. The Friedr. Dick chef's knife blade has exactly the same dimensions as the Forschner. Its seamless handle is made of black polypropylene.

Lemon Zester

We are always fishing for a new or improved citrus zesting device. Just before wrapping up this issue we came upon a catch. Made by Mastrad in Paris, the zester looks peculiar, to say the least. It is arc-shaped with an oval rubber handle on one end and a small plastic beak-shaped tip with a hole through it at the opposite end. With the arc positioned so that it curves upward, you simply drag the tip along the citrus fruit, in this case a lemon, for a perfect strip of zest. Unlike traditional zesters, the Mastrad device requires little pressure. It is also less likely than a traditional citrus stripper to pick up any of the bitter pith. As much as we like this new gadget, we would stand by our recommendation on page 20 to use a coarse grater to make the grated zest in our lemon soufflé recipe. The Mastrad makes perfect zest strips. An additional chopping step will get you minced zest but that still will not release the lemon oils like a grater does. We would recom-mend this new zester to make long, curling zest strips for garnish to the soufflé. This product is quite new and not widely carried in stores. It can be mail-ordered for $6.95 from **Kitchen Arts (161 Newbury Street, Boston, MA 02116; 617-266-8701).** Shipping does cost $6.95, but you can order up to six zesters at this shipping price.

Alder Smoking Chips

Author A. Cort Sinnes found that alder wood smoking chips worked best for the Hot-Smoked Salmon recipe on page 9. Alder is a tree in the birch family that grows in temperate and cold climates; smoking chips made from this wood lend a hint of sweetness to foods. You might have a hard time finding alder smoking chips on the shelves of a nearby store, but you can order a bag of them (about 2 pounds worth) for $2.95 from **People's Woods (75 Mill Street, Cumberland, RI 02864; 800-729-5800; www.peopleswoods.com).**

Eggology

Our Chilled Lemon Soufflé recipe on page 21 contains raw egg whites, which may be of particular concern to pregnant women or anyone with a compromised immune system. Fortunately, there are a few alternative egg white products available for such recipes. We tested two in the recipe we developed for the chilled soufflé. The first was a powdered egg white product known as Just Whites, the second a pasteurized liquid egg white product known as Eggology. Both successfully whipped to soft peaks (Just Whites requires the addition of water). The soufflé made with Eggology produced a soufflé as tall as one made with standard egg whites, while the Just Whites soufflé stood about ½ inch shorter. More important, tasters detected an off flavor in the soufflé made with Just Whites that was not present in the soufflé made with Eggology. Eggology, which contains nothing but fresh egg whites, is pasteurized as well as tested for salmonella. It must be stored in the refrigerator, where it keeps for four months, or in the freezer, where it keeps indefinitely. To find the nearest store location to you that sells Eggology, contact **Eggology, Inc. (2899 Agoura Road, Suite 600, Westlake Village, CA 91361-3218; 888-669-6557).** An 18-ounce jar typically costs $4.19. You can also find the store nearest you by visiting Eggology's Web site (**www.eggology.com**). Or you can order directly from Eggology, Inc., but you have to order a case (four 64-ounce jars) for $75.80.

Polder Thermometer

The *Cook's* test kitchen constantly uses the Polder Cooking Thermometer/Timer, given an honor-able mention in *Cook's* rating of instant-read thermometers (*see* July/August 1997). But we find ourselves in particular appreciation of this device come summertime, when we're spending a lot of time at the grill. With a 45-inch wire connecting the probe to the base unit, you can gauge the internal temperature of meats without having to scorch your hand, which often happens when you are holding a standard instant-read thermometer over the grill fire. In the past couple of years many kitchenware stores have begun to carry the Polder. If you cannot find it, a good source for ordering it is **A Cook's Wares (211 37th Street, Beaver Falls, PA 15010-2103; 800-915-9788; www.cookswares.com).** It sells for $29.99. The item number is 2999.

One-Quart Soufflé Dish

The *Cook's* test kitchen needed to stock up on one-quart soufflé dishes when working on the Chilled Lemon Soufflé recipe on page 21. We were able to purchase them relatively inexpensively at $5.99 each through the catalog services at **Kitchen Etc. (Department TM, 32 Industrial Drive, Exeter, NH 03833; 800-232-4070).** The white porcelain dish has the glazed and ribbed exterior of a traditional soufflé dish. It is 6½ inches in diameter, with sides 3 inches high. It is ovensafe and can also be used for a small pot pie or casserole, or as an attractive serving bowl.

Electric Tea Maker

In our attempts to find the method for making perfect iced tea (page 10), we found that the TeaMate electric tea maker from Chef'sChoice International made an excellent version. The tea maker resembles a drip coffee maker. Standing 12 inches tall and about 7.5 inches wide, the machine can use loose leaf tea as well as bag tea and brews two to eight cups of either hot or iced tea. Tea leaves are first gently steamed, which provides for maximum extraction of flavor and aroma during steeping, according to the manufacturer. Then a portion of boiled water steeps the leaves (or tea bags) to make a strong concentrate. The steeping time can be adjusted from 2 to 15 minutes. After steeping, the concentrate flows into a preheated carafe with additional boiled water. A warming plate keeps the tea warm. Because this appliance is so specialized, it can be hard to find and is not cheap. We found two mail-order sources. The TeaMate comes in white and can be purchased for $99.99 from **Kitchen Glamor Catalogue (39049 Webb Court, Westland, MI 48185; 1-800-641-1252).** The item order number is 690. It is also available from **Sure Source (50 Commerce Drive, Trumbull, CT 06611; 1-888-666-5771)** for $99.95.

RECIPE INDEX

Green Goddess, Smoked Salmon with Dill and Horseradish, and Spinach with Feta and Garlic Dips (clockwise from front) **PAGE 24**

Three-Bean Salad with Cumin, Cilantro, and Oranges **PAGE 18**

Classic Fajitas and Grilled Corn **PAGES 15 AND 7**

Quick, Simple Full-Flavored Iced Tea **PAGE 11**

Hot-Smoked Salmon **PAGE 9**

Individual Summer Berry Pudding **PAGE 23**

PHOTOGRAPHY: CARL TREMBLAY   STYLING : MYROSHA DZIUK

Yellow Brandywine

Flammé

Moskvich

Green Zebra

Wonder Light

Debarao

German

Valencia

Cherokee Purple

Nepal

Great White Beefsteak

HEIRLOOM TOMATOES

COOK'S
ILLUSTRATED

The Ultimate Stuffed Chicken Breasts
Crispy Coating, Perfectly Cooked Interior, and Three Different Fillings

Best Fresh Tomato Sauce
Peel, Seed, and Cook Quickly

Thick-Cut Pork Chops
The Secret to Cooking Tender, Juicy Chops

Double Chocolate Cookies
As Intense as Hot Fudge Sauce

Deep Dish Pizza Comes Home
Surprise Dough Makes The Difference

Taste-Testing Parmesan

The Best Garlic Bread

Rating Salad Spinners

Bean and Pasta Soups

Rustic Apple Tarts

Best American Merlots

$4.95 U.S./$5.95 CANADA

CONTENTS

September & October 1999

COOKING APPLES Apples, like tomatoes, are available in much wider variety today than they were a few years ago. In the course of developing our recipes for apple pie and for baked apples (November/December 1997 and September/October 1995, respectively), we tested dozens of varieties to see which were preferable for each purpose. We found that Baldwin, Northern Spy, Golden Delicious, and Cortland made the best baked apples, firm and flavorful when they emerged from the oven. For apple pies, our regional favorites include Macouns, Empires, Winesaps, Rhode Island Greenings, Galas, and Cortlands. Of the apples that are available nationwide and year-round, we like a combination of McIntosh and Granny Smiths, which we also preferred in the apple tartlet recipe on page 22.

COVER PAINTING: BRENT WATKINSON, BACK COVER ILLUSTRATION: JOHN BURGOYNE.

COOK'S
ILLUSTRATED

PUBLISHER AND EDITOR
Christopher Kimball

SENIOR EDITOR
John Willoughby

SENIOR WRITER
Jack Bishop

ASSOCIATE EDITORS
Adam Ried
Maryellen Driscoll
Dawn Yanagihara

TEST KITCHEN DIRECTOR
Kay Rentschler

TEST COOKS
Anne Yamanaka
Bridget Lancaster
Julia Collin

CONSULTING FOOD EDITOR
Jasper White

CONSULTING EDITORS
Jim Dodge
Pam Anderson

ART DIRECTOR
Amy Klee

CORPORATE MANAGING EDITOR
Barbara Bourassa

EDITORIAL PRODUCTION MANAGERS
Sheila Datz
Nate Nickerson

COPY EDITOR
India Koopman

EDITORIAL INTERNS
Sarah Moughty
Lydia Peelle

MARKETING DIRECTOR
Adrienne Kimball

MARKETING MANAGER
Pamela Caporino

MARKETING ASSISTANT
Connie Forbes

CIRCULATION DIRECTOR
David Mack

FULFILLMENT MANAGER
Larisa Greiner

PRODUCTS MANAGER
Steven Browall

CIRCULATION ASSISTANT
Carrie Horan

VICE PRESIDENT
PRODUCTION AND TECHNOLOGY
James McCormack

SYSTEMS ADMINISTRATOR
Richard Cassidy

PRODUCTION ARTIST
Daniel Frey

PRODUCTION INTERN
Melissa Connors

CONTROLLER
Mandy Shito

OFFICE MANAGER
Mary Connelly

SPECIAL PROJECTS
Deborah Broide

For list rental information, contact The SpeciaLISTS, 1200 Harbor Blvd. 9th Floor, Weehawken, NJ 07087; (201) 865-5800; fax (201) 867-2450. Editorial office: 17 Station Street, Brookline, MA 02445; (617) 232-1000; fax (617) 232-1572. Editorial contributions should be sent to: Editor, *Cook's Illustrated*. We cannot assume responsibility for manuscripts submitted to us. Submissions will be returned only if accompanied by a large self-addressed envelope. PRINTED IN THE USA.

HEIRLOOM SEEDS

When I was young, the farmers in our small Vermont town still mowed hay with a team of horses, corn was harvested with a corn binder pulled by a team of mules, and small fields were often hayed with a pitchfork and wagon. Fields were planted with grain drills—wooden horse-drawn seeders, each with a row of metal cones that made furrows in the soil for the seeds. The outhouse was in use until 1969, most cooking was done on a wood Kalamazoo stove, and wells were dug only after a dowser had located the best spot, using a forked stick made from apple wood, the divining rod moving sharply downward in the presence of underground water.

I am only one generation removed from a time when every family farm was its own factory, churning out butter and cream, provisioning a root cellar, spinning wool, rendering lard, putting up preserves, making dandelion wine, boiling maple sap into syrup, collecting honey, and the like. In those days, farms were full of wood and metal machines, the labor-saving devices of the nineteenth century, which carried over well into the twentieth. There were milk aerators and churns, yarn winders and corn graders, shredders and binders, root cutters and cheese presses, Felloe saws (used for cutting rounds of wood for wheels) and beetles (large mallets), hog hooks and marking gauges, barn scrapers, metal swing churns, cream separators, and the all-purpose Superior stainless milk pails. In the winter ice was sawed, put onto sleds, and then moved by teams of horses to large ice houses where engine-powered conveyors lifted the heavy blocks to the houses' upper levels. The blocks were then packed with sawdust and the ice houses closed;

the heavy 21-inch blocks would last well into summer.

Now, every August, we visit local fairs that often have museums or barns full of old equipment. I dutifully take each of my children past the dog treadmills and the summer hearses (winter hearses had runners), the mailman's buggy with the built-in stove, the snow rollers (five-foot-high wooden rollers pulled by horses to pack down the snow), nickel-plated wood stoves, phaetons and surreys, spinning wheels and yarn winders, and displays showing old kitchens or children's bedrooms or the toolshed built onto the side of a barn. I eagerly enter the "What Is It?" contests or look hard at the old photos, hoping to see one of the old-timers I used to know or what the abandoned train station looked like in 1910, when it was prosperous, an artery pumping the lifeblood of commerce into a small New England town.

I often wonder if along with the fence tighteners and the ice tongs we have also lost a bit of self-reliance and a connection to how beginnings turn into endings. A well-made tool in knowledgeable hands is a wonderful thing; wood is cut and split, cream is churned into butter, a field is mowed in the afternoon sun, swallows swooping low, looking for bugs that have lost their hidey-holes. Farmers have necessarily been men and women of many trades: planters and cultivators, veterinarians and blacksmiths, carpenters and cooks, bakers and weathermen. They could judge a horse or use an Eddy plough or dig a well. They could also teach their sons and daughters, passing along experience

Christopher Kimball

to the next generation. In that world, I think, parents loomed large, for their skills were readily apparent. A man who can grow corn to feed pigs or a woman who can put up tomatoes and beans demonstrates his or her usefulness daily, the kids spectators to the accumulation and value of experience. Today, most parents have diminished roles, their expertise narrow and rarely seen, appreciated only by a small number of coworkers.

So in an age of specialists, perhaps we ought to take the time to be generalists. Let's learn to fix what is broken, master the shovel and the hoe, and become experts on planting and pruning. Each of us should know something about the soil, about compost and lime, about pH levels and organic matter, and about how to get rid of potato bugs. We should know the difference between the bark and leaves of elm and ash and recognize fiddlehead ferns and wild watercress when we see them.

And, in the kitchen, we should know the chuck from the round, a braise from a stew, and a torte from a tart. To sauté, roast, and bake should be second nature, and a whisk ought to be held with casual confidence. Good cooks are masters of many things, improvising and substituting to achieve modest ends. We should stand firm in front of the stove, feet planted in knowledge and experience, not as tourists surrounded by the unfamiliar. Like farmers, we should take the time to learn how to raise a healthy crop, cultivating our children like heirloom seedlings started in a warm, sunny corner of a country kitchen.

ABOUT COOK'S ILLUSTRATED

The Magazine *Cook's Illustrated* (ISSN 1068-2821) is published bimonthly (6 issues per year) by Boston Common Press Limited Partnership, 17 Station Street, Brookline, MA 02445. Copyright 1999 Boston Common Press Limited Partnership. Periodical postage paid at Boston, MA and additional mailing offices, USPS #012487. A one-year subscription is $29.70, two years is $55, and three years is $75. Add $6 postage per year for Canadian subscriptions and $12 per year for all other foreign countries. To order subscriptions in the U.S. call 800-526-8442; from outside the U.S. call 515-247-7571. Gift subscriptions are available for $24.95 each. Postmaster: Send all new orders, subscription inquiries, and change of address notices to: *Cook's Illustrated*, P.O. Box 7446, Red Oak, IA 51591-0446.

Magazine-Related Items *Cook's Illustrated* is available in annual hardbound editions for $24.95 each plus shipping and handling; each edition is fully indexed. Discounts are available if more than one year is ordered at a time. Individual back issues are available for $5 each. *Cook's* also offers a six-year index (1993–1998) of the magazine for $12.95. To order any of these products, call 800-611-0759 inside the U.S. or 515-246-6911 outside the U.S.

Books *Cook's Illustrated* publishes a series of single-topic books, available for $14.95 each. Titles include *How to Make a Pie, How to Make an American Layer Cake, How to Stir-* *Fry, How to Make Ice Cream, How to Make Salad, How to Make Simple Fruit Desserts, How to Make Cookie Jar Favorites, How to Cook Holiday Roasts and Birds, How to Make Stew, How to Grill, How to Make Pizza, How to Make Holiday Desserts, How to Make Pasta Sauces, How to Barbecue & Roast on the Grill, How to Cook Shrimp & Other Shellfish, How to Cook Garden Vegetables,* and *How to Make Pot Pies and Casseroles. The Cook's Bible,* written by Christopher Kimball and published by Little, Brown and Company, is available for $24.95. *The Yellow Farmhouse Cookbook,* also written by Christopher Kimball and published by Little, Brown and Company, is available for $24.95. To order any of these books, call 800-611-0759 inside the U.S. or 515-246-6911 outside the U.S.

Reader Submissions *Cook's* accepts reader submissions for Quick Tips. We will provide a one-year complimentary subscription for each tip that we print. Send your tip, name, address, and daytime telephone number, to Quick Tips, *Cook's Illustrated*, P.O. Box 470589, Brookline, MA 02447. Questions, suggestions, or submissions for Notes from Readers should be sent to the same address.

Subscription Inquiries All queries about subscriptions or change of address notices should be addressed to *Cook's Illustrated*, P.O. Box 7446, Red Oak, IA 51591-0446.

Web Site Address Selected articles and recipes from *Cook's Illustrated*, as well as our bookstore, can be found at www.cooksillustrated.com.

Light Cream

The recipe for Double Chocolate Pudding in our March/April 1999 issue calls for two cups of whole milk and one cup of light cream. It turns out, though, that light cream is a mystery to some of our readers, several of whom contacted us to say they could not find it in their markets. We investigated and found that there is no standard for the national availability of dairy products. Susan Ruland, spokesperson for the International Dairy Foods Association in Washington, D.C., said that supermarkets serving different areas will stock different products, depending on the buying habits of customers. Ruland offered buttermilk as a striking example, noting that while many stores in the Northeast fail to stock it, in the South, you'd be hard-pressed to find a single grocery without it because buttermilk is a standard ingredient in southern cooking. Neighborhood by neighborhood and region by region, stores are most likely to fill their limited shelf space with those products which sell best, and what sells best is different in different parts of the country.

Along with availability, the precise composition of light cream also varies. According to the FDA's *Code of Federal Regulations Title 21*, light cream, which can also be called coffee cream or table cream, may contain anywhere between 18 to 30 percent milk fat. This is a surprisingly wide margin, especially compared with other creams, such as half-and-half, which must contain between 10.5 to 18 percent milk fat, or heavy cream, which must contain at least 36 percent milk fat.

So what do you do about the pudding if you cannot get light cream? To approximate the same percentage of milk fat in the original recipe, we substituted a mixture of one cup whole milk and two cups half-and-half, both nationally available products, for the milk and light cream combination. None of our tasters could detect any significant flavor difference between the two. The consistency of the half-and-half version was a little bit looser than that of the original, but it still set nicely at room temperature, and we did manage to polish off the entire batch without looking back.

Rejuvenating Popcorn

I was told by a popcorn farmer that you can prevent all those unpopped kernels at the bottom of the pot by moistening the raw popcorn. He said to add enough water to a jar with the raw kernels to just cover them, let the jar sit for a minute, and then pour off the water immediately, including any that has pooled at the bottom. Then shake the jar vigorously to make sure all the kernels are wet, and let it sit, covered, for 24 hours. Once rehydrated, almost all the kernels pop and the puffs are more tender.

SARENE WALLACE
CAMARILLO, CALIF.

➤ We tested your method with popcorn that had been sitting in an open bag in one of our editor's cupboards for almost a year. Just as you say, the batch made from kernels moistened using your process was more tender and fluffy, with far fewer unpopped kernels than the batch popped from the plain, unmoistened kernels.

This makes sense because popcorn depends on inner moisture to pop. Lori Warner, marketing manager for the Popcorn Board in Chicago, explained that the optimal degree of moisture in good popping corn is 13.5 to 14 percent. The moisture in each kernel takes the form of a tiny droplet of water stored inside the starch of the kernel. The starch, in turn, is surrounded by a hard outer casing. When the kernels approach boiling temperature, the water within expands quickly and creates internal pressure, as much as 135 pounds per square inch by one estimate, until the outer casing finally explodes and steam is released. The kernel essentially turns inside out, with the starch now on the outside.

The Popcorn Board's Web site (www.Popcorn.org) also offers a considerably less scientific, but equally intriguing, explanation of how popcorn pops. As stated in the Web site, in American Indian folklore, some tribes were said to believe that quiet, contented spirits lived inside of each popcorn kernel. When their houses were heated, the spirits would become angrier and angrier, shaking the kernels until the heat became unbearable, at which point the spirits would burst out of their homes and into the air "in a disgruntled puff of steam."

Dry Roux

I thoroughly enjoyed reading your gumbo article (*see* "Discovering Great Gumbo," May/June 1999, page 6). Having grown up in Louisiana, I will admit that there are as many gumbo recipes as there are Boudreaux's and Thibodeaux's. There are, however, but a few ways to make roux. I was surprised that you did not discuss a method for making a "dry" roux. Simply place the desired amount of flour in a heavy skillet (Creole and Cajun cooks almost always favor cast iron), and brown it just as you would a "wet" roux. Similarly, you must constantly stir the flour to prevent it from sticking and burning. Dry roux will darken several shades when it is added to wet ingredients; I find that when the flour reaches a peanut butter shade of brown, the gravy will have a rich, dark brown color with no loss of the nutty flavor. Also, for the health conscious, some of the unnecessary fat is eliminated from the dish when using a dry roux.

J. KEVIN MARTIN
LAPLACE, LA.

➤ The spirit of gumbo is nothing if not the spirit of culinary improvisation and good-hearted controversy about how it is made best. It was in just this frame of mind that we took to the test kitchen to pit the dry roux against our more traditional, fat-based roux. In addition, we wanted to investigate the possibility of eliminating half a cup of fat from a very rich recipe, though the notion seems to run counter to the nature of gumbo.

Our luck with the dry roux was not as good as yours. Alone in the pan, the flour began to smoke after about 5 minutes—much earlier, even over medium heat, than the wet roux. After the same 20 minutes that we cooked the wet roux, the dry version had browned only to the color of sand, and we had to continue cooking for another 8 to 10 minutes before it reached a light-brown peanut butter shade. We also tried cooking the flour over medium-high and high heat, as recipes for dry roux in several cookbooks recommended, but in both cases there was so much smoke so early in the cooking process that we thought the flour was burning.

While the gumbo made with the dry roux certainly met our minimum standards for depth of color and flavor, tasters noted that it was a shade lighter and somewhat less nutty tasting than the original. Nonetheless, we would consider using a dry roux if we were trying to cut out some of the fat in the gumbo recipe. Remember, though, that a dry roux gumbo could not be considered strictly "low fat" because of the sausage, which we would not be willing to sacrifice.

Filé Safety

I read with interest your gumbo article, particularly the sidebar regarding the use of filé powder as a thickener. On the same day, I read an article in our local newspaper on the popularity of herbal remedies. This article stated that sassafras (the dried leaves of which filé is made from) had been banned by the Food and Drug Administration for use in food because it contains the carcinogen safrole. Another article I read recently said that filé powder should not be used for the same reason.

JACQUELINE AYERS
FAYETTEVILLE, N.Y.

To get an answer to your question, we consulted the FDA's *Code of Federal Regulations Title 21*, FDA food safety experts, and specialists in the fields of botany and herb and spice processing. According to the FDA representative with whom we spoke, filé powder is considered safe for food use. He did say that safrole, as you learned, is prohibited from direct addition to or use as human food, but he also noted that sassafras bark and root contain the greatest concentrations of safrole in the plant. Filé is made from the leaves. We might also add that our recipe for Shrimp and Sausage Gumbo with Filé calls for just 1½ teaspoons of filé powder, which is divided into servings for six to eight people.

Sweet Potatoes and Yams

I enjoyed the sweet potato casserole recipes in your November/December 1998 story "Not-Too-Sweet Potato Casserole." I am not clear, however, about the definitions of "sweet potato" and "yam." The stores where I shop sell "sweet potatoes," which are yellow inside, and "yams" which are orange inside and have a much sweeter, altogether different flavor.

CLINTON FOOTE
VANCOUVER, BRITISH COLUMBIA

Though the labeling of yams and sweet potatoes is often wrong and almost always confusing, we advise that you buy by color. We like the tubers with the dark, orangey-brown skin and the vivid orange flesh within. The flesh cooks up moist, and the flavor is very sweet. Though often labeled as yams, both fresh and canned, these are actually a variety of sweet potato developed in Louisiana in the 1930s. The growers called them yams simply for marketing purposes to set them apart from other sweet potato varieties. In so doing, they have confused consumers to this day.

Other varieties of sweet potato that are widely available commercially are paler in color, with a lighter yellow skin and a light-colored flesh that cooks up drier and tastes somewhat less sweet than the deeper orange variety.

True yams, on the other hand, belong to a completely different botanical family and are much more scarce in North America than sweet potatoes. Generally found in Asian or Latin markets, true yams are often sold in chunks because they can grow to be several feet long. Because there are dozens of varieties of yams, the flesh color can range from white to light yellow to pink and the skin color from off-white to brown. All of them, though, have very starchy flesh.

Windsor Pan

My husband and I were married recently, and we received a Windsor pan as a wedding gift. The pan is very heavy and, unlike our other saucepans, the sides angle gently outward toward the top. Though I have been using it as I would any regular saucepan, we figure that the unusual shape must be intended for a specific purpose, but we don't know what.

ANDREW AND MARIA VINING
TORRINGTON, CONN.

Also called a slant- or flare-sided saucepan, the Windsor saucepan is designed to reduce liquids efficiently. Often used in sauce making where the reduction of liquids is key, the flared sides increase the top surface area to speed evaporation. Our kitchen tests proved this true. We boiled one quart of water over high heat for 10 minutes in both a two-quart straight-sided saucepan with a six-inch top diameter and a two-and-one-half-quart Windsor pan with an eight-inch top diameter. After 10 minutes, the Windsor had evaporated a full cup of water, whereas the straight-sided saucepan had evaporated only three-quarters cup. The flared sides of the Windsor also make stovetop stirring and whisking a little easier. One cookware retailer we contacted mentioned that the Windsor resembles a French pan called a fait tout, except that the fait tout has shorter sides, thereby offering some of the advantages of a sauté pan as well.

According to information we obtained from cookware manufacturer All-Clad Metalcrafters, some sources claim that the Windsor pan was invented by a chef at the medieval Windsor Castle in order to better indulge the king's enthusiastic taste for sauces.

Easy Caramel Cleanup

Yesterday I made the crème caramel from the recipe in the September/October 1998 issue of *Cook's (see* "Classic Crème Caramel," page 24). The custard was phenomenal, but the caramel gave me problems. The finished custards turned out onto the serving plates well and there was an adequate amount of caramel sauce over them, but there were also very hard rims of caramel left stuck in the ramekins. The caramel was set so hard that we had difficulty washing the ramekins clean.

ELIZABETH BURRIDGE
SALT SPRING ISLAND, BRITISH COLUMBIA

Several other readers have contacted us with the same concern about residual caramel. A little bit of hardened caramel left over in the ramekins is, in our experience, normal with this dessert. In fact, in the course of testing the crème caramel recipe, our cooks had the same experience. Though we cannot keep some caramel from sticking to the ramekins, we can suggest a fairly easy cleanup method. Simply cover the ramekins with three or four inches of water in a large Dutch oven or soup kettle and bring to a boil. Use long-handled tongs to occasionally swish the ramekins around in the boiling water, lifting them up, pouring the water in them back into the pot, and immersing them into the boiling water again. It may take as long as 30 minutes, but the caramel will eventually dissolve into the water, leaving the ramekins easy to clean with soap and water.

Summer Pudding

Owing to a printing error, the last line of the Summer Pudding recipe on page 23 of the July/August 1999 issue was cut off. We apologize for any frustration caused by this error. Here is the recipe.

Follow recipe for Individual Summer Berry Puddings through step 1. While berries are cooling, follow illustration 1 to trim bread, spray loaf pan with vegetable cooking spray, and line pan with plastic wrap. Place loaf pan on rimmed cookie sheet. Following illustrations 2 and 3, assemble, cover, and weight the puddings. Following illustration 4, unmold and serve.

WHAT IS IT?

We rented a beach house this summer and found this utensil in one of the kitchen drawers. It looks like a shrimp deveiner. Are the holes for measuring shrimp size?

MAURA ROLLAND
FLORENCE, S.C.

This utensil, called a skeleton knife, is not meant for shrimp but to cut through soft, mushy, or sticky foods, especially soft cheeses. The advantage of the skeleton blade, which has three large holes punched out along its length, is its relative lack of metal— there is less to which sticky foods can cling. Typically, the blade is made of stainless steel with a microserrated cutting edge, and the handle is made of lightly textured black plastic. The prongs at the tip of the blade are for picking up the slices.

We cut slices from blocks of cream cheese, soft Teleme cheese, mozzarella, and chèvre, as well as from raw and cooked potatoes, with both a skeleton knife and a six-inch cook's knife. We found that, indeed, the slices of all the cheeses and the potatoes were much easier to remove neatly from the skeleton knife than from the standard cook's knife. The slices we cut with the skeleton knife also retained their shape a little better than those cut with the cook's knife, which tended to squish down the food. In side-by-side tests of tomato slicing, though, we found the skeleton knife made very little difference. Skeleton knives are available by mail for $19.95 from Professional Cutlery Direct, 242 Branford Rd., North Branford, CT 06471; 800-859-6994. The purchase code is MESSC199.

Quick Tips

Disposing of Excess Fat

Those who cook with bacon, sausage, or ground meat infrequently may not keep a "fat jar" in the refrigerator for easy disposal of excess fat. Madeleine Alexander of Portland, Ore., is always ready for the occasion. She washes out the cardboard containers from half-and-half or heavy cream and saves them under the sink. When she has hot bacon or other fat to throw away, she pulls out one of the stored small cartons, which makes the ideal receptacle.

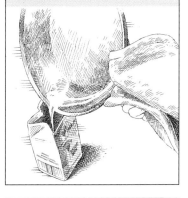

Efficient Coffee Grinding

Many blade-type coffee grinders grind the beans unevenly, producing some powder and some large pieces of bean. Suzanne Albinson of New Haven, Vt., evens out the grind by grasping the coffee grinder with her hand over the hopper, lifting the whole unit off the counter, and shaking it gently while grinding. This moves the beans around and helps the machine to grind more evenly.

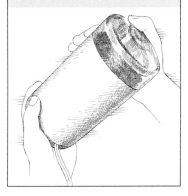

Freezing Cookie Dough

Keeping some frozen dough on hand means you can bake just as many, or as few, cookies as you like without first having to whip up a batch of dough. Test kitchen director Kay Rentschler forms the dough into balls and arranges them on a sheet pan or cookie sheet to freeze. Once the individual balls of dough are frozen, she simply places them in a zipper-lock freezer bag and stows it in the freezer.

Anchoring Parchment

It is irritating when the sheet of parchment covering a cookie sheet slides around as you try to drop a ball of cookie dough onto it. Test cook Bridget Lancaster has an easy way to get around this problem.

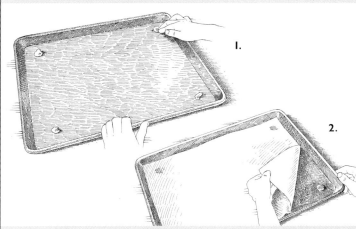

1. Put a small dab of the dough or batter at each corner of the baking sheet, and then press the parchment onto the small bits of dough.
2. The dough pieces secure the parchment to the baking sheet.

Homemade Tiered Shelf Organizer

Small items such as spice jars can get lost at the back of a well-stocked cabinet. Jerry Seaward of Oak Harbor, Wash., stacks two-by-four pieces of lumber, cut to the right length, to create different height levels in his cabinet. This way, items stored at higher levels in the rear are just as visible as those placed in the front.

Interesting Pizza Toppings Always at Hand

Homemade pizza is like a blank canvas for the creative use of myriad toppings. The problem is that you don't always have that many topping options on hand. Kristy Smith of Kalamazoo, Mich., has come up with a simple solution. Whenever she is cooking another dish that might make a good pizza topping, she reserves a little bit in a yogurt or cottage cheese container, labels it, and freezes it. When pizza is on the menu, she can sort through the frozen topping options, defrost the choices in the microwave, and let her creativity flow.

Thawing Frozen Pesto Cubes

The end-of-summer harvest season is the ideal time to transform all that extra basil in your garden into frozen cubes of pesto to use during the winter. But sometimes thawing those cubes takes more forethought than you have to devote to a meal. Shawmir Naeem of Allston, Mass., has developed a method of quickly thawing pesto to be served with pasta. Simply place as many frozen cubes as you need to thaw in a stainless steel mixing bowl and fit the bowl over the pot of cooking pasta, as if it were a makeshift double boiler. The heat from the boiling water melts the cubes just in time to toss with the hot pasta.

ILLUSTRATION: JOHN BURGOYNE

Send Us Your Tip We will provide a complimentary one-year subscription for each tip we print. See page 1 for information.

Smoothing Out Polenta

Every now and then, you may end up with little lumps of cornmeal in your polenta. When Rosalind Foyer of Encino, Calif., faces this problem, she uses her immersion blender to smooth out the mixture. She also uses it to blend in the butter.

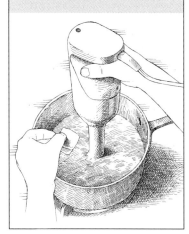

Cooking from Newspaper Recipes

When Karen Toner of Hoboken, N.J., clips recipes from a newspaper, she leaves plenty of head space above the recipe title. This way, she can close the paper in a cabinet door, and the recipe will hang at eye level right in front of her, away from messes on the work surface. With this method, no adhesive from tape ends up sticking to the cabinet door.

Freeing Up Containers

Plastic food storage containers often end up in the freezer along with their frozen contents. Lynette Terzic of La Costa, Calif., found a way to liberate her containers from the freezer.
1. Pass the container under hot running water just long enough to release its contents in a frozen block.
2. Drop the frozen block of food into a freezer bag for storage in the freezer.

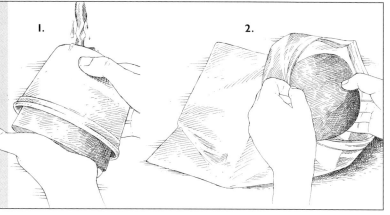

Breaking Spaghetti Strands Neatly

Though we don't usually break strands of pasta that we plan to sauce and eat, we often do break them for casseroles such as turkey Tetrazzini (see "Tetrazzini Revisited," November/December 1998, page 19). However, breaking the spaghetti strands in half before adding them to the pot often results in short shards of pasta flying every which way in the kitchen. You can avoid this problem by following this tip from Liam O'Caoimh of Wilton, County Cork, Ireland.

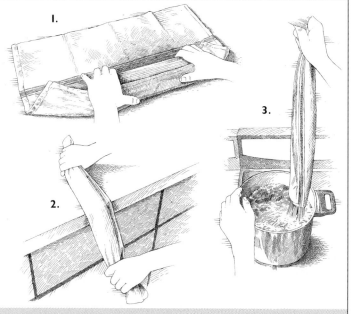

1. Roll up the bundle of spaghetti in a kitchen towel that overlaps the spaghetti by 3 to 4 inches on both ends.
2. Holding both ends firmly, center the rolled bundle over the edge of a table or counter. Push down with both hands to break the pasta in the middle of the bundle.
3. Holding the bundle vertically over the pot of boiling water, release the bottom of the cloth so that the pasta slides neatly into the pot.

Measuring Charcoal for Grilling

Many recipes for charcoal grilling, including those in *Cook's*, call for a particular volume of charcoal. Since volume can be very difficult to judge, Eric Dahl of Quincy, Mass., simplifies the process by fully opening the top of an empty half-gallon carton of milk or juice and using it to get a rough measure.

Safer Ginger Grating

Most cooks who use fresh ginger have scraped their fingers on the grater when the piece of ginger gets down to a tiny nub. Instead of cutting a small chunk of ginger off of a larger piece and then grating it, Alice Gordenker of Arlington, Mass., simply peels the small section of the larger piece that she wishes to grate and uses the rest of the ginger as a handle to keep her fingers safely away from the grater's teeth.

Perfect Goat Cheese Slices

The note in our recipe for Arugula and Radicchio Salad with Warm Goat Cheese and Olive Dressing (November/December 1998, page 18) said that goat cheese rounds can be difficult to slice neatly. Arthur Stone of Port Jefferson, N.Y., finds that dental floss is a good solution to this problem.

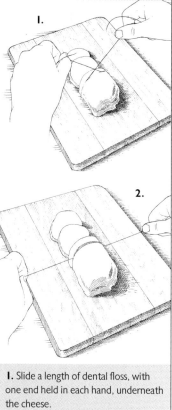

1. Slide a length of dental floss, with one end held in each hand, underneath the cheese.
2. Pull up, crossing the two ends to cut off neat slices.

Quick, Fresh Tomato Sauce

Extensive testing uncovered the secrets of a quick-cooked fresh tomato sauce
that is both hearty and brightly flavored.

≥ BY JACK BISHOP ≤

When tomatoes are good, nothing quite compares with their taste, a study in subtly contrasting sweet and tart flavors. The best fresh tomato sauces for pasta capture this complexity. Another consideration when making fresh tomato sauce is texture: the best of them are hearty and dense. Too many fresh tomato sauces are watery or mealy and have little fresh tomato flavor. If you are going to bother with fresh tomatoes, the sauce should be at least as good (if not better) than something you could make by just opening a can.

So when I set out to make a really good fresh tomato sauce, I knew I would focus on two issues—preserving the fresh tomato flavor and handling the tomatoes in such a way that they would yield a sauce with the proper consistency.

I began by culling about 60 recipes for tomato sauce and analyzing the variables. Most sources followed a simple pattern—heat the oil (and usually some garlic), add the tomatoes, simmer until the tomatoes have broken down into a thick sauce, add seasonings, and toss with pasta.

In some cases, the tomatoes were simply chopped before being added to the oil, but most sources recommended peeling and seeding them before chopping. A few recipes called for seeding the tomatoes but leaving the skins on.

Preparing the Tomatoes

Working with a basic recipe that contained just olive oil, diced fresh tomatoes, and salt, I prepared three batches of sauce—one with tomatoes that I peeled and seeded before dicing, one with tomatoes that I only seeded and diced, and one with tomatoes I neither seeded nor peeled. The results were surprisingly different. The sauce made with peeled and seeded tomatoes was by far the best. It had the best consistency—dense and

A shortened cooking time gives this simple sauce a fresh flavor.

hearty—as well as the brightest, freshest flavor. Both sauces made with unpeeled tomatoes contained hard, unappetizing bits of curled up skin (the skin had separated from the individual tomato cubes as the tomatoes cooked). In addition, these sauces were less fresh tasting.

I also found that the sauce made with peeled and seeded tomatoes had cooked more quickly than the other two sauces. It took just 10 minutes in a sauté pan for peeled and seeded tomatoes to fall apart to the proper consistency. When I left the skins on the tomato cubes, they took 18 minutes to collapse; evidently, the skins help the tomatoes hold their shape. As for the seeds, tasters did not object to them, but the seeds made the chopped tomatoes more watery and thus increased the cooking time. I had uncovered a key element to great fresh tomato sauce—short cooking time. Peeling and seeding speeds cooking and is necessary for this reason, not to mention the fact that the skins mar the texture of the finished sauce.

I was pretty sure about my finding but felt that my hypothesis—that long cooking destroys fresh tomato flavor—needed more testing. After all, my Italian grandmother (as well as countless Italian cookbook authors) insists on simmering tomato sauce for at least an hour, if not longer. I prepared three more sauces with peeled, seeded, and diced tomatoes. I cooked one for 10 minutes (the minimum time necessary for the tomatoes to break down into a sauce), one for 30 minutes, and a third for an hour. The sauce that cooked for 10 minutes had the best flavor. The others reminded me of tomato puree—they were dense and smooth, but left me wondering where the tomato flavor had gone.

No Minimizing

After making so many batches of this sauce, I was beginning to wonder if there was a way to get around peeling, seeding, and chopping before cooking. It was taking me longer to prepare the tomatoes than to cook the sauce.

Many recipes in Italian cookbooks call for peeling and seeding after the tomatoes have been cooked. The tomatoes are cut into quarters, stewed in a casserole until they collapse, and then put through a food mill to remove the skins and seeds. The tomato pulp is then used to make sauce. A variation on this method calls for roasting the tomatoes, then putting them through a food mill. Either way, the food mill allows the skins and seeds to be removed after cooking.

I stewed tomatoes in a casserole with a bit of oil until they collapsed and then ran them through a food mill. The mill removed all the skins and a good amount of seeds. However, the tomato pulp was still pretty watery and needed to be cooked down further. And the color of the pulp was an odd brick red. One taste and I recognized the flavor—the pulp had the strong scorched or roasted flavor I associate with Mexican cooking. (For

many Mexican dishes, whole or sliced tomatoes are seared on a griddle and then peeled and made into sauce.) The same thing happened to tomatoes put in the oven. In both cases, the flesh of the tomato was exposed to the heat and acquired an almost burnt flavor that I did not want in my sauce. Tomato flavor is pretty delicate, and if you add burnt notes, the balance between sweetness and acidity will be lost.

Final Adjustments, Final Touches

In the process of doing my testing, I found that it worked best to use a wide pan (a 10-inch pan is right for a single batch of sauce) to promote quick evaporation. When I tried cooking two pounds of prepared tomatoes in a three-quart saucepan, I had to pile the tomatoes on top of one another because of the smaller surface area. As a result, they took an extra 10 minutes to thicken up and did not taste as fresh. As for the

type of pan, I prefer a sauté pan with relatively high three-inch sides rather than a skillet with sloped sides. The reason is simple—less splattering. Keep the cover off as the sauce cooks to allow the tomato liquid to evaporate, and cook the sauce over a brisk medium heat.

Now I knew how to handle the tomatoes to keep their flavor lively: peel, seed, and chop, then cook them quickly in a sauté pan with oil. Next I had to figure out the other components of the sauce. I tried sautéing various aromatic vegetables in the oil before adding the tomatoes and found that a little garlic (heated with the oil so it would not burn) was the best choice. Onion was good as well (especially when I wanted to play up the sweetness in the sauce), but garlic was my first choice. I found leeks, carrots, and celery too distracting.

My recipe now contained olive oil (I found that extra-virgin oil makes a real difference here), garlic, and tomatoes. Of course, the sauce needed some salt, and I thought an herb would round out the flavors. Basil is the natural choice, but parsley is appropriate as well.

I picked up a few more refinements from Christopher Kimball's story on canned tomato sauces in the May/June 1997 issue of *Cook's*. I saved some of the cooking water from the pasta to help spread this dense tomato sauce over the pasta, and I added a little olive oil to the pasta and sauce for a hit of fresh olive flavor. The result was a sauce that celebrated the flavor of tomatoes, plain and simple.

PASTA AND FRESH TOMATO SAUCE WITH GARLIC AND BASIL
SERVES 4

Any type of tomato may be used in this recipe—just make sure to choose the ripest, most flavorful ones available. Short tubular or curly pasta shapes such as penne or fusilli are well-suited to this chunky sauce. Alternately, before adding the basil, the sauce may be pureed in a blender or food processor so it will coat strands of spaghetti or linguine. The recipe may be doubled in a 12-inch skillet. The sauce freezes well, but add the basil when reheating.

3 tablespoons extra-virgin olive oil
2 medium garlic cloves, minced or pressed with garlic press
2 pounds ripe tomatoes, cored, peeled, seeded, and cut into ½-inch pieces
2 tablespoons chopped fresh basil leaves
   Salt
1 pound pasta (*see* note)

1. Heat 2 tablespoons oil and garlic in medium skillet over medium heat until garlic is fragrant but not browned, about 2 minutes. Stir in tomatoes; increase heat to medium-high and cook

until liquid given off by tomatoes evaporates and tomato pieces lose their shape to form a chunky sauce, about 10 minutes. Stir in basil and salt to taste; cover to keep warm.

2. Meanwhile, bring 4 quarts water to boil in large pot or soup kettle. Add 1 tablespoon salt and pasta. Cook until pasta is al dente (refer to package directions; cooking times vary with different shapes). Reserve ¼ cup cooking water; drain pasta and transfer back to cooking pot. Mix in reserved cooking water, sauce, and remaining tablespoon oil; toss well to combine. Serve immediately.

PASTA AND FRESH TOMATO SAUCE WITH CHILE PEPPER AND BASIL

Follow recipe for Pasta and Fresh Tomato Sauce with Garlic and Basil, heating ¾ teaspoon red pepper flakes with oil and garlic.

PASTA AND FRESH TOMATO SAUCE WITH ANCHOVIES, OLIVES, AND CAPERS

Follow recipe for Pasta and Fresh Tomato Sauce with Garlic and Basil, heating 3 minced anchovy fillets with oil and garlic. Add 8 large brine-cured black olives (such as kalamata), pitted and chopped (about ¼ cup), and 1 tablespoon drained capers to sauce along with basil.

PASTA AND FRESH TOMATO SAUCE WITH ONION AND BACON

Pancetta, unsmoked Italian bacon, can be substituted for American bacon in this variation. Because it is leaner, sauté it in 2 tablespoons of olive oil with the onion.

Mince 1 medium onion and cut 4 strips (about 4 ounces) bacon into ¼-inch pieces. Follow recipe for Pasta and Fresh Tomato Sauce with Garlic and Basil, omitting garlic and heating bacon and onion in 1 tablespoon olive oil until onion begins to brown and bacon begins to crisp, about 6 minutes. Continue with recipe, substituting equal amount minced fresh parsley for basil.

PASTA AND FRESH TOMATO CREAM SAUCE WITH ONION AND BUTTER

This rich sauce is especially good with fresh fettuccine or cheese ravioli.

Follow recipe for Pasta and Fresh Tomato Sauce with Garlic and Basil, substituting melted butter for olive oil and 1 medium onion, minced, for garlic; sauté onion until golden, about 5 minutes. Continue with recipe, adding ½ cup heavy cream to tomatoes after chunky sauce has formed; simmer until cream thickens slightly, 2 to 3 minutes longer. Toss the pasta with sauce and cooking water, omitting the additional oil.

The Ultimate Stuffed Chicken Breast

Here's how to produce a crispy coating, a moist, perfectly cooked interior,
and a bold filling that will not leak out during cooking.

⇒ BY STEPHANIE LYNESS ⇐

O n their own, chicken breasts can be
pretty ho-hum, but when they're
breaded and stuffed with the right
filling, the results can be truly wonderful. The filling coats the chicken with a
creamy, tasty sauce, and the crust makes a
crunchy counterpoint.

But these tasty little bundles pose a number of
problems for the cook. Chicken breasts are tricky
to cook—dry if cooked too long, rubbery if
undercooked—and it's difficult to arrive at a consistent cooking time because breasts vary in size,
one to another, and the pointed end is thinner
than the rounded end. As for the filling, it must
be creamy without being runny, and tasty but not
so strong-flavored that it overpowers the chicken.
Not only that, but if the crust doesn't effectively
enclose the filling, it leaks out.

Solving these problems seemed especially
important because I think of stuffed chicken
breasts as a "special occasion" dish that involves
a fair amount of work. I wanted the recipe to be
virtually foolproof, cooking up perfectly every
time, and absolutely delicious as well.

Charting a Path

There are many ways to make stuffed chicken
breasts, so my first task was to test them all and
find out which basic method worked best. I tried
roasting them, sautéing them, and browning first
then roasting. I tried skin on and skin off,
breaded and not breaded. I tried slipping the
stuffing under the skin, cutting a slit for the stuffing in the thick part of the breast, and spreading
pounded breasts with stuffing, then rolling them
up and securing them with toothpicks. I even
tried one recipe that called for a whole (double)
breast to be stuffed as one piece and baked. When
this orgy of testing came to an end, I had learned
a lot about the issues involved in making this dish
and had a much clearer picture of what I needed
to do to perfect it.

From the beginning my tasters almost unanimously disliked the skin, which did not crisp up
in response to any of the methods used. They did
like the breading, however, which provided a
toasty flavor as well as a crisp complement to the
meat. Since the breading was well liked, I knew I
had to find a cooking method that would crisp
the exterior without overbrowning it before the
center was fully cooked. Deep-frying was the

To serve the chicken breasts, slice them crosswise on a slight diagonal and then fan them out on the plate.

obvious answer, but since that is not an option for
many home cooks, I needed to look further. Two
of the cooking techniques I had tried during the
first round of tests—fully cooking in a skillet on
the stove top and stove-top browning then baking—warranted further exploration.

I ran my first test on top of the stove, sautéing
the breasts in just enough vegetable oil to generously coat the bottom of the sauté pan. This test
revealed a number of problems. First, it was difficult to arrive at a heat that would brown the
chicken without burning it, so the breasts
required constant tending. With attention and
lots of fussing, the top and bottom of the breasts
did brown well, but the sides did not. And the
breasts often stuck to the pan. Furthermore, even
though the three breasts in the pan at any one
time were only of slightly different weights and

shapes, their rates of cooking were different
enough to be a problem.

It seemed logical that the two-step method—
a preliminary pan-frying on top of the stove followed by baking in the even heat of the oven—
would solve the twin problems of overbrowning
and too much fussing. I sautéed the next batch in
oil that came one-third to halfway up the sides of
the chicken, cooking until the chicken was well-
browned all over. Then, to combat the sogginess
I had observed in roasted breasts during the initial round of testing, I baked the chicken on a
wire rack on a jelly-roll pan so that hot air could
circulate underneath the breasts.

The results were much improved: the breasts
didn't stick to the pan; they came out of the oven
evenly browned, with an excellent, crunchy coating; and the meat inside was not soggy but

instead almost uniformly moist, with only the skinny tips of the breasts slightly dry. Because the time in the oven didn't significantly darken the crust, I could rely on this method for a perfect crust every time as long as I carefully supervised the stove-top browning.

Comparing Crumbs

Next I had to figure out what ingredients to use in the crust. The commercial breadcrumb coating I was using tasted OK, but I wanted to make sure that other options wouldn't taste better. I did a side-by-side testing of three breasts, each coated with an anglaise breading (flour, egg, and breadcrumbs) and cooked according to the method above. On one breast I used commercial dried breadcrumbs, on another homemade fresh breadcrumbs, and on the third Japanese packaged, dried breadcrumbs, called panko.

Of the three, I liked the flavor of the fresh crumbs the best, but the hot oil splattered badly on contact with the moisture in the crumbs. I didn't want to give up on the fresh taste, though, and I was willing to do a little extra work to attain perfection, so I dried the bread in the oven for long enough to get rid of some of the moisture, but not so long that the bread toasted; darkened crumbs might burn on the chicken. Several tests later, I got the method and timing right: cubes of bread dried in a very low oven (250 degrees) for about 30 minutes and then ground in the food processor produced crumbs that tasted fresh but didn't splatter or burn.

Getting Stuffing Right

Satisfied with the coating and cooking methods, I turned my attention to perfecting the stuffing technique. During my first round of testing, I had found "pocket-stuffed" breasts to be particularly troublesome. Since this method places the filling in the thickest part of the breast, its shape becomes still more uneven, so the small tapered end is far gone by the time the thicker portion is cooked. And, of course, when you cut into it, the tapered end is disappointingly devoid of filling. Pounding the breasts thin and rolling them up around the filling produced the most even distribution of the filling and the most even cooking of the meat. It was also the only method that prevented the filling from leaking out during cooking. Once cooked, the breasts could be sliced into medallions that looked lovely on the plate.

But there was still a problem. These breasts had to be secured with toothpicks—sometimes multiple toothpicks in a single breast—all of which then had to be removed before the breast was sliced into medallions.

Luckily, getting over this hurdle turned out to be easier than I thought. I reasoned that chilling the stuffed breasts briefly before cooking would inhibit the cream cheese in the filling from melting so quickly and that the chilled

cheese might also hold the roll together. I was right on both counts. Wrapping the breasts in aluminum foil and chilling them for 45 minutes before breading and cooking cooled the cheese enough to hold the roll together. It also kept the cheese from melting out of the crust during baking. This technique also makes it possible to prepare the breasts up to this point and refrigerate them overnight, which is very helpful when entertaining.

I had finally achieved my goal: tender, evenly cooked chicken breasts with a crunchy outer coating and creamy, flavorful fillings that did not leak out during cooking. Next time I wanted a special occasion dish, I knew I would be prepared.

ULTIMATE STUFFED CHICKEN BREASTS
SERVES 4

The fillings made with ham and cheddar cheese and with gorgonzola are simple, requiring very little preparation. The last two fillings are a little more involved, but worth the effort. The chicken breasts can be filled and rolled in advance, then refrigerated for up to 24 hours.

- 4 boneless, skinless chicken breasts (5 to 6 ounces each), tenderloins removed and reserved for another use
  Salt and ground black pepper
- 1 recipe filling (recipes follow)
- 1 cup all-purpose flour
- 4 large eggs
- 1 tablespoon plus ¾ cup vegetable oil
- 1½ cups fresh bread crumbs

1. Place each chicken breast on large sheet of plastic wrap, cover with second sheet, and pound with meat pounder or rolling pin until ¼-inch thick throughout (*see* illustration 1, page 10). Each pounded breast should measure roughly 6 inches wide and 8½ inches long. Cover and refrigerate while preparing filling.

2. Place breasts skinned side down on work surface; season with salt and pepper. Follow illustrations 2 through 4 (page 10) to fill, roll, and wrap each breast. Refrigerate until filling is firm, at least 45 minutes.

3. Adjust oven rack to lower-middle position; heat oven to 400 degrees. Spread flour in pie plate or shallow baking dish. Beat eggs with 1 tablespoon vegetable oil and 1 tablespoon water in second pie plate or shallow baking dish. Spread bread crumbs in third pie plate or shallow baking dish. Unwrap chicken breasts and roll in flour; shake off excess. Using tongs, roll breasts in egg mixture; let excess drip off. Transfer to bread crumbs; shake pan to roll breasts in crumbs, then press with fingers to help crumbs adhere. Place breaded chicken breasts on large wire rack set over jelly-roll pan.

4. Heat remaining ¾ cup oil in medium skil-

let over medium-high heat until shimmering, but not smoking, about 4 minutes; add chicken, seam side down, and cook until medium golden brown, about 2 minutes. Turn each roll and cook until medium golden brown on all sides, 2 to 3 minutes longer. Return chicken rolls, seam side down, to wire rack set over jelly-roll pan; bake until deep golden brown and instant-read thermometer inserted into center of each roll registers 155 degrees, about 15 minutes. Let stand 5 minutes before slicing each roll crosswise diagonally into 5 medallions; arrange on individual dinner plates and serve.

HAM AND CHEDDAR CHEESE FILLING WITH THYME

- 1 tablespoon butter
- 1 small onion, minced
- 1 small garlic clove, minced
- 4 ounces cream cheese, softened
- 1 teaspoon chopped fresh thyme leaves
- 4 ounces cheddar cheese, shredded (about ½ cup)
- 4 slices (about 4 ounces) thin-sliced cooked deli ham
  Salt and ground black pepper

Heat butter in medium skillet over low heat until melted; add onion and sauté, stirring occasionally, until deep golden brown, 15 to 20 minutes. Stir in garlic and cook until fragrant, about 30 seconds longer; set aside. In medium bowl using hand mixer, beat cream cheese on medium speed until light and fluffy, about 1 minute. Stir in onion mixture, thyme, and cheddar; season with salt and pepper and set aside. To stuff breasts, follow illustration 2, page 10, placing 1 slice ham on top of cheese on each breast, folding ham as necessary to fit onto surface of breast.

GORGONZOLA CHEESE FILLING WITH WALNUTS AND FIGS

Two tablespoons dried cherries or cranberries can be substituted for the figs.

- 1 tablespoon butter
- 1 small onion, minced
- 1 small garlic clove, minced
- 2 ounces cream cheese, softened
- 1 teaspoon chopped fresh thyme leaves
- 2 ounces gorgonzola cheese, crumbled (about ½ cup)
- ¼ cup chopped toasted walnuts
- 3 medium dried figs, chopped (about 2 tablespoons)
- 1 tablespoon dry sherry
  Salt and ground black pepper

Heat butter in medium skillet over low heat until melted; add onion and sauté, stirring occasionally, until deep golden brown, 15 to 20 minutes. Stir in garlic and cook until fragrant, about 30 seconds longer; set aside. In medium bowl using hand mixer, beat cream cheese on medium speed until light and fluffy, about 1 minute. Stir in onion mixture, gorgonzola, walnuts, figs, and sherry; season with salt and pepper and set aside. To stuff breasts, follow illustration 2.

ROASTED MUSHROOM AND PROVOLONE FILLING WITH ROSEMARY

10	ounces white mushrooms, washed, stemmed, and quartered
2	tablespoons olive oil
	Salt and ground black pepper
1	tablespoon butter
1	small onion, minced
1	small garlic clove, minced
4	ounces cream cheese, softened
1	teaspoon chopped fresh thyme leaves
1	tablespoon chopped fresh rosemary
4	ounces provolone cheese, shredded (about 1/2 cup)

1. Adjust oven rack to lowest position; heat oven to 450 degrees. Toss mushrooms with olive oil, and season with salt and pepper; spread in single layer on jelly-roll pan and roast until mushroom liquid has almost completely evaporated and mushroom surfaces facing pan are browned, 12 to 15 minutes. Turn mushrooms with metal spatula; continue to roast until mushrooms are browned all over, 5 to 10 minutes longer. Set aside.

2. Heat butter in medium skillet over low heat until melted; add onion and sauté, stirring occasionally, until deep golden brown, 15 to 20 minutes. Stir in garlic and cook until fragrant, about 30 seconds longer; set aside. In medium bowl using hand mixer, beat cream cheese on medium speed until light and fluffy, about 1 minute. Stir in onion mixture, thyme, rosemary, and provolone; season with salt and pepper and set aside.

3. To stuff breasts, follow illustration 2, arranging mushrooms on top of cheese on each breast.

BROILED ASPARAGUS AND SMOKED MOZZARELLA FILLING WITH BALSAMIC VINEGAR

16	medium asparagus spears, trimmed to 5-inch lengths
2	teaspoons olive oil
	Salt and ground black pepper
2	tablespoons balsamic vinegar
1	tablespoon butter
1	small onion, minced
1	small garlic clove, minced
4	ounces cream cheese, softened
1	teaspoon chopped fresh thyme leaves
4	ounces smoked mozzarella cheese, shredded (about 1/2 cup)

1. Heat broiler. Toss asparagus with olive oil and season with salt and pepper; spread in single

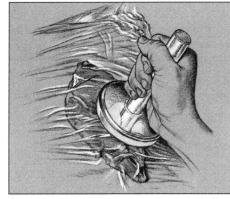

1. Place each trimmed breast between 2 sheets of plastic wrap. Starting in the center of each breast, pound evenly out toward the edges, taking care not to tear the flesh.

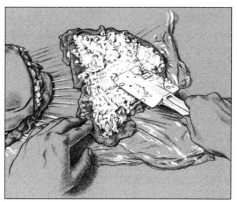

2. Place breasts skinned side down on work surface, season, and spread with one-quarter of the cheese mixture.

3. Roll the cutlet up from the tapered end, folding in the edges to form a neat cylinder.

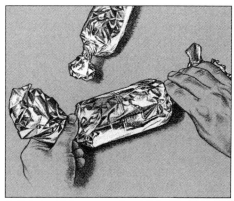

4. To help seal the seams and to chill the filling, wrap the breasts in aluminum foil and twist the ends in opposite directions. Refrigerate for at least 45 minutes.

5. A perfect coating will be thin and uniform, with no tacky areas.

6. Slip the chicken breasts seam side down in the hot oil.

layer on jelly-roll pan and broil 4 inches from top heating element until tender and browned, 6 to 8 minutes, shaking pan to rotate spears halfway through cooking time. Sprinkle with balsamic vinegar; set aside.

2. Heat butter in medium skillet over low heat until melted; add onion and sauté, stirring occasionally, until deep golden brown, 15 to 20 minutes. Stir in garlic and cook until fragrant, about

30 seconds longer; set aside. In medium bowl using hand mixer, beat cream cheese on medium speed until light and fluffy, about 1 minute. Stir in onion mixture, thyme, and mozzarella; season with salt and pepper and set aside.

3. To stuff breasts, follow illustration 2, placing 4 asparagus spears horizontally on top of cheese on each breast, spacing them about 1 inch apart and trimming off ends if necessary.

Pasta and Bean Soups

Make traditional Italian soups in far less time by using canned instead of dried beans. And for the best texture, make the soup ahead and add the pasta at the last minute.

≥ BY G. FRANCO ROMAGNOLI ≤

Italian pasta and bean soups are attractive because of their simplicity. The only time-consuming part of the process is preparing and cooking the beans from scratch, and that step is easily circumvented by using a can opener. Another obstacle to overcome when making these soups is preventing the pasta from becoming soggy. Adding it at the end of the cooking process takes care of this. In fact, any of these soups can be made ahead, covered, and refrigerated for up to two days as long as you heed one caveat: Leave out the pasta when you first make the soup, add it when you reheat it.

PENNE AND CHICKPEA SOUP
SERVES 6 TO 8 AS A MAIN COURSE

- ¼ cup olive oil
- 4 ounces bacon or pancetta, diced fine
- 4 medium garlic cloves, peeled and bruised
- 1 sprig fresh rosemary, plus 1 tablespoon chopped fresh rosemary leaves
- 2 cans (14½ ounces each) diced tomatoes (about 2 cups), with liquid
- 2 cans (15½ ounces each) chickpeas (about 3 cups), drained and rinsed, and 1½ of the 3 cups mashed with a fork
- 2 teaspoons salt, plus extra for seasoning
- 8 ounces penne or other short pasta
  Ground black pepper
  Freshly grated Pecorino Romano cheese
- ¼ cup extra-virgin olive oil (optional)

Heat olive oil in large soup kettle or stockpot over medium heat. Add bacon or pancetta; sauté until browned, 4 to 5 minutes. Add garlic and rosemary sprig; sauté until fragrant, about 2 minutes longer. Add tomatoes with their liquid, whole and mashed chickpeas, 6 cups water, and salt; bring to boil. Reduce heat and simmer to blend flavors, about 10 minutes. Add pasta; cook until tender, about 10 minutes. Remove rosemary sprig and add chopped rosemary; adjust seasoning with salt and ground black pepper, and serve, passing grated cheese and olive oil, if desired, separately.

FETTUCCINE AND WHITE BEAN SOUP
SERVES 6 TO 8 AS A MAIN COURSE

- ¼ cup olive oil
- 4 ounces prosciutto, diced fine
- 1 medium onion, diced fine
- 1 can (14½ ounces) diced tomatoes (about 1 cup), with liquid
- 1 celery stalk, diced fine
- 1 medium potato, peeled and cut into ½-inch cubes
- 2 teaspoons salt, plus extra for seasoning
- 2 cans (15½ ounces each) white beans (about 3 cups), with liquid
- 1½ tablespoons minced fresh sage leaves
- 5 ounces fettuccine, broken into 2-inch pieces
  Ground black pepper

Heat olive oil in large soup kettle or stockpot over medium heat. Add prosciutto and onion; sauté until onion is translucent, 4 to 5 minutes. Add tomatoes with their liquid, celery, potato, salt, beans with their liquid, sage, and 6 cups water; bring to boil and cook until potato is tender, about 5 minutes. Add the fettuccine and cook, stirring occasionally, until pasta is tender, 7 to 8 minutes. Off heat, adjust seasoning with salt and ground black pepper, and serve.

ORZO AND KIDNEY BEAN SOUP
SERVES 6 TO 8 AS A MAIN COURSE

- 2 teaspoons salt, plus extra for seasoning
- 1 pound (about ½ small head) green cabbage, cored and shredded
- 3 tablespoons olive oil
- 1 medium onion, diced fine
- 2 medium leeks, white part only, washed thoroughly and chopped fine
- 1 small carrot, peeled and diced fine
- 1 celery stalk, diced fine
- 3 ounces bacon or pancetta, diced fine
- 1 potato, peeled and coarsely grated
- 1 can (15½ ounces) red kidney beans (about 1½ cups), with liquid
- ¼ teaspoon ground white pepper
- ¼ teaspoon ground cinnamon
- 6 ounces orzo (1 cup)
  Freshly grated Parmesan cheese

1. Bring 4 quarts water to boil in large saucepan. Add 2 teaspoons salt and cabbage; blanch until crisp-tender, about 5 minutes. Drain and rinse under cold water; set aside.

2. Heat olive oil in large soup kettle or stockpor over medium heat. Add onion, leeks, carrot, celery, and bacon or pancetta; sauté until soft-ened and golden, about 5 minutes. Add reserved cabbage, potato, beans, pepper, cinnamon, and 2 quarts hot water; bring to boil. Add orzo, reduce heat to low, and simmer until orzo is tender, 7 to 8 minutes. Adjust seasoning with additional salt, if necessary, and serve, passing grated cheese separately.

MACARONI AND PINTO BEAN SOUP WITH MUSSELS
SERVES 6 AS A MAIN COURSE

- 4 pounds fresh mussels, cleaned and debearded
- 1 cup dry white wine
- ¼ cup olive oil
- 3 medium garlic cloves, peeled and slivered
- ½ teaspoon crushed red pepper flakes
- 1½ tablespoons chopped fresh rosemary leaves
- 2 teaspoons salt, plus extra for seasoning
- 2 cans (15½ ounces each) pinto beans (about 3 cups), with liquid, 1½ of the 3 cups mashed with a fork
- 1 can (14½ ounces) diced tomatoes (about 1 cup), with liquid
- 8 ounces elbow macaroni, penne, or other short, tubular pasta
  Ground black pepper

1. Bring mussels and wine to boil in large cov-ered soup kettle or stockpot; cook until mussels open, 3 to 5 minutes. Transfer mussels to large bowl with slotted spoon, allowing liquid to drain back into pot; cool slightly. Separate meat from shells, reserving meat in small bowl and discard-ing shells. Pour mussel broth into 1 quart mea-suring cup, holding back and discarding last few tablespoons of broth if there is sediment; set broth aside. (Should have about 2 cups.) Rinse and dry pot; return to burner.

2. Heat olive oil, garlic, pepper flakes, and rose-mary in now-empty pot over medium heat until garlic is fragrant but not brown, 2 to 3 minutes. Add 6 cups water, salt, whole and mashed beans with their liquid, tomatoes with their liquid, and reserved mussel broth; bring to simmer, add pasta, and cook until pasta is tender, 7 to 8 minutes. Add reserved mussel meat; adjust seasoning with salt and ground black pepper to taste, and serve.

G. Franco Romagnoli is the author of *Zuppa! A Tour of the Many Regions of Italy and Their Soups* (Henry Holt, 1996).

Bringing Deep-Dish Pizza Home

Can you make better-than-takeout deep-dish pizza at home, in a reasonable amount of time?

⇒ BY ANNE YAMANAKA ⇐

Deep-dish pizza is not something that most people think of making at home. That's not surprising, since it's definitely easier to pick up the phone and order a "pan" pizza. So why make this uniquely American pizza at home? There is one very good, very simple reason: because most deep-dish pizzas out there are not worth eating. I've had moderately good deep-dish pizzas, but most were oily discs of tasteless, soggy, heavy dough overwhelmed by even greasier toppings.

I wanted to devise a deep-dish pizza recipe in which a great crust takes center stage, especially since these pizzas are about 75 percent crust. I wanted that crust to be rich, substantial, and moist, with a tender, yet slightly chewy crumb and a well-developed flavor, like that of a good loaf of bread. In addition, it should be crisp and nicely browned, but not dry or tough. Knowing how time-consuming pizza making can be, I also wanted a pizza dough that could be made in as short a time as possible, without sacrificing quality.

Getting the Dough Right

After scouring various cookbooks, my colleagues and I in the *Cook's* test kitchen made five different pizza doughs and baked them in deep-dish pans. To our disappointment, none delivered the flavorful, crisp brown crust that we felt was needed. Even pizza dough recipes developed exclusively for deep-dish pizzas were terrible.

After these initial tests, we tried dozens of variations. We played around with the ratio of water to flour, the amount of oil, the type of flour, and just about every other variable we could think of. But we weren't satisfied until we finally widened our field of focus and decided to try a recipe for focaccia. In "Foolproof Focaccia" (*Cook's Illustrated*, May/June 1997), Jack Bishop uses boiled, riced potatoes in his focaccia dough to add moisture and flavor. This crust was just what we were hoping for: very wet and yet easy to handle, light, and smooth. When baked, it was soft and moist, yet with a bit of chew, sturdiness, and structure that was not present in the previous doughs. Furthermore, the flavor hit the mark,

Since many home cooks don't have a deep-dish pizza pan, we tried several alternatives, including round cake pans, springform pans, and even skillets. With some timing changes, the cake pans worked as well as the deep-dish pizza pan. The other options, however, did not prove useful.

since the potato added an extra richness and sweetness to the dough. (*See* "Potatoes in Bread? You Bet," page 13.)

Now that I had found a dough that I was happy with, the challenge was to create a rising and baking method suited for deep-dish pizza. I tried an idea suggested by *Cook's* publisher Christopher Kimball, who advised placing the pizza dough in a barely warmed oven for the first rise. This worked like a charm, reducing the initial rising time from 1 hour to 35 minutes and producing dough that tasted no different from the dough that rose at room temperature for a full hour.

Next I tried reducing the amount of time required for a second rise. But I found that the dough that was allowed to rise for the recommended 30 minutes was vastly better than crusts with no second rise or a second rise of only 15 minutes. The flavor was more complex and the texture of the pizza crust was softer and lighter, making this second rising too important to pass up or shorten.

Baking and Topping

After some testing, I discovered that a crust baked at 425 degrees on a baking stone was almost perfect; the bottom and sides of the pizza were well-browned, and the interior crumb was moist, light, and evenly cooked through. While the bottom and sides of the pizza were nicely browned at 425 degrees, though, the exterior of the crust was still slightly tough. To combat this, I began lining the pizza pan with oil. After some experimentation, I found that the pizzas made with a generous amount of oil lining the pan (we found ¼ cup to be optimal) had a far more desirable crust than those made with little or no oil in the pan. Lightly "frying" the dough in the pan made for a rich, caramelized exterior; this added a good amount of flavor and a secondary texture to the crust, without drying it out or making it tough.

Now it was time for the toppings. On most pizzas, the toppings can simply be placed on raw dough and baked, since the crust bakes in about the same time as the toppings.

I was quite skeptical about trying this with the thicker crust of a deep-dish pizza, but I tried it anyway. No surprise. The weight of the toppings prevented the crust from rising in the oven, resulting in a dense, heavy crust, especially in the center of the pie. So I tried prebaking crusts from 5 minutes up to 15 minutes to develop some structure before adding the toppings. The pizza pre-baked for 15 minutes, then topped, was perfect. Not only did the pizza have a chance to have an initial rise in the oven without the weight or moisture of the toppings, but the toppings had just enough time to melt and brown when the crust was baked through.

At last we had deep-dish pizza that was not a tremendous hassle but had a great crust and perfectly cooked toppings. I'm not sure I'll ever order this dish from a pizza shop again.

TESTING | POTATOES MAKE CRUST SPRINGY

Dough with potato (right) produced a much springier, chewier, and softer crust than the same dough without potato (left).

1. Punch dough down and pat into 12-inch circle. Place dough in oiled pan and let rest 10 minutes.

2. Pull the relaxed dough up the sides of the pan to form a standing edge.

3. Sprinkle the topping over the hot crust and slide the pan back onto the pizza stone.

DEEP-DISH PIZZA
MAKES ONE 14-INCH PIZZA, SERVING 4 TO 6

Prepare the topping while the dough is rising so it will be ready at the same time the dough is ready. Baking the pizza in a deep-dish pan on a hot pizza stone or quarry tiles will help produce a crisp, well-browned bottom crust. Otherwise, a heavy rimless cookie sheet (do not use an insulated cookie sheet) will work almost as well. If you've only got a rimmed cookie sheet, turn it upside down and bake the pizza on the flat rimless side. The amount of oil used to grease the pan may seem excessive, but in addition to preventing sticking, the oil helps the crust brown nicely.

1	medium baking potato (about 9 ounces), peeled and quartered
1 1/2	teaspoons rapid-rise yeast
3 1/2	cups unbleached all-purpose flour
1	cup warm water (105 to 115 degrees)
6	tablespoons extra-virgin olive oil, plus more for oiling bowl
1 3/4	teaspoons salt
1	recipe topping (recipes follow)

1. Bring 1 quart water and potato to boil in a small saucepan over medium-high heat; cook until tender, 10 to 15 minutes. Drain and cool until potato can be handled comfortably; press through fine disk on potato ricer or grate through large holes on box grater. Measure 1 1/3 cups lightly packed potato; discard remaining potato.

2. Adjust one oven rack to highest position, other rack to lowest position; heat oven to 200 degrees. Once temperature reaches 200 degrees, maintain heat 10 minutes, then turn off heat.

3. In bowl of standing mixer or in workbowl of food processor fitted with steel blade, mix or pulse yeast, 1/2 cup flour, and 1/2 cup warm water until combined. Cover with plastic wrap and set aside until bubbly, about 20 minutes. Add 2 tablespoons olive oil, remaining 1/2 cup water, 3 cups flour, salt, and potato. If using mixer, fit with paddle attachment and mix on low speed until dough comes together. Switch to dough hook attachment and increase speed to medium; continue kneading until dough comes together and is slightly tacky, about 5 minutes. If using food processor, process until dough comes together in a ball, about 40 seconds. Dough should be slightly sticky. Transfer dough to lightly oiled medium bowl, turn to coat with oil and cover tightly with plastic wrap. Place in warm oven until dough is soft and spongy and doubled in size, 30 to 35 minutes.

4. Oil bottom of 14-inch deep-dish pizza pan with remaining 4 tablespoons olive oil. Remove dough from oven; turn onto clean, dry work surface and pat into 12-inch round (see illustration 1, above). Transfer round to pan, cover with plastic wrap, and let rest until dough no longer resists shaping, about 10 minutes.

5. Line low oven rack with unglazed baking tiles or place pizza stone or rimless cookie sheet on rack (do not use insulated cookie sheet; see note above) and heat oven to 425 degrees. Uncover dough and pull up into edges and up sides of pan (see illustration 2) to form 1-inch-high lip. Cover with plastic wrap; let rise in warm draft-free spot until double in size, about 30 minutes. Uncover dough and prick generously with fork. Bake on preheated tiles, stone, or cookie sheet until dry and lightly browned, about 15 minutes. Add desired toppings; bake on tiles, stone, or cookie sheet until cheese melts, 10 to 15 minutes (5 to 10 minutes for 10-inch pizzas). Move pizza to top rack and bake until cheese is spotty golden brown, about 5 minutes longer. Let cool 5 minutes, then, holding pizza pan at angle with one hand, use wide spatula to slide pizza from pan to cutting board. Cut into wedges and serve.

10-INCH DEEP-DISH PIZZAS

If you don't own a 14-inch deep-dish pizza pan, divide the dough between two 10-inch cake pans. Follow recipe for Deep-Dish Pizza through step 3. Grease bottom of 2 10-inch cake pans with 2 tablespoons olive oil each. Turn dough onto clean, dry work surface and divide in half. Pat each half into 9-inch round; continue with recipe, reducing initial baking time on lowest rack to 5 to 10 minutes and dividing topping evenly in half between pizzas.

FRESH TOMATO TOPPING WITH MOZZARELLA AND BASIL

4	medium ripe tomatoes (about 1 1/2 pounds), cored, seeded and cut into 1-inch pieces
	Salt and pepper to taste
2	medium cloves garlic, minced
6	ounces mozzarella cheese, shredded (about 1 1/2 cups)
1 1/4	ounces Parmesan cheese, grated (about 1/2 cup)
3	tablespoons shredded fresh basil leaves

1. Mix together tomatoes and garlic in medium bowl; season to taste with salt and pepper and set aside.

2. Top partially baked crust evenly with tomato mixture (see illustration 3) followed by mozzarella, then Parmesan. Bake as directed in recipe for Deep-Dish Pizza (step 5). Scatter basil over fully baked pizza before cutting into wedges.

FOUR-CHEESE TOPPING WITH PESTO

1/2	cup homemade or prepared basil pesto
6	ounces mozzarella cheese, shredded (about 1 1/2 cups)
4	ounces provolone cheese, shredded (about 1 cup)
1 1/4	ounces grated Parmesan cheese (about 1/2 cup)
1 1/4	ounces blue cheese (about 1/4 cup, crumbled)

Spread partially baked crust (see illustration 3) evenly with pesto; sprinkle with mozzarella, followed by provolone, Parmesan, and blue cheese. Bake as directed in step 5 of recipe for Deep-Dish Pizza.

Potatoes in Bread? You Bet

Boiled potatoes in this pizza dough had a distinct effect on the flavor and texture of the final crust. The result: a moister, more tender, sweeter, and softer dough than one made with just wheat flour. I wanted to know why the boiled potatoes made such a difference in the pizza dough. According to Dr. Al Bushway, professor of food science at the University of Maine, potatoes contain more starch than wheat flour. Since starch traps moisture during baking, this made for a moister dough. Potatoes also contain less protein than flour. This results in less gluten being formed in the dough, which in turn produces a softer, more tender product. Finally, potatoes add another dimension of flavor in two ways. For one, the free sugars in the potatoes cause faster fermentation, resulting in a more complex flavor in a shorter period of time. Second, the sugars that are not consumed by the yeast in the fermentation process add sweetness to the final dough. —A.Y.

How to Cook Thick-Cut Pork Chops

Today's pork chops are much leaner. Here's how to produce a tender, juicy chop.

⋑ BY KAY RENTSCHLER ⋐

When was the last time you had a really juicy, tender, thick pork chop? These days it is likely to be something you remember, but not something that you've recently enjoyed. In response to American demands for low-fat meat, the pork industry has systematically trimmed down the hefty fat-producing hogs of the past to create today's newer pig, sleek of silhouette and lean of flesh. In fact, today's pork has about 30 percent less fat than it did 20 years ago. Healthy? Yes. Nutritious? Yes. Tasty? We're not so sure.

All of this notwithstanding, I love thick-cut pork chops, and, with the help of *Cook's* test kitchen, I was determined to find a way to cook a juicy, flavorful chop.

After settling on rib loin chops 1½ inches thick (*see* "Which Chop Is Best?" page 15), we needed to figure out the best cooking method. Although our instincts and empirical observations suggested that today's leaner pork might not be responsive to yesterday's cooking strategies, we tried them all anyway. We baked, we breaded, we braised, we sautéed, and we did a combination of sautéing followed by a finish in the oven with the temperature set variously at high, medium, and low. The chops that spent their entire cooking time in the oven were uniformly disappointing, eliciting from our tasters such adjectives as "wan," "cottony," "tough," and "tasteless." Crisp breading, so delectable when coating thin chops or cutlets, did nothing for the thicker chops. Pan-searing, followed by a short braise in stock, wine, or milk—the conventional therapy for tough pork—only made the meat drier and tougher.

In the end we obtained the most promising results by means of straightforward dry-heat methods. A high-heat sear for two or three minutes per side (depending on the number of chops in the pan) followed by about 10 minutes per side of covered stove-top cooking over reduced heat yielded very good results. But we found these chops to be just slightly less tender than those which we started in the frying pan and finished in the oven. There was no demonstrable advantage to using a lower oven temperature (we tried 450, 350, and 250 degrees): the chops simply took longer to cook. In the end, purely for the sake of

To get chops of roughly the same weight, avoid prepackaged chops. Ask your butcher to cut them for you.

expediency, we settled on searing the chops in a sauté pan, then transferring them to a preheated sheet pan in a 450-degree oven to finish cooking.

Now we had found the best cooking method, but the chops were still lacking in flavor and moistness. Owing to their relative absence of fat or collagen (those classic suppliers of flavor and moisture), these chops were clearly perfect candidates for brining.

Most of the recipes we looked at involved relatively long immersion in brines with rather low concentrations of sugar and salt, about ½ cup of each per 2 quarts of water. After trying a number of these for various periods of time—from several hours up to two days—we found that the finished chops, while indeed more moist, had become almost watery, with a webby, hamlike texture. The longer-brined versions did not brown well during the initial searing, while shorter brining produced chops with no palpable improvement in flavor or texture. To try to rectify these problems, we increased the proportions of sugar and salt to liquid to compensate for the shorter brining time. Bingo. Twelve-ounce chops left for one hour in this more concentrated brining solution managed a significantly noticeable improvement in flavor and still achieved a desirable degree of caramelization during pan-searing.

Our final step was to determine the exact relationship between flavor and the internal temperature of the meat. The best-tasting chops we had

tried hovered at an internal reading of 140–145 degrees. But medium-rare pork? What would our mothers say?

One of the reasons so much pork today reaches the table dry and overcooked is the public's residual fear of the trichinosis parasite. But there is actually little cause for concern, because there are very few trichinosis cases in the United States (only 230 cases nationwide in the period from 1991 to 1996, some 40% of them caused by eating wild game.) Moreover, the parasites that cause this disease are destroyed when the pork has reached an internal temperature of 137 degrees. So the notion of medium-rare pork needn't be met with a shudder of horror or revulsion.

After fiddling around with various options, we ultimately committed to the bold maneuver of cooking the chops to a temperature of 125–127 degrees. We were able to do this by letting the chops complete their cooking outside the oven, covering them with aluminum foil while they rested to allow the juices to redistribute throughout the meat. After this five-minute rest, the chops' temperature went up to a perfect 140–145 degrees. Relinquishing a minimum of juice—it all stayed in the chop—and retaining the barest whisper of pink on their interior, the chops were succulent and highly flavorful. This was largely due, we felt, to the fact that cooking by residual heat is a gentler and more precise method of reaching the final serving temperature. Chops left to rest uncovered, on the other hand, not only lost heat but showed little escalation in their internal temperature between pan and plate.

To ensure perfectly cooked chops, an instant-read thermometer is absolutely essential. Time estimates will be just that—estimates—and no amount of prodding or poking with your finger will give you a true reading of doneness.

PAN-SEARED, OVEN-ROASTED THICK-CUT PORK CHOPS
SERVES 4

If you're making one of our pan sauces to accompany the chops, you may opt to use only water, sugar, and salt in the brine and omit the other flavorings. If the chops aren't being cooked immediately after brining, simply wipe off the excess brine, place the them on a wire rack set on top of a rimmed sheet pan, and keep them in the refrigerator, uncovered, to air dry for up to 3 hours. Should you choose to make one of the sauces, have all the

Which Chop Is Best?

In many supermarkets, all pork chops from the loin are simply labeled "loin chops." However, there are significant differences in the four types of chops that come from the loin. Two—the blade chop and the sirloin chop—are less common and more likely to be correctly labeled. The two chops that you are most likely to run into labeled simply "loin chop" are the center-cut chop and the rib chop.

Center-cut Chop   **Rib Chop**

As the name implies, center-cut chops are cut right out of the center of the loin. You can pick them out by the bone that divides them into two sections, giving them a close resemblance to a T-bone steak. Like a T-bone, they have meat from the loin on one side of the bone and a small portion of the tenderloin muscle on the other side. Some people prefer these center-cut chops because the tenderloin portion in particular is extremely tender. They will work fine in this recipe.

Our top choice, though, is the rib chop, cut from the rib section of the loin, slightly closer to the shoulder. It has a somewhat higher fat content, which makes it both more flavorsome and less likely to dry during cooking. The rib pork chop can be distinguished by the section of rib bone along one side.

Sometimes these chops are boneless, making it much more difficult to tell them apart. But since we find bone-in meat juicier, we suggest you look for bone-in chops.   — John Willoughby

ingredients ready before browning the chops, and begin the sauce while the chops are in the oven.

3/4   cup lightly packed dark brown sugar
1/2   cup kosher salt (or 1/4 cup table salt)
10   medium garlic cloves, crushed
4   bay leaves, crumbled
8   whole cloves
3   tablespoons whole black pepper-
    corns, crushed
4   bone-in, 12-ounce, rib loin chops
    1 1/2-inches-thick
2   tablespoons vegetable oil

1. In gallon-sized zipper-lock plastic bag, dissolve sugar and salt in 2 cups hot water. Add garlic, bay leaves, cloves, peppercorns, and 4 cups cold water; cool mixture to room temperature. Add pork chops, then seal bag, pressing out as much air as possible; refrigerate until fully

seasoned, about 1 hour, turning bag once. Remove chops from brine and dry thoroughly with paper towels.

2. Adjust oven rack to lower-middle position, place shallow roasting pan or jelly-roll pan on oven rack, and heat oven to 450 degrees. When oven reaches 450 degrees, heat oil in 12-inch heavy-bottomed skillet over high heat until shimmering but not smoking, about 2 minutes. Place chops in skillet; cook until well-browned and nice crust has formed on surface, about 2 minutes. Turn chops over with tongs; cook until well-browned and a nice crust has formed on second side, about 2 minutes longer. Using tongs, transfer chops to preheated pan in oven. Roast until instant-read thermometer inserted into the center of each chop registers 125–127 degrees, 8 to 10 minutes, turning chops over once halfway through cooking time. Transfer each chop to platter; cover loosely with foil (be sure not to wrap foil tightly around meat), and let rest about 5 minutes. (Check internal temperature; it should register about 145 degrees).

SPICY CITRUS PAN SAUCE
MAKES ABOUT 1 CUP

1/2   cup molasses
1/4   cup juice and 1 1/2 teaspoons zest from 2 limes
1   cup juice from 2 large oranges
2   medium garlic cloves, chopped
4   chipotle chiles en adobo
2   tablespoons cold unsalted butter, cut into
    2 pieces
    Salt and ground black pepper

1. In bowl of food processor, puree molasses, lime juice and zest, orange juice, garlic, and chipotle chiles until smooth. Transfer to small bowl; set aside.

2. Pour off fat from skillet used to brown chops; place skillet over medium-high heat and add molasses mixture, scraping pan bottom with wooden spoon to loosen browned bits. Simmer until thickened and syrupy, about 2 minutes.

Whisk in butter, one piece at a time; season to taste with salt and pepper and serve with pork chops.

SWEET AND SOUR PAN SAUCE WITH BACON AND TOMATOES
MAKES ABOUT 2 CUPS

5   slices bacon (about 5 ounces), cut into 1/4-inch pieces
2   large shallots, minced
    Pinch sugar
1   medium garlic clove, minced
4   medium plum tomatoes, peeled, seeded and cut
    into 1/4-inch pieces
1/2   cup balsamic vinegar
1   cup dry Marsala or sweet vermouth
4   tablespoons cold unsalted butter, cut into 4 pieces
1   tablespoon chopped fresh parsley leaves
    Salt and ground black pepper

Pour off fat from skillet used to brown chops; place over medium-high heat and sauté bacon until crisp, about 6 minutes. Transfer bacon with slotted spoon to paper towel–lined plate; pour off all but 1 tablespoon of bacon fat. Reduce heat to low; add shallots and sugar and cook until softened, about 1 minute (do not brown). Add garlic; cook until fragrant, about 30 seconds. Increase heat to medium-high; stir in tomatoes and vinegar, scraping pan bottom with wooden spoon to loosen browned bits. Add Marsala or vermouth; simmer until reduced by half, about 5 minutes. Whisk in butter one piece at a time. Stir in parsley and bacon, season to taste with salt and pepper; serve with pork chops.

MEAT | BUY THE RIGHT CHOP

Supermarket chops are often cut thick at the bone and thinner at the outer edge, like the one at left above. With such chops, the thinner periphery will overcook before the thicker meat near the bone is finished. Make sure you get chops that are of even thickness, like the one at right above.

STEP-BY-STEP | THE PATH TO PERFECT CHOPS

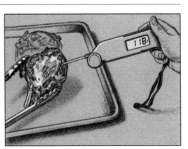

1. To brine, place empty zipper-lock bag in a high-sided bowl. Put the pork chops in the bag and add the lukewarm brining solution, then seal well.

2. Make sure that the chops are well and evenly browned on both sides. Be sure to use a large enough pan so the chops are not crowded while browning.

3. Transfer the browned chops to a preheated baking sheet. To check internal temperature, insert an instant-read thermometer into the center of the chop from the side.

Avoiding Mixing Mix-Ups

The majority of baking recipes are written with an underlying assumption that the reader is well-versed in basic mixing techniques. But most of us learned cooking informally, which often means that we learned some things wrong or picked up bad habits along the way. Through tests and trials, we here at *Cook's* have learned quite a lot about how far awry a recipe can go with just one false step in the mixing process. Cakes, we found, are perfect examples of this principle. Though these two pages focus on tips and techniques for mixing cake batter, much of the information here can be applied to all kinds of baking recipes.

CREAMING

Most butter cake recipes begin by creaming butter. Butter must be creamed so that it can coat the flour and prevent gluten from forming, thus producing a tender cake. In addition, creaming incorporates air into the butter, which is essential for leavening. Correctly creamed butter will create a light, airy cake.

Is Your Butter Soft Enough?

To cream, butter must be brought to a cool room temperature (about 67 degrees Fahrenheit) so that it is malleable but not soft. This is called "the plastic stage," and it is the condition in which the butter will best hold air and be stable. Following are three clues to help you tell if your butter is at the right stage for creaming.

The butter should give slightly when pressed but still hold its shape.

When you unwrap the butter before creaming, the wrapping should have a creamy residue on the inside.

The butter should bend with little resistance and without cracking or breaking.

Creaming Tips

It can take a long time for a stick of chilled butter to reach the right temperature for creaming. If you are in a hurry, you can speed up the softening process by cutting the butter into tablespoon-sized pieces. We found that it will soften to the right stage in about 15 minutes.

If your butter is too cool when creamed, it will look shiny and granular after adding sugar and will not aerate properly. If creamed at the proper temperature, the butter and sugar mixture will look thick, dull, and smooth.

If, despite all precautions, your butter is still too cool, a quick remedy is to the wrap bowl in a warm damp towel and continue creaming.

Cake recipes typically call for adding wet and dry ingredients alternately for even blending. If you're using a handheld mixer, twist a damp towel (right) and form a turban nest for the bowl, thus securing it in place so that you may proceed with mixing.

Adding eggs to creamed butter deflates it a bit. For this reason, it is important to add room temperature eggs one at a time (far right) and cream until each is completely incorporated and the butter has returned to a light, fluffy state.

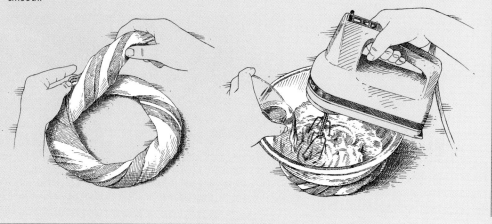

WHIPPING

Recipes for sponge and angel food cakes use whipped egg whites to aerate and leaven their batters. If you are using a handheld or standing mixer to whip, begin on low speed and beat whites until foamy, gradually increasing speed to medium high.

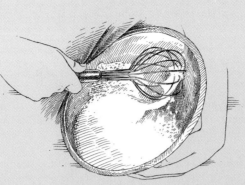
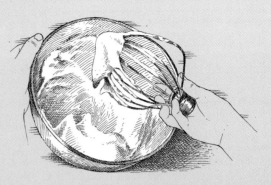

We tried whipping egg whites with a number of whisk types. This peculiarly shaped balloon whisk by Rösle was the hands-down winner. If you hand-whip egg whites often, this whisk is definitely worth having (*see* Resources, page 32).

To hand-whip efficiently, hug the bowl at an angle between your arm and rib cage. Make sure to move the whisk in a circular motion in order to sweep air into the whites. This movement does not need to be fast.

If using a standing mixer to whip egg whites, turn mixer off just shy of proper consistency. Detach whisk attachment and bowl and whisk the last few strokes by hand. Be sure to scrape along the bottom where the beaters may not have reached.

FOLDING

It is important to use a light but quick hand when folding whipped ingredients so that you do not deflate the batter. We tested a number of utensils for folding (including bare hands). While a large flat spatula (about 2¾ x 4½ inches) works very well, the best tool is a flexible dough scraper (below, right). This tool is particularly helpful with foamy batters, such as sponge cakes. Begin folding immediately after whipping egg whites to prevent them from deflating.

Folding comes down to four quick motions. For stiff batter recipes, whisk one third of the whipped whites into the batter and then fold in the rest using the following steps:

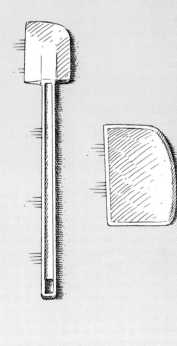

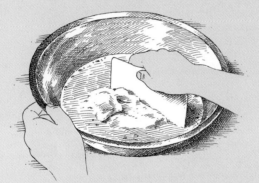

I. Place the whipped whites on top of the batter and cut through the middle of the bowl with the curved edge of a flexible dough scraper.

2. Holding the dough scraper flat against the bowl, scoop along the bottom, then slide up the side of the bowl. Simultaneously begin turning the bowl a third of the way around, counterclockwise.

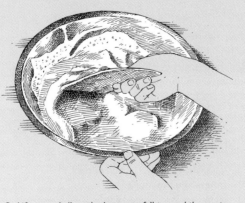
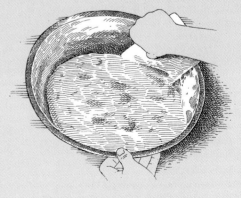

3. Lift up and allow the batter to fall toward the center. Repeat Steps 1 through 3 twice, until egg whites are just incorporated and no white streaks remain.

4. Sweep once around the bowl to incorporate any residual batter that may have clung to the sides.

Illustration: John Burgoyne

Crisp Cabbage Salads

Pre-salting creates pickle-crisp cabbage that is perfect for combining with bold flavors.

⋩ BY EVA KATZ ⋨

Cabbage makes a great salad. Not just as coleslaw or a picnic side dish but a crunchy, flavorful, dress-up kind of salad. Cabbage's natural spicy-sweetness and crunchy texture work well with many strong and unconventional flavor combinations. Dressings with spicy chiles, sweeteners, tangy acids, and strong herbal or spice flavors highlight the natural flavors in cabbage without overpowering them. Also, unlike lettuce salads, cabbage salads can be made well in advance, and leftovers don't have to go to waste—they make a great addition to a sandwich or lunch box.

One problem with cabbage salads is their tendency to become watery and bland when dressed and allowed to sit. This occurs because the cells of the cabbage are full of water that leaches out into the salad, diluting its consistency and flavor. Salting the cabbage and setting it over a colander allows a good bit of this liquid to be drawn out. Salads made with this salted and drained cabbage do not become overly watery, and the flavors of the dressing remain undiluted. Because salting does soften cabbage a bit, these salads won't have the intense crispness of most coleslaws, but their pickle-crisp texture is ideal for forking and eating.

The best way to shred the cabbage, as Pam Anderson discovered in her story on coleslaw in the July/August 1995 issue of *Cook's*, is to quarter the cabbage, core it, then separate the quarters into stacks of leaves that flatten when pressed lightly. At this point you can either put the leaves through a food processor fitted with a slicing disk or slice by hand. To do the latter, use a chef's knife to slice each stack diagonally into thin strips.

SWEET AND SOUR CABBAGE SALAD WITH APPLE AND FENNEL
MAKES ABOUT 5 CUPS, SERVING 6 TO 8

- 1 pound (about 1/2 medium head) green cabbage, shredded
- 1 teaspoon salt
- 1/2 small red onion, chopped fine
- 1 tablespoon honey
- 2 tablespoons rice wine vinegar
- 2 tablespoons olive oil
- 1 teaspoon mustard
- 2 teaspoons minced fresh tarragon leaves
- 1 large Granny Smith apple, peeled, cored, and cut into 1/4-inch pieces
- 1 medium head fennel, cored and sliced thin (about 2 1/2 cups)
  Ground black pepper

1. Toss shredded cabbage and 1 teaspoon salt in colander or large mesh strainer set over medium bowl. Let stand until cabbage wilts, at least 1 hour or up to 4 hours. Rinse cabbage under cold running water (or in large bowl of ice water if serving immediately). Press, but do not squeeze, to drain; pat dry with paper towels. (Can be stored in zipper-lock bag and refrigerated overnight.)

2. Stir together onion, honey, vinegar, oil, mustard, and tarragon in medium bowl. Immediately toss cabbage, apple, and fennel in dressing. Season to taste with salt and pepper; cover and refrigerate until ready to serve.

CABBAGE AND RED PEPPER SALAD WITH LIME–CUMIN VINAIGRETTE
MAKES ABOUT 5 CUPS, SERVING 6 TO 8

- 2 tablespoons juice plus 1 teaspoon grated zest from 1 lime
- 2 tablespoons olive oil
- 1 tablespoon rice wine or sherry vinegar
- 1 tablespoon honey
- 1 teaspoon ground cumin
  Pinch cayenne
- 1 pound (about 1/2 medium head) green cabbage, shredded fine, salted, and drained (*see* step 1 in first recipe)
- 1 red bell pepper, seeded and cut into thin strips
  Salt

Stir together lime juice, zest, oil, vinegar, honey, cumin, and cayenne in medium bowl. Toss cabbage and red pepper in dressing. Season to taste with salt; cover and refrigerate until ready to serve.

CONFETTI CABBAGE SALAD WITH SPICY PEANUT DRESSING
MAKES ABOUT 5 CUPS, SERVING 6 TO 8

- 2 tablespoons smooth peanut butter
- 2 tablespoons peanut oil
- 2 tablespoons rice wine vinegar
- 1 tablespoon soy sauce
- 1 teaspoon honey
- 2 medium garlic cloves, chopped coarse
- 1 piece ginger (1 1/2 inches), peeled
- 1/2 jalapeño chile, halved and seeded
- 1 pound (about 1/2 medium head) green cabbage, shredded fine, salted, and drained (*see* step 1 in first recipe)
- 1 large carrot, peeled, grated, and prepared with cabbage
- 4 medium radishes, halved lengthwise and sliced thin
- 4 medium scallions, sliced thin
  Salt

In bowl of food processor fitted with steel blade, puree peanut butter, oil, vinegar, soy sauce, honey, garlic, ginger, and jalapeño until smooth paste is formed. Toss cabbage and carrot, radishes, scallions, and dressing together in medium bowl. Season to taste with salt; cover and refrigerate until ready to serve.

COLESLAW WITH BACON AND BUTTERMILK DRESSING
MAKES SCANT 5 CUPS, SERVING 4 TO 6

Salting and draining the onion with the cabbage helps mellow harsh raw onion flavors.

- 6 slices bacon (about 6 ounces), cut into 1/4-inch pieces
- 1/2 cup buttermilk
- 2 tablespoons vegetable oil
- 2 tablespoons cider vinegar
- 1 tablespoon caraway seeds
- 1/4 teaspoon dry mustard
- 2 teaspoons sugar
- 1 pound (about 1/2 medium head) green cabbage, shredded fine, salted, and drained (*see* step 1 in first recipe)
- 1 large carrot, peeled, grated, and prepared with cabbage
- 1/2 medium onion, sliced thin and prepared with cabbage
  Salt and ground black pepper

1. Fry bacon in medium skillet over medium heat until crisp and brown, about 6 minutes. Transfer bacon with slotted spoon to plate lined with paper towels; discard fat.

2. Stir together buttermilk, oil, vinegar, caraway, mustard, and sugar in medium bowl. Toss cabbage, carrot, onion, and bacon in dressing. Season to taste with salt and pepper; cover and refrigerate until ready to serve.

Perfecting Garlic Bread

Here's how to get a smooth garlic flavor without a bitter aftertaste.

≥ BY ADAM RIED ≤

Sometimes the simplest foods stir the deepest passions. Garlic bread, for instance, recently turned the conversation at a casual dinner party I was throwing into a heated argument. Everyone at the table had a different method—to which he or she was fiercely devoted—for making it. The debate raged for nearly an hour. Clearly, a fact-finding mission was in order.

So simple to make, yet so often a soggy, greasy disappointment, garlic bread should have a lightly toasted surface with a crisp crust that shatters when bitten. The bread within should be, warm and chewy, light and yet substantial. Butter, which I chose over olive oil for this American-style bread, should be plentiful but not excessive, and the garlic flavor should be full and prominent without being harsh. But garlic bread rarely lives up to this ideal. Sometimes there is so much garlic you can taste it for days, other times there is so little you can't taste it at all. Worse yet, the bread is often totally saturated with butter.

We started out in the usual *Cook's* manner, by tasting several garlic breads made according to different recipes and methods. From this came an interesting revelation: Even though most of the breads had too little garlic oomph (they ranged from a single clove to six per one-pound loaf of bread), every single taster disliked the raw garlic flavor. I'd definitely have to deal with this. Tasters made several other helpful observations. First, there was unanimous preference for wide loaves of bread, such as Italian, which yielded large slices. Second, they preferred their loaf sliced with the insides exposed to the oven to crisp up rather than cut in vertical slices left attached at the bottom, as specified in many recipes. This method left the slices soggy and a bit harsh-tasting.

The Name of the Game

The cry for a full, resonant garlic flavor necessitated the use of many more cloves than the two or three called for in most of the recipes I looked at. But upping the ante created another problem... near overpowering harshness from all that raw garlic. For advice on how to deal with this

Keep the loaf halves intact during preparation, then cut into generous slices for serving.

issue, I called Dr. Susan Brewer, associate professor of food chemistry at the University of Illinois in Urbana. She explained that there are hundreds of chemical compounds in garlic responsible for its flavor and odor. The two harshest tasting and smelling chemical groups, glucose inolates and sulfur-containing isothiocyanates, activate when the garlic cloves are cut, she said, but they are also the first to dissipate when the garlic is heated. Heat, therefore, tames the harshness of garlic, eliminating its unpleasant raw edge and helping to accentuate its sweeter, nutty flavors.

Since the flavor of garlic mellows with heat, precooking the cloves a bit seemed like a good plan. To keep the testing consistent, I used six medium garlic cloves, or about two tablespoons, minced, per one-pound loaf of bread and tried two methods of precooking the garlic. First, I sautéed the minced garlic in butter, but the resulting bread lacked character and depth. It failed to earn any first- or even second-place votes among my tasters. On top of that, I wasn't crazy about the melted butter (more on that later). Second, I tried a method borrowed from *Cook's* July/August 1998 article "Chef's Vegetable Preparation Tips"—namely, toasting the unpeeled cloves in a dry skillet over medium heat until they were just fragrant. This cooks the garlic just enough to highlight its rich, sweet, nutty flavor, and the resulting bread was judged a winner by

every taster. After a few experiments, I settled on 8 minutes of toasting; at 10 minutes the garlic was a little too docile, and at 5 minutes it still had more raw punch than my tasters and I liked.

Toasting allowed me to use far more garlic than most recipes allow. Most tasters favored 10 medium cloves, which equaled three generous tablespoons, minced, for each one-pound loaf. In addition to mincing the toasted garlic, I tried slicing it, pureeing it, and crushing it though a press, but there was no noticeable improvement in flavor. I also tried sprinkling the minced garlic on the buttered bread rather than mixing it into the butter, and again there was no real advantage.

Bread and Butter

Not surprisingly for a dish largely about bread, the type of bread used makes a huge difference. The whole wheat and sourdough loaves I tried tasted out of place, and the long, narrow shape and relatively open texture of French bread produced slices that were too small to be truly satisfying. So I stuck with football-shaped loaves of hearty white Italian bread. But be sure to use the highest quality loaf you can. The sturdy texture, satisfying chew, and well-developed yeasty flavor of the bakery-purchased, artisan Italian loaves I tried made the supermarket variety seem fluffy, unsubstantial, and bland by comparison.

The right amount of butter would make the garlic bread moist, not soggy or saturated. Many recipes call for a stick or more, which made the bread spongy and slightly greasy. Less butter—six tablespoons—did the trick, giving the bread ample richness without marring its texture. Melting the

TECHNIQUE | TOAST IT

Toast the unpeeled garlic cloves in a small, dry skillet over medium-high heat for 8 minutes, tossing frequently.

butter proved unnecessary, while also adding an unnecessary step and utensil (a brush to distribute it on the bread) to the process. Softened butter that I could spread easily with a rubber spatula worked best. I also tried, to no avail, mashing the minced garlic and butter together a couple of hours ahead of time. There was no question that the bread needed salt and pepper, but I stuck to unsalted butter because it allows for precision when determining the amount of salt in a recipe. I also checked out an arsenal of additional ingredients common to many recipes. Red wine, olive oil, paprika, hot pepper sauce, cayenne, garlic powder, garlic salt, mustard, and lemon juice all failed to impress, but two tablespoons of grated Parmesan cheese added depth and complexity without interfering with the garlic flavor. Even for the master recipe, I recommend the cheese. You won't even know it's there but for the subtle flavor boost it gives the bread.

The last areas of inquiry were the cooking method and temperature. Many recipes recommend wrapping the loaf in foil for all or part of its time in the oven. My initial tasting and subsequent tests proved the foil wrapping to be a counterproductive extra step. My tasters and I consistently found the wrapped breads to be soggy, with a slightly harsh flavor and an unwelcome steamed taste. It turned out, as Susan Brewer explained, that exposing the cut-and-buttered surface to the oven heat helped to mellow the garlic's flavor by dehydrating the molecules somewhat. This changes their structure, and with it, their flavor. Wrapping the loaf in foil, or for that matter reassembling it so the cut sides faced each other, deprived the garlic of some heat, thereby diminishing the desirable flavor change.

The oven setting most commonly listed in the recipes I looked at was 350 degrees, but that wasn't hot enough to give the bread the super-crisp, toasted exterior layer I was after. I tested and retested, increasing the temperature by 25 degrees each time until I got to 500 degrees, which produced a beautifully crunchy crust and a nicely browned surface in just nine minutes or so, with no broiling involved. I did find it necessary to set the bread on a baking sheet, though, to avoid scorching the bottom.

By the end of the testing, my tasting crew was downing half a loaf of garlic bread per person without batting an eye. Clearly, I had a recipe that would provide all the heavy artillery I needed to win the next round of the dinner-table garlic bread wars with my friends.

CLASSIC AMERICAN GARLIC BREAD
SERVES 6 TO 8

Garlic bread is best served piping hot, so time it to arrive at the table last, once all the other dishes are finished and ready to serve.

9–10 medium garlic cloves (about the size of a plump cashew nut), skins left on
6 tablespoons unsalted butter, softened
2 tablespoons grated Parmesan cheese
½ teaspoon salt
1 whole loaf high-quality Italian bread (about 1 pound, football-shaped), halved lengthwise (*see* illustration, right)
Ground black pepper

1. Adjust oven rack to middle position and heat oven to 500 degrees. Meanwhile, toast garlic cloves in small skillet over medium heat, shaking pan occasionally, until fragrant and color of cloves deepens slightly, about 8 minutes. When cool enough to handle, skin and mince cloves (you should have about 3 tablespoons). Using dinner fork, mash garlic, butter, cheese, and salt in small bowl until thoroughly combined.

2. Spread cut sides of loaf evenly with garlic butter mixture; season to taste with pepper. Transfer loaf halves, buttered side up, onto baking sheet; bake, reversing position of baking sheet in oven from front to back halfway through baking time, until surface of bread is golden brown and toasted, 8 to 10 minutes. Cut each half into 2-inch slices; serve immediately.

HERB GARLIC BREAD

Follow recipe for Classic American Garlic Bread, mashing 1 tablespoon each minced fresh basil and chives and ½ tablespoon each minced fresh thyme and oregano into garlic butter mixture.

CHIPOTLE GARLIC BREAD

Canned chipotle chiles packed in adobo sauce add a smoky, spicy flavor that was the hands-down favorite of every tester.

Follow recipe for Classic American Garlic Bread, mashing 1½ chipotle chiles en adobo (about 1 tablespoon) and 1 teaspoon adobo sauce into garlic butter mixture. Increase baking time to 10 to 12 minutes.

PARMESAN AND ASIAGO CHEESE GARLIC BREAD

Follow recipe for Classic American Garlic Bread, decreasing salt to ¼ teaspoon, increasing Parmesan cheese to ¼ cup, and mashing ¼ cup grated Asiago cheese and 2 teaspoons Dijon mustard into butter along with garlic.

GOAT CHEESE GARLIC BREAD

Follow recipe for Classic American Garlic Bread, decreasing salt to ¼ teaspoon and mashing 2 ounces softened goat cheese into garlic and butter mixture. Increase baking time to 10 to 12 minutes.

TECHNIQUE | SLICE IT

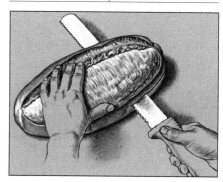

Using a long serrated knife, slice the bread in half lengthwise.

Rustic Free-Form Apple Tartlets

The cream cheese dough, a combination of apples, and a sprinkle of sugar during baking create a tart that combines rich apple flavor, a moist filling, and a tender but sturdy crust.

⇒ BY GREG CASE WITH KAY RENTSCHLER ⇐

Compared with many other desserts that involve pastry, apple pie is actually very easy to put together. That is one of the primary reasons that it is *the* American home dessert. A similar dessert exists in many European cuisines. Italians call it a crostata, and in France it is known as a galette. In America, it is known simply as a free-form apple tart. Made in the shape of a thin, flat round, the free-form apple tart is perhaps the oldest of all pastries. While many cultures have their own particular version, some sweet and others savory, all are rustic, country-style pastries casually put together. To make them, the dough is rolled out in a circle, the filling is piled in the center, and the dough is then gathered up along the edges to form a border around the filling. Because there is only one crust, and even that does not have to be fitted into a pie plate, this tart is actually simpler than a pie. The nature of the beast, however, presents a number of problems.

Because there is no top crust to seal in the moisture, the apple filling can become dried out while baking. Another consideration is the type of dough used to form the tart. It must be sturdy enough to contain the filling while also providing a complementary texture and flavor. Then there is the major role of the apples themselves. Their flavor should be bold and distinct, their texture neither dry nor mealy but supple.

With these considerations in mind, I set out to create a recipe that would be easy to put together, make use of readily available ingredients, and produce a dessert with a rich apple flavor, moist filling, and tender but sturdy crust.

Apple Round Robin

I started with the filling. Obviously, the type of apple used would be key. The method used to prepare and cook the apples would also affect their taste and texture. Should they be sliced thick or thin when placed in the tart? Should they be precooked or raw?

To answer these questions, I gathered together the most commonly available apples: Granny Smith, Gala, McIntosh, Braeburn, Fuji, and Red and Golden Delicious. I tested each type by baking it in a large tart. All of the apples became tough, dry, and leathery except the McIntosh, which baked to the other extreme; they were so moist that they turned to mush.

The dough can be formed into individual tartlets, like this one, or made into one large tart.

Of the varieties tested, I found the Granny Smiths, Galas, and McIntosh to have the most distinct apple flavor after being baked. Working with these three types, my thought was that the moisture in the McIntosh might prevent the Galas or Granny Smiths from drying out, creating a moist balance of taste and texture for the filling. I baked two tarts, one with the McIntosh and Granny Smith apples and one with the McIntosh and Gala apples. The combination of two types of apple did create a filling that was more moist, but it was still a bit dry, and I was not totally satisfied. However, I did find the McIntosh/Granny Smith combination to be more flavorful than the McIntosh/Gala. Since Christopher Kimball reached this same conclusion in his exploration of apples for classic apple pie (*see* "All-Season Apple Pie," November/December 1997), I decided to proceed with this combination, confident that it offered the best flavor.

Testing Texture

Now I wanted to resolve the texture issue. Perhaps, I thought, cooking the apples first would create a more moist filling. I tried sautéing the apples, reducing their cooking juices, and adding the liquid to the tart. This was not a success: the apples had a mushy texture, some of the simple apple flavor I wanted to preserve had been lost in the cooking, and the process was becoming more demanding than necessary.

At this point I returned to the original method of cooking the tart with raw apples. But this time I sliced them thinner and increased the oven temperature. These changes were an improvement; the thinner apple slices cooked more quickly at the higher temperature and were therefore more moist—but they still weren't perfect. At the suggestion of pastry guru Jim Dodge, a *Cook's* consulting editor, I reserved two tablespoons of the sugar in the recipe to sprinkle over the tart halfway through baking. This turned out to be a great idea, helping to keep the apples from drying out while they baked. (*See* "Why Sprinkle during Baking?" right).

The Right Dough

Having cleared the hurdle presented by the apples, I was ready to tackle the problem of finding the right pastry dough. I tested several different doughs in search of the perfect match for the most flavorful apple filling. I first tried a store-bought puff pastry, thinking this would make the dessert easier to prepare. Unfortunately, when baked, the pastry absorbed moisture from the fruit, which caused it to become limp and doughy. I then tried using my own quick puff pastry, thinking it might have more body than the commercial product, but the results were the same.

Abandoning the idea of a flaky butter pastry, I tried what I thought would be a dough with more structure: a pâte sucrée. This dough had a nice flavor that complemented the apples, but the texture was very similar to the texture of the filling. I wanted a pastry that would offer more contrast with the filling. A more traditional pie dough was my next choice. I tried two, one with all butter and another that combined butter and shortening. The all-butter crust tasted good but lacked tenderness; the butter/shortening dough was sturdy but didn't quite provide the flavor that I wanted to pair with the apples.

In search of yet another alternative, I remembered my friend Lora Brody's rugalach, crescent-shaped cookies rolled with fruit and nuts and made with a wonderful cream cheese pastry. I thought this might be just what I was looking for, but I also knew that this tender, flavorful dough might be somewhat hard to handle when making a full-sized tart. So I decided to try my hand at tartlets, which I always like in any case because they look beautiful and because it's nice for each person to get a whole little tart.

Back to the kitchen I went and made tartlets with the cream cheese dough. This was sublime, the perfect marriage of pastry to filling. The dough was moist, very tender, and added great flavor to the dessert.

I also tried making this recipe as one large tart, and it is still a wonderful dessert. So if you are short on time you can make just one large tart. I've included recipes for both the single large tart and six apple tartlets.

The only other word of caution I would offer is to avoid making this dessert in a hot or humid kitchen—the soft, delicate cream cheese pastry won't stand up to it. Otherwise, I do believe that this is a great recipe to put together on short notice. Keeping some dough portioned out in the freezer (it will last for up to a month) would make this dessert a snap to put together.

PREP | THE RIGHT SLICE

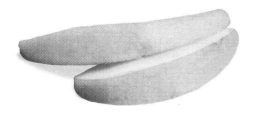

It is important to slice the apples thin (about one-quarter inch) so that they cook all the way through during the relatively short baking time.

Why Sprinkle during Baking?

Sprinkling sugar over the apples while they were baking played an integral role in creating a moist tart. I wanted to have a clearer understanding of why the interaction between the sugar and the fruit caused the final tart to be different, so I called Shirley Corriher, author of *Cookwise* (Morrow, 1997), who advises *Cook's* on food science. Corriher explained that sugar is hygroscopic, which means it tends to attract and combine with moisture. When sugar is sprinkled on top of the fruit during baking, it combines with some of the moisture that the fruit is giving up as it heats and forms a syrup. The syrup doesn't give up water as easily as the apples do, and, as a result, the fruit mixture doesn't dry out as much during baking. To further illustrate, Corriher gave the analogy of beating egg whites with or without sugar. Egg whites that are stiffly beaten without sugar will become dry and unusable if left to stand at room temperature for even a short time. However, egg whites that are stiffly beaten with sugar can stand at room temperature for several hours and still remain moist. Here again, the sugar, by combining with some of the moisture in the egg whites, has formed a syrup that retains the moisture. —G.C.

RUSTIC FREE-FORM APPLE TARTLETS

SERVES 6

The amount of cream cheese and butter used in this dough makes it soft and delicate. For easiest handling, make sure that these ingredients are cold and that your kitchen is cool. Serve the warm tartlets with a scoop of ice cream or with lightly sweetened whipped cream.

Tart Dough

- 1 1/4 cups all-purpose flour
- 2 tablespoons sugar
- 1/4 teaspoon salt
- 8 tablespoons (1 stick) cold unsalted butter, cut into 1/2-inch pieces
- 4 ounces cold cream cheese, cut into 1/2-inch pieces
- 2 teaspoons juice from 1 lemon
- 1–2 tablespoons ice water

Apple Filling

- 1 1/4 pounds Granny Smith apples (about 3 medium)
- 1 1/4 pounds McIntosh apples (about 3 medium)
- 2 tablespoons juice from 1 lemon
- 1/4 cup plus 2 tablespoons sugar
- 1/4 teaspoon ground cinnamon
- 2 egg whites, beaten lightly

1. In bowl of food processor fitted with steel blade, pulse flour, sugar, and salt to combine. Add butter and cream cheese; pulse until mixture is sandy, with small, pebblelike curds, 10 to 12 one-second pulses (mixture should not form cohesive ball). Turn mixture into medium bowl.

2. Sprinkle lemon juice and 1 tablespoon ice water over mixture. With rubber spatula, use folding motion to evenly distribute water and lemon juice into flour mixture until small portion of dough holds together when squeezed in palm of hand (*see* illustration 1), adding up to 1 tablespoon more ice water if necessary. (Mixture will look dry even after liquid is incorporated.) Turn dough onto clean, dry work surface; gather and gently press together into cohesive ball, then flatten into rough disk. With chef's knife or dough scraper, cut dough into 6 equal pieces, shaping each piece into disk about 3 inches wide. Place disks in single layer on flat dinner plate, wrap plate in plastic, and refrigerate until firm, about 30 minutes (can be refrigerated up to 2 days).

3. Remove dough from refrigerator (if refrigerated longer than 30 minutes, let stand at room temperature until soft and malleable). Working one at a time, roll out disks between 2 sheets of lightly floured parchment paper into circles approximately 6 inches wide. Remove top layer of parchment; trim bottom layer of parchment into rectangles about 2 inches larger than dough. Stack rectangles with parchment on plate; cover plate with plastic wrap and refrigerate while preparing fruit.

4. Adjust one oven rack to highest position and other rack to lowest position; heat oven to 400 degrees. Peel, core, and cut apples into 1/4-inch-thick slices and toss with lemon juice, 1/4 cup sugar, and cinnamon. Arrange parchment-lined dough rounds in single layer on work surface. Following illustrations 5 and 6, arrange about 1 cup apple slices, thick edges out, in circular mound, leaving 1-inch border of dough. Fold dough border up over filling, pleating dough to fit snugly around apples. With cupped hands, gently press dough to filling, reinforcing shape and compacting apples (*see* illustration 7). Using parchment lining, slide 3 tartlets onto each of 2 cookie sheets.

5. Bake tartlets until pale golden brown, about 15 minutes. Brush crust with beaten egg whites and sprinkle apples with remaining 2 tablespoons sugar. Return tartlets to oven, switching positions of cookie sheets; bake until crust is deep golden brown and apples are tender, about 15 minutes longer. Cool tartlets on cookie sheets 5 minutes; using wide metal spatula, remove from parchment and transfer to cooling rack. Cool additional 5 minutes; serve.

RUSTIC FREE–FORM APPLE TART
MAKES ONE 9-INCH TART, SERVING 6

This tart, with its large mound of apples, must bake for a longer time at a lower temperature than the tartlets. Use a jelly-roll pan or rimmed cookie sheet so that it will catch any juices released during baking. Doubling the pan on which the tart is baked halfway through baking will shield the bottom crust and keep it from overbrowning.

1. Follow recipe for Rustic Free-Form Apple Tartlets, flattening dough into 6-inch disk in step 2, then wrapping disk in plastic wrap and chilling until firm, about 30 minutes (can be refrigerated up to 2 days).

2. Adjust oven rack to lower-middle position and heat oven to 375 degrees. Remove dough from refrigerator (if refrigerated longer than 30 minutes, let stand at room temperature until malleable). Roll dough between 2 large sheets of lightly floured parchment paper into circle about 15 inches wide. Peel off top layer of parchment and, using parchment lining, slide dough onto jelly-roll pan or rimmed cookie sheet; cover with plastic wrap and refrigerate while preparing fruit as described in step 4 of recipe for Rustic Free-Form Apple Tartlets.

3. Following illustrations 5 and 6, arrange apple slices, thick edges out, in circular mound, leaving 3-inch border of dough. Fold dough border up over filling, pleating dough to fit snugly around apples. With cupped hands, gently press dough to filling, reinforcing shape and compacting apples (see illustration 7).

4. Bake until pale golden brown, about 30 minutes. Place pan with tart onto second pan of same size to insulate bottom crust; brush crust with beaten egg whites and sprinkle with remaining 2 tablespoons sugar. Return to oven and bake until crust is deep golden brown and apples are tender, about 30 minutes longer. Cool tart on pan 10 minutes, loosen parchment where it may have stuck to pan, then, using parchment lining, slide tart onto cooling rack. Place a large, round plate on top of tart, invert tart, peel off parchment, and re-invert tart onto serving platter.

Greg Case is the pastry chef at Hamersley's Bistro in Boston, Mass.

TECHNIQUE | MAKING INDIVIDUAL TARTS

1. Squeeze some dough in the palm of your hand. It should hold together.

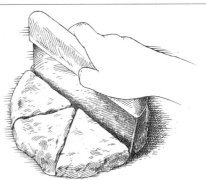

2. Work dough together lightly to form 6-inch disk. Cut disk into 6 equal pieces, then round and flatten each slightly to form small disks, about 3 inches in diameter.

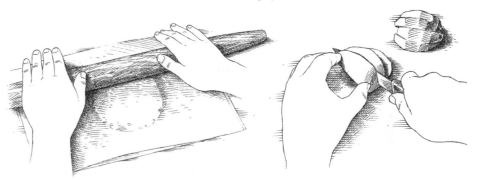

3. Place individual disks between squares of parchment paper and roll out into 6-inch circles. Lift and realign sheets of parchment as dough becomes thinner.

4. Slice apples ¼ inch thick.

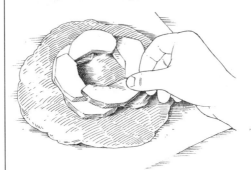

5. Arrange apple slices in even circle over dough, leaving free a 1-inch perimeter of dough for fluted edge.

6. Fill in center with additional slices, lending support to circular wall of apples.

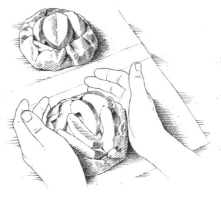

7. Fold outer lip of dough snugly inward over apples and cup with hands to compress and shape.

8. Grasping parchment edges, transfer each tartlet to baking sheet.

Double Chocolate Cookies

The secret of a chocolate cookie with the intensity of hot fudge sauce is a combination of the right kind of chocolate and cocoa powder.

≥ BY CHRISTOPHER KIMBALL ≤

Obsessions often begin with chance encounters, a wry, fetching smile glanced out of the corner of an eye or perhaps one's first taste of a home-grown tomato. One of my greatest obsessions, however, has been the first transcendent bite of the perfect chocolate cookie, still warm out of the oven. The first bite would reveal a center of hot fudge sauce, and the texture would call to mind chocolate bread pudding with a deep, complex chocolate flavor. This would be the sort of confection that creates intense focus while it is consumed, sights and sounds subordinate to taste, overloading the other senses to the point of dysfunction.

The problem is that I have, for years, been trying to perfect this cookie. I have created large, dense cookies that were rich and decadent, but the chocolate flavor was dull and overwhelming, and the texture was, well, on the dry side. I have also experimented with thin, crisp cookies (nice but not intense), chewy cookies (good but not showstoppers), and cakelike chocolate cookies, which tend to be dry and uninspiring. Our test kitchen also made a half-dozen recipes from various cookbooks and discovered a world of difference in texture, flavor, and appearance, from soft mocha-colored disks to thick mounds of pure fudge. This panoply of outcomes gave me pause, since the ingredient lists seemed to have more in common than the cookies themselves. Figuring out what makes a chocolate cookie tick was going to require weeks of testing and a great deal of detective work.

Down to Basics

My first step was to strip the recipes down to their basics to understand the fundamentals. A chocolate cookie is a mixture of melted chocolate, sugar, eggs, butter, flour, baking soda or powder, and salt. Vanilla, coffee, and nuts are extras.

The key issues were how to handle the butter and eggs. The butter can be melted or creamed, and the eggs can be beaten or just whisked into the batter. For the first test batch, we melted the butter and whipped the eggs. The results were

If you like bursts of warm melted chocolate in your cookies, include chocolate chips in the batter.

good, but the cookies were a bit cakey and loose, without any chew. For the next batch we melted the butter and did not beat the eggs. These cookies were a bit dry and cakey. When we started creaming the butter and beating the eggs into it after creaming, we noticed an immediate improvement. However, we finally settled on a modified creaming method with minimal beating to produce moist cookies that were not cakey.

The next issue was one of proportions, that is, the ratio of flour to butter to eggs to sugar to chocolate. This was going to be crucial to the thickness of the cookie, its texture, and the degree to which the taste of chocolate would dominate. Looking over the recipes we had tested, I saw so many permutations that I felt like the British trying to crack the German secret code in World War II.

To organize the facts, I made a chart of the various ratios of eggs, sugar, chocolate, and butter to flour, with related comments on the taste, texture, and shape of each cookie we had tested. I quickly noted that the ratio of eggs and butter to flour was less important than the ratio of sugar and chocolate to flour. The driest cookie used less than one-half cup of sugar per cup of flour; the richest, wettest cookie used three cups. The

cookie with the faintest chocolate flavor and a relatively firm, dry texture used only two ounces of chocolate per cup of flour, whereas other recipes used up to a pound of chocolate with only one-half cup of flour. After many tests designed to balance sweetness and moisture, we settled on one cup of sugar to one cup of flour. More tests ended up suggesting that we use eight ounces of chocolate per one cup of flour. Finally, we had a cookie that had good chocolate flavor and was moist, not dry. Nonetheless, the flavor and texture could be still better, so we moved on to other ingredients.

We started the cookie with all white granulated sugar and then tested a mixture of brown sugar and granulated, which seemed to improve the flavor and added just a bit more moisture. We also tried corn syrup, which had little effect. A small amount of vanilla extract and instant coffee powder rounded out the flavors. Throughout the testing, we had been using all-purpose flour. We decided to try cake flour as well, but the resulting cookie was a bit too delicate. We also varied the quantity of flour throughout the testing process, starting at three cups and eventually working our way down to two cups. To create a thicker, more stable cookie, we tried replacing some of the butter with vegetable shortening (Crisco), but this created an unattractive, greasy-looking cookie with a pale white sheen. I thought that the choice of leavener might be important, so we tested baking powder against baking soda and found that the cookies with the powder were slightly thicker.

TECHNIQUE | SIZE MATTERS!

The balls of raw dough should be about the size of a golf ball. Don't skimp.

Not All Chocolates Are Created Equal

There are many options when it comes to chocolate: unsweetened, bittersweet, semisweet, cocoa powder, and chips. The question is, how are they different?

Unsweetened chocolate, often called baking chocolate or chocolate liquor, is made from roasted cocoa beans and contains about 50 percent solids from the beans and 50 percent cocoa butter. Bittersweet and semisweet chocolates (also called dark chocolates) are made from unsweetened chocolate that is ground with sugar and then further refined. Since bittersweet and semisweet chocolates are about 50 percent sugar, they have less chocolate flavor than unsweetened, which has no added sugar. (Although individual brands may vary, bittersweet averages around 46 percent sugar by weight; semisweet is about 57 percent sugar.) The chocolate flavor they do have, however, is less bitter and more complex, features appreciated by many bakers.

Chocolate chips, as we pointed out in our September/October 1998 tasting, are made from chocolate with relatively little cocoa butter, about 30 percent or even less. (Dark chocolates, by comparison, must have at least 35 percent cocoa butter.) This is because the chips will not hold their shape with more fat. This lower percentage of cocoa butter makes for a less buttery, grainier texture and flavor.

Cocoa powder is made from unsweetened chocolate. Much of the fat is removed by pressing, leaving behind the solids. These leftover solids are then fluffed up and packaged. Dutch-processed cocoa is less acidic than regular cocoa and many people, myself included, feel that this results in a stronger, more interesting chocolate flavor.

Another factor that affects the quality of one brand of chocolate over another is the use of additives. Most processed dark chocolates include vanilla, lecithin (which makes chocolate smoother when poured), and other flavorings, often including soy. In addition, some manufacturers roast their beans for a shorter time on the theory that when the chocolate is baked by consumers it will undergo additional processing.

As for which type of semisweet chocolate is best for a chocolate cookie, we tested four major brands head to head: Nestlé, Bakers, Ghirardelli, and Callebaut. The Bakers turned out a gritty cookie that received low marks, Nestlé had an off, somewhat fruity taste, and the Ghirardelli had a muted but pure chocolate flavor that was quite pleasant. But the Callebaut was our favorite, with a big chocolate flavor that was clean, direct, and full of punch.   —C.K.

The Search for the Ultimate Chocolate Experience

At this point our cookie was thick and very good, but not the sort of thing that would reduce the average adult to tears of joy. The flavor was still a bit dull, and the texture was moist but mono-chromatic. We wondered if we could solve this problem by varying the type of chocolate. We found that unsweetened chocolate, an ingredient often called for in chocolate cookie recipes, added a bit of intensity to the flavor. Unfortunately, we also discovered an aggressive sour note in these cookies, even when the sugar level was adjusted for the bitterness of the chocolate. Semisweet and bittersweet chocolate turned out to be better choices owing to their rounder, less overwhelming flavor. These chocolates undergo more processing than unsweetened, and they also get other flavorings; this no doubt gives them a smoother, richer flavor. (See "Not All Chocolates Are Created Equal," left.)

Our hunt was almost over, but now we wondered if a bit of cocoa powder might add more depth of flavor to our cookie. One-half cup of Dutch-processed cocoa was substituted for the same amount of flour, and the chocolate flavor became both smoother and deeper. (We also tried a batch of cookies made only with cocoa powder—no chocolate—and they were disappointing, having a just faint chocolate flavor.) At last, we had brought my fantasy to life: a double chocolate cookie that was both rich and soft, with an intense chocolatey center that could drive anyone to distraction.

THICK AND CHEWY DOUBLE CHOCOLATE COOKIES
MAKES ABOUT 3½ DOZEN COOKIES

To melt the chocolate in a microwave, heat at 50 percent power for 2 minutes, stir, then continue heating at 50 percent power for 1 more minute. If not completely melted, heat an additional 30 to 45 seconds at 50 percent power. Semisweet chocolate chips may be added for a bigger chocolate punch; if used, they will slightly increase the yield on the cookies. We recommend using a spring-loaded ice cream scoop to scoop the dough. Resist the urge to bake the cookies longer than indicated; they may appear underbaked at first but will firm up as they cool.

2	cups all-purpose flour
½	cup Dutch-processed cocoa powder
2	teaspoons baking powder
1	teaspoon salt
16	ounces semisweet chocolate, chopped
4	large eggs
2	teaspoons vanilla extract
2	teaspoons instant coffee or espresso powder
10	tablespoons (1¼ sticks) unsalted butter, softened but still firm
1½	cups packed light brown sugar
½	cup granulated sugar

1. Sift together flour, cocoa, baking powder, and salt in medium bowl; set aside. Melt chocolate in medium heatproof bowl set over pan of almost-simmering water, stirring once or twice, until smooth; remove from heat. Beat eggs and vanilla lightly with fork, sprinkle coffee powder over to dissolve, and set aside.

2. In bowl of standing mixer fitted with paddle attachment (or with hand mixer), beat butter at medium speed until smooth and creamy, about 5 seconds (15 seconds with hand mixer). Beat in sugars until combined, about 45 seconds (1½ minutes with hand mixer); mixture will look granular. Reduce speed to low and gradually beat in egg mixture until incorporated, about 45 seconds (1½ minutes with hand mixer). Add chocolate in steady stream and beat until combined, about 40 seconds (1 minute with hand mixer). Scrape bottom and sides of bowl with rubber spatula. With mixer at low speed, add flour mixture and mix until combined, about 40 seconds (1 minute with hand mixer). Do not overbeat. (Stir in chocolate chips with wooden spoon, if using.) Cover with plastic wrap and let stand at room temperature until consistency is scoopable and fudgelike, about 30 minutes.

3. Meanwhile, adjust oven racks to upper- and lower-middle positions and heat oven to 350 degrees. Line 2 cookie sheets with parchment paper. Leaving about 1½ inches between each ball, scoop dough onto parchment-lined cookie sheets with 1¾-inch diameter ice cream scoop.

4. Bake cookies until edges have just begun to set but centers are still very soft, about 10 minutes, turning cookie sheets from front to back and switching from top to bottom racks halfway through baking

5. Cool cookies on sheets about 10 minutes, slide parchment with cookies onto wire rack and cool to room temperature; remove with wide metal spatula.

TRIPLE CHOCOLATE COOKIE VARIATION

Add 12 ounces (about 2 cups) of semisweet chocolate chips to the batter after the dry ingredients are incorporated.

Are Cheap Parmesans Any Good?

Is Parmigiano-Reggiano, at $14 per pound, worth the price or are cheaper, domestic Parmesans good alternatives?

⋟ BY MARYELLEN DRISCOLL ⋞

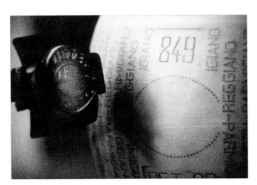

Authentic Parmigiano-Reggiano always has the name stamped on the rind.

For the first 17 or so years of my life, my idea of Parmesan cheese was a whitish powder that came in a jar, just like garlic. I think all those blissfully ignorant years of shaking the jar over a plate of my mother's spaghetti sauce imprinted a notion of this cheese as a simple seasoning— almost like an upscale salt. So while I now buy Parmesan in wedge form, on more than one occasion I have turned a store's cheese display upside down in search of the smallest and thus least costly wedge in the batch. It's a sort of nonsensical nod to frugality.

So it was with some ill ease that I began to research Parmesan products in preparation for a blind taste test. I found that the cost range is wide, with most jarred grated Parmesans and domestic Parmesan wedges ranging from $6.50 per pound to $8 per pound, and the "authentic" Parmigiano-Reggiano at the high end, $13.99 per pound. I had to wonder if the "authentic" Parmigiano-Reggiano would be that much better when tasted side by side with a domestic Parmesan at half the price, which I have long assumed was a reasonable option.

To assemble the products for the tasting I needed to define what constituted a Parmesan-type cheese. After reading various books and articles and talking to Steven Jenkins, general manager (and cheese aficionado) at the Fairway Market in New York City, I had learned that Parmesan is a "grana," a hard, grainy cheese. The grana cheese category is composed mostly of Italian grating cheeses. Parmigiano-Reggiano is the most famous (and expensive) of the granas, and its manufacture dates back 800 years. Parmigiano-Reggiano has become an increasingly

regulated product; in 1955 it became what is known as a certified name (not a brand name). Since that time the name has indicated that the cheese was made within a specific region of northern Italy and approved by a certifying consortium.

American cheese makers have been making Parmesan only since the beginning of the century and need not abide by any more stringent regulations than basic USDA standards. There is no lack of pregrated products, but only a handful of domestic Parmesans come in wedges.

Other granas considered Parmesan types are Grana Padano (from Italy) and Reggianito (from Argentina).

Ultimately, the samples in the tasting included five pregrated Parmesan cheeses (domestic and imported), three wedges of domestic Parmesan, a wedge of Grana Padano, one of Reggianito, and two of Parmigiano-Reggiano. To see if differences in store handling could affect the quality of the latter two, one was purchased at a specialty cheese store that cuts from the wheel per order and has controlled humidity; the other was purchased precut and wrapped in plastic at a large supermarket. All of the cheeses were tasted grated, at room temperature. The 14 tasters consisted of *Cook's* staff and expert cheese tasters from Formaggio Kitchen, a specialty food store in Cambridge, Mass.

To get an idea of what the tasters might want to look for when tasting the different cheeses, I spoke to a number of cheese experts as well as Nancy Radke, U.S. director of communications for the Consorzio del Formaggio Parmigiano-Reggiano. All recommended that the tasters rate the cheeses on the basics: aroma, flavor—particularly depth of flavor and saltiness versus sweetness— and overall texture. The Parmesans should also be left to sit on the tasters' tongues to see if they melt smoothly into creaminess in the mouth. All of the experts I spoke to expressed confidence that Parmigiano-Reggiano would be the hands-down winner.

Tasting Results

As it turned out, this time the experts were correct. Parmigiano-Reggiano had a depth and complexity of flavor and a smooth, melting texture that none of the others could match.

Parmigiano-Reggiano owes much of its flavor to the unpasteurized milk used to produce it, according to Radke. It is a "controlled-district"

cheese, which means not only that it must be made within the boundaries of this zone but also that the milk used to make it and even the grass, hay, and grain fed to the cows that make the milk must come from the district. Consequently, "just like good wine, a lot of character comes from its soil and climate," said Radke. This proved to be true in the tasting. None of the other cheeses had the sweet, nutty, creamy flavor that helped Parmigiano-Reggiano earn its high ratings.

Apart from these flavor differences, we also found that almost all of the cheeses in the tasting— except the Parmigiano-Reggiano—were extremely salty. In fact, Parmigiano-Reggiano contains about two-thirds less sodium than the other Parmesans. Radke believes this is because the wheels of Parmigiano-Reggiano are so large that they do not become as saturated with salt during the brining process that is one of the final steps in making the cheese. (The average wheel is about 9 inches high, 16 to 18 inches in diameter, and weighs 75 to 90 pounds; domestic Parmesan wheels average 24 pounds.)

The low salt content of Parmigiano-Reggiano makes it more perishable than other cheeses once cut from the wheel. Once cut, the cheese will also begin to dry out. This was evident in the Parmigiano-Reggiano sample purchased at the grocery store. Tasters rated this a few tenths of a point lower than the sample purchased at the specialty cheese store because of a chalky finish. This drying effect was even more glaring with the chalky pregrated products, which received consistently poor ratings.

Another benefit of the larger wheel is that Parmigiano-Reggiano can age longer, said Radke. Parmigiano-Reggiano ages for about 24 months, while domestic Parmesan ages for about 10 months. The longer aging allows more complex flavors and aromas to develop.

The aging also makes a difference in texture, creating a distinctive component that tasters described as "crystal crunch." The crunch stems from proteins breaking down into free amino acid crystals during the latter half of the aging process. The crystals are visible, appearing as white dots in the cheese. No other Parmesan had this effect.

Other textural differences are created by the fact that the curds for Parmigiano-Reggiano are cut into fragments the size of wheat grains, which is much finer than the fragments created in the manufacture of domestic Parmesan. The benefit of smaller curds is that they drain more effectively, said Radke. Domestic Parmesans have to be mechanically pressed to get rid of excess moisture. The consequence, as our tasting panel discovered with the domestic Parmesans that were not pregrated, is a cheese that is much more dense. They characterized as it "rubbery," "tough," and "squeaky."

The tasting did not rule out all of the other Parmesans as completely unacceptable—just most. One scored well enough to be recommended. This was Wisconsin-made DiGiorno. So while there is a somewhat more affordable Parmesan option, the Parmigiano-Reggiano was in a class of its own. When added to a dish it acts as more than a seasoning; it can add a complex spectrum of flavor. And, as I found after learning that Italians commonly eat Parmigiano-Reggiano in chunks as a table food, it makes for a tempting snack while preparing a complementary meal.

TASTING PARMESAN CHEESE

The Parmesan-type brand name cheeses were selected for the blind tasting based on national availability. The specialty Parmesan-type cheeses were selected based on recommendations from cheese experts. All were tasted in grated form, with water and plain crusty bread served as palate cleansers. They were judged by aroma, flavor, texture, and melting ability. The panel of 14 tasters consisted of *Cook's* staff as well as cheese experts from Formaggio Kitchen in Cambridge, Mass.

RECOMMENDED

Parmigiano-Reggiano MADE IN ITALY (PURCHASED AT SPECIALTY FOOD STORE)

➤ **$13.99/lb.**

This certified cheese carried a distinctly sweet aroma along with a "roundness of flavor" that was remarkably sweet, nutty, and creamy. Perhaps even more outstanding was its smooth melting quality. It "melted like butter in my mouth," said one taster. When grated, this cheese was fluffy and light, smooth yet substantial with just a bit of crystal amino acid crunch. The fact that the cheese was purchased at a specialty store that keeps the cheese in conditions of perfect temperature and humidity showed up in both texture and flavor.

Parmigiano-Reggiano MADE IN ITALY (PURCHASED AT SUPERMARKET)

➤ **$13.99/lb.**

A close runner-up, this wedge of certified Parmigiano-Reggiano was purchased in the cheese section of a large chain supermarket. It had more fruity flavor notes and was described as having a "full, lingering, pungent, slightly barnyardy flavor." In terms of mouthfeel, it started out smooth but had a dry finish, described by some as "chalky." Despite not living up to the textural superiority of the wedge purchased at the specialty cheese store, this sample had "the depth of a well-aged cheese" and was "a complete delight to taste alone."

DiGiorno Parmesan MADE IN WISCONSIN

➤ **$7.99/lb.**

The only domestic Parmesan to which tasters gave a strong nod of approval. Its "clean" flavor was only moderately salty. Tasters also found it a bit tangy but still sweet and nutty, if only faintly so. While there was "not much body" to this cheese, one expert taster noted that its texture was "more or less correct." "Not a bad cheese, not too intense, but has a nice salty-sweet quality."

NOT RECOMMENDED

Reggianito MADE IN ARGENTINA

➤ **$5.99/lb.**

This South American Parmesan-style cheese had a "strong dairy flavor" but was "overwhelmed by salt" and lacked depth. It was fairly smooth, yet lacking in body, and "disappeared too quickly on the tongue." "There is a caramel-like flavor that I like, but it's overwhelmed by the salt abundance," commented one taster. Available in grocery stores with a wide cheese selection.

Grana Padano MADE IN ITALY

➤ **$10.95/lb.**

This cheese scored surprisingly well in all categories, except when it came to tasters' overall liking. The flavor was "mild" but "complex" with "a little sweet and some toasted nut." The aftertaste was milky and mildly sour. It had a soft, supple mouthfeel, melting readily on the tongue. It "suggests quality cheese … but falls short" and "seemed weak."

Stella Parmesan MADE IN WISCONSIN

➤ **$6.49/lb.**

First off, every taster was taken aback by the aroma, which was described as "burnt," "like fresh-baked bread," "a tiny bit fishy," like "fried chicken," "smoky," and "meaty." Comments on flavor were just as colorful: "Smoky, ham flavor," "strange porklike flavor," "burnt garlic," and "like chicken, seriously." In sum, it was dry and "not Parmesan-y at all."

BelGioso Parmesan MADE IN WISCONSIN

➤ **$6.49/lb.**

A domestic cheese that was "somewhat bright, not very interesting, but OK." The finish was sharp, and salty flavors were dominant. "Texture is also disappointing—leathery." "Tastes really young, like it is aged less than some of the others." (The label states that the cheese was aged a minimum of 10 months.)

Suprema Imported Parmesan MADE IN ITALY

➤ **$3.99 for an 8-oz. container**

This pregrated cheese might be an Italian import but did not make the grade of a certified Parmigiano-Reggiano. There was a sharp edge to its flavor, and it had grainy texture. "Tastes pregrated," noted one taster. Similarly, another said, "Tastes processed, with that shrink-wrapped American cheese kind of flavor."

Horizon Organic MADE IN COLORADO

➤ **$4.05 for a 3.5-oz. jar**

The aroma brought one taster back to "pasta night circa 1973." It "tastes like mild canned cheese," but with a strong aftertaste "like salty metal filings." The texture was powdery and felt pasty on the tongue.

Kraft Grated Parmesan MADE IN ILLINOIS

➤ **$3.79 for an 8-oz. can**

One taster thought this cheese tasted like "Easter candy," while others thought they tasted balsamic vinegar, roasted nuts, cooked hot dogs, beef bouillon, or crackers. All agreed the cheese tasted bitter and dry and felt gritty in the mouth. This Parmesan "could ruin a dish," commented one taster.

4Cs Parmesan MADE IN ITALY

➤ **$2.79 for a 6-oz. jar**

"The only flavors present are unpleasant," wrote one taster. Others described the flavor as sharp and bitter, like "burnt rubber" and "machine oil." More than one likened the texture to gravel. One wrote, in sum: "Terrible flavor, terrible texture—this makes me miserable."

Ronzoni Grated Parmesan LABEL STATES "CONTAINS PRODUCT FROM ITALY AND ARGENTINA"

➤ **$3.29 for an 8-oz. can**

Apparently, it gets worse. Tasters said this Parmesan was like "old, dirty fish," or like "chewing on an old shoe." In less creative terms, it was gritty, salty, and stale.

The Spin Cycle: Rating Salad Spinners

First-rate design can make a helpful gadget even easier to use.

⇒ BY ADAM RIED ⇐

Everyone has their pet peeves, and limp, wet greens in a salad is high on my personal list. One of my favorite methods for drying wet greens is to place them in a cotton pillowcase, go outside, and swing the pillowcase around in circles. Believe it or not, this technique dries the greens very effectively, and the water that isn't thrown off by the swinging movement is absorbed by the material. Fun as it is, though, I realize this method is not practical for every cook; those with limited movement in their hands, arms, and shoulders and those who live in apartments with little or no outdoor access come to mind. The alternative, using kitchen or paper towels to blot the water off the drenched leaves, is a wet, sloppy, arduous task. That's why salad spinners, which use centrifugal force to dry the greens (just like me and my pillowcase), are such a good idea. But which of them works the best? To find out, I bought eight different models and brought them into the *Cook's* kitchen for a full testing.

The basic design of all salad spinners is similar. A perforated basket is fitted into a larger outer bowl, and gears connected to the mechanism in the lid spin the basket rapidly, creating centrifugal force that pulls the greens to the sides of the basket and the water on the leaves through the perforations into the outer bowl. Beyond this, however, there are three important ways in which various models can differ.

First is the lid, some of which are solid and some of which have a hole so water can be run directly into the basket while you spin. Second is the outer bowl, some of which, like the lids, are solid, while others are perforated so water can flow through. The third major difference is the mechanism that makes the baskets spin. Among the eight models we tested, the units from Zyliss and Progressive International operate with a pull cord; the Copco,

Triumph, Norpro, and Better Houseware all have turning cranks; the Copco Turbo model has a lever crank; and the Oxo has a pump knob.

Flow Through? No

To be honest, almost all the spinners did a reasonably good job of drying wet lettuce leaves and parsley, though none dried the greens so thoroughly that they wouldn't benefit from a quick blotting with paper towels before being dressed. In fact, the difference in the amount of water thrown off by the best dryer of the lot, the Zyliss, and the worst, the Norpro, was roughly half an ounce, or a mere tablespoon. Since the differences between them in terms of drying performance are not terribly dramatic, what you really want is a spinner that is well designed, easy to use, and sturdy.

The best way to clean greens thoroughly is to soak them in a large bowl or sink full of water. Though it may require several changes of water, this method allows dirt from the greens to settle on the bottom of the bowl, where it stays if you lift the leaves out gently.

This approach to cleaning greens is the reason I didn't like the Norpro and Better Houseware spinners, both of which have flow-through lids. The greens I cleaned by running water into the basket tended to bruise from the rushing water and never got clean enough. In addition to the flow-through lid, the bowl of the Better Houseware had holes in the bottom so the water could flow right out. Again, I did not consider this a benefit, in part because it assumes you have an empty sink in which to place the spinner, which I, for one, rarely do if I'm cooking a whole meal. Second, I like to use the outer bowl of the spinner to soak the leaves clean, since I'm going to dirty it anyway when I spin them dry.

Get a Grip

The design of the lid was one factor that made some spinners easier to use than others. The rapid spinning of the inner basket and resulting centrifugal force create quite a bit of vibration, so all the spinners but one have to be held down with your free hand to keep them from dancing right across the counter.

The exception to this rule, and the real standout in terms of design and ease of use, was the Oxo. You

The Salad Spinners We Tested

BEST SALAD SPINNERS: 2-WAY TIE

Zyliss Salad Spinner
This solid-feeling spinner is particularly smooth in action.

Oxo Good Grips
Very well designed and the only spinner in the group that we could use with one hand.

Progressive Int'l Cord Salad Spinner
Smooth to use, but capacity is slightly smaller than we like.

Copco Salad Spinner
Considerable vibration in use.

Triumph Salad Spinner, Model M72
Solid and effective, but hard to hold down and a real drag to use.

Copco Turbo Salad Spinner
Design is controversial, and spinner squeaks like a squirrel being electrocuted with every spin. Irritating.

Norpro Deluxe Multipurpose Salad Spinner
Full handle makes for a comfortable grip, but overall feel is exceedingly flimsy.

Better Houseware Salad Spinner
Neither the flow-through design nor the cramped bowl appealed to us.

RATING SALAD SPINNERS

In each spinner, we spun 4 ounces (about half a medium head) of red leaf lettuce leaves—doused in water and then drained for two minutes—and checked for dryness every 15 seconds. We performed the same test using 4 ounces (about 1 medium bunch) of flat-leaf parsley. Grip comfort, ease of use, and drying ability were equally important considerations. We assessed the dryness of the greens by visual and tactile inspection and by blotting the spun leaves on paper towels. We also measured the weight of water thrown off. Finally, we considered capacity, which we measured by loosely packing torn lettuce leaves in the perforated spinner inserts, and overall design and sturdiness. Spinners are listed in order of preference from best to worst.

Brand	Price	Capacity	Mechanism	Flow Through	Grip Comfort	Ease of Use	Drying Ability	Design/ Sturdiness	Testers' Comments
TIED FOR BEST SPINNER Zyliss Salad Spinner	$20.00	5 quarts	Top-mounted pull cord	No	★★	★★★	★★★	★★★	Direction of the basket spin reverses with each pull of cord. Top is very easy to grip, so spinner can be held tight and kept stable during use. Dried the greens exceptionally well in just 30 seconds of spinning.
TIED FOR BEST SPINNER Oxo Good Grips Salad Spinner	$25.00	5 quarts	Top-mounted pump knob	No	★★★	★★★	★★	★★★	Most expensive spinner of the lot had an excellent design with two particularly smart features: a no-skid base on the bowl, and a push-button brake to stop the spinning. Very sturdy, but drying time and performance were a little behind Zyliss.
Progressive International Pull Cord Salad Spinner	$16.99	3 quarts	Top-mounted pull cord	No	★★	★★★	★★★	★★	Easy to use, solid feeling, and dried greens impressively. Bowl felt a little cramped for the parsley, and lots of parsley slipped into outer bowl through the relatively wide slots of the insert.
Copco Salad Spinner	$9.99	4 quarts	Top-mounted turn crank	No	★★	★★	★★★	★★	In use, it shakes, rattles, and rolls like crazy and requires some strength to hold onto and stabilize. Deep, tall bowl was quite spacious for parsley. Hard to stop once it's spinning.
Triumph Salad Spinner, Model M72 (distributed by Mouli)	$14.75	5 quarts	Top-mounted turn crank	No	★	★	★★★	★★	Dried greens well, but very uncomfortable to use. Noticeable resistance made crank handle difficult to turn, and there was really no good place on the lid to grab the spinner and hold it down.
Copco Turbo Salad Spinner	$19.99	5 quarts	Top-mounted lever crank	No	★★	★	★★	★★	Lever crank was controversial; some staffers found it easy to use, while others considered it awkward and difficult. Very squeaky in use, jammed frequently, and hard to stop.
Norpro Deluxe Multipurpose Salad Spinner	$8.95	4 quarts	Top-mounted turn crank	Yes (lid only)	★★★	★★★	★	★	Easy to use and very comfortable to hold because of the handle, but lousy at drying greens. Very noisy in use, and both insert and lid fit poorly.
Better Houseware Salad Spinner	$6.99	3 quarts	Top-mounted turn crank	Yes (lid and bowl)	★★	★★	★★	★★	We see no real advantage to the flow-through design. This noisy spinner turned in a mediocre drying performance.

can actually use the Oxo with only one hand because of its clever no-skid base and the pump knob by which it operates. Pushing the pump down both makes the basket spin and pushes the whole unit down onto the counter. Better yet, the Oxo has a lock to keep the pump knob in the down position, making storage a little easier.

Among the others, the Zyliss, Progressive International, and Copco Turbo lids were easier to grip than the Copco, Triumph, or Better Houseware. The Norpro was the only spinner with a full-fledged handle (on the outer bowl), so it was a breeze to hold in place, but the handle alone was not enough to bump this spinner up from the bottom of the pack when it came to the ratings.

The spinners differed noticeably with regard to their fit, finish, and overall feeling of sturdiness. If the lid, for instance, did not align properly with the basket, it was difficult to get the basket to start rotating, or it might jam as it was spinning. While this was not a disaster, it was annoying because you had to stop and realign the lid for the spinner to work properly. The Zyliss and the Oxo were the sturdiest feeling,

best-fitting spinners of the bunch. The Norpro and the Better Houseware were at the bottom of the list in terms of fit and sturdiness, as both were noisy and flimsy feeling, and the lid of the Norpro fit poorly. Some users found it tricky to fit the lid of the Copco Turbo correctly over the basket, so this spinner was the most prone to jamming. In addition, the Copco Turbo made an annoying squeak while spinning.

Another thoughtful feature of the Oxo was a push-button brake to halt the spinning basket, a task that some of the spinners made more challenging. The baskets in both pull-cord units, the Zyliss and the Progressive International, were also easy to halt because they stopped almost as soon as you stopped pulling the cord.

In the course of all this spinning, I did learn that it's important to spin small batches of leaves, no more than half of a medium head of lettuce. Packing the bowl full does not allow enough room for water to run off thoroughly. It is also a good idea to distribute the leaves evenly in the basket; bunching them on one side makes the spinner wobble more in action. Of the spinners in our group, the easiest to use, by a long shot, was

the Oxo, but the Zyliss got the greens a little drier a little faster. You make the choice. Either way, it will be the right one.

Storing Greens

Storing cleaned and dried greens is another advantage of salad spinners, especially those with solid outer bowls and generous capacity. As a side experiment to this testing, I washed and dried 10-ounce heads of red leaf lettuce and stored them in five different products, including cotton and terry-cloth bags, perforated zipper-lock vegetable storage bags, and two specially designed plastic food storage containers, all intended specifically for storing greens or vegetables. I also stored a batch in the Copco salad spinner. After six days in the refrigerator, the spinner-stored leaves still looked great—fresh, firm, moist, and 100 percent useable. By comparison, the leaves in the zipper-lock bag and plastic storage containers had discolored or gone limp, and those in both the cotton and terry-cloth bags were lifeless and totally spent, fit only to be tossed out. —A.R.

Tasting American Merlots

Once relatively unknown, Merlot is now the best-selling red wine in the United States. But is it worth buying? We tested 25 and liked 16 of them. BY MARK BITTMAN

Merlot has become the hottest selling red wine in the United States. Why? Because, generally speaking, it is soft when it is young, containing few of the harsher components of its cousin, Cabernet Sauvignon. This makes it accessible, smooth, and easy to drink, exactly the qualities that most American newcomers to wine appreciate in a red.

But experienced and perhaps prejudiced wine drinkers have long believed that the very qualities that make Merlot enjoyable—a sweetish bouquet, a readily likable flavor—also make it simple. It lacks, they say, the "backbone" or "structure" of wine that relies on the Cabernet grape. It is the Cabernet grape, they say, that is responsible for making many of the great red wines truly great.

In traditional French winemaking—at least in Bordeaux, the ancestral home of both grapes—neither Merlot nor Cabernet is used alone except in rare instances. In fact, they're frequently combined to take advantage of the lush softness of the first and the austere complexity of the second. But in California, the wine industry continues to focus on "varietals," that is, wines made from a single grape. It is difficult, at this juncture, to justify this practice, especially given that the best California reds are the blends, sometimes called "meritage" wines.

Nevertheless, the practice of making varietal wines continues, even though it often results in the worst of all possible worlds: Cabernet that is too harsh and tannic to drink, and Merlot that is too insipid to be enjoyable, at least for people accustomed to bolder, stronger, more sophisticated French-style wines.

Our tasting, however, would seem to indicate that at least some winemakers have mastered the Merlot challenge. Even the veteran tasters in our group agreed that the majority of the Merlots we tasted had merit and that some of them were surprisingly good. And this sentiment extends beyond the $65 wine from Duckhorn, generally considered California's best Merlot and uniformly acclaimed the best wine of our tasting. There were even a couple of $10-and-under Merlots that, while lacking complexity, offered as much as you could hope for in an inexpensive red wine. In between were a host of well-made wines that belied our preconceived notion that

all Merlots were simple. (There were rejects, of course—9 out of the 25 wines we tasted were considered sub-par.)

The bad news is that you usually get what you pay for: all the losers cost $15 or less, and more than half of the $20-and-under wines

wound up on the reject pile. The good news is that you can find a decent Merlot for less than $20, but if you leave it to chance, you probably won't. And every wine that cost more than $25 was worth drinking—many were even worth their asking price.

RATING THE WINE | AMERICAN MERLOT

The wines in our tasting—held at Mt. Carmel Wine and Spirits in Hamden, Connecticut—were judged by a panel made up of both wine professionals and amateur wine lovers (in this tasting, there was a heavier-than-usual representation of the latter). The wines were all purchased in the Northeast; prices will vary throughout the country.

Within each category, wines are listed in ascending order of price; there are only recommended wines here (those our panel would not recommend are not listed), all of which received near-unanimous approval.

RECOMMENDED MERLOTS, UNDER $20

1997 Hacienda Clair de Lune, $7. If you asked for a glass of Merlot at a bar and were served this you'd be reasonably well-satisfied.

1997 Fetzer Eagle Peak, $10. Not a great wine, with too much oak and not enough fruit, but more than decent at this price.

1997 Forest Glen Barrel Select, $10. Also over-oaked, but again a good simple wine.

1997 Francis Coppola Diamond Series Blue Label, $16. Easily the best relatively inexpensive wine, not as exotic as the best of the tasting but generally loved for its spicy, peppery, clove-y flavors. Well worth the money. **BEST BUY.**

1996 Sebastiani SONOMA **$17.** It's likely there is some Cabernet blended in here because this wine has more structure than most.

1996 Estancia SONOMA **$17.** A wine with a future; good right now, almost certainly better in a couple of years.

1995 Beaulieu Vineyards NAPA **$19.** Good nose of black cherry and eminently drinkable. Very nice stuff.

RECOMMENDED MERLOTS, $20 TO $30

1996 Markham NAPA **$20.** Short on fruit, not terribly well-balanced, but too good overall to reject.

1996 Franciscan Oakville Estate NAPA **$22.** A fine wine with complexity, interest, and loads of different flavors. Well-loved and worth the price.

1996 Michel Schlumberger SONOMA **$22.** Another winner, lighter-weight than the above wine but beautifully balanced.

1995 Chateau St. Jean SONOMA **$25.** Interesting wine that has some guts; more appealing to those used to old-fashioned European wines.

1996 Whitehall Lane NAPA **$26.** Very nice, complex wine that was the best of the price category. **OUR TOP CHOICE.**

1996 Turnbull Merlot NAPA **$26.50.** Too good to reject but not exactly exciting. You can do better.

RECOMMENDED MERLOTS, OVER $30

1996 Cuvaison NAPA **$31.50.** Dark, fruity, and complex wine that would be easy to get excited about at a better price.

1996 Matanzas Creek SONOMA **$45.** Clean nose, delicious fruit, spicy and complex if a little hot. Overpriced.

1996 Duckhorn Vineyards Estate Grown NAPA **$65.** The price is obviously a joke; that aside, this was the best wine of the tasting. Serve only if you must impress someone with an extremely experienced palate.

Culinary Dictionaries

Want to know why certain French earthenware casseroles are called marmites
or how the original peach Melba was served? A rash of new and old culinary
dictionaries can point the way. BY CHRISTOPHER KIMBALL

Thirty years from now, I may be the last living American who still walks over to the small-print (one-volume) edition of the *Oxford English Dictionary* to look up "coxcomb" (a fool), "plash" (a light splash), or "nonce" (the present time). Perhaps it is the fact that I grew up in a house stuffed with books, many of which resided in a library containing glass-fronted bookcases and red leather reading chairs. On the other hand, this may simply be one more sign of my froward (obstinate) nature, preferring, as I do, the touch and feel of a book to the click of a keyboard.

Although there are Web site dictionaries currently devoted to sake and malt liquor, to name just two, the written word is still handiest when researching culinary terms. I have chosen eight culinary dictionaries for this roundup, all of them published in the last 10 years. Some are comprehensive but dry, others are witty but incomplete, and some are the best of all worlds. You choose.

The top dog in this race is clearly the *Food Lover's Companion* (Barron's, 1995) by Sharon Tyler Herbst. A Barron's paperback, it runs 700 pages and contains 4,000 terms. The joy of this book is that it is wide ranging, and the listings expand to handle more complicated subjects. The subject of eggs, for example, too common to merit consideration in most of the other books, takes up a whopping two pages. Here you will learn what the "chalzae" is and how much a dozen "pee wee" eggs weigh, and get information on cholesterol, calories, storage, etc. You can also find definitions for "marmite," "celeriac," "fischietti," and "alkanet." The charts and tables at the back of the book are numerous and useful, including the usual measurements and substitutions but also featuring charts showing cuts of meat, addresses for food boards, and high-altitude adjustments. It also fits nicely in the hand, and the typography is designed for quick and easy use.

A number of other dictionaries provide more concise definitions for thousands of culinary terms, without much discourse or explanation. In this category are *The Chef's Companion* (Van Nostrand Reinhold, 1996) by Elizabeth Riely, *International Dictionary of Food and Cooking* (Peter Collin, 1998) by Charles Sinclair, and *Webster's New World Dictionary of Culinary Arts* (Prentice-Hall, 1977) by Steven Labensky, Gay G. Ingram, and Sarah R. Labensky. *Webster's* is the most complete, with 16,000 listings, but this title was clearly a recycled database project: the editors went into their computers and simply pulled out anything that sounded vaguely like cooking. Along with "Eßstäbchen" (the German word for chopsticks) and "oinochoe" (an ancient Greek pitcher-like vessel), I also found, to my surprise but not delight, definitions for a few business terms, such as "equity" and "estimated sales." At current market prices, I might say that I had "equity" in a piece of tenderloin, but that seems a bit beyond the pale.

The International Dictionary consists of culinary terms from foreign dictionaries. It would be useful to cooks who ply foreign culinary waters but of marginal value to the more xenophobic American cook. The definitions in *The Chef's Companion* are concise to a fault, yet there are no more listings than in the excellent *Food Lover's Companion*.

The Glutton's Glossary (Routledge, 1990) by John Ayto and *The Dictionary of American Food and Drink* (Hearst, 1994) by John Mariani are more heavily annotated than the other volumes, which means fewer but longer listings. Mariani's book, which was originally published in 1983 and revised in 1994, is a fascinating trove of American culinary lore, providing discursive commentary on the origin of the fortune cookie, the fact that there are 353 slang terms for the word "drunk" in the American vernacular, and that "restaurant"

was a French term meaning restorative. Although its 2,000 listings makes it light compared with *Webster's*, Mariani's book makes fascinating reading, contains 500 recipes, and is replete with useful stuff. Who needs the other 4,000 listings?

The Glutton's Glossary is published in England and reflects the culinary view from the other side of the big pond, including definitions for "Chelsea buns," "bloomers" (a long loaf of white bread), and "sack" (a Spanish wine imported and sweetened by the English). You will learn that the dessert peach Melba was named after a soprano, Helen Porter Mitchell, whose stage name was Nellie Melba (1859–1931). Escoffier designed in her name a dessert that consisted of vanilla ice cream and peaches resting on an ice swan covered with a net of spun sugar. Later, he popularized the dessert by reducing it to the fruit, the ice cream, and, in place of the swan and spun sugar, sweetened raspberry sauce.

The last two books in the lineup are reference works but not true dictionaries. *The Book of Food* (Henry Holt, 1980) is a guide to 1,000 ingredients with 200 color photographs. It has some useful meat charts, preparation illustrations (cutting up a rabbit, for example), and photos of ingredients such as grains, spices, and even dried fish. However, other books of ingredients have done a superior job of visual presentation. *The Food Lover's Tiptionary* (Hearst, 1994) by Sharon Tyler Herbst has 4,500 listings and is an odd duck indeed, being a listing of tips and techniques by subject, such as celery, mayonnaise, and "Gifts, Food." You will find some real gems here, some self-evident advice, and a few old chestnuts that could have used some first-hand testing. It is not the sort of book one automatically turns to for advice since it is not a dictionary, but if you can sift the wheat from the chaff, it is worth a look.

RESOURCES

Most of the ingredients and materials necessary for the recipes in this issue are available at your local supermarket, gourmet store, or kitchen supply shop. The following are mail-order sources for particular items. Prices listed below were current at press time and do not include shipping or handling unless otherwise indicated. We suggest that you contact companies directly to confirm up-to-date prices and availability.

Salad Spinners

Of the eight salad spinners tested on page 28, the Oxo Good Grips and Zyliss models were our favorites. Some advantages of the Oxo salad spinner are its no-skid base, push-button stop, and easy single-handed use. It is also dishwasher-safe. Oxo's clever pump handle projects about 2 inches from the spinner's lid but easily locks down into place to make for easy storage at 7 inches in height and 10 inches in diameter. You can mail-order the Oxo Good Grips Salad Spinner for $25.99 from **A Cook's Wares (211 37th Street, Beaver Falls, PA 15010-2103; 800-915-9788; www.cookswares.com).** The Swiss Zyliss salad spinner spins greens with the quick pull of a cord. The cord design works much like a yo-yo. Once the cord is extended, the spinning basket reverses direction, drawing the cord back in toward the lid. The Zyliss has a clear bowl (9.5 inches in diameter, 6 inches high) with a lid that comes in white. It can be ordered by mail (item# 115529) for $19.99 from **Kitchen Etc. catalogue services (Department TM, 32 Industrial Drive, Exeter, NH 03833; 800-232-4070).**

Parmigiano–Reggiano

While Parmigiano-Reggiano is becoming increasingly available in the United States, not every town has a specialty cheese store or grocery store with an extensive cheese display. Even those which do might not have a steady turnover of Parmigiano-Reggiano, which is typically pre-cut and plastic-wrapped in such situations. The result, as we found, can be a drier, less creamy product.

All is not lost, however. Many specialty food stores will ship cheese. If you opt to purchase a wedge of Parmigiano-Reggiano, one mail-order source we recommend is Formaggio Kitchen. This specialty foods store is very serious about cheese, going as far as to have its own on-site cheese cave. Formaggio goes through about two full wheels of Parmigiano-Reggiano each week, so you are guaranteed freshness. According to owner Ihsan Gurdal, the store is also particular about the Parmigiano-Reggiano it buys, selecting only wheels made during certain months and by certain farms. Gurdal says he prefers Parmigiano-Reggiano made in the spring, early summer, and some of the fall months, when the milk solids are highest. As an imported product, the price of Parmigiano-Reggiano can vary. It typically sells for $10 to $14 per pound at **Formaggio Kitchen (244 Huron Avenue, Cambridge, MA 02138; 888-212-3224.)**

Balloon Whisk

There is a certain satisfaction in whipping egg whites by hand, in part because it can be quite a workout. The commonly recommended kitchen tool for this somewhat arduous task is the balloon whisk. For the mixing tips on pages 16–17, we tested hand-whipping egg whites with a few different kinds of balloon whisks as well as with an ordinary kitchen whisk. It was no surprise to find that whipping whites to the firm-peak stage with the smaller, stiffer everyday whisk was a real chore; we actually gave up because it was taking too much time. A stiff balloon whisk and a more flexible balloon whisk (shaped the same but with different tension in the wires) each whipped whites to firm peaks in about the same amount of time, but we found the more flexible whisk to be physically less taxing.

The tool we found most remarkable, though, was the unusual round balloon whisk made by Rösle, a German manufacturer that has a line of more than 20 whisks. Shaped like a hot air balloon, this whisk whipped whites in half the time taken by a regular balloon whisk. The wires in the Rösle whisk are cemented into the barrel handle with a polyresin, giving the handle a weight and grip desirable for whipping. The 10½-inch Rösle balloon whisk also has a very polished appearance—it's made of 18/10 stainless steel, which helps it to hold its shine and makes it dishwasher-safe. It sells for $19.95 (item #0185) at **Sur La Table (Catalog Division, 1765 Sixth Avenue South, Seattle, WA 98134-1608; 800-243-0852).** Sur La Table also sells a set of three Rösle whisks (item #6742)—the balloon whisk, a basic whisk, and a flat whisk—for $39.95 (a $49.95 value).

Flexible Dough Scraper

All the care and energy that can go into properly whipping egg whites can go to pot if you improperly fold them into the bowl of batter, as shown on page 17. While a large rubber spatula works fine, we found that a flexible dough scraper does an even better job at folding. And it's a great all-around kitchen tool to boot. We frequently use it for dividing dough, scraping counters, and getting the last bits of cookie batter out of a bowl. **Sweet Celebrations (P.O. Box 39426, Edina, MN 55439-0426; 800-328-6722),** a mail-order company specializing in baking supplies, sells a plastic scraper (5¾ inches long, 3¾ inches wide) for just 65 cents.

Callebaut Chocolate

The Sweet Celebrations catalog (*see* above) also carries Callebaut semisweet chocolate, which we recommend as the best chocolate to use in our recipe for double chocolate cookies on page 24. Callebaut was also highly recommended in our rating of bittersweet and semisweet chocolates (*see* "Are Expensive Chocolates Worth the Money?" November/December 1994). A block weighing two pounds, two ounces, sells for $14.75. Fortunately, Callebaut semisweet chocolate is a popular item in many gourmet food stores; receiving chocolate by mail order during warm months can be chancy.

Deep–Dish Pizza Pan

For the recipe on page 12, we tried several different styles of deep-dish pizza pan. We were exceptionally satisfied with Chicago Metallic's Professional Deep Dish Pizza Pan, an anodized heavy-duty aluminum pan, coil-coated with a Silverstone nonstick finish. While we would not recommend using a knife or steel pizza cutter on this pan (we removed our pizzas to a cutting board to slice them), the nonstick finish is tough: it is applied at 700 degrees so that it forms a particularly strong bond with the pan's base material. Many nonstick finishes, on the other hand, are simply sprayed on, which is why they tend to chip, crack, and rust. This U.S.-made pan also has satisfactory heft, weighing about two pounds, and is about 14 inches in diameter with sides that are 2 inches high, making it useful for dinner rolls, a large country loaf, or even coffee cake. It is also dishwasher-safe. You can order this pan by mail for $24.95 from **King Arthur Flour's Baker's Catalogue (P.O. Box 876, Norwich, VT 05055-0876; 800-827-6836; www.kingarthurflour.com).** Make sure you order item # 5014.

Cinnamon Chips

We often call the folks at King Arthur Flour with questions about baking. We were surprised to find out that one of the top-selling items in their Baker's Catalogue is cinnamon chips. So we bought a bag—a good excuse to whip up scones at the start of a workday. It is no wonder these sweet, aromatic chips are driving blueberries out of scones and muffins in cafés and bakeries all over, but it seems as if they have yet to make a grocery shelf debut. A pound sells for $3.95 in **King Arthur Flour's Baker's Catalogue (P.O. Box 876, Norwich, VT 05055-0876; 800-827-6836; www.kingarthurflour.com).**

RECIPE INDEX

Free-Form Apple Tartlets **PAGE 22**

Thick-Cut Pork Chops **PAGE 14**

Double Chocolate Cookies **PAGE 25**

Macaroni and Pinto Bean Soup with Mussels **PAGE 11**

Ultimate Stuffed Chicken Breasts **PAGE 9**

Deep-Dish Pizza **PAGE 13**

PHOTOGRAPHY: CARL TREMBLAY   STYLING : MYROSHA DZIUK

Winesap

Golden Delicious

Northern Spy

Rhode Island Greening

Cortland

Empire

Gala

Granny Smith

Baldwin

Macoun

McIntosh

FAVORITE COOKING APPLES

NUMBER FORTY-ONE

NOVEMBER & DECEMBER 1999

COOK'S
ILLUSTRATED

Grill-Roasted Turkey
The Best Methods for
Gas and Charcoal

How to Buy & Bake
Supermarket Ham
We Investigate What to Buy and
the Best Way to Prepare It

Dinner Rolls
Simplified
Better Flavor, Simpler Technique

Rating Cake Pans
A $4 Pan Beats $80 Competitor

Real Sweet Potato Pie
We Reinvent a Classic Southern Dish

Better Cranberry Sauce
Ultimate Cream of Tomato Soup
Holiday Potato Casserole
Gingerbread Cookies Worth Eating
The Secret of Spiced Nuts
Best Cranberry-Nut Bread

$4.95 U.S./$6.95 CANADA

CONTENTS

November & December 1999

www.cooksillustrated.com

PUBLISHER AND EDITOR
Christopher Kimball

SENIOR EDITOR
John Willoughby

SENIOR WRITER
Jack Bishop

ASSOCIATE EDITORS
Adam Ried
Maryellen Driscoll
Dawn Yanagihara

TEST KITCHEN DIRECTOR
Kay Rentschler

TEST COOKS
Bridget Lancaster
Julia Collin

CONSULTING FOOD EDITOR
Jasper White

CONSULTING EDITORS
Jim Dodge
Pam Anderson

ART DIRECTOR
Amy Klee

CORPORATE MANAGING EDITOR
Barbara Bourassa

EDITORIAL PRODUCTION MANAGERS
Sheila Datz
Nate Nickerson

COPY EDITOR
India Koopman

EDITORIAL INTERN
Lydia Peelle

MARKETING DIRECTOR
Adrienne Kimball

MARKETING MANAGER
Pamela Caporino

MARKETING ASSISTANT
Connie Forbes

CIRCULATION DIRECTOR
David Mack

FULFILLMENT MANAGER
Larisa Greiner

PRODUCTS MANAGER
Steven Browall

CIRCULATION ASSISTANT
Carrie Horan

VICE PRESIDENT
PRODUCTION AND TECHNOLOGY
James McCormack

SYSTEMS ADMINISTRATOR
Richard Cassidy

PRODUCTION ARTIST
Daniel Frey

PRODUCTION INTERN
Melissa Connors

CONTROLLER
Mandy Shito

OFFICE MANAGER
Mary Connelly

SPECIAL PROJECTS
Deborah Broide

For list rental information, contact The SpeciaLISTS, 1200 Harbor Blvd. 9th Floor, Weehawken, NJ 07087; (201) 865-5800; fax (201) 867-2450. Editorial office: 17 Station Street, Brookline, MA 02445; (617) 232-1000; fax (617) 232-1572. Editorial contributions should be sent to: Editor, *Cook's Illustrated*. We cannot assume responsibility for manuscripts submitted to us. Submissions will be returned only if accompanied by a large self-addressed envelope. Postmaster: Send all new orders, subscription inquiries, and change of address notices to: *Cook's Illustrated*, P.O. Box 7446, Red Oak, IA 51591-0446. PRINTED IN THE USA.

WHOLE BAKING SPICES Spices used in baking tend to have rather perfumey flavors often described as "warm." Among the more familiar of such spices are cloves, cinnamon, and nutmeg, all of which originated in Southeast Asia and are highly aromatic. Less familiar (and less potent) is mace, which is a lacy covering found on the outside of the nutmeg. Saffron, the stamens of a particular type of crocus, is very often used in breads, while licorice-flavored star anise and crystallized ginger more often appear in cakes and cookies. Cardamom, a member of the ginger family that is used in many types of bread, may be white, green, or black, depending upon how it is processed. Baking spices that originated in the Americas include allspice berries and vanilla, which is a bean from an orchid plant native to Mexico.

COVER PAINTING: BRENT WATKINSON,   BACK COVER ILLUSTRATION: JOHN BURGOYNE.

GHOST STORIES

Every small town in Vermont has its own special ghost story. (Many of them have been recorded by Joseph Citro in *Green Mountain Ghosts and Green Mountain Dark Tales*.) These hand-me-down visitations make good bedtime fare, the kids begging for a scary story, but nothing too spooky to ruin the sleep of a jumpy four-year-old. Our part of Vermont is no different. A nearby inn has a haunted room, number 329, which, according to Mr. Citro, was visited by poltergeists. An employee was called to the room by a couple and their two kids. When he got there, he found the rocking chairs rocking, the lamp shades spinning, and the bed walking across the floor. The kids were crying, the parents were huddled in a corner with eyes wide as headlights, and the employee took one look, turned on his heels, and left a lot faster than he came in. This is the same establishment in which employees have reported hearing strange voices, feeling ghostly taps on the shoulder, and sensing unexplained footfalls, the air becoming chill as the unseen walks past.

My own family has plenty of ghost stories as well, some old and some recent. My four great-aunts often summered in rural Maryland at a house that had a long gravel driveway. In the middle of the night they often heard the sound of a four-in-hand driving up to the front door, horses breathing hard, with the distinctive sound of wagon wheel on stone. Of course, the driveway was always empty. A cousin of mine once lived in a large house just outside Baltimore with friends and went up to explore the large attic. There was a woman at the other end, dressed in old clothes, rummaging through suitcases. My cousin mentioned this at dinner, described the woman, and was told that the person in question

was the original owner, who had died years ago. This was the same house in which a closet door once opened to reveal a spectral staircase that was never seen again. (None of the witnesses had the courage to enter.)

We are all haunted by different visions. I once met a Vermonter who told me his dreams were filled with the scent of the two-fisted baking-powder biscuits his mom used to bake in the wood cookstove, the aroma drifting out

Christopher Kimball

over the fields, calling the men to breakfast. He said they never tasted the same baked in a modern oven. A farmer acquaintance of mine is often visited by the memory of burnt cookies, the farm's cook selling the good ones to the local country store. He got to like the taste after a while and is now never quite satisfied with the pale, "underbaked" variety. My own memories are haunted by the yellow farmhouse of my childhood, the green Kalamazoo wood stove burning even in summer, bread rising on the proofing shelf, and the sudden appearance of ghostly figures at the screen door, the sun at their backs, their approach having gone unnoticed in the half-light of the small front parlor.

In the country, old men sit on sofas and front porches, dreaming of ghosts who haunt their waking dreams, young sons sitting beside them in the cab of an old pickup, traveling down dirt roads long since paved and decorated with outlet stores. They remember the throaty growl of the exhaust and the warm breeze that rustled the thick, sun-bleached hair of their sleepy traveler, head crooked and resting on the brown vinyl door

panel. But cooks remember ghosts of kitchens, grandmothers at the stove, sturdy and cheerful, stirring pots and rolling out thin sheets of dough, kids at their feet. Kitchens of the past were always simple rooms, filled with confidence and the bustle of hard work, not the empty showpieces of today, linoleum replaced by granite, a whisk made obsolete by machinery. Cooks also lie awake at night with the ghosts of foods remembered: a large bowl of homemade peach ice cream, sweet-and-sour fish cooked in a shack on a deserted island beach, a glass of cool Sancerre at a Left Bank bistro, the season's first batch of new potatoes steamed and served with fresh chives.

The drumbeat of the new century is just around the corner, and I wonder if our ghosts will be buried at last, unable to visit us at the witching hour. Our eyes will be unable to detect a smoky wisp of spirit, ears too dull to hear the swish of a long black skirt as a phantom disappears around the corner, the sound of her dress the only hint of her passing. We will write off ghostly visitations as "an undigested bit of beef, a blot of mustard, a crumb of cheese, a fragment of underdone potato," as Dickens's Scrooge attempted to do with Marley's specter. And if we are one day unable to call to mind these ghosts, so too will we be unable to come back to visit the next generation, reassuring them with happy memories of our dead century. We would do well to lie awake at night and listen for the sound of ghostly footfalls overhead or the aroma of pot roast from another age. After all, we are only listening for ourselves.

ABOUT COOK'S ILLUSTRATED

The Magazine *Cook's Illustrated* (ISSN 1068-2821) is published bimonthly (6 issues per year) by Boston Common Press Limited Partnership, 17 Station Street, Brookline, MA 02445. Copyright 1999 Boston Common Press Limited Partnership. Periodical postage paid at Boston, MA and additional mailing offices, USPS #012487. A one-year subscription is $29.70, two years is $55, and three years is $75. Add $6 postage per year for Canadian subscriptions and $12 per year for all other foreign countries. To order subscriptions in the U.S. call 800-526-8442; from outside the U.S. call 515-247-7571. Gift subscriptions are available for $24.95 each. Postmaster: Send all new orders, subscription inquiries, and change of address notices to: *Cook's Illustrated*, P.O. Box 7446, Red Oak, IA 51591-0446.

Magazine-Related Items *Cook's Illustrated* is available in annual hardbound editions for $24.95 each plus shipping and handling; each edition is fully indexed. Discounts are available if more than one year is ordered at a time. Individual back issues are available for $5 each. *Cook's* also offers a seven-year index (1993–1999) of the magazine for $12.95. To order any of these products, call 800-611-0759 inside the U.S. or 515-246-6911 from outside the U.S.

Books *The Best Recipe*, which features 700 of our favorite recipes from the pages of *Cook's Illustrated*, is available for $24.95. *Cook's Illustrated* also publishes a series of single-topic

books, available for $14.95 each, which cover pie, American layer cake, stir-frying, ice cream, salad, simple fruit desserts, cookie jar favorites, holiday roasts and birds, stew, grilling, pizza, holiday desserts, pasta sauces, barbecuing and roasting on the grill, shrimp and other shellfish, cooking garden vegetables, pot pies and casseroles, and soup. *The Cook's Bible*, written by Christopher Kimball and published by Little, Brown and Company, is available for $24.95. *The Yellow Farmhouse Cookbook*, also written by Christopher Kimball and published by Little, Brown and Company, is available for $24.95. To order any of these books, call 800-611-0759 inside the U.S. or 515-246-6911 from outside the U.S.

Reader Submissions *Cook's* accepts reader submissions for Quick Tips. We will provide a one-year complimentary subscription for each tip that we print. Send your tip, name, address, and daytime telephone number to Quick Tips, *Cook's Illustrated*, P.O. Box 470589, Brookline, MA 02447. Questions, suggestions, or submissions for Notes from Readers should be sent to the same address.

Subscription Inquiries All queries about subscriptions or change of address notices should be addressed to *Cook's Illustrated*, P.O. Box 7446, Red Oak, IA 51591-0446.

Web Site Address A searchable database of recipes, testings, and tastings from *Cook's Illustrated*, plus our ever-expanding online bookstore, information on great holiday gifts and gift subscriptions, and more can be found at **http://www.cooksillustrated.com**.

Defending Garlic Powder

I agree with most of what I read in *Cook's*, but I do have one small and quibbling lamentation—I am not happy about your recent use of powdered garlic.

ROGER MARTIN
NEW YORK, N.Y.

➤ We heard from several readers who wondered about our use of garlic powder in the May/June 1999 recipes for Rich and Creamy Blue Cheese Dressing (*see* page 15) and Best Oven-Fried Chicken (*see* page 19). It is very rare that we choose powdered garlic over fresh, but we felt it was appropriate in both of these recipes for three reasons.

First, in neither of these recipes were we looking for a pronounced garlic flavor. Instead, garlic played a supporting part, enhancing the flavors of the main seasonings by adding a little extra depth. Since the flavor of garlic powder is mellower than that of raw garlic, the powder was well suited for this role. Second, the amount of garlic powder in both recipes was very small—⅛ teaspoon in the dressing and ¼ teaspoon in the chicken. Both amounts equal less than one small clove of garlic minced, and because both of the recipes are quick and easy to make, it hardly seemed worth the trouble of skinning and mincing the garlic for such a tiny amount. Third, garlic powder is just that—a powder, which distributes evenly and virtually disappears into the overall texture of the dish, leaving behind no tiny pieces, as minced garlic sometimes does. This characteristic was a benefit in both dishes, especially the dressing.

Even though garlic powder is widely available in supermarkets, it is one seasoning that we do go to the trouble of mail-ordering from Penzeys Spices (P.O. Box 933, W19362 Apollo Drive, Muskego, WI 53150; 800-741-7787; www.penzeys.com). The flavor of Penzeys garlic powder is much more true to the real article than any of the supermarket powders we sampled alongside. Penzeys granulated Californian garlic powder comes in a variety of package sizes and types; the four-ounce plastic bag costs $2.79. (For additional information on supermarket garlic substitutes, *see* "The Many Faces of Garlic," September/October 1999, page 20).

Storing Potatoes with an Apple

I appreciated the article inset on storing potatoes (*see* "Stress-Free Spud Storage," September/October 1998, page 9) and wanted to pass along a method that I've learned. While I store potatoes out of the sun's reach, I also include an apple in my pile of spuds. I've kept a bag of potatoes for many weeks in this manner, always firm and sprout-free. When I forget the apple, I end up with sprouts in no time.

JENNY MCDANIEL
OMAHA, NEB.

➤ In the "Stress-Free Spud Storage" sidebar to our September/October 1998 article on homemade hash browns, we found that potatoes remained in the best condition after four weeks when stored in a cool, dark spot as opposed to warm, well-lit, or refrigerated conditions. Your idea about the apple was intriguing, so we set up an experiment to see if we could improve on our original results. We stored two 5-pound bags of russet potatoes, one with an apple and the other without, in a dry, dark, cool, well-ventilated spot and checked on both bags every other day for eight weeks. The potatoes in both bags looked fine until the three-week point, when one of the potatoes stored without the apple began to sprout. Two weeks later all but one of the potatoes stored without the apple had sprouted.

By comparison, the potatoes stored with the apple remained firm and free of sprouts, though a great deal of condensation had built up in the bag. At the eight-week point, when this response to your note was written, the potatoes without the apple were largely soft, shriveled, and sad looking. The potatoes stored with the apple, on the other hand, were mostly firm (small soft spots had developed on two of them) and looked good.

Dr. Greg Porter, associate professor of agronomy, and Dr. Alfred Bushway, professor of food science and human nutrition, both at the University of Maine in Orono, concurred that the ripe apple gives off ethylene gas as it respires. Simply put, the ethylene gas, as well as other organic alcohols emitted by the apple, suppresses the elongation of the potatoes' cells, which is what causes the sprouts to form.

Scoring Flank Steak

I enjoyed your article about grilling flank steak (*see* "How to Grill Flank Steak," July/August 1999, page 14) but was surprised that it didn't mention a technique I've used for years, namely, scoring the meat with a sharp knife before cooking it.

SUE NIRENBERG
NEW YORK, N.Y.

➤ Even after thoroughly researching flank steak recipes while developing our article, we did not run across a single reference to the scoring technique. So we called Marlys Bielunski, director of food communications for the National Cattleman's Beef Association in Chicago. Bielunski had indeed heard of the technique, which she said was more common in the 1950s and 1960s, back when flank steak was an unpopular cut. She was right; we did find references to scoring when we went back to cookbooks from that era. She posited that scoring originated as a technique for tenderizing the meat, by cutting across its long fibers, and for helping the marinade to penetrate deeper into the meat. Bielunski added, though, that the Beef Association's test kitchen had tested the scoring technique extensively and found that it really did not improve the steak.

Our test kitchen concurred. We grilled scored and unscored flank steaks side by side and then repeated the test with a single steak, split down the middle, with one half scored and the other half unscored. In neither instance did our tasters feel that the scored portion was any more tender or flavorful than the unscored. The scored steak did curl somewhat less on the grill, but the difference was minimal and all but eliminated when the unscored steak was placed on the cutting board curled side down before serving. Last, we noted that scoring did not change the cooking time at all.

What really does affect tenderness is the way you slice the steak. This is not a steak you want to cut into large pieces. Instead, cut very thin slices, on the bias and across the grain, as we direct in the recipe.

Warming Holiday Dishes

I like to pull out all the stops when it comes to cooking and serving holiday meals. One particularly nice touch I learned years ago from a caterer friend is to heat the dinner plates by rinsing them and then running them through the dishwasher drying cycle just before dinner is served. It's an easy flourish, and friends and family are always wowed when their food is served on warm plates.

LESLIE PAGNOTTA
RYE, N.Y.

➤ Our test kitchen director, Kay Rentschler, uses the same trick for warming dinner plates before a special meal; it works like a charm. We suggest placing the plates in the top rack, if they fit, because that is where most of the heat is. We also suggest having a dish towel handy to wipe off any water that may not have dried in the machine.

Reconsidering Apple Pie Air Space

In the November/December 1998 "Notes from Readers" section, I was interested to note your solution to the problem of air space between the top crust and the apples in apple pie. You approached the issue from the standpoint of the crust. Instead, I approach it from the apples, which I sauté in a large skillet over medium heat until they just begin to get tender. When they are cooled, I mix them with the seasonings and proceed with the rest of the recipe. For me, this system has always produced beautiful pies, with the top crust snug against the apples.

K. MONTGOMERY
BREWARD, N.C.

➤ Many readers agree that precooking the apples is the key to preventing a space between the apples and the top crust in the pie. In fact, we heard from readers who sauté the apples almost fully, who sauté them until about half-cooked, who sauté them just until the first wisps of steam appear, who microwave them, and who macerate them overnight with sugar and spices. Though we were pleased with the solution we wrote about in the original November/December 1998 "Notes from Readers," we decided to test the precooking method that has worked so well for so many. For these pies, we chose the firm crust variation of our American Pie Dough recipe (*see* September/October 1996, page 24), which has 7 tablespoons of fat, versus 10 tablespoons in the master recipe. We knew that a crust with the smaller amount of fat would form a dome over the apples if we did nothing to prevent it.

Testing for the original apple pie article (*see* "All-Season Apple Pie," November/December 1997, page 19) proved that we were not fans of macerating. Our tasters felt the apples suffered in both texture and flavor. The pie made with apples that had been sautéed until just softened (about 12 minutes) and then cooled looked beautiful. The top crust was married to a compact apple filling, and the pie produced neat, sharp slices. The flavor of this pie was good, but all of our tasters gave a slight edge to the pie made with uncooked apples, which we thought had a slightly brighter, truer flavor. And encasing them in a pastry made with slightly more fat made for a snug fit between filling and top crust.

Quick-Clean Drip Pan

When I need to place a cookie sheet beneath a pie or casserole to catch drips as it bakes, I make sure to line the sheet with baking parchment first. This basically eliminates cleanup.

SUSAN RUTHERFORD
SALT LAKE CITY, UTAH

➤ Indeed it does. When we tried this, we simply whisked the parchment with its sticky, caramelized drippings right off the cookie sheet and into the trash. Absolutely no scrubbing was necessary.

Pouring Oil Smoothly, Continued

I read your May/June 1999 Quick Tip for pouring oil smoothly from gallon containers (*see* "Quick Tips," May/June 1999, page 4) by punching an extra hole in the can opposite the spout. I believe that I have a better solution: forget the extra hole and pour with the existing spout at the top. Then you get a smooth, controllable flow without an extra hole in the container to close up in some manner.

HARVEY JETMORE
ROELAND PARK, KANS.

➤ This Quick Tip elicited tremendous reader response, and most every letter agreed with you, asserting that we should have poured with the spout facing up (counterintuitive as that may be) rather than punching a hole in the container and pouring with the spout pointed down. So we tried it, and still found the flow to be less smooth than it was with the extra hole and the spout at the bottom. Readers also pointed out that the extra hole compromises the integrity of the container and its ability to protect the oil from light and air. We found a small wad of plastic wrap to be a quick, easy, effective plug for the hole.

Five-Spice Powder

Some recipes I've seen call for five-spice powder. What is this?

DEVAN SCOTT
RICHMOND, VA.

➤ Used as a seasoning in Chinese cooking, five-spice powder is typically a blend of cassia cinnamon, star anise, Szechuan peppercorns, cloves, and either fennel or anise seeds. Another very common variation substitutes ground ginger for the Szechuan pepper, and still others add dried orange peel or omit the cloves.

We tried both the Szechuan pepper and the ginger versions in sautéed breaded chicken breasts. In this savory application, tasters slightly preferred the powder with Szechuan pepper, though the ginger version was also deemed perfectly suitable and delicious.

Five-spice powder is now commonly available in the spice aisle at many supermarkets, but if you want to order some by mail, try either the Spice Merchant (4125 S. Highway 89, P.O. Box 524, Jackson Hole, WY 83001; 800-551-5999), which sells the Szechuan peppercorn version, $2.95 for a two-ounce package, or Penzeys Spices (P.O. Box 933, W19362 Apollo Drive, Muskego, WI 53150; 800-741-7787; www.penzeys.com), which sells the ginger version, $4.79 for a four-ounce package.

WHAT IS IT?

While going through my father's estate recently I came across this contraption, and it has me baffled. I thought it would make a good candidate for a *Cook's* "What Is It?"

GEORGE KLIMPKE
CAMPBELLSPORT, WIS.

➤ We guess that ham was popular in your father's home because this device is a carving stand, used most often for ham, and sometimes for roast leg of lamb. Also called a ringed ham holder, the stand is a strong metal frame with open rings into which the shank end of a cooked ham or roast is placed. This way, the meatier portion is held upright and exposed for easier trimming and slicing. The carving stand is about six inches high, so it effectively stabilizes the ham or roast by accommodating roughly 40 percent of it at the shank end. One source we consulted said that ham stands are common equipment in large delicatessens, while another expert said that there are some models in which the rings can be adjusted to fit different sizes.

We used the stand while carving an eight-pound shank-end ham and found it to be a mixed blessing. Though the ham was held stable, we encountered difficulties on several fronts. First, the angle at which the ham sat in the stand required us to hold the carving knife in an awkward, uncomfortable position. This actually made the knife more difficult than usual to maneuver. Second, we had to readjust the position of the ham in the stand several times as we removed slices of meat. Otherwise, the knife would be blocked by the top ring in the frame. Last, the rack itself slid very easily on the work surface. Based on this experience, we'd suggest some practice in the kitchen before attempting to carve adroitly in front of guests. A fixed model, chromed steel carving stand, called a "ham rack" in the catalog, is available by mail order for $9.99 from the Kitchen Glamour catalog (39049 Webb Court, Westland, MI 48185-7606; 800/641-1252; www.KitchenGlamour.com). The item number is 292.

Quick Tips

Melting Chocolate

The microwave is one of our favorite tools for melting chocolate, but, as Janet Bellini of Florence, Italy, points out, not all readers own one. Instead of microwaving, Janet uses an equally simple technique. She simply places the chocolate in a small, heatproof bowl, covers the surface with plastic wrap, and places the bowl on the burner plate of her coffee maker. She then turns on the maker, and the gentle heat of the burner melts the chocolate without burning it.

Organizing Cookie Decorations

A busy schedule during the holiday season or baking with kids often means that you can't get a whole batch of cookies decorated in a single sitting. Julie Buyon of White Plains, New York, keeps her decorations in a muffin tin, which makes them easy to both store and move around the kitchen.

ILLUSTRATION: JOHN BURGOYNE

Securing a V-Rack in a Roasting Pan

If your V-rack and your roasting pan are not well matched in size, or if you have a nonstick roasting pan, the V-rack and its heavy contents can slide around in the pan, throwing off your balance and increasing the chance of dropping the whole thing. Leslie Shaw of Aiea, Hawaii, has discovered a way of stabilizing the rack in the pan. She makes four ropes of twisted tin foil (as described in the January/February 1999 Quick Tip "Making a Flame Tamer") and twists two onto each end of the V-rack base to fasten. She then feeds the free ends of the ropes through the pan handles and twists to fasten them around the handles.

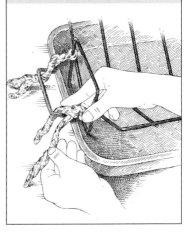

Preventing Pepper Grinder Mess

Cooks who use a mill to grind pepper know that it invariably leaves a mess of ground pepper on the surface where it is set down. To avoid this nuisance, Danielle Vallee of North Vancouver, British Columbia, uses a small ceramic dish, such as a ramekin or Japanese soy sauce dish, as a base for the grinder. This way, the excess pepper ends up in the dish, not on a counter.

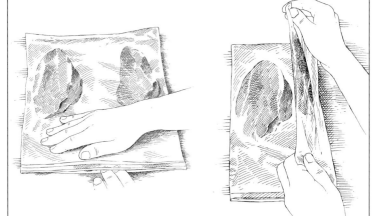

Freezing Smaller Portions of Meat

For cooks who are feeding small families, or perhaps just one person, freezing meat in smaller batches is sometimes necessary. Rosemary Johnson of Irondale, Alabama, has found a good method.
1. Place two pieces of meat, whether chicken breasts, small steaks, or portions of ground meat, at different locations inside a large zipper-lock freezer bag. Flatten out the bag, forcing the air out in the process, so that the meat portions do not touch.
2. Then fold the bag over in the center and freeze it. This way, you have the choice of using one or both frozen meat portions.

Forcing Out the Air

Karen Gale of Andover, Massachusetts, recently came up with an especially efficient way to force the air out of a bag of food prior to freezing (or rolling to crush crackers or cookies). With the food bunched at the bottom of the bag, press the plastic tight against the food and simply twist the bag around and around from the bottom up. If closing the bag with a twist tie, just fasten it around the twisted plastic near the food.

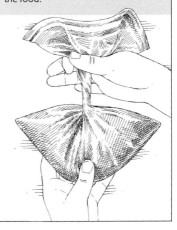

Send Us Your Tip We will provide a complimentary one-year subscription for each tip we print. See page 1 for information.

Steaming—and Storing—Roasted Peppers

Bonner Evarts of Austin, Texas, has a great idea for steaming skins off roasted peppers. She steams them in a plastic Tupperware bowl with a tight-fitting lid. This way, she can store any of the peppers not used immediately in the same container.

Chilling a Whipped Cream Bowl without a Freezer

For many cooks, the freezer is either too small or too full to accommodate a large bowl to be chilled before making whipped cream. To get around this problem with her own tiny freezer, Gail Black of Memphis, Tennessee, improvised on a trick she learned to chill a champagne bucket.

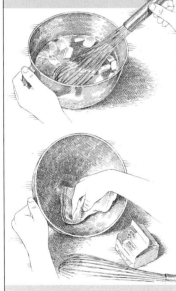

1. At least 15 minutes before whipping the cream, fill the bowl with ice cubes and cold water, place the whisk in the ice water, and put the bowl into the refrigerator to chill.
2. When you whip the cream, simply pour out the ice water, then dry the bowl and whisk quickly. The bowl stays cold and the cream whips beautifully.

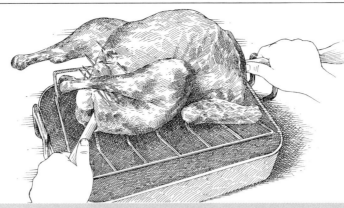

Turkey-Lifting Leverage

Lifting a hot turkey from the roasting rack onto the carving board can be a messy, precarious maneuver. Brian Linzie of Minneapolis, Minnesota, makes the transfer a little easier by using two sturdy, long-handled wooden spoons. Insert the bowl ends of the spoons into either end of the bird's cavity so that the handles stick out. Grasp the handles, really choking up on them so your hands are right next to the turkey, and lift the bird off the rack (which you may have to hold in place with the help of a passerby in the kitchen).

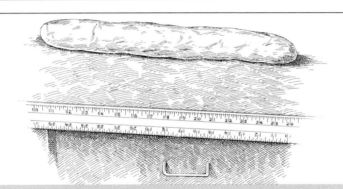

Measuring Bread and Pastry Doughs

Those who work frequently with bread and pastry doughs know that you often have to measure out the doughs to ensure that they'll fit in their pans or yield as many pieces as the recipe indicates. Rather than fumbling to find a ruler each time she has to measure, Elizabeth Suttle of Homer, Alaska, has affixed a yardstick to the front of her countertop. It's not obtrusive, and it is always there when she needs it.

Keeping Pasta Dough Moist

Often when you make fresh pasta, you are working with only a small portion of the dough at a time. Rather than simply leaving the rest of the dough sitting on the counter where it can dry out, *Cook's* test kitchen director Kay Rentschler covers it with an overturned bowl to keep it moist and pliable.

Drying Fresh Pasta

If you have ever made fresh pasta in long shapes, you know the challenge of finding enough space for the pasta to dry. Richard Piro of San Francisco, California, dug a couple of brooms out of his closet, unscrewed the broom heads, cleaned off the broomsticks, and set them between two chairs. Then he dusted the sticks with flour and hung the pasta out to dry.

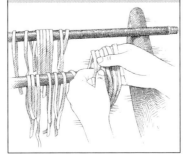

The Raw and the Hard-Boiled

Many recipes for hard-cooked eggs recommend adding a little vinegar to the cooking water to help control floaters as well as any strands of cooked egg white that result when the shells crack. Alex Leo of Portland, Oregon, discovered that adding a little bit of inexpensive balsamic vinegar tints white eggshells slightly, helping him to tell the cooked eggs apart from the raw once they are stored in the refrigerator.

Making Ginger Juice

Sharon Weil of Ra'anana, Israel, is a big fan of the flavor of fresh ginger but not a big fan of grating it. So she doesn't grate it anymore, using this trick instead.

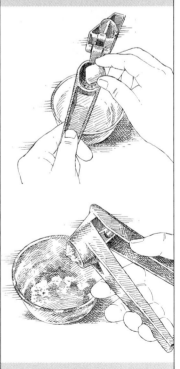

1. Cut off a small piece of ginger, about the size of a large garlic clove, peel it, and place it in a garlic press.
2. Extract the juice in one easy movement.

The Secret of Spiral-Sliced Hams

Holiday hams are usually dry and dull. For a moist, juicy, and flavorful ham, ignore the package directions and bake it in a bag.

≥ BY DAWN YANAGIHARA ≤

I've always been fond of ham. I love its toothy, meaty chew and its unique combination of sweetness, saltiness, and smokiness. But even being the devoted ham fancier that I am, I have to admit that the versions that appear on most holiday tables are far from ideal. Very often they are dry as dust or mushy as a wet paper towel. I decided to find the best possible way to prepare a pre-cooked supermarket ham so that it could live up to its full potential.

Our tasting (*see* page 26) revealed spiral-sliced ham to be the favorite ham among those available in the average supermarket. As for "cooking" (really, only heating) these fully cooked hams, it's a no-brainer—which is why, I'll bet, that hams appear on many holiday tables nationwide. The problem is that heating instructions for spiral-sliced hams differ from package to package. To add to the confusion, there are discrepancies in recommended final internal temperatures. Such imprecision wouldn't be such an issue if these hams didn't readily dry out and turn to jerky when improperly heated.

What's the Temp?

One factor that had to be decided at the outset was the internal temperature to which the ham should be heated. Spiral-sliced hams are fully cooked, and so long as the sell-by date hasn't come and gone, the ham can be served straight out of the package. While most cooks would still elect to heat the ham before serving, there is no consensus as to what temperature it should reach before being brought to the table. The label of one package says 120 degrees. The National Pork Producers Council says 140 degrees. Two manufacturers didn't include a temperature in their heating directions, so I called to inquire and was told 150 degrees by one and 155 degrees by the other. This discrepancy is unfortunate, because heating the ham to the proper internal temperature is critical to helping it retain its juices.

Place the ham cut-side down as it bakes, then turn it on its side, as shown, for slicing. Keeping the cut side down during baking will keep the first few slices moist as the ham sits in the juices it releases rather than being directly exposed to the oven's heat.

When I heated a ham to 140 degrees it lost a large amount of liquid and was dry. Heating to 130 degrees was an improvement, but I found that taking the ham to only 100 degrees was better yet. The outer inch of the ham registered at about 145 degrees, and residual heat caused the internal temperature to continue rising as the ham rested, covered, after coming out of the oven. After 40 minutes it peaked at 120 to 125 degrees, which had been my original goal. Though this may sound like a low temperature, the ham was warm to the touch and, most important, had remained moist and juicy. And, after all, we are dealing with a precooked cut of meat here.

Putting the Ham in the Bag

Having settled on the final temperature, I needed to figure out exactly how to get there. My first task was to determine the proper oven temperature. I quickly found that a high (400 degrees) or

even a moderate (325 degrees) oven was no good. Though the hams were covered with foil for protection, when subjected to these temperatures they lost an astounding amount of liquid (up to 2 cups); the meat was dry and leathery and the slices torqued and splayed.

I then began experimenting with low oven temperatures. These worked much better, but cooking time now became an issue. At the low end of the scale, an average nine-pound ham heated in a 225-degree oven was both juicy and moist and held its shape, but it took a grueling 3¼ hours to heat up. In a 250-degree oven, the ham was just as good, but it heated in 2¾ hours, shaving 30 minutes off the cooking time.

Although easy, this was still a long process, so I sought means to speed it up. I tried different combinations of high and low temperatures, but they were either detrimental to the moistness of the ham or effected no improvement in the swiftness of its heating.

The test kitchen then suggested a plastic oven bag instead of the foil cover. Quite to my astonishment, this simple, flimsy looking accoutrement—relatively new to supermarket shelves—cut off a few minutes per pound. It may sound insignificant, but this can translate into a 20- to 30-minute differential when cooking a piece of meat the size of a ham. I posited that the oven bag, wrapped tightly around the ham, eliminated the air space—an insulation of sorts—that is formed between the foil and the ham, thereby giving the ham direct exposure to heat and speeding its heating. A call to food scientist Shirley O. Corriher confirmed this. Corriher explained that the oven bag simply forms a tight seal that helps encapsulate the heat, whereas the heat easily escapes through the loose seal between baking dish and foil.

Another step that speeds the heating process is letting the ham stand at room temperature for 90 minutes before putting it in the oven. This, too, takes off a couple of minutes per pound.

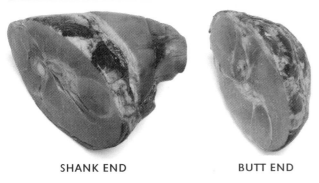

SHANK END   **BUTT END**

For easy carving, look for a shank-end ham (left) with the tapered pointed end opposite the cut side. The butt end (right) has a rounded, blunt end.

By using an oven bag and letting the ham stand at room temperature I had whittled the heating time down to about 2¼ hours, with a 40-minute rest out of the oven. Protracted though this process may seem, it's great in that it frees the oven for other tasks.

Sauces and Shanks Preferred

In addition to proper cooking technique, two other important factors come into play in getting the ham you really want: what you use for sauce and which half of the ham you buy.

Most spiral sliced hams come with an enclosed packet of glaze. I tossed them all aside because I have found that glazes, whether prepackaged or homemade, do little to enhance a ham. Instead, they tend to sit on the surface like a layer of gooey candy. Though this appeals to the child in me, I much prefer to make an interesting, flavorful sauce to accompany the ham. The sauce, since it doesn't use any pan drippings, can be made ahead and reheated. It dresses up the ham, making it look and taste more elegant, and it also adds moisture to

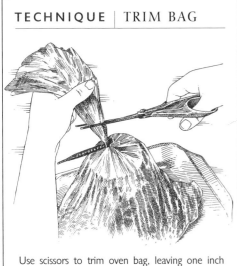

Use scissors to trim oven bag, leaving one inch above tie.

carved ham slices, which tend to dry out somewhat as they sit uncovered on a serving platter, waiting for guests to reach for seconds.

I also discovered that the shank end of the ham is substantially easier to carve than the butt end because of the bone configuration. The packages aren't labeled as such, but the shank can be identified by the tapered, more pointed end opposite the cut side. The butt, on the other hand, has a very blunt, rounded end. If you can't find a shank half, however, don't despair; both halves taste equally good. Your knife will just encounter a few more bumps and curves while carving.

HOW TO PREPARE SPIRAL-SLICED HAM

You can put the ham in the oven cold, bypassing the 90-minute standing time. If you do, add a couple of minutes per pound to the heating time. If using an oven bag, cut slits in the bag so it does not burst. Allow about 3 to 4 servings per pound for a bone-in ham. Most half hams range in size from 7 to 10 pounds, serving 20 to 30. We recommend buying a shank portion because the bone configuration makes it easier to carve; look for the half ham with the tapered, pointed end. The Polder Cooking Thermometer/Timer is the perfect tool for monitoring the ham's temperature; leaving it in the ham while the ham is in the oven and setting it to alert you when the ham has come up to temperature will save you from having to constantly check the oven to see when the ham is "done."

1. Unwrap one 7- to 10-pound spiral-sliced half ham, preferably shank end; remove and discard plastic disk covering bone. Place ham in plastic oven bag, tie bag shut, and trim excess plastic (see illustration, left). Set ham cut-side down in 9 x 13-inch baking dish and cut four slits in top of bag with paring knife. Alternatively, place unwrapped ham cut-side down in baking dish and cover tightly with foil. Let stand at room temperature 90 minutes.

2. Meanwhile, adjust oven rack to lowest position and heat oven to 250 degrees. Bake ham until center of ham registers about 100 degrees on instant-read thermometer, 1½ to 2½ hours (about 14 minutes per pound if using plastic oven bag, about 17 minutes per pound if using foil), depending on size of ham. Remove ham from oven and let rest in baking dish in oven bag or with foil cover until internal temperature registers 115 to 120 degrees on instant-read thermometer, 30 to 40 minutes. Cut open oven bag or remove foil, place ham on carving board, and slice, fol-

Silence of the Hams

We rounded up as many bone-in, spiral-sliced hams as we could find in the average supermarket and tasted them all to discern the good and the bad. All hams were heated according to the directions given in the accompanying recipe.

RECOMMENDED

Cook's Spiral Sliced Hickory Smoked Honey Ham
Almost all tasters appreciated this ham's simple "clean" and "meaty" flavor, though a few were left wanting stronger sweet, salt, smoke, and spice flavors. Overall, it's an "honest ham" that "doesn't seem processed" or "taste like it's pumped full of chemicals."

Hillshire Farm Spiral Sliced Brown Sugar Cured Ham
Most tasters noted a pleasant balance of salt and sweet, but others thought the flavor insubstantial and "lacking much assertion." As for the texture, many found it to be a bit chewy and dry, while a couple of tasters said these qualities make this a "real man's ham."

NOT RECOMMENDED

Hillshire Farm Spiral Sliced Honey Cured Ham
Almost every taster remarked on the pock-marked meat of this ham. Its appearance, coupled with the rubbery, wet, very "pumped" texture, made this very sweet ham "look and taste like a sponge."

Carando Spiral Sliced Hickory Smoked Ham
(SOLD AS FARMLAND IN THE MIDWEST AND ON THE WEST COAST)
"Sour" and "acidic," "old" and "musty," yet without much flavor, most tasters griped. The meat verged on dry but was tender, with a coarse, crumbly, "fall-apart" quality.

Thorn Apple Valley Honey and Brown Sugar Cured Spiral Sliced Ham
(SOLD AS COLONIAL IN NEW ENGLAND AND WILSON IN THE MIDWEST)
Most tasters agreed that this ham tipped the salty scale, though a few found the salt level to their liking. Several tasters noticed the overwhelming presence of spice, and others noted an "off" plastic or chemical flavor.

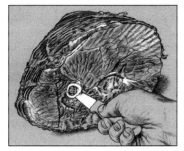

1. With the tip of a paring or carving knife, cut around the bone to loosen the attached slices.

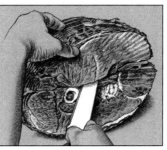

2. Using a long carving knife, slice horizontally above the bone and through the spiral cut slices, toward the back of the ham.

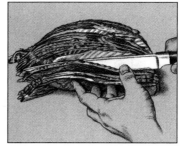

3. Pull the cut portion away from the bone and cut between the slices to separate them fully.

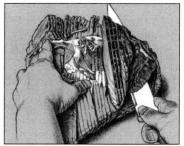

4. Beginning at the tapered end, slice above the bone to remove the remaining chunk of meat. Flip the ham over and repeat the procedure for the other side.

lowing illustrations 1 to 4 above. Serve immediately with one of the following sauces, if desired.

DRIED CHERRY AND STOUT SAUCE WITH BROWN SUGAR AND ALLSPICE
MAKES ABOUT 4 CUPS

Stout is a strong, dark beer made from toasted barley. Here, it makes a rich, full-bodied sauce with subtle smoky notes and a characteristic bitter finish.

1	cup chicken stock or canned low-sodium chicken broth
2	tablespoons cornstarch
2	tablespoons unsalted butter
3	medium shallots, chopped fine
1/8	teaspoon ground allspice
4	cups stout
1/3	cup packed brown sugar
1	cup dried tart cherries (about 5 ounces)
1 1/2	tablespoons balsamic vinegar
	Salt and ground black pepper

Whisk together chicken stock and cornstarch; set aside. Heat butter in 12-inch skillet over medium heat until foaming; add shallots and sauté until softened, about 3 minutes. Stir in allspice; cook until fragrant, about 30 seconds. Add stout, brown sugar, and dried cherries; increase heat to medium-high, bring to simmer, and cook until slightly syrupy, about 10 minutes. Whisk chicken stock and cornstarch mixture to recombine, then gradually whisk into simmering liquid; return to simmer to thicken sauce, stirring occasionally. Off heat, stir in balsamic vinegar; season to taste with salt and pepper. (Can be cooled to room temperature and refrigerated up to 2 days. Reheat in medium saucepan over medium-low heat.) Serve with ham.

MUSTARD SAUCE WITH VERMOUTH AND THYME
MAKES ABOUT 3 1/2 CUPS

The Dijon mustard lends a creaminess to this sauce, while the whole-grain mustard adds texture and visual appeal.

1 1/2	cups chicken stock or canned low-sodium chicken broth
2	tablespoons cornstarch
2	tablespoons unsalted butter
3	medium shallots, chopped fine
2	cups dry vermouth
1	tablespoon packed brown sugar
1/2	cup Dijon mustard
1/4	cup whole-grain mustard
1	tablespoon chopped fresh thyme leaves
	Salt and ground black pepper

Whisk together chicken stock and cornstarch; set aside. Heat butter in 12-inch skillet over medium heat until foaming; add shallots and sauté until softened, about 3 minutes. Stir in vermouth and sugar; increase heat to medium-high and simmer until alcohol vapors have cooked off, about 4 minutes. Whisk chicken stock and cornstarch mixture to recombine, then gradually whisk into simmering liquid; return sauce to simmer until thickened, stirring occasionally. Off heat, whisk in Dijon and whole-grain mustards and thyme; season to taste with salt and pepper. (Can be cooled to room temperature and refrigerated up to 2 days. Reheat in medium saucepan over medium-low heat.) Serve with ham.

A Ham Glossary

"Ham" is quite a confusing term. Technically, it refers to the hind leg of a pig, from the shank to the hip, that has been preserved by curing and/or smoking. Within that definition, however, there are many possibilities, ranging from the the type of pig to the curing method to the smoking time to the region in which the ham is made. Sometimes ham is even used to refer to a different cut of pork entirely. The following are brief definitions of some of the many types of hams.

COUNTRY HAM is traditional in the southeastern United States and is the result of a long curing process in which the ham is smoked over fragrant hardwoods and aged for up to one year. No water is added during this process, resulting in a highly flavored, salty ham.
SMITHFIELD HAM, touted by many as the premier American country ham, is a country ham that is cured and processed in Smithfield County, Virginia.
TASSO, a Creole and Cajun specialty from Louisiana, is a heavily spiced ham that is cured in a salt brine and then cold-smoked.
PROSCIUTTO is an Italian ham that is salted and air-dried but not smoked. It is usually not cooked after being cured and is served in paper-thin slices.
SERRANO is a an air-cured Spanish ham similar to prosciutto, with a rich flavor and firm texture.
BLACK FOREST HAM is a strongly brined, heavily smoked German ham that is dipped in beef blood to create a black outer coating.

WESTPHALIAN HAM is another well-known high-quality German product. It is dry-cured and smoked with juniper berries and beechwood. Like prosciutto, serrano, and Black Forest, after being cured this ham is usually eaten with no further cooking.
CANNED HAM is made from either a whole piece of meat or "formed" smaller pieces of meat. It is brine-cured, pressed, and molded, often with the addition of gelatin to help retain natural juices. The ham is then vacuum-sealed. These hams are precooked and need only to be reheated.
DAISY HAM is not really a ham, since it does not come from the pig's leg. Instead, it is a preserved boneless cut from the neck and shoulder. It is also known as "smoked Boston shoulder" or "cottage ham."
FRESH HAM is another term that refers to a cut from the shoulder of the pig. It is uncooked and has a delicate pork flavor that lacks the smokiness or saltiness of cured hams.   – Lydia Peelle

Ultimate Cream of Tomato Soup

We found a way to make a soup with rich, perfectly balanced tomato flavor and silken texture even when fresh tomatoes are not available.

⇒ BY KAY RENTSCHLER WITH BRIDGET LANCASTER ⇐

Rainy Saturdays in late winter bring to mind the grilled cheese sandwiches and tomato soup of my childhood. The sandwiches were made with squishy white bread and cheese from an oblong box. As for the soup, it came in a can, of course—and we all know which can.

Long after our affection for other soups sealed within the small red and white icons has waned, our nostalgia for Campbell's cream of tomato soup persists. Few of us really eat canned tomato soup these days, but some of us do have a vision of the perfect tomato soup. Here at *Cook's*, our vision was a soup of Polartec softness, rich color, and a pleasing balance of sweetness and acidity.

To get a good dose of reality, we opened a can of Campbell's. Though rich and tomatoey, it was cloyingly sweet, not unlike a cream of ketchup soup. So we moved on to a soup that would actually be as good as we remembered.

For our first set of tests, we used fresh out-of-season tomatoes. Arriving in the test kitchen, the tomatoes were cosmetically peerless, with gleaming red skins and crisp upright stems. But their taste was a very different matter. Without exception, the soups they produced were anemic and completely lacking in tomato flavor. Those containing flavor boosters such as carrots, celery, and onions failed perhaps even more strikingly to suggest a tomato soup. One made with a roux had the characteristics of a tomato gravy.

Not content to develop a recipe that would be worth making only during the one or two months of the year when tomatoes are in prime form, we turned to canned tomatoes. For our soup we selected fine canned organic diced tomatoes and added shallots, a bit of flour to give the finished product some body, a spoon of tomato paste and canned chicken broth to enrich the flavor, a splash of heavy cream and sherry for refinement, and a pinch of sugar for good measure. Though the resulting soup was dramatically better than those made with fresh winter tomatoes, it failed to make the cut; the flavor simply wasn't robust enough.

So, how do you get bigger flavor from canned tomatoes? If they were fresh and ripe, you might roast them: the caramelization of sugar in the skins that occurs during roasting concentrates and intensifies the flavors. In the *Cook's* test kitchen, where any experiment is considered worth trying,

we decided to roast canned tomatoes. We hoped that intense dry heat might evaporate the surface liquid and concentrate the flavor.

Leaving the above recipe largely unchanged, we switched from diced to whole tomatoes for ease of handling, drained and seeded them (reserving the juice for later), then laid them on a foil-covered sheet pan and sprinkled them with brown sugar, which we hoped would induce a surface caramelization. Only minutes after sliding our tray of tomatoes into a 450-degree oven, the test kitchen was filled with real tomato fragrance, and we knew we had done something right. The roasting made an extraordinary difference, intensifying the tomato flavor and mellowing the fruit's acidity. The rest of the soup could be prepared while the tomatoes roasted, knocking down the overall stove time to about 20 minutes.

Only one minor visual detail marred our efforts. The intense flavor we'd achieved by roasting the tomatoes was not mirrored in the soup's color. The deep coronation red we admired while the soup simmered on the stovetop gave way to a faded circus orange following a round in the blender. The mechanical action of combining solids and liquids had aerated the soup and lightened the color. This wouldn't do. We decided to leave the rich tomato broth behind in the saucepan while pureeing the solids with just enough liquid to result in a soup of perfect smoothness. A finish of heavy cream and our tomato soup vision had come to life.

TECHNIQUE | OVEN-DRIED

Let the tomatoes cool slightly before peeling them off the foil.

ULTIMATE CREAM OF TOMATO SOUP
MAKES ABOUT 5½ CUPS, SERVING 4

Make sure to use canned whole tomatoes that are not packed in puree; you will need some of the juice to make the soup.

- 2 cans (28 ounces each) whole tomatoes (not packed in puree), drained, 3 cups juice reserved, tomatoes seeded
- 1½ tablespoons dark brown sugar
- 4 tablespoons unsalted butter
- 4 large shallots, minced
- 1 tablespoon tomato paste
  Pinch ground allspice
- 2 tablespoons all-purpose flour
- 1¾ cups chicken stock or canned low-sodium chicken broth
- ½ cup heavy cream
- 2 tablespoons brandy or dry sherry
  Salt and cayenne pepper

1. Adjust oven rack to upper-middle position and heat oven to 450 degrees; line jelly-roll pan or rimmed cookie sheet with foil. Spread tomatoes in single layer on foil, and sprinkle evenly with brown sugar. Bake until all liquid has evaporated and tomatoes begin to color, about 30 minutes. Let tomatoes cool slightly, then peel them off foil (*see* illustration); transfer to small bowl and set aside.

2. Heat butter over medium heat in medium nonreactive saucepan until foaming; add shallots, tomato paste, and allspice. Reduce heat to low, cover, and cook, stirring occasionally, until shallots are softened, 7 to 10 minutes. Add flour and cook, stirring constantly, until thoroughly combined, about 30 seconds. Whisking constantly, gradually add chicken stock; stir in reserved tomato juice and roasted tomatoes. Cover, increase heat to medium, and bring to boil; reduce heat to low and simmer, stirring occasionally, to blend flavors, about 10 minutes.

3. Strain mixture into medium bowl; rinse out saucepan. Transfer tomatoes and solids in strainer to blender; add 1 cup strained liquid and puree until smooth. Place pureed mixture and remaining strained liquid in saucepan, add cream, and heat over low heat until hot, about 3 minutes. Off heat, stir in brandy or sherry; season to taste with salt and cayenne, and serve immediately.

Foolproof Turkey on the Grill

How to take the guesswork out of grill-roasting the holiday bird over either charcoal or gas.

≥ BY JACK BISHOP ≤

I can still remember the first time I cooked a whole turkey in a covered grill. I lit the charcoal, banked the coals to one side, added some wood chips, and placed a small turkey over the cool part of the grill. Two hours later, I had the best-looking and best-tasting turkey of my life—the crispiest skin imaginable coupled with moist meat that had been perfumed with smoke.

Unfortunately, I can also remember the second time I tried this feat. I must have built the fire a little too hot; when I checked the bird after the first hour, the skin was burnt. I continued on because guests were coming that summer night. Some cosmetic surgery to remove the charred skin from my blackened bird and some juicy mango salsa to camouflage the overcooked breast meat saved the meal.

I have continued to grill-roast turkeys over the years not only because the bird sometimes turns out to be fantastic but also because using the grill for the turkey frees up the oven for all the other components of the holiday meal. But the results have been consistently inconsistent. Part of the problem is the inherent unpredictability of grill-roasting over charcoal. Sometimes the fire can be too hot, other times it can be too cool. If the day is particularly windy, the fire will cool down faster than on a hot, sultry night. Because you are cooking with the cover down to conserve fuel (frequent peeking will cause the fire to die down and is a no-no), it's hard to know what's happening inside the grill.

I decided to get serious and figure out what the variables are when grill-roasting a turkey and then devise a method for controlling these variables. My goal was simple: I wanted a bird with crisp, browned skin, moist meat, and a good smoky flavor—every time.

Gas Is Good

Because gas grilling involves fewer variables than charcoal grilling, I decided to start with gas. I quickly learned that a small turkey (less than 14 pounds) works best when grill-roasting. Even on a really large gas grill, I found that the skin on a large bird burns by the time the meat comes up to temperature. For the same reason, you can't cook a stuffed turkey on the grill. A stuffed bird takes longer to cook through, and this added time almost guarantees that the skin will blacken.

Following the lead of previous turkey recipes developed for *Cook's*, I also confirmed that brining the turkey is a must for a tender, juicy bird. Grilling is even more punishing on delicate breast meat than oven roasting. The bird's proximity to the heat source, coupled with all that smoke (which tends to dehydrate foods), puts brining in the position of making a real difference in the quality of the white meat. If you can't be bothered with brining, season the bird liberally with salt just before grilling and be prepared to serve the white meat with plenty of gravy or chutney.

Next I turned to the question of trussing. *Cook's* test kitchen generally ties the legs of the turkey together to keep them from splaying open as they roast. When I tried this, I noticed that the inner thigh cooked more slowly than the rest of the bird. Trussed birds needed an extra 10 to 15 minutes on the grill to get the shielded portion of the thigh up to the correct internal temperature. While this may not sound like much extra time, it translated into overcooked breast meat. Even worse, the skin burned. When I abandoned any trussing or tying of the legs, the temperature in the thighs and breasts was equalized and the skin extremely crisp and dark brown, but not black.

My next set of experiments centered on turning the bird. As with oven roasting, I found it best to start the bird breast-side down. After an hour, I flipped the bird breast-side up for the remainder of the cooking time. I noticed that the side (wing and leg) closest to the fire was cooking faster than the other side of the bird. To eliminate this problem, I found it necessary to rotate the bird twice—once when it is turned breast-side up, and once when the cooking is almost completed. Each time, I turned the bird so that the opposite wing and leg faced the heat source.

I next focused on whether to cook the bird right on the grill grate or on a rack. I found that the turkey placed in a nonadjustable V-rack cooked more evenly and with less scorching of the skin than the bird placed right on the grate. But a rack with a sturdy metal base is essential. If the V-rack rests on just two little legs, those legs can fall between the grill grates and the turkey can topple over.

My last area of investigation on the gas grill was its temperature. Clearly, I needed to grill-roast the bird over indirect heat, with one burner lit and the other burner off. My question was how to keep the heat on the lit burner. I tested this recipe on three grills—two models with two burners and one model with three burners. I found it best to leave the lit burner turned to high in each case. At lower settings, there was not enough heat to cook the bird properly. The temperature

Grill-roasting the turkey in a V-rack ensures good air circulation.

gauges on the three grills I worked with ranged from 300 to 350 degrees during the entire cooking time. Total cooking time for a 12- to 14-pound bird varied from 2 to 2½ hours. (Count on the longer time if the weather is cool or windy.)

Charcoal Is Better

Turkey cooked on a gas grill is delicious. The recipe is foolproof, and the skin becomes especially crisp and richly colored. But getting smoke flavor into a gas-grilled bird is not so easy. While adding wood chips before lighting the grill helped some, the resulting smoke flavor was mild. A mildly smoked bird may be fine for some meals, but I think if you are going to bother with grilling you might as well get the added benefit of a stronger smoke flavor. The problem with gas grills is that there's no way to add chips once the fire is going (see "Chips and Chunks," right). I concluded that removing the turkey, trying to lift off the hot, heavy cooking grate, and then placing another packet of chips over the lit burner was much too dangerous.

Charcoal is another matter. I quickly realized that I had to add fuel to the fire at the halfway point anyway, so I could add more wood at the same time. I came to this conclusion after producing yet another blackened bird. I foolishly thought I could build a really big fire on one side of the grill, put the turkey on the cool side, throw on the cover, and come back two hours later. While it's possible to get the meat up to temperature with this method, the intense initial heat (upward of 425 degrees) causes the skin to burn.

I found it far better to build a moderate fire, bank the coals to one side of the grill, and cook the turkey breast-side down for one hour, just as I had on the gas grill. After an hour, the temperature inside the grill drops from a high of 350 to 375 degrees to somewhere around 275

degrees. At this point, the grill needs more fuel to finish cooking the turkey. Since I was removing the cooking grate anyway, I decided to add another packet of chips along with a dozen unlit briquettes. (Unlike the very heavy gas grate, you can lift a charcoal grate with heavy-duty tongs. You can also simply toss wood into a pile of charcoal; for gas, you must position the foil tray over the burner, an impossible task when the grill is hot.)

At about this point I began experimenting with chunks of wood versus wood chips. I found that chunks, although not suitable for use with a gas grill, were far superior and easy to use with a charcoal grill (see "Chips and Chunks," above). To avoid raising the temperature inside the grill too much, though, I found I needed to skip the extra briquettes altogether when using wood chunks; adding the wood chunks alone after the first hour of grilling did the job of raising the temperature inside the grill as much as needed.

So would I cook my next turkey over gas or charcoal? Gas is certainly more convenient and more reliable if the weather is especially cold or windy. However, the extra smoky flavor that only charcoal and wood chunks can deliver makes the kettle grill my first choice for grill-roasting a turkey.

GRILL–ROASTED TURKEY FOR CHARCOAL GRILL
SERVES 10 TO 12

Charcoal gives you the opportunity to add wood twice—at the outset of grilling and when the bird is turned breast-side up at the one-hour mark—for a stronger smoke flavor. If you're using wood chips, don't forget to add fresh briquettes at the same time you add the second packet of wood chips. Wood chunks throw off enough heat as they burn to make additional bri-

Tucking the wings will prevent them from burning on the grill.

quettes unnecessary. Hickory and mesquite are widely available in chunk and chip form; both work well in this recipe. Hardwood charcoal burns faster and hotter than briquettes, so be sure to use briquettes in this recipe. The total cooking time is 2 to 2½ hours, depending on the size of the bird, the ambient conditions (the bird will require more time on a cool, windy day), and the intensity of the fire. Check the internal temperature in the thigh when rotating the bird at the 1-hour-and-45-minute mark. If the thigh is nearly up to temperature (the final temperature should be 175 to 180 degrees), check the temperature again after about 15 minutes. If the thigh is still well below temperature (145 degrees or cooler), don't bother checking the bird again for at least another 30 minutes.

- 2 cups kosher or 1 cup table salt
- 1 turkey (12 to 14 pounds), giblets and tail removed, rinsed thoroughly, and wings tucked (*see* illustration, above)
- 6 wood chunks (each about 3 inches long) or 6 cups wood chips
- 2 tablespoons unsalted butter, melted

1. Dissolve salt in 2 gallons water in large (at least 16-quart) stockpot or clean bucket. Add turkey and refrigerate, or set in a very cool spot (between 32 and 40 degrees), 12 hours or overnight (or use the shorter, more intense brine described on page 16).

2. Toward end of brining time, soak wood chunks in bowl with cold water to cover for 1 hour and drain. Alternatively, place half the chips on 18-inch square of heavy-duty aluminum foil and seal to make a packet. Use fork to tear about six holes in foil to allow smoke to escape. Repeat with remaining 3 cups wood chips and another sheet of foil; set aside. Fill 1 large chimney generously with charcoal (about 70 briquettes) and ignite; burn until briquettes are completely covered with light gray ash.

Chips and Chunks

Gas adds no smoke flavor to a turkey, and charcoal briquettes add little. (Hardwood lump charcoal produces more smoke flavor than briquettes, but it burns too hot and too quickly for the task of grill-roasting a turkey.) For a decent smoke flavor, you must add wood chips or chunks.

Chips work on either gas or charcoal. I tried soaking the chips to slow down the rate at which they burn. (Ideally, wood should smolder and give off smoke for as long as possible.) Even when soaked overnight, however, chips were spent in just five minutes when added directly to a charcoal fire or sprinkled over a gas burner. To slow down the burning, chips must be shielded from the fire. In the case of a charcoal fire, this means wrapping the unsoaked chips in an aluminum foil packet. (Tear some holes in the packet to allow the smoke to escape.) A foil packet doesn't work all that well on gas—I found it shielded the chips too much. What works much better is an open foil tray placed over the gas burner destined to remain on during the entire grilling time. An uncovered foil tray blocks enough heat to prevent the chips from igniting in seconds while also freeing the smoke to flavor the turkey.

But for real smoky flavor, wood chunks are the best option because they burn more slowly than chips. Unfortunately, wood chunks are too large to catch fire and smolder in a gas grill. They are designed to be nestled into a lit pile of charcoal. Soaking the chunks slows down the rate at which they burn and increases the smoke output. I found that soaking for an hour keeps chunks the size of a tennis ball smoldering for about 45 minutes. —J.B.

ILLUSTRATION: ALAN WITSCHONKE

TURNING THE BIRD

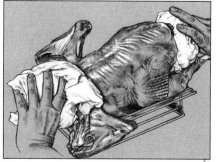

1. With wad of paper towels in each hand, grasp turkey on either end and roll it toward you like a barrel, flipping it breast-side up on the rack.

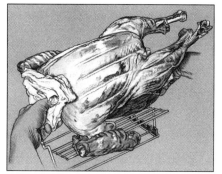

2. The thigh that has been closer to the fire will now face you and should be away from the fire when the turkey is replaced on the grill.

3. Meanwhile, spray V-rack with nonstick cooking spray. Remove turkey from brine and rinse inside and out under cool running water to remove all traces of salt. Pat turkey dry with paper towels; brush both sides with melted butter. Set turkey, breast-side down, in V-rack.

4. Empty coals into grill and pile onto one side. Place 3 soaked wood chunks or 1 wood chip packet on top of coals (*see* illustration for grilling on charcoal, right). Position grill rack over coals and place V-rack with turkey over cool part of grill; open grill lid vent halfway and cover, positioning vent over turkey. Cover and grill-roast 1 hour.

5. Remove lid from grill. Using thick potholders, transfer V-rack with turkey to rimmed cookie sheet or roasting pan. Remove grill rack and add 3 remaining soaked wood chunks or 12 new briquettes and remaining wood chip packet on top of coals; replace grill rack. With wad of paper towels in each hand, flip turkey breast-side up in rack (*see* illustration 1, above). Return V-rack with turkey to cool side of grill so that leg and wing that were facing coals are now facing away (*see* illustration 2). Cover and grill-roast 45 minutes.

6. Using thick potholders, carefully turn V-rack with turkey (breast remains up) so that leg and wing that were facing coals are now facing

away. Insert instant-read thermometer into each thigh to check temperature and gauge how much longer turkey must cook (*see* note on previous page). Cover and continue grill-roasting until thermometer inserted into thigh registers 175 to 180 degrees, 15 to 45 minutes more. Remove turkey from grill, cover loosely with foil, and let rest 20 to 30 minutes; carve and serve.

GRILL-ROASTED TURKEY
FOR GAS GRILL
SERVES 10 TO 12

Because it's not possible to add more wood during the cooking process, a turkey grill-roasted over a gas fire will not taste as smoky as one roasted over charcoal. As with the charcoal recipe, check the internal temperature in the thigh when rotating the bird for the final time to get an idea of how much longer it needs to cook.

- 2   cups kosher or 1 cup table salt
- 1   turkey (12 to 14 pounds), giblets and tail removed, rinsed thoroughly, and wings tucked (*see* illustration, page 11)
- 3   cups wood chips
- 2   tablespoons unsalted butter, melted

1. Dissolve salt in 2 gallons water in large (at least 16-quart) stockpot or clean bucket. Add turkey and refrigerate or set in a very cool spot (between 32 and 40 degrees) 12 hours or overnight (or use the shorter, more intense brine described on page 16).

2. Toward end of brining time, soak wood chips in bowl with cold water to cover for 30 minutes, then drain. Make foil tray for chips with 12 x 18-inch square of heavy-duty foil: To do so, make a 1-inch fold on one long side. Repeat 3 more times and turn fold up to create a sturdy side

that measures about 1 inch high. Repeat process on other long side. With short side facing you, fold in both corners as if wrapping gift. Turn up inside inch or so of each triangle field to match rim on long sides of foil tray. Lift pointed end of triangle over rim of foil and down to seal. Repeat process on other short side. Place chips in foil tray.

3. Meanwhile, spray V-rack with nonstick vegetable cooking spray. Remove turkey from brine and rinse inside and out under cool running water to remove all traces of salt. Pat turkey dry with paper towels; brush both sides with melted butter. Set turkey, breast-side down, in V-rack.

4. Position tray with chips on top of burner that will remain on during entire cooking time (*see* illustration for grilling on gas, below right). Turn all burners to high, close lid, and heat grill until chips begin to smoke, 10 to 15 minutes. Turn off burner(s) without chips; leave one on high. Place V-rack with turkey over cool part of grill; cover and grill-roast, regulating lit burner as necessary to maintain temperature between 300 and 350 degrees, for 1 hour.

5. Open lid; with wad of paper towels in each hand, flip turkey breast-side up (*see* illustrations 1 and 2, left). The leg and wing that were facing the lit burner should now be facing away from it. Close lid and continue grill-roasting for 45 minutes.

6. Using thick potholders, carefully turn rack with turkey (breast remains up) so that leg and wing that were facing lit burner are now facing away. Insert instant-read thermometer into each thigh to check temperature and gauge how much longer turkey must cook (*see* note in Grill-Roasted Turkey for Charcoal Grill, page 11). Close lid and continue grill-roasting until thermometer inserted into thigh registers 175 to 180 degrees, 15 to 45 minutes more. Remove turkey from grill, cover loosely with foil, and let rest for 20 to 30 minutes; carve and serve.

TECHNIQUE | POSITIONING THE WOOD CHIPS

Grilling on Charcoal Place soaked and drained wood chunks or a foil packet filled with wood chips on top of the coals. Set the top grate in position, heat briefly, and then scrape the grate clean with a wire brush. You are now ready to cook over the cool part of the grill.

Grilling on Gas When using a gas grill, place the soaked chips in a foil tray and set tray over burner you plan to leave on during cooking process (in this case, the front one—we call this the primary burner). Make sure the tray is resting securely over the burner and will not tip. Replace the grill rack and preheat the grill as directed.

Improving Cranberry Sauce

Back-of-the-bag recipes aren't bad, but we found a way to make a dramatic improvement.

⇒ BY ADAM RIED WITH DAWN YANAGIHARA ⇐

Although cranberry jelly, molded in the shape of the can and sliced into neat disks, is one of my culinary guilty pleasures, it's usually not my first choice for the holiday table. There, a soft, tart-sweet sauce with plenty of whole berries reigns. The best cranberry sauce has a clean, pure cranberry flavor, with enough sweetness to temper the assertively tart fruit but not so much that the sauce is cloying or candylike. The texture should be that of a soft gel, neither too liquidy nor too stiff, cushioning some softened but still intact berries.

Because simple cranberry sauce has only three ingredients—cranberries, sweetener, and liquid—the variables to test were relatively straightforward. Though many of the recipes I researched called for 1 pound of cranberries, I wanted to base mine on 12 ounces of berries simply because all the bags I saw in the stores were that size; I couldn't see the point of opening a second bag to use only a third of it.

Most cranberry sauce recipes use granulated sugar as a sweetener, but I also tried other possibilities, including brown sugar, honey, maple syrup, and corn syrup. Granulated sugar was my tasters' favorite because it balanced the tartness of the berries with a direct sweetness, without adding a strong flavor profile of its own. The corn syrup tasted flat and bland, while the flavors of the maple syrup, brown sugar, and honey were too pronounced, compromising that of the berries. The amount of sugar called for in the recipes I turned up during my research ranged from ⅜ cup to 1½ cups for 12 ounces of berries. In my tests, tasters unanimously favored 1 cup of sugar. I also tested the assertion in one recipe that adding the sugar after the berries and liquid have cooked together prevents the berry skins from toughening, but not a single taster noticed any difference.

The liquids used to make the sauce ran a wide gamut. I tried batches made with apple juice and cider, white and dark grape juice, orange juice, pineapple juice, cranberry juice cocktail, 7-Up, red wine, white wine, port, and champagne. Except for the port and champagne, which are used in the recipe variations, my tasters and I agreed that none of these liquids—even the orange juice, which is traditional—offered a significant flavor advantage over plain water. In testing different amounts of water, I found that ¾ cup provided the ideal sauce-to-berry ratio once the sauce had reached serving temperature.

Tests of the various cooking times revealed that less is more. About five minutes over medium heat was all it took to achieve a supple, just-firm-enough set in the cooled sauce. Cranberries are high in pectin, a naturally occurring carbohydrate in many fruits. In the presence of sugar and acid (cranberries contain both), the large pectin molecules bond with each other to produce the characteristic jelled consistency. Since pectin molecules are released as the cells of the fruit break down during cooking, the longer the fruit cooks, the more pectin is released (and the more liquid is evaporated), and the stiffer the finished gel becomes. Cooking the sauce for 10 minutes, for instance, resulted in a gel you could slice with a knife. I also tested using a skillet instead of a saucepan and high heat rather than medium heat. I could see no advantage either way and decided to leave well enough alone.

The last round of tests focused on seasoning. Many recipes call simply for cranberries, water, and sugar, while others specify additions such as lemon juice, almond or vanilla extract, and salt. Lemon juice was much too tart, and both extracts left my tasters cold, but we were amazed by the dramatic improvement a little salt could make. Just one-quarter teaspoon of salt revealed heretofore unknown sweetness in the cranberries and heightened the flavor of the sauce overall, letting loose a full range of high and low flavor notes.

SIMPLE CRANBERRY SAUCE
MAKES 2¼ CUPS

The cooking time in this recipe is intended for fresh berries. If you've got frozen cranberries, do not defrost them before use; just pick through them and add about 2 minutes to the simmering time.

- ¾ cup water
- 1 cup sugar
- ¼ teaspoon salt
- 1 12-ounce bag cranberries, picked through

Bring water, sugar, and salt to boil in medium nonreactive saucepan over high heat, stirring occasionally to dissolve sugar. Stir in cranberries; return to boil. Reduce heat to medium; simmer until saucy, slightly thickened, and about two-thirds of berries have popped open, about 5 minutes. Transfer to nonreactive bowl, cool to room temperature, and serve. (Can be covered and refrigerated up to 7 days; let stand at room temperature 30 minutes before serving.)

CRANBERRY–ORANGE SAUCE

Orange juice adds little flavor, but we found that zest and liqueur pack the orange kick we were looking for in this sauce.

Follow recipe for Simple Cranberry Sauce, heating 1 tablespoon grated orange zest with sugar mixture. Off heat; stir in 2 tablespoons orange liqueur (such as Triple Sec or Grand Marnier).

CRANBERRY SAUCE WITH PEARS AND FRESH GINGER

Peel, core, and cut 2 medium-sized firm, ripe pears into ½-inch chunks; set aside. Follow recipe for Simple Cranberry Sauce, heating 1 tablespoon grated fresh ginger and ¼ teaspoon ground cinnamon with sugar mixture and stirring pears into liquid along with cranberries.

CRANBERRY SAUCE WITH CHAMPAGNE AND CURRANTS

Follow recipe for Simple Cranberry Sauce, substituting champagne for water and adding 3 tablespoons dried currants to liquid along with cranberries.

What's in a Name?

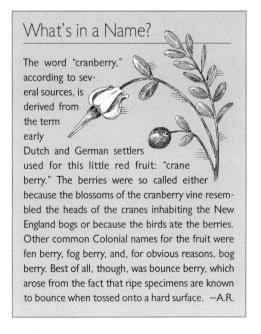

The word "cranberry," according to several sources, is derived from the term early Dutch and German settlers used for this little red fruit: "crane berry." The berries were so called either because the blossoms of the cranberry vine resembled the heads of the cranes inhabiting the New England bogs or because the birds ate the berries. Other common Colonial names for the fruit were fen berry, fog berry, and, for obvious reasons, bog berry. Best of all, though, was bounce berry, which arose from the fact that ripe specimens are known to bounce when tossed onto a hard surface. —A.R.

The Best Dinner Rolls Made Easy

We improved the texture and flavor of the American dinner roll and updated the shape.

⇒ BY JEANNE MAGUIRE WITH KAY RENTSCHLER ⇐

I can't imagine a more welcoming sight at any dinner table than a basket of warm, fresh bread. But in these times of ripping at crusty European loaves, I have found myself craving a soft, rich, buttery American dinner roll. My mouth watered for one of those light-as-a-feather pillows, straight from the oven, encased in a soft, floury crust. With this objective in mind, I marched into the kitchen, making a detour into the pantry to gather a few American cookbook classics.

Two major facts were revealed during my research. First, I would need only the most basic of ingredients: flour and yeast, butter and milk, salt and sugar, and a bit of water. Unfortunately, my second revelation disappointed: I would need to set aside 3½ hours to make any of these recipes. My mission now became more focused. I wanted to produce an updated, simplified version of the classic dinner roll that would neither take half the day in the making nor demand that I first obtain a degree in the science of baking. After thinking about it a bit more, I realized that what I wanted was a recipe that would appeal to cooks who ordinarily thought that making dinner rolls was either too difficult or just too much trouble.

I began by making a few of the recipes I had found. Though none was bad, neither did any of them produce the dinner roll I was craving. One recipe was heavy and doughy, one was on the dry side, one was not sweet enough, and they all lacked flavor. So, taking what I thought was the best of each, I put together my own working recipe and began my in-the-kitchen research.

Quick Yeast, Quick Rolls

My first foray into testing was a resounding success. I made one batch of rolls using regular active dry yeast and another using rapid-rise yeast. The rolls made with the regular yeast took 90 minutes to double in volume for their first rise, while those made with rapid-rise yeast took a mere 45 minutes. Excited by this development, I shaped the rolls and put them aside for their second rise. These results were even better. The dough made with the active dry yeast took a full 45 minutes to

Unlike European-style rolls, these have a soft crust.

complete its second rise, while its rapid-rise counterpart, remarkably, took only 20 minutes. After baking the rolls, I compared them for flavor, loft, and texture. It was impossible to tell them apart. I had already reached a milestone—dinner rolls in half the time.

Flour was next on the list for investigation. I settled on testing bleached all-purpose flour, unbleached all-purpose flour, and bread flour, each of them from companies with national distribution. While the bleached all-purpose flour resulted in a roll with very nice texture, I thought the taste was a bit off. As I expected, the rolls made with bread flour were tough and chewy. The rolls made with unbleached all-purpose flour, however, were soft and airy and married well with the other flavors in the recipe. (I might also add that this is a particularly nice dough to work with—smooth and soft and obedient. The suppleness of the dough, I felt, would be particularly important to the novice bakers I wanted to attract to this recipe.) To be sure of my conclusions, I made one more batch of rolls, this time using a ratio of 3 parts unbleached all-purpose flour to 1 part bread flour. These rolls had a bit more chew

than those made exclusively with all-purpose flour. I ended up preferring the softer quality of the latter.

With two of the main ingredients established, I felt I was well on my way, but the rolls were not as rich or as buttery as I wanted. Up to this point I had been using 4 tablespoons of butter to 3½ cups of flour. I decided to make batches of rolls using 6, then 8, and even a whopping 10 tablespoons of butter, softened so it would be easy to work into the dough. The rolls made with 6 tablespoons of butter were an improvement on my original recipe, and the rolls made using 8 tablespoons were still better. But I guess it is possible to have too much of a good thing, because the rolls made with 10 tablespoons produced a dough that was very messy. For the optimal balance of great taste and ease of handling, I settled on 8 tablespoons of unsalted butter.

Now I turned to the liquid. All of the recipes I dug up listed water as a portion of the wet ingredients, but I had a notion that replacing the water with milk, with its additional fat, would result in a softer dough. I was right. This small adjustment contributed richness as well as softness, and the extra fat also caused the rolls to bake to a beautiful golden-brown color.

Getting into Shape

The shaping of the dinner rolls was an area in desperate need of a facelift. The old cookbooks I'd been using had instructions for cloverleaf, fan, and croissant shapes, adding time I did not wish to spend. I had been rolling the dough into balls, a method in which I was by now quite proficient. That said, my technique still took a fair amount of time and a great deal of manipulation. "Rounding" dough, as it is called, relies on the friction created between the moisture in the dough and the work surface. Guided by a cupped palm, the piece of dough is rolled with resistance along the work surface so that its upper surface tightens and the surface underneath rolls itself into a tight ball. If the interior of the roll lacks the structure created by rounding, the results will prove unsatisfactory to the eye as well as the tooth.

PHOTOGRAPHY: CARL TREMBLAY

My first thought was to simplify the shaping process by baking the rolls in muffin tins. Unfortunately, they didn't brown evenly and looked distressed.

Inspired by the fanciful pillow-shaped rolls I had seen cut from long baguette forms—usually made of doughs far leaner than mine—I next decided to give my retro dinner rolls a brave new look. Hand-squaring the proofed dough and then rolling it tightly by hand to create a long, narrow cylinder provided just the internal structure achieved by rounding, but with much less effort. From there I used a metal bench scraper to cut triangular "pillows." A liberal dusting of flour before their final rise gave the baked rolls a lovely rustic finish, far more appealing than a traditional milk or egg glaze. The plump pillows have just the right soft, chewy denseness to sink your teeth into.

At last I had the soft and feathery dinner rolls I'd imagined. Best of all, they have been nicely modernized, as testified by their reduced preparation time and sleek appearance.

RICH AND TENDER AMERICAN DINNER ROLLS
MAKES ABOUT 2 DOZEN TRIANGULAR ROLLS

To ensure the softest, most tender rolls, avoid flouring the work surface during hand kneading; if necessary, flour your hands instead. The flour that you use to dust the work surface during shaping stays on the surface of the dough and is meant to give the rolls a soft, delicate look. The dough is best made in a standing mixer; there is too large a quantity of soft dough for a food processor, and it is difficult to make by hand. You will need four cookie sheets for this recipe.

- 1 1/4 cups whole milk
- 2 tablespoons sugar
- 1 package rapid-rise yeast
- 1 large egg, beaten lightly
- 3 1/2 cups all-purpose unbleached flour, plus extra for work surface and dusting rolls
- 1 1/2 teaspoons salt
- 8 tablespoons (1 stick) unsalted butter, cut into 8 pieces and softened

1. Adjust oven rack to low position and heat oven to 200 degrees. Once oven reaches 200 degrees, maintain oven temperature 10 minutes, then turn off oven heat.

2. Microwave milk and sugar in microwave-safe measuring cup or bowl at full power until warm (about 95 degrees). (Alternatively, heat milk and sugar in small saucepan over medium heat until warm; remove from heat.) Whisk to dissolve sugar. Sprinkle yeast over surface of liquid, cover with plastic wrap, and set aside for 10 minutes to soften yeast. Whisk egg into milk mixture, dissolving yeast.

3. Combine flour and salt in bowl of standing mixer fitted with paddle attachment; mix on lowest speed to blend, about 15 seconds. With mixer running, add milk mixture in steady stream; mix on low speed until flour is just moistened, about 1 minute. With mixer running, add butter one piece at a time; increase speed to medium and beat until combined and dough is scrappy, about 2 minutes. Replace paddle with dough hook and knead dough until smooth but still sticky, about 4 minutes. Scrape dough out onto work surface. Knead by hand until very smooth and soft but no longer sticky, about 1 minute; do not add more flour. Transfer dough to large bowl, cover with plastic wrap, and place in warm oven until dough doubles in bulk, about 45 minutes.

4. Line two cookie sheets with parchment paper. Punch down dough, replace plastic wrap, and let dough rest 5 minutes. Turn dough onto lightly floured work surface and follow illustrations 1 through 8 to shape and cut into triangles. Transfer rolls to cookie sheet, then cover with clean kitchen towels and let rise until almost doubled in bulk, 20 to 30 minutes. Meanwhile, adjust oven racks to upper- and lower-middle positions; heat oven to 375 degrees.

5. Slide each cookie sheet with rolls onto another cookie sheet to prevent bottom crust from overbrowning; bake until golden brown, about 15 minutes, rotating cookie sheets front to back and switching positions from top to bottom halfway through baking time. Transfer rolls immediately to wire rack; cool 5 minutes and serve.

Jeanne Maguire lives and cooks in Massachusetts.

STEP-BY-STEP | FORMING THE ROLLS

1. Lightly flour work surface, and pat dough into 9-inch square. Fold dough into thirds, folding upper 3 inches down and lower 3 inches up. Pinch together edges to seal.

2. Using the side of your outstretched hand, firmly press an indentation along the length of the dough.

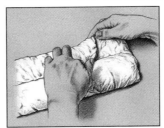

3. Fold and roll upper sealed edge of dough toward center indentation, pressing firmly with your fingertips to seal.

4. Pull the upper edges of the dough down over the thick portion to meet the seam, pressing with your fingertips to seal. Repeat 5 or 6 times. The dough will lengthen and form a taut, narrow cylinder about 17 inches long.

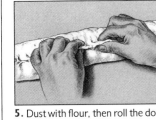

5. Dust with flour, then roll the dough seam-side up and pinch firmly to seal.

6. Press an indentation into the length of the dough along the seam with the side of your open hand. Repeat steps 4 and 5 to form a long, taut cylinder.

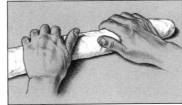

7. Gently stretch and roll the dough cylinder until it measures 36 inches long and about 2 1/2 inches wide.

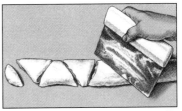

8. Holding the bench scraper at a 45-degree angle to the cylinder, lop off one end. Cut triangular-shaped rolls along dough, alternating the scraper 45-degrees to right and left. You should get 24 rolls.

ILLUSTRATION: ALAN WITSCHONKE

Turkey-Roasting Basics

The problem with roasting turkeys of any size is that the breast is done long before the thighs, resulting in tough, dry white meat. After roasting countless turkeys, we have found two things to be most important in overcoming this problem. First, roasting the bird breast-side down for a majority of the time shields the breast meat and slows its cooking, while exposing the thighs to the heat necessary to finish on par with the breast. Second, brining the bird before roasting supplies it with added moisture, which helps to keep the breast meat from drying out even if it does overcook slightly. Below you'll find step-by-step instructions for roasting a turkey. If you plan to roast a stuffed turkey, we rec-ommend a 12- to 15-pound bird. If you must roast a bigger bird to feed a large crowd, we suggest using an unstuffed 18- to 20-pound bird and baking the stuffing separately; large stuffed birds pose a challenge because the internal temperature of the stuffing lags behind as the breast and thigh meat overcook. BY DAWN YANAGIHARA AND KAY RENTSCHLER

BRINING

Brining your turkey will produce a moist, well-seasoned bird. Before brining, remove the giblets, neck, and tail piece and reserve for gravy. To brine overnight, dissolve 1 cup table salt or 2 cups kosher salt in 2 gallons cold water in a large stockpot or clean bucket, submerge the bird in the solution, and refrigerate for 8 to 12 hours. If your refrigerator space is at a premium—as it is for many of us during the holidays—try using a more concentrated, and therefore quicker, brine along with some disposable frozen ice packs, as explained below.

Double the amount of salt in the solution, place 4 or 5 large clean frozen ice gel packs in the brine with the turkey, tie the bag shut, cover the container, and place it in a cool spot for 4 hours. For ease of cleaning, you can line the brining vessel with a turkey-sized oven bag. After 4 hours, remove the turkey from the brine, rinse well under running water, and pat dry inside and out with paper towels.

Illustration: John Burgoyne

STUFFING AND TRUSSING

Preheating in a microwave gives the stuffing a head start on cooking so that the turkey does not overcook as it waits for the stuffing to reach the proper internal temperature of 165 degrees. Just before stuffing the turkey, heat about 6 cups stuffing in microwave-safe bowl at full power 6 to 8 minutes, until it reaches 120 to 130 degrees. A homemade cheesecloth bag makes easy work of removing the stuffing when it's time to carve the bird, and you can simply preheat the stuffing right inside the bag.

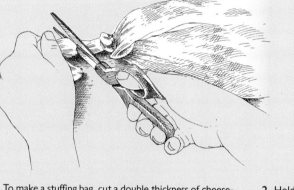

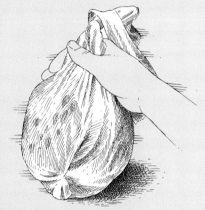

1. To make a stuffing bag, cut a double thickness of cheesecloth approximately 15 x 24 inches. Mound about 6 cups of stuffing into a rough 8 x 11-inch log on top of the cheesecloth. Fold long sides of cheesecloth in, overlapping them by about 1½ inches in the center of stuffing mound. Knot one end of the cheesecloth and trim the excess with scissors.

2. Holding the bag by the untied end of cheesecloth, lift and shake gently to compact the stuffing. Knot the end and trim excess with scissors. The bag should measure about 6 x 9 inches. Heat the stuffing bag following the directions above and fit into the body cavity, leaving one knotted end peeking out for easy removal. Wearing clean rubber gloves will make the hot stuffing bag easier to handle.

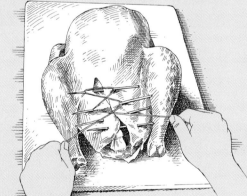

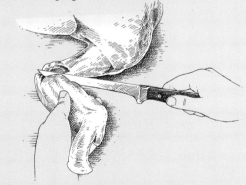

3. If you're not using a stuffing bag, you must close the cavity to prevent the stuffing from spilling out. A simple way to do this without a trussing needle is to snip 4 long wooden skewers into 5-inch lengths. Push the skewers through the skin on either side of the cavity. Use a 20-inch piece of heavy kitchen twine to lace the cavity shut, as if lacing a pair of boots. Trim the excess twine and tie the legs together loosely at the ankles.

4. If you are roasting a large bird, we recommend removing the first 2 joints of the wing, leaving only the drumette attached. Otherwise, the wings may extend over the edge of the roasting pan and drip onto the oven floor, causing smoke. Reserve the wings for use along with the neck, tail, and giblets when making gravy.

ROASTING

Every oven comes with a broiler pan and rack. We discovered that this simple piece of equipment makes a fine turkey-roasting pan. The flat slatted surface of the rack performs a dual function: unlike other racks, it doesn't cut into or disfigure the breast when the turkey is started breast-side down; the slats also provide drainage for the turkey drippings and protect the vegetables from surface evaporation. Coarsely chop 2 medium onions, 1 medium carrot, and 1 medium rib celery and place them in the bottom of the roasting pan along with 2 cups water. While the turkey is roasting, make a broth with the giblets, neck, tail piece, and (if you have them) wings. (*See* box below.)

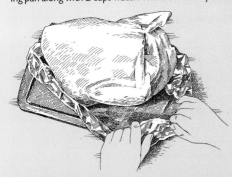

1. Place 2 sheets of aluminum foil, each measuring 18 x 25 inches, on top of the rack, then place the bird breast-side down. Roll and crush the edges of the foil up around the sides of the turkey to keep the breast from listing to one side. Brush the back with melted butter and roast following directions in box, below right.

2. When it's time to turn the turkey breast-side up, make thick wads from several sheets of paper towels, moistening them with water to keep them from sticking to the skin of the bird. Use the paper towels to support each end of the bird as you lift it out of the roasting pan, leaving the foil behind. (Use the same paper towels again when you return the bird, breast-side up, to the pan.)

3. With the bird out of the roasting pan, turn it breast-side up onto a rimmed sheet pan. Loosen the foil sheet and allow juices to run off into the broiler pan; discard the foil. Lift the broiler pan rack carefully and add ½ cup water to the pan. Using a wooden spoon, scrape to loosen the browned meat bits stuck to the pan. Replace the broiler pan rack, then transfer the turkey to the rack, breast-side up. Continue to roast, following directions in box below.

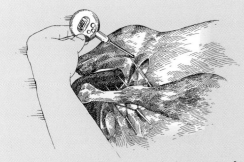

4. An instant-read thermometer is the best means of telling when the turkey is done. Take the internal temperature of the bird in the thickest part of the thigh; it should register 175 to 180 degrees. The stuffing should register about 165 degrees. Again, using wadded paper toweling, transfer the bird to a carving board or rimmed sheet pan, cover it loosely with foil, and let it rest 20 to 30 minutes while preparing gravy.

Turkey-Roasting Times and Temperatures

Stuffed 12- to 15-Pound Turkey

Serves 10 to 12. Roast breast-side down at 400 degrees for 1 hour. Reduce oven temperature to 250 degrees and continue to roast 1¾ hours longer. Turn bird breast-side up, brush with 1 tablespoon melted butter. Increase oven temperature to 400 degrees and continue to roast until thigh registers 175 to 180 degrees and stuffing registers 165 degrees on instant-read thermometer, 1 to 1¼ hours longer.

Unstuffed 18- to 20-Pound Turkey

Serves 18 to 20. Roast breast side down at 250 degrees for 3 hours. Turn bird breast side up and brush with 1½ tablespoons melted butter; roast 1 hour longer. With bird still in oven, increase oven temperature to 400 degrees and roast until thigh registers 175 to 180 degrees, about 1 hour longer.

Giblet Gravy

A broth made from the neck, tail, and giblets combined with pan drippings makes a rich, flavorful gravy. Simmer the broth while the turkey is roasting. While the turkey is resting, prepare the pan drippings following illustrations at right.

For the broth: Coarsely chop 2 medium onions, 1 medium carrot, and 1 medium rib celery. Place vegetables in large saucepan with giblets, neck, tail piece, 6 sprigs fresh thyme, and 1 bay leaf; cover with 8 cups water and simmer, uncovered, to make flavorful broth, about 2 hours. Strain broth into large glass measuring cup or bowl (discard solids); set aside (you should have about 4 cups broth).

For the gravy: In now-empty saucepan, heat 4 tablespoons reserved turkey fat over medium heat until bubbling, about 1 minute; stir in ¼ cup all-purpose flour and cook, stirring constantly, until combined, about 1 minute. Gradually whisk in defatted pan drippings and reserved broth; bring to boil, reduce heat to low and simmer, stirring occasionally, until thickened, about 5 minutes. Off heat, season to taste with salt and ground black pepper. Makes about 4 cups.

PREPARING THE DRIPPINGS FOR THE GRAVY

1. Remove the broiler pan rack and place the pan bottom over two burners set at medium heat. Add 1 cup dry white wine to the pan and bring the liquid to a simmer; with a wooden spoon, scrape the pan bottom to loosen browned bits.

2. Strain this liquid into a glass measuring cup and discard the solids in the strainer. Let the liquid settle so that the fat separates to the top; then, tilting the measuring cup, use a wide, shallow soup spoon to skim the fat off the surface. Reserve the fat for making the roux to thicken the gravy.

Holiday Potato Casserole

We wanted a casserole that featured the flavor of potatoes,
yet was still rich and elegant enough for a holiday side dish.

⇒ BY MARYELLEN DRISCOLL ⇐

Occasionally there's a recipe being developed in the *Cook's* test kitchen that is as irresistible as it is rich. This was especially the case last summer when the test kitchen was developing a potato casserole recipe for a book in *Cook's* master series, *How to Make Pot Pies and Casseroles.* Slices of potato were swathed in heavy cream and grated Gruyère cheese, with crisp bacon interspersed to punctuate the dish's full flavor. In between daily heapings, I realized this "scalloped" or "gratin" style of potato casserole is the only type I have made at home. But for all its rightful goodness, there were times when I felt that this particular casserole might not be ideal for every situation. It would fit beautifully alongside ham, but I was not sure if its creamy base would match up well with a turkey, say, or perhaps even a roast beef. Because there are no rigid rules for making casseroles, and because potato dishes are enduringly popular at just about every table, I decided to explore making a potato casserole that was not based on cream. I figured there must be a way to revise this beloved classic so that the potato could speak its piece clearly, yet still have enough poise to be served as a side dish if necessary at a holiday dinner.

After many experiments, we discovered how to create a casserole with densely-packed layers that didn't slither apart at the touch of a fork.

It Was the Baker's Wife

To be certain there was not a potato casserole recipe already out there, I began scouring cookbooks. In my research, I homed in on French cuisine, which is perhaps at its most innovative when it comes to transforming the potato. In the end, two gratin dishes caught my attention. One, called Potatoes Boulangère (the Baker's Wife's Potatoes), consists of layers of sliced, seasoned potatoes and onions cooked in stock. A similar dish, Potatoes Savoyarde, came from the province of Savoy. Here layered potato slices are cooked in a stock and topped with melted Gruyère.

I tried a number of versions of both recipes with disappointing results. If the potatoes were not swimming in a pool of stock, they were completely parched, the liquid having cooked off too quickly. Even in the one recipe in which the ratio of stock to potatoes was balanced, the flavors of the stock and potatoes were much too distinct, disconnected, and dull. Not only that, but there was nothing that held the potatoes together. The slices slipped all over the place when I tried to pierce through the layers. Despite the disappointment, there remained plenty of promise, because this style of potato casserole was everything the dairy-ful mainstay was not. It just seemed to be a matter of finding a middle ground.

Thick as a Brick

I focused first on the texture issue. I wanted the potato layers to pack densely so that they wouldn't slip every which way when sliced into. I thought this could be done by using a cooking technique that manipulated as much starch out of the potato and into the broth as possible, creating a pasting effect. I tried many different approaches, including parboiling the potatoes in water and in stock, and cooking them covered and uncovered in the oven. Whatever I did, I ended up with a sort of slippery sauce that prevented the potatoes from packing together. I then decided to try varying the amount of starch in the dish. The potatoes I first used were high in starch. Switching to lower-starch potatoes helped some with the slither effect, but they lacked the potatoey flavor I wanted. Medium-starch all-purpose potatoes were unpalatable. After some investigating, I found out that the potato starch I had hoped would pull this dish together was in fact aggravating the problem. (*see* "The Science of Slither," right.)

Because it became clear that some other thickening agent would be necessary, the test kitchen tried dotting a blend of butter and flour between the layers. It didn't help at all. I also tried placing foil-covered bricks on top to physically pack the slices together, to no avail. So we agreed to take a more sophisticated route and make a velouté, a sauce in which stock is thickened with white roux. The velouté rounded out the flavor and mouthfeel of the dish, which was thin when made with only seasoned broth. The potatoes, however, still did not hold together. It became time to resort to a surefire solution—cheese, lightly grated in between the potato layers. This sealed the layers of potato into a cohesive casserole.

I confess the addition of cheese seemed a bit deviant considering "the mission" of minimizing the dairy in the dish. But while there was enough cheese to give the dish a flavor boost, it neither weighed down the svelte, stock-based sauce nor stole the show from the potatoes. It was also quite different from the milk base I was trying to avoid. As for the type of cheese, my tasters and I found that the mild and creamy flavor of Gouda played an effective supporting role. Gruyère, which is commonly used in potato casseroles, became stringy when melted, which I did not like.

For convenience' sake, we conducted most of the tests using canned stock. We did try the recipe with homemade chicken stock, which made for a much cleaner flavor and, owing to the collagen in homemade stock, gave the "sauce" more body. Ultimately, we decided the recipe was flavorful enough from other influences that the use of a low-salt canned stock was permissible.

As for the choice of potato, I found the high-starch russet potato to be preferable because it added to the dense texture I was seeking and tasted more potatoey than a low-starch potato, such as a round white. I also tried mixing in Yukon gold potatoes and found them to be

TECHNIQUE
PROPER POTATO LAYERING

Layer the two potato types alternately, creating three to four snug rows of densely overlapping slices.

worth the minor fuss. They added a welcome layer of succulent flavor to the dish. Because there is a lot of slicing to do in this recipe, I wanted to see if I could prep the potatoes well ahead of cooking by slicing them and soaking them in water. Unfortunately, it didn't work. Slicing exposes a lot of potato surface from which a lot of starch can leach. A compromise is to peel the potatoes in advance and soak them whole in water until it is time to assemble the casserole.

Finally, all that remained was the ultimate test: the approval of my tasters. The outcome was a hit. They cleaned out the entire casserole dish before I could get a second helping.

HOLIDAY POTATO CASSEROLE WITH GOUDA, GARLIC, AND THYME
SERVES 8 TO 10 AS A SIDE DISH

The potatoes can be quickly sliced in a food processor fitted with a slicing disk. Whole peeled potatoes can be placed in water to prevent discoloring; once sliced, however, do not immerse them, because they will leach the starch necessary for thickening the sauce. The large, coarse grains of kosher salt make sprinkling easy, which is why we use it here instead of table salt. If you can find it, try substituting rich, creamy Italian (not Danish) fontina cheese for the Gouda.

8	ounces Gouda cheese, shredded (about 2 cups)
4	medium garlic cloves, minced (about 1 ½ tablespoons)
4	teaspoons minced fresh thyme leaves
2	tablespoons unsalted butter
¼	cup all-purpose flour
3½	cups chicken stock or canned low-sodium chicken broth
1	bay leaf
2	pounds Yukon gold potatoes, peeled and sliced ⅛ inch thick
2	pounds russet potatoes, peeled and sliced ⅛ inch thick
¾	teaspoon kosher salt
¾	teaspoon ground black pepper

1. Adjust one oven rack to lower-middle position and second oven rack to highest position; heat oven to 400 degrees. Toss together cheese, garlic, and thyme in small bowl; set aside.

2. Heat butter in medium saucepan over medium heat until foaming; whisk in flour and cook until golden and bubbly, about 30 seconds. Whisking constantly, gradually add chicken stock. Increase heat to high, add bay leaf, and bring to boil. Reduce heat to medium and simmer, stirring occasionally, until mixture thickens, about 2 minutes. Off heat, remove and discard bay leaf; cover to keep sauce warm.

3. Alternating Yukon Gold and russet slices, arrange a third of potatoes in overlapping rows (*see* illustration at left). Sprinkle potato layer

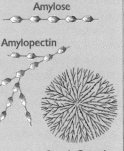
evenly with ¼ teaspoon salt, ¼ teaspoon pepper, and a third of cheese mixture. Make a second layer with same amount of potatoes, salt, pepper, and cheese. Make a third layer with same amount of potatoes, salt, and pepper, but reserve remaining cheese. Pour warm sauce over potatoes, tilting pan side to side to distribute evenly. Cover with foil and bake on lower-middle rack 45 minutes. Remove foil and continue to bake until potatoes are tender, about 45 minutes longer. Remove potatoes from oven and sprinkle with remaining cheese; bake on highest rack until cheese is golden brown, about 5 minutes. Cool 10 minutes and serve.

Sweet and Savory Spiced Nuts

We discovered how to get maximum flavor with minimum mess.

BY ADAM RIED

At holiday parties, spiced nuts usually disappear faster than the host can replenish the bowl. But most spiced nuts are made with a heavily sugared syrup, which can leave your hands sticky and cause the nuts to clump together in blotchy, indelicate clusters.

Finding the right coating method required a good deal of testing. The most common technique, boiling the nuts in a heavy sweetened and seasoned syrup, was out of the running because it made the nuts sticky. Another popular method, toasting or sautéing the nuts in butter or oil before tossing them with spices, dulled the finish of the nuts and made them taste bland or oily. A third option, coating the nuts with a spiced egg white mixture, created such a chunky, candylike coating that the nuts themselves were barely visible.

Our answer came when we adapted a technique from *Martha Stewart's Hors d'Oeuvres Handbook* (Clarkson Potter, 1999). This time around, we made a light glaze for the nuts from very small amounts of liquid, sugar, and butter. It worked like a charm. This treatment left the nuts shiny and just tacky enough for a dry spice coating to stick perfectly, giving the nuts both a consistent, beautiful appearance and plenty of flavor.

Kosher salt is important here because it adds crunch and has a clean flavor. If you can, make the nuts ahead of time; as they sit they will better absorb the flavorings.

WARM-SPICED PECANS WITH RUM GLAZE
MAKES ABOUT 2 CUPS

2 cups raw pecan halves (8 ounces)

Warm Spice Mix
2 tablespoons sugar
3/4 teaspoon kosher salt
1/2 teaspoon ground cinnamon
1/8 teaspoon ground cloves
1/8 teaspoon ground allspice

Rum Glaze
1 tablespoon rum, preferably dark
2 teaspoons vanilla extract
1 teaspoon light or dark brown sugar
1 tablespoon unsalted butter

1. Adjust oven rack to middle position and heat oven to 350 degrees. Line rimmed cookie sheet with parchment paper and spread pecans in even layer; toast 4 minutes, rotate pan, and continue to toast until fragrant and color deepens slightly, about 4 minutes longer. Transfer cookie sheet with nuts to wire rack.

2. *For the spice mix:* While nuts are toasting, stir together sugar, salt, cinnamon, cloves, and allspice in medium bowl; set aside.

3. *For the glaze:* Bring rum, vanilla, brown sugar, and butter to boil in medium saucepan over medium-high heat, whisking constantly. Stir in toasted pecans and cook, stirring constantly with wooden spoon, until nuts are shiny and almost all liquid has evaporated, about 1½ minutes.

4. Transfer glazed pecans to bowl with spice mix; toss well to coat. Return glazed and spiced pecans to parchment-lined cookie sheet to cool (can be stored in an airtight container for up to 5 days).

MEXICAN-SPICED ALMONDS, PEANUTS, AND PUMPKIN SEEDS
MAKES ABOUT 2 CUPS

1¼ cup sliced almonds (4½ ounces)
2/3 cup roasted unsalted shelled peanuts (3 ounces)
1/4 cup raw pumpkin seeds (1 ounce)

Mexican Spice Mix
1 tablespoon sugar
1 teaspoon kosher salt
1/4 teaspoon ground cinnamon
1/4 teaspoon ground cumin
1/4 teaspoon ground coriander
1/8 teaspoon cayenne
1/8 teaspoon garlic powder

Simple Glaze
2 tablespoons water
1 teaspoon light or dark brown sugar
1 tablespoon unsalted butter

1. Adjust oven rack to middle position and heat oven to 350 degrees. Line rimmed cookie sheet with parchment paper and spread almonds in even layer. Toast 4 minutes, rotate pan; add peanuts and pumpkin seeds, spreading in even layer. Continue to toast until fragrant and color deepens slightly, about 4 minutes longer. Transfer cookie sheet with nuts to wire rack.

2. *For the spice mix:* While nuts and seeds are toasting, stir together sugar, salt, cinnamon, cumin, coriander, cayenne, and garlic powder in medium bowl; set aside.

3. *For the glaze:* Bring water, brown sugar, and butter to boil in medium saucepan over medium-high heat, whisking constantly. Stir in toasted nuts and seeds and cook, stirring constantly with wooden spoon, until nuts are shiny and almost all liquid has evaporated, about 1½ minutes.

4. Transfer glazed nuts to bowl with spice mix; toss well to coat. Return glazed and spiced nuts to parchment-lined cookie sheet to cool (can be stored in an airtight container for up to 5 days).

INDIAN-SPICED CASHEWS AND PISTACHIOS WITH CURRANTS
MAKES ABOUT 2 CUPS

1¼ cup raw cashews (6 ounces)
1/2 cup raw unsalted shelled pistachios (2 ounces)
2 tablespoons currants

Indian Spice Mix
1 tablespoon sugar
1 teaspoon kosher salt
1 teaspoon curry powder
1/4 teaspoon ground cumin
1/4 teaspoon ground coriander

Simple Glaze
2 tablespoons water
1 teaspoon light or dark brown sugar
1 tablespoon unsalted butter

1. Adjust oven rack to middle position and heat oven to 350 degrees. Line rimmed cookie sheet with parchment paper and spread cashews in even layer; toast 4 minutes, rotate pan, and toast 4 minutes longer. Add pistachios, spreading in even layer; continue to toast until fragrant and color deepens slightly, about 2 minutes longer. Transfer cookie sheet with nuts to wire rack; add currants.

2. *For the spice mix:* While nuts are toasting, stir together sugar, salt, curry powder, cumin, and coriander in medium bowl; set aside.

3. *For the glaze:* Bring water, brown sugar, and butter to boil in medium saucepan over medium-high heat, whisking constantly. Stir in nut mix and cook, stirring constantly with wooden spoon, until nuts are shiny and almost all liquid has evaporated, about 1½ minutes.

4. Transfer glazed nuts and currants to bowl containing spice mix; toss well to coat. Return glazed and spiced nuts to parchment-lined cookie sheet to cool (can be stored in an airtight container for up to 5 days).

The Best Cranberry-Nut Bread

The proper mixing method and the right combination of leaveners gave us the perfect texture and flavor.

⇒ BY ANNE TUOMEY AND ANN FLANIGAN ⇐

We don't make cranberry-nut bread just for ourselves. We make it for the kindergarten teacher, the mail carrier, and anyone else who deserves something homemade rather than store-bought for the holidays.

The problem is that this simple bread is often sub-par, sunken in the middle or too dense or so overly sweetened that the contrast between the tart berries and what should be a slightly sweet dough is lost. We wanted to avoid these problems, and we had some other goals in mind as well. We were looking for a crust that was golden brown and evenly thin all the way around and a texture that was somewhere between a dense breakfast bread and a light, airy cake. And, for convenience' sake, we wanted a recipe that fit easily into a standard 9 by 5-inch loaf pan. After looking at almost 60 recipes, it seemed evident that the mixing method and the leavening were the most important factors in getting the quick bread we were after.

First we tackled mixing. Some recipes called for the creaming method, in which the butter and sugar are creamed together and then mixed with eggs and flavorings. Dry and wet ingredients are then alternately beat into this aerated mixture. Other recipes used the quick bread method. In this technique, the butter is melted and added to the wet ingredients. Wet and dry ingredients are then mixed together just enough to moisten the dry ingredients. This method helps to avoid the development of gluten and a tough crumb.

We made several loaves using each of these two methods. While the creaming method did give us a marginally more tender bread, we quickly determined that it was too light and airy. We liked the denser, more compact texture produced by the quick bread method. An added advantage of the quick bread method is, as its name implies, that it is very fast.

Next we moved on to the question of leavening. When we looked back at our testing, we noted that 75 percent of the recipes combined baking powder with baking soda to leaven the bread. The rest used all baking powder or all baking soda. We tried every option we could think of using these two leaveners, both alone and together. We found that baking powder seemed to enhance the flavor, while baking soda supported the structure; finding the right balance was tricky. Eventually, we came to the decision that one-quarter teaspoon of baking soda combined with one teaspoon of baking powder gave us the bright flavor and rather dense texture we were looking for.

With our mixing and leavening methods settled, we focused on ingredients. We quickly determined that we liked the flavor that butter provided over that of oil, margarine, or vegetable shortening. More than one egg made the bread almost too rich and caused the interior to turn somewhat yellow. After testing different amounts and types of sugar, we stuck with one cup of granulated sugar, which provided the right amount of sweetness. Orange zest added not only to the flavor but to the interior appearance as well.

We also tinkered with the liquid component. Many recipes called for water or even boiling water, but freshly squeezed orange juice was usually mentioned and offered the best flavor. We compared fresh, home-squeezed orange juice with commercially prepared juices made from both fresh oranges and from concentrate; home-squeezed juice was the winner, hands down.

Not every recipe called for dairy, but we tested everything from heavy cream to sour cream. Both buttermilk and yogurt provided the moistness and tang we were looking for, with buttermilk edging out yogurt by a hairbreadth.

Last but not least were the cranberries. The cranberry harvest begins just after Labor Day and continues through early fall, which means that by mid- to late January, no fresh berries are available. Cranberries freeze beautifully, so grab a few extra bags to have on hand and freeze them until ready to use. We found no discernible difference in the finished product whether using fresh or frozen cranberries.

PREP | CHOP, CHOP

Coarsely chopped berries such as these look and taste best.

CRANBERRY-NUT BREAD
MAKES ONE 9-INCH LOAF

We prefer sweet, mild pecans in this bread, but walnuts can be substituted. Resist the urge to cut into the bread while it is hot out of the oven; the texture improves as it cools, making it easier to slice. To toast pecans, heat griddle over medium heat. Add pecans, chopped coarse; toast, shaking pan frequently, until nuts are fragrant, 3 to 5 minutes.

1/3	cup juice plus 1 tablespoon grated zest from 1 large orange
2/3	cup buttermilk
6	tablespoons unsalted butter, melted
1	large egg, beaten lightly
2	cups all-purpose flour
1	cup sugar
1	teaspoon salt
1	teaspoon baking powder
1/4	teaspoon baking soda
1 1/2	cups cranberries (about 6 ounces), chopped coarse (*see* illustration)
1/2	cup toasted pecans, chopped coarse

1. Adjust oven rack to middle position and heat oven to 375 degrees. Grease bottom of 9 x 5-inch loaf pan. Stir together orange juice, zest, buttermilk, butter, and egg in small bowl. Whisk together flour, sugar, salt, baking powder, and baking soda in large bowl. Stir liquid ingredients into dry with rubber spatula until just moistened. Gently stir in cranberries and pecans. Do not overmix.

2. Scrape batter into loaf pan and spread with rubber spatula into corners of pan. Bake 20 minutes, then reduce heat to 350 degrees; continue to bake until golden brown and toothpick inserted in center of loaf comes out clean, about 45 minutes longer. Cool in pan 10 minutes, then transfer to wire rack and cool at least 1 hour before serving.

Anne Tuomey and Ann Flanigan live and write in Wellesley, Massachusetts.

Real Sweet Potato Pie

The problem with most sweet potato pies is that they are pumpkin pies in disguise. Our challenge was to create a blue-ribbon dessert that still tasted like sweet potatoes.

≥ BY CHRISTOPHER KIMBALL ≤

There are two kinds of southern cooking: lady food and down home food. Sweet potato pie stems from the latter category, since historically sweet potatoes were cheap and available and the recipes for this dessert were short on eggs, milk, and white sugar. Instead of scarce white sugar, country cooks relied more heavily on the natural sweetness and texture of the sweet potatoes themselves, combined with sorghum syrup or molasses. This resulted not in the custard-like pie we know today but in a toothier pie, something more akin to a delicate version of mashed sweet potatoes.

But all that is history. The question for the *Cook's* test kitchen was how to create a distinctive sweet potato pie, a recipe that honored the texture and flavor of sweet potatoes while being sufficiently recognizable as a dessert. Neither a custardy, pumpkin-style pie nor mashed-potatoes-in-a-crust would do.

A review of more than 30 recipes led us to five distinctive approaches to this dish, ranging from mashed sweet potatoes with a modicum of milk and eggs to Paul Prudhomme's Sweet Potato Pecan Pie, which he soaks in a sweet syrup, to the "typical" pumpkin pie, with sweet potatoes substituted for the pumpkin. Some recipes separated the eggs and whipped the whites, some used evaporated or condensed milk, others used a combination of white and sweet potatoes, and most of them used a profusion of spices. To my surprise, all of them had abandoned molasses or sorghum for either white or brown sugar.

Although the classic pumpkin-pie style was good, our tasters were drawn to more authentic recipes, especially one published in Dori Sanders's *Country Cooking* (Algonquin Books of Chapel Hill, 1995), which had more sweet potato flavor. One problem with all of these recipes, however, was their mashed-potatoes-in-a-crust quality. We wanted a recipe that would work as a dessert, not a savory side dish to a turkey dinner. This would require some fiddling with the amount of milk, eggs, and sugar as well as with the method of preparing the potatoes. Another problem with these recipes was the likelihood they had been modernized (for example, they all used white sugar), and I wondered if a bit of detective work might bring the sweet potato pie back to its roots, making it a dessert with more character than the white tablecloth pie it has become.

Be sure to bake this pie just until the edges start to set up; it will continue baking once it is out of the oven.

The first step was to determine the best method of preparing the sweet potatoes. One group of tasters was keen on slicing cooked potatoes and then layering them in the pie shell. This method was quickly discarded, since its product bore little resemblance to a dessert. We also gave up on using a food processor to beat the cooked potatoes; this resulted in a very smooth, custardy texture. We finally settled on coarsely mashing the potatoes, leaving a few small lumps (*see* illustration 3, page 23). This also simplified the recipe, precluding the need to pass the potatoes thtough a sieve to remove fibrous strings, a step called for in some of the more refined recipes. We also decided on microwaving as the easiest method of precooking the sweet potatoes. It took just 10 minutes, without having to first boil water or preheat an oven.

Next, we discarded the notion of using a bit of white potato in the recipe (a technique often used by traditional southern cooks to lighten the texture). This made the pie more complicated and a bit grainy as well. Separating the eggs and whip-

ping the whites, another common procedure, produced an anemic, fluffy dessert lacking in moisture and flavor. Sweetened condensed milk did not improve the flavor, and we ended up preferring regular milk over half and half. We added two yolks to three whole eggs to properly moisten the texture. Orange zest and lemon juice were tried and discarded because they detracted from the delicate flavor of the sweet potato itself; a bit of bourbon helped to pick up the flavor.

A major problem with modern sweet potato pies is that they call for the usual pumpkin pie spices, which overwhelm the taste of the sweet potato. The solution was to use only a modest amount of nutmeg. White sugar was fine, but since older recipes often call for molasses (some also used sorghum syrup, cane syrup, dark corn syrup, and even maple syrup), we decided to test it. The results were mixed, so we settled on one tablespoon of molasses as optional. This boosts flavor without overpowering the pie with the distinctive, malt taste of molasses. (Even two tablespoons of molasses were too many.)

At this point we had a pie that we liked a lot, with real sweet potato flavor and enough custardy richness to place it firmly in the dessert category. But something was still lacking. The pie tasted a bit vegetal; it needed more oomph. Based on Paul Prudhomme's notion of adding pecan pie flavorings to the mix, we made a few pies to see if we could create two layers—one of sweet potato filling and one similar to the sweet filling in a pecan pie—to jazz things up. Creating two separate layers presented a challenge until I came upon the idea of baking the pecan pie filling first, until it set in the shell, about 20 minutes, and then adding the sweet potato filling on top. This worked like a charm and made a stupendous pie. Even so, many taster found the process a little unwieldy. After more experiments, we came up with an easy-as-pie technique for adding a separate bottom layer: we simply sprinkled the bottom of the crust with brown sugar before adding the filling.

Now we had something really special, a pie with an intense, thick, pure-sweet-potato filling, perfectly complemented by a layer of melted brown sugar just beneath. Its unique nature is reflected in the color of the filling, which is a fantastic orange rather than the dull brown that results from the use of too much molasses and too many spices. This was a sweet potato pie that any southern cook would be proud of.

THE BEST SWEET POTATO PIE
MAKES ONE 9-INCH PIE, SERVING 8 TO 10

For prebaking the pie shell, we prefer metal or ceramic pie weights because of their heft and ability to conduct heat. Remove the foil lining and weights only after the dough has lost its wet look and has turned straw-colored from its original yellow hue. This will prevent the sides of the pie shell from slipping down and losing their shape. The sweet potatoes cook quickly in the microwave but can also be pricked with a fork and baked uncovered in a 400-degree oven until tender, 40 to 50 minutes. Some tasters preferred

a stronger bourbon flavor in the filling, so we give a range below. If you like molasses, use the optional tablespoon; a few tasters felt it deepened the sweet potato flavor. Serve the pie with whipped cream.

Pie Dough
1¼	cups all-purpose flour
½	teaspoon salt
1	tablespoon sugar
4	tablespoons chilled unsalted butter, cut into ¼-inch pieces
3	tablespoons chilled all-vegetable shortening
4–5	tablespoons ice water

Sweet Potato Filling
2	pounds sweet potatoes (about 5 small to medium)
2	tablespoons unsalted butter, softened
3	large eggs plus 2 yolks
1	cup sugar
½	teaspoon grated nutmeg
¼	teaspoon salt
2–3	tablespoons bourbon
1	tablespoon molasses (optional)
1	teaspoon vanilla extract
⅔	cup whole milk
¼	cup packed dark brown sugar

1. In food processor bowl fitted with steel blade, pulse flour, salt, and sugar to combine. Scatter butter pieces over flour mixture; cut butter into flour with five 1-second pulses. Add shortening and continue cutting in until flour is pale yellow and resembles coarse cornmeal, with butter bits no larger than small peas, about four more 1-second pulses. Turn mixture into medium bowl.

2. Sprinkle 4 tablespoons ice water over mixture. With rubber spatula, use folding motion to evenly distribute water into flour mixture until small portion of dough holds together when squeezed in palm of hand; add up to 1 tablespoon more ice water if necessary. Turn dough onto

clean, dry work surface; gather and gently press together into cohesive ball, then flatten into rough 4-inch disk. Wrap in plastic and refrigerate at least 30 minutes, or up to 2 days, before rolling.

3. Remove dough from refrigerator (if refrigerated longer than 30 minutes, let stand at room temperature until malleable). Roll dough on lightly floured work surface or between two large sheets of plastic wrap to 12-inch disk about ⅛ inch thick. Fold dough in quarters, then place dough point in center of 9-inch pie plate; unfold dough.

4. Working around circumference of pan, ease dough carefully into pan corners by gently lifting dough edges with one hand while pressing around pan bottom with other hand. Trim edge to ½ inch beyond pan lip. Tuck rim of dough underneath itself so that folded edges are about ¼ inch beyond pan lip; flute dough. Refrigerate pie shell for 40 minutes, then freeze for 20 minutes. (This two-step process helps to reduce shrinkage of the crust during baking.)

5. Meanwhile, adjust oven rack to middle position and heat oven to 375 degrees. Press doubled 18-inch square of heavy-duty foil inside shell and fold back edges of foil to shield fluted edge; evenly distribute about 2 cups metal or ceramic pie weights over foil. Bake, leaving foil and weights in place until dough dries and lightens in color, 17 to 20 minutes. Carefully remove foil and weights by gathering sides of foil and pulling up and out. Bake until light golden brown, about 9 minutes longer. Remove from oven; reduce oven temperature to 350 degrees.

6. Prick sweet potatoes several times with fork and place on double layer of paper towels in microwave (see illustration 1). Cook at full power for 5 minutes; turn each potato over and continue to cook at full power until tender, but not mushy, about 5 minutes longer. Cool 10 minutes. Halve each potato crosswise; insert small spoon between skin and flesh, and scoop flesh into medium bowl (see illustration 2); discard skin. (If potatoes are too hot to handle comfortably, fold double layer of paper towels into quarters and use to hold potato half). Repeat with remaining sweet potatoes; you should have about 2 cups. While potatoes are still hot, add butter and mash with fork or wooden spoon; small lumps of potato should remain (see illustration 3).

7. Whisk together eggs, yolks, sugar, nutmeg, and salt in medium bowl; stir in bourbon, molasses (if using), and vanilla, then whisk in milk. Gradually add egg mixture to sweet potatoes, whisking gently to combine.

8. Heat partially baked pie shell in oven until warm, about 5 minutes. Sprinkle bottom of pie shell evenly with brown sugar. Pour sweet potato mixture into pie shell over brown sugar layer. Bake until filling is set around edges but center jiggles slightly when shaken, about 45 minutes. Transfer pie to wire rack; cool to room temperature, about 2 hours, and serve.

STEP-BY-STEP | PREPARING THE SWEET POTATOES

1. In preparation for microwaving, lay the sweet potatoes out in a fan shape on a double thickness of paper towels.

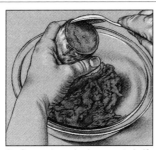

2. Cut each cooked potato in half crosswise, then scoop out the pulp into a mixing bowl with a small spoon.

3. Mash the cooked potatoes coarsely with a fork or spoon. Some small lumps of potato should remain.

Gingerbread Cookies Worth Eating

Most recipes turn out dough that is best used for building material. Is there a way to make gingerbread cookies that actually taste as good as they look?

⇒ BY STEPHEN SCHMIDT ⇐

Gingerbread cookies are ubiquitous at holiday time—stuffed into stockings, propped up around candles to make centerpieces, and hung in windows and on Christmas trees. Only rarely, though, do gingerbread cookies appear on cookie trays, and when they do most people pass them by. People know from experience that gingerbread cookies, no matter how pretty they may be, are usually hard and dry. But this outcome is not inevitable. I have discovered that by using the right proportions of ingredients, it is possible to produce gingerbread cookies that are a pleasure to eat.

There are actually two types of gingerbread cookie. When you roll the dough thick and bake the cookies only briefly, you get soft, moist, gently chewy cookies—or at least that is what you want to end up with. If you roll the dough thin and bake the cookies somewhat longer, you get buttery tasting, snapping-crisp cookies, a type of gingersnap, really. Thick gingerbread cookies are primarily suitable for the cookie tray. Thin gingerbread cookies also make delicious tray cookies, but, because they are sturdy and keep well, they are also the cookies you want to use to decorate the tree. In setting out to develop a perfect recipe for gingerbread cookies, I focused on the thick ones, which are more difficult to produce. In my experience, any dough that will make good thick gingerbread cookies can be adapted to make delicious thin ones.

A review of the recipes in contemporary cookbooks quickly revealed to me the root of the problem with most gingerbread cookies. Any experienced cookie baker knows that cookies made with less than four tablespoons of fat to a cup of flour will be dry. Yet many of the recipes I examined called for as little as two or three tablespoons of butter or shortening to a cup of flour. The writers of these recipes were not concerned with holiday waistlines. Rather, they wanted to make sure the dough would be firm enough to handle and then cut into intricate shapes. Fat makes doughs soft. From the standpoint of convenience, the less fat in a gingerbread cookie dough, the better.

But what about taste? Surely there was a middle ground. After a little searching, I discovered several recipes that called for the requisite one-quarter cup of fat to a cup of flour. I made one of these. The cookies turned out soft and fairly moist, but I didn't really like them. They were

Just because these gingerbread cookies taste great doesn't mean they can't also be decorative.

pale, bland, and generally uninteresting. After doing some thinking and calculating, I added 50 percent more brown sugar and molasses. The resulting cookies were delicious: flavorful, pleasantly sweet, and moist and chewy.

But they still were not perfect. Instead of rising flat and level, they looked a little bumpy. This would not be a problem if the cookies were presented plain, but decorations would be marred by the cookies' uneven surface. I knew where the problem lay. The extra sugar I had added to the dough was absorbing too much of the available liquid. Sugar is hydroscopic—that is, it soaks up liquid. This is why very sugary cookies, such as wafers and tuiles, bake up so crisp and dry and also why the same cookies, unless very tightly covered, tend to go soft and tacky again after just a few days' keeping. The sugar absorbs moisture from the air. The extra sugar I had added to my dough was not quite sufficient to make the cookies hard and dry, thank goodness, but it was still having an effect.

By absorbing the liquid in my dough, the sugar, evidently, was preventing the formation of gluten, a tough, stretchy molecule that develops when flour proteins are moistened. Gluten creates a net-

work of air-trapping spaces in doughs that bakers refer to as structure. When doughs have a great deal of structure, they puff dramatically. When they have none, they do not puff at all. And when they have just a little, as was the case with my gingerbread cookies, they tend to puff a little but then deflate, the dough being too "weak" to hold its form after it has risen.

It is easy to understand this basic principle of baking if you compare cookies and cakes. They are fundamentally similar in their basic ingredients, and most cookie doughs and cake batters are mixed in the same way—the butter, eggs, and sugar are "creamed," and the flour and liquid are then added alternately. So what accounts for the very different textures of cookies and cakes? It is, of course, the amount of liquid. Cookies, being relatively dry, form little gluten and therefore puff only a little and are, to one degree or another, firm. By contrast, cakes, being moist, form a good deal of gluten, and the gluten network traps and holds air, causing cakes to rise and become puffy and soft.

What I needed to do, I realized, was make my gingerbread, which was close to becoming a crisp, nonpuffing cookie, slightly more akin to a puffy cake. The obvious solution was to add a couple of tablespoons of milk. I feared, however, that the dough, already chock-full of butter, brown sugar, and molasses, would surely be too soft to handle if I tried to sneak in some liquid.

But I simply had no choice. I tried the dough as before, with the full complement of all the good stuff, plus two tablespoons of milk. To my delight, the dough proved quite manageable when handled in the usual way—chilled, then rolled on a lightly floured surface—and downright obliging when rolled between sheets of parchment. And the cookies were perfect: smooth, even, and delightful to eat, whether rolled thick or thin.

To make the process of rolling out the cookies even easier, I also altered the usual mixing method. Most recipes for gingerbread cookies call

People like to add candied and fresh ginger to gingerbreads, and I was curious to know if there was any point in using either in gingerbread cookies. The answer, I think, is yes—but with qualifications.

Candied ginger gives gingerbread cookies a nice pungency without imparting a harsh bite. I found that a full half-cup, or about 2½ ounces, was required to make a difference in flavor. The ginger must be ground very fine, or the dough will be difficult to cut into neat shapes. First, if your ginger comes in chunks, slice it into thin flakes with a knife. Then combine the ginger and the brown sugar called for in the recipe in the food processor and process until the ginger practically disappears, about two minutes. Add the remaining dry ingredients, process to blend, and proceed with the recipe. Do not decrease the ground ginger; the cookies will be bland if you do.

Fresh ginger proved to be more problematic. On the one hand, much to my surprise, I really liked the lively, almost tingly flavor that it imparted. On the other hand, I would not use it in thick gingerbread cookies that I intended to decorate. Perhaps because it is moist, fresh ginger makes thick gingerbread cookies puffy and wrinkly. (Thin gingerbread cookies made with fresh ginger looked fine, and their flavor was altered, though only marginally.) You will need a lot to make an impact—a good three ounces, or a piece roughly six inches long and one inch wide. Peel the ginger and grate it to a pulp. You need to end up with one-quarter cup of pulp. Add the pulp with the molasses to the batter and omit the milk. Again, do not decrease the amount of ground ginger.

Of course, the easiest way to make your gingerbread cookies more gingery is simply to add more ground ginger. If you want really hot, spicy gingerbread cookies, you will want to add a full ounce, or about one-quarter cup.   —S.S.

---

for making the dough by creaming softened butter and sugar, then adding the dry and liquid ingredients, as if making a cake. When mixed in this manner, the dough is inevitably quite soft and must be refrigerated for several hours, even overnight, before being rolled and cut. I prefer instead to mix the dough in the food processor, first blending the dry ingredients, then cutting in slightly softened butter, and, finally, adding the molasses and other liquid ingredients, as if making a pie crust. When mixed in this way, the dough is firm enough to be used at once, though I prefer to roll it between sheets of parchment paper and then chill it briefly before cutting to make sure the cookies will maintain a perfect shape when transferred to the sheets. Even assuming that you do take the time to chill the dough before cutting, you will still save some time by using the food processor to mix the gingerbread—a welcome convenience during the hectic holiday season.

THICK AND CHEWY GINGERBREAD COOKIES
FOR ABOUT TWENTY 5-INCH GINGERBREAD PEOPLE OR THIRTY 3-INCH COOKIES

If you plan to decorate your gingerbread cookies and make ornaments out of them, follow the directions for Thin, Crisp Gingerbread Cookies. Because flour is not added during rolling, dough scraps can be rolled and cut as many times as necessary Don't overbake the cookies or they will be dry. Store soft gingerbread in a wide, shallow airtight container or tin with a sheet of parchment or waxed paper between each cookie layer. These cookies are best eaten within one week.

3	cups all-purpose flour
¾	cup firmly packed dark brown sugar
1	tablespoon ground cinnamon
1	tablespoon ground ginger
½	teaspoon ground cloves
½	teaspoon salt
¾	teaspoon baking soda
12	tablespoons (1½ sticks) unsalted butter, cut into 12 pieces and softened slightly
¾	cup unsulphured molasses
2	tablespoons milk

1. In food processor workbowl fitted with steel blade, process flour, sugar, cinnamon, ginger, cloves, salt, and baking soda until combined, about 10 seconds. Scatter butter pieces over flour mixture and process until mixture is sandy and resembles very fine meal, about 15 seconds. With machine running, gradually add molasses and milk; process until dough is evenly moistened and forms soft mass, about 10 seconds. Alternatively, in bowl of standing mixer fitted with paddle attachment, stir together flour, sugar, cinnamon, ginger, cloves, salt, and baking soda at low speed until combined, about 30 seconds. Stop mixer and add butter pieces; mix at medium-low speed until mixture is sandy and resembles fine meal, about 1½ minutes. Reduce speed to low and, with mixer running, gradually add molasses and milk; mix until dough is evenly moistened, about 20 seconds. Increase speed to medium and mix until thoroughly combined, about 10 seconds.

2. Scrape dough onto work surface; divide in half. Working with one portion of dough at a time, roll ¼-inch thick between two large sheets of parchment paper. Leaving dough sandwiched between parchment layers, stack on cookie sheet and freeze until firm, 15 to 20 minutes. (Alternatively, refrigerate dough 2 hours or overnight.)

3. Adjust oven racks to upper- and lower-middle positions and heat oven to 350 degrees. Line two cookie sheets with parchment paper.

4. Remove one dough sheet from freezer; place on work surface. Peel off top parchment sheet and gently lay it back in place. Flip dough over; peel off and discard second parchment layer. Cut dough into 5-inch gingerbread people or 3-inch gingerbread cookies, transferring shapes to parchment-lined cookie sheets with wide metal spatula, spacing them ¾ inch apart; set scraps aside. Repeat with remaining dough until cookie sheets are full. Bake cookies until set in centers and dough barely retains imprint when touched very gently with fingertip, 8 to 11 minutes, rotating cookie sheets front to back and switching positions top to bottom halfway through baking time. Do not overbake. Cool cookies on sheets 2 minutes, then remove with wide metal spatula to wire rack; cool to room temperature.

5. Gather scraps; repeat rolling, cutting, and baking in steps 2 and 4. Repeat with remaining dough until all dough is used.

THIN, CRISP GINGERBREAD COOKIES
FOR 2½ TO 3 DOZEN GINGERBREAD PEOPLE OR 4 TO 5 DOZEN COOKIES

These gingersnap-like cookies are sturdy and therefore suitable for making ornaments. If you wish to thread the cookies, snip wooden skewers to ½-inch lengths and press them into the cookies just before they go into the oven; remove skewers immediately after baking. Or, use a drinking straw to punch holes in the cookies when they're just out of the oven and still soft (*see* illustration below). Store in an airtight container. In dry climates, the cookies should keep about a month.

Follow recipe for Thick and Chewy Gingerbread Cookies, quartering rather than halving the dough, rolling each dough quarter ⅛-inch thick, reducing oven temperature to 325 degrees, and baking cookies until slightly darkened and firm in center when pressed with finger, about 15 to 20 minutes.

Stephen Schmidt is a cooking teacher and the author of *Dessert America* (Scribner, 1997).

TECHNIQUE
POKING HOLES

If you want to use the gingerbread people as decorations, use a straw to poke a hole in each one right after they come out of the oven.

Bone-In Supermarket Hams Sweep Tasting

Our tasting revealed that while many commercial hams make good holiday centerpieces but bad eating, bone-in hams are a good bet.

⇒ BY MARYELLEN DRISCOLL ⇐

Life changed for me when I turned 30. I suddenly began thinking about investments and savings, such as purchasing my very first ham. I liked the idea that it could provide many meals over the course of a typically busy week. There was just one problem with this scenario: whenever I looked at the many varieties of ham at the supermarket, I would walk away confused and empty-handed.

I ultimately shared my frustration with a number of ham company representatives. All were sympathetic, conceding that the number of choices was overwhelming and that "the industry" had done a poor job of educating consumers on the differences between them. A well-stocked supermarket can offer as many as a dozen different kinds of ham to choose from, not to mention the many different brands out there. It made perfect sense to sort matters out.

Because there are so many kinds of supermarket ham to choose from, the editors at *Cook's* agreed that a blind tasting that compared different types of hams would be more useful than our usual approach of rating various brands. To understand how supermarket hams can differ, you need to know just what constitutes a ham, how it is made, and how differences in processing translate into differences in labels.

But What Is a Ham?

Starting with the elementary, a ham is, by definition, a pig's hind leg that typically has been cured and/or smoked for preservation and flavor. Curing, one of the oldest forms of meat preservation, was originally done by rubbing salt into the meat or packing the meat in barrels of salt. Eventually, it was discovered that curing with a brine—a solution of water, sugar, and salt—was faster and made for a more flavorful product. Nowadays supermarket hams are simply injected with a brine solution that is often used more for flavor than preservation (nitrites are added for preserving) and can even include smoke flavor, thus replacing another traditional step in the ham-making process. Almost all supermarket hams are sold fully cooked and are so labeled.

A whole ham tends to be massive—weighing about 15 pounds. So, for manageability, hams are increasingly cut in half and sold in two pieces, the butt and the shank (*see* "Is Buying by the Pound Best?" below). Whether half or whole, though, the differences in supermarket hams come down to what bones, if any, have been removed and how much water, if any, has been added.

Of course hams can be sold with the bone left in. There are also semiboned hams, in which the aitchbone (pronounced H-bone), a bone from the pelvis, and the knuckle are removed for easier carving, leaving only the round leg bone. For easier carving yet, ham manufacturers came up with boneless hams, which are sold in cylindrical loaf shapes of various sizes.

All of these forms of ham vary in terms of the amount of water added during the curing process. According to the U.S. Department of Agriculture, if the finished product—after curing, smoking, and/or cooking—exceeds the original weight of the ham, known as the green weight, it must be labeled in accordance with the amount of water that has been added. A ham that has no added water is labeled just plain "ham." While some manufacturers still make these hams, they can be very hard to find in supermarkets, particularly at times other than the holidays. "Ham with natural juices" (as the label would state) has 7 to 8 percent water added; "Ham—water added" has 12 to 15 percent water added; and "ham and water product" contains more than 15 percent added water. The more water a ham contains, the less expensive it is per pound. The flip side is that you can end up paying for more than a pound of water when buying a seven-pound "ham and water product."

Testing the Hams

Once I was familiar with all of the choices, I was ready to hold a blind tasting. The samples consisted of nearly every supermarket ham that could be found in late spring, when the tasting took place (*see* chart, "Tasting Supermarket Hams," right). I could not find a plain bone-in ham with natural juices on the Eastern seaboard. According

---

Is Buying by the Pound Best?

Increasingly, people are purchasing half hams over whole ones. If they are not spiral-sliced, according to Mike Lewis, manager of the meat department at Star Market in Allston, Massachusetts, it makes a difference which half you buy because of the different configurations of bone and meat.

The rounded butt can be meatier (or sometimes may just seem that way), but it actually contains less desirable meat. That's partly because the butt contains a bone from the pelvis known as the aitchbone. This bone is what has given ham its reputation for being difficult to carve. The meat around it is not only difficult to carve or even pull off the bone but also contains a lot of membrane, fat, and gristle.

The bones in the shank portion are easier to work around. The muscles in this half contain less fat and gristle. Ironically, the shank typically costs 20 to 30 cents less per pound than the butt. Lewis said that this is because the bones in this half tend to be larger.

Some companies will actually indicate on the label which half of the ham is in the package. But for those that don't, a consumer can still readily tell by the shape.

If you opt to purchase a bone-in shank that is not spiral-sliced, we recommend pulling the large muscles off the shank after cooking (wear gloves to avoid burns). The seams between the muscles are visible and loosen easily when hot. Once removed, the sections can be carved individually. A five- to seven-pound shank half will feed six to eight people.   —M.D.

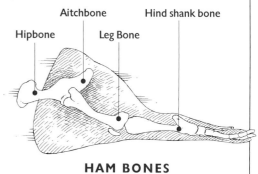

HAM BONES

TASTING SUPERMARKET HAMS

The hams listed below (in order of ranking) were served reheated to a panel of 15 tasters from the magazine staff. Slices were carved from each ham and served to the tasters separately so that they could not see if a slice came from a traditional bone-in ham or not. The tasters rated each ham on flavor and texture characteristics as well as their overall liking of each. Bread and water were served as palate cleansers. We found that the prices of hams tested vary significantly according to the season and availability. Prices can also differ significantly from brand to brand.

BONE-IN HAM WITH NATURAL JUICES, SPIRAL CUT
➤ Sold for $2.69 per pound.
This favorite ham had "good bite, not that yielding, spongy texture commonly found in hams," as one taster commented. Overall, the flavor was more balanced than that of any of the other hams—"not too strong or salty or offensive," "real meaty," and slightly sweet. Also the easiest ham to carve and serve.

BONE-IN HAM, WATER ADDED
➤ Butt end sold for $1.49 per pound. Shank sold for $1.29 per pound.
The general consensus was that this ham was bland. To its credit, though, there were no off or chemical flavors. Many tasters described the texture as "spongy" or "like a watered-down pork chop." For some it was a pleasant compromise—"not chewy, not gummy"—between the texture of the natural juice bone-in ham and the water product bone-in ham.

BONELESS HAM WITH NATURAL JUICES
➤ Sold for $3–4 per pound.
This ham had a strong flavor punch that may have been simply salt overkill. The texture was decent—chewy and meaty—but extremely dry. One taster said the texture reminded her of Canadian bacon.

BONE-IN HAM AND WATER PRODUCT
➤ Sold for 98 cents per pound.
Our tasters were not fooled by this ham. The "damp texture is very off-putting, like damp paper towels." "It has a rubbery feel that's not nice." The flavor was artificial and bland. It also had a processed appearance.

SEMIBONELESS HAM, WATER ADDED
➤ Sold for $2.49 per pound.
This ham looked questionable from the start, compressed and spongy, with an interior littered with pock marks. It was criticized for tasting waterlogged and having a mushy or rubbery texture.

SEMIBONELESS HAM WITH NATURAL JUICES
➤ Sold for $2.69 per pound.
Deemed "Spam's cousin" by one taster. The texture was described as rubbery, spongy, "plasticized," and flabby.

BONELESS HAM, WATER ADDED
➤ Sold for $3–4 per pound
This ham looked like processed, compressed meat and had such a soft texture that one taster said it dissolved in his mouth. The flavor was bland, off, and artificial. "Tastes like a slice of roasted hot dog—and a bad dog at that."

BONELESS HAM AND WATER PRODUCT
➤ Sold for $2.79 per pound.
"Did someone say Spam?" wrote one taster. Another called it "Jello-ham." It was gelatinous and glistening, and it looked as if it came from a can—shaped as such but packaged in plastic wrap. This ham had a suspicious oily sheen and dark red blotches. Many tasters could tolerate only one bite.

---

to a few butchers at large chains, these tend to be offered only around the holidays. But there was no lack of such hams in a spiral-sliced version, a sample of which was included in the tasting.

The tasting results were almost predictable: more bone and less water seemed to make for the tastiest hams.

The reason why the hams with natural juices were preferred to those with water added—or with so much water added that the ham is called a "water product"—seemed readily apparent. The more water, the more diluted the ham flavor and the more chemical and "off" the hams tended to taste.

According to Larry Borchert, a professor of muscle biology and meat science at the University of Wisconsin at Madison, hams do not naturally hold water. The two proteins that make up the muscles of a ham, actin and myosin, bind together to form a complex protein known as actomyosin. Actomyosin is not water-soluble, but it is salt-soluble. Thus ham manufacturers must inject sodium phosphate into supermarket hams to enable the muscles to retain water. The advantage of this treatment can be that a ham does not end up completely dehydrated after processing. The disadvantage, however, is that the ham can be so pumped up with water, or "highly extended," as Borchert phrased it, that it takes on an unpalatably damp, spongy texture and a watered-down flavor. This was the case with all of the "water product"

hams and, to a lesser degree, the "ham—water added" products.

The other key finding was that hams seem to be better off when the bone is left in. While there is all sorts of speculation as to why keeping the bone contributes to flavor, the reasons for this have not been scientifically ascertained. Borchert proposed that the question be reversed—that is, what is it about the process of making a boneless product that compromises the overall appeal of a ham?

Roll It and Pat It
As convenient as it might be to carve a boneless ham, the downside is that boneless hams must be subjected to a lot of processing so that the loose pieces of meat pulled from the bone will hold together. Some boneless hams consist of large pieces of muscle that are sectioned and formed. According to Dr. Dennis Buege of the University of Wisconsin at Madison, these hams must be tumbled and bound to fill the hole left from the bone. Boneless hams can also consist of ground meat that is injected with salt so that the proteins dissolve and then coagulate and bind together while being tumbled and kneaded into a ham form. This inevitably changes the original texture of the meat.

In accordance, our tasters' biggest quibble with the boneless hams, as well as the semiboned, was that they lacked the texture of "real" ham. At best, it was reminiscent of Canadian bacon.

"Compressed" and "processed" were also common terms of complaint.

When all was said and done, it was the spiral-sliced ham with natural juices that stood out as the best ham to buy. It is neither overly pumped up with water nor packed into a cylindrical loaf shape. And for the test kitchen staff, who had to carve all of the hams before the tasting, it was hands-down the most convenient of the bone-in hams.

Such convenience has to be taken into consideration because it is the particular difficulty of carving a ham that triggered the introduction and popularity of the boneless ham. Yet all of the ham manufacturers interviewed reported that with the advent of the spiral-slicing machine, consumers are increasingly returning to what we found to be the best all-around ham.

The spiral-sliced ham is also the most expensive of the bone-in hams—averaging at least a dollar more per pound than the runner-up, an unsliced bone-in ham with water added. All of the dozens of spiral-sliced hams we purchased for our tasting were made with natural juices, which automatically means a more expensive ham. One manufacturer said that spiral-sliced hams are not being made into water-added and water product hams simply because they are too spongy for the spiral slicer to do its work. So while it is fortuitous for the consumer that the latest in technology requires the preservation of ham texture and flavor, such innovation has come at a price.

$4 Cake Pan Wins Testing

We tested all the options, including one pan that retails for around $80, and found that cheap pans work just fine.

⇒ BY ADAM RIED ⇐

Along with birthdays, anniversaries, and graduations, the holidays are cake time for many people. Cakes can be temperamental, though, open to influences ranging from the temperature of the ingredients to the method used to mix them. We wondered if the pan used to bake the cake might also have a significant influence on the outcome, so we assembled a collection of 11 different pans and baked nearly 50 plain and chocolate butter cakes to find out.

Like much bakeware, cake pans come in a variety of shapes and sizes. We focused on round pans, 9 inches in diameter and 2 inches deep (or as close to it as we could find from a particular manufacturer), because they're a common choice for baking basic American layer cakes. When the shopping was done, we had nine typical pans from familiar bakeware manufacturers, including Kaiser, Ekco, Revere, T-Fal, WearEver, Chicago Metallic, Wilton, and Calphalon, and two somewhat unusual entries from All-Clad and Demarle. The main differences in the pans fell into three categories: the materials from which the pans were made, including tinned, stainless, and aluminized steel and aluminum; their weight, which ranged from a low of 5.2 ounces per pan to a whopping 22.7 ounces (heavier pans were labeled "commercial" or "professional" weight); and special features such as nonstick coatings and insulation (an airspace sandwiched between two layers of metal).

The two more curious contenders were a preproduction prototype of an ultra-expensive pan from All-Clad's brand new line of bakeware and a completely flexible pan made of silicon-coated fiberglass mesh from Demarle, the French company that makes Silpat nonstick baking sheet liners.

Initially, we wondered how the pans would affect the texture of the cakes.

The Cake Pans We Tested

BEST CAKE PAN

Ekco Baker's Secret Non-Stick Round Cake Pan
Inexpensive pan excelled in every category—and has handles.

RECOMMENDED

All-Clad Bonded Bakeware
Exorbitant, but the last you'd ever have to buy.

Calphalon Nonstick Professional
Decent performer suffered from only fair release.

Kaiser Backform
Cakes were high, but disappointingly pale.

T-Fal Resistal Homebake
Very slick bottom, slides across oven rack.

Chicago Metallic Village Baker
Performance does not justify persnickety drying.

Chicago Metallic Commercial
A solid, middle-of-the-road pan.

NOT RECOMMENDED

Wilton Enterprises Performance Pans
Produces good cakes, but releases them poorly.

Revere Stainless Steel Professional
Poor browning and release.

WearEver CushionAire
Mediocre performance, cumbersome cleaning.

Demarle Flexipan
Strange pan with no instructions for use.

Frankly, we were a little surprised to find that the cakes baked in all of the pans had a tender, lovely texture. We inspected and tasted each one very carefully, and no one could detect any noticeable differences from pan to pan. Convinced that the pan itself had little effect on the crumb, we moved on to other tests. For each pan, we rated three performance traits. Most important was the way it released the cake, followed by how it browned the crust, and, finally, by the cake's overall appearance.

Removing a cake from its pan can be difficult. Portions of the crust—or, worse yet, whole chunks of cake—can stick to the pan. And if the side crust left on the cake is crumbly or shredded, frosting it neatly can be tricky. In truth, all of our pans but one released their cakes adequately. Only the Demarle Flexipan retained a large chunk of the cake. The best of the lot, however, were the Ekco and All-Clad pans, nonstick and stick-resistant, respectively, which released both yellow and chocolate cakes very well every single time.

When it came to browning the crusts, there were dramatic differences in the pans. Before baking, we learned that leading bakers and cookbook authors consistently advise against using pans with dark finishes, such as the nonsticks, because they tend to overbrown the crusts. When all was said and done, we disagreed. Three out of our four dark-surfaced pans—the Ekco, Calphalon, T-Fal, and Demarle—did produce very deeply browned crusts, but we considered none of these cakes to be overbrowned or undesirable. In fact, we enjoyed the richer flavor of the dark crusts when eating these cakes unfrosted, and we also found that their sturdiness and resistance to crumbling made them easier to frost.

The only dark pan that produced a poor crust was the Demarle Flexipan. Although the browning was adequate, the silicon surface promoted a slick, glass-smooth, high-gloss crust that

RATING CAKE PANS

We tested eleven 9-inch (or very close to it) round cake pans and rated them according to the criteria listed below, baking at least three cakes in each pan. All ingredients were weighed, the batter was consistently mixed and portioned by weight (18 ounces) into each pan by the same person, and all the cakes were baked on the same rack, in the same oven, and rotated at the same point during the baking process. In addition, all pans were greased with a moderate coating of nonstick cooking spray and then floured. Performance differences in the pans that did well were minor enough to allow us to recommend any of them. Therefore, the pans are listed in two categories: Recommended and Not Recommended. The ease with which the pan released the cake and the condition in which it left the crust was our most important test, followed by the depth and degree of browning and the overall shape and appearance of the cake.

Brand	Price	Material/Finish	Size	Release	Browning	Appearance	Testers' Comments
BEST CAKE PAN **Ekco** Baker's Secret Non-Stick Round Cake Pan	$3.99	Tinned steel/Medium gray nonstick coating	8⅞" diameter by 1½" deep	★★★	★★★	★★★	With handles for easy lifting and turning and a nonstick finish for perfect release and easy cleaning, this pan's a winner.
RECOMMENDED **All-Clad** Bonded Bakeware 9-Inch Round Cake Pan (pre-production sample)	$80.00 (est.)	Five ply—three inner layers aluminum with two outer layers stainless steel/"Stick-resistant"	9" diameter by 2" deep	★★★	★★★	★★	Release and browning were very good, but the cakes were not as high as some of the others, and for this kind of money, we expect perfection. Along with the Ekco, this was the only pan with handles.
Calphalon Nonstick Professional Bakeware 9-Inch Round Cake Pan	$18.99	Aluminized steel/Matte black nonstick coating	9" diameter by 2" deep	★★	★★★	★★★	Pretty good performance, though a small amount of crust did stick in the pan after each cake was released.
Kaiser Backform Round Cake Pan	$4.99	Tinned steel/Shiny silver	9" diameter by 2" deep	★★	★★	★★★	Produced a nice, high cake with a moderate hump in the middle. The crusts were disappointingly pale.
T-Fal Resistal Homebake Layer Cake Pan	$7.99	Aluminum with nonstick coating and honeycomb-textured bottom surface/Dark black	9" diameter by 1½" deep	★★	★★★	★★	Manufacturer directions suggest "reducing usual cooking temperature and duration," without specific recommendations for how much.
Chicago Metallic Village Baker Commercial Weight 9-Inch Round Cake Pan	$10.40	Tinned steel/Shiny silver	9" diameter by 2" deep	★★	★★	★★★	Cakes baked in this pan attained good height, but were not matched by the browning.
Chicago Metallic Commercial 9-Inch Round Cake Pan	$12.50	Aluminized steel/Matte silver	9" diameter by 2" deep	★★	★★	★★	Pan turned in a fair, but not stellar, performance all around.
NOT RECOMMENDED **Wilton Enterprises** Performance Pans, 9-Inch Round	$10.99 for set of two	Aluminum/Matte silver (anodized)	9⅛" diameter by 1¾" deep	★	★★★	★★	The height of the cakes and the browning of the crusts were decent, but it took a lot of fiddling to get the cakes out of the pan.
Revere Stainless Steel Professional Weight Round Cake Pan	$12.99	Stainless steel/Shiny silver	9" diameter by 1½" deep	★	★	★★	Cakes baked in this pan had nice height but very poorly browned crusts, which were largely ruined by poor release. Wide rim eases handling.
WearEver CushionAire Nonstick Insulated Bakeware Round Baking Pan	$13.99	Two sheets of aluminum with an air layer in between/Nonstick finish in medium gray	9" diameter by 1¾" deep	★	★	★	This pan turned out rather pale, unremarkable cakes. Side crusts shredded when removing cake from pan.
Demarle Flexipan	$20.70	Silicon-coated knitted glass fabric/Shiny black	8¾" diameter by 2⅜" deep	★	★★	★	All of the cakes baked in this pan had very slick, glossy, unnatural looking bottoms and side surfaces and a faint rubbery flavor. Pan must be laid on a rack or grill, for baking, freezing, or carrying when full.

looked totally unnatural and had a noticeably off flavor. The two pans that did a particularly good job of browning, the All-Clad and the Wilton, were made of aluminum (the All-Clad has a three-ply aluminum core). The ability of aluminum cake pans to brown their contents deeply and evenly also made them a favorite among the pros whose books we consulted. Aluminum owes its success in this area to the fact that it conducts heat efficiently, quickly, and evenly. By the same token, the pros warned against using pans made from stainless steel, which, because it is an inferior heat conductor, does not promote browning. Our stainless steel Revere pan proved their warnings to be true.

Last, we noted the overall appearance of the cake, which we judged on the basis of its height, shape, and evenness as well as on the angle of the cake's sides. The height of the cakes was very consistent. Most of the cakes baked in most of the pans measured within ⅛ inch of 1¼ inches. The tallest was a 1½-inch cake baked in the Kaiser pan, and the most squat were 1-inch cakes baked in the insulated WearEver and the Demarle Flexipan. Likewise, almost all of the cakes baked evenly, without a noticeable hump in the middle. Last, some cooking authorities mentioned that pans with straight sides (which from our group was all but the Ekco, Kaiser, T-Fal, Wilton, and Revere) produced neater looking cakes than those with flared sides. Again, this didn't seem like a big deal to us. Any angle in the side of the cake could easily be hidden with frosting when the cake was iced.

One more benefit shared by the Ekco, which was the least expensive of the lot at just $4, and the All-Clad, which at around $80 was the most expensive, was handles. Only these two pans had them, and we loved them for it. When transferring a batter-filled pan to the oven or rotating it part way through baking, we found that the handles made it much easier to grab the pan without landing a corner of the pot holder in the batter.

The light, cheap Ekco was the only pan to earn a "good" rating in all three tests: release, browning ability, and appearance of the cake. Add to that its handles and rock-bottom price tag, and it looks pretty good. Of course, the Ekco may prove less durable than some of its heavier competitors. In fact, just in the course of our testing, it picked up two small dents. But for the price of the next best pan, the gorgeous $80 All-Clad, you could afford to replace the Ekco 20 times, should the need arise.

KITCHEN NOTES

Editor's Note: Welcome to Kitchen Notes, a new section of the magazine that features advice, test results, buying tips, and updates on *Cook's* articles from the staff of our test kitchen. We will also include updates on our equipment-testing articles, letting you know how the models that won top ratings have stood up to 12 months or more of hard use in our test kitchen. We also invite your comments about featured cookware items. If you own a KitchenAid Ultra Power (KPF 600) or Cuisinart Pro Custom 11 (DLC-85) food processor or a Krups Pro Aroma 12 Time Model 453 or Black & Decker Kicthentools Model TCMKT800 coffee maker, drop us a note or leave comments at our Web site (www.cooksillustrated.com). Thanks.

—Christopher Kimball, Publisher and Editor

Guacamole Wrap

In our recipe for Chunky Guacamole (May/June 1999), we suggest pressing a sheet of plastic wrap directly on the surface of the guacamole to deter discoloration for up to one day. Sparked by Harold McGee's findings on guacamole storage in his book *The Curious Cook* (North Point Press, 1990), we mashed some avocados and covered the surfaces with six different plastic wraps—Handi-Wrap, Reynolds Plastic Wrap, Glad Cling Wrap, Top Crest Premium Cling Wrap, Saran Wrap, and a food service–quality plastic wrap. For the first several hours, none browned. After 48 hours all had turned a putrid brown except for the one covered with Saran Wrap, which remained bright green. According to McGee, Saran Wrap is the only one made from polyvinylidene, which better retards discoloration because it is much less permeable to oxygen than the compounds used to make most other wraps. Saran Wrap does cost about 80 cents more per 100 feet than the other plastic wraps.

Bad Wraps

While we were testing guacamole storage, we also tested the clingability of the various storage wraps in the manner suggested on the side of the Reynolds box. We filled a drinking glass with one cup of water, covered the mouth with plastic wrap, turned the glass upside down, and gave it 10 good shakes. We're happy to report that most brands held securely in place with no leaks except for Glad Cling Wrap, which loosened after being turned upright, and Handi-Wrap, which unsealed and soaked us.

Wrap Alternatives

Of course, there are plenty of alternatives to plastic wrap, including those old-time vinyl bowl covers that resemble shower caps. The Vermont Country Store (P.O. Box 3000, Manchester Ctr., VT 05255-300; 802-362-8440) still sells these 1950s covers. They might look silly, but they can spare you from having to transfer leftovers to a sealed container. The eight-piece set fits bowls from 3 to 14 inches across and costs $8.95.

Kitchen Speak

Ever wondered about the difference between boiling and blanching? We encountered that question in "Classic Three-Bean Salad Updated" (July/August 1999). Boiling is a method in which food is cooked fully in boiling liquid, as are the beans in our recipe. In blanching, food is briefly placed in boiling liquid, then removed and immediately "shocked," or placed in cold water, to stop the cooking. Blanching is typically part of the preparation process, whether it is to loosen skins for peeling, to set colors, to make food more tender, and/or to remove unwanted flavors. Most blanched foods are used in other preparations or cooked further. For example, when we cooked broccoli rabe (*see* "Taming Broccoli Rabe" in our January/ February 1999 issue), we found that blanching before sautéing with other ingredients removed much of the bitterness from this vegetable.

Steely Numbers

If you are shopping for stainless steel kitchen utensils or cookware, you may notice that many pieces display a stamp or mark of "18/8" or "18/10." We turned to books and the makers of All-Clad cookware for a translation. The "18" refers to the percentage of chromium in the steel, which primarily protects against corrosion. The "8" or "10" denotes the percentage of nickel, which provides luster and some additional corrosion resistance. You will pay more for 18/10 stainless steel, but basically all this buys you is shinier cookware.

Advice for Seasonal Bakers

If you check your cupboard in preparation for holiday baking and find your brown sugar has hardened up, you might try a couple of tricks we have come to rely on to make it soft and fresh once again. One option: Place one or two bread slices in an airtight container with the sugar and let it sit overnight. A speedier method: Place the hardened sugar and bread in a microwave-safe container, cover it with plastic wrap, and place in microwave set to full power for 10 to 20 seconds. Why does this work? Sugar is hydroscopic, so it draws in moisture from the bread and softens.

Preserving the Page

We have no qualms with minor splatters on our cookbook pages. The real problem occurs when messy hands scramble to hold the pages open. In the *Cook's* test kitchen, we work from photocopies tacked to a standing clipboard (found in most office supply stores). Without all the advertising that bulks up most magazines, *Cook's* is actually light enough to be held on one of these clipboards. Just clip a plastic sheet protector (available at stores that sell school supplies) over the page for added protection. If you want a "real" cookbook holder, there are all sorts out there, half of which, we found, either don't work or work only for books of one particular size. We did, however, find one cookbook holder worth considering. *See* Resources, page 32.

Allspice but None

This season of pumpkins, squash, and sweet potatoes means warm aromatic spices take center stage, too. More than once we have found ourselves out of allspice when we needed it. We have tried lots of cookbook concoctions for substitutes, which typically consist of combinations of cinnamon, nutmeg, and clove, but none captured the essence of the real thing. Allspice is a pea-sized berry that comes from the evergreen pimiento tree, which is grown primarily in Jamaica. Cinnamon, nutmeg, and clove—the spices commonly believed to be blended to make allspice—are from Asia. Part of the confusion is caused by the spice's name, another part by the fact that all four spices contain the volatile oil eugenol, which is essentially what gives allspice its fragrant yet distinct character.

Spud Spots

While peeling and slicing dozens upon dozens of potatoes for the holiday casserole recipe on page 18, we often ran up against little (and sometimes not so little) gray splotches on the surface of the potatoes. According to Greg Anthony, who produces Irish Eyes with a Hint of Garlic, a mail-order seed catalog specializing in spuds, the spots are typically bruises (starches that start turning to sugar) that result from rough handling by large-scale harvesting and processing equipment. He said it is fine to just cut out the bruised parts and discard them, which we found easy enough to do with the wedged tip of a vegetable peeler.

Culinary Dictionary

As much satisfaction as one might get from turning to the securely bound pages of a dictionary, the Web can also be an excellent source of information. We learned that the entire contents of the *Food Lover's Companion* (Barron's, 1995), the culinary dictionary we rated as best in the *Cook's* September/October '99 issue, can be accessed on line at the Epicurious Web site (http://food.epicurious.com/find/food).

Another Look at Italy

Two new cookbooks show that there is, in fact, something new
to say about Italian cooking. BY CHRISTOPHER KIMBALL

The Italian Country Table

Lynne Rosetto Kasper

(Scribner, 1999)

In this book, Lynne Rosetto Kasper, author of the acclaimed *The Splendid Table* (Morrow, 1992), travels back to Italy to fully explore the cooking and culture of several regions, among them Alto Adige, the region of Italy that borders on Austria. (Her first book focused on the Emilia-Romagna region.) Not just an assemblage of carefully collected and tested recipes, this book is a poem to country life, to the goatherds and vintners, to the days of the central town oven that brought together the women of the village to bake bread, roast chicken, and swap stories. It will guide you gently into the past but leave you with a vision of the future: good food simply prepared with a deep sense of cultural integrity, an ingredient that is sadly lacking in most modern American cuisine.

Kasper's cooking is informed by the Italian term *nostrano*, which means both "local" and "ours," the implication being that food must have a sense of place and history to be worth eating. This 400-page book is also a lot of fun, containing fascinating anecdotes (fava beans were always served with the skins on to make the men stronger in both the fields and the marriage bed) and descriptions of locals who provide the link between country life and the country table: the last shepherds in Puglia or the old woman at a grain shop who still sells the old-fashioned grain known as farro. Because we reviewed this book in galley form, we cannot comment on the color photography or page layout.

PROS: Even a cursory read of her new book immediately identifies Kasper as a skilled writer and cook who also spends the time and effort to do original research. This lovingly conceived work elevates her into the very highest ranks of cookbook writers, those who successfully combine enthusiasm with rigorous investigation to produce seminal works. Almost as a bonus, the recipes are fascinating, fresh, and perfectly suited to the American table in their simplicity and lack of hard-to-find local Italian ingredients. If you purchase only one book this year, make it *The Italian Country Table*.

CONS: Aside from a few minor complaints about recipe directions, this book is nearly perfect.

RECIPE TESTING: We found only one misstep in the 20 recipes we tested; the balance had the ring of authenticity and were generally simple to prepare, calling for only an occasional adjustment. The beauty of the these recipes is the happy marriage of simplicity and culinary originality. Cantaloupe served with black pepper, olive oil, and vinegar was divine; a stuffed-under-the-skin butterflied chicken is now part of my midweek repertoire; grilled chicken in Sicilian mint sauce was dead simple to make and the flavor combinations were refreshing. The only loser in the bunch was a spiced cauliflower with ziti that turned out a bit dry, with flavors that did not seem to integrate well. With very few exceptions, the author has translated these recipes expertly for the American kitchen, requiring few, if any, ingredients that have to be mail-ordered from some boutique or artisan in Alto Adige, the downfall of many "authentic" regional Italian cookbooks.

The Mediterranean Feast

Clifford Wright

(Morrow, 1999)

Shifting gears from *The Italian Country Table* to *The Mediterranean Feast* was like moving from a divine bed and breakfast to the world's largest five-star hotel. The historical sweep of the latter is vast, beginning with the Arab agricultural revolution of the ninth through twelfth centuries (an antidote to the culinary status quo—famine), the age of exploration that followed in the fifteenth and sixteenth centuries (which introduced new foods), and, finally, the Renaissance (which introduced a new age of culinary aesthetics). The point of this complex, detailed tome is that only by understanding the great sweep of history can one truly understand and appreciate Mediterranean cuisine. By implication, the author admonishes other culinary historians for their narrow view of what he considers to be an enormously complex issue—the development of a heterogeneous cuisine that is an amalgam of complex historical trends. Recipes are presented for novices and food historians alike as they might be in a college textbook, as a means of sampling the cultural events and references printed on the page. The author makes no claim for simplicity in his recipe selections but rather offers them in their historical context. The book runs to 750 pages. We also reviewed this book in galley form and so cannot comment on photography or layout.

PROS: The good news is that this book has many fascinating recipes as well as an incredible depth of historical fact and numerous anecdotes. Recipes come from Greece, Croatia, Venice, Provence, Andalusia, Languedoc, Sardinia, and elsewhere. One learns that Venetian harlots were quite erudite, having to cater not only to the physical but also the philosophical needs of their clients. During the Spanish Inquisition, a test of one's conversion to Christianity was the public consumption of pork, forbidden to true Muslims and Jews. Such historical tidbits seem virtually countless, and the range of recipes is almost equally broad, offering unusual and intriguing combinations of ingredients.

CONS: This is an academic work at heart, lacking the personal warmth of Kasper's writing. But then a thousand-year tour of the entire Mediterranean region hardly gives one time to delve deeply into the daily life of any one locale. One also gets the feeling, after much recipe testing, that the author is less a cook than he is a writer and historian.

RECIPE TESTING: We had our share of problems with these recipes; about half of the dozen that we tested were not deemed worth a second shot. A recipe for tuna with tomatoes turned out overcooked fish but displayed interesting flavors; penne with asparagus yielded mushy asparagus, and the accompanying raw egg sauce was not a crowd pleaser; a Sardinian cheese soup failed on all counts; and the intriguing roasted macaroni turned out to be no more than a dry, dull American casserole. But there were winners as well. The baba ghanoush (eggplant dip) was excellent; a phyllo pudding was interesting and easy to make, and it had supporters in the test kitchen; a potato sauce was excellent, although perhaps mistitled—it has plenty of tomatoes and peppers as well; and braised oxtails were good if a bit too sweet from too many carrots. Even though many of these recipes needed adjustment, we found plenty to like here, a real treasure trove of recipes that are worthy of exploration by anyone skilled and patient in the kitchen.

RESOURCES

Most of the ingredients and materials necessary for the recipes in this issue are available at your local supermarket, gourmet store, or kitchen supply shop. The following are mail-order sources for particular items. Prices listed below were current at press time and do not include shipping or handling unless otherwise indicated. We suggest that you contact companies directly to confirm up-to-date prices and availability or to request a catalog.

Cake Pans

In our search for the best cake pan (*see* story on page 28), we were pleasantly surprised with the low-priced Ekco Baker's Secret Non-Stick round pan. It was the only pan to receive a perfect score for cake release, browning, and appearance. Its side handles are an added bonus, since they make it easy to turn the pan during baking and to lift it hot out of the oven. Manufactured in the United States, the Ekco cake pan is made of tin-plated steel with a nonstick coating. The suggested retail price of the Ekco pan is a mere $3.99. It is available at most major discount chains and grocery stores. You can call the manufacturer at **1-800-367-3526** to find the nearest retailer in your area that carries Ekco products. Our second-place finisher, the All-Clad Bonded Bakeware round cake pan, falls at the opposite end of the price spectrum at $80. The pan is made from triple layers of aluminum and dual outer layers of stainless steel that are bonded to a champagne-colored, stick-resistant surface. All of this makes this pan particularly stunning in appearance; it also happens to bake cakes well. The All-Clad is available through **Sur La Table (1765 Sixth Avenue, Seattle, WA 98134-1608; 800-243-0852; www.surlatable.com)** for $79.95 and **The Baker's Catalogue (King Arthur Flour, P.O. Box 876, Norwich, VT 05055-0876; 800-827-6836; www.kingarthurflour.com)** for $80. The Baker's Catalogue item number is 5175.

V-Racks for Grilling

The most important feature of a V-rack used for grilling poultry is its base, which must be substantial enough to keep the rack from slipping through the bars of a gas grill. The next consideration is the height of the rack, which must be low enough to allow it to fit fully inside the closed grill. For this issue's grilled turkey recipe (*see* page 11), our test kitchen used an adjustable roasting rack with a four-sided rectangular base (10 inches by 7¼ inches) that rests securely on the grill. The V angle of the rack can be adjusted to six different positions, ranging from 30 degrees to about 150 degrees. The larger angles are designed to accommodate larger birds, but they also make it possible for the rack and bird to fit easily under a grill cover. This style of roasting rack is common in general houseware stores, but we have found that the models found in those locations tends to be flimsy. We purchased ours for $12.95 from **Sur La Table (1765 Sixth Avenue, Seattle, WA 98134-1608; 800-243-0852; www.surlatable.com)** and found it to be much more sturdy. The item number is 0162.

Ginger Grater

The Greater Zester continues to impress us with its diverse uses and delicate grating ability. It works wonders with hard-to-grate ginger in this issue's gingerbread cookie recipe, and it is also a whiz at finely grating cheese and zesting citrus fruits and chocolate. Its style and shape, which make it resemble a toothed metal ruler, make for easy handling, and its length, which exceeds that of most other graters, makes for fewer sweeps and less work. The Greater Zester should be washed by hand with soap and warm water. Order by mail for $13.50 from **Cooking by the Book, Inc. (13 Worth Street, New York, NY 10013; 212-966-9799).**

Cookbook Holder

While there are a number of ways to rig a cookbook to stand up or stay open, it is ideal to have a reliable stand that can prop up and position the pages of a cookbook of any size. After testing about a half-dozen styles of cookbook holders, we found most to be dismally ineffective or at best inflexible. One, however, did warrant a sound recommendation. Known as the Folding Oak Bookstand, this stand is sold through the Levenger catalog, which specializes in "tools for serious readers." The stand adjusts to three angles (70, 60, and 52 degrees) and can fold flat for easy storage. Along the front half of the stand is a series of holes used to position page restraint pegs, which allow books of different sizes to be held open. We were able to prop up our smallest paperback cookbook and our largest hardbound tome perfectly with a simple adjustment of the pegs. Made in the United States from native oak, the Folding Oak Bookstand can be ordered by mail for $29.95 from **Levenger (420 South Congress Avenue, Delray Beach, FL 33445-4696; 800-544-0880; www.levenger.com).**

Gingerbread Cookie Cutters

Gingerbread cookie cutters come in all shapes and sizes, and some are sturdier than others. In the gingerbread cookie recipe on page 25, we found that it is important to use a cutter that is deep enough to press cleanly all the way through thick dough. **Sur La Table (1765 Sixth Avenue South, Seattle, WA 98134-1608; 800-243-0852; www.surlatable.com)** carries 2-inch- and 3-inch-tall tinplate cutters of men and skirted women for $1.00 each, as well as a 5-inch-tall man for $1.25. **N.Y. Cake & Baking Distributor (56 West 22nd Street, New York, NY 10010; 800-942-2539)** carries 5-inch-tall men and skirted women aluminum cutters for $1.99 each.

Great Sweet Potatoes

Virtually all of the yams sold in American supermarkets are in fact sweet potatoes. Real yams are thick, tropical-vine tubers that can grow up to 7 feet long, depending on the species. Although many southern growers refer to their crops as yams, they are in fact sweet potatoes—edible roots that are part of the morning glory family. There are two basic types of sweet potato grown in the United States: those with light-colored flesh and thin skins and the darker-skinned varieties that are often erroneously labeled yams. We used the latter type for our sweet potato pie recipe (page 23) because it was more readily available. If you would like to purchase high-quality sweet potatoes from a southern grower, contact **Garber Farms (3405 Des Cannes Highway, Iota, LA 80543; 318-824-6328)**. We taste-tested their sweet potatoes and found them superior to those found in local Boston markets. (We also taste-tested a supermarket jewel yam grown in California, which was a bit fibrous, toothsome, and not very sweet, and a garnet yam from California, which was sweet but very starchy, almost a cross between a regular potato and a sweet potato.) Garber Farms sells sweet potato gift boxes during the holiday season.

Crystallized Ginger

If you like to add crystallized ginger to your gingerbread cookies for an extra-spicy kick, we recommend Williams-Sonoma's Australian crystallized ginger. It tastes fresh and peppery with, of course, a sweet candy edge. A one-pound can sells for $13.50. You can find this product at Williams-Sonoma stores or order it from their catalog **(Williams-Sonoma Mail Order Department, P.O. Box 7546, San Francisco, CA 94120-7456; 800-541-1262)**. The mail-order item number is 94-47266.

Baking Spices

While many of the spices on this issue's back cover can be found in supermarkets, some spices, such as black, white, and green cardamom pods, are more of a specialty item. One of our favorite sources for such items (as well as for everyday spices) is the **Penzeys Spices catalog**. Not only does Penzeys carry an impressive variety of spices, it also explains the differences between them. You can request a copy of the company's catalog by calling **800-741-7787** or by visiting its Web site **(www.penzeys.com)**.

RECIPE INDEX

Cranberry-Nut Bread **PAGE 21**

Grill-Roasted Turkey **PAGE 11**

Holiday Potato Casserole **PAGE 19**

Ultimate Cream of Tomato Soup **PAGE 9**

Rich and Tender American Dinner Rolls **PAGE 15**

The Best Sweet Potato Pie **PAGE 23**

PHOTOGRAPHY: CARL TREMBLAY   STYLING : MYROSHA DZIUK

Cloves

Black Cardamom

Green Cardamom

Allspice

Star Anise

White Cardamom

Saffron

Dried Mace

Cinnamon Sticks

Mace Covering Nutmeg

Crystallized Ginger

Nutmeg

Vanilla Beans

WHOLE
BAKING SPICES